American Encounters/Global Interactions
A series edited by Gilbert M. Joseph
and Emily S. Rosenberg

This series aims to stimulate critical perspectives and fresh interpretive frameworks for scholarship on the history of the imposing global presence of the United States. Its primary concerns include the deployment and contestation of power, the construction and deconstruction of cultural and political borders, the fluid meanings of intercultural encounters, and the complex interplay between the global and the local. American Encounters seeks to strengthen dialogue and collaboration between historians of U.S. international relations and area studies specialists.

The series encourages scholarship based on multiarchival historical research. At the same time, it supports a recognition of the representational character of all stories about the past and promotes critical inquiry into issues of subjectivity and narrative. In the process, American Encounters strives to understand the context in which meanings related to nations, cultures, and political economy are continually produced, challenged, and reshaped.

DUKE UNIVERSITY PRESS   *Durham and London* 2001

FRAGMENTS OF A GOLDEN AGE

The Politics of Culture in Mexico Since 1940

Edited by Gilbert M. Joseph, Anne Rubenstein,

and Eric Zolov

© 2001 Duke University Press
All rights reserved
Printed in the United States of America on acid-free paper ∞
Typeset in Galliard by Wilsted & Taylor Publishing Services
Library of Congress Cataloging-in-Publication Data appear
on the last printed page of this book.
Frontispiece: Painting by Juan O'Gorman, *La ciudad de
México,* 1949. Temple/Masonite. 66 × 122 cm. Used by
permission of the Museo de Arte Moderno (Instituto
Nacional de Bellas Artes), Mexico City.
"Corazón de Rocanrol" was previously published in
The Other Side. Copyright 1992 by Rubén Martínez.
Originally published by Verso Books. Reprinted by
permission of Verso Books, London, UK. All rights reserved.

Contents

List of Illustrations

Foreword: Taking Mexican Popular Culture by Storm

This book celebrates Mexican culture, turning it into part of the country's mystique. It analyzes Mexico's popular movements as fundamental to an appreciation of the deeply rooted, moral sensibilities of Mexicans. These essays examine the originality of strategies of social movements whose many voices never appear in the newspapers. What these scholars know is that to listen to street voices is a way of making history, not the *petite histoire* of European court gossip, but the painful, dark, and deep history of those who have nothing and still are able to create their own idols, the myths of their culture, the saints of their devotion.

In a country that floats adrift like ours, to analyze the social and cultural movements of a society in the process of organizing—as the Mexican cultural critic Carlos Monsváis has done—is to give that society a keel, or maybe an anchor. In this way, ordinary people come to realize that they too belong to the world and that their values, even the most disdained of them—such as the culture of poverty—have universal meaning. Anne Rubenstein gives us a Pedro Infante we had forgotten, and she rescues him from the titillating pages of yellow journalism and the shouting of two wives to reinsert him in national culture, thereby transforming him into a pillar of our collective imaginary. Seth Fein does the same for the golden age of Mexican cinema, as does Heather Levi with her delightful essay on wrestling.

In Mexico, farsighted scholars now study popular culture because they know that the behavior of the masses is crucial for understanding humankind. Interest in this topic increased after 1980. With the growth of the academic field, urban popular culture has become indispensable to the analysis of society. Is popular culture present everywhere, or only in those poor nations that still value the work of artisans, autochthonous dances, rituals, and traditions? The unique features of Mexican popular culture make it a source of insight into the national identity. In the chronicles of the past, "Indians" managed to save themselves almost every time; today the city and modernity contaminate the air of the countryside, debasing indigenous popular arts. An example of this is the aesthetics of bad taste, so widespread in Mexico and known under the category of *lo naco*. Lo naco arises simultaneously with mass culture, which Theodor W. Adorno and Max Horkheimer saw as a threat to the authenticity of art in their *Dialectic of Enlightenment*. In Mexico, however, lo naco and great art feed each other and occasionally become fused. Mexican popular culture swallows the whole of society without contradicting the essence of art.

Carlos Monsiváis, celebrated by the fifteen contributors to *Fragments of a Golden Age*, took on the task of recognizing and observing the importance of the details of popular life in the formation of Mexico. Better than anyone else, Monsiváis knows that history is not made just in Congress, but in the public square, in the street, in the tenements, in one's own home, in the movies, and even in kitchens. If in the wealthy neighborhoods of Las Lomas de Chapultepec and El Pedregal de San Angel, everything petrifies and rituals all seem the same, popular culture forms part of Mexico's constant transformation. As Jeffrey M. Pilcher reminds us, "Food served to communicate anger as well as love; a wife could burn her husband's tortillas if she suspected him of infidelity." As all the scholars involved in this volume recognize, the work of Monsiváis remains one of the clearest examples of the argument that popular culture constitutes the essential motor of transformation and of permanence. What is popular culture? Monsiváis answers: "In Mexico popular culture used to be defined as anything related to rural and indigenous communities, and that meant dances, religious festivals, herbal medicine, regional cuisines, etc. By 1970, because of the influence of North American academia and the popularizing effect of magazines, popular culture was redefined to include urban culture, including such products of the cultural industry as cinema and pop songs. At this point what is known as 'the golden age of Mexican cinema' acquires a new level of prestige and importance, with its long parade of genres—especially melodrama and *ranchera* comedy—and its gallery of sacred cows: Cantinflas, Dolores del Río, María Félix, Pedro Armendáriz, Tin Tan, Joaquín Pardavé, Ninón Sevilla, Arturo de Córdova . . ."

This book opens the doors to a Mexico that is only beginning to be recognized, even when the evidence of its strength is overwhelming. It is a world almost unknown abroad, despite the fact that popular cultural expressions such as wrestling (*lucha libre*) cross borders and become an essential item of life in cities like Los Angeles. It was also in Los Angeles that Superbarrio broke popularity records, as artists of the stature of Juan Gabriel and Lola Beltrán had done before him.

The death of Pedro Infante as a political spectacle, rock 'n roll, soap operas, life in a small Mayan village where TV arrives only through cable, photojournalistic magazines, Mexican cinema, the small screen, postcards, and erotic totemism, all form a collage and are sources of inspiration to be taken into account if we want to know "deep Mexico." Not only the "deep Mexico" of Guillermo Bonfil, but the Mexico that invades the stadiums, the one that journeys to the Villa de Guadalupe and crowds to see the Pope, the one that shouts in political rallies and in markets, the one that sits in front of television on an empty stomach, the one that listens to the radio, travels by subway and shouts "¡olé!" at bullfights and "¡gol!" at soccer games, the one that makes waves, the one that lives in the "belts of misery," the one that gets drunk and loses or wins without even betting.

The Mexico of losers is far more essential than the Mexico of businessmen, whose culture is an exact copy of the American one. There was always more originality in the twelve ropes of the lucha libre ring in which El Santo wrestled and in the locks of the Blue Demon than in the imitations of the "American way of life" of the residents of Las Lomas de Chapultepec and El Pedregal. The life of a Mexican forced to emigrate as a *bracero* is more valuable because it is a crushing, hapless life compared with that of an entrepreneur who represents 1 percent of the population.

The lives of "deep Mexico" are influenced by history, but also, as the main thesis of this book asserts, they influence history and change the course of events. This is clear, especially in the last few years, when we find an increasingly active civil society that is more and more conscious of its own power. Until recently, it has exploded only a few times since 1910: 1958, 1968, 1985. John Mraz speaks of the caravan of hunger of 1951 when fifteen thousand miners and their families marched from Nueva Rosita to Mexico City to present their plight to Miguel Alemán, president of the Republic. At that time, the newspapers never carried chronicles of life in popular neighborhoods or photographs of the so-called humble and needy. Quite the opposite. One must remember that in those years writers like Carlos Fuentes and Juan Rulfo worked as movie censors under the orders of then national director of Cinematographic Affairs Jorge Ferretis, preserving Mexico's "good image." Censorship consisted of shouting "cut" each time a scrawny dog walked on the set because its presence denigrated Mexico.

No matter what direction Mexico follows during the new administration, one has to underscore the political satisfaction of millions of Mexicans who voted against the official party, the PRI. It is commonplace to say that there are many Mexicos. It is true that many Mexicos concern us, but they all form a unique culture that is in constant evolution. Any cultural phenomenon is a fact for history; and in the last analysis, all human activity is cultural in the anthropological sense, since no one can transcend culture. Nobody fails to create a second nature. If structurally and physiologically we are imperfect beings, weak in comparison to other species, it must be that the instinct for survival is sharpened in countries threatened by hunger. Mexico is an ingenious nation that has found the way of mitigating the assault of neoliberalism, responding with social mobilization. One example is that of the Zapatista Army of National Liberation in Chiapas, springing out of indigenous experience but already a part of our popular culture. The ski mask is now an emblem of resistance of the most novel and most bellicose Mexico. Like the rest of the Latin American world, we have found a way of going from mere subsistence to existence, from eating and keeping ourselves warm to movies, television, and popular idols—and out of these we construct our cultural life as people.

The theme of popular culture is difficult, and we can deal with it like St. Augustine answering questions on the problem of time: "If they ask me what it is, I do not know; if nobody asks me, I know." In the same way, I know what popular culture is, but a general definition that encompasses all of its elements is not self-evident. The efforts of these authors, however, form a ray of light that allows us to understand that strange phenomenon: Mexico's *cultura popular*.

Elena Poniatowska, Mexico City
Translated by Aurora Camacho de Schmidt
and Arthur Schmidt

Acknowledgments

Like many collaborative projects, this one began as scribblings on a hotel napkin, made during the American Historical Association meeting in Chicago in January 1995. At that time, Mexican cultural studies in the United States was still in its infancy and Anne Rubenstein and Eric Zolov hoped to contribute to a field on the verge of a vibrant transformation. During this early stage, they received timely encouragement from Bill Beezley, who, from the start, has been an avid fan and supporter of the project. As they began to search for an appropriate venue to put together a conference on the subject, they joined forces with Gil Joseph, a kindred spirit in studies of Mexican cultural politics who brought experience as an organizer and editor of projects that likewise sought to move Mexican and Latin American historiography in new directions.

The conference that launched this collection, "Representing Mexico: Transnationalism and the Politics of Culture Since the Revolution," was held in Washington, DC, in November 1997 at the Woodrow Wilson International Center for Scholars of the Smithsonian Institution. Featuring some twenty-five scholars working on cultural politics in post-1940 Mexico across disciplines and academic generations, the event was jointly sponsored by the Latin American Program of the Woodrow Wilson Center and Yale's Council on Latin American Studies, with major funding provided by the Hewlett Foundation and additional support contributed by the History Departments of Georgetown University and Allegheny College.

Needless to say, the editors are particularly grateful to those colleagues whose ideas and energy ensured the success of the 1997 conference and made this volume possible. In addition to the writers and artists whose work appears in these pages, we wish to thank the following people who contributed research findings and commentaries in Washington: José Agustín, Roger Bartra, Bill Beezley, Aline Brandauer, Blanca de Lizaur, Joanne Hershfield, David Lorey, Julio Moreno, Aviel Roshwald, John Tutino, and Mark Wasserman. Finally, the spirited participation of audience members, including graduate students from Georgetown University, Yale University, and Rutgers University, helped ensure an especially fruitful encounter.

As the proceedings of the conference metamorphosed into a volume over the next two and a half years, we incurred other debts. Our editorial labors were underwritten by additional Hewlett funds administered by Yale's Council on Latin American Studies. John Tutino and Bill Beezley read the manuscript with characteristic care and made critical recommendations. Anu Mande and Seth Cook ably assisted in the preparation of the final manuscript. The Frederick W. Hilles Publication Fund of Yale University and the Dean's Office of Franklin and Marshall College underwrote the cost of obtaining a variety of permissions. A draft of the introduction received a painstaking vetting from a junior faculty reading group at Allegheny College (thanks are especially due here to Sergio Rivera Ayala, Shannan Mattiace, Pat Moynagh, and Barbara Riess) and also benefited from presentation at a session sponsored by the Conference of Latin American Historians during the American Historical Association meeting in Chicago in January 2000.

Finally, we take great pleasure in thanking our extraordinary editor at Duke, Valerie Millholland. Valerie supported and oversaw the project from its earliest days, helped us over the rough spots, and encouraged us to think boldly about the integration of visual materials. She continues to set the standard for editorial excellence in our field.

One last note is in order. As this volume went into production, Mexicans elected Vicente Fox of the Partido Acción Nacional (PAN), Mexico's oldest opposition party, over the official presidential candidate of the ruling Partido Revolucionario Institucional (PRI). This collection testifies to the strength of the cultural project orchestrated by the PRI during its more than seventy years in power. But it also bears witness to the creativity and resilience of the diverse Mexican society that was shaped by that project yet, in the end, unbowed by the authoritarianism that often sustained it. As scholars of Mexico, we are left to ponder the impact of this momentous political transition on the cultural fabric and lived identities of the Mexican nation. Will the categories of analysis and inquiry suggested in many of these essays cease to be relevant in a post-PRI era? Or will the impact of the PRI's cultural projects indeed continue to shape the terms of debate and identity politics even as the PRI searches for its own role as a party in opposition? Either way, it is clear that we are living in a transformative historical moment. We hope this book will further an understanding of the postrevolutionary cultural project in Mexico and even of how it might shape the unpredictable future.

Gilbert M. Joseph, Anne Rubenstein, and Eric Zolov

I

RECLAIMING THE HISTORY
OF POSTREVOLUTIONARY
MEXICO

Assembling the Fragments:
Writing a Cultural History of Mexico Since 1940

Gilbert M. Joseph, Anne Rubenstein, and Eric Zolov

Fragments are the only form I trust. —Donald Barthelme,
Unspeakable Practices, Unnatural Acts

Fragmentation, ambiguity, and disjuncture are features of complex systems . . . [but] the task remains to understand the complex architecture of parts and whole. —Fernando Coronil, foreword to *Close Encounters of Empire*

There is a historical narrative about Mexico after the Revolution that everyone knows. It could be a mural, one so familiar that we buy postcards of it without bothering to visit it first. Three scenes would occupy the foreground of this imaginary fresco. On the left would be the 1940 inauguration of President Manuel Avila Camacho, with his signature declaration *Soy creyente* (literally, "I am a believer," but by implication, "I am a Catholic") scrolling from his lips, indicating an end to the Revolution's anticlericalism and radical fervor. In the center we'd see the brutal 1968 massacre of student demonstrators by government agents at Tlatelolco Plaza, rendered in blood red and the black of despair. And at the right of the mural, marking the end of one era and the onset of the next, we would have President Carlos Salinas de Gortari, luridly depicted in *chupacabras* regalia, of course, and his neoliberal allies George Bush and Bill Clinton signing the 1994 NAFTA accord, with the Zapatista leader of Chiapas, Subcomandante Marcos, posing threateningly behind them, laptop in hand. This mural's background might feature jagged lines on a graph to represent a national economy that had cycled several times between miraculous expansion and disastrous collapse; or perhaps smoggy crowd scenes to suggest the massive population boom and staggering urbanization of Mexico City and the country at large after 1940; or maybe even ranks of faceless bureaucrats with outstretched hands to evoke the increasing power, centralization, and corruption of the state.

Our imaginary mural depicts the "revisionist" history of the postrevolutionary era that has held sway in Mexican studies since the 1970s. As Arthur Schmidt documents in his contribution to this volume, such dark-hued accounts have interpreted the trajectory of the decades since 1940 as one of "Revolution to Demolition," inverting the "Revolution to Evolution" narrative told by an earlier generation, which had depicted the postrevolutionary period in essentially benign terms to validate the Mexican state's own Whiggish tale. That earlier orthodoxy had asserted—and celebrated—Mexico's gradual attainment of political stability and a modicum of democratization, as well as an impressive threshold of economic development, all under the aegis of a modernizing, nationalist postrevolutionary regime. Challenges to this neat teleology began even as it was being formulated. Especially in the late 1950s and 1960s, novelists, artists, art critics, and journalists joined peasant organizers and unionists in resisting and rewriting the official version of the past. But the Revolution to Evolution story dominated the popular imagination as well as most scholarship until 1968, when it was shattered in the wake of the state's repressive tactics at Tlatelolco and the tumultuous, cyclical shocks that have dragged down an economy previously believed to have "taken off." Few now argue with revisionism's general political-economic critique of the Institutional Revolution's trajectory and deficiencies.

Yet many scenes, great and small, don't fit revisionism's broadly brushed mural. Consider just a few of the incongruous episodes that lack a place in the conventional picture.

It is 1947. The archbishop of Mexico City strides through Mexico's very first Sears Roebuck store, pronouncing blessings on the new enterprise as incense censers swing, shop-girls genuflect, and press photographers explode flashbulbs to publicize the thoroughly modern event.[1]

It is 1956. A year-end report on ticket sales in Central American movie theaters announces that the top three movies for the year are all Mexican-made (and all musical comedies starring Pedro Infante). Meanwhile, Che Guevara, Fidel Castro, and their small band of Cuban revolutionaries have commenced training in the techniques of guerrilla warfare in Mexico City. They gather each day for their clandestine practice in front of the popular Lindavista movie palace, strengthening themselves by their long walks through the city to and from the cinema; later, Che would claim that he modeled his self-effacing public persona after Cantinflas, Mexico's king of comedy. To oversee their physical training the exiles choose a Mexican, the professional wrestler Arsacio Vanegas, who will weep when they finally leave him behind as their rickety boat sails from a beach near Tuxpan.[2]

It is 1961. Soon Gabriel García Márquez will arrive in Mexico City to write the meditation on Colombia's past that will eventually earn him the Nobel Prize: *Cien años de soledad* (*One Hundred Years of Solitude*). Carlos Fuentes, meanwhile, has already left for Havana, where he is completing the definitive statement of revisionist historical narrative, his novel *La muerte de Artemio Cruz* (*The Death of Artemio Cruz*).[3] Although Fuentes depicts the Mexican Revolution and the Mexican state using the image of a dying rich man's putrefying body, the novelist will go on working at a high level in the Mexican diplomatic corps for another decade.

It is 1969. The village of Huautla de Jiménez, Oaxaca, has long since developed a reputation among adventurous youth from the United States and other wealthy nations as a good place to find hallucinogenic mushrooms and peaceful rural isolation. More recently, these foreigners have been joined by Mexico's own *jipitecas*, who are searching for forms of cultural rebellion in the aftermath of the destruction of the student political movement at Tlatelolco. But the Mexican state, too, is looking for a way out of the resulting political stalemate, and some within the government hope to encourage national unity by blaming the tumult of 1968 on foreign agitators. Thus, the federal and local police raid Huautla and find twenty-two foreigners they can deport, all with long hair, many with bare feet and guitars (simultaneously, the police also jail sixty-four Mexican members of a local commune). But it is already too late to stop the wave of cultural change. The gringo hippie style has become *jipi* fashion, and Mexico's middle-class urban youth are doing the previously unthinkable: dressing in "Indian" beads, embroidered shirts, and sandals. Through association with the rebels from the United States, then, the children of the social sector most likely to express contempt for Mexico's indigenous people begin borrowing the Indians' distinctive dress.[4]

It is the late 1970s, and although Chicano cultural and political groups remain active in southern California, more and more Mexicans and Mexican Americans in Los Angeles find themselves drawn to gangs that express ethnic identity and pride in the face of an increasingly hostile Anglo society. Each organization develops complex rules for communal and individual self-display, but all share one regulation: no woman may have herself tattooed with the image of the Virgin of Guadalupe. That picture belongs on male bodies only.[5]

It is 1980. In Nayarit, a group of Huichol Indians declares that they will rename their town after the man they most admire: assassinated Chilean president Salvador Allende.[6]

It is the late 1980s. Tzotzil-speaking Indians from the highland village of San Juan Chamula in Chiapas toast during festivals with Pepsi-Cola rather than beer or pulque.[7]

It is the early 1990s. A group of restless Mayan teenage girls in a small village in Yucatán assert their "modern" identities and gain a measure of local respect when they start to imitate a rock group on a popular Televisa variety show.[8]

It is 1994. New immigration laws in the United States find physical expression in a huge new metal gate at the Tijuana border, and almost overnight the muralist movement, discredited in Mexico's official culture since the middle of the 1950s (which saw both the death of Diego Rivera and the publication of José Luis Cuevas's manifesto against muralism, "La Cortina de Nopal"), revives itself to cover the gate with a wordless tale of danger, anger, and sorrow.[9]

It is 1997. The city council of Tijuana declares itself scandalized by Tijuana's terrible public image, created by media coverage of the wretched conditions there both for would-be border crossers and, even more, for the migrants from southern Mexico who come seeking work in the unregulated *maquiladoras* that cluster near the border. The council responds by taking out a patent on "the good name of the city of Tijuana." But even with NAFTA's new standards for enforcement of international copyright laws, the council will find it impossible to prevent local, national, and global exposure of the worsening conditions there.[10]

It is the end of the century, and the economy, despite or because of neoliberal reforms, is collapsing (again). Small groups of children stop traffic in the largest cities to earn tiny sums as rewards for performing stunts—eating fire, building human pyramids, shouting out popular songs—much as kids might have done on the same streets a century before. Only now, these impoverished street urchins masquerade as Carlos Salinas and Bart Simpson.

These fragments of stories suggest that the familiar narrative of post-1940 Mexico fails to accommodate the numerous contradictions and nuances embedded within the daily life of the period. Cultural and political relations among Mexicans themselves, between Mexicans and their government, between Mexicans and a host of actors and agencies in the United States, and between Mexicans and the rest of Latin America are far more complicated and ambiguous than the revisionist metanarrative will allow. Although these relationships were typically asymmetrical, they were also invariably multifaceted, and power was rarely fixed on one side or another. And rather than the story of postrevolutionary Mexico being that of the outright betrayal or slow death of the Revolution, the era is often recollected by the people who lived through it as a "Golden Age" (at least, that is how they often describe the years prior to the economic shocks of the mid-1970s). This volume seeks to excavate the cultural fragments of that golden age and, once they are dusted off and scrutinized from a variety of methodological and disciplinary perspectives, to begin to assemble them within a broader framework of historical analysis. It is our contention that such an analysis must integrate political-economy and cultural studies approaches and examine the intersection of local, national, and transnational realms.

To return to Fernando Coronil, whose epigraph introduces this essay:

> One consequence of the various "turns" (discursive, linguistic) and "posts" (postmodernism, postcoloniality) has been the tendency to identify political economy with modernist master narratives and cultural studies with postmodern fragmented stories. While one approach typically generates unilinear plots, unified actors, and integrated systems, the other produces multistranded accounts, divided subjects, and fragmented social fields. Yet there is no reason why social analysis should be cast in terms that polarize determinism and contingency, the systemic and the fragmentary. The critique of modernist assumptions should lead to a more critical engagement with history's complexity, not to a proliferation of disjointed vignettes and stories. . . . [T]he analytical inclusion of fluid subjects and unstable terrains must be complemented by the analysis of their articulation within encompassing social fields.[11]

Unfortunately, until now, the cultural history of postrevolutionary Mexico has often been discussed in terms of a bounded nationalism celebrated for its authenticity and idiosyncrasy but epitomized by the amorphous concept of *lo mexicano* (the Mexican way). Part official construct, part popular narrative, lo mexicano emerged in the 1920s as the organizing motif for a society devastated by revolutionary turmoil and in search of a unifying identity. The images, language, colors, songs, and ultimately the martyred leaders of the vanquished popular revolutionary armies were appropriated, sanitized, and then celebrated with gusto by the victorious middle-class Constitutionalist faction and their caudillo allies. Embodied politically in the new, one-party state orchestrated by the Partido Nacional Revolucionario (which was founded in 1929 and rebaptized as the Partido Revolucionario Mexicano in 1938 and the Partido Revolucionario Institucional in 1946), Mexicans across class, regional, ethnic, race, gender, and generational lines were exhorted by their rulers to feel part of the new "Revolutionary Family" to which they belonged by birth and which spoke in their name.

These processes did create a common discourse of national belonging, which was firmly in place by the time Manuel Avila Camacho became president in 1940. In the following decades, a shared mythology drawing on a pantheon of popular idols and icons—military and political heroes like Benito Juárez, figures from mass media like the wrestler El Santo, villains like La Malinche, and above all, the Virgin of Guadalupe—helped unify the nation as never before in its history. But, as we shall see, this cultural-political construct was shaped, resisted, and ultimately negotiated by a multitude of actors and interests, and lo mexicano came to serve counterhegemonic impulses as well as regime projects.

The Politics of Culture During the "Golden Age" (and Beyond)

Mexican historiography usually identifies 1940 as a turning point. The year is held to mark the beginning of the end to the revolutionary promise, embodied particularly in the now mythic figure of Lázaro Cárdenas, whose *sexenio* (six-year presidential term) ended in 1940. Although closer historical scrutiny of the Cárdenas period indicates a conscious turn to the right following the 1938 oil nationalization, 1940 still remains a convenient historical signpost of the shift in revolutionary politics away from Cárdenas's radical redistribution of wealth toward Avila Camacho's policy of intensive capital accumulation. Moreover, despite (and, in important ways, owing to) the economic dislocations generated by World War II, 1940 is often also hailed as the onset of the country's prolonged "miracle" of economic growth, which continued through the 1960s.

It is not surprising, therefore, that 1940 has been identified, retrospectively, in elite memoirs and mainstream histories alike as the beginning of

Mexico's Golden Age. This rubric is often used by scholars in connection with Mexico's "classic" period of cinematic production, which roughly spanned the years from 1940 to 1960, though it has also been taken up by memoirists, journalists, and others.[12] In this volume, however, we propose to extend the metaphor to encompass other aspects of cultural production and reception—consumer culture, print journalism, television, and tourism—during roughly the same period. Moreover, we use the phrase Golden Age as a metonym for a nostalgically depicted bygone era, a period when lo mexicano still invoked a series of roughly shared assumptions about cultural belonging and political stability under a unifying patriarchy. That patriarchy, as John Mraz contends in his contribution, which analyzes the popular illustrated magazines of the day, was anchored by "the untouchable core of the nation," *El Señor Presidente* himself. He presided over a formidable cultural state in which "the wealthy and powerful were to be emulated, the underdogs made picturesque or ignored completely or demonized if they did not follow the rules, [and] the nation was one, indivisible and homogeneous." The essays that follow, through their examination of the cultural fragments of this era, post facto representations of it, and the phenomena that constitute its legacy (latter-day *telenovelas*, well-remembered songs, the recycled images of movie stars and other popular heroes), illuminate the politics of cultural production and consumption that played a pivotal role in the construction of Mexican nationalism throughout the second half of the twentieth century.

With the Mexican state's shift to the right after 1940 came a heightened sense of patriotism. The PRI fueled nationalistic sensibilities in a variety of cultural arenas, inculcating what Mary Kay Vaughan calls "social citizenship" through public schooling, a ritualized politics of public celebrations, and the promotion of nationally validated, regional tourist sites (for example, Acapulco and Chichén Itzá) and folkloric displays (the *jarabe tapatío*, the *china poblana*).[13] These strategies enabled the party to reap ideological (and material) benefits by making an explicit connection among itself, the nation's epic Revolution, and the colors of the national flag. Mexico's entry into World War II in May 1942 reinforced this process of patriotic identification: Seth Fein's essay suggests how, in responding to the state's rallying around the flag in the cinematic fight against fascism, Mexicans also inadvertently strengthened the centralizing, authoritarian aspects of one-party rule.

The market powerfully complemented the state in the production of social citizenship; indeed, in many of the essays below, it is difficult to discern where one domain begins and the other ends, so intertwined are the two. Mexicans' attachments to the *patria grande* were enhanced by the massification of culture and the commodification of everyday life, which increasingly bound rural and urban Mexicans together in common (if still unequal) rituals of consumption.

Yet there were also certain identifiable junctures during which the state, in its increasingly protective relationship with capitalist actors, nurtured the growth and influence of a monopolistic commercial media. One such important juncture was the formation of Telesistema Mexicano in 1955, a mass media conglomerate that was the result of a merger between two of Mexico's most powerful media figures: Rómulo O'Farrill, a confidant of former president Miguel Alemán, and Emilio Azcárraga Vidaurreta, whose dominance over commercial radio paved the way for his control over television. Azcárraga quickly dominated the new relationship, consolidating a mass media dynasty that would dominate commercial production of culture in Mexico (and throughout parts of Latin America) for the next four decades. While Telesistema dominated radio and the new medium of television, a state-protected commercial cinema also flourished in the post-1940 period, directly contributing to the popularity of national icons of the silver screen, who now took their rightful place alongside imported Hollywood idols with whom Mexicans were already deeply familiar.

Thus, through such common terms of reference as movie star Jorge Negrete, radio station XEW, *fotonovelas* (comic books), and Sabritas (a popular brand of Mexican junk food), Mexicans came to share in a consumer language forged through state-sponsored cultural nationalism, import-substitution industrialization policies, and, ironically, closer ties with the United States. In effect, the forties, fifties, and sixties constituted a Golden Age of consumption, and thus of belonging. As the essays by Anne Rubenstein and Eric Zolov make clear, certain icons and referents of national identity (such as Pedro Infante and the Ballet Folklórico) were successfully exported by this powerful alliance of state and private sector; internationally they projected a colorful but increasingly cosmopolitan (and *safe*) image of Mexico.

At the same time, aspects of U.S. mass culture were "Mexicanized," further blurring the line between the foreign and the local. Consider the curious ascendancy of Pan Bimbo, Mexico's Wonder Bread clone, as a distinctly national staple. Pan Bimbo acted as the distributor for state-sponsored, "educational" comic books about Mexican history in the 1970s and for *cancioneros revolucionarios*, illustrated leaflets reprinting collections of revolutionary-era songs, in the 1990s. By doing so, it offered itself as a kind of bridge between the traditional and the modern and, even more important, between lo mexicano and the American Dream. Such processes of transculturation were especially pronounced in the popular realms of cooking, rock music, and professional wrestling, as the evocative chapters by Jeffrey Pilcher, Rubén Martínez, and Heather Levi demonstrate.

This volume argues, in effect, that Mexico's identity as a modernizing nation was directly tied to the celebration of its Golden Age at home and abroad. As the country became increasingly urban and consumer-oriented, it was imperative that the state reallocate—though by no means displace—the emphasis it gave to the countryside, which had of course been the *fuerza motriz* of the Revolution of 1910. As the chapters by Pilcher, Alex Saragoza, Zolov, Rubenstein, Steven Bachelor, Alison Greene, and Vaughan illustrate, Mexican modernity during the second half of the twentieth century came to be defined by the delicate discursive balance between rural and urban cultures. Whereas once a minuscule and insecure cosmopolitan elite eschewed rural culture as barbaric and "Indian," now enlarged middle and upper classes flaunted their internationalism while simultaneously embracing a rural culture that had been conveniently mesticized and mainstreamed. Indeed, the postrevolutionary discourse of the state identified a seemingly timeless rustic landscape as an important wellspring of Mexican cultural "authenticity." This complex intertwining of rural and urban cultural sensibilities became a hallmark of lo mexicano in the 1940s and 1950s and was integral to its Golden Age representations. Political culture illustrates the juxtaposition of rural and urban frames, as in the term *charro* (cowboy), which came to describe corrupt union bosses. In politics and other arenas, the PRI made explicit its commitment to an institutionalized revolution that encompassed both rural and urban needs, myths, and utopias. At home and abroad, Mexican identity was celebrated—and scrutinized—for its cultural and political "idiosyncrasy."[14] This penchant for "exceptionalism" provided a false sense of security for Mexicans (and foreign observers) who confided in the PRI's ability to carry out its oxymoronic project of an "institutionalized revolution."

The cultural consensus that held sway after 1940 was broken in the transformative events of the 1968 student movement and subsequent massacre at

Tlatelolco. Although societal values and attitudes toward the political regime were clearly changing prior to 1968 (witness the paralyzing strike galvanized by railroad workers in 1958[15] and Fuentes's withering critique of the Institutional Revolution in *La muerte de Artemio Cruz* in 1962), it is still possible to see the events of 1968 as the close of Mexico's Golden Age. Gone in the wake of the student massacre was any sense of coherence to the official "revolutionary" project; gone was the shared concern with international reputation, which reached its epitome with the 1968 Mexico City Olympics; gone too was any willingness to accept the PRI's rhetoric of revolutionary promise.

The students' challenge to the state's patrimonial authority and the latter's brutal response also dealt a mortal blow to the *patriarchal* culture that had been the very essence of Golden Age identity. Reassembling the patriarchal ideal of the Revolutionary Family would prove difficult, if not impossible, in the decades that followed. Some observers, ranging from anthropologist Matthew Gutmann to cultural critic Carlos Monsiváis, have noted that the disintegration of the Revolutionary Family model for the patriarchal state coincided with a whole complex of changes in family structures and daily behavior, including the discrediting of the *casa chica* (a second, informal family/household for men who could afford to keep them), greater involvement by men in child care, growing participation by women in organized feminist groups, and even the beginnings of a gay and lesbian movement.[16] Other scholars agree that recent changes in discourse around love, sex, and family have been quite impressive, but they are less sure that actual behavior (either after 1968 or before it) follows discourse in any predictable pattern.[17] But in either case, it remains clear that the end of the Revolutionary Family metaphor, which cast the state as the wise, gentle, all-providing father, was congruent with the end of the ideal of such a patriarch in ordinary Mexican families, too.

The 1970s afforded a last, somewhat desperate attempt on the part of the PRI to reassemble the shattered elements of belonging created in the wake of 1968. President Luis Echeverría's (1970–1976) unlikely return to the populist style of governance and redistributive policies of Mexico's foundational revolutionary patriarch, Lázaro Cárdenas, was a forceful reminder of the latent power of a revolutionary discourse. This populist reprise, continued under President José López Portillo (1976–1982), was underwritten by the speculative profits suggested by large discoveries of petroleum on the one hand, and the unchecked borrowing of OPEC-generated "petrodollars" on the other, which wrapped Mexico's political elites in a protective cocoon of unrestricted revenues. New public works projects, the Mexicanization of moribund industries, and a newfound public largesse for the arts, all clothed in the discourse of a rejuvenated revolutionary nationalism, purchased an extension of the public legitimacy that the PRI had lost as a result of 1968. Yet the wealth generated by oil also brought massive indebtedness, corruption, and vast economic inefficiencies that collectively set the stage for a meltdown of the nation's economy in 1982—and for the start of a debt crisis that was to plague Mexico and much of the rest of Latin America for nearly a decade.

Thus, despite the dramatic efforts by the PRI during the 1970s to reclaim center stage in the negotiation over national identity, by the early 1980s an embracing, comforting narrative of national belonging had lost its force. With the economy and the political system seeming to hover permanently on the verge of collapse (and the word *crisis* used so pervasively in daily life that it came to describe the routine pattern of Mexican life), critics on both ends of the political spectrum doubted the capacity of the PRI state to maintain its once potent legitimizing rationales of modernization and national unity. A variety of commentators began to suggest that Mexico had entered a new, "postmodern" period in which, as one political scientist provocatively observed in 1988, "the national unity forged by the PRI is unraveling, and the mosaic of civil society can no longer be ordered neatly along 'corporatist' lines. Rather, it is necessary to consult another social and political map, one which expresses Mexico's characteristic fragmentation by region, locality, class, gender, and ethnic group."[18]

In the wake of the herculean grassroots mobilization that dug Mexico City out from under the terrible earthquake of 1985, civil society seemed poised to seize the initiative from a hegemonic state in crisis; but it soon became apparent that the even more tumultuous shocks of neoliberalism were outpacing the welter of local forces that militated for democratization. The final years of the century revealed a national polity fragmented as much in terms of cultural identity as of political affiliation. As the essays by Greene and Omar Hernández and Emile McAnany suggest, the Golden Age's shared sense of imagined community has been steadily eroded under the onslaught of domestic political crisis and scandal; rampant crime and judicial impotence; international trading blocs, multinational corporate culture, "hot money" investment and flight; and the proliferation of transnational mass media, migrant circuits, and identities. Meanwhile, social movements in Chiapas and elsewhere, like artists and performers in Mexico City, have made their own claims on the national symbols, myths, and icons. But while performance artist Astrid Hadad, playwright Jesusa Rodríguez, rock band Café Tacuba, cartoonists Jis y Trino, and Subcomandante Marcos—in their own ways—have refashioned the official stories of Mexico, the PRI continues to recycle them, too, often using its powerful links to the nation's culture industries. This volume, therefore, offers both glimpses beneath the haze of nostalgia into Mexico's Golden Age and a vantage point on the postmodern reassembly of national identity in present-day Mexico.

The Challenge of Writing a New Cultural History of Post-1940 Mexico

This collection also represents the first real attempt to relate issues of representation and meaning to questions of power in a history of Mexico since 1940. In fact, to date it is one of the few academic histories that exists in English for post-1940s Mexico.[19] What explains the reluctance of professional historians to transcend the cardenista divide? Some Mexicanists may fear that to study the latter half of the twentieth century is to *lose Mexico*— to encounter little more than crass transnational capitalism, an all-too-familiar McWorld set down on the Zona Rosa. Moreover, unlike earlier eras of the nation's history, the post-1940 period offers the historian few documents to undertake a comprehensive study of politics (or at least of "high politics"); these remain classified by the state. At the same time, historians may fear being overwhelmed by the amount of print from the period, from true-crime tabloids to scholarly journals, that awaits them in the archives. This type of source material, both because of its sheer volume and the disreputable aura that clings to it, can also leave scholars in a panic over authenticity. What is "real" in the world of fanzines, *teleguías*, dittoed manifestos from obscure political groups that perhaps existed only on paper, maps to metros still unbuilt? And when has a historian read enough of the infinite supply to begin to analyze it?

Thus, for very plausible reasons, historians seem to have calculated that the period was best left to journalists of greater or lesser reliability, politicians with axes to grind, social scientists and policy makers with models to perfect, and postmodern cultural theorists in search of hybrid art forms. Of course, many scholars from these fields have made contributions of lasting value: Elena Poniatowska, Carlos Monsiváis, Guillermo Bonfil Batalla,

Néstor García Canclini, José Agustín, and Roger Bartra, among others, have provided maps to the territories into which historians have, thus far, refused to enter.[20] But this does not excuse historians from their own responsibility to investigate and interpret this elusive, dazzling, and confusing Golden Age—and its aftermath.

The contributors to this volume (historians and historically inspired social scientists and cultural critics) refuse to cede the field to others. We contend that the politics of culture constitutes one of the keys to understanding Mexico after 1940; that the PRI's economic and political project would surely have failed if the cultural project had not been in place; and that the PRI's cultural regime was inextricably bound up with the political economy of the nation. We further assert that the volume's focus on cultural history provides the best and *sometimes the only* window onto crucial aspects of the post-1940 Mexican experience, particularly the negotiation of postrevolutionary national and local identities and the nation's multistranded participation in transnational commodity culture; it also enables us to gain a more than superficial understanding of the relative continuity of political practice and the relative stability of social hierarchies prior to the 1990s.

And because our attention is not focused primarily on the upper levels of the state, the relative absence of "official" archival materials does not cripple our enterprise. Indeed, traditional caches of documentation and the conventional methods of political and social history would not prepare us to ask or answer the kinds of questions regarding the politics of cultural production, dissemination, and reception that lie at the heart of this project. Moreover, as the essays that follow attest, there is an abundance of business records and audiovisual materials from the culture industries themselves; a host of nongovernmental organizations, including the mainstream and alternative press, as well as private archives, offer access to photo collections, recipe books, and other less traditional sources; and scholars of the post-1940 period have recourse to oral history and ethnographic techniques.

Although the volume's contributors represent diverse disciplinary, generational, and national perspectives and might disagree with one another regarding the manner in which structural and poststructural approaches should be deployed, we nonetheless have discovered that we form a discursive community. Most of us also share formation in the U.S. academy, either through graduate training or as professors or both. Perhaps Néstor García Canclini's celebration of "hybrid culture" appeals to so many of us because of our own mixed identities, as we slide among transnational, national, regional, local, ethnic, religious, political, generational, or professional subject positions. As Quetzil Castañeda has appropriately suggested elsewhere, sometimes Chihuahua appears just outside our front doors in Connecticut or Pennsylvania, and sometimes we imagine ourselves to be in Mexico when we're really only in Mexico City.[21]

The volume's lineage can be traced through a recent movement in Latin American and Mexican studies to conceptualize *culture* within a broad Gramscian, even Foucauldian, tradition, one that examines the links between culture and power.[22] The contributors to *Fragments of a Golden Age* all understand "culture" to mean something including but not limited to institutional or "high" culture, but beyond that, it would be very difficult for all of us to agree on a definition of this most vexed term. Some of us view culture, following E. P. Thompson, as a social process; others might prefer a more explicitly Geertzian position, defining culture as the shared understandings, symbols, and meanings embedded in the daily practices of elite and popular (or foreign and local) groups. But that definition includes a firm refusal to specify—in checklist fashion—the contents of those understandings, symbols, and meanings, a static and reductionist undertaking at best.[23]

All of us, being historically minded, are interested in the ways that elite/foreign and popular/local understandings are constantly being remade. At once socially constituted (it is the product of present and past activity) and socially constituting (it is part of the meaningful context in which activity takes place), culture never represents an autonomous domain. Instead, popular and elite (or local and foreign) cultures are produced in relation to each other through a dialectic of encounter that takes place in arenas and contexts of unequal power and entails reciprocal borrowings, expropriations, translations, misunderstandings, negotiations, and transformations.[24] In the essays that follow, cultural practices, artifacts, institutions (markets as well as museums), and "contact zones" (culture industries, tourism, cuisine, sports, riots, and leisure pursuits) are accompanied by the broader cultural realm of aspirations, narratives, ideas, values, attitudes, tastes, and habits.[25] Thus, the manifestations of post-1940 Mexican culture are many and diverse, but their history is invariably interwoven with power-laden intentions and consequences.

The volume's contributors agree on the importance of writing a history of post-1940 Mexico that features a variety of actors possessing multiple identities that were often ambiguous and contradictory. We are mapping pathways of historical change that are rarely neat or linear and typically involve multiple domains of social life. Thus, even though Mexico's modernizing state had a penchant for dichotomizing discourses (lo mexicano vs. *lo extranjero*) and binary constructs (its trumpeting of a Golden Age of nationalism and consumerism itself presupposed a more "traditional" and problematic revolutionary epoch), we are committed to unpacking these state projects and forms. Several of the essays examine how the state and ordinary Mexicans, working sometimes in opposition to and sometimes in collaboration with each other, used these dichotomies for their own divergent or overlapping purposes, often redefining the binaries in the process.

As we have unpacked the false oppositions of nationalist rhetoric, so we have attempted to undo a false opposition seemingly inherent in the field of cultural studies: the neat division between studies of "production" and studies of "reception." This naturalized distinction, particularly central to scholarship on mass media, seemed to obscure more than it clarified. Consider the most popular cable TV programs in present-day Mexico, many of them made in the United States, some in Brazil, a few others in Japan. Who can be said to produce them? Who, precisely, is receiving them? By the time these shows appear on Mexican television sets they have been through a complex process of translation, informal censorship, reediting, and dubbing, along with the adding and subtracting of musical sound tracks, sound effects, laugh tracks, and advertisements—all of which have radically altered them from the form they once had in their countries of origin. The meaning of these TV shows, furthermore, is not produced by the foreigners who make the shows, nor by the state and private enterprises that control the shows' entry into the Mexican market, nor even by the individual members of the audience, but by all of these cultural actors in relationship with one another. The line between "production" and "reception," then, cannot be drawn without dividing our understanding of this delicate cultural process in half. Several contributors to this volume are working more or less consciously toward creating new models for studying culture that do not rely on this false distinction.

Read together, this volume's essays contrast the robust cultural state of the 1940s and 1950s with its diminished successor in later decades. It was not that the Mexican state forfeited its claim to produce and regulate national culture; rather, it lost its grip in the face of escalating internal demands for inclusion, deepening economic crisis, and the formidable cultural challenge posed by multinational corporations. Without denying the negative and culturally homogenizing effects that increasing North American penetration has had on Mexico, these essays also underscore its empowering and culturally differentiating consequences.[26] Yet even as the contributors attempt to historicize the state's cultural project in the context of shifting political-economic trends and the new subjectivities these helped produce, they also draw our attention to divisions within the state itself. The state was far from monolithic; some might argue that a coherent cultural project, other than the survival of the state itself, never really existed over the long term. Not only did the cultural policies of post-1940 presidential administrations differ markedly in their prevailing emphases; there was significant competition (and often bitter argument) among the cultural dependencies of each administration. To cite but one example, at the height of the Golden Age's frenzy of consumption, dissident leftists on the government's Censorship Commission for periodicals argued the need to propagate "socialist culture" among Mexico's youth, lest disturbing, unchecked trends in the nation's culture industries turn the nation's children into North Americans.[27]

Of course, given the exploratory nature of this volume, there are obvious limits to its ability to flesh out Mexico's complex politics of culture. The essays are stronger on the fashioning and dissemination of Golden Age cultural projects than on the manner in which they were appropriated at the grass roots; similarly, the volume's coverage of cultural politics is much richer for Mexico City than for provincial, rural, and indigenous Mexico. Finally, although the contributors pay a good deal of attention to international flows and encounters and the process of transculturation that ensued in a variety of contexts, the collection lacks a sustained focus on the process of migration to and from the United States. In short, there is much work to be done as historians, anthropologists, cultural critics, and others reclaim Mexico's present and recent past from the policy sciences and seek to elaborate analyses that integrate issues of meaning and representation with questions of politics and power.

This is necessary work, but also, we hope, work that will bring some pleasure both to those who create it and those who read it. There is a great deal of room for play here. The phrase Golden Age itself has many valences; contemporary writers and artists sometimes employed the term sarcastically to point up its political uses by the official party and its complacent ally, the new middle class. In *The Death of Artemio Cruz*, Carlos Fuentes wrote: "Hah: imagine yourselves . . . you hypocrites, saving penny by penny to buy a car on time . . . making little monthly payments on some scrubby lot somewhere, sighing for a refrigerator, sitting in a cheap neighborhood movie every Saturday . . . eating out once a month: imagine yourselves subscribing to all the phoniness . . . having to shout, Why there's no place like Mexico! in order to feel alive; having to be proud of serapes and Cantinflas and mariachi and *mole poblano* in order to feel alive!"[28]

In the face of this fierce catalog of all that is phony and hypocritical in Fuentes's version of Mexico circa 1960, we insist that Cantinflas, and refrigerators, and the people who used them to define themselves as Mexican citizens deserve respectful attention. Against the broad brush strokes of official and revisionist depictions of the Golden Age, the contributors to this volume together have assembled a mosaic of our own, finding new meanings in mariachi and mole poblano, agreeing that such tesserae can have dangerously sharp edges, but also can delight and, when joined together carefully, enlighten us.

Notes

1   See the paper presented by Julio Moreno, "Constructing the Mexican Dream: Consumer Culture in Mexico City and the Reconstruction of Modern Mexico in the 1940s," at the conference Representing Mexico: Transnationalism and the Politics of Culture Since the Revolution, Woodrow Wilson Center, Washington, DC, November 1997.

2   For Infante's enormous popularity, see Anne Rubenstein's essay in this volume. For the cultural politics of *lucha libre*, Mexican professional wrestling, see Heather Levi's contribution. For the story of the Cubans' years in Mexico, their involvement with Vanegas, and Che's use of the Cantinflas persona, see Paco Ignacio Taibo II, *Ernesto Guevara también conocido como El Che* (Mexico City: Editorial Planeta, 1996), 113–37 (edición bolsillo).

3   Gabriel García Márquez, *One Hundred Years of Solitude*, trans. Gregory Rabassa (New York: Harper and Row, 1970), originally published in Spanish in 1967; Carlos Fuentes, *The Death of Artemio Cruz*, trans. Sam Hileman (New York: Farrar, Straus and Giroux, 1964), originally published in Spanish in 1962.

4   See Eric Zolov, *Refried Elvis: The Rise of the Mexican Counterculture* (Berkeley: University of California Press, 1999), 140–45.

5   "Revered Catholic Icon Becomes Mysterious Target of Vandals in Los Angeles," *New York Times*, 24 October 1999, section A; Mary Jo Dudley, commentary presented at the conference Transforming Cultures in the Americas, Cornell University, February 1998.

6   Eduardo Galeano, *Memory of Fire: Century of the Wind*, trans. Cedric Belfrage (New York: Pantheon/Random House, 1988), 277–78.

7   See the chapter by Jeffrey Pilcher in this volume.

8   See the chapter by Alison Greene in this volume.

9   See Néstor García Canclini, "Latins or Americans: Narratives of the Border," *Canadian*

Journal of Latin American Studies 23, no. 46 (1998): 125–26. For "La Cortina de Nopal" in English translation, see José Luis Cuevas, "The Cactus Curtain," *Evergreen Review* 2 (1959): 111–20.

10   García Canclini, "Latins or Americans."

11   Fernando Coronil, foreword to *Close Encounters of Empire: Writing the Cultural History of U.S.–Latin American Relations*, ed. Gilbert M. Joseph, Catherine LeGrand, and Ricardo Salvatore (Durham, NC: Duke University Press, 1998), ix.

12   Julia Tuñón, who defines the *edad de oro* of Mexican cinema as the period 1939–1952, points to a broader definition used by other film scholars of "the mid-thirties to the mid-fifties." See Tuñón, *Mujeres de luz y sombra en el cine mexicano* (Mexico City: El Colegio de México, 1998), 13, n. 1. Manuel Magaña Contreras, in his memoir of Mexico City life, identifies the Golden Years of the city as beginning in the early 1930s and ending sometime around 1960. See Magaña Contreras, *Ciudad abierta: Los años de oro* (Mexico City: Análisis y Evaluación de Prensa, 1996), 3.

13   See Vaughan's essay in this volume, as well as the essays by Eric Zolov, Alex Saragoza, and Quetzil Castañeda. The *jarabe tapatío* is a traditional dance from the Jalisco region that features vigorous footwork. The *china poblana* is a folkloric representation of women from Puebla as a mestiza in picturesque dress; it is said to have originated in the sixteenth century.

14   The two most famous treatments of Mexican identity are Octavio Paz, *The Labyrinth of Solitude: Life and Thought in Mexico* (New York: Grove Press, 1961), and Oscar Lewis, *The Children of Sánchez* (New York: Vintage Books, 1961), but there are hundreds of more obscure examples of this genre.

15   The strike is discussed by Vaughan and by Steven Bachelor in his essay on the militant consumer culture of Golden Age autoworkers.

16   See Matthew C. Gutmann, *The Meanings of Macho: Being a Man in Mexico City* (Berkeley: University of California Press, 1996); Carlos Monsiváis, "Los que tenemos unas manos que no nos pertenecen," *Debate Feminista* 16 (October 1997): 11–33, and "Lo masculino y lo femenino al final del milenio," in *Masculino/femenino al final de milenio*, ed. Dulce María López Vega (Mexico City: APIS, 1998), 7–24.

17   See Ana María Amuchástegui Herrera, "Virginidad y iniciación sexual en México: La sobrevivencia de saberes sexuales subyugados frente a la modernidad," *Debate Feminista* 18 (October 1998): 131–51; Kaja Finkler, *Women in Pain: Gender and Morbidity in Mexico* (Philadelphia: University of Pennsylvania Press, 1994), 25–39; and Manuel Fernández Perera, "El macho y el machismo," in *Mitos mexicanos*, ed. Enrique Florescano (Mexico City: Editorial Aguilar, 1995), 179–84.

18   Alberto Aziz Nassif, "Modernización y vacío," paper delivered at the colloquium Modernization and Postmodernity in Mexico, Center for U.S.-Mexican Studies, University of California at San Diego, February 1988.

19   For a review of the existing literature, see Schmidt's essay in this volume; also see Stephen R. Niblo, *Mexico in the 1940s* (Wilmington, DE: Scholarly Resources, 1999). Niblo's introduction summarizes all previous historical research on the period as follows: "The historiographical landscape for the final three-fifths of the twentieth century looks bleak" (xviii).

20 A (very incomplete) list of such important contributions to the study of Mexico after 1940 would have to include José Agustín, *Tragicomedia mexicana*, 3 vols. (Mexico City: Editorial Planeta, 1990, 1992, 1998); Roger Bartra, *The Imaginary Networks of Political Power*, trans. Claire Joysmith (New Brunswick, NJ: Rutgers University Press, 1992); Guillermo Bonfil Batalla, *México profundo*, trans. Philip Dennis (Austin: University of Texas Press, 1996), and *Pensar nuestra cultura* (Mexico City: Alianza Editorial, 1991); Jorge G. Castañeda, *La herencia: Arqueología de la sucesión presidencial en México* (Mexico City: Editorial Alfaguara, 1999); Jean Franco, *Plotting Women: Gender and Representation in Mexico* (New York: Columbia University Press, 1989); Néstor García Canclini, *Culturas híbridas* (Mexico City: Grijalbo, 1990), and *Transforming Modernity*, trans. Lidia Lozano (Austin: University of Texas Press, 1993); Carlos Monsiváis, *Días de guardar* (Mexico City: Biblioteca Era, 1970), and *Los rituales del caos* (Mexico City: Biblioteca Era, 1995); Carlos Monsiváis and Carlos Bonfil, *A través del espejo: El cine mexicano y su público* (Mexico City: Ediciones el Milagro, 1994); Elena Poniatowska, *Nobody, Nothing: The Voices of the Mexico City Earthquake*, trans. Aurora Camacho de Schmidt and Arthur Schmidt (Philadelphia: Temple University Press, 1995), and *La noche de Tlatelolco* (Mexico City: Biblioteca Era, 1971); Annick Prieur, *Mema's House, Mexico City: On Transvestites, Queens, and Machos* (Chicago: University of Chicago Press, 1998); Sara Sefcovich, *La suerte de la consorte* (Mexico City: Océano, 1999), and *México: País de ideas, país de novelas* (Mexico City: Grijalbo, 1987); Josefina Zoraida Vázquez, ed., *Historia de la lectura en México* (Mexico City: El Colegio de México, 1988).

21 Quetzil Castañeda, "A Mystery Theatre in Chichén Itzá: Erotics, Totemism, Postcards, Ruins," paper presented at the conference Representing Mexico: Transnationalism and the Politics of Culture Since the Revolution, Woodrow Wilson Center, Washington, DC, November 1997. An odd but indisputable fact: nearly all the most important (re)formulations of Mexican identity and the Mexican condition of the past half-century, at least, have been created by artists, writers, and scholars whose own *mexicanidad* has been made questionable by immigrant status, residence or training outside the country, sexual orientation, Judaism or Protestantism or atheism, or some combination of the above. Like Frida Kahlo (the bisexual daughter of immigrants), Tina Modotti (herself an immigrant), Carlos Fuentes (who spent his childhood and much of his working life in Europe and the United States), García Canclini (an immigrant), and Monsiváis (a Protestant), most of the contributors to this volume are self-conscious outsiders. Which, of course, is not to deny that most of us also speak from a privileged position in the United States.

22 This lineage in Latin American studies includes many important collections of essays. We have drawn special inspiration from Daniel Balderston and Donna Guy, eds., *Sex and Sexuality in Latin America* (New York: New York University Press, 1997); Brenda Jo Bright and Liza Bakewell, eds., *Looking High and Low: Art and Cultural Identity* (Tucson: University of Arizona Press, 1995); William H. Beezley, Cheryl English Martin, and William E. French, eds., *Rituals of Rule, Rituals of Resistance: Public Celebrations and Popular Culture in Mexico* (Wilmington, DE: Scholarly Resources, 1994); Gilbert M. Joseph and Daniel Nugent, eds., *Everyday Forms of State Formation: Revolution and the Negotiation of Rule in Modern Mexico* (Durham, NC: Duke University Press, 1994); Gilbert M. Joseph, Catherine C. Legrand, and Ricardo D. Salvatore, eds., *Close Encounters of Empire* (Durham, NC:

Duke University Press, 1998); and the recent issue of the *Hispanic American Historical Review* 79 (May 1999) devoted to "The New Cultural History of Mexico."

23 Florencia Mallon, participating in the recent heated debate in the *Hispanic American Historical Review* 79 (May 1999) regarding the practice of Mexican cultural history, defined "culture" as "a series of arguments over values and standards of behavior, rather than as a discrete set of norms and values that guide all kinds of conduct in society." See Mallon, "Time on the Wheel: Cycles of Revisionism and the 'New Cultural History,'" 345.

24 See Gilbert M. Joseph, "Close Encounters," in *Close Encounters of Empire*, ed. Joseph, LeGrand, and Salvatore, 3–46, especially 8.

25 The notion of "contact zones" is drawn from Mary Louise Pratt, *Imperial Eyes: Travel Writing and Transculturation* (New York: Routledge, 1992).

26 See particularly the essays in this volume by Bachelor, Greene, Pilcher, and Vaughan.

27 See, for instance, Anne Rubenstein, *Bad Language, Naked Ladies, and Other Threats to the Nation: A Political History of Comic Books in Mexico* (Durham, NC: Duke University Press, 1998), chap. 4.

28 Fuentes, *The Death of Artemio Cruz*, 79.

Making It Real Compared to What?
Reconceptualizing Mexican History Since 1940

Arthur Schmidt

The six decades of Mexican life since 1940 have ceased to be the exclusive property of essayists, journalists, and practitioners of the policy sciences and are now passing into the realm of historical studies.[1] Only a generation ago, Charles Cumberland's history of Mexico relegated most of the experience after the Mexican Revolution to posthistory. Entitled "At Last," the final chapter to his *Mexico, the Struggle for Modernity* remained both devoid of periodization and smugly content. Cumberland concluded that although "Mexico by the mid-1960s had not yet arrived in the Promised Land . . . at long last the leaders of the Mexican nation had come to realize that the greatest natural resource available to any society is its people, who with proper training and stimuli can do wondrous things. With that recognition the battle was half won, and it was this realization which gave President [Gustavo] Díaz Ordaz the confidence with which he assumed office in 1964."[2]

Since those words were written, Mexico has moved out from under the "shadow of the Mexican Revolution" into a time of great uncertainty. The country's deeper incorporation into the globalizing world economy has been fraught with suffering and instability. Mexican statecraft, far from treating the "people" as "the greatest natural resources available," has been more inclined to manipulate than to trust civil society. There has been little of the confident march toward progress envisioned by Cumberland. Various "political reforms" as well as an economic "Second Revolution" have taken place, yet Mexico has not completed the much heralded "transition" to political democracy and steady market-based economic growth.[3] Mexico today must simultaneously construct a democratic political system out of nondemocratic traditions, promote economic growth through market economic policies, narrow the widening gap between rich and poor, and create an authentic rule of law.[4] It remains far from certain whether Mexico will be able to bring about constructive change in the midst of the powerfully creative yet powerfully destabilizing forces of economic globalization. As Héctor Aguilar Camín notes, Mexicans today "are living through a change of historical period that transforms yesterday's defining realities into relics of the past."[5] In the retrospective view of some, the three decades after 1940 have become a departed "Golden Age" of stability and prosperity, the object of nostalgic lamentations over *el México que se nos fue* (the Mexico that we lost).[6]

The need for perspective on Mexico's crisis makes the present moment opportune for revising historical understanding of the country's recent past. Mexico's processes of change are so complicated and unpredictable that they engulf the writing of history itself. Today, as in the past, the fundamental reinterpretations of Mexican history must originate in a moment of frightful crisis, from the seeming "sensation of finding oneself facing the foreseeable end of a civilization, a country, a nation."[7] Keeping faith with this inventive interpretive tradition requires going beyond the "regime history" that has characterized the writing about contemporary Mexico.[8] Although this emphasis on national decision-making sectors has inevitably constituted a first step in converting the domain of "current events" into a historical past, it has ceased to serve as an adequate basis for understanding the rich complexities of Mexico since 1940.

As Fernando Coronil observed in a passage cited by the editors of this volume in their introduction: "The critique of modernist assumptions should lead to a more critical engagement with history's complexity, not to a proliferation of disjoined vignettes and stories. . . . Fragmentation, ambiguity, and disjuncture are features of complex systems, rather than their opposite. Lest we miss the forest for the trees, the task remains to understand the complex architecture of parts and whole."[9] A deeper and more dynamic comprehension of Mexico's experience since 1940 requires approaches that will integrate culture, economics, society, and the state into patterns of interaction with one another in a variety of settings: local, regional, national, and global.[10] New approaches will have to embrace a sense of change at their core. The writing of post-1940 Mexican history must exhibit sensibilities of method and interpretation that can cope with indeterminate, ambiguous outcomes instead of fitting any established "master narrative."

Mexico: Revolution to Evolution to Demolition

Two broad master narratives may be said to have framed Mexico's contemporary history over the past several decades, outlooks that might be informally termed the "Revolution to Evolution" and "Revolution to Demolition" schools. They emerged to interpret the two principal political economies that have governed Mexico since 1940: import-substitution industrialization (1940–1982) and neoliberalism (1982–present).

Revolution to evolution
A rosy and often ahistorical view of post-1940 Mexico, the Revolution to Evolution perspective derived from the "nation-building" legacies of the Mexican Revolution (*forjando patria* in Manuel Gamio's apt phrase) and the post–World War II concerns of policy sciences in the United States.[11] It emphasized Mexico's development, the stable process of nation building and material progress that seemed to characterize the country for nearly three decades after 1940. It stressed as well the new patterns of friendship and cooperation that first emerged between U.S. and Mexican governing circles during the Second World War.[12] U.S. social scientists during the cold war, including some historians such as Howard Cline, Stanley Ross, and Frank Tannenbaum, responded to Third World pressures for decolonization, anti-imperialism, and radical social change by defining Mexico's as the "preferred revolution." In their search for anticommunist models, they contended that "the Mexican experience afforded a preferred solution for the hemispheric problem of change and development" and had "much to offer the world."[13]

Naturally, such opinions enhanced the self-image of decision-making circles in Mexico. Post-1940 Mexican economic and political elites viewed "modern Mexico as the negation of its past."[14] U.S. political scientist Frank Brandenburg codified their outlook when he defined what he called "The Mexican Proposition": "Revolution in Mexico, the permanent revolution, is a dynamic political, social, and economic fact. First unleashed in 1910, its perennial goal is striking in its simplicity: Social justice for all Mexicans.

Many routes have been tried, some followed, some expanded, some abandoned, but all have been directed toward achieving the over-all goal. . . . Revolution for this modern Mexican is more than an ideal: It is the continuing struggle to transform his society into the shape of an ideological image. The Mexican sees himself as part of this struggle."[15]

The claim of the ongoing Revolution provided an important unifying myth that offered legitimacy to the post-1940 political system and defined the *mestizo* as the incarnation of the national citizen to whom the future belonged.[16] Mestizo nationalism and modernity went hand in hand to transform the "Indian problem" into innumerable "unique, particular, and concrete" matters that analysts assumed would be resolved by economic development.[17] Lively discussions might take place in Mexican magazines and newspapers about the meaning of *lo mexicano* and *mexicanidad*, but their impact on social thought ultimately proved static as the subtleties of essayists such as Samuel Ramos and Octavio Paz disappeared amid essentialist popularizations of dubious psychological or historical validity.[18] Mexican national character was said to have "successfully amalgamated with the main traditions of Western-style political democracy," producing "a coherent pattern of attitudes and mechanisms that form a unique New World 'Middle Way.' "[19]

The Revolution to Evolution perspective had particular praise for Mexico's economic growth and political stability in the decades after 1940. In a world context favorable to the concept of national development, Mexico's industrial growth proved outstanding. Between 1940 and 1970, the Mexican economy expanded more than sixfold, and manufacturing output rose by a factor of ten. Foreign capital, especially from the United States, readily invested within the protective tariff walls of the Mexican market, playing an especially strong role in the growth of modern manufacturing.[20] Political and economic elites in Mexico formed understandings that allowed for high levels of private capital formation and rapid economic expansion in a context of low inflation and orderly government finances, particularly during the years of "stabilizing development" from 1955 to 1970.[21] Mexico was said to have broken with the archaic monopoly interests that had controlled economic life prior to 1910, creating in their stead "a socially responsible class of Mexican entrepreneurs" that knew how to work in partnership with state participation in the economy. "Private capital, management, and personnel, no less than their counterparts in the public sector, are forcefully building the nation," wrote Brandenburg.[22]

Steady material expansion and the orderly transfer of presidential power from one *sexenio* to the next encouraged observers to see constructive change as emanating from the actions of Mexico's economic and political elites rather than from the society at large. Brandenburg discussed the country's stable political change as a product of the actions of the "Revolutionary Family" composed at the top by the president—the "liberal Machiavellian"—and about twenty political leaders; at the second level by an "inner council" of about two hundred figures from the major private and public bureaucracies; and at the third level by "the formal political apparatus." This "family" even had its own "revolutionary creed" rooted in concepts of nationalism and social justice by which it brought modern improvement to the rest of Mexico.[23]

Post-1968

Ultimately, domestic and international events made it impossible for the Revolution to Evolution interpretation to recruit a second generation of adherents. The 1968 Tlatelolco massacre dramatically showed the intolerant, autocratic character of the political system, and increased income inequality undermined the notion of a perpetual Revolution that brought "social justice." Instability became more common as both the global and domestic economic systems faced structural upheavals. During the populist presidency of Luis Echeverría Alvarez (1970–1976) the old understandings between political and economic elites broke down. Echeverría sought unsuccessfully to raise the tax burdens on the wealthy enough to pay for ambitious new programs aimed at overcoming social inequities and winning back popular support for the regime. The private sector resisted, seeking greater economic autonomy. More mature and self-confident, it profoundly distrusted the economic statism at the core of the government's response to rapidly changing domestic and international conditions.[24]

A heavy dependence on foreign capital and a growing external disequilibrium constituted problematic features of Mexico's import-substitution model.[25] First under Echeverría and subsequently even more under José López Portillo (1976–1982), when Mexico's proven oil reserves gained it global recognition as a "newly industrializing country" on the rise, the state borrowed extensively abroad to cover its growing internal and external shortfalls. Governed by its own insatiable appetite for oil, the United States pressured Mexico to export as much petroleum as possible. International bank circles, flush with recycled petrodollars after the oil price rises of 1973, were more than willing to accommodate Mexico's profligate borrowing through profligate lending. By the early 1980s, however, the López Portillo government suddenly found itself with its back against the wall. Anti-inflation policies in the United States had helped provoke global recession. Reduced petroleum demand, high international interest rates, an overvalued peso, and growing capital flight forced the Mexican government in August 1982 to declare that it could no longer meet its foreign debt payments.[26]

Despite López Portillo's last-ditch populist flourish in nationalizing the Mexican banking system in September, the country's international financial breakdown in 1982 marked the end of its post-1940 economic system. By that time, analysts from all ideological perspectives had long since rejected the smooth gradualist visions of national development inherent in the Revolution to Evolution interpretation. Economic and political uncertainty had induced writers as varied as Daniel Cosío Villegas, Pablo González Casanova, Roger Hansen, Judith Hellman, Kenneth Johnson, and Gabriel Zaid to produce critical analyses of the previously much praised "Mexican system."[27] Yet, from the vantage point of the present, one is struck by how much of the Revolution to Evolution approach survived in later scholarship. The focus of research continued to be primarily the upper decision-making realms of the political system as the concept of the Revolutionary Family gave way to more detailed analyses of Mexican elite patterns. Roderic Ai Camp generated a vast compendium of valuable biographical material and analyzed the linkages between educational background and achievements in politics. Peter Smith worked with over six thousand individuals who held prominent national office after 1900 to document patterns of political mobility, the structured influence of political *camarillas* (factions), and the existence of separate entrepreneurial and political elites in Mexico.[28] As with these two examples, much of this scholarship constituted fundamentally important and excellent work. Significant for historical interpretation, however, a largely unstated, collective assumption developed that "Mexico's political stability and resilience" could be understood "as a function of unilateral state power," and that the state acted "as the sole initiator of social reforms."[29] Even radical new initiatives came from the top, as in the case of the shift toward economic neoliberalism undertaken by the state technocratic elite under Carlos Salinas de Gortari (1988–1994), a shift that "would have been impossible without the prior existence of such a well-calibrated authoritarian machine."[30]

The influence of Southern Cone studies further encouraged this concentration on the power of the state, bringing the terms "corporatist" and "authoritarian" into discussions of the "Mexican system" to explain its lack of change.[31] As depicted, this "essentially inclusionary" civilian system successfully controlled issues of access and succession, dominated elections, and created a vast network of adherents to the country's "successful one-party authoritarian regime."[32] Even in studies that looked at the local content of political life, "the fight was always basically the same and the state always won."[33] Continuity and a lack of change were said to characterize Mexican political life, in contrast to the rest of Latin America.[34] Radical scholars in Mexico and the United States focused on the powerful co-optive and coercive capacities of the system to prevent change and to promote the conditions most suitable for capitalist accumulation.[35] The concentration on state power and the emphasis on the effectiveness of corporatism marginalized society from any explanatory processes. Mexican people did not act as a causal force in their own history. Even the dominant legacy of Lázaro Cárdenas was said to be social pacification and the creation of the instruments of state hegemony: "Short of rebellion, Cárdenas had returned popular classes he had mobilized in the mid-1930s to powerlessness, within the party and in the general electorate. . . . They were to be solely beneficiaries, dependent upon an exclusive ruling group, acting through a growing institutional apparatus which alone determined and addressed their needs."[36]

While rejecting the Revolution to Evolution interpretation, post-1968 analysts nevertheless succumbed to its "nationalization of society," the tendency to "subordinate the existence of individuals of all classes to their status as citizens of the nation-state, to the fact of their being 'nationals.'"[37] Like writers from the Revolution to Evolution school, their views, although far more critical, fell within the nation-building tradition of historical writing that emerged in Mexico from the Reforma onward. This tradition lauded the formation of a state capable of dominating the country's territory, defending it internationally, and transforming its inhabitants into modern citizens.[38] Although Mexico after Tlatelolco experienced an era of major crisis, political conflict and change were still seen as anomalies in post-1968 treatments of contemporary Mexican history.[39] Studies paid little attention to local or regional patterns and almost none to culture, other than in the static mold of the "civic culture."[40] Although they rejected the glossy superficiality of the Revolution to Evolution scholarship, most analyses still neglected the give and take of political life, ignored differences between national and local politics, and generally excluded society, particularly the popular classes, from any significant influence on political decisions.[41] Even in the world of anthropology, culturalist explanations for poverty retained their intellectual and political preeminence until at least the 1970s, reinforcing a top-down view of post-1940 Mexico experience in both "traditional" rural and "modern" urban areas.[42]

Revolution to demolition

Many of these deficiencies continued under the aegis of "transition to democracy" interpretations after 1982. The governments of Miguel de la Madrid (1982–1988), Carlos Salinas de Gortari (1988–1994), and Ernesto Zedillo (1994–2000) converted Mexico's political economy to a "neoliberal" model, first through an International Monetary Fund austerity program, and subsequently through initiatives to liberalize domestic prices, international trade, and investment as well as to privatize state enterprises, including the nationalized banks. The centerpiece of economic reform was the negotiation of the North American Free Trade Agreement (NAFTA), which went into effect in January 1994. The nearly two decades of neoliberal reform in Mexico have been ones of great hardship for most Mexicans: austerity and low oil prices brought a precipitous drop in living standards in the mid-1980s that has still not been fully recovered; the peso devaluation crisis of 1994–1995 resulted in a 6.2 percent plunge in the GDP; and economic growth rates on the average still rank below those of the import-substitution years.[43] A recent evaluation argues that Mexico's "bigger economic pie has meant very little for a majority of the population. . . . Unfortunately, what's missing—wage and employment gains, improvements in income distribution, and sustainable growth—may never follow 'naturally' from the new market model."[44]

Nevertheless, many commentators have assumed an inevitable success for the way Mexico has been integrated more fully into the world economy. They posit a natural correlation between "free markets" and "free societies." As economic reform changed Mexico, so their thinking has gone, Mexico would naturally undergo a transition to democracy. The informational requirements and social flexibility necessary for economic competitiveness would promote democracy, and in due course, higher standards of living would create a structure of legal norms and human rights capable of coping with rapid cultural change.[45] Mexico has not yet followed any of these transition scripts, however. For some writers, such as Enrique Krauze, the stagnated transition has fostered an impatient conversion of the transition to democracy thesis into a Revolution to Demolition interpretation of contemporary Mexican history. As a veteran of the 1968 movement, Krauze has turned the post–World War II modernizing elite perspective upside down, crafting a withering critique of public authority in Mexico in which "nation destroying" has replaced "nation building." For him, state power has been willful, capricious, and ultimately destructive, an immense burden from which society must be freed. "Power was the essential business" of the contemporary Mexican political system, Krauze writes, "the great national industry" within which "politicians, most especially the President of the Republic, . . . behaved with almost total impunity." The architect of the "Mexican miracle," both economically and politically, was Miguel Alemán, the *cachorro* (cub) of the Revolution who set out to rebuild Mexico as a modernized *patria* while simultaneously enriching himself and his friends. Alemán established himself as the "hub of power" around whom "whirled the wheel, that is the people. The hub moved and moved the people. . . . The wheel of power became a fiesta of disguises. Some dressed up through cynicism; others were not even aware that they were wearing costumes; some sincerely believed that they were not. The wheel grew until it included almost the entire country. The Revolution had died, but in the Zócalo the crowd shouted: *Viva la Revolución!*"[46]

In an engaging fashion, *Mexico, Biography of Power* guides the reader through a story of inevitable national disaster. Krauze depicts an all-powerful system that co-opted and suppressed the reform efforts attempted after 1958 by laborers, teachers, doctors, and students, culminating in the Tlatelolco massacre of 1968. President Díaz Ordaz was no "tolerant, liberal Machiavellian" in the Brandenburg mold, but rather a Mexican "Nero." He "saw enemies or detractors everywhere, and when he did not see them he invented them." In Díaz Ordaz, "the system had attracted, favored, and created the politician it required . . . an agent of the court, a prosecuting attorney, a man with the temperament of a police chief or authoritarian general. This was Díaz Ordaz's historical role."[47] As presidents after Díaz Ordaz sought to restore the Revolution's lost legitimacy, they destroyed much of the country's stability and standard of living. Revolution became demolition: "Though the deep-seated cult of authoritarian government in Mexico would not recognize the fact, 1968 was both its highest point of authoritarian power and the real beginning of its collapse. That decline has lasted twenty-nine years, with multiple twists and turns. Though the direction now is clear—toward the bankruptcy of the system and its inevitable transformation—the process is still an open one, in a sense a free fall."[48] In Krauze's narrative, democracy emerges defined as Mexico's central historical task: the demolition of presidential autocracy.

Mexico, Biography of Power offers too conveniently simple an interpretation, one that "anthropomorphizes national history" and shrinks back from the full-scale revision that contemporary Mexican history requires.[49] Like much of the social science scholarship on Mexico since 1968, Krauze's arguments play to excess a one-note song, that of the "Leviathan state" and the "imperial presidency." His interpretation of the country's entire history as a search for democracy takes too many liberties with the realities of Mexico's experience. "Although democracy has been a significant political issue during most of Mexico's modern history, it has often not been the principal political aim or site of contention," Claudio Lomnitz observed in an acrimonious exchange of views with Krauze.[50] Those who would write the contemporary history of Mexico should be wary of such sweeping a priori master narratives. They often bespeak more of present-day intellectual fashion than of substantive historical grounding. Yesterday, Mexico's experience was said to be a "search for modernity"; today, it is declared to be the pursuit of democracy. Both the Revolution to Evolution and Revolution to Demolition interpretations have fixed an enduring focus on the state, rendering the members of society largely the objects rather than protagonists of their own experience. In the fashion of many nineteenth-century liberals, Krauze believes that "the best allies" of tyranny in Mexico are mass "apathy and ignorance." "The true heart of the system," he writes, "rests on the traditional, premodern political culture of the majority of Mexicans, for whom *politicians are the legitimate owners not only of power but of the nation*."[51] Like the Revolution to Evolution thesis that it upends, the Revolution to Demolition interpretation fails as a framework for contemporary Mexican history because it postulates an invisible, complacent society over the past six decades.

Change has been at the center of the contemporary historical experience of Mexico. Mexicans today are five times as many in number, far more urban, and considerably younger on the average than they were in 1940. Systems of mass communication and consumption have revamped their daily lives, forging new patterns of identity and interests. Large numbers of Mexicans currently live or have lived in the United States. Historical interpretations can no longer presume a single national direction in all of these changes. If those who would write the history of Mexico since 1940 are to follow Coronil's injunction to attempt to "understand the complex architecture of parts and whole," in this case to trace the complex relations that underlie the living construct of "Mexico," they will have to employ more diverse methods that offer less emphasis on the unity of the nation-state than those followed by past scholarship. Mexico's future at the turn of the millennium remains highly uncertain.[52] New interpretations of Mexico's contemporary history will have to embrace indeterminacy, stressing the multiple patterns of interaction that take place among culture, economics, politics, society, and the globe at large. Two lines of approach merit particular attention: decentering the previous emphasis of scholarship on the nation-state, and examining popular culture as a vital force in historical change.

Ya lo ves como el destino todo cobra y nada olvida[53]

The uncertain character of Mexico's current condition suggests that a prolonged time of troubles better fits Mexican contemporary history than any memory of a past Golden Age.[54] The highly successful industrialization after 1940 "modernized the country without lifting it from underdevelopment."[55] In reality, the fulfillment of the Mexican state-nationalist project lasted barely a generation. The "stabilizing development" years featured high economic growth rates, low inflation, a steady foreign exchange rate, and considerable advances in manufacturing. At the same time, however, they exhibited serious financial, distributional, and international problems that have since remained fundamental ingredients of the contemporary crisis. "Even if the student demonstrations that took place in 1968 had not occurred," as Roberto Newell and Luis Rubio have written, "the model of Stabilizing Development would have had to be modified or replaced by something else."[56] The foreign borrowing under Echeverría and López Portillo did not constitute the starting point of Mexico's crippling foreign debt problem. Their measures simply augmented the burden of what clearly was present in the heart of the stabilizing development years: the inability of the state to finance itself from domestic resources, the unwillingness of the private sector to agree on any new tax system, structural shortfalls in the international current account, and the severe dependency of Mexico on outside capital and technology. In addition, the period of Mexico's most rapid economic expansion could not combine growth with equity. An acutely unequal distribution of income became one of the enduring structural characteristics of Mexican economic life.[57]

These less than golden qualities of Mexico's political economy after 1940 indicate the importance of "decentering" historical analysis away from its past emphasis on national development. Such a shift of focus accords with trends in contemporary historical analysis that are attempting to construct frameworks other than the national as prisms for understanding the human experience. As one commentator recently stated: "Two centuries ago the modern practice of history began to focus history's basic concern with change and continuity around narratives about the fate of nations, to try to persuade people to interpret their lives in nation-centered terms. . . . We have so naturally assumed that nations will order the details of history that we miss other ways of organizing narratives of change and continuity."[58] New forms of creating Mexico's "narratives of change and continuity" since 1940 will have to look both outward, grasping the role of global forces within domestic Mexican life, and inward, examining types of social and political expression at the local and regional levels.

The global within the domestic

"National development" was highly international from the start. Mexico remained dependent on the United States for a large share of its international trade, tourism, capital investment, and technology. Beginning with the advent of the Bracero Program in 1942, important segments of the Mexican workforce relied on seasonal and later more permanent employment in the United States. Even national cultural industries like the Golden Age of Mexican cinema emerged from wartime patterns of cooperation in production, marketing, and finance between the United States and Mexico. The national decision-making autonomy enjoyed by Mexican elites in part derived from the willingness of the United States to refrain from attempting to manage economic and political affairs in Mexico, a restraint that would not persist in the absence of stability and the end of the cold war.[59] The previously underemphasized international aspects of Mexico's political economy after 1940 should not be taken to mean that nothing has changed under current globalization. Fundamental historical changes often consist of significant shifts in matters of degree. Just as the post–World War II world economic system gave birth to the distinct era of globalization, so with the advent of neoliberalism, a qualitatively new extension of past external linkages has emerged: "The neoliberal project implies a break with the past, and with past social pacts. Even if driven—at the outset—by autonomous state initiative, its eventual destination is a tight dependence of state and society on international capital. . . . If there is a 'dominant class' in Mexico today, it is that often anonymous, tentacular 'dominant class' whose interests now straddle the globe, defying strict definition or regulation. There are Mexicans—like Slim or Azcárraga—who arguably belong to that class; but the logic of their action is global rather than Mexican."[60]

Those engaged in Mexican contemporary history will now have "to think forwards,"[61] to interpret the experiences of Mexicans over the past six decades in the light of the denationalizing global forces that have become increasingly predominant toward the end of the twentieth century. Mexico's post-1940 Golden Age situated itself in a global context conducive to Third World state nationalism. The disintegration of this "national project" has coincided in time with the articulation of highly intense global networks that, in the view of some, constitute the foundation of an entirely new historical age. The English social scientist Martin Albrow argues that "the modern project"—the territorial and social expansion of the nation-state, the rationalization of social behavior, the premise that identity and fulfillment would be found primarily within the bounds of the nation-state, and the univeralization of this system ultimately leading to "the end of history"—has come to an end. In his view, the termination of the modern age has brought a global age, not as the culmination of modernity, but rather as a break from it: "Globalization then is the term which becomes prevalent in a transitional period of history, not a single overall process of change. It characterizes the beginning of the Global Age simply because the weight of reference to globality displaces modernity from its prior position in characterizing the configuration, but it has no inherent direction or necessary end-point."[62]

Albrow's ideas alert students of Mexican history to the need to identify the globalizing patterns that have played significant roles in the internal history of the country since 1940 and, in particular, to identify the shift that has taken place from "national project" to "global project." His views stress the linkage between internal sociocultural change and global factors that must constitute a principal thread in the weaving of contemporary Mexican history: "When we invoke the Global Age we jettison three centuries of assumptions about the direction of history. We move from seeing globalization as yet another stage of modernity . . . to seeing it as the preparation for the global becoming part of life and globality becoming a constitutive fac-

tor in potentially any sector, sphere or institution. . . . The globe has become a normal reference point. The transformations that have taken place
lodge globality in everyday life. . . . It is the facticity of the social which provides the basis for the narrative history of the Global Age."[63]

Neoliberalism may have been a top-down policy pushed by the central
state after 1982, but its articulation rested not just on state power or the force
of external capital. It drew strength from its connections to the ways in
which "globality" was "lodged in everyday life" in Mexico, a reality that
the economic policies, cultural industries, consumer patterns, and migra-
tory movements of the Golden Age did much to create. For example, the
increased competition that Omar Hernández and Emile McAnany find
among private cultural enterprises in the aftermath of NAFTA responds not
only to the trade agreement but also to the deep penetration of U.S. business
and culture into Mexican life that took place in the decades after 1940.

The corollary of a diminished emphasis on a nation-state–centered narrative is the adoption of a pluralistic "Greater Mexico" definition of Mexican
identity. This notion places new emphasis on unearthing the transnational
dimensions that are embedded within many of the aspects of contemporary
Mexican history and to see in particular the influences that Mexico and the
United States have had and continue to have within each other's domestic
sphere.[64] Post-1940 Mexican migration to the United States offers a powerful demonstration of the role of global forces in transforming the internal
structures and patterns of daily life in Mexico, and of the capacity of Mexican culture to remake external influences into a syncretic adaptation of its
own practices.[65] In the midst of the growing influence of migration, popular Mexican identity patterns have remained strong and appear to adapt well
to the global age. Roger Rouse and Michael Kearney provide examples of
villages that have transformed themselves into transnational communities,
incorporating settlements of out-migrants in the United States (many of
whom are involved in patterns of circular migration) into active community consciousness and ritual.[66]

Retablos (ex-votive paintings) demonstrate the incorporation of the issues of migration (the dangers of travel to the United States, fear of immigration officials, illness, travel and work accidents) into an existing popular
form of religious culture.[67] Migration to the United States has constituted
a central element in the history of Mexico since 1940, one that has revealed
the ability of ordinary Mexicans to act as historical protagonists provoking
significant changes both at home and abroad. The early years of World War

II precisely mark the point of departure of the contemporary mass migration of Mexicans to and from the United States, provoking increased Mexicanization of the United States and the transnationalization of a significant proportion of the Mexican labor force.[68] Nevertheless, relatively few general treatments of contemporary Mexican history have seen fit to integrate migration as a subject matter with other, more standard versions of events.[69] This failure to see the intimate linkage between the global and forms of daily life in Mexico will have to change if the period since 1940 is to be comprehended fully.

A less than almighty state

The concept of a Greater Mexico set of identities calls for the writing of Mexican history since 1940 to realize the full implications of a contemporary rereading of the title of Leslie Byrd Simpson's 1941 classic, *Many Mexicos*.[70] Steve Stern has asked: "In what sense may we speak of 'Mexico'? The regional heterogeneity of Mexico is dramatic, even notorious. The variety of languages, ethnic and cultural contexts, regional economies, and regional political cultures dazzles both the superficial tourist and the assiduous scholar. The ever growing mountain of superb regional histories corroborates the sense that 'Mexico' is a half-fiction, a patchquilt of 'many Mexicos' stitched together as much by political fiat and cultural proclamation as by unity of experience, memory, and identity."[71] The "many Mexicos" of today would include, but not be limited to, those identified by residence in the nation-state, regions, local settlements ranging from grand metropoli to small hamlets, different areas outside the nation-state (especially in the United States); by personal traits and patterns of identity shaped by age, gender, sexual orientation, class status, occupation, educational experience, political views, cultural tastes, consumer habits, religious affiliation, organizational memberships, and so on ad infinitum. Conventional analyses of political life have usually presented state and society as separate spheres, one the domain of the "public," the other of the "private," a dichotomy that poorly represents the interpenetration of state and society so characteristic of the Mexican "state-party" regime.[72] New accounts have come to question this conception of two spheres and of the Leviathan state, both of which were so prominent in the Revolution to Evolution and Revolution to Demolition theses. Lorenzo Meyer has disputed the historical emphasis on a "strong state" in contemporary Mexico, contending that its institutional weaknesses are as much a part of its fundamental characteristics as its dominant presidency.[73] Alan Knight suggests a trade-off between strength and stability in the case of the Mexican state. Under what he calls the "Hapsburg" pattern, stability predominated during the *desarrollo estabilizador* years (1954–1970) as a "structural feature of state-civil society relations" that "did not reflect mere presidential temperaments." Although the state was not without some measure of autonomy, its patterns of interaction with society generally "pandered to the interests of [the] bourgeoisie" through low taxes, high tariffs, and severe restrictions on labor and agrarian militancy.[74]

Historical accounts of contemporary Mexico should remain attuned to the efforts of the state to create the patria, but they also need to become more sensitive to issues of central state weakness than they have previously. Throughout the post–World War II era, states all over the world expanded in size and expenditure, but not all such growth reflected strength. Mexico, like many Third World states, remained "weak," unable to establish and enforce rules against powerful sectors of domestic society.[75] Mexico provides a salient example of what Balibar calls "the relative indeterminacy of the process of constitution and development of the nation form."[76] It may be somewhat unfair to call the PRI a "ramshackle institution"; nevertheless, it often has been barely more "institutional" than it has been "revolutionary."[77] A well-rooted legal infrastructure to govern the transactions of everyday life never developed in post-1940 Mexico.[78] The unsatisfactory service capacity of the government bureaucracy is revealed by the fact that fully a third of public employees in 1975 had no secondary education.[79] These weaknesses of what today are sometimes called microeconomic institutions and services possess as much significance for daily life in Mexico at the end of the twentieth century as the more widely discussed fact that "the project of rational, democratic power that should replace [*presidencialismo*] has not yet developed."[80] Politics in contemporary Mexico must be seen through interaction between state and society at multiple levels.

Nation and region

By decentering Mexican contemporary history, new scholarship has created possibilities for more diverse and meaningful periodizations and for more complex patterns of mutual influence between state and society, including taking regionalism seriously. For too long, writers have tended rather unimaginatively to frame the history of Mexico since 1940 in terms of presidential sexenios or in terms of two discrete time periods, 1940–1970 and

1970–present, neither fashion a very helpful way of viewing the events of six decades of the twentieth century. Such periodizations have contributed to an "analytical homogenization" that has made the post-1940 Mexican experience into a "bland two-dimensional backdrop against which today's images of crises and modernization are projected to dramatic effect."[81] Although the macroeconomic growth of the decades from 1940 to 1970 remains a highly impressive achievement, these years were never as quiescent, successful, and internally coherent as the bipolar periodization implies. For one thing, the years in which the "Mexican system" operated in a stable fashion with all of its fundamental features in place were relatively few, largely the Ruiz Cortines presidency from 1952 to 1958, and certainly not the three decades from 1940 to 1970. Rubin, for example, sees the demise in the late 1950s and early 1960s of regional *cacicazgos* (power domains) dating from the 1930s as underlying many of the political conflicts over representation and authority that emerged in the 1980s–1990s. This perspective creates a variation in periodization that "directly contradicts the relative homogeneity of political process and outcome postulated by the state-centered approach."[82]

In short, "regime history" since 1940 can now be broadened beyond state policy decisions into an examination of the socioeconomic context of decision making, breaking down abstract general frameworks (e.g., "capitalist industrialization") into more precise political and economic strategies linked to different interest groups and other structures of power.[83] Already scholars have begun to do this, burrowing within society and institutions, exploring resource issues and social conflict,[84] questioning the supposed docility of labor,[85] and examining those sectors that have been ruled out of preexisting versions of post-1940 history, such as the army, the church, and scientific bodies.[86] Steven Bachelor's essay in this volume, for example, demonstrates the many ways in which workers at the General Motors factory in Mexico City sought to shape their own destiny: organizing a union, going out on strike, setting up their own social services, establishing a new neighborhood, and making contacts with other unions both in Mexico and in the United States. "At the heart of autoworkers' emerging political consciousness," writes Bachelor, "was the insistence that they should have a role in deciding the course of corporate and state modernization projects." The workers had their own view of what "modern" working-class life should be, distinct from the corporate paternalism of General Motors or the "revolutionary nationalism" of the Mexican state. Nor is their case an isolated one.

The auto industry constituted a strategic centerpiece in post-1940 Mexico's import-substitution industrialization. Labor activism in the railroads and other sectors left a strong stamp on the generation after World War II.[87]

Alternative visions of Mexico's post-1940 experience are also visible at the regional level. Historical scholarship over the past quarter century has explored how powerful a "luxuriant and confusing" regional variety has been "in the evolution of Mexico's history and in the consciousness of Mexicans as portrayed in their politics, art, social thinking, and *mentalidad*."[88] Yet, as far as Mexico's contemporary history was concerned, regions were taken to be retrograde nests of prenational factionalism. In the words of Carlos Monsiváis: "Until very recently, to speak of Mexican regionalism was to refer almost exclusively to realities blurred by mythology. The fatalistic faith in the omnipotence of the center (the peak of power in Mexico City) was such that to mention regionalism was most often to conjure up legends of the bewildered fringes and the feudal realities of backwardness."[89] Regional economic growth and urbanization as well as the expansion of mass communications systems now make it impossible for the old views to prevail. Region and nation in Mexico are no longer seen as being in binary opposition. Lomnitz has argued that the nation-state does not supersede regions, as earlier modernization approaches would have assumed. Cultural and social diversity constitutes a bedrock reality in a country the size of Mexico. "There exists," he writes, "a spatial dimension of cultural differentiation which allows us to understand cultural fragmentation as something other than a complete lack of cultural unity or identity."[90] His studies of Morelos and the Huasteca emphasize "the space in which a culture of interrelations is negotiated" and the cultural "symbolic elements" (e.g., zapatismo, in the case of Morelos) involved in both regional power relations and the hegemony of the central state.[91] Central states can rarely exercise all power directly, a fact true of contemporary Mexico even if it was resolutely ignored by the Revolution to Evolution scholarship. As Bryan Roberts has noted, "The Mexican state must often work through political intermediaries who control significant local resources."[92] Even though the size and scope of the federal bureaucracy grew in the decades after 1940, the authority of the state continued to be subject to the vested interests and deal-making power of local caciques, provincial elites, and the domestic private sector. The vaunted corporatist organizations only penetrated society unevenly while remaining plagued by notable cases of caciquismo as well.[93] "Contrary to the assumptions about power inherent in the corporatist state analysis of Mexico," argues Rubin, "incompleteness, instability, and domination are intimately connected."[94] Though the specifics of their analyses differ, both Rubin and Lomnitz see regional political and cultural dynamics as exercising significant influence over what has been previously analyzed as simply "national" life.

The interaction they perceive between regions and the nation-state in the realm of politics also proves true in the world of social history. Jeffrey Pilcher's contribution to this volume, for example, shows how local dietary traditions have interacted with changes in food production technology and new national and international influences, in general resisting homogenizing tendencies while selectively reaffirming some local dishes and adopting some new ones from the outside. *La comida mexicana* came into being as a "combination of regional dialects" under the nationalist ideology of the state, the influence of tourism, and the expansion of consumer markets and mass communications.[95] Regional cuisines were not obliterated, yet "the construction of a national cuisine inevitably reduced complex regional dialects into a few stereotyped dishes."[96] A similar pattern of reduction of regional features into a set of nationally accepted standards took place in the construction of the tourist industry and in the formation of such institutions as the Ballet Folklórico.[97] A national tourist industry demanded a centrally regulated infrastructure and definition of lo mexicano, something that could come about only through regional interests being able to negotiate a place for themselves within the new cultural constructs of official nationalism.

State, society, and culture

Emphasis on the interplay of the regional with the national, whether in politics, tourism, or food, suggests that analysts of post-1940 Mexican history should heed the warning of English sociologist Bob Jessop against "focusing on the state alone—even assuming one could precisely define its institutional boundaries."[98] It is evident that the postrevolutionary Mexican state can be usefully understood, not as an institutional monolith but as "an ensemble of practices, institutions, and ideologies of rule" unevenly intermeshed with society.[99] "The powers of the state are always conditional and relational," notes Jessop, and therefore, "the state must be related not only to the broader political system but also to its wider social environment."[100] Three important conclusions flow from this. First, reexaminations of Mexican political life after 1940 imply far more than just filling out an incomplete picture, painting in the rest of the numbers, as it were. By obliging new periodizations, new relationships between the state and other political actors, and new interpretations of the interactions between the center and the provinces, the historicizing of contemporary Mexico also requires much greater appreciation of popular agency. There will certainly still be room for writing that looks at Mexican politics in terms of the nation and its top decision makers, but analysts must ultimately conceive of the dynamics of post-1940 Mexican history as rooted in the assertion of social groups as well as in the dealing in high-level offices. Rubin argues, for example, that the renovation of politics in the provinces was "understood, debated, and acted on in routine and extraordinary ways by ordinary Mexicans. Their actions, often at the regional level and in arenas outside of formal politics, shaped and challenged the policies of state actors by providing vetoes, new languages, changing cultural and political forces, and alternative institutional arrangements."[101] Such a statement amounts to a major reversal in orientation to Mexican contemporary history where society served only as a passive backdrop or, as in the case of Krauze's *Biography of Power*, a corrupted impediment to progress.

Second, the historical trajectory of the Mexican state and of its principal national projects should be envisioned as taking place in the context of a society characterized by multiple inequalities and subordinations, not united in a single destiny. The vocabulary and symbols used by diverse elements of this society are thus crucial to comprehending Mexican historical patterns after 1940. These immense transformations of culture and society in Mexico over the past six decades mean that state-society relations have to be interpreted as dynamic rather than static, open to both the influences of the temporal context and the initiatives springing from elements in society themselves. In this context, the concept of hegemony becomes a highly valuable one if understood as "struggle, the ways in which the words, images, symbols, forms, organizations, institutions, and movements used by subordinate populations to talk about, understand, confront, accommodate themselves to, or resist their domination are shaped by the process of domination itself. What hegemony constructs, then, is not a shared ideology but a common material and meaningful framework for living through, talking about, and acting upon social orders characterized by domination."[102] Students of contemporary Mexican history must examine popular cultures and characteristics of the state in relation to one another, something that has been undertaken all too infrequently in Latin American history, not just in the experience of Mexico since 1940.[103]

Third, writers of post-1940 Mexican history will have to be sensitive to what Aguilar Camín has labeled *subversiones silenciosas*, the multiple and profound changes in social custom and behavior that have taken place in Mexico throughout the past six decades.[104] These "subtle and continuous revampings of personal pathways, decisions, and obstacles" constitute a "silent revolution," in the view of Stern.[105] Many of these changes are of a social and cultural nature, something that must be understood if writers of contemporary Mexican history wish to begin their analysis, in the words of Arturo Escobar, "with people's self-understanding, with giving an account of people as agents whose practices are shaped by their self-understanding."[106] This is particularly important because, as James Scott has noted, "social and historical analyses have, almost inevitably, the effect of diminishing the contingency of human affairs."[107] Attention to popular cultures provides an important corrective to this abstracting, determinist quality of structural analysis, facilitating examination of perception, language, popular agency, and contingency.[108] Mexico, like the rest of Latin America, finds itself "in an age of traditions that have not vanished, a modernity that never quite arrives, and a postmodern questioning of the evolutionary projects that enjoyed hegemony during this century."[109] Sociohistorical examination of contemporary Mexico that lacks an awareness of popular cultures risks sculpting a two-dimensional object.[110]

No hay nada completo[111]

Incorporating popular culture into the study of history counters the false sense of completeness claimed by post-1940 modernizing historical narratives. The Revolution to Evolution tradition ordered everything within a national framework that, on the one hand, reached deeply into the past, and on the other, pointed to a glorious future. The historical gaze of postrevolutionary Mexican nationalism extended into the remote pre-Hispanic times, ultimately anchoring itself in the "*monumentalization* and *nationalist ritualization* of culture" of the National Museum of Anthropology.[112] Revolutionary nationalism's vision of the future was one of modern prosperity. Postwar Mexican governments regularly proclaimed the country *en vías del desarrollo* (on the road to development). A "'prospective nationalism,' a vanity associated with the inevitable Mexico to come," attempted to sustain public faith during the Golden Age.[113]

Yet no national ideology can own the past or shape the future to its taste. In its rendering of both the past and the future, Mexican state nationalism after 1940 became a species of "Mystery Theatre," to borrow the words Quetzil Castañeda uses in this volume to describe Chichén Ítza.[114] The regime's "inevitable Mexico" of historical destiny never arrived. Instead, Mexicans found that they had to cope with greater inequality, political repression, economic collapse, and natural catastrophe. Ultimately, a more diverse and complex Mexico shook off the "demobilizing power" of official nationalism and became "the society getting organized,"[115] one characterized by a wide array of effervescent forms of group expression that have surpassed the capacity of the formal political system or official ideology to encompass them. Politics in present-day Mexico includes but goes far beyond parties and elections. Political life involves a vibrant civil society pushing for its rights and programs, seeking to open avenues of opportunity within very unequal structures of power. Popular cultures actively influence these struggles. After all, the definition of the concept of popular cultures demonstrates a fundamental connection to networks of unequal power: "Popular cultures . . . are formed through a process of unequal appropriation of the economic and cultural property of a nation or ethnic group by some of its subordinate sectors, and through both a symbolic and real understanding, reproduction, and transformation of general as well as particular living and working conditions. . . . In short, popular cultures are the product of unequal appropriation of cultural capital, the people's own reflections about their living conditions, and conflict-ridden interaction with hegemonic sectors."[116]

National culture and cultural diversity

Much of the history lived by the majority of Mexicans after 1940 can be told in the expansion of the country's cultural industries and in the ways popular cultures coped with the messages emanating from mass communications media. The rapid growth of print and photojournalism along with the electronic media of radio, cinema, and television proved instrumental in both the hegemony of official state nationalism after 1940 and its subsequent demise. Mass communications interpreted a time of rampant urbanization and industrialization for the public. The postrevolutionary "modern" nation-state and the production of mass culture required each other's existence. The efforts of the Mexican state to forge the cultural fabric of a strong national identity included not only a system of public education and new government cultural institutions but also encouragement of the modern mass media of magazines, radio, cinema, advertising, and television.[117] Comic books circulated widely, offering stories that mixed national discourses of urbane progress and conservative tradition, at times accompanied by idealized drawings of Mexican regions and famous sites. Controversies about the morality and civic value of comic book content only made them more popular. "Through arguments like those that swirled around *historietas*, the state reproduced and legitimized itself" and promoted a "modern" national culture.[118] As John Mraz discusses in this book, photo magazines like *Hoy, Rotofoto*, and *Mañana* carried alluring images of the socially glamorous of the day and the politicians of officialdom. The radio and the phonograph brought regional musical forms into contact with one another, creating a set of national music styles that accompanied a society in transition. Radio beamed the voices of *locutores* and singers into homes and workplaces across urbanizing Mexico, popularizing the music of composers such as Agustín Lara and José Alfredo Jiménez and such singers as Jorge Negrete, Pedro Infante, and Lola Beltrán.[119]

At the same time, Mexican cinema, "more than any other cultural form, modernised tastes and prejudices and refashioned the idea of the nation by transforming nationalism into a big spectacle."[120] As Mexico became an urban society "united and transfigured by melodrama," the film industry shaped the ways migrants from the countryside adapted to urban life.[121] In discussing Emilio "El Indio" Fernández's 1947 film *Enamorada*, Jean Franco notes that the cinema "provided a powerful technique for shoring up the family (at least in theory) at a time in which large numbers of immigrants were drifting into the city and finding themselves without the social censorship and the religious and political control that prevailed in the provinces."[122] The postrevolutionary Mexican public went to the movies "not to dream, but to learn," a significant process for both the "expanding and ascendant middle class" and those beneath them on the social scale.[123] Movie idols such as Pedro Infante provided the lessons, in some cases acting out the transition from the rural world to the city. As Anne Rubenstein notes in this volume, Infante's career "began with his playing a character from an imagined past, an invented tradition of the rural north, but it ended in a series of comic and equivocal depictions of modern city life." Cinema facilitated a common urban cultural patrimony whose symbols were absorbed in varied ways by unequal social sectors. In the words of Monsiváis about Cantinflas: "The poor applaud in him what is close and familiar to them and, whether they realize it or not, become enthusiastic about a not-so-very-strange fact: the festive and vindictive representation of poverty. The rich are grateful for the opportunity to laugh at demagogues and the poor, and at the last gasp of small-town rural comedy."[124]

The emergence of a mass consumer society provided Mexicans in the generations after 1940 with a widely diffused but unevenly appropriated package of symbolic and material goods. Simplistic interpretations emphasized the harmonious blending of the traditional and the modern in a supposedly unique, Mexican way. Yet Mexico's complex social and cultural changes would prove neither uniform nor harmonious. The modernization process itself soon outstripped the original imaginary framework of Mexican state nationalism and the cultural industries. The activities of women, for example, ranged beyond the limits of the classical narrative lines still pursued by Mexican films of the 1940s.[125] More experienced with city life and somewhat better educated, urban social groups by the mid-1950s no longer identified in the same fashion with earlier cultural messages. As the cultural and political myths of the Mexican Revolution waned, foreign investment, U.S.-style consumer goods, and new communications technologies, especially television, expanded North American cultural influence in Mexican daily life. Diversified technologies, diversified messages, and diversified audiences interacted to produce more complex cultural mixtures. The "folkloric" quality of "traditional" crafts gave way to new adaptations of form as artisan production expanded rather than retreated as expected in the face of modernization. Cultural life became dynamically, often unpredictably hybrid in character and meaning. At the same time, the gap between the "cultured" and the "popular" no longer remained "defined as it had been until the second half of [the twentieth] century in terms of social class, as the division between an educated elite and an illiterate or semi-literate majority. High culture became the domain of a small fraction within the bourgeoisie and middle classes, while most of the upper and middle classes, along with almost all of the working class, became subject to the mass programming of the cultural industry."[126]

How audiences received and acted on the messages they received from this mass programming could not be easily predicted.[127] U.S. government evaluators found it hard to determine the impact of the propaganda films they disseminated widely in Mexico with the assistance of the Mexican government in the late 1940s and early 1950s.[128] The late Emilio Azcárraga, head of Televisa, the most powerful of Mexican television networks, saw programming simply as the means of pacifying and consoling the suffering lower classes. "Mexico is a nation with a class of humble people who've been screwed and will continued to be screwed," he said in 1993. "Television has the obligation to entertain this people and take them out of their sad reality and difficult future."[129] Azcárraga presumably would have agreed with the wall graffiti proclaiming *Televisa idiotiza* (Televisa stupefies), but the popular impact of television and other mass media could often be hard to elucidate. "Do the televised church services from the Basilica of Guadalupe renew our Mexican identity," asks Monsiváis, "or do they simply integrate the credo with satellite dishes?"[130] Mass cultural programming can produce unanticipated results, as essays in this volume demonstrate. Alison Greene finds that a stronger sense of mexicanidad resulted from the exposure of rural Yucatecos to global television programming once they received cable; Anne Rubenstein depicts the conflicts that ensued between popular understandings of the film messages of Pedro Infante and the actions of state bureaucracies; Heather Levi discusses the contentious results of television's attempts to reshape a popular form of public entertainment for middle-class viewing audiences. Levi's essay reflects many of the issues stemming from the increased privatization of cultural production and consumption that has taken place in Mexico, particularly since the debt crisis in 1982. The Mexican state has diminished its participation in cultural production, leaving mass programming to private forces.[131] At the same time, changing technologies such as video have combined with the greater physical insecurities and dispersed settlement patterns of urban life to diminish the importance of public space. Cultural consumption has become more and more of a home-bound, private activity rather than something that inherently involved congregation in public areas such as museums, cinemas, or plazas.[132]

It remains a major challenge for analysts to discern the ways in which highly visible social and cultural changes intersect with the issues of political power and economic policy. Uncovering the history of Mexico since 1940 will require careful historical use of a concept such as agency. Culture can work both as a constraint and a catalyst to action. Social groups often appropriate cultural symbols in fashions that emphasize accommodation to an existing order, as many argue happened in postrevolutionary Mexico. At the same time, societies do not always move in a single direction, and questions of cultural receptivity are seldom one-way matters. Hegemony is a relational concept rooted in the notion of struggle. Popular cultures form in opposition to the dominant order. They are capable of rendering the content of mass communication in novel ways, injecting meanings that serve to promote self-assertion and resistance, thus creating wholly new historical protagonists.

The so-called Golden Age after 1940 was not simply a time of mass acculturation and widespread acquiescence in a new order. There remains an as yet unwritten history of "a people whose anonymity included the refusal of all concessions, the unknown militants who chose prison or losing their jobs rather than giving up, the feminists who suffered decades of insults and ridicule, but just kept on fighting all the same, the railroad workers and electricians sacked just weeks before their retirement because they refused to sign up for the corrupt official union."[133] Mass communications engender mixtures of acquiescent and resistant behavior within systems of domination and inequality. Mexican young people from the expanding middle class appropriated rock music from the United States and Europe, ultimately inventing their own versions that gained listeners throughout Latin America. Initially accepted by the state and commercialized by the private sector, "rock music established itself as a crucial reference point in Mexican society, a signifier of cosmopolitan values and a bearer of disorder and wanton individualism."[134] Rock expressed a new youth culture that rejected the stifling order of Mexican state nationalism. As Rubén Martínez notes in this volume, rock became the setting for a "battle for the cultural soul of Mexican youth." Though not a direct cause of the student movement of 1968, rock played in the background and continued to nurture an oppositional counterculture both repressed and co-opted by the state in the years following Tlatelolco as well as exploited commercially by private cultural industries. Rock's transformation from an imported cultural influence to a means of expression of the internal conflicts of Mexican society continued as appropriations of rock by urban lower-class elements hardened its oppositional qualities further. "It might be true that rock began in the North," Martínez is informed by his friend Roco, "but now it's all ours."

Yet change is seldom uniform, and the story of rock music culture illustrates the importance of avoiding dichotomies in historical analysis of Mexico since 1940, in this case between dominant and subaltern. Society did not simply divide between the upholders of the old order and resistant youth. Individuals and social groups have more than one identity and, therefore, more than one pattern of historical interaction. "There are times and places," writes Coronil, "where subjects appear on history's pages as subaltern actors, just as there are times or places in which they play dominant roles. Moreover, at any given time or place, an actor may be subaltern in relation to another, yet dominant in relation to a third."[135] Mexican male youth articulated a gendered subalternity. They found themselves in discontented subordination to the state and to their parents, yet they attempted to maintain a position of superiority toward women of their own generation. Young women experienced *La Onda* (Mexico's rock counterculture) differently from men. They were "expected to adhere to a higher standard of morality than were men," not only by their parents but by their male peers. "While rock had challenged older hierarchies and in doing so had invented new participatory spaces for women, patriarchy was not destroyed by the rock counterculture (despite rhetoric to the contrary), simply reinvented."[136] In this context of sociocultural upheaval, women rejected this reinvented patriarchy. Women's organizations and publications sprang up in Mexico with great intensity beginning in the early 1970s, creating a widespread movement with a long list of demands, from workplace equality to freedom from sexual violence.[137]

Cultural creativity and popular agency

These sociocultural changes offer important markers for understanding the historical fabric of life in post-1940 Mexico. Gender issues constitute a meaningful arena of change, one that is both complex to analyze and subtly linked to local, national, and global contexts in Mexican contemporary history.[138] They contain the underlying varieties within society that are distinct from yet interact with the prevailing patterns of "national culture" as defined by the cultural industries. The aftermath of the Mexican revolution offered a setting in which machismo was elevated into "a definitive and defining characteristic of what it meant to be Mexican," a distorting process in which the mass media, consumer society, and intellectuals all participated.[139] Yet, in reality, acting "macho" constituted only one form of male behavior, one that did not necessarily correlate either with other attributes of Mexican national culture or with popular agency.[140] Some of the workers in the GM plant that Steven Bachelor writes about lived out this stereotype of male behavior, but many did not. Not all definitions of manliness among the workers derived from machismo. Other attributes of what it meant to be a man influenced the job performance and self-definition of these skilled workers far more.[141] Being macho in a stereotypical sense had little to do with union participation and no significant connection with attitudes toward other aspects of Mexican national culture. Both workers who acted macho and those who did not engaged in union activities that defied state nationalism.

Analysis of post-1940 Mexico needs to employ a distinction between agency understood as cultural creativity and agency understood as resistance. Renderings of contemporary Mexican history should appreciate but not exaggerate forms of resistance. It would constitute an overpoliticization to craft the post-1940 story exclusively as one of widespread popular resistance to diverse forms of domination. Agency is not always identical with resistance.[142] "Cultural creativity," notes Matthew Gutmann, "is a far more productive concept than resistance in analyzing the inventiveness of the popular classes, because it emphasizes not only the desire of ordinary people to react to their life situations, but, more importantly, the active ways in which men and women seek to shape their lives every day."[143] In the case of Bachelor's essay, agency in the form of acts of resistance (union organizing, going on strike, demonstrating to obtain urban services in the new neighborhood) depended on a whole complex of other forms of agency as cultural creativity, as GM workers adapted to the city, formed families, learned industrial jobs, and constituted their own definition of an appropriate modern way of life. These manifestations of popular cultural creativity constitute essential threads in the fabric of the country's post-1940 experience, more widespread than overt forms of resistance.

The present-day zapatista uprising in Chiapas demonstrates both an unusual level of resistance and an inventiveness indicative of the potential of popular cultural creativity to link together matters of culture, economics, society, state, and globe. A fall in globally determined coffee prices, the perceived implications of NAFTA, historical patterns of oppression, and culturally sensitive indigenous organizing all figure among the causes of the revolt. In the wake of the rebellion, the insurgents have attempted to sustain their position in part through an international mobilization of sympathizers and through a highly creative use of contemporary communications technology, particularly the Internet. Cultural issues figure heavily in zapatista demands, but they do so not in an abstract sense of "folklore" but rather in terms of culture's organizing power when fused to matters of political representation and economic sustenance. The rebellion has created a focal point highlighting the reality that Mexico—as a nation, as a culture, as a society—does not consist of a single "historical project," and that "modernity" cannot exist in Mexico without cultural pluralism and without offering an economically viable future for the immense number of Mexicans left outside its narrative.[144] Throughout Mexico, indigenous peoples have been engaged in a process of reassertion that has become an influential feature of contemporary society and culture, far different from the roles anticipated for them by the *indigenismo* of earlier generations, many of whose forms were shaped by the hand of the postrevolutionary state.[145]

Popular cultures and future scholarship on contemporary Mexico
Future examinations of contemporary Mexican history should explore popular cultural issues that have not yet been extensively engaged. Popular cultures, for example, can include expressions of antisocial behavior. At the turn of the millennium, Mexico exhibits an intriguing mixture of change (regional rebellion, popular movements, opposition electoral victories, particularly the election of President Vicente Fox), continuity ("neoliberal" economic policy, the presence of the United States, concentrated wealth), and social disintegration (rampant crime, diverse and expanding forms of violence, institutional debility, worsening inequalities, domestic militarization). The reality of rural and urban Mexico since 1940 includes complex mixtures of lawlessness, corruption, and clientelism that should give pause before the assumption is made that all forms of popular creativity are constructive. Popular cultures can devise all manner of destructive types of behavior, as Mexico's experience with youth gangs, narcotrafficking, street children, and urban crime indicates. Staying alive often exacts a frightening price in human behavior. Elena Poniatowska points out in a recent essay on Mexico City street children that "drugs and delinquency are their means of survival."[146] Analysts will have to make careful judgments about positive and negative impacts of popular cultures and their interrelations with other historical forces in Mexican life. This will involve distinguishing between biased representations of subaltern behavior, such as the assumption that all youth gangs consist of hoodlums, and behavioral patterns themselves.[147]

Too often analysts of popular cultures have forgotten about economic matters, either assuming that they are simply part of a dominant order that subalterns resist or seeing them as inherent in structuralist forms of explanation that they reject. Such an approach "privileges the cultural sphere, transforming the economic, political, and social spheres into epiphenomena— that is, into phenomena that are not basically symbolic in nature, but that can be fully explained by what happens in [the] cultural sphere."[148] The goal of cultural analysis should be to enrich and diversify existing forms of analysis, to engage with them, not to supplant them. The essays in this volume consistently show the strong linkages between economic issues and culture in Mexico since 1940, particularly for mass cultural production. Future work on post-1940 Mexican history will have to continue examination of the interrelationships of popular cultures with economic patterns. On the one hand, scholars must delve into matters of high-level state economic policy and the market dynamics of cultural production. On the other, they must examine through the lens of cultural creativity how popular groups refashioned mass cultural influences and their own cultural perceptions in order to cope with economic considerations. The families of GM autoworkers, for example, could aspire to "modern" images of domesticity because of their relatively high wages. Plunging wages after 1982 forced families to redefine gender relations, change their diets, and resort more to the informal economy.[149] Matters of cost have shaped popular forms of cultural consumption. The appeal of comic books, for example, was facilitated by their cost of no more than a quarter to a third of what an average worker made in an hour, a ratio that publishers worked to keep constant even in times of inflation.[150] In one of Oscar Lewis's "case studies in the culture of poverty," the Gutiérrez family charged neighbors in their *vecindad* a few centavos each day for the privilege of watching their large television, still protectively wrapped in its original carton, as a means of paying for it and adding to household income.[151] Scholars have just begun the process of indicating how popular cultural creativity connects popular economic circumstances with the "imaginary networks" laden with "myth and national culture" that legitimize the Mexican state.[152] These examinations will have to continue, both for the immediate post-1940 Golden Age and for the period of privatization of cultural production and consumption increasingly characteristic of more recent years.

Religion constitutes another neglected area in the history of contemporary Mexico where popular cultural creativity intertwines complex domestic and global networks of unequal power. University-based intellectuals, especially North Americans, do not always find themselves as inherently familiar with matters of religiosity as they might be with issues involving television or tourism, for example. Contextual blinders should not lead students of contemporary Mexican history to neglect the vital wellspring of religious belief and practice in looking at popular cultural creativity in Mexico. Comprehending the zapatista rebellion in Chiapas, to take one salient case, would be impossible without understanding popular religious issues.[153] Scholars have provided insight into rural political movements such as *sinarquismo* through comprehension of the religious aspects of their social and cultural content.[154] The recent experience of the Catholic Church in Mexico involves a realignment of state-church relations in which the Vatican and Mexican bishops have often played conflicting roles. At the same time, popular religious cultures have given voice to social and political activism, reflecting the impact of Vatican II, the Latin American bishops meeting at Puebla in 1978, new Latin American religious thinking, and numerous other domestic and global influences.[155] The Catholic Church in Mexico will have to be understood in the history of contemporary Mexico as one composed of different popular cultures and centers of agency, not just in terms of an institutional hierarchy. Moreover, Mexico can no longer be assumed to be simply a "Catholic country," as Protestant evangelical faiths have spread considerably over the past few decades, creating much greater popular religious diversity.

The expansion of Protestantism demonstrates that the augmented presence of the global within Mexico signifies more than what is usually meant by the "Americanization" of society. Cultural approaches to the study of international relations and to globalization have demonstrated that power, although it is manifestly unequal, does not simply flow in a one-way direction.[156] The old dichotomous analysis between the national and popular on the one hand, and the foreign and elite on the other can no longer be sustained.[157] In the words of Coronil: "Imperial encounters entail the transcultural interaction of the domestic and the foreign under changing historical conditions. This process does not involve the movement of discrete entities from one bounded body to another across fixed borders, but rather their reciprocal transformation. The borders between the dominant and the subaltern are multiple—from the physical frontiers that separate them to the 'contact zones' where imperial and subaltern actors interact. In imperial-subaltern encounters, bodies and borders are mutually defined and transformed through asymmetrical processes of transculturation."[158]

The growth in population, power, and cultural influence of the Mexico-U.S. border region confirms this argument. This region, whose expansion should constitute an important historical theme in the fate of post-1940 Mexico, concentrates within itself the dynamics of economic globalization and the unpredictable popular cultural creativity embodied within the concept of "hybridization." It contains the major social inequalities of class, gender, and ethnicity as well as an increasing militarization that appear to be influential trends in the transnationalization of societies.[159] The analysis of Monsiváis stresses the importance of popular cultural creativity in the process of reconstitution of Mexican identity on both sides of the border. From Houston, he reports the formation of *un pueblo al instante* (an instant people) at a Los Tigres del Norte concert.[160] In his view, "not all Americanization is negative, nor is Mexican society defenseless. The vitality of our society has already 'Mexicanized' much of the Americanization, as evidenced in the behavior of middle-class sectors, youth subcultures (from *cholos* to punks), women's attitudes, etc. . . . And in Mexico we assimilate by incorporating what is assimilated into our identity; we are an 'Americanized' country that 'Mexicanizes' its Americanization. This is not a play on words, nor is it a tragedy. It is a potential road to modernity, which pays no heed to the orthodoxies of official nationalism (which does not believe in them anyway)."[161]

In Mexico, as in many other areas of the Third World where exposure to globalized communications media has rapidly demonstrated an impact on popular culture, "simple notions of homogenization, ideological hegemony or imperialism fail to register properly the nature of these encounters and the interplay, interaction and cultural creativity they produce."[162]

Conclusion

The global interactivity of culture does not mean that students of post-1940 Mexican history should let their analysis be a contented one in the fashion often heard in Mexican governmental and high-media circles. Satisfaction over the export of Mexican *telenovelas* (soap operas), for example, hardly does justice to the issues of unequal cultural influence.[163] Many contentious questions remain over cultural policy in Mexico and over the impact of elite-dominated as well as heavily Americanized systems of mass communication. These provide windows for investigation into the history of Mexico since 1940. Elite domination over the mass communications media remains a problem in both the United States and Mexico despite the new levels of intra-elite competition within Mexico.[164] Recent research has shown that border-area television programming and management respond more to class factors than to differences in nationality between Mexicans and North American audiences.[165] This renovation of the transnational elite cultural pact that began in the context of World War II Mexican cinema does not necessarily mean the end of potentially serious misunderstandings between influential circles in the United States and Mexico.[166] Contemporary historical analysis will have to sort out the interplay between common interests and disagreements. It will need to assess how much a concentration of U.S. media influence may reinforce an economic structure that does not value popular cultural creativity, diminishing Mexico's capacity for self-renovation.[167]

Historical reinterpretation of Mexico since 1940 will have to weigh these matters carefully. In providing a much-needed departure from the old analyses that concentrated on elite visions, state power, and official nationalism, new work should not neglect the enduring preoccupation that has existed for generations about Mexican national identity and sovereignty. Certainly the lives of nation-states involve remarkable amounts of fantasy: myths, symbols, dreams, and "histories." Benedict Anderson has called the nation-state an "imagined community," and Coronil has used the term "magical state" in his account of twentieth-century Venezuelan history.[168] But, as the idea of cultural hegemony postulates, sociocultural constructions involve patterns of popular and elite interaction. Mass "imagining" has been a substantial force in Mexico's history. As essays in this volume indicate, contemporary Mexican history evidences diverse popular concepts of the nation and national identity in tourist projects, cinema, food, labor relations, and mass communications. Much of Mexico's history in the nineteenth and twentieth centuries has been influenced by having to reconcile contradictory internal characteristics and external pressures. The pursuit of a national culture, one "necessarily *dominant and popular* at the same time," should not be taken as an old-fashioned pursuit, now dated by the globalizing tendencies of the late twentieth and early twenty-first centuries.[169] If anything, globalizing forces make such a task even more imperative in order to deal with the multiplying issues of political order and security that are emerging within Mexico and in the U.S.-Mexican relationship.

Any strengthening of Mexican national identity will have to derive from more equitable systems of representation and participation—cultural, political, and economic—than have thus far existed. Historical reevaluation of Mexico since 1940 can contribute to revitalizing national identity, not in the old manner of forjando patria, through a single tale of modernization and national cultural uniqueness, but through a deep-seated appreciation of popular cultural creativity. Such an appreciation must rest, not on romanticization, but on careful delineation of the complex and sometimes contradictory interactions of popular culture with unequal structures of political and economic power, regional, domestic, and global. This approach offers a way of defining the "what" against which Mexican history since 1940 can be "made real."

Notes

1   A partial list of some of the recent works that have begun to explore Mexico's post-1940 experience as history includes the relevant volumes of the Colegio de México, *Historia de la Revolución Mexicana*, 23 vols. (Mexico City: El Colegio de México, 1977–1995), and of Enrique Semo, coord., *México, un pueblo en la historia*, 8 vols. (Mexico City: Alianza Editorial Mexicana, 1981–1990), as well as Héctor Aguilar Camín and Lorenzo Meyer, *In the Shadow of the Mexican Revolution: Contemporary Mexican History, 1910–1989*, trans. Luis Alberto Fierro (Austin: University of Texas Press, 1993); Viviane Brachet-Márquez, *The Dynamics of Domination: State, Class, and Social Reform in Mexico, 1910–1990* (Pittsburgh: University of Pittsburgh Press, 1994); Alan Knight, "The Rise and Fall of Cardenismo, c. 1930–c. 1946," in *Mexico Since Independence*, ed. Leslie Bethell (New York: Cambridge University Press, 1991), 241–320; Kevin J. Middlebrook, *The Paradox of Revolution: Labor, the State, and Authoritarianism in Mexico* (Baltimore: Johns Hopkins University Press, 1995); two recent works by Stephen R. Niblo, *War, Diplomacy, and Development: The United States and Mexico, 1938–1954* (Wilmington, DE: Scholarly Resources, 1995), and *Mexico in the 1940s: Modernity, Politics, and Corruption* (Wilmington, DE: Scholarly Resources, 1999); Ian Roxborough, "Mexico," in *Latin America Between the Second World War and the Cold War, 1944–1948*, ed. Leslie Bethell and Ian Roxborough (Cambridge, England: Cambridge University Press, 1992), 190–216; and Peter Smith, "Mexico Since 1946: Dynamics of an Authoritarian Regime," in *Mexico Since Independence*, ed. Bethell, 321–96. All unattributed translations are mine.

2   Charles C. Cumberland, *Mexico, the Struggle for Modernity* (New York: Oxford University Press, 1968), 323 and, more broadly, 273–323.

3   Mexico legislated electoral reforms in 1976, 1987, 1990, 1993, 1994, and 1996. See Sergio Sarmiento, "Elecciones," *Reforma*, 7 July 1997. On the revolutionary magnitude of the shifts in economic policy, see M. Delal Baer, "Mexico's Second Revolution: Pathways to Liberalization," in *Political and Economic Liberalization in Mexico: At a Critical Juncture?*, ed. Riordan Roett (Boulder, CO: Lynne Rienner, 1993), 51–68.

4   Lorenzo Meyer, "Mexico: Economic Liberalism in an Authoritarian Polity," in *Market Economics and Political Change: Comparing China and Mexico*, ed. Juan D. Lindau and Timothy Cheek (Lanham, MD: Rowan and Littlefield, 1998), 156.

5   Héctor Aguilar Camín, *Subversiones silenciosas: Ensayos de historia y política de México* (Mexico City: Aguilar, 1993), 195–96.

6   Alan Knight, "Historical Continuities in Social Movements," in *Popular Movements and Po-*

litical Change in Mexico, ed. Joe Foweraker and Ann L. Craig (Boulder, CO: Lynne Rienner Publishers, 1990), 93; Juan Gabriel, *El México que se nos fue*, Bertelsmann de México CDP 743212 95802 7.

7   Héctor Aguilar Camín, "Historia para hoy," in *Historia, ¿para qué?* (Mexico City: Siglo XXI Editores, 1980), 148.

8   This essay variously uses terms such as "contemporary Mexico," "post-1940 Mexico," and "Mexico since 1940" to refer to Mexican history after 1940. It generally avoids using the word "modern," as Daniel Cosío Villegas linked it to the history of the Restored Republic and Porfiriato. See *Historia moderna de México*, 8 vols. (Mexico City: Editorial Hermes, 1955–1972).

9   Fernando Coronil, foreword to *Close Encounters of Empire: Writing the Cultural History of U.S.–Latin American Relations*, ed. Gilbert M. Joseph, Catherine C. LeGrand, and Ricardo D. Salvatore (Durham, NC: Duke University Press, 1998), xi. Néstor García Canclini, *La globalización imaginada* (Mexico City: Paidós, 1999), 48–49, makes similar observations.

10   Limitations of space require mentioning many topics that cannot be explored in depth. In this essay, "state" may be taken to mean that institutional entity and set of networks that have (a) the exclusive authority to make laws or rules; (b) the monopoly of violence with which to enforce them; and (c) the cultural power that lends this authority and enforcement the quality of moral regulation. "Society," in this case, designates all those persons who consider themselves Mexican in some fashion (wherever they live) and all those who reside within the boundaries of the Mexican Republic. "Culture" may be said simply to be the set of symbols and perceptions exhibited in the daily practices of groups of people by which they make sense of the world and express that sense. "The globe" and "global" refer to those transnational forces, whether of a state or a nonstate nature, that have exercised significant influence on Mexican society.

11   The designation Revolution to Evolution derives from the title of Howard Cline, *Mexico: Revolution to Evolution, 1940–1960* (New York: Oxford University Press, 1963). The sources within Mexico that shaped the construction of official history after the Revolution were numerous and varied. For an examination of the use of hero cults in the building of official history, see Ilene V. O'Malley, *The Myth of the Revolution: Hero Cults and the Institutionalization of the Mexican State, 1920–1940* (Westport, CT: Greenwood Press, 1986). For two recent accounts of the interplay between state "cultural projects," particularly education, and local popular cultural forms, see Alan Knight, "Popular Culture and the Revolutionary State in Mexico, 1910–1940," *Hispanic American Historical Review* 74, no. 3 (1994): 393–444; and Mary Kay Vaughan, *Cultural Politics in Revolution: Teachers, Peasants, and Schools in Mexico, 1930–1940* (Tucson: University of Arizona Press, 1997). Alex Saragoza's contribution to this volume discusses the construction of an official historical imagery for the purposes of tourism.

12   Early indications of this cooperation can be found in Arthur P. Whitaker, ed., *Mexico Today* (Philadelphia: American Academy of Political and Social Science, 1940). See also Niblo, *War, Diplomacy, and Development*, as well as two essays in this volume: Seth Fein's coverage of U.S.-Mexican wartime cooperation in cinema production and Eric Zolov's examination of the refashioning of Mexico's image in postwar tourism.

13 Stanley Robert Ross, "Mexico: The Preferred Revolution," in *Politics of Change in Latin America*, ed. Joseph Maier and Richard W. Weatherhead (New York: Praeger, 1964), 140; Frank Brandenburg, *The Making of Modern Mexico* (Englewood Cliffs, NJ: Prentice-Hall, 1964), xi. See also John A. Britton, *Revolution and Ideology: Images of the Mexican Revolution in the United States* (Lexington: University Press of Kentucky, 1995), 196–99. From a much later vantage point, Mexican historian Enrique Krauze denounced the process of self-deception that enveloped this generation of U.S. social scientists. "There were professors in the United States," he notes with a tone of irony, "who wound up viewing [the Mexican system] as the politicians wanted them to see it: not as a sham but as reality—an eccentric, revolutionary, one-party democracy." See Krauze, *Mexico, Biography of Power: A History of Modern Mexico, 1810–1996*, trans. Hank Heifetz (New York: HarperCollins, 1997), 549–50.

14 Lorenzo Meyer, "Historical Roots of the Authoritarian State in Mexico," in *Authoritarianism in Mexico*, ed. José Luis Reyna and Richard S. Weinert (Philadelphia: Institute for the Study of Human Issues, 1977), 3.

15 Brandenburg, *The Making of Modern Mexico*, 1.

16 Daniela Spenser and Bradley A. Levinson, "Linking State and Society in Discourse and Action: Political and Cultural Studies of the Cárdenas Era in Mexico," *Latin American Research Review* 34, no. 2 (1999): 245. Frank Tannenbaum, *Mexico, the Struggle for Peace and Bread* (New York: Knopf, 1950), 51, wrote that "the *mestizo* is generally the only Mexican who has a sense of the nation. . . . To him will go the credit of having created a common people out of the many diverse groups on Mexican soil."

17 Arturo Warman, "Indigenist Thought," in *Indigenous Anthropology in Non-Western Countries: Proceedings of a Burg Wartenstein Symposium*, ed. Hussein Fahim (Durham, NC: Carolina Academic Press, 1982), 92. In the view of anthropologist Oscar Lewis, the "Indian problem" had become a "limited and regional one" whose "redemption" was a major goal of the Mexican revolution. See Lewis, "Mexico Since Cárdenas," in *Social Change in Latin America Today: Its Implications for U.S. Policy* (New York: Harper and Brothers for the Council on Foreign Relations, 1960), 260.

18 José Agustín, *Tragicomedia mexicana* (Mexico City: Planeta, 1990), 1:144–45, 203–26; Carlos Monsiváis, "Notas sobre la cultura mexicana en el siglo XX," in *Historia general de México*, ed. El Centro de Estudios Históricos, El Colegio de México (Mexico City: El Colegio de México, 1976), 4:401. As an example of trivialization, see, the comments of T. B. Irving in his introduction to Samuel Ramos, *Profile of Man and Culture in Mexico*, trans. Peter G. Earle (Austin: University of Texas Press, 1962), xix: "Mexico is on the road up, the errors of youth are giving way to the experience of maturity. Mexicans no longer need to learn how to die; they may now even plan how to live." Paz's study of *mexicanidad* in *The Labyrinth of Solitude*, trans. Lysander Kemp (New York: Grove Press, 1961), influenced others to write Mexican national character profiles, such as chapter 1 of Alan Riding, *Distant Neighbors: A Portrait of the Mexicans* (New York: Knopf, 1984). On the origins of lo mexicano thought, see Henry C. Schmidt, *The Roots of Lo Mexicano: Self and Society in Mexican Thought, 1900–1934* (College Station: Texas A&M Press, 1978). John Mraz's essay in this volume discusses the world of magazine journalism.

19 Howard F. Cline, *United States and Mexico*, rev. ed. enlarged (New York: Atheneum, 1963), 6.

20 Aguilar Camín and Meyer, *In the Shadow of the Mexican Revolution*, 172–73; Richard S. Weinert, "The State and Foreign Capital," in *Authoritarianism in Mexico*, ed. Reyna and Weinert, 109–28. On the post–World War II world economic context, see Eric J. Hobsbawm, *The Age of Extremes: A History of the World, 1914–1991* (New York: Pantheon, 1994), chap. 9.

21 Miguel Ramírez, "Mexico," in *The Political Economy of Latin America in the Postwar Period*, ed. Laura Randall (Austin: University of Texas Press, 1997), 118–20.

22 Brandenburg, *The Making of Modern Mexico*, 219, 221. On Mexico's "two distinct and competitive elites," the economic and the political, see Peter H. Smith, "Does Mexico Have a Power Elite?" in *Authoritarianism in Mexico*, ed. Reyna and Weinert, 129–51.

23 Brandenburg, *The Making of Modern Mexico*, 4–18, 165.

24 Ramírez, "Mexico," 120–26.

25 René Villarreal, "The Policy of Import-Substituting Industrialization," in *Authoritarianism in Mexico*, ed. Reyna and Weinert, 96.

26 Ramírez, "Mexico," 126–30; Judith Teichman, *Policymaking in Mexico: From Boom to Crisis* (Boston: Allen and Unwin, 1988), 87–142.

27 Daniel Cosío Villegas, *El sistema político mexicano* (Mexico City: Joaquín Mortiz, 1975); *El estilo personal de gobernar* (Mexico City: Joaquín Mortiz, 1974); *La sucesión presidencial* (Mexico City: Joaquín Mortiz, 1975); *La sucesión: Desenlace y perspectivas*, 2d ed. (Mexico City: Joaquín Mortiz, 1976); Pablo González Casanova, *Democracy in Mexico*, trans. Danielle Salti (New York: Oxford University Press, 1970); Roger D. Hansen, *The Politics of Mexican Development* (Baltimore: Johns Hopkins University Press, 1971); Judith Adler Hellman, *Crisis in Mexico* (New York: Holmes and Meier, 1978); Kenneth F. Johnson, *Mexican Democracy: A Critical View*, rev. ed. (New York: Praeger, 1978); Gabriel Zaid, *El progreso improductivo* (Mexico City: Siglo XXI Editores, 1979); *La economía presidencial* (Mexico City: Editorial Vuelta, 1987); and *La nueva economía presidencial* (Mexico City: Editorial Grijalbo, 1994).

28 Roderic Ai Camp, *Mexican Political Biographies, 1935–1975* (Tucson: University of Arizona Press, 1976), and *Political Recruitment Across Two Centuries: Mexico, 1884–1991* (Austin: University of Texas Press, 1995); Peter H. Smith, *Labyrinths of Power: Political Recruitment in Twentieth-Century Mexico* (Princeton, NJ: Princeton University Press, 1979).

29 Brachet-Márquez, *Dynamics of Domination*, 7.

30 Miguel Angel Centeno, *Democracy Within Reason: Technocratic Revolution in Mexico* (University Park: Pennsylvania State University Press, 1994), 33.

31 For example, Stephen D. Morris, *Political Reformism in Mexico: An Overview of Contemporary Mexican Politics* (Boulder, CO: Lynne Rienner Publishers, 1995), 18.

32 Jonathan Hartlyn and Arturo Valenzuela, "Democracy in Latin America Since 1930," in *The Cambridge History of Latin America*, ed. Leslie Bethell (Cambridge, England: Cambridge University Press, 1994), 6:107.

33 Jeffrey W. Rubin, "Decentering the Regime: Culture and Regional Politics in Mexico," *Latin American Research Review* 31, no. 3 (1996): 97.

34 Ruth Berins Collier and David Collier, *Shaping the Political Arena: Critical Junctures, the Labor Movement, and Regime Dynamics in Latin America* (Princeton, NJ: Princeton University Press, 1991), 574.

35   See, for example, Bo Anderson and James D. Cockcroft, "Control and Co-optation in Mexican Politics," in *Dependence and Underdevelopment: Latin America's Political Economy*, ed. James D. Cockcroft, André Gunder Frank, and Dale L. Johnson (Garden City, NY: Doubleday Anchor, 1972), 219–44; and two works by Arnaldo Córdova, *La formación del poder político en México* (Mexico City: Era, 1972), and *La política de masas del cardenismo* (Mexico City: Era, 1974).

36   Stuart F. Voss, "Nationalizing the Revolution: Culmination and Circumstance," in *Provinces of the Revolution: Essays on Regional Mexican History, 1910–1929*, ed. Thomas Benjamin and Mark Wasserman (Albuquerque: University of New Mexico Press, 1990), 301.

37   Etienne Balibar, "The Nation Form: History and Ideology," in *Race, Nation, Class: Ambiguous Identities*, ed. Etienne Balibar and Immanuel Wallerstein, trans. Chris Turner (London: Verso, 1991), 92.

38   For a short introduction to the history of Mexican nationalism, see Héctor Aguilar Camín, "La invención de México," *Nexos*, July 1993, 49–61.

39   Viviane Brachet-Márquez, "Explaining Sociopolitical Change in Latin America: The Case of Mexico," *Latin American Research Review* 27, no. 3 (1992): 91.

40   Gabriel A. Almond and Sidney Verba, *The Civic Culture: Political Attitudes and Democracy in Five Nations* (Princeton, NJ: Princeton University Press, 1963). On the important relationship of culture to political power in Mexico, see Rubin, "Decentering the Regime," especially 85–86, 96–98, 103–19; and Gilbert M. Joseph and Daniel Nugent, "Popular Culture and State Formation in Revolutionary Mexico," in *Everyday Forms of State Formation: Revolution and the Negotiation of Rule in Modern Mexico*, ed. Gilbert M. Joseph and Daniel Nugent (Durham, NC: Duke University Press, 1994), 15–23.

41   Diane E. Davis, *Urban Leviathan: Mexico City in the Late Twentieth Century* (Philadelphia: Temple University Press, 1994), 11–12, 320–24.

42   Cynthia Hewitt de Alcántara, *Anthropological Perspectives on Rural Mexico* (London: Routledge and Kegan Paul, 1984), 69, 174.

43   One historian has noted that Mexico's average annual rate of real GDP growth was 6 percent in 1940–1979 and 0.18, 3.16, and 2.7 percent during the past three sexenios, respectively. See Enrique Semo, "La izquierda y las elecciones: Globalidad humanizada," *Proceso*, 6 February 2000, 50.

44   Manuel Pastor Jr. and Carol Wise, "Mexican-Style Neoliberalism: State Policy and Distributional Stress," in *The Post-NAFTA Political Economy: Mexico and the Western Hemisphere*, ed. Carol Wise (University Park: Pennsylvania State University Press, 1998), 43, 80.

45   Baer, "Mexico's Second Revolution,"; William Perry, "Mexico and NAFTA: The Politico-Security Dimension in Historical Perspective," in *Assessments of the North American Free Trade Agreement*, ed. Ambler H. Moss Jr. (New Brunswick, NJ: Transaction Publishers, 1993), 33–51.

46   Krauze, *Mexico, Biography of Power*, 529.

47   Ibid., 734–35.

48   Ibid., 736–37.

49   Claudio Lomnitz accuses Krauze of "anthropomorphizing national history" in "An Intellectual's Stock in the Factory of Mexican Ruins," *American Journal of Sociology* 103, no. 4 (1998): 1055.

60   *Arthur Schmidt*

50   Ibid. For the Krauze-Lomnitz interchange, see *Milenio*, 11 May 1998–1 June 1998.

51   Krauze, *Mexico, Biography of Power*, 553; emphasis in the original.

52   David Thelen and Lorenzo Meyer, "A Conversation with Lorenzo Meyer about Mexico's Political Transition: From Authoritarianism to What?" *Journal of American History* 86, no. 2 (1999): 603.

53   "You see how fate gets you for everything and forgets nothing," a line from "Cuando el destino," a song written by José Alfredo Jiménez. For a version sung by Pedro Infante, *José Alfredo Jiménez y sus interpretes*, Ofreón JDC-055.

54   On present-day Mexico's condition as a time of troubles, see Jorge G. Castañeda, *The Mexican Shock: Its Meaning for the United States* (New York: New Press, 1995), 141–45.

55   Jeffrey Bortz, "The Effect of Mexico's Postwar Industrialization on the U.S.-Mexico Price and Wage Comparison," in *U.S.-Mexico Relations: Labor Market Interdependence*, ed. Jorge A. Bustamante, Clark W. Reynolds, and Raúl A. Hinojosa Ojeda (Stanford, CA: Stanford University Press, 1992), 229.

56   Roberto Newell G. and Luis Rubio F., *Mexico's Dilemma: The Political Origins of Economic Crisis* (Boulder, CO: Westview Press, 1984), 111.

57   Clark W. Reynolds, "Why Mexico's 'Stabilizing Development' Was Actually Destabilizing (With Some Implications for the Future)," *World Development* 6, nos. 7–8 (1978): 1007, 1012; Carlos Tello, "La economía mexicana: Hacia el tercer milenio," *Nexos*, July 1996, 48; Manuel Pastor and Carol Wise, "State Policy, Distribution, and Neoliberal Reform in Mexico," *Journal of Latin American Studies* 29, no. 2 (1997): 421–29.

58   David Thelen, "Rethinking History and the Nation-State: Mexico and the United States," *Journal of American History* 86, no. 2 (September 1999): 440.

59   Thelen and Meyer, "A Conversation with Lorenzo Meyer," 606.

60   Alan Knight, "The Modern Mexican State: Theory and Practice," paper delivered at the Twentieth Congress of the Latin American Studies Association, Guadalajara, Jalisco, Mexico, 17–19 April 1997, 19.

61   Stuart Hall, "Cultural Studies: Two Paradigms," in *What Is Cultural Studies? A Reader*, ed. John Storey (London: Arnold, 1996), 48.

62   Martin Albrow, *The Global Age: State and Society Beyond Modernity* (Stanford, CA: Stanford University Press, 1996), 95.

63   Ibid., 106, 107.

64   José E. Limón, *American Encounters: Greater Mexico, the United States, and the Erotics of Culture* (Boston: Beacon Press, 1998), 3, defines the idea of "Greater Mexico" as encompassing "all Mexicans . . . from either side, with all their commonalities and differences" as well as the processes of "internalization" of Mexican influences within the United States and U.S. influences within Mexico. The *Journal of American History* 86, no. 2 (1999) devoted a special issue, entitled *Rethinking History and the Nation-State: Mexico and the United States as a Case Study*, to a more global conception of history. This issue may be found at <http://www.indiana.edu/~jah/mexico> (9 March 2000).

65   On the importance of Mexican migration in Mexican life, see Jorge Durand and Douglas Massey, "Mexican Migration to the United States: A Critical Review," *Latin American Research Review* 27, no. 2 (1992): 3–42.

66   See Roger Rouse, "Mexican Migration and the Social Space of Postmodernism," in *Be-*

tween Two Worlds: Mexican Immigrants in the United States, ed. David G. Gutiérrez (Wilmington, DE: Scholarly Resources, 1996), 247–63; and Michael Kearney, *Reconceptualizing the Peasantry: Anthropology in Global Perspective* (Boulder, CO: Westview Press, 1996), chaps. 1, 8.

67   See Jorge Durand and Douglas Massey, *Miracles on the Border: Retablos of Mexican Migrants to the United States* (Tucson: University of Arizona Press, 1995).

68   Manuel García Griego offers an account of the historical evolution of the Bracero Program in "The Importation of Mexican Contract Laborers to the United States, 1942–1964," in *Between Two Worlds*, ed. Gutiérrez, 89–117.

69   For example, Krauze, *Mexico, Biography of Power*, ignores the subject. Smith, "Mexico Since 1946," and Aguilar Camín and Meyer, *In the Shadow of the Mexican Revolution*, offer only the shortest of mentions. The Colegio de México's *Historia de la Revolución Mexicana* does discuss migration, but generally only as an aspect of Mexican diplomatic issues with the United States. Multivolume histories such as *México, un pueblo en la historia* and Pablo González Casanova, coord., *La clase obrera en la historia de México*, 17 vols. (Mexico City: Siglo XXI Editores, 1980–1981), place Mexican international migration in separate volumes, defining the experience of Mexican migrant labor as a subject external to Mexico itself whose social history takes place only within the bounds of the United States.

70   Leslie Byrd Simpson, *Many Mexicos*, 4th rev. ed. (Berkeley: University of California Press, 1966).

71   Steve Stern, *The Secret History of Gender: Women, Men, and Power in Late Colonial Mexico* (Chapel Hill: University of North Carolina Press, 1995), 23–24. On the plurality of Mexican culture, see also Carlos Fuentes, *Nuevo tiempo mexicano* (Mexico City: Aguilar, 1994), 81–93.

72   Fernando Coronil, *The Magical State: Nature, Money, and Modernity in Venezuela* (Chicago: University of Chicago Press, 1997), 63–65, offers a critique of this conventional liberal formulation.

73   Lorenzo Meyer, "Agencia Ciudadana," *Reforma*, 7 September 1995.

74   Alan Knight, "State Power and Political Stability in Mexico," in *Mexico: Dilemmas of Transition*, ed. Neil Harvey (London: The Institute of Latin American Studies, University of London and British Academic Press, 1993), 42, 52, 54, 57.

75   See Joel S. Migdal, *Strong Societies and Weak States: State-Society Relations and State Capabilities in the Third World* (Princeton, NJ: Princeton University Press, 1988).

76   Balibar, "The Nation Form," 91.

77   For the phrase "ramshackle institution," see Knight, "Historical Continuities in Social Movements," 95.

78   See Luis Rubio, "El talón de Aquiles de la reforma económica," *Vuelta*, July 1993, 36–39.

79   Laurence Whitehead, "State Organization in Latin America Since 1930," in *The Cambridge History of Latin America*, ed. Bethell, 6:34.

80   Carlos Monsiváis, "Ya no semidiós, sino un funcionario: El ocaso del presidencialismo," *Universidad de México*, July–August 1995, 21.

81   Knight, "Historical Continuities in Social Movements," 93.

82   Rubin, "Decentering the Regime," 99, 103–12, 235.

83   Sylvia Maxfield, *Governing Capital: International Finance and Mexican Politics* (Ithaca,

NY: Cornell University Press, 1990), shows the influence of the banking sector on Mexican state economic policy.

84 See, for example, Bonfil Batalla, *México Profundo: Reclaiming a Civilization*, trans. Philip A. Dennis (Austin: University of Texas Press, 1996); Vivienne Bennett, *The Politics of Water: Urban Protest, Gender, and Power in Monterrey, Mexico* (Pittsburgh: University of Pittsburgh Press, 1995); John Gledhill, *Casi Nada: A Study of Agrarian Reform in the Homeland of Cardenismo* (Albany: State University of New York Press, 1991); Frans J. Schryer, *Ethnicity and Class Conflict in Rural Mexico* (Princeton, NJ: Princeton University Press, 1990); Lane Simonian, *Defending the Land of the Jaguar: A History of Conservation in Mexico* (Austin: University of Texas Press, 1995).

85 See Brachet-Márquez, *The Dynamics of Domination*, and Middlebrook, *The Paradox of Revolution*.

86 See, for example, Roderic Ai Camp, *Generals in the Palacio: The Military in Modern Mexico* (New York: Oxford University Press, 1992), and *Crossing Swords: Politics and Religion in Mexico* (New York: Oxford University Press, 1997); and Joseph E. Cotter, "Before the Green Revolution: Agricultural Science Policy in Mexico, 1920–1950" (Ph.D. diss., University of California at Santa Barbara, 1994).

87 Jorge Medina Viedas, *Elites y democracia en México* (Mexico City: Cal y Arena, 1998), 291–95. See also Carlos Monsiváis, *Días de guardar* (Mexico City: Editorial Era, 1970).

88 Eric Van Young, "Introduction: Are Regions Good to Think?" in *Mexico's Regions: Comparative History and Development*, ed. Eric Van Young (La Jolla: Center for U.S.-Mexican Studies, University of California at San Diego, 1992), 1.

89 Carlos Monsiváis, " 'Just Over That Hill': Notes on Centralism and Regional Cultures," in *Mexico's Regions*, ed. Van Young, 247.

90 Claudio Lomnitz-Adler, "Concepts for the Study of Regional Culture," in *Mexico's Regions*, ed. Van Young, 84.

91 Ibid., 73, 76. See also Claudio Lomnitz, *Exits from the Labyrinth: Culture and Ideology in the Mexican National Space* (Berkeley: University of California Press, 1992).

92 Bryan Roberts, "The Place of Regions in Mexico," in *Mexico's Regions*, ed. Van Young, 227.

93 Jeffrey W. Rubin, "Popular Mobilization and the Myth of State Corporatism," in *Popular Movements and Political Change in Mexico*, ed. Foweraker and Craig, 248–49.

94 Rubin, "Decentering the Regime," 121. See also his *Decentering the Regime: Ethnicity, Radicalism, and Democracy in Juchitán, Mexico* (Durham, NC: Duke University Press, 1997).

95 See Pilcher in this volume as well as his *¡Que vivan los tamales! Food and the Making of Mexican Identity* (Albuquerque: University of New Mexico Press, 1998), especially chap. 6.

96 Pilcher, *¡Que vivan los tamales!*, 156.

97 See the essays of Alex Saragoza and Eric Zolov in this volume.

98 Bob Jessop, *State Theory: Putting the Capitalist State in Its Place* (University Park: Pennsylvania State University Press, 1990), 367.

99 Coronil, *The Magical State*, 4, uses this phrase to describe Venezuela, but it also aptly applies to contemporary Mexico.

100 Jessop, *State Theory*, 365.

Making It Real Compared to What?   63

101 Rubin, "Decentering the Regime," 99.

102 William Roseberry, "Hegemony and the Language of Contention," in *Everyday Forms of State Formation*, ed. Joseph and Nugent, 360–61.

103 Joseph and Nugent, "Popular Culture and State Formation in Revolutionary Mexico," 3.

104 Aguilar Camín, *Subversiones silenciosas*.

105 Stern, *The Secret History of Gender*, 327.

106 Arturo Escobar, "Culture, Economics, and Politics in Latin American Social Movements Theory and Research," in *The Making of Social Movements in Latin America: Identity, Strategy, and Democracy*, ed. Arturo Escobar and Sonia E. Alvarez (Boulder, CO: Westview Press, 1992), 63.

107 James C. Scott, *Seeing Like a State: How Certain Schemes to Improve the Human Condition Have Failed* (New Haven: Yale University Press, 1998), 4, 344, 346. Scott warns against the "high-modernist ideology" inherent in a great deal of social science and advocates paying attention to "the skills, intelligence, and experience of ordinary people."

108 Carlos Monsiváis, who cautions against the conflation of popular cultures into one popular culture, also makes careful distinctions among shared tastes and experiences on the one hand, and cultures on the other. See Monsiváis, *Mexican Postcards*, ed. and trans. John Kraniauskas (London: Verso, 1997), 190.

109 Néstor García Canclini, "Modernity after Postmodernity," in *Beyond the Fantastic: Contemporary Art Criticism from Latin America*, ed. Gerardo Mosquera (Cambridge, MA: MIT Press, 1996), 46–47.

110 One recent historical work that appreciates popular cultures in a useful fashion is Mary Kay Vaughan's *Cultural Politics in Revolution* (196–98). Although the book focuses on the years 1930–1940, Vaughan offers some highly important observations for students of the post-1940 period, particularly those centering around how, "in the negotiation of cultural politics through schooling in the 1930s, a shared language for dissent and consent was forged." This interaction between elements of the state and society created a "notion of the cultural nation as a multiethnic one made up of a multiplicity of local cultures." These cultural and social constructs remained alive, serving as the means by which elements of society negotiated their compliance with the "long period of social development, differentiation, and maturation" after 1940.

111 "There's Nothing Complete," a song written by Bulmaro Bermúdez and Rodrigo Montoya Cedillo and sung by Vicente Fernández, *El número uno*, Columbia CDDE 950.

112 Néstor García Canclini, *Hybrid Cultures: Strategies for Entering and Leaving Modernity*, trans. Christopher L. Chiappari and Silvia L. López (Minneapolis: University of Minnesota Press, 1995), 120; emphasis in the original.

113 Monsiváis, *Mexican Postcards*, 22. Another version of "recycling the future" returned with the future-oriented rhetoric surrounding the neoliberal policies of Carlos Salinas. See Eduardo Barrera, "The U.S.-Mexico Border as Post-NAFTA Mexico," in *Mass Media and Free Trade: NAFTA and the Cultural Industries*, ed. Emile G. McAnany and Kenton T. Wilkinson (Austin: University of Texas Press, 1996), 197.

114 Coronil, *The Magical State*, 3, likens the pretense of historical completeness to a magic show in which "what is forgotten screens what is remembered."

115 Carlos Monsiváis, *Entrada libre: Crónicas de la sociedad que se organiza* (Mexico City: Edici-

ones Era, 1987). The extraordinary activity of Mexican civil society has been of keen interest to anthropologists, sociologists, writers of fiction, and chroniclers of social testimony. Just a few of the titles available are Judith Adler Hellman, *Mexican Lives* (New York: New Press, 1994); Sarah LeVine, *Dolor y Alegría: Women and Social Change in Urban Mexico* (Madison: University of Wisconsin Press, 1993); Carlos Monsiváis, *Los rituales del caos* (Mexico City: Ediciones Era, 1995); Elena Poniatowska, *Massacre in Mexico*, trans. Helen R. Lane (Columbia: University of Missouri Press, 1991), and *Nothing, Nobody: Voices of the Mexico City Earthquake*, trans. Aurora Camacho de Schmidt and Arthur Schmidt (Philadelphia: Temple University Press, 1995); and Rafael Reygadas Robles Gil, *Abriendo veredas: Iniciativas públicas y sociales de las redes de organizaciones civiles* (Mexico City: Convergencia de Organismos Civiles por la Democracia, 1998).

116 Néstor García Canclini, *Transforming Modernity: Popular Culture in Mexico*, trans. Lidia Lozano (Austin: University of Texas Press, 1993), 21–22; the extensive italics in the original text have been removed.

117 See the contributions in this volume by Seth Fein, Heather Levi, John Mraz, Anne Rubenstein, Alex Saragoza, and Eric Zolov. Néstor García Canclini notes the formation of the Instituto Nacional de Bellas Artes y Literatura, the Museo de Artes Plásticas, the Academias Mexicanas de la Danza y la Opera in 1947, the Instituto Nacional Indígenista in 1948, and the Museo Nacional de Artes e Industrias Populares in 1951. See "La cultura mexicana hacia el próximo milenio," in *México hacia el 2000: Desafíos y opciones*, coord. Pablo González Casanova (Caracas: Editorial Nueva Sociedad, 1989), 385.

118 Anne Rubenstein, *Bad Language, Naked Ladies, and Other Threats to the Nation: A Political History of Comic Books in Mexico* (Durham, NC: Duke University Press, 1998), 31, 42, 164. Eighty percent of the comic book production in Mexico is of domestic origin, according to William Rowe and Vivian Schelling, *Memory and Modernity: Popular Culture in Latin America* (London: Verso, 1991), 112.

119 Carlos Monsiváis has labeled José Alfredo Jiménez "the poet of marginal desolation" in "'Les diré que llegué de un mundo raro,'" *La Jornada Semanal*, 30 May 1999.

120 Carlos Monsiváis, "Mythologies," in *Mexican Cinema*, ed. Paulo Antonio Paranaguá (London: British Film Institute, 1995), 127. See also Carlos Monsiváis and Carlos Bonfil, *A través del espejo: El cine mexicano y su público* (Mexico City: Ediciones El Milagro/Instituto Mexicano de Cinematografía, 1994).

121 Monsiváis, *Mexican Postcards*, 447.

122 Jean Franco, *Plotting Women: Gender and Representation in Mexico* (New York: Columbia University Press, 1989), 152. Julia Tuñón argues that in his films, "Fernández unconsciously represented the problem of the transition from a traditional communitarian social model to an individualistic modern world." See Tuñón, "Emilio Fernández: A Look Behind the Bars," in *Mexican Cinema*, ed. Paranaguá, 189.

123 Monsiváis, "Notas sobre la cultura mexicana," 446.

124 Monsiváis, *Mexican Postcards*, 100.

125 See Joanne Hershfield, *Mexican Cinema/Mexican Woman, 1940–1950* (Tucson: University of Arizona Press, 1996).

126 García Canclini, "Modernity after Postmodernity," 40. See also his "La cultura mexicana hacia el próximo milenio," 385–87.

127   García Canclini notes how little research has been done in Mexico on the consumption of material and cultural goods. See "El consumo cultural y su estudio en México: Una propuesta teórica," in *El consumo cultural en México*, coord. Néstor García Canclini (Mexico City: Consejo Nacional para la Cultura y las Artes, 1993), 15.

128   Seth Fein, "Everyday Forms of Transnational Collaboration: U.S. Film Propaganda in Cold War Mexico," in *Close Encounters of Empire*, ed. Joseph, LeGrand, and Salvatore, 423–33.

129   Quoted in Waldir Jose Rampinelli and Nildo Domingos Ouriques, eds., *Os 500 anos: A conquista interminavel* (Petropolis, Brazil: Editora Vozes, 1999), 88–89. I am indebted to my colleague Philip Evanson for bringing this quotation to my attention. For a recent study of the life of Azcárraga, see Claudia Fernández and Andrew Paxman, *El tigre: Emilio Azcárraga y su imperio Televisa* (Mexico City: Grijalbo, 2000).

130   Carlos Monsiváis, "Cultural Integration in Latin America at the Millennium," in *A New Moment in the Americas*, ed. Robert S. Leiken (New Brunswick, NJ: Transaction Publishers, 1994), 86.

131   García Canclini, "La cultura mexicana hacia el próximo milenio," 388–92.

132   García Canclini, "Culturas de la ciudad de México: Símbolos colectivos y usos del espacio urbano," in *El consumo cultural en México*, coord. García Canclini, 43–85.

133   Monsiváis, *Mexican Postcards*, 23.

134   Eric Zolov, *Refried Elvis: The Rise of the Mexican Counterculture* (Berkeley: University of California Press, 1999), 11.

135   Coronil, *The Magical State*, 16.

136   Zolov, *Refried Elvis*, 196–97.

137   Julia Tuñón Pablos, *Women in Mexico: A Past Unveiled*, trans. Alan Hynds (Austin: University of Texas Press, 1999), 110–13.

138   Matthew C. Gutmann, *The Meanings of Macho: Being a Man in Mexico City* (Berkeley: University of California Press, 1996), 9, 48, 170.

139   Monsiváis, *Mexican Postcards*, 14–15; Gutmann, *The Meanings of Macho*, 27.

140   Gutmann, *The Meanings of Macho*, 79, 88, 236, 244, 263.

141   In a more recent setting, Gutmann (ibid., 79, 88) found that many men defined responsibility for their children's care and upbringing as an important characteristic of their definition of manliness.

142   On matters of agency and popular culture, see the *Hispanic American Historical Review* 79, no. 2 (May 1999) devoted to "the new cultural history."

143   Gutmann, *The Meanings of Macho*, 260.

144   Amid the voluminous literature on Chiapas that has resulted since 1994, see Neil Harvey, *The Chiapas Rebellion: The Struggle for Land and Democracy* (Durham, NC: Duke University Press, 1998), and Ejército Zapatista de Liberación Nacional (EZLN), *Documentos y comunicados*, 3 vols. (Mexico City: Ediciones Era, 1994–1997). For a long-term historical perspective on issues of indigenous identity in Mexico, see Enrique Florescano, *Etnía, estado y nación: Ensayo sobre las identidades colectivas en México* (Mexico City: Aguilar, 1997).

145   Alan Knight makes this point in examining the ideas concerning race of Gonzalo Aguirre Beltrán, Alfonso Caso, Manuel Gamio, and José Vasconcelos. See Knight, "Racism, Rev-

olution, and *Indigenismo,*" in *The Idea of Race in Latin America, 1870–1940*, ed. Richard Graham (Austin: University of Texas Press, 1990), 71–113. See also Warman, "Indigenist Thought," 75–96.

146 Elena Poniatowska and Kent Klich, "In the Street," *DoubleTake* (winter 1998): 118. Poniatowska was responsible for the text, Klich for the photographs.

147 See Héctor Castillo, Sergio Zermeño, and Alicia Ziccardi, "Juventud popular y bandas en la ciudad de México," in *Cultura y pospolítica: El debate sobre la modernidad en América Latina*, comp. Néstor García Canclini (Mexico City: Consejo Nacional para la Cultura y las Artes, 1991), 273–94. For some of the complex problems of urban popular cultures, see Monsiváis, *Los rituales del caos*.

148 Barrera, "The U.S.-Mexico Border," 191–92.

149 See LeVine, *Dolor y Alegría*, chap. 6; Lourdes Benería, "The Mexican Debt Crisis: Restructuring the Economy and the Household," in *Unequal Burden: Economic Crises, Persistent Poverty, and Women's Work*, ed. Lourdes Benería and Shelly Feldman (Boulder, CO: Westview Press, 1992), 83–104; and Mercedes González de la Rocha, "Family Well-Being, Food Consumption, and Survival Strategies During Mexico's Economic Crisis," in *Social Responses to Mexico's Economic Crisis of the 1980s*, ed. Mercedes González de la Rocha and Agustín Escobar Latapí (La Jolla: Center for U.S.-Mexican Studies, University of California at San Diego, 1991), 115–27. For a recent study of street vending that would benefit from more attention to matters of popular culture, see John C. Cross, *Informal Politics: Street Vendors and the State in Mexico City* (Stanford, CA: Stanford University Press, 1998).

150 Rubenstein, *Bad Language, Naked Ladies, and Other Threats to the Nation*, 14.

151 Oscar Lewis, *Five Families: Mexican Case Studies in the Culture of Poverty* (New York: Wiley, 1962), 125–209.

152 Roger Bartra, *The Cage of Melancholy: Identity and Metamorphosis in the Mexican Character*, trans. Christopher J. Hall (New Brunswick, NJ: Rutgers University Press, 1992), 163.

153 See John Womack Jr., "Chiapas, the Bishop of San Cristóbal, and the Zapatista Revolt," in *Rebellion in Chiapas: An Historical Reader*, ed. John Womack Jr. (New York: New Press, 1999), 1–59.

154 Jean Meyer, *El sinarquismo: ¿Un fascismo mexicano?, 1937–1947* (Mexico City: Joaquín Mortiz, 1979). Sinarquismo was a right-wing Catholic movement that operated chiefly in the 1930s and 1940s to resist the domestic social agenda of the Revolution and to promote traditional values and political action among Mexico's rural population.

155 See Camp, *Crossing Swords*, and Michael Tangeman, *Mexico at the Crossroads: Politics, the Church, and the Poor* (Maryknoll, NY: Orbis, 1995).

156 Gilbert Joseph, "Close Encounters: Toward a New Cultural History of U.S.-Latin American Relations," in *Close Encounters of Empire*, ed. Joseph, LeGrand, and Salvatore, 18.

157 García Canclini, "La cultura mexicana hacia el próximo milenio," 387.

158 Coronil, foreword to *Close Encounters of Empire*, ed. Joseph, Le Grand, and Salvatore, x.

159 Amid the enormous literature on the border, see Timothy J. Dunn, *The Militarization of the U.S.-Mexico Border: Low-Intensity Conflict Doctrine Comes Home* (Austin: Center for Mexican American Studies, University of Texas, 1996); García Canclini, *Hybrid Cultures*, chap. 7; Lawrence A. Herzog, ed., *Shared Space: Rethinking the U.S.-Mexico Border Envi-*

ronment (La Jolla: Center for U.S.-Mexican Studies, University of California at San Diego, 1999); Kathryn Kopinak, *Desert Capitalism: Maquiladoras in North America's Western Industrial Corridor* (Tucson: University of Arizona Press, 1996); Oscar J. Martínez, *Border People: Life and Society in the U.S.-Mexico Borderlands* (Tucson: University of Arizona Press, 1994); Ramón Eduardo Ruiz, *On the Rim of Mexico: Encounters of the Rich and Poor* (Boulder, CO: Westview Press, 1998); Susan Tiano, *Patriarchy on the Line: Labor, Gender, and Ideology in the Mexican Maquiladora Industry* (Philadelphia: Temple University Press, 1994).

160   Carlos Monsiváis, "Se crea un 'pueblo' al instante," *Reforma*, 22 June 1999.

161   Monsiváis, " 'Just Over the Hill,' " 250.

162   David Held, David Goldblatt, Anthony McGrew, and Jonathan Perraton, *Global Transformations: Politics, Economics, and Culture* (Stanford, CA: Stanford University Press, 1999), 374.

163   See the comments of, for example, Alejandra Lajous Vargas, director of Channel 11 in Mexico City: "Mexico: Culture and Identity in the Information Age," in *Identities in North America: The Search for Community*, ed. Robert L. Earle and John D. Wirth (Stanford, CA: Stanford University Press, 1995), 102–14.

164   See the discussion in this volume by Hernández and McAnany of the competition between Televisa and Televisión Azteca. Mexican fiction has appreciated the power of mass media control. Artemio Cruz, the fictional character created by Carlos Fuentes to symbolize the transformation of the popular uprising of the Mexican revolution into a system of oligarchic domination, was a mass communications mogul. See Fuentes, *The Death of Artemio Cruz*, trans. Alfred MacAdam (New York: Noonday Press/Farrar, Straus and Giroux, 1991). On issues of concentrated mass media control in the United States, see Robert W. McChesney, *Rich Media, Poor Democracy: Communication Politics in Dubious Times* (Champaign: University of Illinois Press, 1999).

165   Barrera, "The U.S.-Mexico Border," 207–9.

166   See Sergio Aguayo Quesada, *Myths and (Mis)Perceptions: Changing U.S. Elite Visions of Mexico*, trans. Julian Brody (La Jolla: Center for U.S.-Mexican Studies, University of Califonia at San Diego, 1998).

167   See Néstor García Canclini, "North Americans or Latin Americans? The Redefinition of Mexican Identity and the Free Trade Agreements," in *Mass Media and Free Trade*, ed. McAnany and Wilkinson, 142–56.

168   Benedict Anderson, *Imagined Communities: Reflections on the Origin and Spread of Nationalism* (New York: Verso, 1983); Coronil, *The Magical State*.

169   Bartra, *The Cage of Melancholy*, 165.

II

AT PLAY AMONG

THE FRAGMENTS

Mexico's Pepsi Challenge:
Traditional Cooking, Mass Consumption,
and National Identity

Jeffrey M. Pilcher

The Tzotzil Indians of San Juan Chamula may never appear on television commercials in the United States, but they nevertheless form part of the Pepsi Generation. Though Mexicans usually celebrate religious festivals with beer or tequila, in this highland Chiapas community toasts are invariably made with Pepsi-Cola. The Tzotzil devotion to soft drinks illustrates the ubiquitous presence of industrial processed food in even the most remote indigenous regions—and the fact that the cacique (political boss) controls the Pepsi distributorship.[1] The neighborhood store, with its refrigerator full of ice-cold Pepsi, therefore provides not only a watering hole for Chamulans but also a meeting place among global capital, national politics, and local cultures. This essay examines the dramatic transformation of Mexican foodways in the twentieth century and the resulting contests over markets, gender, and national identity.

The challenge posed to Mexicans by the growth of mass culture in all its forms has been to realize the possibilities of nationalism and industrialization in a democratic manner that preserves the distinctiveness of local cultures. Few areas can claim greater urgency in this regard than food policy. The history of postcolonial Africa and India clearly demonstrates the need for democratic governance of food distribution. Despite a rapidly growing population, India has been spared from famine not because of the agricultural gains of the so-called Green Revolution, but rather through political mechanisms for ensuring that the hungriest people get food. Starvation in

Africa meanwhile has resulted largely from the actions of armed bands who confiscated and sold food aid shipments and locally grown crops, leaving people to die.[2]

Ensuring the nutritional health of the poor is equally difficult without respect for local cooking traditions. Peasant cultures throughout the world have developed nutritionally balanced diets of complementary vegetable proteins, for example, rice and soybeans in Asia, or maize and beans in the Americas, to replace expensive animal proteins. Industrial processed foods such as powdered milk can supplement these diets in important ways, but the devaluation of traditional cooking through transnational advertising and misplaced ideals of modernity has primarily increased the consumption of junk foods based on fats and sugars. The gravest risks lie in the transition between traditional and industrial diets, as poor Mexicans substitute *alimentos pacotilla* (packaged foods) for vegetable proteins, but cannot afford the meats that supply protein to the diets of the rich.[3]

Nevertheless, food processing moguls do not alone dictate the industrialization of foodways, a point clearly demonstrated by the role of women in the transformation of Mexico's staple, the corn tortilla. Women labored endlessly to grind maize by hand on the pre-Hispanic *metate* (saddle quern), yet they adopted mechanical mills only with great hesitancy in the twentieth century. Their skepticism about the new technology reflected not a reflexive peasant conservatism but justifiable concerns about the costs of using the mills and about their own identity within the family. And when a cottage industry of tortilla factories finally replaced household production on a daily basis, it was threatened in turn by the monopolistic efforts of the Maseca corporation to sell *masa harina* (dehydrated tortilla flour). But once again many women rejected any changes in their tortillas, despite the company's insistent advertising campaigns.[4]

Although resistance to Maseca affirms the vitality of local cooking traditions, the corporation's massive growth illustrates an equally important point for cultural studies. The homogenizing effects of national food-processing companies may pose as great a threat to local cultures as the more visible cultural imperialism represented by Ronald McDonald. Maseca executives dream of a day when their gleaming factories process all the maize in Mexico, removing the "imperfections" that many people believe give tortillas their character. Global corporations meanwhile have learned that to compete successfully in national markets they need to modify their products to suit native consumers. A Big Mac with fries may taste exactly the same in Mexico City, Beijing, and Oak Brook, but even McDonald's has adapted to local markets, either by serving salsa with the fries or by posing the eponymous clown as Buddha.[5] No doubt the world will continue to grow more like the United States, as the Cassandras of cultural imperialism have warned, but the converse is equally true, as ever more people in the United States eat Maseca tortillas.

Traditional Cooking and Female Identity

The film adaptation of Laura Esquivel's novel *Like Water for Chocolate* illustrated the rich expressiveness of traditional Mexican cooking as a performance art. The heroine, Tita, forbidden to marry her beloved Pedro, carried on an illicit affair through the medium of cooking. In one of the more provocative scenes of the movie she prepared *mole poblano* (turkey with chile pepper sauce) on the traditional grinding stone, and the sight of her gracefully swaying body nearly gave him a heart attack. This section examines the intimate connections between female identity and traditional cooking, particularly grinding corn on the metate, as a prelude to discussing twentieth-century changes in Mexican cuisine.

Pre-Hispanic people would certainly have understood the European aphorism "You are what you eat." The basically vegetarian diet eaten by all but a small nobility clearly justified such identification. Even though maize provided as much as 80 percent of the daily intake, when combined with beans, chiles, and squash it formed the basis for a nutritionally balanced diet. The complementarity between corn and beans, each of which supplied amino acids missing in the other, ensured a regular supply of high-quality proteins in the absence of European domesticated animals such as cattle, pigs, and chickens. The Aztec Empire supported a population of as many as 25 million people, but only through the hard of work of farmers and cooks.[6]

The labor-intensive cooking techniques developed by pre-Hispanic *campesinos* continued to dominate the nineteenth-century Mexican kitchen. At its center stood the metate, a rough black tablet of volcanic rock, sloping forward on three stubby legs, used to grind corn for tortillas and tamales, chiles and seeds for sauces, and fruits and chocolate to drink. The Spanish *fogón* (brick stove) distinguished well-equipped kitchens from the *comal* (griddle) laid over an open fire in popular barrios, but both rich and poor cooked in the same earthenware *ollas* (pots) and *cazuelas* (bowls).

Everyday staples had long been commercialized in Mexico City, where the wealthy ate wheat bread from professional bakers and more modest housewives purchased corn tortillas from what were essentially metate sweat shops. But in the countryside and in poor urban neighborhoods, women spent up to five hours each day preparing tortillas to feed their families. Elite stereotypes of Native Americans as long-suffering wretches owed much to the image of women kneeling at the metate. To understand the backbreaking work of wielding a heavy stone *mano* (muller), one can look to the heavily muscled triceps and backs of the Indian women depicted by the muralist Diego Rivera. Women could not gain sufficient leverage to grind corn standing up, so swollen knees became a painful side effect of feeding a family.[7]

Within the family, at least, a woman gained status and identity through her skill at the metate. Historian Wendy Waters has examined these social implications using the field notes of anthropological studies conducted from the 1920s to the 1940s in Tepoztlán, Morelos. Tortilla making was so essential to domestic life that no woman in the village became eligible for marriage until she had demonstrated this skill. Men complimented women by praising their tortillas, and some even claimed to be able to identify the unique taste and texture of corn ground on their wives' metate. Women expressed affection through their role of feeding the family, offering favorite children extra helpings of beans or reserving for them the best tortillas. As a result, children were sensitive to the size of their portions and to the order in which they were fed. Food served to communicate anger as well as love; a wife could burn her husband's tortillas if she suspected him of infidelity.[8]

The symbolic connections between cook and food, already present in the daily preparation of tortillas, beans, and chile peppers, grew exponentially during festive meals, along with the work required. Tamales survive as one of the oldest ceremonial foods in the Western Hemisphere—and one of the most time-consuming—made by spreading *nixtamal* dough inside corn husks, adding chile sauce and bits of meat or beans, folding them up into dumplings, and steaming them in an olla. Mole poblano, another venerable dish served at religious and family celebrations, comprised turkey and a complex sauce of chile peppers, nuts, seeds, and spices. The elaborate concoction achieved such intense flavors through the technique of toasting the ingredients first on the comal, then grinding them separately on the metate, before simmering them all together in a cazuela, a process that could take days to complete. Women undertook such arduous work to help ensure the stability of the entire community. Indeed, memories of mole continue to draw modern migrant workers home every year to participate. And women gained respect and authority for the physical labor they performed in feeding the community.[9]

Changes in the twentieth century placed enormous strain on traditional cooking and the communities it helped preserve. The spread of railroads during the dictatorship of Porfirio Díaz (1876–1911) and of highways under the revolutionary governments that followed (1911–1940) opened subsistence agricultural communities to international market forces. The developmentalist ideology that guided both regimes encouraged the growth of urban manufacturing at the expense of the countryside. The resulting accommodations among the Mexican people, their government, and the food-processing industry is the subject of the next section.

Replacing the Aztec Blender

Entering the market economy required entirely new forms of kitchen performances, as a group of nineteen women living near the shores of Lake Pátzcuaro, Michoacán, discovered one evening in the spring of 1936. Led by Delfina Jazo, they formed the Women's Anticlerical and Anti-Alcohol League of Rancho Las Canoas, and proceeded to draft a petition to President Lázaro Cárdenas. The women respectfully asked for help to obtain a mechanical mill to grind corn for making tortillas, and in this way to liberate them from the "bitter, black stone with three feet called the *metate*."[10] Replacing the "Aztec blender," as the metate came to be called, was the first step in replacing household cooking with mass production. Corn mills freed women from a daily routine of hard labor, but those hours had to be spent earning cash to pay the mill charges. Traditional peasant lifestyles gradually gave way to modern mass production, a process that was actively encouraged by postrevolutionary governments. The women of Las Canoas acknowledged the magnitude of this transformation, at least implicitly, when they formed an anticlerical association to petition for a food-processing appliance.

Mexican women had long resisted technological innovation in cooking. Water-powered grain mills had come into use in Europe before the birth of Christ, yet most campesinas still prepared corn by hand in the early twentieth century, leading one Mexican politician to exclaim that "we still live in the Stone Age!"[11] The first barrier to be overcome in the spread of commercial nixtamal mills to Mexican villages was the challenge to women's established domestic roles. Technical flaws in the early mills allowed women to demonstrate their superiority over machines and assert their place within the family. Because villages lacked electricity, early models operated on gas engines, which caused the tortillas to come out tasting like high-octane fuel. Even when gas generators were separated from electric motors, the corn acquired a metallic taste and rough texture. Women could avoid these unpleasant side effects by briefly regrinding the masa on the metate, yet many refused to patronize the mills, indicating deeper social concerns about grinding corn. Gossip in the village of Tepoztlán questioned the femininity of anyone who carried her corn to a commercial mill. Many women feared that neglecting the metate would lead to a dangerous swelling of the joints called "laziness of the knees."[12]

Whereas the arrival of a nixtamal mill often worried village women, it absolutely infuriated men. Many forbade their wives and daughters from patronizing the new establishments, fearing a direct challenge to their patriarchal authority. Without the discipline of the metate, some believed women would become lazy and promiscuous. As one old-timer from the Yucatán explained, the mill "starts early and so women go out before dawn to grind their own corn the way they used to at home. They meet boys in the dark and that's why illegitimacy is caused by the *nixtamal*." To prevent such danger, the men of one agricultural cooperative that received a mill locked it away from their wives. In another case, a group of women who attempted to organize for their right to a mill were physically assaulted by disgruntled men.[13]

Some of the first rural women to patronize the new mills were those who had fled the countryside during the decade of revolutionary fighting (1910–1920) and discovered the convenience of machine-ground corn in cities or towns. Financial considerations also helped determine who took their corn to the mill. Relatively poor women whose families held little land, contrary perhaps to expectations, often had the greatest incentive to pay for machine-ground corn. Although this service required a few centavos, it freed women from several hours of daily work. They could use that time to engage in artisanal crafts or to become petty merchants, traveling to nearby towns to buy cheaper products, and thus earn enough money to offset the cost of the mill. The acceptance of the mill as a natural tool therefore helped draw subsistence farmers into the money economy. Wealthier families who could easily afford the added expense of the mill were often the last ones to give up the metate. Some considered home-ground corn a status marker, a way of asserting that they lived better than their neighbors because they ate better tortillas. But they could also pay poorer women to do the actual grinding.[14]

Political as well as economic issues influenced the reception of mechanical mills in rural Mexico. Established caciques often enriched themselves by asserting monopolistic control over nixtamal mills, and aspiring populist leaders used them as a form of patronage, like *ejido* land grants, to organize supporters. President Cárdenas, for example, used grants of nixtamal mills to encourage membership in the official party and to discourage rival church organizations. Women learned to phrase their requests for mills within the dominant developmentalist discourse; thus, the use of anticlerical and anti-alcohol rhetoric by the women of Lake Pátzcuaro may have reflected political expedience rather than popular attitudes about either pulpit or *pulque*.[15]

The urban industrialization of food production continued through the 1950s and 1960s with the gradual development and acceptance of automatic tortilla makers. Mexican inventors first attempted to duplicate the subtle skills of the *tortillera* in the Porfirian era, but workable models did not emerge until the 1920s, and an industrial census of 1945 recorded just 2,215 tortilla factories in the entire country. Engineers finally resolved technological problems in the 1950s, and over the next two decades, manufacturers sold more than 60,000 machines, placing tortilla factories conveniently in neighborhoods throughout the Republic. Tortilla aficionados clearly recognized the difference between artisanal and factory tortillas. Relatively wealthy peasant women, who could afford to devote themselves exclusively to domestic work, rejected machine-made tortillas as "raw" because they stuck together. Ordinary campesinas began to purchase tortillas for everyday consumption and used the time saved to earn outside income; the metate and comal came out for festive occasions, when only a philistine would eat tortillas that "tasted like electricity" because they had not been cooked over a wood-burning fire.[16]

The shift from the cardenista emphasis on the countryside to the postrevolutionary "Golden Age" and its single-minded pursuit of industrialization brought a far more profound change through the replacement of this new cottage industry of tortilla making to the mass production of masa harina or nixtamal flour. Roberto M. González opened the first dehydrated nixtamal factory in 1949 in Cerralvo, Nuevo León, under the trade name Molinos Azteca, S.A. (Maseca), followed a year later by a rival state-supported enterprise, Maíz Industrializado, S.A. (Minsa), in Tlalnepantla, Mexico. Nixtamal flour, like corn mills and tortilla machines, required decades of research and development before yielding a marketable product. Maseca and Minsa did not begin to expand their operations and build new processing plants until the mid-1960s. Nevertheless, in 1975, tortilla flour production surpassed 500,000 tons, 5 percent of all the corn consumed in Mexico, and by the 1990s the industry had tripled its output, reaching 1.5 million tons and placing Maseca's president on the Forbes list of billionaires.[17]

The steady increase of masa harina sales resulted not only from Maseca's heavy advertising budget but also from active state intervention. The state firm, Minsa, far from competing with its private counterpart, has cooperated on both research and marketing. Moreover, the Ministry of Commerce and Industrial Development boosted the industry's market share by requiring many corn millers to sell masa harina despite vigorous protests about the inferior quality of such tortillas.[18] Officials justified support for the industry by pointing out the potential nutritional benefits of tortilla flour. For the nominal cost of $10 a ton, Maseca could enrich its masa harina with enough protein and vitamins to satisfy minimum daily requirements, but the company has nevertheless resisted implementing the strategy. Although vitamin and protein enrichment would make little difference in taste beyond the already significant change from fresh to dehydrated corn, the politically powerful company feared that any additives would undermine its market share.[19]

The industrialization of the tortilla was a singularly Mexican enterprise, but technology for manufacturing many other foods already existed in the United States and Western Europe. The spread of refrigerated meats, canned vegetables, comestible oils, and bottled drinks therefore depended primarily on the growth of incomes and infrastructure. All of these food-processing businesses emerged in the Porfirian industrial boom of the 1890s, yet their expansion was limited to small urban markets. Creating an infrastructure of rural marketing networks for processed foods required significant investments. Pre-Hispanic merchants had carried on an extensive trade in nonperishable, relatively high-value goods such as cacao and dried chiles, supplemented in the colonial period by coffee, sugar, and spices, but it was more difficult to transport Pepsi by mule. Fortunately for businessmen, revolutionary governments of the 1920s and 1930s placed a high priority on road building to unify the country and its markets. Soft drink and beer distributors were among the first entrepreneurs to take advantage of these highways to send glass bottles from regional plants to consumers and then to return the empties safely for refilling—an essential step to keep prices affordable. Both Coke and beer arrived in the village of Tepoztlán within six years after the opening of a road from the state capital in 1936. The appearance of Pepsi in the 1940s and the growth of national breweries helped foster competition in local markets.[20]

Food distributorships therefore developed in a hybrid fashion, combining modern and traditional marketing methods. The first Mexican supermarket chains, SUMESA and Aurrera, opened in the 1940s and 1950s, but even today they remain concentrated in upper-middle-class neighborhoods. Manufactured foods reached the rest of the population through small-scale grocers, often in municipal markets, and ambulant vendors. These merchants depended on corporate distributors for credit as well as business supplies such as display cases and refrigerators.[21] One shopkeeper considered the Coke deliveryman so important to his livelihood that he invited the driver to his daughter's fifteenth birthday party.

The costs of establishing and maintaining these delivery routes encouraged the centralization of Mexican food processing within large industrial groups. The largest Coke franchise in the world, for example, Fomento Económico Mexicano S.A., also included Cervecería Cuauhtémoc within the Monterrey-based Garza Sada conglomerate. Pepsico meanwhile diversified into the complementary snack food industry, merging with Frito-Lay in the United States, then acquiring Mexican chip makers Sabritas and Bali.[22] As in the case of tortilla flour, the government encouraged the growth of these companies through ostensibly competitive state food corporations. Rural stores established in the 1960s and 1970s by the National Company for Popular Subsistence (CONASUPO) stocked products such as animal crackers and soft drinks, either produced by state factories or purchased from private groups, thereby helping incorporate rural consumers into larger national markets.[23]

Mexican politicians meanwhile have forgone many potential health benefits that their economic ventures might have achieved. They conceded to food manufacturers the educational power of the mass media, allowing massive advertising campaigns for soft drinks and snack candies, with small-print advice to eat fresh fruits and vegetables as the only concession to public health.[24] Programs to supplement processed foods, including tortilla flour, have been raised periodically but never carried through. Perhaps the most nutritionally irresponsible example of state assistance to private enterprise lay in the subsidies on flour and sugar given to snack food producers, which made this business, in the words of one health official, a *negociazo* (scam).[25]

The twentieth-century trend removing production from household to factory has placed ever greater emphasis on women's roles as consumers. Though less labor-intensive than grinding corn on the metate, the liberating effects of this transformation are limited by the selection of goods that manufacturers make available in stores. Maseca will never mass-produce the artistry of Oaxacan tortillas, for example, nor will bottled mole poblano compare with homemade versions. The meanings of food within Mexico's expanding consumer society are considered in the following section.

A Golden Age of Mexican Cooking

The Mexico City newspaper *Excelsior* represented one possible future for the national cuisine in a 1945 advertisement for Aunt Jemima brand pancake mix. The first scene portrayed a cartoon figure suspiciously eyeing a stack of pancakes; in the next panel he chewed the foreign food thoughtfully; finally, he broke into a broad grin of approval. Within a decade, this advertiser's dream had become a reality for many middle-class families who had replaced the traditional fried beans, tortillas, and chiles with the breakfast food of their neighbors to the north.[26] The postrevolutionary era witnessed tremendous changes in food consumption, with serious nutritional consequences for the lower classes. Yet cultural imperialism has not overwhelmed traditional Mexican cooking. At worst, a form of hybridization took place as Mexicans incorporated foreign foods into established eating patterns. Balanced against this have been the efforts of patriotic cooks to create a unified cuisine as part of a self-conscious nationalist program.

Cookbooks made an important, if everyday, contribution to the postrevolutionary artistic renaissance that helped forge a national consensus and contributed to stability and growth for three decades beginning in the late 1930s. Cultural icons such as mariachi music, *charro* horsemen, *indigenista* murals, and *china poblana* beauties were exalted, or created, as authentic representations of *lo mexicano*. Cookbooks likewise identified mole poblano as a symbol of the national identity, complete with mythic origins in the convents of colonial Puebla, where Sor Andrea de la Asunción supposedly combined seasonings from the Old World with chile peppers from the New to form a culinary emblem of the mestizo "cosmic race."[27]

But the question remains how many people actually cooked out of these books. The expansion of culinary literature might well have represented another of Eric Hobsbawm's "invented traditions," giving women a sense of nostalgia in times of rapid change. Urbanization clearly affected eating habits, making it impossible for most workers to enjoy a traditional afternoon *comida* and siesta with the family, forcing them to carry their lunch or buy it in a restaurant. Fruit- and seed-flavored *aguas frescas* (fresh waters) meanwhile lost favor to carbonated soft drinks; by 1990 the average Mexican consumed a little more than one twelve-ounce soft drink a day. Sales of *alimentos chatarra* (snack foods) likewise boomed at the expense of corn-based snacks called *antojitos* (little whimseys) such as enchiladas and quesadillas.[28]

The urban middle classes have adopted many North American–style foods beyond pancakes. Misguided consumers abandoned crusty *bolillos* (rolls) fresh from neighborhood bakeries in favor of chewy, plastic-wrapped *pan de caja* (bread from a box). The Ideal Bakery came out with the first Mexican version of Wonder Bread in the 1930s, but after 1945 it lost customers to the current market leader, Bimbo bread. Housewives not only began making geometrically precise sandwiches instead of *tortas compuestas* overflowing with pork, beans, and avocados, they also conducted bizarre experiments with mass-produced ingredients to create such hybrid dishes as shrimp and cornflakes, calf brains with crackers, macaroni and milk soup, and pork loin in Pepsi-Cola.[29]

These examples may well illustrate a dark side of mass production, but they do not depict the annihilation of Mexican gastronomy. Cultural differences make it risky to generalize between the Mexican middle classes and their counterparts in the United States. Simple household appliances demonstrate subtle but important distinctions. For example, Mexicans used their newly purchased refrigerators to store soft drinks and beer instead of a week's worth of groceries. And whereas the most valuable appliances north of the border may have been electric toasters and cake mixers, Mexicans preferred the electric blender, the juice press, and the pressure cooker. The blender's facility in grinding chile sauces relegated the metate to the status of a kitchen curiosity, and the juicer turned Mexico's ubiquitous oranges into daily glasses of fresh juice. The pressure cooker solved the age-old problem of boiling water at high altitudes in central Mexico. Beans could now be prepared in less than an hour, saving on fuel costs as well as time, and the toughest beef could be made edible in minutes.

Even these innovations could be used to demonstrate the relative "underdevelopment" of Mexican kitchens: housewives continued to shop for groceries every day and spurned such conveniences as canned beans and frozen orange juice concentrate. Yet the Mexican woman's skepticism of the doctrine that time is money may reflect a more realistic view of the limitations of household technology. Ruth Schwartz Cowan observed that mechanizing housework in the United States had the ironic effect of creating "more work for mother." Time saved by laundry machines, for example, was spent in the automobile working as the family chauffeur. Mexican women at least had the satisfaction of feeding their families fresh food.[30]

Moreover, many foreign manufacturers won customers by demonstrating the utility of their products for making national dishes. Glasbake Cookware ran a series of newspaper advertisements featuring recipes for Mexican regional dishes such as *mole michoacano*. Appliance makers depicted giant cazuelas simmering on top of their modern stoves, and an advertisement for pressure cookers made the justifiable claim that "Mexican cooking enters a new epoch with the *Olla presto*." Even Coca-Cola appealed to Mexican customers with nostalgic scenes of picnics at Chapultepec Park.[31]

Mexicans also appropriated elements of foreign culture to their own purposes. Domestic soft drink manufacturers such as Mundet competed with Coke and Pepsi by introducing lines of soda flavors adapted to Mexican tastes for orange, mango, and apple cider. The habit of eating eggs for breakfast, when transferred from the United States to Mexico, stimulated creative experimentation rather than slavish imitation. In searching for national counterparts to eggs Benedict, Mexican chefs served *huevos rancheros* (ranchstyle eggs) fried with tomato-and-chile sauce, *huevos albañiles* (bricklayers' eggs) scrambled with a similar sauce, and *huevos motuleños* (from Motul, Yucatán) fried with beans, ham, and peas. Soon, no hotel with pretensions to luxury could neglect having its own "traditional" egg dish on the breakfast menu.

The modern desire to preserve traditional Mexican cooking, or to create new traditions when appropriate ones could not be found, also inspired a flurry of folkloric studies in the countryside. Josefina Velázquez de León brought together the country's diverse regional cuisines for the first time in a single work, *Platillos regionales de la República Mexicana* (Regional dishes of the Mexican Republic, 1946). Virginia Rodríguez Rivera published another classic volume, *La cocina en el México antiguo y moderno* (Cooking in ancient and modern Mexico, 1968), of nineteenth-century dishes drawn from oral history interviews. Mexican women thus displayed a mania for preserving their culinary past, even as it began to slip away. Nevertheless, they had mixed success in preserving traditional cooking. Attempts to construct a national cuisine reduced complex regional cooking styles to a few stereotyped dishes, which often misrepresented the foods eaten in those areas. Even an author as sensitive as Velázquez de León adapted traditional village recipes to the needs of urban cooks. For the *zacahuil*, the giant Huastecan tamal cooked in a pit and capable of feeding an entire community, she instructed readers to use a scanty three kilograms of maize and to bake it in the oven.[32]

But by the same token, transnational advertising campaigns had equal difficulty instilling North American and Western European values in the Mexican countryside. The example of Pepsi in San Juan Chamula illustrates the ways that modernizing societies adapt consumer products to fit their cultures. Rather than drinking Pepsi as a daily snack in imitation of the middle classes in either Mexico or the United States, the Chamulans incorporated the soft drink into the community's ritual life, for example, giving cases of Pepsi as dowries for brides. Religious leaders celebrated church services with Pepsi instead of wine, telling parishioners that carbonation drives off evil spirits and cleanses the soul. The natives even hung Pepsi posters in their homes beside the family crucifix, for as one person explained to an anthropologist, "When men burp, their hearts open."[33]

The resilience of local customs has not offset the nutritional damage of the transition from traditional to industrial diets. Studies by the National Nutrition Institute and by numerous anthropologists from the 1960s to the 1990s have documented a fundamental trend toward the replacement of corn and beans by sugar and fats. Well-to-do Yucatecan peasants and working-class Mexico City residents both derive an average of 20 percent of their calories from processed foods, including soft drinks, beer, chips, and candy. The rural poor, unable to afford such snacks except on special occasions, dump heaping spoonsful of sugar into weak coffee. So pervasive has sucrose become that one study recommended vitamin-enriched sugar as the most efficient means of improving rural nutrition.[34] The convenience of processed foods often came at the expense of nutrition, as when cooks used dried consommé instead of tomatoes and onions, in effect replacing vegetables with salt. Poverty further distorted the diets of campesinos subsisting on the fringes of the market economy. The rising price of beans forced many poor families to buy cheaper wheat pasta with grave dietary consequences. Whereas corn and beans together provided high-quality protein, corn and spaghetti did not.[35]

The food-processing industry has waged a century-long campaign to remove consumers from the source of their nourishment, to make packaged foods seem natural and living plants and animals untouchable. For example, transnational executives hoping to establish modern chicken-packing plants in Mexico expressed the long-term goal of persuading consumers that poultry tastes best when purchased from a plastic bag in the refrigerated section.[36] The combination of manufactured foods and traditional cooking styles has had mixed results, introducing valuable new sources of protein to poor consumers, but also destabilizing their nutritional intake. It remains to be seen how successful the chicken packers will be in convincing Mexicans that "parts are parts." The next section will examine the fate of Mexican food in the corporate marketplace of the United States.

Swallowing NAFTA

Culinary hybridization has a long history in Mexico. The enormous vogue of things French in the nineteenth century produced a host of Parisian-sounding banquet menus and cookbooks, which, on closer inspection, displayed a distinctive process of Mexicanization; for example, a recipe for *bifstec à la Chateaubriand* appears to foreigners to resemble fajitas with French fries.[37] Mexican foods also yielded hybrids in the United States under such names as Tex-Mex, New Mex, and Cal-Mex. These foods derived from the regional cooking of northern Mexico, which is what the Southwest was before 1848. Like their neighbors in Sonora and Chihuahua, Mexican Americans often prefer wheat to corn tortillas and eat more beef than chicken or pork. The spread of Mexican foods in the United States demonstrates that though corporate marketing may create further hybrids, traditional Mexican can take root even in foreign soils.

Non-Hispanics in the Southwest had long eaten at chili stands in San Antonio and Mexican restaurants in California, but these ethnic foods expanded out of the region to build national markets only in the 1980s. In 1992 salsa sales surpassed those of catsup, up from just 10 percent a decade earlier. Taco Bell, which opened in California in 1962 and went public in 1969, spread across the country in the 1980s. Southwestern moved upscale in restaurants such as Coyote Café and Abiquiu, becoming so trendy that in 1987

M. F. K. Fisher declared, "If I hear any more about chic Tex-Mex or blue cornmeal, I'll throw up."[38] Nevertheless, tortillas were still a marketing hit in 1997, which advertisers dubbed the year of wrap, as they came to outsell all other ethnic breads, including bagels and pita.

This success often came by separating Mexican foods from their ethnic roots. Mexican restaurants in the East are often run by Greek immigrants, and the leading salsa manufacturers have been bought up by corporate giants Campbells Soup, Pillsbury, and Frito-Lay. Taco Bell transformed the soft corn tortilla into a hard "taco shell," causing many people mistakenly to think that "soft" tacos are always made with wheat tortillas. The techniques developed by poor Mexican Americans to cook the cheap but tough beef flank (*fajitas* in Spanish) have been transformed by fashionable restaurants, creating the oxymoron "chicken fajitas." As the market grows for "wraps," product differentiation has led to tortillas flavored with cinnamon or pesto.

Such corporate innovation had little appeal for Hispanics, who often told the marketers of flavored tortillas that "Grandma would turn over in her grave if she saw what you are doing." Frito-Lay displayed an egregious degree of corporate insensitivity when, in the 1960s, it attempted to reach the Hispanic market with the Frito Bandito. One of the great advertising disasters of all time, this campaign conveyed a host of negative stereotypes about Mexicans. The company recognized that Fritos had irrevocably alienated the Hispanic market, and started over with first Doritos and then Tostitos. Taco Bell, meanwhile, ignored the Hispanic market altogether, concentrating instead on males age eighteen to thirty-four.[39]

But these experiences did not prove that corporations cannot produce genuine Mexican food. Mission Foods, the tortilla market leader, has always given priority to the Hispanic market; but then, the company is a subsidiary of Maseca, the Mexican conglomerate. The Irvine, California–based chain El Pollo Loco likewise sought to provide authentic *tacos al carbón*, and advertised this with scenes of open-air street vendors filmed in Mexico. Upscale establishments such as Zarela Martínez's eponymous New York restaurant and Rick Bayless's Frontera Grill in Chicago distinguished themselves from Chi Chi's by offering esoteric dishes such as *cuitlacoche* (Mexican truffles) and by specializing in regional Mexican cuisines, a path earlier taken by Szechuan Chinese and northern Italian restaurants. So, while Taco Bell readily admits they do not sell the real thing, the marketer's quest for product differentiation will provide a niche for authentic Mexican in the United States.

Conclusion: The Grail of Authenticity

Mexicans have long represented their collective identity through the art of cooking. From the corn tamales prepared for pre-Hispanic rituals to the bottles of Corona raised at the World Cup, eating the appropriate foods has been an essential part of civilized behavior. Nationalist champions in particular have attached great importance to authenticity because a "genuine" work of art, however humble, demonstrates a nation's cultural autonomy, and this distinctiveness in turn justifies its claims to political sovereignty. As a result, different groups have struggled to define the authentic national cuisine, particularly in times of rapid technological and cultural change.[40] This essay has attempted to untangle the complex negotiations of identity and markets proceeding among traditional peasant cooks, progressive urban gourmets, food-processing corporations, and an unfortunately partial state.

Connections between food consumption and elite identity can be seen in the current fad for the so-called *nueva cocina mexicana*. Chefs have turned to Native American plants and animals to claim an equal standing with the great cuisines of Europe and Asia, but prepare these ingredients with the difficult techniques of European haute cuisine to maintain their cultural distinction from the popular masses. Thus, Arnulfo Luengas, chef of the Banco Nacional de México's executive dining room, created avocado mousse with shrimp, beef Wellington with chiles, and chicken supreme with cuitlacoche.[41] Some might question the *mexicanidad* of such dishes, but the prominent cookbook author Alicia Gironella De'Angeli insisted that this was "the same food we serve at home. It is one of two tendencies in Mexican cooking. The other is the popular Mexican food, the kind with the grease and cheese and everything fried. It is the traditional food that we are reinterpreting." She asserted that the new dishes actually derived from pre-Hispanic origins: "We did not have the lard and the grease that most people think of as Mexican in our roots. The Spaniards brought the pigs."[42] In this way, she appropriated Aztec authenticity for elite cuisine and associated lower-class foods with the villainous conquistadors.

But the popular sectors would not allow her to have such international sophistication and eat it with a nationalist flourish, too. They formulated their own diverse ideas of what constituted authentic Mexican food. Maize of course constituted the quintessential cuisine of rural Mexico. During a drought in the Huasteca, when corn shipments arrived from the United States to relieve local shortages, campesinos claimed that even the pigs turned up their snouts at the imported grain.[43] But authenticity meant something entirely different to cooks patting out tortillas by hand in restaurants on scenic Janitzio Island, Lake Pátzcuaro, where they started with Maseca-brand masa harina, then reground it on the metate for the tourists' benefit.

Authentic Mexican dishes even jostled for space on city streets in the United States. Mexican vendors, long a fixture of San Antonio and East L.A., began selling *birria* on 22nd Street in Chicago and tamales from pushcarts circling Yankee Stadium. Mario Ramírez, an immigrant from Puebla who started washing dishes in New York hotels, worked his way up to souschef at the Russian Tea Room before opening the Rinconcito Mexicano on 39th Street in Manhattan. There he disdained trendy nouvelle Mexican, preferring instead to sell honest tacos to Mexican workers in the Garment District as well as to midtown businesspeople. "When New Yorkers taste my cooking," he claimed proudly, "they know the real Mexico and they like the real Mexico and they don't want unreal Mexico anymore."[44]

The government has likewise had its say in defining Mexican cuisine through an often contradictory set of food policies. The National Nutrition Institute developed programs to improve the health of rural and urban poor through educational campaigns about the best ways to use both traditional staples and vitamin and protein supplements. The state food agencies also provided infrastructure to assist small farmers in selling corn to lucrative urban markets and thus preserving their livelihoods. But far more of the government's resources went to promoting domestic manufacturers, even to the point of subsidizing the junk food industry.

Businesses have tried to adopt the mantle of authenticity, even when they represented foreign owners. Advertising billboards informed Mexicans "Tortillas taste good, and better with Maseca." Transnational corporations meanwhile adapted their products to Mexican tastes to face off local competitors. Bags of Sabritas *chicharrones* (pork rinds) shared counter space with Fritos corn chips, and Mundet *cidral* (carbonated apple cider) sat in the refrigerator with Pepsi-Cola. Which goes to show that Macario, the Tzotzil Faust, does not need a North American Mephistopheles to sell his soul. And yet, as with so many contests for hegemony, victories are incremental, individual, and always contested in the struggles between rich and poor, producer and consumer, business and regulator, ruler and subject. Fortunes are made while people go hungry, biodiversity is sacrificed to economic growth, but ordinary cooks, seeking only to feed their families, nevertheless preserve the fragments of a Golden Age of Mexican cooking.

Notes

1   Matt Moffett, "Mexicans Convert as a Matter of Politics," *Wall Street Journal*, 1 June 1988; Jan Rus, "The 'Comunidad Revolucionaria Institucional': The Subversion of Native Government in Highland Chiapas, 1936–1968," in *Everyday Forms of State Formation: Revolution and the Negotiation of Rule in Modern Mexico*, ed. Gilbert M. Joseph and Daniel Nugent (Durham, NC: Duke University Press, 1994), 292. Translations mine unless otherwise noted.

2   Jean Drèze and Amartya Sen, *Hunger and Public Action* (Oxford: Clarendon Press, 1989), 68, 91, 122.

3   Alberto Ysunza Ogazón et al., *Dietas de transición y riesgo nutricional en la población migratoria* (Mexico City: Instituto Nacional de Nutrición, 1985); Lucia Batrouni et al., *Situación de barrios marginados de Teziutlán* (Mexico City: Instituto Nacional de Nutrición, 1983); Adolfo Chávez et al., *La nutrición en México y la transición epidemiológica* (Mexico City: Instituto Nacional de Nutrición, 1993).

4   Adriana Cópil, "La guerra de las tortillas," *Contenido* (July 1992): 42–47.

5   See the fascinating studies in James L. Watson, ed., *Golden Arches East: McDonald's in East Asia* (Stanford, CA: Stanford University Press, 1998).

6   On the nutritional value of the pre-Hispanic maize complex, see William T. Sanders, Jeffrey R. Parsons, and Robert S. Santley, *The Basin of Mexico: Ecological Processes in the Evolution of a Civilization* (New York: Academic Press, 1979), 376; Hector Arraya, Marina Flores, and Guillermo Arroyave, "Nutritive Value of Basic Foods and Common Dishes of the Guatemalan Rural Populations: A Theoretical Approach," *Ecology of Food and Nutrition* 11 (1981): 171–76. The population estimate comes from Woodrow Borah and Sherburne F. Cook, *The Aboriginal Population of Central Mexico on the Eve of the Spanish Conquest* (Berkeley: University of California Press, 1963).

7   Margaret Park Redfield, "Notes on the Cookery of Tepoztlan, Morelos," *American Journal of Folklore* 42, no. 164 (April–June 1929): 167–96; Nathan L. Whetten, *Rural Mexico* (Chicago: University of Chicago Press, 1948), 305; Oscar Lewis, *Life in a Mexican Village: Tepoztlán Revisited* (Urbana: University of Illinois Press, 1951), 72.

8   Wendy Waters, "Roads, the Carnivalesque, and the Mexican Revolution: Transforming Modernity in Tepoztlán, 1928–1943" (M. A. thesis, Texas Christian University, 1994), 165–70.

9   Lynn Stephen, *Zapotec Women* (Austin: University of Texas Press, 1991), 186.

10   Archivo General de la Nación (AGN), Ramo Presidentes, Lázaro Cárdenas, exp. 604.11/83.

11   *El Universal*, 11 November 1933.

12   Quote from Redfield, "Notes on Cookery of Tepoztlan," 182; *El maíz, fundamento de la cultura popular mexicana*. Mexico City: Museo Nacional de Culturas Populares, 1982, p. 82.

13   AGN, Cárdenas, 604.11/21, 149, 155; quote from Arnold J. Bauer, "Millers and Grinders:

Technology and Household Economy in Meso-America," *Agricultural History* 64, no. 1 (winter 1990): 16.

14   Waters, "Roads and the Mexican Revolution," 167, 173.

15   AGN, Cárdenas, exp. 604.11/67, 91, 92, 121; Dawn Keremitsis, "Del metate al molino: La mujer mexicana de 1910 a 1940," *Historia Mexicana* 33 (October–December 1983): 297.

16   Robert V. Kemper, *Migration and Adaptation: Tzintzuntzan Peasants in Mexico City* (Beverly Hills: Sage Publications, 1977), 29, 152; Maria da Glória Marroni de Velázquez, "Changes in Rural Society and Domestic Labor in Atlixco, Puebla, 1940–1990," in *Creating Spaces, Shaping Transitions: Women of the Mexican Countryside, 1850–1990*, ed. Heather Fowler-Salamini and Mary Kay Vaughan (Tucson: University of Arizona Press, 1994), 223; Jaime Aboites A., *Breve historia de un invento olvidado: Las máquinas tortilladoras en México* (Mexico City: Universidad Autónoma Metropolitana, 1989), 39, 47; *El maíz*, 82.

17   Nacional Financiera, *La industría de la harina de maíz* (Mexico City: NAFINSA, 1982), 13–14; *La industria de maíz* (Mexico City: Primsa Editorial, 1989), 108–14; Cópil, "La guerra de las tortillas," 42–47; Aboites, *Breve historia de un invento*, 50–51; *Forbes*, 15 July 1996.

18   Clara Jusidman, "El maíz, en los procesos de globalización y modernización," *Cuadernos de Nutrición* 16, no. 1 (January–February 1993): 41–42; *La industria de maíz*, 128–30; Cópil, "La guerra de las tortillas," 43–47.

19   Nacional Financiero, *La industría de la harina de maíz*, 51; Ana Naranjo B., *Informe de programas y proyectos de doce años, 1976–1987* (Mexico City: Instituto Nacional de Nutrición, 1987), 225–26; Enrique C. Ochoa, "The Politics of Feeding Mexico: The State and the Marketplace Since 1934" (Ph.D. diss., University of California, Los Angeles, 1993), 245.

20   Waters, "Roads and the Mexican Revolution," 78; J. C. Louis and Harvey Z. Yazijian, *The Cola Wars* (New York: Everest House, 1980), 46, 60.

21   Fernando Rello and Demetrio Sodi, *Abasto y distribución de alimentos en las grandes metropolis* (Mexico City: Nueva Imagen, 1989), 68–80; Ochoa, "The Politics of Feeding Mexico," 44–45.

22   José Antonio Roldán Amaro, *Hambre y riqueza en la historia contemporanea de México*, vol. 1 of *Historia del hambre en México*, ed. Pablo González Casanova (Mexico City: Instituto Nacional de Nutrición, 1986), 40; Carol Meyers de Ortiz, *Pequeño comercio de alimentos en colonias populares de Ciudad Nezahuacóyotl: Análisis de su papel en la estructura socioeconómica urbana* (Guadalajara: Editorial Universidad de Guadalajara, 1990), 33; Matt Moffett, "A Mexican War Heats Up for Cola Giants," *Wall Street Journal*, 26 April 1993, B1, 6; Young and Yazijian, *The Cola Wars*, 133.

23   Ochoa, "Politics of Feeding Mexico," 273.

24   David Márquez Ayala, "Las empresas transnacionales y sus efectos en el consumo alimentario," in *Transnacionales, agricultura, y alimentación*, ed. Rodolfo Echeverría Zuno (Mexico City: Editorial Nueva Imagen, 1982), 218; Naranjo, *Informe de programas*, 228–34.

25   Quote from "La entrevista: Dr. Adolfo Chávez Villasana," *Cuadernos de Nutrición* 6, no. 9 (July–September 1983): 12–16.

26   *Excélsior*, 9 February 1945; Oscar Lewis, *Five Families: Mexican Case Studies in the Culture of Poverty* (New York: Basic Books, 1959), 306.

27   Jeffrey M. Pilcher, *¡Que vivan los tamales! Food and the Making of Mexican Identity* (Albuquerque: University of New Mexico Press, 1998), 138–40.

28 Leticia Serrano Andrade, "El consumo de alimentos industrializados en una comunidad rural de la Zona Norte del Estado de Veracruz" (Thesis, Escuela de Salud Pública de México, 1984), 5; Moffett, "Mexican War for Cola Giants," B1; Chávez, *La nutrición en México.*

29 Pilcher, *¡Que vivan los tamales!*, 127.

30 Ruth Schwartz Cowan, *More Work for Mother: The Ironies of Household Technology from the Open Hearth to the Microwave* (New York: Basic Books, 1983).

31 *Excélsior*, 15 April, 14 July, 1 September, 16 December, 1945; 2 June 1947.

32 A similar process has been identified by Arjun Appadurai, "How to Make a National Cuisine: Cookbooks in Contemporary India," *Comparative Studies in Society and History* 30, no. 1 (January 1988): 3–24.

33 Moffett, "Mexicans Convert as a Matter of Politics."

34 Gilberto Balam, "La alimentación de los campesinos mayas del estado de Yucatán (Primera parte)," *Cuadernos de Nutrición* 16, no. 6 (November–December 1993): 41; Chávez, *La nutrición en México*, 33, 78; Jesús Ruvalcaba Mercado, *Vida cotidiana y consumo de maíz en la huasteca veracruzana* (Mexico City: Centro de Investigaciones y Estudios Superiores en Antropología Social, 1987), 31, 39.

35 K. M. DeWalt, P. B. Kelly, and G. H. Pelto, "Nutritional Correlates of Economic Micro-differentiation in a Highland Mexican Community," in *Nutritional Anthropology: Contemporary Approaches to Diet and Culture*, ed. Norge W. Jerome, Randy F. Kandel, and Gretel H. Pelto (Pleasantville, NY: Redgrave Publishing, 1980), 213; Serrano Andrade, "El consumo de alimentos industrializados," 29; Chávez, *La nutrición en México*, 28; Balam, "Alimentación de los campesinos mayas," 43.

36 Personal communication from John Hart, Mexico City, 16 July 1997.

37 Hortensia Rendón de García, *Antiguo manual de cocina yucateca: Fórmulas para condimentar los platos más usuales en la península*, 7th ed., 3 vols. (Mérida, Mexico: Librería Burrel, 1938 [1st ed., 1898]), 55.

38 Quoted in Sylvia Lonegree, *Fashionable Food: Seven Decades of Food Fads* (New York: Macmillan, 1995), 378.

39 Donna R. Gabaccia, *We Are What We Eat: Ethnic Food and the Making of Americans* (Cambridge, MA: Harvard University Press, 1998), 165; quote from Margaret Littman, "Wrap Up Profits with Tortillas," *Bakery Production and Marketing* 31, no. 16 (15 November 1996): 40.

40 JoAnn Martin, "Contesting Authenticity: Battles over the Representation of History in Morelos, Mexico," *Ethnohistory* 40, no. 3 (summer 1993): 438–65.

41 *El universo de la cocina mexicana: Recetario* (Mexico City: Fomento Cultural Banamex, 1988), 18, 40, 48.

42 Quoted in Florence Fabricant, "Mexican Chefs Embrace a Lighter Cuisine of Old," *New York Times*, 3 May 1995, B3.

43 Ruvalcaba Mercado, *Maíz en la huasteca*, 85.

44 Molly O'Neill, "Mexicans Show New York Their Real Food," *New York Times*, 25 August 1993.

The Selling of Mexico:
Tourism and the State, 1929–1952

Alex Saragoza

By means of our small rural schools we are trying to integrate Mexico. . . . That means to teach the people of the mountains and isolated valleys, the millions that are of Mexico but are not yet Mexicans.—A rural schoolteacher, quoted in *Mexican Folkways*, 1927

With the standardization of the Jarabe and the teaching of it in all of the federal government schools, it is even being adopted in the Indian villages. But it will never be the same dance with them, for they will interpret it in their own fashion and weave it into their own patterns of expression.—*Mexican Folkways*, 1930

The historic importance of tourism in Mexico rests largely on its economic impact, as the industry has generated a large proportion of foreign earnings for the country, particularly in the post-1940 era.[1] Yet, the significance of tourism extends beyond its economic consequences, as the early development of the industry also illuminates the workings of an authoritarian regime, including its ideological and cultural project. In this latter regard, tourism in the postrevolutionary era reflected the gradual, selective appropriation of cultural forms to "image" the country through the articulation of notions of national identity and its attendant heritage. In concert with segments of the private sector, the state figured crucially in shaping the cultural expectations of tourists through the construction of an apparatus and infrastructure that undergirded the industry. In this sense, tourism contributed substantively to the nationalization of cultural expression in Mexico and its projection outside of the country.

Nonetheless, Mexican tourism held an intrinsic domestic dimension, often blurred by the centrality of foreign visitors to the industry and its post-1940 development. Rather, the formative stage of tourism in Mexico took place within the context of an intensely nationalist cultural project that marked the state-building efforts of the new postrevolutionary government. The initial thrust of the tourist industry built on the state's drive to construct a sense of nation—or, as Manuel Gamio put it, *forjando patria*—expressed in an essentialist vocabulary of national identity, that of *lo mexicano, mexicanidad, el pueblo mexicano*, and related terms. This nascent phase of state-sponsored cultural formation was far from monolithic in character nor a complete departure from prerevolutionary nationalist thinking, but it proved decisive to the discursive repertoire of the new state from the 1920s through the following decade.[2] Despite the dominance of foreign tourism to the industry, particularly after 1940, the imaging of Mexico manifested the imprint of that earlier, heritage-based preoccupation of the state's cultural project.

In this fitful, irregular process, a discernible shift was evident by the conclusion of the Cárdenas administration (1934–1940). In the years prior, the state's fledgling and diffuse cultural project showed much experimentation and flux. But the war years and their immediate aftermath witnessed the consolidation of a tightly organized tourist policy under the aegis of Miguel Alemán Valdés from 1940 to 1952, first as head of the Ministry of Gobernación that supervised national tourism, and then as president from 1946 to 1952. The state's desire, and Alemán's ambition, to "modernize" Mexican tourism after 1940, however, found it impossible to escape the cumulative effects of the discursive practices of the previous period.

An uneasy accommodation ensued. Selected forms of heritage for the presentation of mexicanidad commingled with a tourism based on sun, beaches, and recreation. In this move, an array of cultural forms identified with the "typical" in Mexico congealed into ubiquitous, nearly standardized representations, perhaps most colorfully captured in the performance of the *jarabe tapatío* to mariachi music as a quintessential expression of Mexican music and dance. Still, this shift conceded much of its imaging to the previous incorporation of the local into the more encompassing category of lo mexicano framed by the state's policies, agencies, and programs.

In brief, the selling of Mexico for touristic consumption involved a complex, negotiated process that enjoined the public and private sectors with the local in the construction of lo mexicano.[3] Local entities developed specific and at times distinctive responses to federal initiatives that impinged on the tourist industry. Thus, regional and municipal authorities worked to foment a sense of *patria*, but one at times with a local inflection. Clubs, antiquarian societies, and volunteer organizations contributed as well to enhancing or to building heritage sites that paralleled government-supported displays in Mexico City. And the private sector, especially the entertainment business, contributed to the imaginary of mexicanidad. Furthermore, restaurant owners, merchants, hoteliers, and the like produced their own images of *lo típico*: waitresses and waiters in "traditional" garb; the selling of curios and artifacts in stores; the "Mexican-style" architecture of lodging establishments and their attendant interiors. Nevertheless, in this multilayered presentation of Mexican heritage and culture, the state's project served as a vital if not essential catalyst.

Néstor García Canclini has proposed persuasively that one effect of tourism is to turn the particularities of ethnic cultural expression into a larger category of "type." That is, what is unique to a specific region or ethnic group becomes "typically" Mexican: the cultural expression, display, or artifact of that group—the local—loses its particularity and authenticity. "The need to homogenize and at the same time preserve the attraction of the exotic dilutes the specificity of each village or town," García Canclini argues, "not into the common denominator of the ethnic and Indian but into the (political) unity of the state—Michoacán, Veracruz—and each state into the political unity of the nation."[4]

Yet, the process described by García Canclini unfolded unevenly over time and space, subject to political interests, policy shifts, economic conditions, and the vagaries of specific situations and communities. In this respect, the importance of the state lay less in its ability to dictate or to impose its definition of mexicanidad and more in its capacity to provoke or to channel a response to the government's cultural initiatives. Indeed, the efficacy of the state's cultural project varied, complicated by the circumstances that surrounded the transition from the populism of cardenismo to the conservative regimes that followed. In the presence of the local, the state framed a capacious definition of lo mexicano that proved resilient in the touristic display of Mexican culture and heritage.

Among several scholars, Mary Kay Vaughan has masterfully depicted the contentious negotiation that marked the relations between federal educational programs and local communities during the Cárdenas years, underscoring the regional differentiation in the receptivity to state cultural policies following the Revolution.[5] In this sense, the center found it difficult to impose easily its policies on the periphery. On the other hand, the state's cultural directives also emanated from sources less vulnerable to direct resistance. In this vein, from 1937 to 1939 the Departamento Autónomo de Prensa y Publicidad (Independent Department of Press and Publicity)

(DAPP), for example, produced thousands of posters, pamphlets, leaflets, advertisements, musical shows, and the like. These activities by DAPP reinforced the movie shorts and radio programs of the Secretaría de Educación Pública (SEP), such as its broadcasts of *música folklórica nacional* and *música selecta nacional*. DAPP, along with the SEP and other government agencies, extended the reach of the state in ways less susceptible to face-to-face negotiation and/or outright elimination through physical means by local powers.[6]

Furthermore, the interactions between the state and the local took place in a tense, fluid milieu that belied the clarity of the overt conflicts between government cultural agencies and rural villages or towns. In this regard, Marjorie Becker made an insightful point in her study of the peasantry of Michoacán and the cardenista regime, when she noted that "Mexican peasant cultures can in no way be viewed as static oases of calm."[7] The gathering momentum of migration in the Bajío region, including Michoacán, indicated but one source of this erosion of "calm" in the countryside. In fact, if the Mexican scholar Jesús Arroyo is correct, over 60 percent of Mexican immigrants to the United States in 1926 derived from the Bajío region.[8] Moreover, this human movement toward urban centers and/or the northern border intensified with the Cristero rebellion of the late 1920s. The majority of these migrants consisted of young, able-bodied men (and many women as well) with unsettling effects on the sociocultural solidity of sending communities. In addition, many migrants returned and, it appears, often left again to test their fortunes elsewhere, leaving behind the cultural residue of their stays outside of their native villages and towns. If Cárdenas intended a "cultural transformation of the countryside," to employ Becker's terms, his scheme "to revise peasant assessments of the world" proceeded in an arena fissured by sources of change beyond cardenista-inspired teachers, schools, and curricula.[9]

The relationship of the state to the local was made more complex by the urbanized cultural forces that filtered into rural areas. The lyrics of Agustín Lara, who had his own radio show by 1930, quickly spread beyond the limits of Mexico City soon thereafter, as the widening embrace of commercial radio followed the reach of electrical lines into the smallest of hamlets. And the first recording of the Mariachi Cocutla in 1933 immediately made its debut outside the vicinity of cities, as phonograph sets were readily available even in remote rural villages. Equally significant, the instant popularity of sound film and its presentation of mexicanidad was not restricted to the imaginary of urban middle and upper classes. The highly romanticized view of the countryside, for instance, in *Allá en el rancho grande* (1936), proved to be as entertaining in the primitive movie houses of small rural towns as it was in the sumptuous cinemas of Mexico City. Or, more to the point of this essay, when the comic Mario Moreno (Cantinflas) included a satirical scene involving American tourists in the film *Ni sangre, ni arena* in 1940, it is hard to believe that the humor was appreciated only by movie audiences of the metropolis.[10]

As Carlos Monsiváis has suggested, local cultural authority in the 1930s underestimated or misunderstood the deepening inroads of urban-based media on a population irreversibly moving away from a society presumably based on the persistence of pristine rural communities: "The modernization of the public is partial and restricted, but undeniable, and can be seen in neighborhood dance styles, a new sense of humor, the 'look' of women and in the renewal of melodrama."[11] Radio, cinema, recordings, comic books, and the like expanded their presence in the midst of the cultural encounters between the state and the local.

In short, from the 1920s through the 1930s the local was implicated in the permeable construction of lo mexicano that spanned instrumental forms, such as the public schools, to the codification of the "typical" by the mass media. This essay can only be suggestive of this dense, multivalent process that also involved legislation, municipal agencies, bureaucratic structures, educational institutions, cultural exchange programs, government-private sector groups, local organizations, and more. In this bulky mix, four elements were salient in the interplay between the state and the local in the essentializing representation of Mexico: the discourse of *indigenismo*; the monumentalist component of the government's cultural project; the concern for the "folkloric"; and the intellectual debate over the meaning of mexicanidad. In this ungainly enterprise, the state took the lead and increasingly conditioned the interaction among these four elements with the local. And as state authority thickened, the profitability of tourism attracted the avarice and ambition of powerful political actors, reinforcing the role of government in the tourist industry, including its representational dimension.

The significance of indigenismo to the nationalist discourse of the state held an inherently local dimension. Although the official celebration of Mexico's indigenous past was fraught with confused if not contradictory views (and often at odds with everyday government practice), indigenismo remained a key ingredient of the new state's promotion of a national identity.[12] Though these federally funded efforts found their most public expression in major archaeological projects in selected sites, many regional and municipal governments paralleled the campaign, aided by locally based societies, clubs, and private donors. Thus, while the "great" civilizations (Aztec, Mayan, Zapotec) were at the center of the state's indigenista vision, the optic was not exclusive but encompassed, for example, the Purépecha (Tarascan) of Michoacán and Veracruz's attention to its Olmec heritage. To put it briefly, the state's indigenismo was often mediated by locally defined notions of indigenous roots that gave specific attention to native forms of cultural production, including proximate archaeological zones; in fact, it was not unusual for such sites to receive federal funds for their restoration or to improve their formalized presentation.[13]

A second cohering linkage between the local and the state derived from the building or refashioning of museums or monuments, which allowed for the material display of the nation's heritage. The remodeling of the national museum after the Revolution, for instance, was reproduced in several states with the establishment or expansion of regional museums that emphasized their area's material culture and history. Some states virtually started from scratch in this regard; other institutions built on their established collections, such as the museum of Michoacán located in Morelia, or that of Veracruz in Jalapa.[14] Similarly, the rehabilitation of vintage buildings, statuary, and plazas in Mexico City was imitated in many parts of the country, from newly minted plaques dedicated to local heroes to the improvement of historic architectural sites, such as the so-called *obispado* in Monterrey, Nuevo León, a complex of buildings harking back to the colonial era. In this sense, the notion of "old Mexico," based largely on the country's colonial architectural patrimony, often drew from local initiatives, such as the Amigos de Taxco, a group dedicated to the promotion of the former mining town as a tourist site.[15]

Third, the state's promotion of the recovery and performance of "authentic" Mexico perforce encompassed the enormously diverse localized "folklore" of the nation. This specific quest for the essential Mexico was not confined to the color and pageantry of the capital's Xochimilco gardens or its notable marketplaces. Publications such as *Mexican Folkways* highlighted the immense variety of the country's folkloric expression. Handicrafts, clothing, games, textiles, and the like frequently made their way into expositions sponsored by local authorities, usually in conjunction with traditional fiestas or civic holidays, that sustained a local inflection, dutifully recorded by a growing legion of observers and students of Mexican popular arts.[16]

In many cases, these local forms of cultural expression made their way to Mexico City for periodic display at government request and cost, including dance troupes and musical groups. As early as 1921, José Vasconcelos, head of SEP at the time, orchestrated a display of Mexican handicrafts, and in a subsequent and ostentatious display of the "traditional" in 1924, Vasconcelos brought "folkloric" groups from throughout the country to perform their regionally specific dances.[17] In a corresponding and academic manner, journals, books, and scholarly conferences celebrated the diverse, localist manifestations of Mexican folklore. Thus, the local was literally brought to the center of the state's cultural project, facilitated by the fascination for popular culture among prominent writers, artists, and academics.

The intellectual ferment stimulated by the postrevolutionary concern for a new sense of national identity constituted a fourth element connecting the local with the state. Indeed, a major current in this discussion was a near obsession among intellectuals for the popular, the folkloric, the vernacular for much of the 1920s and into the 1930s.[18] The interest in el pueblo mexicano spurred the exploration of the nation's heritage into obscure corners of the country, as pioneering researchers recorded the music, folk songs, and tales of village composers, singers, and storytellers. These efforts provided unprecedented recognition to the particularities of Mexican culture and led to a surge of activities that focused on local history and lore. In this endeavor, the leadership of men such as Narciso Bassols, director of the National Museum for several years and who also served for a time as the head of the Ministry of Education, proved crucial to the incorporation of a large array of regionally specific forms of *artes populares*, for instance, to the Museo Nacional.[19] And it was not uncommon for prominent curators in Mexico City to have their trainees move on to provincial posts, enhancing the ties between local institutions and state-sponsored heritage programs. In this vein, the heads of regional museums took advantage of the state's funding of cultural initiatives to highlight the local, as in the improvement of the regional museum of Michoacán. While the anthropologist Alfonso Caso, for instance, garnered national and international fame for his work at Mexico's Monte Albán site, there emerged a number of unsung cultural workers—curators, ethnographers, and *cronistas* (essayists)—who gave localized expression to the professional, scholarly notoriety of the state's cultural project and its leading figures.[20]

These four elements—the discourse of indigenismo, the monumentalist dimension of the state's cultural project, the celebration of the folkloric, and the general intellectual interest in the vernacular—contributed crucially to the foundational representation of Mexican culture and heritage. For much of the 1920s and 1930s, this process implicated the local, and the cultural production of mexicanidad had an assembled, patchwork, "invented" quality, rather than that of a seamless, cohesive whole.[21] Slowly, then with greater momentum, the relationship between the local and the state gradually coalesced through the maturation of a government-led cultural apparatus anchored in the Ministry of Education. Founded in 1939 and placed in SEP, the Instituto Nacional de Antropología e Historia (INAH) culminated and centralized a multifaceted and widely deployed campaign to recover and present Mexico's heritage with manifest consequences for touristic display. Preceded by various loosely tied agencies, offices, bureaus, and commissions, INAH constituted a capstone to the evolution of an organizational structure for the government-sanctioned presentation of Mexican history and culture.[22] More important, the force of INAH and its institutional ancillaries lay in its resources and influence, rather than on heavy-handed controls or directives on cultural presentation.

The thickening linkages between the state and the local moved the nationalist cultural project along increasingly convergent lines by the late 1920s and into the next decade. The notion of the indigenous became associated with monumentalist forms that testified to the "greatness" of pre-Columbian societies, where visibly impressive architectural remains gave heightened testimony to the achievements of pre-European contact cultures. Where possible, therefore, the affirming proximity of imposing archaeological remnants provided the focal point for localist attention to the indigenous. In the absence of grand pre-Columbian monumentalist forms, localist heritage displays sought alternatives in colonialist monuments, and, in the best of circumstances, local presentations of heritage contained native and Spanish architectural attractions. In a similar manner, performed in ostentatious costume and charged by the spirited music of the mariachi, the jarabe tapatío offered exuberant if not showy proof of the distinctiveness of Mexican popular culture that overwhelmed other, less theatrical examples of vernacular musical expression—and engendered the performance of regional dances that approximated the flashy *sones* of Jalisco. In the same vein, folklore and its localist observation gravitated to pageantry and drama, such as the *día de los muertos* or the high-flying *voladores* (flying dancers) of Pa-

pantla.[23] In short, the presentation of local heritage resonated with the center's propensity to foreground color, drama, and spectacle in the representation of mexicanidad. Subtle, delicate, and less imposing cultural forms receded to decorative background or marginal display.

The financial constraints on local institutions served to facilitate the ability of federal agencies to frame localist responses to the production of heritage and its display. Moreover, the definition of lines of inquiry sponsored by INAH and related agencies influenced to a growing extent the parameters for anthropological projects, heritage publications, and cultural exhibits. These state-funded programs channeled support to selected sites and activities, spearheaded by spectacular archaeological excavations, such as that of Monte Albán by Alfonso Caso. Although such large-scale projects received the lion's share of notoriety (and monies), federally funded research encompassed an extensive number of villages and towns and their singular forms of cultural expression, as evidenced in the flood of articles (by Mexican scholars usually trained at state-supported schools and institutes) that appeared in various government-sponsored publications.[24] In addition, federal laws and regulations prodded the convergence of local cultural work with that of the state. The recuperation of historic buildings, for example, was subject to the approval of an agency of the postrevolutionary government as early as 1925. Omnibus legislation of this sort was passed in 1930, amplified subsequently in 1934, and extended with the act that authorized the establishment of INAH.[25] If for no other reason, the locus of authority in shaping the representation of Mexican culture and heritage moved inexorably toward the state as a consequence of the juridical limits on localist heritage institutions and their supporters.

The cultural authority of the state was further reinforced by the celebration of Mexico's cultural project by foreign writers, scholars, and artists; magazines, tourist trade publications, and newspaper stories added to the luster of the government's cultural policies at a time when "things Mexican were in vogue."[26] Lavishly illustrated publications, such as *Mexican Folkways* (subsidized in part by the Mexican government), tended to focus on the recovery of Mexico's localist customs, handicrafts, festivals, and related forms of "folklore." Tourist-oriented magazines often followed suit, as their correspondents traced much the same paths of cultural discovery and retrieval as government-funded researchers. Foreign trade publications, such as *Travel*, contained (if only inadvertently) the blend of the local and the state, as its periodic articles on Mexico featured "quaint" villages and "colorful" practices in Mexico's hinterland with pictures and illustrations, punctuated at times by an interview with a state-supported anthropologist working on a local project.[27]

Tellingly, however, in the same magazine government-funded tourist advertisements revealed the slide toward the use of "stock" images of Mexican culture and life, for example, Mexican maidens in *china poblana* costume.[28] Despite the attention to specific, localized forms of Mexican cultural expression, certain images gradually assumed primacy in the representation of mexicanidad. As a consequence, the diverse nature of Mexico's indigenous cultures distilled into a predominantly Aztec or Mayan reference as a pyramid became the icon of the country's indigenous heritage. Similarly, "old" Mexico and its colonial trappings crystallized into a handful of buildings in Mexico City; away from the capital, the cathedral of Taxco, the narrow winding streets of Guanajuato, and the churches of Puebla augmented the privileged monumentalist repertory of the country's colonialist architecture. In a related manner, the jarabe tapatío became emblematic of Mexican folkloric music and dance—pushing aside other styles—to showcase the stomping steps, gilded sombreros, swishing skirts, and the charro-clad mariachi as the essence of *música netamente mexicana* (authentic Mexican music).[29]

This slide toward the stereotypic was without any central agency or coordination, and was one in which the private sector played a complicit role. In 1930, for instance, the radio program *Así es mi tierra* debuted on radio station XEW to great public response, bringing the vernacular forms of Mexico's diverse regional musical heritage to the capital and calling it *música típica*, the music typical of Mexico. Still, the signature musical style of the show became that of the mariachi that resonated with the nationalizing propensity of the state's cultural project. And with enormous popularity, especially by the 1930s, films frequently pictured Mexicanness in essentialist ways, where once again the china poblana style, for example, acted as the template of "traditional" Mexican female attire. In brief, the media paralleled in many respects the state's selective appropriation of the local into a nexus of symbols that constituted the basis for the representation of mexicanidad.[30]

For the Mexican tourist business, the cumulative effects of these developments gave the industry a particular look, feel, and sound. Tourist guidebooks, for instance, employed certain images to denote Mexicanness, such as serape-clad, guitar-strumming male figures in sombreros; young women in "peasant" blouses and braids; marketplaces festooned with calla lilies à la Diego Rivera; and the identification of architectural sites that consistently included the national cathedral and the pyramids of Teotihuacán.[31] In this sense, through the 1930s the tourist gaze toward Mexico narrowed, lessening its attention to variety and texture, and focused increasingly on formalized displays to represent the culture of the country. As a consequence, the visibility of the local contracted, its multiplicity blurred by an advancing essentialist myopia. This process accelerated as the rising economic importance of tourism pushed the state toward a greater promotion of the industry.

The state's maturing cultural apparatus provided much of the material intended to attract travelers to Mexico. From the beginning, the state's promotion of tourism involved the consonant development of an appealing image for the country. In July 1929, the government formed a commission, housed in the Secretaría de Gobernación, that aimed to ease the entry of visitors along the U.S.-Mexico border.[32] Though the legislation authorizing the agency encompassed both foreign and domestic tourism, its thrust indicated the desire early on to lure American tourists. Shortly thereafter, as part of a reorganization of the government's tourist bureaucracy, an interagency committee was formed to improve coordination and communication among those offices that impinged importantly on travel and tourism, such as transportation, public health, customs, and immigration authorities. Clearly, in the financially strapped conditions of the early 1930s, tourism provoked a more concerted policy.

The election of Lázaro Cárdenas in 1934 led to a substantial expansion of the state's role in tourism: the regulation and licensing of hotels, travel agencies, tourist guides, and restaurants. To enforce the rules of the commission, a fine structure was instituted for violators of the new regulations. Moreover, the agency was authorized to establish tourist offices outside and inside the country, signaling the growing importance of tourism for government revenues. Within Mexico, regional tourist offices were to work with the governors toward promoting the tourist trade.

By presidential decree in December 1939, the state's tourist bureaucracy was restructured on the heels of the first major hemispheric gathering of government-sponsored tourist agencies and their private counterparts in San Francisco, California, in April of that year. Influenced by the discussions at that meeting, Mexico's tourist office was to take on a more "mod-

ern" appearance and organization, emphasizing the state in the more efficient development and promotion of tourism. Mexico City hosted the
second hemisphere-wide tourist conference in early 1941, a sign of the swelling significance of the heritage industry. In the midst of the Good Neighbor
Policy of the Roosevelt administration, the meeting was prefaced by a large-
scale government campaign to market Mexico to American tourists. The
war in Europe pressed Mexico's interest in travelers from the United States,
as the turmoil across the Atlantic forced American tourists to consider other
destinations for vacations. Mexico was determined, it seems, to garner a
large share of that market, as well as that remaining of Europeans able to flee
the troubles on the continent.[33]

The importance of Americans to the heritage industry underscored the
benefits of Mexico's improving infrastructure: the construction and rehabilitation of roads, modernized bus facilities, better railway service, up-
dated airports, new sanitation works, and the expansion of gasoline service
stations. With the surge in foreign tourism after 1940, and more so from the
United States after the war, these infrastructural projects especially served
the needs of Americans, particularly those traveling via automobile. Guidebooks, for instance, from year to year registered the changes generated by
the appearance of new, government-sanctioned tourist sites and services,
testimony to the extension of roads and the reach of autos and buses, the
proliferation of hotels and convenient eateries, as well as the production of
heritage sights by local and federal authorities, merchants, and other purveyors of an area's specific cultural patrimony.[34]

Tourism produced substantial financial dividends for Mexico in these years,
drawing the inevitable attention of powerful, opportunistic political and
economic interests. In this respect, the 1940s represented a critical period
for the tourist business due to the role of Miguel Alemán Valdés. This essay
can provide only a cursory treatment here, but his importance merits at least
brief attention. Alemán forcefully used his political muscle during his tenure as the head of Gobernación from 1940 to 1946, and later his presidential
powers from 1946 to 1952, to promote Mexican tourism. During these
years, Alemán attempted to "modernize" Mexican tourism, to give it a sleek
contemporary style, to refashion the image of Mexico away from quaint
peasants, curio shops, and village marketplaces toward one that was more
metropolitan, up to date, and businesslike. In this broad endeavor, Alemán

made much headway, but he was forced to accede in large measure to an image of mexicanidad forged from the past.

The stakes were high at this point in the history of Mexican tourism, punctuated by the vast amounts of money generated by the rising industry, nowhere more dramatically than in the glittering growth of Acapulco during the war years and the decade that followed.[35] Those were the golden years of Acapulco. The material benefits of the Mexican wartime economy accelerated the expansion of the country's middle class and ballooned the affluence of Mexican elites, allowing an increasing number of Mexicans the means to participate in the lure of Acapulco. Furthermore, famous movie actors, well-known writers, eminent artists, and the socially prominent made Acapulco their playground, adding a unique social patina to the port city. Particularly for residents of the capital, visiting Acapulco became a virtual sign of social status, provoking a weekend exodus of autos and buses from Mexico City for much of the year to the port's beaches, hotels, dance clubs, nightlife, and restaurants. And thousands of foreigners made their way to the bayside city for vacations made impossible elsewhere because of the war. The end of hostilities brought an enormous wave of tourist activity, making Acapulco a resort mecca of international proportions. As a budding, attractive, opulent spot for influential Mexicans—as well as foreign tourists—Acapulco invited intrigue, greed, corruption, and a deepening commercialization of Mexico's "official culture."

Early on in his political career, Alemán came to appreciate the economic potential of tourism in his home state of Veracruz. As the campaign manager of the 1940 presidential campaign of Manuel Avila Camacho, Alemán therefore brought a keen eye to the holdings of the opposition candidate, Juan Andreú Almazán. Prior to his grab at the presidency in 1940, Almazán was a prominent political and military figure who had parlayed his connections and position to build a sizable fortune by the time of his candidacy. As a cabinet member in 1930, Almazán had pushed the rebuilding of the antiquated, arduous road linking Mexico City to Acapulco with the intent of nurturing the port's tourist possibilities. With this in mind, Almazán invested in real estate in the port city's beachfront, including the building of new hotels.

When Almazán lost the election and fled the country, it was Alemán who plotted the confiscation of Almazán's properties and turned them over to a government-appointed group, allegedly to improve infrastructure and facilities in the port city. In fact, this group acted as a front organization for Alemán's designs for making Acapulco a centerpiece of Mexico's post-1940 tourist campaign. At the helm of Gobernación, with oversight of the government's tourist bureaucracy, Alemán held considerable power over Mexico's tourist policies. (Throughout his scheme for Acapulco, the personal economic motives of Alemán were rarely far from the surface.) More important, the port and its still pristine waters and beaches had assumed a much more prominent place in the conceptualization of tourism in Mexico. The combination of foreign and domestic visitors, coupled with the end of the war, made a boom town of Acapulco, as the development of the port went on at a furious rate through the 1950s. The rise of Acapulco as a major tourist center disclosed a salient turn in the industry.

The mix of Acapulco's significance and Alemán's influence forced a reconciliation of the "modern" tourism exemplified by beachside resorts with the heritage-based approach of the 1930s. The marketing of Acapulco required an emphasis on sunny beaches, exotic locales, recreational activities, and "good times" all rolled into one package. The port was basically devoid of impressive indigenous archaeological remains, majestic colonial buildings, or recognized folkloric traditions: no pyramids nearby; no romantic *callejones* (cobblestoned alleyways); no día de los muertos.[36]

In contrast to the heritage-laden publicity of the past, by the 1940s the state's tourist effort modified its picture of Mexico, reducing the focus on culture and lore for greater attention to romantic, sensual settings and leisure in the midst of the modern amenities and style of post-1940 Mexico. Nonetheless, for all of the state's drive (and that of Alemán) for "modernizing" Mexican tourism, the foundational effect of the cultural project of the previous era endured in the touristic representation of Mexico. Space constraints prohibit a detailed examination of the awkward accommodation, but a few examples clearly suggest the nature of the reconciliation: the juxtaposition of the "traditional" (i.e., the essentialist) depiction of Mexico with the contemporary (see Figures 1 and 2).

In a 1939 publication of the Asociación Mexicana de Turismo, the section on travel featured a picture of a sombrero-clad man beside his burro, framed by a large cross and Mexico's famed Popocatépetl volcano, though the text noted the country's modern transportation systems, "making it possible for the traveler to visit the principal places of interest in perfect convenience and comfort." Aimed at foreigners, the inside cover of the pamphlet consists of

1. In an advertisement paid for by Mexico's tourist agency, the female image in folkloric attire creates a selective crescent that arcs from the modern to the indigenous past. Note the suggestion that sun, sand, and romance can be combined with access to Mexico's diverse traditional culture. *New York Times*, 17 February 1952, X59.

a simplified map of Mexico in which only three archaeological sites are highlighted: Teotihuacán's pyramids, the Maya complex of Chichén Itzá and Uxmal, and Oaxaca's Monte Albán and Mitla sites. In one corner of the cover is a figure of a man in a large sombrero (sans full charro regalia), and in the other corner is an illustration of a woman in china poblana–like costume. As evidenced by this publication, the state's notion of tourism remained focused on Mexico City as a hub of activities for visitors. In the text, Acapulco merits only passing reference and a small picture (predictable palm trees and beach) with a caption that describes it as "Mexico's Waikiki." In this respect, Tlaxcala, Puebla, and Huejotzingo receive as much descriptive attention in the pamphlet as the port city. The imaging of Mexico in that 1939 publication was studded with pictures of Mexican women in folkloric dress in "traditional" settings, where everything is "so incredibly inexpensive."[37]

Hospitality keynotes gracious living in Mexico... Land of contrast and charm.

Here you will find romance and excitement; sightseeing, resting and relaxing amidst exotic, colorful surroundings.

You will experience unforgettable thrills exploring vestiges or ancient civilizations and when shopping in picturesque villages for unbelievably, beautiful handmade arts and crafts.

Everywhere ideal, springlike weather, and colonial cities with 20th Century conveniences.

And... travel is so very inexpensive in Mexico.

your travel agent will tell you!

2. A demure and hospitable female image is used here by Mexico's tourist agency to emphasize the accommodating graciousness of Mexico in offering a wide range of activities for tourist enjoyment. Female imagery overwhelmingly dominated the representation of Mexico for tourist consumption. *New York Times*, 4 May 1952, X40.

Much of this "folkloric" optic of Mexico persisted in the September 1941 publication by the government's tourism agency.[38] The frontispiece consists of an *india bonita* framed by cactus and flowers. The most notable difference from the 1939 publication is perhaps best captured in the scenes that border the introduction. A photo of Xochimilco is placed beside that of a mariachi group arrayed along the top of the page, while the bottom includes two photos: one of dancers in stylized jarabe tapatío costume, and the second of a woman in a resplendent charra outfit riding a horse. The bottom of this frame is cornered by two drawings, each containing a woman (with an uncanny resemblance to actress María Félix) in "traditional" dress gazing out somewhat flirtatiously at the reader. This publication features much larger pictures and less text than its 1930 counterpart: tourism had become literally more picturesque.

A revealing subtext marks these publications: the contrast between "traditional" Mexico and "modernity." The desire of Mexico to signify its contemporary face along with its "traditional" mask is explicitly stated in the opening lines of the 1939 pamphlet: "Mexico is a contrasting fusion of the fifteenth and twentieth century civilizations—of stately medieval palaces and ancient cathedrals flanked by modernistically [*sic*] designed office buildings, of ox-carts and airplanes." Still, the focus remained on "old" Mexico City and its environs. Despite the attention to the theme of contrasts, the reconstruction of the past continued to be accentuated. Thus, the 1941 publication maintains sections on costumes, folkloric dance, archaeological monuments, venerable colonial buildings, wonderful vistas, and natural wonders. (As a nod to Alemán's home state, Veracruz received decidedly greater coverage than that found in earlier brochures of this type.) Only the concluding sections of the 1941 publication make a direct effort to point out the modern features of Mexican life, marked by scenes with women prominently pictured in smart, contemporary outfits.

A 1943 government-funded tourist publication differed substantially from its predecessors.[39] The later pamphlet begins traditionally with the first section (of seven) celebrating the country's colonial architecture. But the following section displays the Escuela Preparatoria with its colonial arches framing poses of an athlete in training and a young woman "reviewing her anatomy lesson." The next section focuses on the Paseo de la Reforma and gives much play to women in modern attire; scant notice is given to the avenue's well-known historical monuments. The jarring contrast with the former publications is particularly obvious in the sandwiching of photos of the government printing office and its up-to-date technology between sections on Totonac art and pictures of the famous volcanoes of the valley of Mexico. In brief, the heritage-inflected presentation of Mexico persisted, including the prominence of Mexico City, but now interspersed noticeably by a more contemporary current.

About a decade later, a government-funded advertisement reflected the manifest negotiation between two distinct approaches to the promotion of Mexican tourism (see Figure 1).[40] Culture persisted in the selling of Mexico. The woman's attire privileges the folkloric (braids, shawl, and sandals), including an artifact at her feet. A pyramid punctuates the association with traditional Mexico (and a bullfight scene is added for further authenticity). Yet, the exotic is embedded in the picture (the pineapple as a sign of the tropical, Waikiki-like implication). In the background, the allusion to Acapulco-like settings appears clearly: a marlin leaping out of the water (recreation) and a couple on a beach (sun, sand, and romance). The image creates a crescent, where modernity begins at the top and "heritage" composes the other end. The text in fact attempts to meld the disparate elements together: from "modern" hotels to "unspoiled 17th century cities," and from "very inexpensive" shopping in "colorful Indian villages" to fun in the "tropical" sun, the latter a transparent reference to the sensual possibilities of Mexico, including the lure of "friendly" women who beckon from "out-of-the-way" locations. In folkloric dress, the woman's look is modest, muted, almost shy, conveying a sense of innocence and expectations: she awaits a suitor.

In another advertisement in the same year (1952; see Figure 2), an overarching female figure centers the illustration, as she bows demurely in a long, richly embroidered dress, her face framed by two thick braids reaching down to her bare shoulders. Above this picture, a slogan touts the "hospitality of beautiful Mexico." Drawings on each side of the full-page advertisement mix images of singing mariachis and colonial churches with a woman playing golf. The text of the advertisement contains references to "romance and excitement," the "exotic," and "unforgettable thrills" along with "gracious living" amid the remnants of "ancient civilizations" and access to "beautiful handmade arts and crafts."

In brief, the tourist had available captivating beaches and modern hotels with a special cultural experience, that is, one uniquely "Mexican." The touristic promotion of Mexico by the 1940s signified the transition from essentialist cultural depiction to one less reliant on the appeal of authenticity, monumentalism, and folklore. Pyramids and cathedrals shared the staging of Mexican tourism with golf courses and sportfishing, as the imaging of the country became largely codified, its formulas refined, and its scripts well honed. Tourists eager to experience "Mexican culture" found an infrastructure to provide it (government-regulated), ready-made availability (licensed packaged tours), accessibility (state-approved multilingual guides), and the exotically different (the institutionalized performances of the Ballet Folklórico of Amalia Hernández in 1952). For tourists who found such cultural packaging inconvenient, the experience was brought to them in formalized displays of "Mexican culture." And the package was usually delivered by a smiling staff dressed in "typically Mexican" uniforms of one type or another, eager to please.[41]

The resilient promotional emphasis on "Mexican" culture took place in the context of the growing entry of foreigners that amplified the difference between "them" (most often Americans) and "us" (Mexicans). Residual forms of culture concretized this fundamental distinction, where the daily display of mexicanidad underscored the difference for both tourists and Mexicans. The film historian Ana López has noted the popularity of melodrama in Mexican cinema of the 1940s, including the "drama of identification." Cultural production in this era afforded opportunities for Mexicans to understand themselves "as they were," but also "to learn how they should 'become.'"[42] In this sense, tourism presented the dramatic making of the nation, and other sources of cultural formation "refashioned the idea of the nation by transforming nationalism into a big spectacle."[43] Through its privileged architecture, ritualized displays, and folkloric forms, tourism fused the drama and spectacle of nation with imposing monuments (canonized buildings, museums, archaeological sites), celebrations of heritage (music, dance, costumes), and glorious historical moments (hallowed battlegrounds and heroes).

The government policy of free admission on Sundays to state-run heritage sites, therefore, was more than benevolence by the managers of Mexico's tourist gaze. For Mexicans who trooped through officially consecrated space, who took in elaborate exhibits, and who marveled at ancient artifacts, the meanings of such experiences were magnified by the absence or relative weakness of alternative views of national identification. The representations of mexicanidad in the domestic sphere and its tourist manifestations converge to reify the cultural differences of a generalized cultural binary of "them" and "us." In this sense, tourism constructed the nation as "an assertion of its opposition to other communities and identities" where "to assert 'identity' in this *relational* form [was] to display 'difference' forcibly in the public sphere."[44] In this context, the local was subsumed and selectively deployed within the inclusive narrative of the nation. At this historical juncture, tourism possessed the capacity to generate sentiments conducive to a sense of national identity, furthering as a consequence the cultural and nationalizing project of the Mexican state.

This interpretation argues against a view that defines tourism as simply the commodification of "Mexican culture," as merely capitalist incorporation and manipulation. Rather, tourism was capable of cultural affirmation, an effect deepened by the fact that most tourists were foreigners and, not insignificantly, primarily Americans. As the anthropologist Regina Bendix has observed: "Economic motivations are one part of the story. . . . But wished-for economic benefits do not sufficiently explain why such events are continued for decades. A close examination . . . of new, traditionalized displays points instead toward an affirmation of local and national cultural identity in the face of seasonal mass foreign invasion."[45]

From the 1920s and into the 1940s, the representation of Mexican culture and heritage reflected the progressive conflation of the local into an encompassing but selectively expressed definition of mexicanidad. Tourism contributed importantly to this complicated essentializing process that resonated with the state's nationalist project. Granted, for men like Alemán, tourism was an enterprise primarily for profit and entertainment, and less a construct of legitimation. In his discussion of the populist nationalism of the Cárdenas years, Alan Knight has suggested that "the civilians and técnicos of the Alemán sexenio . . . quarried the rubble of Cardenismo and utilized the material" left behind, "but the ground-plan was their own."[46] One piece of that rubble was a tenacious notion of mexicanidad that yielded large material rewards for the state and its managers in the post-1940 era. But the selling of Mexico also produced valuable, if intangible, benefits for a regime still mining the emotional substance of Mexican nationalism.

Notes

1 For a brief overview of Mexican tourism, see Mary Lee Nolan and Sidney Nolan, "The Evolution of Tourism in Twentieth-Century Mexico," *Journal of the West* 27 (October 1988): 14–25. For a discussion of the statistics regarding Mexican tourism prior to 1960, see G. Donald Jud, "Tourism and Economic Growth in Mexico Since 1960," *Inter-American Economic Affairs* 28, no. 1 (summer 1974): 19. All translations are mine otherwise unless noted.

2 On the inconsistencies of postrevolutionary thinking, including the porfirian intellectual residue on nationalism, see Mauricio Tenorio-Trillo, *Mexico at the World's Fairs: Crafting a Modern Nation* (Berkeley: University of California Press, 1996), especially 243–53.

3 This interpretation reflects to a large extent the work of Ricardo Pérez Montfort, *Estampas de nacionalismo popular mexicano: Ensayos sobre cultura popular y nacionalismo* (Mexico City: CIESAS, 1994); his views are summarized in his essay, "Una región inventada desde el centro: La consolidación del cuadro estereotípico nacional, 1921–1937," in *El nacionalismo y el arte mexicano* (Mexico City: UNAM, 1986), 114–35. For an overview of the relations between the private and public sectors in this period, particularly after Cárdenas, see Ricardo

Tirado, "La alianza con los empresarios," in *Entre la guerra y la estabilidad política: El México de los 40*, ed. Rafael Loyola (Mexico City: Grijalbo, 1986), 195–221. For a collection of essays that discuss several aspects of this process, see Gilbert Joseph and Daniel Nugent, eds., *Everyday Forms of State Formation: Revolution and the Negotiation of Rule in Modern Mexico* (Durham, NC: Duke University Press, 1994), especially the essay by Joseph and Nugent, 3–23. This essay reflects the conceptual understanding of tourism expressed in John Urry, *The Tourist Gaze: Leisure and Travel in Contemporary Societies* (London: Sage, 1990).

4   Néstor García Canclini, *Transforming Modernity: Popular Culture in Mexico* (Austin: University of Texas Press, 1993), 65.

5   See Mary Kay Vaughan, *Cultural Politics in Revolution: Teachers, Peasants, and Schools in Mexico, 1930–1940* (Tucson: University of Arizona Press, 1997). On this point, see also Alan Knight, "Popular Culture and the Revolutionary State in Mexico, 1910–1940," *Hispanic American Historical Review* 74, no. 3 (1994): 433–34.

6   See Fernando Mejía Barquera, *La industria de la radio y la televisión y la política del estado mexicano (1920–1960)* (Mexico City: Fundación Manuel Buendía, 1989), 64–71.

7   Marjorie Becker, *Setting the Virgin on Fire: Lázaro Cárdenas, Michoacán Peasants, and the Redemption of the Mexican Revolution* (Berkeley: University of California Press, 1995), 8.

8   Jesús Arroyo Alejandre, *El abandono rural: Un modelo explicativo de la emigración de trabajadores rurales en el occidente de Mexico* (Guadalajara: Universidad de Guadalajara, 1989), 161–87.

9   Becker, *Setting the Virgin on Fire*, 8–9.

10   See Carlos Monsiváis, "Sociedad y cultura," in *Entre la guerra y la estabilidad política*, ed. Loyola, 259–78. On the notion of lo mexicano and the mass media in Mexico in this period, see Roger Bartra, *La jaula de la melancolía: Identidad y metamorfosis del mexicano* (Mexico City: Grijalbo, 1987), especially 145–51. Also see Carlos Martínez Assad, "El cine como lo ví y como me lo contaron," in *Entre la guerra y la estabilidad política*, ed. Loyola, 339–60.

11   Carlos Monsiváis, "All the People Came and Did Not Fit onto the Screen: Notes on the Cinema Audience in Mexico," in *Mexican Cinema*, ed. Paulo Antonio Paranagua (London: British Film Institute, 1995), 151. On the reconstruction of "community" in rural communities subject to large-scale migration, see Roger Rouse, "Mexican Migration and the Social Space of Postmodernism," *Diaspora* 1, no. 1 (1991): 8–23.

12   On the initial discussion of national identity after the Revolution, see Ramón E. Ruíz, *Mexico 1920–1958: El reto de la pobreza y del analfabetismo* (Mexico City: Fondo de Cultura Económica, 1977), 146–64. For a discussion of indigenismo and its intellectual evolution, see Alan Knight, "Racism, Revolution, and *indigenismo*: Mexico, 1910–1940," in *The Idea of Race in Latin America, 1870–1940*, ed. Richard Graham (Austin: University of Texas Press, 1990), 71–113.

13   See Daniel F. Rubin de la Borbolla, "Valoración de las artes populares en Mexico, 1900–1940," in *El nacionalismo y el arte mexicano*, 360.

14   By 1923, regional museums for Zacatecas, Veracruz, and Queretaro had appeared. The site of a famous battle during the U.S.-Mexican War was also initiated in the same year. See Miguel Ángel Fernández, *Historia de los museos de México* (Mexico City: Banamex, 1987), n.p.

15 See Helen Delpar, *The Enormous Vogue of Things Mexican: Cultural Relations Between the United States and Mexico, 1920–1935* (Tuscaloosa: University of Alabama Press, 1992), 67.

16 For a penetrating and critical assessment of this multifaceted movement, see Irene Vásquez Valle, *La cultura popular vista por las élites* (Mexico City: UNAM, 1989), especially 2–6.

17 For a discussion of this general process, see Rafael Tovar y de Teresa, *Modernización y política cultural* (Mexico City: Fondo de Cultural Económica, 1994).

18 See Vásquez Valle, *La cultura popular vista por las élites*, 2–3.

19 See Tovar y de Teresa, *Modernización y política cultural*, 40–41.

20 Fernández, *Historia de los museos*, 181–94.

21 See Ricardo Pérez Montfort, "Indigenismo, hispanismo y panamericanismo," in *Cultura e identidad nacional*, ed. Robert Blancarte (Mexico City: Fondo de Cultura Económica, 1994), 346–62, for a discussion of this process, including the role of indigenismo, on the importance of the media, the role of foreigners, and the development of archetypes.

22 Under the legislation that created INAH, the institution absorbed the National Museum and the department that managed historical monuments. The origins of INAH were laid down importantly by Manuel Gamio, who in 1925 established the Dirrección General de Monumentos and put it under the control of SEP. INAH attempted to establish a regional museum network, but resources delayed the successful establishment of this project until 1952. The formation of INAH also witnessed its absorption of a key training ground for researchers, the National School of Anthropology and History. See Julio Cesar Olive-Negrete and Augusto Urteaga Castro-Pozo, eds., *INAH, una historia* (Mexico City: INAH, 1988), 15–22. It should be emphasized that the heritage policies and programs of the 1920s and 1930s were inconsistent, subject to the views of the leaders of the heritage bureaucracy, such as Manuel Gamio, Narciso Bassols, and Alfonso Caso, among others. Space constraints do not allow further examination of this issue. On the concept and development of "official culture," see Roger Bartra, *Oficio mexicano* (Mexico City: Grijalbo, 1993), 31–44.

23 On these issues, see the excellent collection of essays in *El nacionalismo y el arte mexicano*.

24 One example of this type of effort was the government-subsidized book publisher Fondo de Cultura Económica, which was established in 1934. Also see Vásquez Valle, *La cultura popular vista por las elites*, 13. A crucial governmental initiative on cultural publications was the series *Anales* of INAH, initially edited by Alfonso Caso. On the importance of publications on culture, see Albert Dallal, "El nacionalismo prolongado: El movimiento mexicano de danza moderna, 1940–1955," in *El nacionalismo y el arte mexicano*, 332.

25 In 1934, the Mexican Congress passed new legislation to protect and conserve "monumentos arqueológicos e históricos, poblaciones típicas y lugares de belleza natural." The department in charge was given broad powers over the protection of the country's cultural patrimony. See Salvador Díaz-Berrio Fernández, *Conservación de monumentos y zonas monumentales* (Mexico City: SEP, 1976), 149–69. This legislation was a revision of the law passed in 1930 that established the Departamento de Monumentos Históricos, Artísticos y Coloniales de la República.

26 See Delpar, *The Enormous Vogue of Things Mexican*, 55–90. Also see Pérez Montfort, "Una región inventada desde el centro," in *El nacionalismo y el arte mexicano*, especially 113–27. The role of foreigners, and their responses to the local-state relationship, raise a number of

112   *Alex Saragoza*

complex issues that cannot be addressed in this essay. For probing, insightful analyses of these complexities, see Gilbert M. Joseph, Catherine C. LeGrand, and Ricardo Salvatore, eds., *Close Encounters of Empire: Writing the Cultural History of U.S.–Latin American Relations* (Durham, NC: Duke University Press, 1998), especially the introductory essays by Joseph and Stern.

27 See *Travel* (January 1929): 7–11, 41; (May 1933): 28–31, 46; (November 1935): 4–10, 42; (June 1938): 6–11, 44. In its edition of October 1928 (pp. 26–27, 49–50), *Travel* featured an article on the pyramids of Teotihuacán outside of Mexico City and included comments by Manuel Gamio, who was leading an archaeological dig at the site.

28 See the advertisement for the Mexican railways in *Travel* (March 1936): 47, where the ad, which prompted Guanajuato, features dancers in jarabe tapatío trappings. According to Yolanda Moreno Rivas, three factors led to the essentialist representation of cultural expression by the 1930s: first, the growth of urbanized cultural formations; second, the spread of the mass media, radio and film in particular; and third, the awareness of the profits to be made from the commercialization of popular music due to radio and recordings. See *El nacionalismo y el arte mexicano*, 59–60. The china poblana references a style of mestiza female dress and presentation dating to colonial Puebla, and which took on national symbolic importance during the Wars of the Reform in the mid-nineteenth century. A fusion of indigenous dress and European fashions, the china poblana included a colorful, sequined-lined skirt, a finely embroidered white blouse, a *rebozo* (shoulder scarf), and thickly braided hair interwoven with ribbons. Today the china poblana can be found in a stylized version of this older fashion.

29 According to an article in *Mexican Folkways* 6, no. 1 (1930): 33–35, the origins of the jarabe tapatío as the "official" dance of Mexico began in the 1920s, when, under Vasconcelos, SEP began staging folk dances through its department of physical culture. The stylization of the dance was credited to Nelli Campobella and her contemporaries into one that was described as a dance created by "the Mexican of the cities." On the basis of this stylization, the dance was standardized through its teaching at government schools and its staging by government-sponsored cultural events. For a similar discussion and conclusion, see Dallal, "El nacionalismo prolongado," 331–34; see also Pérez Montfort, "Una región inventada," 117–19.

30 The famous composer and music arranger Ignacio Fernández Esperón started as a researcher of popular music for SEP; Fernández would then become the musical director of the *Así es mi tierra* radio program. See Yolanda Moreno Rivas, "Los estilos nacionalistas en la música culta: Aculturación de las formas populares" in *El nacionalismo y el arte mexicano*, 62. On film and its nationalist content, which spanned the silent era to that of sound in the early 1930s, see the excellent discussion in Aurelio de los Reyes, *Medio siglo de cine mexicano (1896–1947)* (Mexico City: Ed. Trillas, 1987), 116–32.

31 See *Down Mexico Way in Your Car* (Mexico: DAPP, 1938). This publication was typical of those done by the federal government for American tourists, with maps to guide them to particular sites. The private sector contributed in various ways to promote tourism. For example, El Aguila cigarette company published a guidebook, with the authorization of the government's tourism department, entitled *Along the Road of Romance Land* in 1939.

32 The interests of Abelardo Rodríguez, interim president of Mexico, were involved in this

move. Ex-governor of Baja California Norte, Rodríguez was a patron of border tourism based largely on Americans crossing over to indulge in prostitution, gambling, race track betting, and, until the end of prohibition, alcohol consumption. The early years of the Depression also led to an effort from 1931 to 1934 to promote Mexican economic and cultural nationalism. The state spearheaded the so-called Campaña Nacionalista that was generally echoed outside of Mexico City. This campaign included the making of highly patriotic movie shorts, public events extolling nationalism, and the promotion of Mexican-owned businesses as opposed to those with foreign connections. See José Manuel López Victoria, *La campaña nacionalista* (Mexico City: Ed. Botas, 1965), 243–46. For a discussion of how *día de la raza* became a national holiday in the 1920s with regional support, see "El 12 de ocubre: Entre IV y V centenario," in *Cultura e identidad*, ed. Blancarte, 145–46.

33 For a brief description of the history of government tourist activity, see Luis Chavez Aldape, "Algunas consideraciones sobre política turística," in Consejo Nacional de Turismo, *Memoria: Consejo Nacional de Turismo, 1973* (Mexico City: Ed. Talleres, 1974), 105–8; Consejo Nacional de Turismo, *Memoria: Consejo Nacional de Turismo, 1975* (Mexico City: Ed. Talleres, 1976), 165–82; Hector Manuel Romero, *Enciclopedia Mexicana de Turismo*, 3 vols. (Mexico City: Ed. Limusa, 1986). See also *New York Times*, 18 January 1942, X3.

34 It should be noted that the government-controlled Mexican oil company PEMEX after 1939 was also involved in the promotion of auto-based tourism, including its own promotional advertisements, guidebooks, and related material. In the early development of the tourist business, the problems of transportation and amenities for travelers were serious obstacles to easy travel. On this point for the Mayan pyramids at Chichén Itzá and for reaching Acapulco, respectively, see *Travel* (March 1929): 26–30, 44, 46; (June 1935): 28–32, 48–49.

35 The changes in Acapulco as a result of the wartime boom are noted in virtually all of the articles on the resort area throughout the war years and subsequently. For an early example, see *New York Times*, 4 February 1940, X7. For a discussion of the wartime boom and its social impacts, see Stephen Niblo, *War, Diplomacy, and Development: The United States and Mexico, 1938–1954* (Wilmington, DE: Scholarly Resources Press, 1995), 123–62. The descriptions of Acapulco filled the pages of many editions of mainstream American travel publications and travel sections of major newspapers by the end of the war years. The citations are too many to enumerate here; suffice it to say that every year, usually in February, the *New York Times*, for example, published a special travel supplement that invariably included an article on Mexico, where Acapulco was a frequent object of attention.

36 In an early article on Acapulco in a travel magazine for Americans, there is a telling neglect of interesting sites to visit other than to tout the resort attractions of the port city; see *Travel* (June 1935): 28–32, 44, 46. The article also noted the difficulty of reaching Acapulco given the limitations of transportation to the beachside haven. For an exceptional early advertisement that promoted Acapulco and other beachside destinations, see *Travel* (October 1935): 45, where an ad by the Mexican railways emphasized the "warm, enchanting sands" of Veracruz, Acapulco, and Manzanillo.

37 Asociación Mexicana de Turismo, *Mexico: The Faraway Land Nearby* (Mexico City: Asociación Mexicana de Turismo, 1939), 5; on the passing reference to Acapulco, p. 24.

38 Secretaría de Gobernación, *Revista México: Así es México* (Mexico City: Departamento de

Turismo de la Secretaría de Gobernación 1941). This was a special edition of this publication in observance of the Interamerican Tourist Congress held in Mexico City in September 1941.

39 Departamento de Turismo, *Revista México* 1, no. 1 (1943). This was a bilingual publication, (English-Spanish), slated primarily for foreign consumption.

40 On the process of tourism and its impacts on cultural displays and performances, see García Canclini, *Transforming Modernity*, 40–44. The illustration and text comes from the *New York Times*, 17 February 1952, X59. The other illustration (a piece of a full-page advertisement) and portions of the text comes from the *New York Times*, 4 May 1952, X40. It is beyond the scope of this essay to discuss the centrality of female figures to the promotion of tourism in Mexico, but clearly the sexualized images of tourist activities and the like were crucial to the overall strategy of selling Mexico.

41 As one writer in the *New York Times* put it describing the demeanor of Mexican waiters at a Mexican hotel: "and possesses Chuchu and Carlos, the two handsomest, nimblest waiters in all Mexico" (*New York Times*, 31 October 1943, B11). Tour promoters in the United States in their ads made mention of the sites, sounds, and events included in their packages. For an example, see *New York Times*, 5 July 1953, B21.

42 See Joanne Hershfield, *Mexican Cinema/Mexican Woman, 1940–1950* (Tucson: University of Arizona Press, 1996), 43. Also see Ana M. López, "Tears and Desire: Women and Melodrama in the 'Old' Mexican Cinema," in *Mediating Two Worlds: Cinematic Encounters in the Americas* (London: British Film Institute, 1993), 152–53.

43 Carlos Monsiváis, "Mythologies," in *Mexican Cinema*, ed. Paranagua, 127.

44 Erica Carter, James Donald, and Judith Squires, *Space and Place: Theories of Identity and Location* (London: Lawrence and Wishart, 1993), x.

45 Regina Bendix, "Tourism and Cultural Displays: Inventing Tradition for Whom?," *Journal of American Folklore* (April–June 1989): 132. On the notion of inventing tradition, see Eric Hobsbawm and Terence Ranger, eds., *The Invention of Tradition* (Cambridge, England: Cambridge University Press, 1983). See also Benetta Jules-Rosette, *The Messages of Tourist Art: An African Semiotic System in Comparative Perspective* (New York: Plenum Press, 1984), 3.

46 Alan Knight, "The Rise and Fall of Cardenismo, c.1930–c.1946," in *Mexico Since Independence*, ed. Leslie Bethell (New York: Cambridge University Press, 1991), 320.

Today, Tomorrow, and Always:
The Golden Age of Illustrated Magazines
in Mexico, 1937–1960

John Mraz

Visual culture has been a key site for constructing political power in Mexico. According to Serge Gruzinski, pictures exercised a notable role in the discovery, conquest, and colonization of the New World, initiating a "war of images which has been perpetuated for centuries and does not appear to have concluded today."[1] Religious icons, painted murals, photography, cinema, and television have been fundamental elements in forging cultural identity. Moreover, singular forms of graphic expression have entered into the visual economy of production, circulation, and consumption, acquiring substantial if short-lived significance within particular historical moments.[2] A prime example is offered by the enormously popular *tarjetas de visita*, the first mass-produced photographs, which "generated and generalized a code for representing individuals" in Mexico between 1862 and 1880.[3] Picture postcards were a later and similar phenomenon: in the early twentieth century the market for postcards of the Mexican Revolution reached such proportions that one photographer was producing five thousand cards daily.[4]

From the mid-1930s to the mid-1950s, illustrated magazines established themselves as the newest version of the tarjetas de visita and the picture postcards, sharing the visual culture sphere with more lasting graphic expressions, such as cinema and comic books. Though there were a number of illustrated magazines, *Hoy, Rotofoto, Mañana*, and *Siempre!* seem to have been the most important and are those remembered today. Like their U.S. and

European counterparts—*Life, Picture Post*, and *Vu*—they enjoyed significant popularity.[5] The Mexican magazines were almost certainly bought by members of the new middle classes born of postrevolutionary economic development. Literacy campaigns had created readers for articles by important intellectuals, both foreign and Mexican; they included international figures—Thomas Mann, Leon Trotsky, Pio Baroja, André Gide, Gabriela Mistral, Arnold Toynbee—as well as Mexican thinkers: Samuel Ramos, José Vasconcelos, Vicente Lombardo Toledano, Alfonso Caso, José Revueltas, Salvador Novo, Carlos Fuentes, and Leopoldo Zea. However, what made the magazines different from their predecessors was their visuality: photo reportage and photo essays acquired an autonomy previously unknown in Mexican publications, and the striking imagery of photographers such as Nacho López, the Hermanos Mayo, Ismael Casasola, and Héctor García was provided a space in which to appear. Then, around the middle of the 1950s, in a process that occurred throughout the world, illustrated magazines in Mexico were displaced by the arrival of television.

Though the picture supplements of Porfirian newspapers are in some sense antecedents, the modern illustrated magazines began during the regime of Lázaro Cárdenas (1934–1940).[6] The Mexican press's master editor of graphic publications, José Pagés Llergo, founded *Hoy* in 1937 along with his cousin, Regino Hernández Llergo. Modeled on *Life*, which had begun publishing the year before, *Hoy* was to be "the modern magazine which has been lacking in our country, with objective and fundamentally visual news."[7] Cárdenas carried out the effective centralization of power, but his rule was not marked by the unquestioning complicity of the press with the president, which was increasingly the case after 1940. Rather, the pluralism of his regime can be appreciated in the fact that *Hoy* was the magazine most loved by the private sector and "the leading champion of the opposition."[8] One instance of *Hoy*'s struggle against *cardenismo* was its publication of some sixty-two studies by the Instituto de Estudios Económicos y Sociales, a right-wing think tank, during 1938 and 1939.[9] Though *Hoy* began under Cárdenas, its political leanings made it much more appropriate for the post-1940 period, when, like its baby brother, *Mañana*, it became the unconditional ally of the government. For that reason, these two publications are considered together below.

The magazine most expressive of the give-and-take during Cárdenas's regime was *Rotofoto*, founded by Pagés Llergo in 1938. Reflecting back on the experience of this experiment in press freedom, Pagés Llergo wrote in 1951,

3. Anonymous photographer. Ramón Beteta, Undersecretary of Foreign Relations, in *Rotofoto* 9 (17 July 1938): cover. Courtesy of collection of Armando Bartra.

"*Rotofoto* was a destructive periodical. If Mexico lived the same epoch today I wouldn't hesitate a moment to repeat the adventure. With Cárdenas, we had left behind the night of oppression. Avid of freedom, like waters that overflow a river's banks, the periodicals threw caution to the wind. *Rotofoto* was the culminating expression of that climate."[10]

Rotofoto dealt with the powerful in a way that no Mexican publication would until the 1970s. In sharp contrast to other periodicals, it demonstrated a distinct irreverence toward presidentialism: its first cover featured a photo of Cárdenas sitting on the ground and eating with *campesinos*; later issues showed him on the beach in a swimming suit and in his underwear after bathing in a river.[11] Though the magazine avoided placing an undressed Cárdenas on its cover, it felt free enough to do so with Ramón Beteta, Undersecretary of Foreign Relations and a powerful member of Cárdenas's cabinet (see Figure 3).

Sometimes the magazine went beyond irreverence to a biting iconoclasm that ridiculed politicians in "indiscreet photos," such as the cover graced by a prominent senator stretching his mouth so that a large hunk of food would fit; the title was "Senator Padilla clings tenaciously to his bone [job]"[12] Images taken in the Chamber of Deputies showed congressmen sleeping—"Don Luis V. León is an idealistic deputy; more than an idealist, a dreamer"—or scratching a leg with a sock lowered: "They say that Representative Miguel Martínez is a man of few fleas but, from the photo, we can see that he has quite a few."[13]

Rotofoto's indiscreet photos were probably inspired by the candid images taken during the late 1920s and early 1930s by German photojournalists such as Erich Salomon and Tim Gidal. Magazines such as the *Berliner Ilustrirte* showed political figures in informal situations with the intention of demonstrating the fundamental equality of all human beings in the fragile democracy of the Weimar Republic. This was not the case in *Rotofoto*, where irreverent photos were sometimes used for a different political purpose. During the 1930s a fierce war waged between the followers of communism and of fascism. Pagés Llergo was an admirer of Hitler and Mussolini; his political sympathies led him to mercilessly denigrate and ridicule the great labor leader Vicente Lombardo Toledano. *Rotofoto* was implacable in its attacks; for example, in its second issue appeared an "intimate" profile of Lombardo Toledano that ridiculed his family relations, his opulent office, and his ideological intransigence. In one photo, Lombardo Toledano appears to ignore his daughters who play nearby as he looks away from them while smoking; the caption reads: "The leader sucks well and peers among the trees to see that no agents of the reaction lie in ambush there."[14] In later issues they accused him of being ignorant, a blabbermouth, a hangman, calumnious, and arbitrary. He declared a Confederación de Trabajadores de México (CTM) boycott against the publication and demanded the cancellation of its permission. In the next (the eleventh and last) issue, a photo of Lombardo Toledano appeared on the cover, his right arm raised as if signaling; the caption is, "The most conspicuous traffic cop in Mexico attempts to detain the circulation of *Rotofoto*. We're sorry to be in a hurry and are determined to continue committing infractions" (see Figure 4).[15]

In spite of the editor's intentions, *Rotofoto* was not permitted any more transgressions. Various leaders of CTM syndicates declared strikes against the publication, and police detained Pagés Llergo in his house while labor goons burned down the offices and destroyed the machinery. I believe that the incessant attacks on Lombardo Toledano were the determining factor in *Rotofoto*'s untimely demise.[16] If this is so, Lombardo Toledano's power to

4. Anonymous photographer. Vicente Lombardo Toledano, in *Rotofoto* 11 (31 July 1938): cover. Courtesy of collection of Armando Bartra.

eliminate the publication demonstrates the dependence of Cárdenas on organized labor, as well as the lack of (and perhaps the lack of interest in) the
well-oiled machine of national domination that came into existence under
Miguel Alemán (1946–1952). Whoever was behind the destruction of *Rotofoto*, the magazine remains even today the great legend of Mexican photojournalism and the prototypical example of censorship among cultural critics such as Carlos Monsiváis and Armando Bartra, as well as working
photojournalists such as Pedro Valtierra and Francisco Mata. Usually they
ascribe its end to presidentialism, reading back anachronistically through
the lens of the all-powerful *presidenciato* established by Alemán.

The Mexican government's turn to the right in 1940 is perhaps most
easily encapsulated in the term *alemanismo*, since Alemán converted the
supposedly temporary abandonment of revolutionary social goals by Manuel Avila Camacho (1940–1946) into a new national project, which, it could
be argued, is only today beginning to loosen its grip on the country. The
increase of readers, the growth of the middle class, and the development of

new forms of communication such as illustrated magazines created a situation where the press was an ever increasing power in the country, and it played a fundamental role in maintaining the "social peace" so necessary to Alemán's project of industrialization. Under alemanismo the press had, with few exceptions, "an accentuated conservative tone, when it wasn't frankly reactionary."[17] This political position corresponded to its socioeconomic interests, as well as the government's policy of *pan o palo* (bread or a beating). The destruction of *Rotofoto* had created a dangerous precedent and, together with the asphyxiation of the magazine *Presente* in 1948 for publishing exposés on alemanista corruption, these cases demonstrated to Mexican journalists that they could follow the president's mandates *por lo bueno o por lo malo* (for better or for worse). The media owners' interests were at one with the state apparatus, a situation precisely described in 1953 by the eminent Mexican journalist Francisco Martinéz de la Vega: "The magnates of the press are businessmen, publicity agents, industrialists. And they have a very peculiar, but very concrete, opinion which is expressed in wooing the cash box. Having surrendered themselves in body and soul to submission, they demand their chains of gold. We could say that in Mexico newspapers can be free. But the sad case is that, with very few exceptions, they seem determined to reject that freedom; the chains of gold are necessary so that the industry prospers and balances are satisfactory. The general tone of our great press is that of a lamentable, persistent servility which makes it impossible to freely examine the country's problems."[18]

The press was "always at the service of the Señor Presidente, whoever and however the Señor Presidente was."[19] José Pagés Llergo, founder of all the important illustrated magazines and probably one of the most tolerant editors (in spite of his early fascistoid affinities), expressed in a definitive way the limitations he placed on his journalists: "They can write whatever they want, as long as they don't touch the President of the Republic or the Virgin of Guadalupe."[20]

The taboo against any portrayal that was not entirely complimentary was absolute: "It was always risky to say anything about the President of the Republic."[21] Nonetheless, the fear of possible consequences was not the only consideration; important as well was the complete absence of any notion of the separation, and mutual checking, of powers. The fact that a division between the authority of the executive and the press was seen as neither necessary nor necessarily desirable can be perceived in the 1951 speech by Ignacio Lomelí Jáuregui, subdirector of the García Valseca publication chain, during a luncheon that was the rehearsal for the *Día de la Libertad de Prensa* (Press Freedom Day), a tradition that continues today: "When the goal of the government, to serve the people, coincides with that of the press; when press and government keep vigil for the nation's dignity, acts such as this occur. Government and press fulfill the common aspiration to serve Mexico."[22]

José Agustín has intelligently commented on the "empire of formalism" that so characterized alemanismo.[23] One way of imposing appearances to camouflage reality was to foment nationalism at the same time that an ever greater dependency on the United States was being established; another was to subsidize a cinema full of films such as Ismael Rodríguez's trilogy, which romanticized the working class while the state carried out a systematic campaign to subdue it.[24] In the press, this formalism was manifested in the creation of the Día de la Libertad de Prensa. A year after the press magnates had offered their luncheon to thank Alemán "for having made possible the freedom of press," they established the 7th of June as the official day for unabashedly rendering homage to the president, who in return reaffirmed his support for them.[25] The photojournalists quickly copied the directors and institutionalized *their* day to lunch with the president as January 15. They were rapidly followed by the newspaper and magazine vendors, who had to have *their* annual banquet with the president. In an irony that seems to have escaped the press magnates, the Press Freedom Days are the clearest indication that such liberty is nonexistent.

Notwithstanding its ruse of journalistic liberty, this day of praise for the president also provided the entrepreneurs of the press with an opportunity to express their desires. They asked for protection against the "invasion of magazines printed outside Mexico which inhibit the development of Mexican publications" and insisted on the necessity of building more paper factories for newsprint.[26] The articulation of these wishes makes it clear that the press's acquiescence to the government was not only a result of shared interests and ideology. The government can choose to protect Mexican publications from their foreign competitors, or to leave them vulnerable. It can also use its power to pardon taxes, both domestic and for the imporation of equipment, or subject publications to the hopelessly byzantine and totally arbitrary tax system. Further, until recently it had control over paper through its agency, Productora e Importadora de Papel (PIPSA). Mexican journalists seemed curiously unconcerned about how the government might abuse its monopoly on paper; in 1938, PIPSA was described as "another guarantee for the freedom of the press."[27]

However, the most important source of government control was realized through the use of public funds for publicity. Prior to 1976, the survival of periodicals depended a good deal more on government subsidies, both federal and state, than on sales or commercial advertising. As Julio Mayo stated categorically in talking about the illustrated magazines, "Circulation didn't matter. Advertising didn't matter. The only thing that really mattered was publishing what government functionaries did. Every dependency had money to pay for public relations, and they paid for every mention of anything that had been done and could be related to a particular functionary, for example, public works."[28]

This "news" (for that is how it was published) took the form of picturing federal and state functionaries at the inauguration of new industrial accomplishments, meeting with international business leaders, or announcing social programs carried out by politicians of the official, Partido Revolucionario Institucional (PRI).[29] Though these *gacetillas* are difficult to recognize, they probably constituted some 60 percent of the total magazine pages in *Hoy* and *Mañana*.[30] Moreover, government advertising went much further than subsidizing self-praise for its functionaries; given the vast number of nationalized businesses—the lottery, the oil and telephone companies, the railroads and airlines, the banking and insurance industries—the government was easily the country's largest advertiser. Moreover, providing rich subsidies for the printing of "special editions" was another way of making sure that the image of the country that the PRI wanted to give was published in the illustrated magazines.[31]

Government subsidies, of course, were just a sophisticated form of bribery, a vice in which all were steeped, from the owners and editors in chief to the lowly press photographers.[32] The process of institutionalization under Alemán included the *embute* (bribe), and it became so common a feature of the Mexican scene that Pagés Llergo declared, "In Mexican journalism it is more difficult to be honorable than to be a crook, because the problem of the journalist who wants to be honest is less that of refusing money of a dubious origin, than in making sure they don't literally shove it in his pockets."[33]

The regime's interference in periodicals was not limited to placing favorable "news"; it also made sure that certain things did not see the light of day.

For that reason, there are great lacunae in the press of this period, the most conspicuous being investigations of the almost ostentatious venality of government officials during Alemán's presidency. The "open corruption" of Alemán's regime was so notorious that when Ruíz Cortines (1952–58) entered office he found it necessary to propose a reform of the laws relating to the responsibility of public functionaries to avoid illicit enrichment.[34] Its flagrancy notwithstanding, alemanista fraud is almost unmentioned in the press; this is surely but one example of what the journalist Roberto Blanco Moheno was referring to when he said, "Profits in journalism don't come so much from what is published as from what is NOT published."[35]

Though commercial advertising was evidently less important than government subsidies in financing the magazines, it nonetheless opens a panorama onto the world of their readers. In general, the advertising is clearly directed toward the new middle classes. Airlines, both domestic and foreign, appear regularly, as do ads for elegant department, furniture, and jewelry stores, new residential neighborhoods in Mexico City and Acapulco, expensive cars, French perfumes, Spanish brandies, California wines, Scotch whiskeys, Swiss watches, Arrow shirts, and Parker pens, as well as products by Mennen, Revlon, and Bayer. Alka Seltzer is also announced, presumably to deal with the indigestion caused by such imported modernization. It is important to note, however, that even commercial advertising was related to government activities. For example, when a magazine focused on a state governor, it would publish a long photo essay on his activities, paid for from state monies. But it would also use the opportunity to recruit ads from public agencies and private businesses in the state, as well as paid insertions of congratulations for the governor by individuals who were obviously hoping for a *hueso* ("political bone"). The same process of securing local advertising was followed when the president arrived on one of his innumerable tours of the country.

The magazines that dominated the era from 1937 to 1960 are *Hoy, Mañana*, and *Siempre!* All of these were founded by José Pagés Llergo, whose career contains many of the contradictions present in an ostensibly free press under the thumb of a presidentialist and party dictatorship. Having been cofounder of *Hoy* in 1937, Pagés Llergo left the magazine's masthead to start up *Rotofoto* in 1938. When *Rotofoto* was destroyed, he returned to *Hoy* as an important collaborator until his admiration for the fascist regimes was found to be unacceptable by the imperial power: the magazine was placed on the U.S. State Department's "unofficial black list" in 1941, affecting its advertising revenue.[36] Apparently moved by the criticism of Pàges Llergo's pro-fascist stance, *Hoy* reluctantly marked its distance from him by publishing an evidently painful disclaimer in which it declared that the world tour of the "brilliant Mexican journalist" was "absolutely personal."[37] In 1943, Pagés Llergo founded *Mañana*, again together with his cousin, Regino Hernández Llergo. Pagés Llergo left *Mañana* in 1947, returning to *Hoy* as its director general; however, when the owners of *Hoy* attempted to censor a photo in 1953, creating a cause célèbre of Mexican journalism, he resigned and founded *Siempre!*

Hoy and *Mañana* were cut from very similar patterns, as was to be expected from magazines created by the same team of Pagés Llergo and Hernández Llergo. In the final analysis, perhaps *Hoy* was less superficial than *Mañana* above all during the periods when Pagés Llergo was the editor. The two publications were generally quite conservative, a result both of alemanismo's repressive context and the cousins' ideology. Pagés Llergo considered the fascists to be the "new creators of History," and Hernández Llergo was described by Blanco Moheno (himself very conservative) as "always reactionary"; both cousins were devout Catholics.[38] Moreover, because of the money problems that constantly afflicted Hernández Llergo, Maximino Avila Camacho entered into *Hoy* in the early 1940s. A ruthless caudillo and a fervent antileftist, Maximino was the Secretary of Communications and Public Works during his brother's presidency. Having designs to follow his brother in office, Maximino attempted to acquire influence through dallying in the press. His presence transformed *Hoy*'s oppositional position under Cárdenas into an unconditional support for the presidency (and, says Blanco Moheno, it also changed Hernández Llergo from a journalist into a businessman whose only interest was "living opulently").[39]

The cornerstone of *Hoy* and *Mañana*'s ideology was presidentialism, and each fawned over the occupant of the office in turn. Tours, banquets, meetings, the inaugurations of public works, decorations received from foreign governments, and any number of other presidential activities filled their pages. In fact, around one fourth of the illustrated articles published in these magazines dealt with the president in some way, and there were entire issues dedicated to him that could be up to three times as long as issues normally were.[40] The president's public relations office had unlimited resources, and the inevitable result was the unquestioning adulation that the press heaped on this figure. Such sycophancy—as well as the conflation of presidentialism and nationalism—can be seen in the photograph of Miguel

Alemán and Daniel Morales, the director general of *Mañana*, which was taken when Morales visited Alemán to thank him for his letter of congratulations on the magazine's seventh anniversary.[41] The cutline stated: "Licenciado Miguel Alemán, President of the Republic, extended to *Mañana* a courtesy which honors us and makes us proud. With a spirit of political intelligence and an affability which causes us limitless satisfaction, the Señor Presidente outlined in his letter to *Mañana* what could be considered a message and a norm of conduct for the country's press. In the photo, Daniel Morales renews the intention to continue working incessantly for the country's benefit, which has been, is and will be the ideology of *Mañana*. An ideology of national spirit."[42]

The president served as the great patriarch of a culture still dominated by a traditional family structure. The magazines' portrayal of what a successful man ought to be was encapsulated in this figure, as well as in its infinite replicas: the cabinet members, state governors, and innumerable functionaries who paid for photo essays on their activities. The visual message of these men in suits and ties (when not dressed to provoke populist identification)—inaugurating public works, sitting in banquets, appearing in political gatherings, or pictured in visits by photojournalists to their "private lives"—was clear: men should be important, and the clearest path to such public recognition was to be contributing members of the PRI dictatorship, finding their place on the ladder of patriarchal dominion. Women's role was defined within this apparatus: they should be wives of important men. The primordial example was offered by the First Lady, whose public presence was essentially a reaffirmation of domestic values: she was her husband's shadow at his public appearances, and when she was pictured without him her role as wife and mother was demonstrated in inaugurating child care centers, distributing cooking items, and handing out presents to poor children for Christmas or the Day of the Good Kings. Interesting exceptions to the rule included a *Mañana* series in the early 1950s, "Ellas también hacen la historia" (They also make history), which focused on important women such as Eleanor Roosevelt and Evita Perón, but the patriarchal pattern was usually undisturbed.

The presidentialism of *Hoy* and *Mañana* went hand in hand with an unbridled admiration for the ruling classes. "The week's outstanding social events" were regular features in every issue: images of and notes about the privileged *acomodados'* anniversaries, birthdays, breakfasts, and banquets were as ubiquitous as the "news" of "elegant religious weddings" and "distinguished civil nuptials" of "beautiful and distinguished people" who married in "aristocratic temples and chapels." Too, there was the ever present advice on fashion and hairstyles for women, sections obviously directed at those who could take advantage of this information; a good encapsulation is *Hoy*'s weekly column dedicated to "The Art of Dressing," in which Cecilia Gironella ("Bambi") visited the wives of well-known men so that they could parade their clothes. Aside from the regular features on alemanismo's winners, an entire issue was dedicated yearly to the bankers' convention.

These magazines were a good deal less generous with the *humildes* (lower classes). In relation to the working class, they generally followed the tendency of "industrialist photography," where machines and structures dominated images from which workers were often excluded. Union leaders were an exception to this rule, though they sometimes appeared as the object of ferocious attacks, particularly during the ideological wars of the 1930s; Vicente Lombardo Toledano was drawn to look like Napoleon, and on one occasion a photograph of Enrique Díaz was published on *Hoy*'s cover in which one teacher effusively embraces another because he had yelled at Lombardo Toledano that he was a "cynic" for having converted to Marxism.[43] A constant tactic of the magazines' antiworker line was to associate union leaders with communism. The ridiculous extremes to which this was carried can be seen in the cutline of a 1943 photo where Fidel Velázquez, the individual most responsible for facilitating government control of the Mexican unions, was described as "a man of such firm convictions that he preaches communism everywhere and all the time."[44]

The magazines found union corruption an easy target, although they usually left the officialist leaders alone to concentrate on the organizers of those groups whose independence represented a threat to the established order; thus, they redirected what would have been a well-founded criticism against the very individuals who were engaged in attacking the problem. A revealing example is offered by *Mañana*'s coverage of the 1951 "Caravan of Hunger": 5,000 miners, accompanied by 15,000 family members, marched from Nueva Rosita in the country's north to Mexico City in hopes of presenting their case directly to the president. This movement was the last gasp of the miners' struggle against the takeover of their union by *charros* (union bosses) imposed by the government.[45] Alemán had utilized all his familiar tactics to destroy the workers' organization: the creation of a phantom union that was then recognized as legitimate thanks to judiciary collaboration that declared the strike "nonexistent," accompanied by army occupa-

5. Anonymous photographer. Miners from the "March of Hunger," Basílica de Guadalupe, Mexico City, in *Mañana* 394 (17 March 1951): 8-F. Courtesy of Hemeroteca Nacional.

tion to control the situation. After their condition had turned critical in the mining towns, the marchers walked for fifty days through winter cold to Mexico City, where they were placed in a sports complex that had been conditioned as a "concentration camp" for them.

Their rank-and-file leaders shared the hardships of the march and the camp, but an article in *Mañana* alleged that the leaders "came in luxurious automobiles, arriving at the most luxurious suites in the swankiest hotels, where they uncork the most aromatic cognac and toast the proletariat."[46] *Mañana* followed the line of most of the press, alternately defaming the marchers or ignoring the *caravana*.[47] When the miners arrived in Mexico City, *Mañana* published a photo of them in the Basílica de Guadalupe, with the title "Forgive them Lord, for they know not what they do" (see Figure 5).[48] The editorial facing the photo contained the expected pleas to nationalism, asserting, "The clan of antinational machinations must be satisfied. Few times has it had the opportunity to use a group of genuine workers such as these against the country's tranquility." The priest who presided over the mass of the miners had a different take: "They ask not for riches, but bread for themselves and their children. Bless them, Virgin of Guadalupe, as you have blessed so many just and noble causes."[49]

The antilabor stance of the magazines was played out in different ways. For example, workers were insidiously contrasted with soldiers in several 1938 photo essays composed of images by Enrique Díaz that "demonstrated" that soldiers could meet the need for labor without the accompanying problems of unions. Beneath a photo of soldiers engaged in road construction—these "simple and silent Proletarians who demand nothing"—ran this caption: "Workers would have deserted or gone on strike or asked for indemnification, etc. Soldiers neither complain nor ask for anything. Like men who know how to do their duty, they continued working."[50] Another photograph was called on to testify on behalf of soldiers: "Though union leaders have said that the soldier is a lazy bum, these photos show the contrary: a soldier building a house from the foundation up."[51] What the photo montage as a whole shows is even more revealing: the magazine's undemocratic orientation is embodied in the disproportionately large figure of an officer who looms over the scene to command the soldier and ensure the completion of the task—the antithesis of democratic self-direction.

Things did not go any better for campesinos and Indians, who were portrayed in the picturesque style of Porfirian photography; Enrique Díaz's images of happy peasants on market day and smiling families of fishermen in Pátzcuaro were a staple fare.[52] The exotic approach also provided the publications with a form of soft pornography. For example, the "Indian problem" was depicted by Rafael Carrillo through various images of bare-breasted *indígenas* in "the marvelous landscape of Cosoleacaque," one of them on the cover of *Hoy* (see Figure 6).[53]

As a symbol of the nation, Indians were crucial to presidentialism. For example, in a photo essay on "The President and His People," an Indian is shown shaking hands with Alemán. The president is presented with his face to the camera, extending his hand to the Indian, who, photographed from behind, has no personal identity. The caption states: "This photograph is more eloquent than two hundred words. The spontaneous exaltation of a representative of our humble Indian class to reach out his hand to the First Leader of the Nation who has so profoundly occupied himself with the problems of Mexican agriculture. The Association of Harvesters gave a medal to Lic. Miguel Alemán in recognition for his labor on behalf of the workers of the countryside."[54]

6. Rafael Carrillo. Indígena in Cosoleacaque, in *Hoy* 76 (6 August 1938): cover.
Courtesy of Hemeroteca Nacional.

Presidentialism was central to the Mexican political culture portrayed in
the photographs of the illustrated magazines. It may be useful to compare
the discursive cores of the graphic press in other countries, because publications such as *Life* in the United States and *Picture Post* in Great Britain were
fully as important in those nations as were *Hoy, Mañana*, and *Siempre!* in
Mexico. All these societies passed through disquieting social and cultural
anxieties in the postwar period. This instability was addressed by the formulation of national identities, and the illustrated press was a crucial medium for this. In her study of *Life*, Wendy Kozol has outlined how the representative family served as the pivot of identity in the United States. She
argues that "ordinary" families—white, middle class, heterosexual, and patriarchal—were the vehicle for defining what it meant to be an "American,"
and notes that "news coverage of some of the most critical issues facing
Americans in the post-war period relied on domestic iconography that
blurred the boundaries between public and private spheres and shaped national identity in the process."[55]

In Great Britain, *Picture Post* grew out of the experience of the "people's war" against fascism, which the magazine had portrayed in a spirit of collective effort rather than from the perspective of high policy and grand strategy.[56] This carried over into the postwar years when, with a Labor government in power, a British documentary style developed that was based on the democratization of the photographed subject. As Stuart Hall affirms: "*Picture Post* captured for the still commercially-produced 'news' photograph a new social reality: the domain of everyday life. . . . People here do not require to be surprised off-guard, caught in candid poses, imitate themselves for the camera, perform or pull special faces. . . . The *Picture Post* camera finds them interesting enough, complex enough, expressive enough in the detail of their routine everyday lives. It lends the dimension of significance, intensity to the commonplace."[57]

In Mexico, however, the family was not undergoing the dissolution that was occurring in the much more rapidly modernizing United States, and no "people's war" had required the mobilization of populist imagery as in Britain. *Life* legitimized the "American" way of life through a recourse to "ordinary people" in a mythical family, and *Picture Post* recast British identity in terms of everyday life unlinked to public events; but in Mexico this process of identification with the larger entity was carried out through the figure of the president. The Revolution, that tiger Francisco I. Madero had turned loose back in 1910, had to be tamed. Who better than the supreme patriarch who every six years inherited the mantle of power from the revolutionary pantheon of Madero, Zapata, Villa, Carranza, and Obregón, and ruled with absolute authority throughout his *sexenio*?

Of course, it was necessary to vary the magazines' fare a bit and dilute the propaganda for the president and the PRI. Culture offered a relatively risk-free way to do that. Regular sections in *Hoy* and *Mañana* were dedicated to movies, literature, books, art, history, archaeology, science, music, and the radio, although these were smaller than the feature articles and tended to appear toward the back of the magazines. Those photo essays on culture that were given prominence of place, as well as a number of pages and photos, often focused on individual celebrities, usually movie stars, although the "private" lives of muralists such as Diego Rivera and David Alfaro Siqueiros furnished good material as well. According to Carlos Monsiváis, the 1940s in Mexico was the beginning of the "faith in personages, in celebrities, in Sacred Cows."[58] One of the many U.S. imports flooding Mexico, the fame fabricated by mass media became an "instrument of psychological control," and the magazines' photojournalists such as the Hermanos Mayo played their part in manufacturing this phenomenon: "The Celebrities! The forties is the decade of celebrities, and the Mayo document this irreproachably. Not famous or well-known people, but something different, the new concept imported from the United States: the Celebrity."[59]

The many articles on Mexican cinema focused largely on stars such as María Félix, Pedro Infante, Jorge Negrete, Pedro Armendariz, and Dolores del Río, most often with a typically trivial emphasis on the "personal lives" of the screen idols. One aspect of the publications' general conservatism can be seen in the large number of photo essays on Cantinflas as opposed to the few that were published on Tin Tan, his principal comic rival. Cantinflas was a well-respected figure whose characterization of the *peladito* had won him a huge following in the Spanish-language world for his capacity to turn the tables on the rich and powerful. In 1944, Salvador Novo wrote that Cantinflas was the "representation of the Mexican subconscious."[60] At his best, this comic symbolized those who know how to survive with dignity through quickness of wit in a highly stratified and hierarchical, but ostensibly democratic, society: a colonized being who carves out his own reality in response to a situation in which he is dominated. However, during the 1950s, Cantinflas became increasingly officialist, and one of the ways this was expressed was in a chauvinistic rejection of Tin Tan's character of the *pachuco*. In a pivotal Cantinflas film, *Si yo fuera diputado* (1951), a sign outside a barbershop reads, "Pachucos not served, because I don't like them."[61]

Cantinflas was safe for the magazines because, despite his characteristic play with words, he was never attacked for corrupting the Spanish language. Tin Tan received much criticism for incorporating English phrases, no doubt a result of the fact that in the 1950s, the pachuco symbolized transculturation, modernity, urbanization, the breakdown of traditional values, and a general unease with the suffocating nationalist homogeneity of Alemán's regime.[62] Thus, pachucos were viewed with disdain by both traditional Mexican society and the nouveau riche of alemanismo, who regarded them as social no-accounts and mutilators of the mother tongue, while the ever more officialist (and ever less funny) Cantinflas was lauded with honors by the state apparatus, including the press.

The conservatism of *Hoy* and *Mañana* was also reflected in their portrayal of international news. For example, during the Spanish Civil War, a photo of women committed to Franco's cause was published in *Hoy* with the following caption: "You can see the *señoritas'* enthusiasm; happy as can be, they give the fascist salute while holding bread and canned goods in their arms."[63] Though *Hoy* differed with Cárdenas's support for the Spanish Republic—providing yet another instance of that government's pluralism—this magazine (and all the others) followed the official line for World War II. There was much coverage of this conflict, an event that offered the opportunity to publish a great number of traumatic and spectacular photos of violence. But wars and civil strife were not the only source of morbid, and ultimately insignificant "shock photos"; pictures of ghoulish executions, spectacular suicides, grisly murders, and gory accidents were published constantly.[64] The directors' Catholicism was reflected in regular features on the Church throughout the world, and photos from international agencies of a more inane character were another constant, especially cute animals, picturesque curiosities, and cuddly babies.

A great deal of the imagery of international events turned around the political leaders of the world, often with a strong dose of anticommunism. When it was not overtly political, the "news" centered on the doings of kings and queens, for example, the king of England's visit or the death of Rumania's Queen Maria. This interest in kings and queens found its U.S. counterpart in Hollywood's celluloid stars. Clark Gable and Carole Lombard graced *Hoy*'s first cover, and the magazine claimed proudly to be "the only Spanish-language periodical in the world to have a complete and exclusive editorial staff in Hollywood."[65] In this first issue, *Hoy* set the stage for the future with articles on "The Private Life of the Stars" and "Hollywood Speaks," antecedents of ubiquitous columns such as "How the Hollywood Stars Live," as well as articles that appealed to the ever lurking erotic interest by describing how "Hollywood Makes Love." Hollywood stars were constantly called on to legitimize the magazines; for example, when *Mañana* was founded in 1943, copies had evidently been sent to screen idols to receive responses from them. Thanks to the studios' press agents, *Mañana* soon had autographed photos of the stars expressing their congratulations for the new publication, which it then ran in issue after issue.[66] This legitimation process was extended to the political sphere: movie stars were linked to the Mexican ruling class in typical images such as the full-page photo of Mickey Rooney with President Manuel Avila Camacho, taken by the "premier photojournalist" of *Hoy*, Enrique Díaz.[67]

It was an atypical photo that led to the birth of *Siempre!* In spite of José Pagés Llergo's innate conservatism and his profound commitment to the established order, he had a relatively critical perspective and really believed in the freedom of expression.[68] In 1953, he was the director of *Hoy* when a picture with explosive possibilities arrived over the international photo services. The image had been sent to all the major Mexican periodicals, but only Pagés thought of publishing it. Taken in the Lido, a famous Parisian cabaret, the photo was composed of three key planes: in the foreground was a seminude dancer; immediately behind her was Carlos Girón Jr., a Mexican who observed the woman's body with evident admiration; in the background was Girón's young wife, Beatriz Alemán Velasco, the much-loved daughter of a powerful president who had left office only five months before.[69] Beatriz looks at her recently acquired husband—they were on their European honeymoon—bewildered, hurt, and jealous.

Perhaps Pagés Llergo felt that the time had come to open up new critical spaces in the Mexican press, or maybe he just could not resist the temptation to publish a sensational image; whatever the reason, the editor confronted presidentialism head-on by placing the photo in *Hoy*.[70] However, when the magazine's owners found out that the image had appeared in their periodical, they informed Pagés that henceforth, "everything that was to be published—photographs and written pages—would first be submitted to their censorship."[71] Pagés Llergo resigned from *Hoy* and founded *Siempre!*, the first issue of which appeared seven weeks later with the controversial photo and the following caption:

> BUT WHAT'S WRONG WITH THIS PHOTO? We only publish this photo because the birth of *Siempre!* is closely linked to it. If a photographer would not have been present at the precise moment in which this scene occurred, this magazine would never have seen light. However, *Siempre!* desires to make it clear that, in publishing this photo, José Pagés Llergo does not have—nor could have—the slightest desire to annoy anybody. If someone wants to judge with political criteria what is merely a journalistic document, that's something outside the jurisdiction of he who was yesterday the director of *Hoy* and is today the director of *Siempre!* To Doña Beatriz Alemán de Girón and Don Carlos Girón Peltier, our respects.[72]

Many of *Hoy*'s best collaborators left the magazine with Pagés Llergo and joined *Siempre!*: Francisco Martínez de la Vega, Vicente Lombardo Toledano, Antonio Rodríguez, Luis Gutiérrez y González, Antonio Arias Bernal, Rafael Solana, and Roberto Blanco Moheno.[73] With them, and others attracted by the opportunity to work in real journalism, Pagés created the beginnings of a genuinely pluralist press in place of the "depoliticized" monotony that had characterized *Hoy, Mañana*, and other publications of the period. The question of *mexicanidad* that so dominated the era formed part of Pagés's decision to create a different magazine; rather than copy *Life* or any of the Mexican "foreign-inspired [*extranjerizante*] magazines and newspapers," Pagés wanted to blaze his own trail. He found that in a format that emphasized articles of opinion, no doubt recognizing that investigative journalism was not an option under alemanismo.[74] Moreover, he made it clear that the nation was not the property of those in power: "No party or power monopolizes Mexican thought. The cult of the Homeland is not exclusive to this or that group. Mexican thought lives and breathes in the traditional right, in the center which aspires to moderating equilibrium, and in the impatient and passionate left."[75]

The importance of *Siempre!* cannot be overstated, for it represented a crucial attempt to shrug off the "chains of gold" and create an independent journalism; at its peak, it may have been the best magazine of its kind in the Western Hemisphere.[76] However, it is worth mentioning that, although Pagés had been willing to challenge presidentialism once, he evidently did not want to tempt fate: when the image from Paris was published again on the first anniversary of *Siempre!*, the photo was cropped so as to eliminate the figure of Beatriz Alemán, and reversed to veil the manipulation.[77]

From the mid-1930s to the mid-1950s, photography enjoyed an uncommon prestige in the magazines. The periodicals fought among themselves to project an image of their visuality; *Hoy*, for example, touted itself as "The Supergraphic Magazine." The photojournalists generally received credit for their work, above all the "aces" such as Enrique Díaz, Rafael Carrillo, Ismael Casasola, Nacho López, Walter Reuter, Héctor García, and the Hermanos Mayo.[78] However, as the fifties wore on, the declining importance of photojournalism in the three major Mexican magazines reflected the growth of television in that country, just as occurred with *Life* and *Look* at the same time in the United States and with *Picture Post* in Britain. *Hoy* abandoned visual articles around 1955, and thereafter employed images only for illustrating political essays. *Mañana* held on a little longer, but by 1959 the magazine essentially ceased to publish photo reportage or photo essays. Although *Siempre!* began with a notable interest in photography, it very quickly stopped being of any importance in a magazine much more focused on opinion than on news, and a curiously conservative form of using images became predominant: almost every article consisted of two facing pages, one with a photo and the other with text. The photos were rarely interesting and, what is more, they used the same ones, largely images of the article's author, time and again. Perhaps Pagés Llergo felt that he could not compete with the technological perfection of magazines such as *Life*, and decided to emphasize articles of opinion that, written by the best Mexican journalists, did have a public. Too, it may be that he understood that the days of the illustrated magazines were numbered because of television's competition. The fact is that *Siempre!* abandoned the idea of being an illustrated magazine before either *Hoy* or *Mañana*.

Although the magazines always maintained a large number of photos, they were increasingly tied to simple illustrationism. The decline of photojournalism can be traced most easily in the photo reportage and photo essays, articles in which images are the narrative's core and that have an autonomy evidenced in the fact that photos can be the origin of an essay and not simply pictures utilized to make texts more palatable. From the magazines' inception and up through the first half of the 1950s, they published many photo reportage and photo essays; the photojournalists received credit for the photos and, at times, for the text as well. After around 1955, photo reportage and photo essays became ever scarcer, replaced by articles in which the image was merely an illustration, and photojournalists were credited less often.

An analysis of the photo reportage and photo essays in *Hoy* and *Mañana* enables us to decipher the politics of picturing in those illustrated magazines, which we can later compare to *Siempre!* Here, the concept I use to differentiate between photo reportage and photo essay is the degree to which the subject is somehow "news." That is, I define photo reportage as something whose importance is related to an event that is presented as being ostensibly "newsworthy." The most obvious case would be that of "hard news," for example, catastrophes such as the 1943 eruption of Paricutín and its immediate effects on the population. Other instances of photo reportage, according to my definition, include the coverage of important historical incidents such as Saturnino Cedillo's revolt of 1938, the 1958–1959 strikes, and the Cuban Revolution. I have also categorized as photo reportage those events that are presented as if they had the same importance as hard news: presidential addresses, tours and campaigns, and the banking conventions, as well as cultural and sporting events such as bullfights, and the openings of art exhibits and films. Photo reportage constitutes around one third of all illustrated articles in *Hoy* and *Mañana*.

What I describe as photo essays usually have little to do with "news"; they are often defined as "features" in U.S. journalism.[79] Their significance is not related to a historical occurrence: they do not depict an event that has occurred but rather a situation that exists. They originate in an idea that someone—an editor, a photographer, a reporter—has to tell a story about something of "human interest," often related to culture or travel. Approximately two thirds of the illustrated articles in *Hoy* and *Mañana* are photo essays, and among the predominant themes are visits of photojournalists to Indian communities, churches, and a great variety of tourist attractions within and outside of Mexico. They also deal with actresses and actors, figures from the sporting world, religious acts, and Mexican flora and fauna.

The predominant subject of the illustrated articles in *Hoy* and *Mañana* is, overwhelmingly, the president. Photo reportage on his tours (*giras*) of the country, his campaigns, his presidential addresses (*informes*), his public appearances—above all, in relation to the industrial development of Mexico—and photo essays on different facets of his life (ad nauseam!) constitute around one quarter of the total number of illustrated articles. Photo reportage about the president are to a great extent created media events; that is, they are not really newsworthy but simply propaganda acts armed to grandstand the president and his programs, as well as demonstrate his personal support for governors and other functionaries.

After the presidency, the upper class is the theme most often covered in the photo reportage of *Hoy* and *Mañana*. A large number of these picture the banking conventions that took place every year, although the wealthy's weddings, funerals, banquets, birthdays, and christenings also appear incessantly. The magazines also published photo reportage about human tragedies, from floods and earthquakes to murders and suicides. Cultural photo reportage principally include the openings of exhibits and spectaculars, as well as the first nights of plays and films. There is very little photo reportage in which the working class appears, and this is generally limited to showing the unions parading in gratitude to the president in May Day marches or to their rare historical appearance in rebellion during the street struggles of the 1958–1959 strikes (obviously presented from a very conservative perspective).

Because I have classified the immense majority of the illustrated articles on the president as photo reportage, the presence of the government in the category of photo essay is not so great. There are more photo essays in *Hoy* and *Mañana* on religion, Indians, sports, and actresses than on the government, which appears largely in articles about the army or public works. Tourism, the arts, and medicine are well represented. Women, too, receive attention, although it is generally related to fashion or to showing them in bathing suits, underwear, or pajamas—or with even less clothing in the case of the bare-breasted indígenas. Actors appear about half as much as actresses, which is a little more often than Mexico's flora and fauna. There are also photo essays on dance, theater, literature, science, business, and cinema. Children do not get much space, but they do appear more than workers, to whom are dedicated around the same number of photo essays as lepers.

Among those that could be considered exceptional photo essays in *Hoy* and *Mañana*, either for their critical element or for their uncommon theme, are several that deal with the poor in urban slums, almost always with the collaboration of Nacho López or the Hermanos Mayo. Antonio Rodríguez was the author of both photos and text for several wrenching articles on extreme poverty in the Mezquital. There are a few pieces on poor children, often published a little before Christmas to play on sentimental chords. The photo essays that differ from the common pattern constitute some 5 percent of the total, and there is almost no critical photo reportage.[80] In sum, the general panorama of illustrated articles in *Hoy* and *Mañana* is almost always reactionary in political terms, aesthetically conservative, and thematically monotonous.

A *Mañana* report on the 1952 May Day battle between the official unions and independent workers offers a fascinating glimpse of how the magazines transformed news about the working class through recontextualizing images.[81] Under alemanismo, May Day had been converted from a march of worker protest into a parade of banners thanking the president for his unceasing efforts on their behalf. This reached at least one of its acmes in 1951, when Miguel Alemán marched arm in arm with Fidel Velázquez, lifetime leader of the CTM, through the Zócalo; the image was published in *Mañana* over this caption: "The first worker of Mexico: Miguel Alemán" (see Figure 7).[82]

Whether such arrogant flouting of the government's control of organized labor was responsible or not, the next year saw an exceptionally bloody struggle between CTM goons and the independent workers who attempted to enter the official parade near the Bellas Artes concert hall. Trying to take back May Day was a yearly custom among the unaffiliated, but, as

7. Anonymous photographer. Miguel Alemán and Fidel Velázquez, May Day march, Mexico City, May 1, 1951, in *Mañana* 402 (12 May 1951): 8. Courtesy of Hemeroteca Nacional.

the last year to protest against the president who had created *charrismo*, 1952 resulted in a particularly brutal confrontation.

The 1952 melee was covered by two of the Hermanos Mayo, Faustino and Julio.[83] One of Faustino's images was given a full page in the photo report-age on the tumult: it is a young girl, probably overcome by tear gas, who is being treated by a nurse; the caption describes her as an "innocent victim" of "the Red Provocation." Another Mayo photo—it is unclear whether it is Faustino's or Julio's—shows a badly beaten man who is evidently being taken into custody (see Figure 8). This would indicate that he must be one of the independent workers who, having been attacked by the CTM guards, is now being conducted to jail by plainclothes police. The caption gives this photo a very particular meaning: "A group of senseless anti-patriotic provo-cateurs attempted to lessen the force of the Mexican workers' formidable and vigorous unity with the Government of the Republic presided over by Miguel Alemán, causing fratricidal violence in a battle with the May Day

8. Hermanos Mayo. Dissident worker attacked by police and members of the CTM, Mexico City, May 1, 1952. Courtesy of Fondo Mayo, Chronological Section 3959, Archivo General de la Nación.

parade marchers in front of Bellas Artes. This photograph of tremendous drama reveals the instant in which one of the communist *pistoleros* [thugs] is detained by the inflamed multitude. The workers' serene and measured comportment kept the street battle from becoming a bloody tragedy, without precedent, without name."

Although *Mañana* published three Mayo images of this conflict, it did not publish what I consider the best of the Hermanos Mayo's five million negatives: the image taken by Julio Mayo of the mother grieving over her dead son in the Cruz Verde after he, an independent unionist, was killed by CTM goons (see Figure 9). Those photos that were printed could be given a reactionary interpretation through the captions and text, but that of the grieving mother is too powerful and speaks too much for itself to permit its meaning to be transformed through an "extraneous conceptual framework."[84] It could not be included in the reportage on May Day, 1952, at any rate, but with the passage of time, this photo was recontextualized; thus tamed, it appeared in a 1955 photo essay on the "Most Journalistic Mayo Photos."[85] There, the image was stripped out of its real matrix and, with a cynicism that relied on the ambiguity of even the most powerful photos, was assigned a fabricated significance, transforming a historical instance of the struggle against charrismo into a timeless and recurrent phenomenon of

9. Julio Mayo. Mother grieving for dissident worker killed in May Day battle, Mexico City, May 1, 1952. Courtesy of Fondo Mayo, Chronological Section 3959, Archivo General de la Nación.

daily life: "Who is she? Who is he? Their simple names, from the *pueblos*, are condensed in this brief eloquence: mother and son. The mother destroyed by pain, the son knocked down by death. The scene: the *Cruz Verde* some day in 1950. Any day in which drama can occur. The moment which Julio Mayo etched cannot be more moving."[86]

Siempre! represented the first lasting challenge to presidentialism, something that is apparent in the magazine's layout. The media events—for example, the president's tours and opening of public works, as well as the activities of other PRI politicians—are found in the back pages of *Siempre!*; this identified them as paid insertions rather than, as was common in *Hoy* and *Mañana*, presenting them as if they were news. Among *Siempre!*'s photo reportage there is a goodly percentage on the president, but these generally deal with news such as *informes* and meetings with foreign heads of state. Though there are quite a few on the campaign of Adolfo López Mateos (1958–1964), it is useful to point out that there were essentially the same number of photo reports on international events. Visual reports on the Cuban Revolution, the government of Jacobo Arbenz in Guatemala and its overthrow, racial strife in the United States, and the Suez crisis give an indication of *Siempre!*'s seriousness, although there are also "photo shock" images: executions, suicides, macabre deaths, sensationalist crimes, and catastrophes. Some of the more published subjects in *Siempre!*'s photo essays are life in Mexico City (sometimes relying on staged scenes) and Indians (often offering the opportunity to show bare-breasted indígenas).

Perhaps the presidentialist adulation of *Hoy* and *Mañana* was replaced in *Siempre!* by a "womanizing" obsession.[87] The magazine's birth had been the result of a curious knot of presidentialism and pictured female nudity, however much Pagés Llergo attempted to displace the political significance of his decision to publish the cabaret photo by emphasizing the erotic element to make it appear that objections to it had been for the seminude woman and not for the presence of Alemán's daughter. *Time* magazine characterized the incident as "Don Quijote vs. Venus," and Pagés Llergo appeared on the cover of *Siempre!*'s fifth anniversary issue as a Don Quijote painting a woman in a bikini.[88] Almost every issue contained the modest equivalent of a *Playboy* centerfold: the central pages are color photographs of actresses, dancers, and *vedettes*, breasts pouring out of half-unbuttoned blouses, legs tantalizingly exposed as they frolic negligee-clad in bed or lie next to swimming pools in bathing suits. The first issue of *Siempre!* without such images is number 69, and every once in a while thereafter the "centerfold" was occupied by sections such as "Masterworks of the Great Painters"; needless to say, there are always one or two nudes among the paintings. Notwithstanding what today looks like shameless sexploitation, Pagés Llergo's insistence on the erotic can also be seen as an important alternative to the prudish moralism of President Adolfo Ruiz Cortines (1952–1958).

Pagés Llergo's *Siempre!* also offered the opportunity to Nacho López to create what is arguably the most powerful photo essay published in any Mexican illustrated magazine, "Sólo los humildes van al infierno" (Only the poor go to hell).[89] The critique that "Sólo los humildes" makes of the police, and by extension of the Mexican class system, had few precedents in Mexican mass-circulation journalism. Under Pagés Llergo, both *Hoy* and *Siempre!* had published similar editorials, calling the police "El cancer de México," but I have yet to find any other critical essays on the police in *Hoy, Rotofoto, Mañana*, or *Siempre!* during the period 1937 to 1960.[90] Nacho López must have entered into this project with great enthusiasm; evidently it was the photo essay to which he gave the most of himself, as the article's subtitle notes that he dedicated "four weeks to visiting *delegaciones* in order to show readers a hell that Dante forgot."[91]

The title itself is explicitly critical, for "only the humble" end up in these infernos. The rich can always pay the police off in the street, so that they are

10–15. Nacho López. "Sólo los humildes van al infierno," in *Siempre!* 52 (19 June 1954). Courtesy of Hemeroteca Nacional.

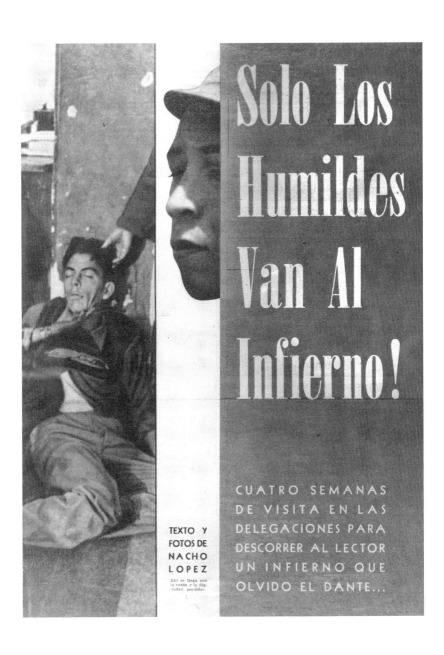

Solo Los Humildes Van Al Infierno!

CUATRO SEMANAS
DE VISITA EN LAS
DELEGACIONES PARA
DESCORRER AL LECTOR
UN INFIERNO QUE
OLVIDO EL DANTE...

TEXTO Y
FOTOS DE
NACHO
LOPEZ

Ahí se llega con
la razón y la dig-
nidad perdidas.

not taken to the delegación; moreover, they have the social and economic resources that make it unnecessary for them to have recourse to the police to settle problems. The text underlines class difference in relation to who goes to these hell holes: "The cement [of the police station's floor] is not for those who commit the real robberies and frauds for thousands and millions

DESAMPARO Cada noche, mil historias distintas con un común denominador; el hambre, la ignorancia, el desamparo. Hombres y mujeres sin más apoyo que una débil, inconsistente esperanza. Una madre cuyo retoño ha sido golpeado por un padre vicioso. Es entonces cuando la justicia quiere ser implacable...

ILUSIONES También, ahí en las antesalas del infierno, surgen las escenas sentimentales, amorosas, de tipo sexual. El rapto, salpicado de ilusiones, promesas y proyectos. Después, el arrepentimiento, el engaño y finalmente, la acusación brutal sin otra alternativa que la iglesia o la cárcel...

RUTINA Para otros, la visita nocturna a una delegación, es ya el paseo acostumbrado y periódico. Es, para muchos —los rateros profesionales, los viciosos, los carteristas, los borrachos—, un enfrentarse a lo que ellos piensan que es su destino inexorable; es parte de su vida, rutina incambiable. ... Derecha: Hasta la Cárcel de la Ciudad —El Carmen—. llegan día a día interminables colas de hombres y mujeres procedentes de todas las delegaciones. Todos son gentes humildes, sin amparo.

22

of pesos, nor is it for those who hand out bills to avid hands, nor is it for those who have 'influence' and count on lawyers to defend them."

The photographs are a nightmarish tour of the delegaciones, peopled by drunks, beaten wives and children, deceived women, common criminals, drivers who have had an accident, gigolos, and policemen who threaten or

EL DOLOR, LA
ANGUSTIA Y
LA MISERIA
EN UNA CASA

"Si nada más fué un ronón, jefe..." El lenguaje reducido, inconvincente brota temeroso y sin fuerza ahí frente a la barandilla del juez calificador. No hay palabras ni esperanza. Es como si para estas gentes humildes existiera una permanente maldición de la que ya no pueden escapar. — Abajo: El desfile de pasiones más impresionante. El odio, la ira, el rencor, la ternura, el amor... todo surge ahí sin freno, primitiva, brutalmente. Junto al espectáculo del criminal nato y sin escrúpulo, el gesto dulce y amoroso de la madre que todo lo perdona. Sobre las frías lozas, la espera angustiosa con el viejo par de zapatos, testigos de un caminar sin destino!

23

sleep: "Every night, a thousand different stories with the same common denominator: hunger, ignorance, defenselessness. Men and women with no succor except a weak, flickering hope."

The delegaciones' annihilating atmosphere is marvelously reproduced by policemen who hover over their victims in the frame, visually crushing

146   *John Mraz*

DOLOR Y LAGRIMAS ¿Qué sabe la sociedad de los humildes? ¿Qué del hambre, la soledad y los conflictos de estas gentes? ¿da. Ella no sabe de estas cosas sucias, denigrantes, incómodas, ofensivas. Como que las delegaciones, o el llanto de estas mujeres marcadas ya para siempre! cárcel, sólo fueron hechas para los desamparados. ¡Cuántas noches interminables se escuchan los gri — Derecha: otro tipo que vive al margen de las leyes, por ignorancia, por necesidad. El "gigoló" de barr morador permanente de salones de baile, billares y cantinuchas, etc.

YA NADA LOS CONMUEVE Son los pies de los humildes y los desamparados que tienen su propio espíritu y su pro lenguaje. Es como si tuvieran dignidad y se avergonzaran de pisar esos centros don rantes de la comodidad; pies que cargan el peso de la ignorancia, el hambre, la miseria, las pasiones. Ah, y nunca se han encontrado ahí con unos pies elega temente calzados, cobijados. — Abajo, izquierda: La policía, los jueces calificadores, en las delegaciones, parece como si hubieran perdido todos los sen mientos humanos. Nada los conmueve: ni las lágrimas de una mujer. — Abajo derecha: Para este hombre —como para tantos otros— todo le es igual; q lo encierren, que lo pongan en libertad. Como que la vida, su vida, es precisamente la cárcel.

them. López's criticism of the police reaches its culmination in his image of the sleeping guardian of order. His caption is as damning as the photo: "Even in hell these 'little angels' sleep, indifferent to and detached from the pain of the *humildes*. Later, they will wake up insolent, insulting and ill-humored to take out their bad mood on the victims who have have come to

HISTORIAS DE LA CIUDAD No es acaso una nueva experiencia, para esta pobre mujer, el haberse encontrado en una atmósfera hostil, sucia, amenazante de la delegación. Pero aún así, el ambiente la aniquila, como aniquila a todos los que llegan a caer ahí. Es el infierno temido. ¿Su delito? Una riña de vecindad por un motivo sin importancia. ¿Pero —cabe preguntar— ése es el auténtico origen? Los sociólogos seguramente lo negarían. — Derecha: El desfile interminable continúa. Ahora es la mujer que ha sido golpeada por el marido borracho, irresponsable, inconsciente, y con el que, al salir, volverá irremediablemente.

DESFILE DE PASIONES Aún en el infierno, estos "angelitos" duermen, indiferentes y ajenos al dolor de los humildes. Después despertarán insolentes, groseros, malhumorados y descargarán su mal humor sobre las víctimas que caen en las delegaciones. El atropellado, el apuñalado, los viciosos, el borracho, un marido desobligado, el escandaloso, el ratero, el carterista, el que tuvo la mala fortuna de violar un reglamento. A todos por igual. Aun sobre la infeliz mujer del pueblo que ha sido golpeada —abajo izquierda.— Pero así está la vecindad. Y por lo tanto, en esa atmósfera asfixiante y deprimente, continúa el desfile de pasiones: el odio, el rencor, la ira, el amor, la ternura. Cada noche, en las lúgubres delegaciones policiacas, se escribe una amarga, breve, ignorada historia de las gentes humildes que habitan en una bella, moderna y progresista capital.

25

the *delegaciones*. The person hit by a car or stabbed, the vicious, the drunks, the irresponsible husband, the public disturbance, the thief, the pickpocket, the individual who had the bad luck to get caught breaking a law. They will fall on all of them equally."

This essay is a landmark in the history of Mexican photojournalism.

16. Nacho López. "Gigolo" arguing with police in delegación, Mexico City, 1954. Courtesy of Fondo Nacho López, 405667, Fototeca del Instituto Nacional de Antropología e Historia.

Nonetheless, the question remains: What stories were not told? I believe that the most important of the missing narratives is the representation of resistance and solidarity among the humildes. Although these elements are to some extent implicit in the text, they are absent from the published photographs. Nonetheless, they are revealingly apparent in several negatives. For example, resistance is clearly present in two images that were either left out or cropped and recontextualized: those in which the "gigolo" (Figure 16) and the "abductor" (Figure 17) are shown arguing with the police, vehemently insisting on their rights. This aspect of the gigolo did not appear in the magazine, though one was included in which he is considerably less vehement.[92] The image of the abductor in a defiant attitude was published, but it was drastically cropped, and the silhouette was placed beneath the image of the man appealing to the police; this converted a challenge to authority into a plea for mercy.[93]

Lack of solidarity among the *desamparados* (foresaken ones) is expressed graphically through the visual structures of the images: in almost all of the published photos, the humildes are either alone or in the company of the police. When they do appear with others of their condition, they usually

17. Nacho López. "Abductor" arguing with police in delegación, Mexico City, 1954. Courtesy of Fondo Nacho López, 405680, Fototeca del Instituto Nacional de Antropología e Historia.

stare in opposite directions, evidencing alienation. Nonetheless, it is clear from the archive negatives that López must have intended to include images of solidarity. Some 20 percent of the total negatives for the essay present the humildes in situations of mutual aid, a demonstration of his design to go beyond denouncing individual problems to graphically represent collective struggle (which, at any rate, is a fact of life within the delegaciones). Why they were not published is difficult to say. It is worth considering that the two silhouettes that are published in "Sólo" have been cut out from two of the negatives that manifest, respectively, solidarity and resistence: the "on-looker" of the essay's second page (Figure 18) and the defiant "abductor" (Figure 17). Their appearance in the essay could indicate that they were pre-selected by Nacho López for incorporation in the article, but were put to a use that dramatically transformed their meaning. This would seem to suggest that the decision was not his to make; it may have been taken out of his hands by the magazine's directors, who decided that it was one thing to criticize the problem of police corruption and impunity—which everybody in Mexico knew then (and still knows) to be intolerable—but quite another to

18. Nacho López. People making declarations in delegación, Mexico City, 1954. Courtesy of Fondo Nacho López, 405668, Fototeca del Instituto Nacional de Antropología e Historia.

propose the organized resistance of the humildes. Whichever the reason, and from whatever source came the decision, the effect of the published images is to portray the humildes as helpless objects of society, rather than representing their capacity to be the subjects of their own histories.

In the end, "Sólo los humildes van al infierno," the most critical photo essay published in the Mexican illustrated magazines, both exemplifies the individual brilliance of Nacho López and demonstrates the complex constraints of journalism in Mexico. The illustrated magazines functioned within the very specific, if never explicitly articulated, limits established during the Golden Age: the president was the untouchable core of the nation; the wealthy and powerful were to be emulated; the underdogs must be made picturesque or ignored completely or demonized if they did not follow the rules; the nation was one, indivisible and homogeneous. Mexican journalism had to choose between pan o palo: either publications would be subsidized by state advertising and individuals would receive their embutes or the periodicals would be closed. The subtle controls of the PRI's "perfect dictatorship," as Mario Vargas Llosa recently characterized it, maintained such a convincing façade of a free press that many believed it to be true. Only with the establishment of a genuinely independent journalism in the 1970s was the mask finally torn from the official face of the "lamentable and persistent servility" that was Mexico during the Golden Age.[94]

Notes

I am grateful to Gil Joseph, Eric Zolov, and Eli Bartra for their critical observations, and to the Fototeca of INAH for having provided the equipment and personnel to copy the magazine covers and photo essay.

1   Serge Gruzinski, *La guerra de las imágenes: De Crístobal Colón a "Blade Runner" (1492–2019)* (Mexico City: Fondo de Cultura Económica, 1994), 12. All translations from Spanish are mine.

2   On the concept of visual economy, see Deborah Poole, *Vision, Race, and Modernity: A Visual Economy of the Andean Image World* (Princeton, NJ: Princeton University Press, 1997).

3   See Patricia Massé Zendejas, *Simulacro y elegancia en tarjetas de visita: Fotografías de Cruces y Campa* (Mexico City: INAH, 1998), 15.

4   On the picture postcards, see Paul Vanderwood and Frank Sampanaro, *Border Fury: A Picture Postcard Record of Mexico's Revolution and U.S. War Preparedness, 1910–1917* (Albuquerque: University of New Mexico Press, 1988).

5   Circulation figures for Mexican periodicals are notoriously inexact, and simply unavailable for the illustrated magazines. However, interviews with individuals in both Mexico City and various provincial capitals indicate that *Hoy, Mañana*, and *Siempre!* were much read. For example, a letter from Luis G. Olloqui (librarian of Monterrey, Nuevo León), which was published on the back cover of *Hoy*, indicates the acceptance that the magazine had in that city: of the 142 magazines available in the library, *Hoy* was the most solicited, and had reached a total of 27,385 readers. See *Hoy* 49 (29 January 1938).

   Even information about today's publications is untrustworthy; see Raymundo Riva Palacio, "A Culture of Collusion: The Ties That Bind the Press and the PRI," in *A Culture of Collusion: An Inside Look at the Mexican Press*, ed. William Orme (Miami: University of Miami Press, 1997). Perhaps the popularity that *Life* enjoyed gives us an idea of the acceptance that Mexican magazines may have received: the inaugural issue of *Life* was sent out to 225,000 charter subscribers, and another 200,000 copies sold out within hours of appearing on newstands; within three months it was selling a million copies weekly. Circulation reached a peak of 5.8 million subscribers, and market studies placed the total number of readers at 20 million. See Wendy Kozol, *Life's America: Family and Nation in Postwar Photojournalism* (Philadelphia: Temple University Press, 1994), 35; Glenn G. Willumson, *W. Eugene Smith and the Photographic Essay* (Cambridge, England: Cambridge University Press, 1992), 312; and *Life 60th Anniversary* (October 1996), 13.

6   A more immediate precedent may be the magazine *Todo*, which began to publish in 1933. See Rebeca Monroy Nasr, *Fotografía de prensa en México: Un acercamiento a la obra de Enrique Díaz, Delgado y García* (Ph.D. diss. Historia del Arte, UNAM, 1997). Even Monroy

concedes that *Hoy* fundamentally transformed magazine journalism in Mexico by giving priority to images (348).

7   Cited in Flora Lara Klahr and Marco Antonio Hernández, *El poder de la imagen y la imagen del poder: Fotografías de prensa del porfiriato a la época actual* (Chapingo, Mexico: Universidad Autónoma de Chapingo, 1985), 17. This text does not appear in *Hoy* 1 (27 February 1937); it must be taken from preceeding materials, as Mexican periodicals often publish an issue to announce a new magazine.

8   Roberto Blanco Moheno, *Memorias de un reportero* (Mexico City: Libro-Mex Editores, 1965), 86.

9   See Stephen Niblo, *War, Diplomacy, and Development: The United States and Mexico, 1938–1954* (Wilmington, DE: Scholarly Resources, 1995), 6.

10 José Pagés Llergo, "Le entrego la bandera," *Rotofoto* (new ed.) 1 (4 August 1951): 8.

11 *Rotofoto* 1 (22 May 1938); 9 (17 June 1938); 10 (23 June 1938). It is worth noting that even in the present climate of freedom granted Mexican photojournalists, they are forbidden to take images of the president while he is eating. This cover is reproduced in John Mraz, "Photographing Political Power in Mexico," in *Citizens of the Pyramid: Essays on Mexican Political Culture*, ed. Wil Pansters (Amsterdam, Netherlands: Thela Publishers, 1997), 159. I am grateful to Armando Bartra for permitting me to consult and make photographic copies from his issues of *Rotofoto*, a magazine almost impossible to find.

12 *Rotofoto* 6 (26 June 1938). *"El señor senador Padilla resuelve aferrarse al hueso." Aferrarse al hueso* is a typically Mexican play on words. *Aferrarse* means literally to seize, grasp, or bite, but its figurative meaning is "to cling." A *hueso* is a bone, but it is also Mexican slang for a position that is given to one through political connections. Hence, the title translates to an assertion that Padilla is intent on clinging to the privileged position he has received as a result of personal connections. See this image in Mraz, "Photographing Political Power," 160.

13 *Rotofoto* 3 (5 June 1938). *"El general y diputado Miguel Z. Martínez, de quien se dice que es hombre de pocas pulgas, pero que, como se ve las posee en abundancia."* Again, it is necessary to translate Mexican slang. *Tener pocas pulgas* means to have little patience, and so here the play is between the figurative and literal meaning of the phrase.

14 *Rotofoto* 2 (29 May 1938).

15 *Rotofoto* 11 (31 July 1938).

16 There are other opinions as to the cause of this publication's end. See Mraz, "Photographing Political Power," 152.

17 Blanca Torres, *Historia de la Revolución Mexicana, 1940–1952: Hacia la utopía industrial,* (Mexico City: Colegio de México, 1984), 21: 171.

18 Francisco Martínez de la Vega, "Libertad, si . . . para encadenarse: Ha pasado un congreso," *Siempre!* 18 (24 October 1953): 16–19.

19 Blanco Moheno, *Memorias,* 294.

20 Carlos Monsiváis, "Pagés Llergo defendió la tolerancia y auspició la libertad de expresión," *Proceso* 686 (25 December 1989): 47.

21 Roberto Blanco Moheno, *La noticia detrás de la noticia* (Mexico City: Author's edition, 1966), 325.

22 Cited in Rafael Rodríguez Castañeda, *Prensa vendida: Los periodistas y los presidentes. 40 años de relaciones* (Mexico City: Grijalbo, 1993), 21.

23 José Agustín, *Tragicomedia mexicana 1: La vida en México de 1940 a 1970* (Mexico City: Planeta, 1991), 72.

24 *Nosotros los pobres* (1947), *Ustedes los ricos* (1948), *Pepe el toro* (1952).

25 Rodríguez Castañeda, *Prensa vendida*, 15.

26 Ibid., 31, 59. A paper factory had been built during World War II. According to Stephen Niblo, this wartime measure had "a profound impact on the government's ability to control the media to the present day" (*War, Diplomacy, and Development*, 113).

27 *Hoy* 60 (15 April 1938): 4.

28 Interview by John Mraz, 20 January 1999.

29 These are commonly referred to as *gacetillas*, and until recently even opposition newspapers continued to run them. In *La Jornada*, for example, they were indicated by putting the headline in italics. On this form of "news," see Joe Keenan, "*La Gacetilla*: How Advertising Masquerades as News," in *A Culture of Collusion*, ed. Orme, 41–48.

30 Since the gacetillas were disguised as news in *Hoy* and *Mañana* and are difficult to recognize even for a trained eye, I consider them together with other illustrated articles in my analysis below.

31 On the enormous profits that could be made on the "special editions," see Blanco Moheno, *Memorias*, 273.

32 On bribes to reporters, see Blanco Moheno, *La noticia*, 125, 172, 188.

33 Miguel Angel Mendoza, "Pagés Llergo: Reportero estrella," *Mañana* 392 (3 March 1951): 29.

34 Olga Pellicer de Brody and José Luis Reyna, *El afianzamiento de la estabilidad política (1952–1960)*, vol. 22 of *Historia de la Revolución Mexicana* (Mexico City: El Colegio de México, 1978), 13, 17–18.

35 Blanco Moheno, *Memorias*, 94.

36 José Luis Ortiz Garza, *México en guerra: La historia secreta de los negocios entre empresarios mexicanos de la comunicación, los nazis y E.U.A.* (Mexico City: Planeta, 1989), 93.

37 *Hoy* 236 (30 August 1941): 4.

38 Monsiváis, *Proceso*, 47; Blanco Moheno, *Memorias*, 13, 86.

39 On the relationship of Maximino Avila Camacho and *Hoy*, see Blanco Moheno, *Memorias*, 87–88. Maximino is also considered in Agustín, *Tragicomedia mexicana*, 47; and Luis Medina, *Historia de la Revolución Mexicana, 1940–1952: Civilismo y modernización del autoritarismo* (Mexico City: El Colegio de México, 1979), 20: 17. Blanco Moheno recounts in various parts of *Memorias* that Hernández Llergo's "craze for women" required him to earn enormous amounts of money.

40 See, for example, *Mañana* 355 (17 June 1950), which is composed of 310 pages on Alemán's trip to the southeast; issues were normally around 100 pages. Two months later, another entire issue was dedicated to Aleman's gira to the north: *Mañana* 362 (5 August 1950).

41 See this image in Mraz, "Photographing Political Power," 161.

42 *Mañana* 366 (2 September, 1950): 6.

43 *Hoy* 75 (30 July 1938); 91 (19 November 1938).

44 *Mañana* 2 (11 September 1943): 18.

45 The term *charro* is widely used in Mexico to describe union leaders who are serving the government rather than their constituency. It is derived from Jesús Díaz de León, who was

imposed as the leader of the railroad union in the 1948 *charrazo*. Because he liked to dress in charro (Mexican cowboy) outfits, the term became synonymous with "sold-out" leaders. See the interview with Guillermo Treviño in John Mraz, *Made on Rails: A History of the Mexican Railroad Workers*, videotape, 1988, distributed by the Cinema Guild, New York.

46 *Mañana* 388 (3 February 1951): 4.

47 See Luis Reygadas, *Proceso de trabajo y acción obrera: Historia sindical de los mineros de Nueva Rosita, 1929–1979* (Mexico City: INAH, 1988), 119; and *La caravana del hambre: Ismael Casasola* (Puebla, Mexico: Universidad Autónoma de Puebla and Fototeca del INAH, 1986), 60. Great exceptions were the two photo reports published in *Hoy* during February before the caravan arrived in Mexico City, with José Revueltas's texts and Ismael Casasola's images; see *Hoy* 730 (17 February 1951); 731 (24 February 1951). The texts are reproduced in the book on Ismael Casasola, along with a number of his photos.

48 *Mañana* 394 (17 March 1951): 8-F.

49 Cited in Daniel Molina, *La Caravana del Hambre* (Mexico City: Ediciones El Caballito, 1982), 68.

50 *Hoy* 75 (30 July 1938): 31–32.

51 "Los soldados del Ejército Nacional son también cumplidos trabajadores," *Hoy* 78 (20 August 1938): 23–24.

52 *Hoy* 77 (13 August 1938).

53 *Hoy* 76 (6 August 1938): 28–33.

54 *Mañana* 422 (29 September, 1951): 14.

55 Kozol, *Life's America*, 6.

56 See Stuart Hall, "The Social Eye of Picture Post," *Working Papers in Cultural Studies* 2 (spring 1972): 70–120.

57 Ibid., 83.

58 Carlos Monsiváis, "Sociedad y cultura," in *Entre la guerra y la estabilidad política: El México de los 40*, ed. Rafael Loyola, (Mexico City: CNCA y Grijalbo, 1990), 274.

59 Carlos Monsivaís, "Los Hermanos Mayo: . . . y en una reconquista feliz de otra inocencia," "La cultura en México" (special ed.), *Siempre!* (12 August 1981): 4.

60 Salvador Novo, *La vida en México en el periodo presidencial de Manuel Avila Camacho* (Mexico City: CNCA-INAH, 1994), 136.

61 "Para pachucos no hay servicio porque me caen gordos." This is the first film for which Cantinflas wrote the script, something he would not do again until *Su excelencia* (1966). His attitude here is no doubt conditioned by the popularity of the pachuco character developed by Tin Tan, above all in his films of the late 1940s, *Calabacitas tiernas* (1948) and *El rey del barrio* (1949).

62 See John Mraz, "Lo gringo en el cine mexicano y la ideología alemanista," in Ignacio Durán, Iván Trujillo, and Mónica Verea, eds. *México–Estados Unidos: Encuentros y desencuentros en el cine* (Mexico City: UNAM-IMCINE, 1996), 83–92.

63 *Hoy* 75 (30 June 1938): 24.

64 On "shock photos," see Roland Barthes, "The Photographic Message," in *Image, Music, Text*, trans. Stephen Heath (New York: Hill and Wang, 1977), 31.

65 *Hoy* 1 (27 February 1937): 5.

66 See *Mañana*, issues 5–10 (October–November 1943).

67   *Hoy* 218 (26 April 1941): 38. See this image in Mraz, "Photographing Political Power," 162.

68   Years later, in 1976, Pagés Llergo would provide Julio Scherer with a floor of the *Siempre!* building to help Scherer start up *Proceso*.

69   See this image in Mraz, "Photographing Political Power," 164.

70   *Hoy* 844 (25 April 1953).

71   José Pagés Llergo, "Así nació *Siempre!*" *Siempre!* 1 (27 June 1953): 54.

72   Ibid., 57. Pagés Llergo may in fact have been founding, along with *Siempre!*, the current practice of destroying ex-presidents. It is said that Adolfo Ruiz Cortines provided funds for the creation of this magazine, perhaps as a way of distancing himself from his predecessor.

73   With the end of the ideological struggles of the 1930s and the incorporation of Lombardo Toledano into the system, he became a regular contributor to the illustrated magazines.

74   Essays of opinion remain the strength of Mexican journalism. The only publication known for investigative reporting is *Proceso*, founded in 1976 by Julio Scherer.

75   Pagés Llergo, "Así nació *Siempre!*," 54.

76   Pagés Llergo argued explicitly that the Mexican press preferred freedom to "the slavery of chains of gold" in *Siempre!*'s first editorial: *Siempre!* 1 (26 June 1953): 8.

77   *Siempre!* 53 (26 July 1954): 33.

78   Humberto Musacchio maintains that only with the arrival of the Hermanos Mayo in 1939 does "the press photographer, until then anonymous, begin to receive the credit his work deserves." See "Apuntes para un árbol genealógico," in Miguel Angel Granados Chapa, Humberto Musacchio, and Herón Alemán *Fotografía de prensa en México: 40 reporteros gráficos* (Mexico City: Procuraduría General de la República, 1992), 94. Nevertheless, that is not the case in *Hoy*, where the photojournalists generally received credit in the 1930s, above all, the "stars."

79   See Brian Horton, *The Associated Press Photo-Journalism Stylebook* (New York: Addison Wesley, 1990).

80   Among the very few exceptions to the rule is the above-mentioned photo reportage by José Revueltas and Ismael Casasola on the "Caravan of Hunger."

81   *Mañana* 454 (10 May 1952): 4-A, 10-A.

82   *Mañana* 402 (12 May 1951): 8.

83   *Mañana* 454.

84   I have taken this concept from Robin Anderson's "Images of War: Photojournalism, Ideology, and Central America," *Latin American Perspectives* 16 no. 2 (1989): 110.

85   The photo of the mother and son was originally published in a photo essay, "13 instantáneas," *Mañana* 627 (3 September 1955): 105. There, those images that had been selected as the thirteen best Mayo photos were arranged year by year, from 1943 to 1955, as if they had been taken in the year to which they were assigned. The magazine's disregard for journalistic truth can be seen in the fact that some of the photos, particularly this one of the mother and her son, were not taken in the year listed; further, the date of the first photo (1943) is, coincidentally, the year of *Mañana*'s founding rather than 1939, the year of the Mayos' arrival in Mexico.

David Alfaro Siqueiros later incorporated the photo of the grieving mother and dead son into a mural in the Jorge Negrete Theater, which he was commissioned to paint by the

National Union of Actors in 1959. However, the mural provoked such controversy among the union members that he was never able to finish it; it was covered by a wall and destroyed. See Antonio Rodríguez, *A History of Mexican Mural Paintings* (London: Thames and Hudson, 1969), 407–8, where photographs of the mural are reproduced in plates 221, 222, 223. On the Hermanos Mayo, see John Mraz, "Foto Hermanos Mayo: A Mexican Collective," *History of Photography* 17, no. 1 (spring 1993).

86 I recently questioned Julio Mayo about the use made of this image. Although he is usually passionate and outspoken, he just shrugged and indicated that this was so common as to make commentary unnecessary.

87 Images of scantily clad women appear to be standard fare of illustrated magazines in general. See the first cover of *Picture Post* (1938), with its leggy girls leaping in the air.

88 *Siempre!* 262 (3 July 1958): cover. The incident was evidently much commented on in the press throughout the Americas; see Rodríguez Castañeda, *Prensa vendida*, 18.

89 *Siempre!* 52 (19 June 1954): 20–25. On Nacho López, see John Mraz, *Nacho López y el fotoperiodismo mexicano en los años cincuenta* (Mexico City: INAH-Océano, 1999). An earlier article was published in English: "Nacho López: Photojournalist of the 1950s," *History of Photography* 20, no. 3 (autumn 1996): 208–19.

90 "La policía, cancer de México," *Hoy* 665 (19 November 1949): 7; "La policía, el cancer de México," *Siempre!* 40 (27 March 1954): 8. Ismael Casasola participated in several photo essays for *Hoy* on prisons for children and women during May and June 1938, but they lack the critical aspect of the López reportage.

91 Mexico City is divided into political-judicial areas called *delegaciones*. When someone is arrested, jurisdiction over them is assigned to the delegación in which they committed their crime. The police stations within the delegaciones are essentially holding cells.

92 See the "gigolo" in the photo at the top right-hand corner of Figure 14.

93 See Figure 13.

94 On Mexican photojournalism since 1976, see John Mraz, *La mirada inquieta: Nuevo fotoperiodismo mexicano, 1976–1996* (Mexico City: CNCA-Centro de la Imagen-Universidad Autónoma de Puebla, 1996); a later version was published in English: "The New Photojournalism of Mexico, 1976–1998," *History of Photography* 22, no. 4 (winter 1998): 313–65.

Myths of Cultural Imperialism and Nationalism in Golden Age Mexican Cinema

Seth Fein

¡Qué viva panamericanismo y el acercamiento de las americanas!
—Pedro Infante's character, Luis Antonio García, in *Los tres García*

This proposition quickly leads to a dilemma: do we recreate national culture in accordance with a "true" popular culture, or do we accept the transnational invasion of the new mass culture? But these alternatives rapidly reveal themselves as false, because national culture today is precisely the amalgam of these two options, and therefore complementary.—Roger Bartra, "Mexican *Oficio*: The Miseries and Splendors of Culture"

In *Los tres García* (1946), the character Luis Antonio García offers a populist critique of Mexico's Good Neighbor relations with the United States, just after World War II had ended and just as the *alemanista* state was about to begin its pursuit of institutionalized *entendimiento* with its northern neighbor. When he encounters two U.S. motorists (a Mexican stereotype of a blonde [*güera*], played by Marga López, and her stout gringo father, played by Clifford Carr) passing through his provincial town, the mischievous *charro* conflates sexual with political conquest in uttering his *albur* (double entendre), which provides this essay's first epigraph.[1] The boisterous macho, played by Pedro Infante, facetiously praises Pan-Americanism, the U.S.-led movement for a hemispheric community of nations based on a supposedly shared regional political history uniting Anglo and Latin Americans, which culminated in the official support (if not popular enthusiasm) offered the United States by Latin American states during the Second World War.

Revising a wartime convention of Mexican cinema, Luis Antonio regenders U.S.-Mexican relations by inverting ostensible inequalities in the international relationship, when, in place of the growing political closeness of the Americas, he salutes the increased accessibility of U.S. women. Where wartime Mexican film offered cross-national romance as a respectful representation of international friendship through remasculinization of Mexican identity (i.e., revision of Hollywood's depiction of U.S.-Mexican gender relations), Luis Antonio's exuberant exclamation humorously expresses mild nationalist resentment.[2] The two visitors whom he (incorrectly) assumes are tourists represent the commodification of Mexico for the more prosperous, car-owning U.S. masses. But their geographical penetration and Mexico's dependence on the U.S. economy, symbolized by the rise of tourism and Mexico's own marketing of Mexican stereotypes, including the provincial charro, is resisted, ironically, through the persistence of cultural nationalism, repackaged for U.S. consumption and more aggressively through Mexican machismo's ability to defend its nation's women while seducing those of invading gringos.[3]

This masculinist message was no doubt deemed, by its producers, useful salve for postwar Mexican national identity; close economic and political relations with the United States would not diminish *lo mexicano*. For Mexican audiences, Luis Antonio's sentiments would form part of a discourse of machismo associated with Infante, for example, memorably in his portrayal of an urban charro, the *motociclista* policeman Pedro Chávez, in *A toda máquina* (1951) and its sequel *Que te ha dado esa mujer* (1951), in which he made explicit the international dimension crucial to his Mexican machismo through his seduction of a visiting gringa. That is, Infante's figure made visible the usually invisible but never absent "other" (the United States) crucial to dominant Mexican discourses, whether disseminated through official rhetoric or popular entertainment. Marcia Landy's observations about how the movie star's gendered public persona "overflows the frames of the narrative" to shape popular reception of history through film is helpful in conceptualizing how Infante's public figure (intertextually constituted among his films and his off-screen media representations) influenced how spectators, across class lines, interpreted postwar U.S.-Mexican relations through his on-screen characterizations.[4]

These more aggressive assertions of nonradical anti-Americanism coincided with two (perhaps) seemingly opposite forces that were (and remain) inextricably linked within the dialectic of U.S.-Mexican relations since the beginning of the 1940s: official invocation of nationalism and state policies fomenting transnationalism. As Mexico, despite the self-proclaimed nationalism of the state's import-substitution industrialization, embarked half-knowingly, in the 1940s, on the road to the North American Free Trade Agreement's (NAFTA) full-throttle economic and political integration, official (cultural and political) expressions of criticism of the United States became more prominent than they had been during World War II. Of course, there had been earlier postrevolutionary rhetorical assaults on the United States; the difference was that in the postwar era this was increasingly at odds with not only the regime's foreign but also its domestic policies. This pattern is particularly notable with regard to film, as the postwar cinematic critique of the United States converged with a decline in U.S. support for Mexican film production and distribution, which had surged during World War II. The loosening of those material bonds also loosened the self-censorship of Mexican producers and intervention of Mexican officials with regard to representing the United States.

Infante's career coincided exactly with the Golden Age of Mexican cinema, which began during the Second World War.[5] In fact, as this essay will show, this icon of Mexican identity (of anti-Yankee, or at least non-Yankee, machismo) was not only forged during a period of intense U.S.-Mexican collaboration in the film sector, but developed through one of the prime pro-war propaganda features produced in the Mexican industry to satisfy Mexican and U.S. officials' shared desire for a nationalist rendering of anti-Axis collaboration. This is not to reduce Infante's career, or the characters he portrayed, to instruments of U.S.-Mexican relations, but simply to recognize the transnational origins of that career and those images and the significance of those origins for coming to terms with Golden Age Mexican cinema and postwar U.S.-Mexican relations.

No matter the force of its discourse, as several contemporary commentators have noted, "globalization" has not erased national (and other) differences. Moreover, the transnational logic of today's cultural economy, both in terms of modes of production and the representational codes of the products themselves, is not an entirely new phenomenon. However, where some postmodern thinking has helped to better conceptualize the current situation as well as to reconceptualize the past, it has not completely eradicated, at least to a historian's eyes, the need to understand the logic of power between states and within nations. That is, as we (necessarily) decenter our approach to transnational culture, recognizing that it neither conforms to simple political and economic dependence at the level of production nor social homogenization (e.g., the still too common assertion of an ever expanding Americanization) at the level of reception, we must come to terms with historical processes, precursors to globalization, if you will, that locate the study of representations within a broader political and economic field of international relations. In doing so, we must abandon the overposited, pointless dichotomy between nationalism and cultural imperialism. Empirical research, not only about the political economy of culture industries but also issues involving historical representation (and reception), undermines such facile formulations, opening the way to a more comprehensive understanding of the interaction of images, ideas, and entertainment with political economy in the story of transnationalization.[6]

Recent events well illustrate the persistence of these historical patterns. President Carlos Salinas de Gortari promoted Mexico's economic integration with the United States through NAFTA as a self-proclaimed form of nationalism supposedly suited for the twenty-first century. The year 1993 was the height of *salinismo*—of the perceived success of the regime's economic project (symbolized by the signing of NAFTA)—which seemed to have reestablished the state-party's credibility after a decade of uninterrupted crises: 1982's debt-induced depression, the government's inadequate and corrupt response to Mexico City's massive 1985 earthquake, and the appallingly fraudulent 1988 presidential election that brought Salinas to power. In 1993, as the regime prepared for NAFTA's implementation—the culmination of its outward-looking economic project on which Salinas's technocrats had gambled the PRI's (Partido Revolucionario Institucional) political capital—it issued postage stamps commemorating the Golden Age of Mexican cinema (see Figure 19). Reflecting the epoch's importance for national identity, the stamps commemorated leading stars: Infante, Mario Moreno (Cantinflas), Dolores del Río, Pedro Armendáriz, María Félix, Jorge Negrete. The conjunction of NAFTA and the postage stamps offers a revealing juxtaposition of symbols for coming to terms with the specific relationship between U.S.-Mexico relations and the hybrid foundations of the Golden Age of Mexican cinema. It demonstrates, too, official uses of "nationalist" mythology—symbolized by, reproduced in, but not limited to cinema—which attempt to conceal international collaboration and dependence with discourses and icons (themselves products, I argue, not of national but transnational, although not instrumentally imperialist, modes of production).[7]

The wartime situation is particularly rich for our understanding of the postrevolutionary state's connections to mass media because it provides a lens through which to view the interaction of national and international forces that reproduced postrevolutionary official discourse in popular cul-

19. Mexican postage stamp of Pedro Infante, issued in 1993. Part of the Salinas regime's deployment of nationalist nostalgia to screen its intense neoliberalism, yet an ironic screen, because the Golden Age of Mexican cinema that created Infante was itself rooted in transnational industrial and cultural processes and U.S.-Mexican political collaboration.

ture: how prewar mass media and corporatist political machinery producing *cardenismo*'s leftist cultural populism transmuted into a system that instituted the postwar rightist ideological synthesis expressed through *alemanismo*. The role of the state in guiding mass cultural production remained constant; the shift in ideological paradigms did not represent international subversion of the regime's role in cultural production but rather the adoption of new discursive practices to maintain its nationalist ideological veneer in an era of transnationalization. In the ideology of some exceptional examples of wartime film propaganda we can read signs of transnationalism immanent in the entire film industry's development and that more broadly pervaded postwar Mexican political economy, culminating in today's neoliberalism (domestically) and NAFTA (internationally). Dialectically linked to the Mexican state's increasing collaboration with the United States, these political-cultural movements are not simply reflected in the shimmering images projected by film; they formed the means of cultural production itself. As we tour the sound stages of Golden Age Mexican cinema, then, we encounter not only Pedro Infante and María Félix but also the interplay of representational and material forces at the transnational nexus of postrevolutionary Mexico's political economy and mass culture.

World War II gave rise to the Golden Age of Mexican cinema. Commercially and culturally, this period of growth has been commonly credited, with reason, as an exceptional epoch during which the Mexican industry challenged Hollywood's international hegemony throughout the Western Hemisphere. Elsewhere I have examined the international political economy that allowed for this industrial situation.[8] I have argued that the Golden Age of Mexican cinema resulted not from nationalist (as usually asserted) but collaborative policies that evolved out of the particularities of U.S.-Mexican interactions at a variety of transnational and intergovernmental levels between the 1930s and 1950s. Chief among these was the direct intervention of the U.S. government in Mexican film production organized by Nelson Rockefeller's Office of the Coordinator of Inter-American Affairs (OCIAA), responsible for U.S. cultural and economic relations with Latin America during World War II.[9]

From the outset of its operation in 1940, well prior to official U.S. entry into the Second World War, Rockefeller's office undertook wide-ranging initiatives to institutionalize Good Neighbor themes and Latin American locales in Hollywood films. Special consultants advised the studios, for example, about their Latin American production (both proactively, encouraging propaganda, and restrictively, regarding censorship). The studios also formed the Motion Picture Society of the Americas (MPSA) as a liaison organization with the OCIAA's Motion Picture Division (MPD), headed by Hollywood producer, Rockefeller associate, and motion picture philanthropist John Hay ("Jock") Whitney.[10] Leading studio executives sat on the MPSA's board, overseeing its wide-ranging promotional and production activities.

With President Avila Camacho's declaration of war in May 1942, following German attacks on the Mexican oil tankers *Potrero del Llano* and *Faja de Oro*, covert forms of Mexican military and economic cooperation with the United States gave way to public displays of alliance with the United Nations, bilateral diplomatic and military planning, and deeper economic collaboration.[11] This transformation affected not only industrial and agricultural development, for example, the modernization of Mexican railroads to better facilitate U.S. exploitation of Mexican resources and labor during the war, but also ideological production. In the case of film, both initiatives converged in the modernization of the Mexican film industry and in the collaborative production of film propaganda within it. However, the obvious differences between cinema and other U.S. programs to stimulate Mexican production (mainly of raw materials) and modernize infrastructure should be noted: film was a manufactured good oriented toward Latin American consumer markets, not only U.S. producers. Unlike the rest of Mexico's booming national manufacturing sector during the war, film was not limited to domestic consumption. Dissemination of Mexican movies cultivated audiences throughout Latin America, affecting popular culture and the image of Mexico throughout the region.[12]

Initially, the OCIAA considered interventions in several Latin American film industries, even unfriendly Argentina's, as a way to squeeze out direct and indirect Axis influence and co-opt foreign producers through patronage. This was similar to other OCIAA culture initiatives. In the areas of print news and radio, for instance, the OCIAA simultaneously disseminated U.S. propaganda through foreign commercial mass media as well as removed pro-Axis information through economic and political pressure, such as buying up all available air time and advertising space in Latin American media markets.[13]

The U.S. modernization of the Mexican industry, to produce pro-war "Latin American" mass entertainment (and censor or preempt any critical ideological interventions), represented acknowledgment by U.S. officials of the already considerable commercial and artistic accomplishments of Mexican cinema (since the mid-1930s) on the one hand, and the limited impact of Hollywood's own Good Neighbor propaganda on the other. Now the U.S. industry, owing to its (albeit often uneasy) wartime partnership with U.S. foreign policy, would help develop Mexican production. U.S. officials believed their ideological agenda could better be served through the Latin Americanization of U.S. propaganda within the Mexican industry than it had been through Hollywood's Latin American–aimed representations of Washington's messages. As U.S. Ambassador George Messersmith aptly observed, "Although we would always be able to produce better pictures at Hollywood—facilities and conditions in Mexico were more favorable to the production of Spanish-language pictures. With American technicians and artistic and technical guidance, excellent pictures could be produced here through existing motion picture companies. Spanish-language pictures produced in Mexico would have a much more acceptable reception in the other American Republics than those produced in the United States."[14]

What had been conceived initially as a limited plan aimed at utilizing foreign film production metamorphosed into a full-scale program of industrial modernization based in Mexico City's two main studios, Cinematográfica Latinoamericana S.A. (CLASA) and Azteca. In early 1942, MPD consultant Frank Fouce (operator of Spanish-language movie houses in Los Angeles and sometime consultant to Hollywood studios about how to represent Latin America in their films)[15] and RKO vice president Joseph Breen (formerly director of Hollywood's self-censorship agency, the Production Code Administration of the Motion Picture Producers and Distributors of America) toured Mexican facilities "to investigate the motion picture industry and the possibilities of effecting a plan of cooperation with the motion picture industry in the United States."[16] By April, Francis Alstock, Jock Whitney's deputy (soon his successor) and a former RKO producer, was openly coordinating plans for Hollywood aid to the Mexican industry.[17] Initial ideas focused on "buying a 49 percent interest in the entire Mexican motion picture industry," estimated at $2 million and installing U.S. "technicians, modern equipment and assistance in distributing films." Rockefeller and Whitney encouraged the undertaking by circulating "a rumor that if United States interests do not come into the Mexican film industry [then] German interests may endeavor to do so."[18] RKO, a studio in which Nelson Rockefeller had large investments until World War II, would serve as an instrument of U.S. foreign policy by establishing Mexican facilities to produce commercial propaganda feature films "suitable for distribution not only in Mexico but also in the United States and other American Republics."[19]

In fact, the initial rationale for Hollywood intervention in the Mexican film industry had less to do with preventing pro-Axis Mexican movie production than with formulating a transnational mode of entertainment production to serve U.S. ideological interests. Although in the short term such a government-led initiative could work against Hollywood's own commercial interests, especially during a period of reduced wartime production more narrowly focused on war-related films (officially perceived as unpopular with Latin American audiences), in the long term U.S. media planners viewed such a program as beneficial to Hollywood's collective business interests. This would be true especially for the studio(s) that took the lead as Hollywood's "chosen instrument"[20] to expand film consumption south of the Rio Grande. Long-term U.S. commercial and cultural interests, OCIAA officials believed, would be served by their modernization project: "The plan would further the Good Neighbor policy by developing a local industry for the expression of local thought. This local industry can do a more effective piece of work in the other republics than can the United States industry because the pictures they would produce would have local backgrounds acceptable to and better understood by the peoples of these republics. Such pictures would supplement those aimed to serve the same purpose which are produced in the United States. Strong local industries would build audiences for motion pictures in the other republics and consequently increase the outlets for films produced in this country."[21]

Concern over the mass culture implications of Argentina's neutralist wartime foreign policy motivated prophylactic U.S. policies aimed to marginalize the South American nation's film industry rather than co-opt it. To prevent the Argentine industry from becoming a direct or indirect source of Axis propaganda, U.S. foreign policy crippled it by denying access to raw film stock, a commodity that the U.S. monopolized and controlled allocation of in the wartime Western Hemisphere. More ambitiously, the OCIAA sought to develop the Mexican industry as a counterweight to Argentine production. On the one hand, the MPD proposed facilitating transfer of virgin film, which even Hollywood had limited access to during the war, to Mexican producers. (By 1944, for example, Mexico received a quota of 45 million feet, whereas pro-U.S. Brazil received 12 million for its smaller, limited, Portuguese-speaking market, and Argentina none.)[22] On the other hand, MPD chief Whitney and his zealous assistant, Alstock, explored expanding the already commercially proven Mexican industry through industrial intervention: "Mexico once held the leading place in the production of Spanish-language pictures, but that position is now held by Argentina. Mexico has been selected as the first country to be assisted under the plan because (a) of its proximity to the United States, (b) its motion picture industry can be developed to a point of major importance in the other American republics, (c) friendly relations exist between the Mexican and our governments, and (d) the Mexican government has already appointed a commission to develop its motion picture industry which is prepared to invite the assistance of the United States through whatever channels may be established to serve the purpose."[23]

Mexican producers were anxious to take advantage of the possibility of U.S. aid. Attempting to solve some of the bottlenecks that had stalled production since the late 1930s, Mexican government officials, producers, and organized labor had begun to coordinate resources in 1942 to exploit favorable trade conditions created by the war. As in other industries, the war gave

rise to increased commercial possibilities for Mexican motion pictures owing to reduced Hollywood exports as well as an almost complete cessation
of European (not to mention Argentine) distribution in the Western Hemisphere. Moreover, because Mexican motion pictures were an international
commodity with loyal Latin American (and U.S. Latino/a) audiences, the
war presented international possibilities for intraregional trade.[24]

In 1942 the Banco de México, with the support of the central government
and national producers, finally organized a Banco Cinematográfico, a national investment project that had been still-born during the Cárdenas
years. To supplement that initiative, the Secretaría de Gobernación (Interior Ministry), under future president Miguel Alemán, formed a Comité
Coordinador y de Fomento de la Industria Cinematográfica Mexicana
(Committee for Coordinating and Fomenting the Mexican Film Industry)
that aimed to foster collaboration among state, capital, and labor. The Comité's tripartite leadership included the nation's most acclaimed director,
Fernando de Fuentes (representing studio interests); the Interior Ministry's chief of its Dirección General de Cinematografía (Office of Cinematographic Affairs), Gregorio Castillo; and Enrique Solís, official leader of studio workers within the powerful Sindicato de Trabajadores de la Industria
Cinematográfica (STIC), an affiliate of the state-aligned Confederación de
Trabajadores de México (CTM).

Solís's participation was particularly significant, because it signaled the
pro-production orientation of the Comité's work, derivative of the integra-
tionist "nationalism" (compelling labor's support of industrialization and
capital accumulation) espoused by *avilacamachismo* in the name of national
development and security during World War II. The controversial labor
official (often accused of corruption by rank-and-file union members) also
had strong personal financial ties to Azteca Studios and encouraged cooperation between skilled labor and producers in the interest of raising motion
picture output and consumption. Solís's position also signaled his rehabilitation by the CTM, which supported Avila Camacho's pro-war foreign policy and production-oriented economic agenda. In 1938, then CTM chief
Vicente Lombardo Toledano had removed Solís as head of an earlier film
workers union for not being sufficiently aggressive in challenging the power
of producers. Now, during the war (when Lombardo Toledano was no
longer head of the ever more conservative CTM), Solís was reinstalled as the
studio workers' leader and chosen to represent organized labor on the Comité. The formation of the national film bank and the development com-

mittee, each aimed at strengthening Mexican motion picture production, also facilitated the implementation of U.S. aid. They streamlined the Mexican industry's collaboration with the OCIAA (by focusing the interests of a range of Mexican producers), but also integrated national production within a Hollywood-led international system.

The OCIAA explained its Mexican program as an extension of the U.S. culture industries' international war effort; it deserved supplies based on its role in waging the (transnationalized) phase of U.S. mass media warfare.[25] Producer goods not directly related to the war ceased production as industrial capacity was put to other uses. Because celluloid was a strategic material, the production and allocation of raw film stock was controlled by the War Production Board (WPB). After a decade of international expansion and artistic progress, Mexican film officials feared that the war would mean an end to industrial growth, the loss of its inchoate foreign markets throughout the Spanish-speaking Americas, reconquest by Hollywood. The agreement between the OCIAA and the Comité Coordinador represented an opportunity not only to sustain production through access to virgin film but also to initiate badly needed modernization of outdated equipment and the expansion of existing capacity. Solís, for one, credited the work of Rockefeller, Alstock, and Fouce with saving the Mexican film industry at a critical moment in its development.[26]

In the interest of maintaining its close relationship with Washington, Hollywood mobilized to expand a competitive national industry that previously it had sought to undermine. In selling his agency's plan to the U.S. studios, the MPD's Alstock believed that wartime assistance was not at odds with the U.S. industry's long-term interests, because it would spread film culture to new markets that U.S. producers would naturally dominate after the war.[27]

The Mexican government, represented by Alemán and the Comité Coordinador, negotiated the framework for U.S. intervention with MPD officials, led by Whitney, in 1942. The agreement outlined the operation of U.S.-Mexican collaboration; U.S. aid would be implemented by Hollywood's MPSA through the Banco de México. The final contract called for a survey by U.S. experts of the Mexican industry to "determine the kind and quantity of machinery and equipment required by the Mexican cinema industry." The OCIAA would use the MPSA's analysis "to employ its resources and influence in placing said machinery at the disposal of the Mexican cinema industry through existing studios or those which may be built for the purpose." It endorsed the Comité Coordinador's plan to consolidate Azteca with the struggling Stahl studios (within the former's administration). The expanded and reorganized Azteca would then be modernized along with CLASA as Mexico's central filmmaking facilities, "equally capacitated to render effective service to all producers of national films." The agreement also proposed construction of a third studio, with Mexican capital (and U.S. equipment and expertise), if demand necessitated further expansion. Equipment provided the Mexican industry with wartime priorities obtained by the OCIAA would be paid for in installments. In addition, "to assure the best use of and profit from the machinery and equipment . . . the Office of the Coordinator shall do everything in its power to provide the services of the experts needed by the Mexican Studios, for the time necessary for training national technicians."[28]

Beyond facilitating the expansion of Mexican film production within a structure dependent on U.S. support, the agreement called for U.S. subsidization through Mexican institutions of specific propaganda films. The Bank of Mexico was to create a special cinema division "to be the channel through which the Office of the Coordinator may take part in the financing of Mexican films which, by reason of their theme, educational value, or other special merits it might be difficult to produce commercially, but which would serve to bring about better InterAmerican understanding, imbue the peoples of the continent with ideas of liberty and patriotism, or make known to the nations of America the history and traditions of the American Republics. The selection of the films to be produced under these conditions, as well as the amount of financing, shall be determined by the Mexican Committee with the approval of the Office of the Coordinator." Moreover, the OCIAA would "guarantee the Cinema Department . . . against any loss which might be incurred in financing said films, having the right to appoint a representative to approve the budgets and financial arrangements." Any profits made would "be exclusively for the producers . . . to stimulate them towards the InterAmerican activities which it is desired to foment."[29] In addition to developing production, the plan arranged for Hollywood to overcome the Mexican industry's "inadequate distribution in the other American republics," so that "with improved production full advantage may be taken of Spanish-language pictures thru distribution through the other American republics and thus increase support of our war effort as well as to combat Axis directed or sponsored Spanish-language propaganda pictures."[30]

U.S. operatives were blunt in assessing the instrumental and structural control over production and censorship they attained through the transfer of Hollywood technology, expertise, and supplies and the way that aid was implemented within Mexican studios. No film could be made without at least tacit U.S. approval. And any project could be stopped through the centralized control exercised by Mexican and U.S. authorities. However, coercion was hardly necessary; Mexican producers went out of their way to please U.S. and Mexican officials.[31] What U.S. planners viewed as part of a sophisticated program of Pan-American propaganda Mexican political and film elites perceived as an opportunity to develop their nation's film industry.

Nationalizing Internationalism

Re-visioning the past is central to every state's self-presentation. As Fernando Coronil has eloquently shown in his recent study of Venezuela's "magical state," analysis of *how* a regime retells the story of national development, *how* it naturalizes its political project historically, allows not only a peek at the inner workings of official discourse but also a glimpse at the transnational dynamics of material development itself.[32] In the case of Golden Age Mexican cinema, the industry's economic and social ties to the state set parameters for representation. And from the outset of sound film production in Mexico in the early 1930s, Mexico's ruling regime subsidized historical movie making as a source of national socialization and ideological rationalization.[33] The accelerating convergence of the state's cultural project with U.S. interests in the late 1930s changed dramatically the course of Mexican cinema's industrial production.[34]

In 1939, Warner Bros. released *Juarez* as an instrument of the late Good Neighbor policy, a prototype of the more massive U.S. film propaganda program initiated during the Second World War.[35] As propaganda, *Juarez* failed miserably in the judgment of its promulgators. U.S. diplomats monitored its reception throughout Latin America; the general response was disinterest, as audiences viewed it as a "Hollywood" production with little meaning for contemporary international relations. Not surprisingly, in Mexico the response was more strident. There were instances of popular rejection of what was seen as denigrating details, as well as elite resentment (from a conservatively nationalist position) of Hollywood's co-optation and perversion of Mexican history. Most unconvincing was the film's attempt to sell a liberal version of U.S. imperialism as a means to enlist Mexico in an unfolding world conflict that did not threaten the nation's sovereignty and seemed only to strengthen long-term U.S. control. The film reproduces, as historical allegory, the post-1938 Cárdenas program, which moved to the center domestically and into alliance with the United States internationally. Signaling future policies, as well as the ever deepening ideological convergence in U.S.-Mexican state-to-state relations, the Cárdenas administration endorsed *Juarez*—including its highly publicized Mexico City premiere in the Palacio de Bellas Artes, Mexico's most important theater. Demonstrating the impact of the period's popular frontism, CTM chief Lombardo Toledano, earlier a strident advocate of anti-Yankeeism, publicly supported the film as part of Mexico's fight against fascism. Despite such official support (Cárdenas himself had endorsed the movie's message during a personal pre-premiere screening provided by a U.S. consul), the movie's refashioning of the Monroe Doctrine as an instrument of defense of Mexican sovereignty rather than of U.S. imperialism was discredited at both elite and popular levels.[36]

The film's failure as propaganda—its ineffective attempt to muster support for the antifascist front led by Cárdenas and Roosevelt through historical allegory, to personify U.S.-Mexican alliance through Lincoln-Juárez friendship, to demonstrate that European rightism and its Mexican collaborators threatened national sovereignty and social progress—provided space for Mexican cinema's reinvention of the Juárez myth as the basis of a "nationalist" pro-war message. That message, in ways not necessarily intended by its producers, was, for Mexican audiences, "essential for understanding the changing character of the present," as Landy put it in analyzing a different case of historical filmmaking.[37]

¡Mexicanos al grito de guerra!, historia del himno nacional (1943) reconfigured Mexican nationalism to support the war effort in ways that reveal the interconnections between World War II (as a transnational process) and the development of official Mexico's ideology. The eventual realization of a Rodríguez Hermanos project first brought to the OCIAA in 1942, it transformed the Mexican national anthem from the framing musical theme for a story based on the (recent sinking of the) *Potrero del Llano*, to the subject of a full-length feature focused on the liberal struggle against conservatives and French intervention in the mid–nineteenth century. Written by Alvaro Gálvez y Fuentes, the project retained the title originally submitted to U.S.

officials in 1942.[38] As does Warner Bros.' *Juárez*, the Rodríguez Hermanos film opens in Paris, where Napoleon III contemplates his New World adventure. Again, rightist nineteenth-century European imperialism threatens Mexican sovereignty; the United States' conquest of half of Mexico's national territory fifteen years prior to the French intervention is absent from this historical allegory's explication of the international dangers faced by the nation. However, unlike the U.S. version, except for a brief scene showing Juárez in exile in Texas,[39] the United States is inconspicuous in *¡Mexicanos al grito de guerra!*; there is no personification, for example, of U.S.-Mexican alliance through friendship between Juárez and Lincoln, as in Hollywood's version. The Rodríguez Hermanos production invokes *juarista* resistance to French intervention to propagandize a nationalist, rather than Warner Bros.' internationalist, rationale for supporting the Allied cause.

This conformed to the OCIAA's intentions regarding its Mexican film program. *¡Mexicanos al grito de guerra!* responded to U.S. propaganda officials' desire to overcome negative Latin American (especially Mexican) reception of the Warner Bros. film with a local version of the Juárez myth that would stimulate popular patriotism against internal and external fascist threats.[40] The film dramatizes the story of the development of Mexico's *himno nacional*, its national anthem, a mainstay of the state's mass culture program since the late 1930s (when it opened the government's Sunday evening radio program, *La Hora Nacional*).[41] Its introductory credits underline its relationship to the regime's project by thanking President Avila Camacho, Secretary of Defense (and ex-president) Lázaro Cárdenas, Secretary of Communications Maximino Avila Camacho (the president's brother), and a lengthy list of military leaders. The opening sequence is punctuated with a concluding shot of the Mexican flag.[42] Beyond justifying Mexico's war mobilization to a skeptical public, the film's message served the regime's domestic security needs as it battled rightist dissent ranging from urban Gold Shirts to provincial Sinarquistas to the pro-clerical rightist mainstream represented by the Partido Acción Nacional (PAN), formed in 1939. Its historical emplotment strove to transcend all political opposition, to legitimize the state's claim to embody the nation.

The narrative relates the parallel triumphs of the himno as Mexico's national anthem and the liberal defense of the nation's sovereignty against the French in 1862. To this end, the film offers a reading of the reciprocal relationship between war and nationalism, relevant for contemporary politics. It recounts the collaboration of Mexican poet Francisco González Bocanegra (played by Carlos Riquelme) and the Catalán expatriate composer Jaime Nunó (Salvador Carrasco) in the late 1850s. Pedro Infante, soon to be the Mexican screen's foremost male sex symbol, plays the film's protagonist, Luis Sandoval, a student of Nunó's who encourages his teacher to compose music for González Bocanegra's poem. This telling of the himno's story conflates *juarismo*'s liberal nationalist mythology with avilacamachismo's progressive centralist ideology. The film's dissemination of the nation's anthem itself formed part of the regime's project of political socialization, which disseminated historical symbols through popular culture and mass communication: to create the nation as (Anderson's) "imagined community" through (Hobsbawm's) "invented tradition."[43] To this end, the film offers a reading of the reciprocal relationship between war and nationalism. The anthem's development, as depicted by the film, represents the postrevolutionary regime's ideology of social inclusion, promoting *mestizaje* (the notion of Mexican national identity as a mixture of indigenous and Hispanic genealogies) as the official culture.[44] In doing so, the narrative well illustrates Jesús Martín Barbero's observations about how twentieth-century Latin American states utilized "mass mediations" to conflate state and nation: "A new nationalism emerged, based on the idea of national culture which would be the synthesis of different cultural realities and a political unity bringing together cultural, ethnic and regional differences. The nation absorbed the people."[45]

The film links the contemporary state's nationalism with the mid-nineteenth-century liberal struggle. In doing so, it revised juarismo to conform to wartime ideology, especially as regards race and class. *¡Mexicanos al grito de guerra!* presents the liberal cause as an integrative movement—for national unity and international liberation—led by middle-class mestizos who inhabit (and negotiate) the cultural terrain between neo-European white economic elites and poor Indians. Racist aspects of the liberal project (e.g., the forced acculturation of Indians, expropriation of collectively held *ejidos* [communal lands], elite emulation of U.S. and European values and styles) are erased, replaced by a natural disposition toward popular culture as lo mexicano.

The film's depiction of the himno's collaborative composition underlines its populist nationalism. Nunó struggles to find an appropriate melody until he turns his ear to the sounds emanating through his window from the street. The composer assimilates a Mexican folk tune sung by an Indian woman selling flowers outside his window; in his melody, the popular mixes with the classical, the Mexican with the European.[46] The himno's music, then, is a product of cultural mestizaje: a combination of the classically trained composer's European background and the street culture of the peasant migrant to Mexico City (a timely theme, given the heightened rural migration to the capital during the Second World War). In a parallel scene, González Bocanegra similarly struggles for inspiration. Finally the poet's gaze fixes on paintings hung on his study's walls (conveyed through a close-up of each tableau) depicting Father Hidalgo's leadership of the 1810 campesino rebellion by landless mestizos—initiated by his legendary call to arms (*grito*)—that ignited the complicated processes that led to Mexican independence.[47] The film thus draws historical parallels between 1810 (opposition to Spanish colonialism), 1862 (resistance to French imperialism), and 1942 (defense against Axis aggression); social justice and national sovereignty, mestizo society and progressive elite leadership, popular and high culture, indigenous and neo-European expression merge in struggles against Old World control. Father Hidalgo's grito, his call to arms against Spanish colonialism and Mexican reaction, forms the core myth for the development of juarista nationalism against French imperialism and its conservative Mexican allies, which, in turn, becomes an allegory for Avila Camacho's move against domestic opposition in the name of national sovereignty. In the wartime telling of Mexican history, 1910 was left out; the pro-war nationalist narrative excludes the Revolution, because U.S. interventions, not to mention Mexican revolutionary radicalism, would muddle the message (which invoked antifascism to promote the state's rhetoric of progress and independence). Alliance with the United States, unaddressed in the film (despite widespread mobilization for the U.S. effort) was presented (or unpresented through its notable absence) as a marriage of convenience that served Mexican nationalism, not U.S. Pan-Americanism.

The himno, then, becomes in *¡Mexicanos al grito de guerra!* (and in the government's other wartime propaganda campaigns promoting the national anthem) the unifying historical symbol for avilacamachismo's mobilization against the Axis. The film, as we will see, produced history to mobilize the very masses its narrative created. It exemplifies Homi Bhabha's description of how through dual discursive movements "the nation turns from being the symbol of modernity into becoming the symptom of an ethnography of the 'contemporary' within modern culture. Such a shift in perspective emerges from an acknowledgement of the nation's interrupted address articulated in the tension between signifying the people as an a priori historical presence, a pedagogical object; and the people constructed in the performance of narrative, its enunciatory 'present' marked in the repetition and pulsation of the national sign."[48]

The title's multiple historical meanings demonstrates this double shift in temporality. *¡Mexicanos al grito de guerra!* is the first line of Mexico's national anthem commemorating Hidalgo's grito and written to support Juárez's movement (as the film explains). But in the context of 1943, the film's title (and message)—*as popularly received*—referred to Mexican President Manuel Avila Camacho's controversial declaration of support for the Allied cause following the sinking of Mexican oil tankers in the Gulf of Mexico by German submarines in May 1942. The Cárdenas administration's 1938 nationalization of foreign oil interests made the German attacks a particularly potent nationalist symbol on which to justify mobilization. It was also an ironically problematic one, with implications for film censorship as well as production, because the industry had been expropriated from U.S. and Anglo-Dutch corporations.[49] Yet these events allowed Avila Camacho to bring public discourse in line with his regime's already considerable covert cooperation with the U.S. war effort. This pro-war message, controversial because of general Mexican disinterest in the conflict and popular antipathy for the United States, was in turn utilized also to construct political consensus for the regime's domestic project.

The War of the Reforma, between conservatives and liberals (1858–1861), provides the story's principal historical framework. After conservatives force the Juárez regime from Mexico City, two governments (represented in one sequence by a split screen) claim sovereignty: one led by Benito Juárez in Veracruz, the other headed by Miguel Miramón in Mexico City.[50] Sandoval and his two mentors meet to discuss current events in the poet's study beneath the tableaux of Hidalgo.[51] They conclude that the liberal struggle is a replay of the earlier independence movement. Their analysis of Mexican politics equates democracy with international independence and progressive social policy; absent is any scrutiny of internal political processes. In fact, instead, political instability—the numerous changes in central governments since independence—is the greatest obstacle to Mexico's achievement of national greatness. These were useful definitions for the wartime state. Avila Camacho, Cárdenas's hand-picked successor, came to power in an openly violent and corrupt 1940 election; his administration sought to legitimize its rule, in part, on the basis of the need for national solidarity in the face of international insecurity. Much like the elites who produced the film, its on-screen protagonists seek to use popular culture to forge national identity as an expression of a particular political movement's claim to the state.[52] Having earlier been rebuffed by Santa Anna in their attempt to have their creation adopted as Mexico's anthem, Nunó and González Bocanegra authorize Sandoval to present the himno to Juárez.[53]

The film blames the conservatives' self-interested corruption for fiscal irresponsibility (the antithesis to Juárez's just and frugal administration) for forcing the government to default on foreign debts after the liberals and Juárez regain control of Mexico City in 1861. The new leader's suspension of payments (recalling recent Mexican policy during the Great Depression) brings intervention from Mexico's foreign creditors: Spain, Great Britain, and France. Luis, who has already enlisted in the liberal army, presents Juárez a copy of the himno. General Ignacio Zaragoza (played by Miguel Angel Ferriz) interrupts the encounter with news of the European intervention, and Juárez adopts the himno as Mexico's national anthem.[54] (Similarly, in Warner Bros.' *Juarez*, the reception of a document stimulates the Mexican hero to action. But in Hollywood's tale, it is a letter and portrait sent by Lincoln that provides ideological inspiration for the Mexican leader as he crafts his movement's manifesto).[55] Spain and Great Britain recognize Juárez's regime and withdraw, while France remains.[56]

In a visually and narratively didactic scene, Juárez (played by Miguel Inclán) addresses the national legislature, and in so doing travels to the present by invoking Avila Camacho.[57] This scene, shot on location in the National Palace, echoes images in widely disseminated U.S. and Mexican films of Avila Camacho declaring Mexico's support for the United Nations' cause. For example, *¡Espionaje en el golfo!* (1943), another pro-war Mexican feature produced within the OCIAA-supported system, concludes with a montage of newsreel-style footage of military preparedness featuring a clip of Avila Camacho's war declaration in the Chamber of Deputies as the sound track blasts martial music. Like *¡Mexicanos al grito de guerra!*'s opening, which foregrounded current events, this similarly didactic concluding segment ends with a shot of the Mexican flag. The film's fictionalized account of Axis espionage within Mexico and the "real-life" sinking of Mexican oil tankers in the Gulf of Mexico links that movie's narrative not only to contemporary events and to the state's war mobilization but also intertextually to *¡Mexicanos al grito de guerra!*'s (and other media's) depiction of Avila Camacho as Juárez. The Chamber of Deputies' mise-en-scène featuring Avila Camacho,

20. The U.S. Office of War Information distributed this photograph of Avila Camacho's 1942 declaration of war against the Axis in the Chamber of Deputies in
news "packets" to privately operated print media worldwide. It reproduces the dominant trope of Mexican moderation, progress, and nationalist internationalism disseminated in numerous U.S. and Mexican wartime propaganda films and which
¡Mexicanos al grito de guerra! reconstructs as mise-en-scène in dramatizing Juárez's
declaration of defense against European intervention. Record Group 208, National
Archives Still Picture Branch.

and which informed reception of Juárez's declaration of war in *¡Mexicanos
al grito de guerra!*, also leaked into U.S. mass media. It became a dominant
visual trope of Mexico's political transformation during the war toward
moderate domestic policies and pro-U.S. foreign relations, justifying U.S.
aid and responding to the Mexican state's desire to be presented more positively (than during the 1930s) to the U.S. public. The image, for example,
was reproduced in print propaganda generated by the U.S. government (see
Figure 20).

This dissemination was not limited to strictly government propaganda.
It also permeated, for example, the pseudo-documentary, newsreel-style

March of Time (which collaborated closely with the OCIAA). Its "Tomorrow's Mexico" (1946) issue, produced in consultation with the Mexican government, reproduced the same footage of Avila Camacho's speech, which the narrator explained represented the Mexican state's shift rightward from cardenismo's leftist nationalism, disparaged in earlier *March of Time* releases: "There stepped into office in 1940 a political moderate, Manuel Avila Camacho. As he took over, the new president was hailed as a man with a middle-of-the-road position, likely to slow down the tempo of reform and consolidate the gains of his predecessor. But the course of Avila Camacho's administration was to be altered by the spread of war to the Western Hemisphere." The film then segues to a poster proclaiming "El Grito de Guerra" and then to pro-war Mexican military parades and public rallies (reminiscent of *¡Espionaje en el golfo!*'s concluding sequence) as the narrator explains how the war shifted public opinion toward the United States: "As Mexico declared war on the Axis, its people found themselves fighting not against the United States, which they had so long feared, but side by side with it." The twenty-minute film then goes on to detail Mexico's economic and diplomatic cooperation with the United States.[58] And in so doing, Mexican and U.S. authorities appropriated and transformed the centralist wartime discourse of official nationalism, reproduced in *¡Mexicanos al grito de guerra!*, to support internationalism (and tourism) in "Tomorrow's Mexico" and other audiovisual productions.[59]

Like Warner Bros.' *Juarez*, *¡Mexicanos al grito de guerra!* depicts Mexican conservatives as protofascists who exhibit racist attitudes toward Indians and mestizos. In a scene set in Chapultepec Park, Luis, accompanied by a group of indigenously attired musicians, serenades the object of his desire, Ester (played by Lina Montes), the niece of a French official in Mexico, the aristocrat Conde Dubois. Whiter than the musicians, his gesture locates liberal constructions of Mexican nationality in popular culture and indigenous society. Sandoval studies European music but his soul is Mexican; he personifies the liberal fusion of Western and indigenous ideals. By contrast, Alberto (Núñez Keith), the conservative creole who escorts Ester, derides the local music. The dandy further insults Luis by tossing him some coins to share with the musicians for their song. Standing for the supposed egalitarian individualism of the liberal cause, Luis returns his romantic rival's insult, dismissing the fop and his crowd as "los aristócratas."[60] In the liberal meritocracy, according to the film, social mobility includes love; a man from Luis's common (economic and ethnic) station can compete for the affection of an upper-class, white *extranjera*, just as he can earn a superior education, despite his humble background.

Although the United States is absent, the international romance foregrounds France (underlining Mexico's wartime mobilization in support of its liberation) by personifying it as a beautiful woman whose ideals and affections lead her not only to choose Luis over Alberto but also to support Mexico over France. This technique of sexualizing international relations paralleled Hollywood's practice of offering positive, but subordinate, representations of other nations.[61] Demonstrating a pervasive intertexuality, it was prevalent in Mexico's pro-war films, too, typically employed to personify the United States in a favorable light while remasculating Mexican identity. It was a counterdiscourse to Hollywood's dominant prewar and wartime genderings of Mexico, Mexicans, and cross-cultural encounters with U.S. Anglos: prior to the war most Mexicans and Mexican Americans were lowly males; during the war more positive representations featured female characters, beautiful, light-skinned latinas who personified Latin America more positively, now as objects of desire rather than derision (but in a passive role that gendered the United States as male subject and the Latin Americans as female objects, thereby reproducing international power in less denigrating but no less unequal terms as had earlier Hollywood practice). Meanwhile, Mexican cinema inverted political and economic relations via gendered representational practices that had Mexican males conquer gringas (Mexican American women) and retain the attraction of mexicanas wooed by visiting gringos (as, for example, in *¡Espionaje en el golfo!*).[62]

Ester defies her uncle (and her native country) to risk her life to inform Luis of the impending French invasion. Similarly, Luis has defied the conservative politics of his father to join the liberals, demonstrating that national honor (or, at least, political identity) supersedes family ties.[63] His filial loyalty to his Catalán mentor Nunó preserves his position as good son, and also serves as a metonymy for the Cárdenas administration's welcome of thousands of Republican Spanish refugees following Franco's fascist victory a few years earlier. The film thus further links the state's contemporary antifascism (not a point of popular consensus) to traditional signs of Mexican patriotism through its construction of the himno's history.

In contrast to upper-class creoles, the film portrays mestizo workers as naturally inclined toward the linked values of nationalism and liberal reform. A street peddler (played by Armando Soto la Marina) plants himself outside a salon where conservative conspirators plot how to use Mexico's debt, accumulated by their rightist leaders, to provoke their French allies to overthrow Juárez. As with Alberto's attitude toward popular music, the traitorous elites disdain the vendor's Mexican snacks. A born nationalist, the *ambulante* eavesdrops on the reactionaries' meeting. He finds his way to Benito Juárez's headquarters where, in contrast to conservative president Miramón, the liberal leader (of Zapotec extraction) is accessible to the average man: "Are you not a president for the people? I am of the people," the plebeian addresses Juárez before informing him of the plot hatched by "enemies of the *patria*."[64]

In seeking official permission to develop its film, Producciones Rodríguez Hermanos explained to Avila Camacho that, in contrast to the film's self-important symbol of reaction, Santa Anna, "the great Indian from Guelatao, Don Benito Juárez, will be presented in the film with his strong reformist figure."[65] Neither the liberal expropriation of peasant lands in the name of economic progress (which led some Indian communities in central Mexico to contribute forces to conservative armies during the French intervention),[66] nor juarismo's radical anticlericalism and expropriation of Indian lands, which likewise alienated peasants, are addressed. In fact, the film actually links its nationalist allegory to pro-clerical sentiment. As González Bocanegra lies on his deathbed just prior to liberal triumph, he gazes not at images of Hidalgo (which had earlier inspired his verse) but at a figure of Christ on the crucifix, which appears in close-up.[67] (Earlier, his future wife, Lupe, lit a candle in front of an icon of the Virgin of Guadalupe as she prayed for the adoption of her *novio*'s work as the nation's anthem.)[68] More than simply comparing the poet's death to Christ's martyrdom, the image suggests the coexistence of Catholicism and liberal nationalism, thereby expanding the film's message of social and ideological inclusion.[69] This fit well with Avila Camacho's own attempts (signaled by his campaign declaration *Soy creyente*) to demonstrate his abandonment of anticlericalism—central to the revolution's ideology and postrevolutionary state's policies during the preceding Calles and Cárdenas epochs. As the administration sought to expand its support among pro-clerical constituencies, the war provided an opportunity to accelerate the state's accommodation of the Church. Popular culture provided the means to propagandize that shift.[70]

The film also offers historical examples, relevant for World War II, of how nationalism produces political conversions. When the French invasion begins, a few prominent conservatives join liberals to defend their common patria, including Luis's romantic rival, Alberto. Although he has lost Ester to the middling mestizo, the creole now joins Luis in defense of the nation against foreign intervention. Alberto's political transformation demonstrates that the struggle for sovereignty takes precedence over social, ideological, and personal differences, forging unity in the cause of national honor. European intervention, then, is the catalyst for cross-cultural and cross-class alliances demonstrated in the film's representation of the liberal army's Cinco de Mayo victory at Puebla in 1862. The film's screenwriter promised Avila Camacho that the defense of a just and progressive state against foreign intervention would be spectacularly dramatized in "the battle of 5 May, glorious historic epic to which we are dedicating very special care."[71] The climactic fifteen-minute sequence's reenactment of the legendary conflict draws on examples from a range of social stereotypes to emphasize the liberal army's composition as a cross-section of citizen volunteers, including entire Indian communities, urban mestizos, and various creole elites. The sequence highlights social inclusion and national consensus through its personification of patriotic sacrifice, as key characters fall on the field of battle: the upper-class criollo (Alberto), the acculturated middle-class mestizo (Luis), the lower-class mestizo (the food peddler), and finally the elder Luis Sandoval, who is shot in the back by "the evil French" when he finally heeded the call of the nation and abandons the traitorous conservatives. Identification with the himno expresses their common national identity. When a youth is shot dead while playing the himno, Luis picks up his bugle and completes the anthem, drowning out the "Marseillaise" and inspiring wounded and tired patriots to fight on. Only with the anthem performed and victory assured does Luis succumb to a French bullet. In the final scene, he dies in the arms of Ester, who has (of course) rushed to him, and beside his father: past and future reconciled—through war—in the name of national unity and the liberal state.

Unlike earlier cinematic representations of the Juárez myth, whether Warner Bros.' production or two earlier Mexican interpretations, Miguel Contreras Torres's *Juárez y Maximiliano* (1933) and its English-language Good Neighbor remake *The Mad Empress* (1939),[72] *¡Mexicanos al grito de guerra!* ends with the 1862 victory over the French, well short of the eventual 1867 defeat (and execution) of Emperor Maximilian, which concluded the earlier U.S. and Mexican features. By preempting France's imposition of the

Hapsburg Emperor Maximilian, the story sidesteps some ideologically messy issues: Maximilian's social progressivism, his execution on Juárez's orders, and how the liberal victory at Puebla (led by the young general Porfirio Díaz) paved the way for the Porfirian state, the overthrow of which by the Mexican Revolution gave birth to the present-day system (the film supports). The film's premiere at rising Mexican media magnate (and OCIAA collaborator) Emilio Azcárraga's Cine Alameda underlined its importance for the contemporary situation and the deepening links between the state and film sector in constructing political propaganda.[73] President Avila Camacho, members of his cabinet, foreign diplomats, and a contingent of cadets from the Colegio Militar attended the festive opening.[74] *¡Mexicanos al grito de guerra!*, however, also exemplified the transnational industrial and ideological web that surrounded Mexican film production during World War II. It typified the wartime state's emphasis on patriotism as a way both to sell a skeptical public its pro-U.S. foreign policies through nationalist imagery and to weave a domestic political consensus from the frayed social fabric of the 1930s (and the popularly contested 1940 "election"). As Luis Medina has put it: "If it is true that the government of Manuel Avila Camacho has been characterized as an epoch of conciliation and unity, in which the forces of the right were counterbalanced by those of the left, almost always to the detriment of the militancy and combativeness of the latter, it is also true that all had been produced by a situation of international emergency."[75]

¡Mexicanos al grito de guerra!'s premiere coincided with the nation's most important holiday, its commemoration of independence from Spain (the himno's very theme). As residents of Mexico City prepared for the president's annual midnight reenactment of Father Hidalgo's 16 September 1810 grito de guerra, they also read an array of newspaper advertisements announcing a special one-day (15 September 1943) preview prior to its first run a month later (see Figure 21). Its premiere preceded by two days that of *¡Espionaje en el golfo!*, another feature (also focused on foreign intervention near Veracruz) that even more directly than *¡Mexicanos al grito de guerra!* presented antifascist nationalism to justify political consensus in support of the regime. Its run began on 17 September, the day after the Independence celebration (see Figure 22). At the same time that Mexico City residents could read side-by-side ads for *¡Mexicanos al grito de guerra!* and *¡Espionaje en el golfo!*, they also saw listings for U.S.-produced antifascist propaganda, such as Warner Bros.' *Misión en Moscú* (*Mission to Moscow*), based on ex-

21. October 1943
newspaper ads for
¡Mexicanos al grito de
guerra!'s first run an-
nounced its successful
special premiere a
month earlier, on the
eve of Mexico's annual
independence celebra-
tions. Excélsior, 18 October 1943, sec. 1, p. 12.

ambassador Joseph Davies's pro-Soviet memoir of his tenure as Franklin
Roosevelt's envoy to Stalin (see Figure 23). Hence, ¡Mexicanos al grito de
guerra!'s reception must be understood in the context of other antifascist
Mexican and U.S. propaganda across various mass media. The film's producers were sensitive to popular resistance to such U.S. connections; from
the start of ¡Mexicanos al grito de guerra!'s first run, its newspaper ads dis-
claimed: "It is not a propaganda film, it is the supreme glorification of the
himno" (see Figure 23).

The himno itself became the subject of a wartime campaign that promoted the anthem as a source of political integration. Mass culture, particularly film, was mobilized in this effort. Numerous U.S. and Mexican
government-made, nontheatrical shorts (on a wide variety of subjects) cli-
max with the anthem.[76] And the Secretaría de Educación Pública (SEP)
oversaw production and dissemination of documentaries about the music
itself. (The song's control by the state was such that the producers of Escua-
drón 201 [1945], dramatizing the efforts of Mexican pilots over the Philip-

pines, petitioned Avila Camacho to intervene with the SEP to obtain permission to use the music in their film's sound track.)[77] The himno (and Juárez), prerevolutionary symbols of patriotic consensus (less controversial than revolutionary signs), were utilized in Mexican cinema to propagandize the state's wartime foreign and domestic policies and its broader claim to define nationalism. In so doing, the film illustrates Mexican cultural critic Roger Bartra's observations about how the postrevolutionary state has manipulated popular culture to effect legitimacy through an "explosion of myths," promoting "the idea of a fusion between the masses and the state, between the *Mexican* people and the *revolutionary* government."[78] To sell such a myth, to invent such a tradition, to foment national mobilization in support of alliance with the very government whose previous violations of Mexican sovereignty were at the core of prewar official ideology, wartime propaganda turned to a prerevolutionary allegory. That allegory intended to conceal the transnational changes underway in Mexican development and especially the state's role in promoting those transformations linking Mexico to the United States with profound sociocultural as well as economic and political consequences.

22. Newspaper advertisement announcing *¡Mexicanos al grito de guerra!*'s special one-day premiere at Emilio Azcárraga's Cine Alameda. It was timed to coincide with 1943's grito celebration, as was *¡Espionaje en el golfo!*'s first run. The *¡Mexicanos!* ad announces that the producers "Present the signal work of national cinema." *Excélsior*, 15 September 1943, sec. 1, p. 12.

23. Side-by-side advertisements for Mexican and Hollywood commercially produced pro-war features. This publicity both marked and masked the transnational
system of production and international collaboration that linked the two nations'
film industries. *¡Mexicanos al grito de guerra!*'s ad insists "No es una película de
propaganda, es la suprema glorificación del Himno" (It's not a propaganda film; it's
the supreme glorification of the National Anthem). *Excélsior*, 22 October 1943, sec.
2, p. 4.

Final Threads: Los Dos Luis

Yet it is not simply as an example of international propaganda that *¡Mexicanos al grito de guerra!* instructs. The film projects other processes under-
girding mass cultural production in Mexico onto the screen of history. The
Golden Age nationalism of Mexican cinema was, at neither industrial nor
cultural levels, a nationalist project, unless one accepts official definitions of
nationalism that justify the rule of the state party. This is not to reduce film
relations to a simple structuralist refashioning of cultural imperialism. It
was not. It *is* to recognize the value of Argentine film theorist Octavio Getino's observations about the internalization of external forces in the development of seemingly national cinemas in Latin America, without suc-
cumbing to what I see as a too simple equation of dependent industrial

production with sociocultural subjugation. Nor, in the same vein, should we overestimate (or romanticize) the possibility, or even value, of a purely Mexican or Latin American (or for that matter African, Asian, European, or North American) cinema.[79]

At the level of audience reception, however, the mass entertainments of Mexican cinema did produce a popular nationalism, one engendering at times counterhegemonic readings, not just in response to the overtly subversive parodies of Cantinflas, but also less obviously (and maybe more devastatingly) in the machismo of Infante's galanos. This space was potentially more significant than, say, the highly stylized official iconography produced by Emilio Fernández or, for that matter, the populist versions of official discourse directed by Alejandro Galindo (so often praised in First and Second World War postwar film culture). Those films, in terms of content and form, took on the project of ¡Mexicanos al grito de guerra!, the legitimation of the state's project.[80] They did so by means of the Spanish-speaking world's most important film industry in the 1940s, which was a key source of international prestige and an officially promoted sign of cultural and economic modernity, as well as a dominant form of political communication for the postwar state.

To focus only on producers (far easier to research than consumers) of mass culture is to miss the significance of the postage stamps, with which we began, for untangling the dense knot of national reception of Golden Age Mexican cinema (regardless of its hybrid machinery, vocabulary, ideology). The development of national popular culture was (and is) distinct from its origins in a transnational matrix of economic and political forces. And the contemporary impact of Mexican cinema of the 1940s defies its production. One thing that is clear is that the project to advance Mexican film production during the war, in order to produce propaganda such as ¡Mexicanos al grito de guerra!, furthered the development of an already thriving transnational audience for Mexican film. The spectator, ultimately, constructs meaning. As the cultural historian Roger Chartier has put it, "Reading, viewing and listening are, in fact, so many intellectual attitudes which, far from subjecting consumers to the omnipotence of the ideological or aesthetic message that supposedly conditions them, make possible reappropriation, redirection, defiance, or resistance."[81]

If at the level of production ¡Mexicanos al grito de guerra! can be read as part of the separate but related histories of international propaganda and the Mexican film industry's development, at the level of the audience it was a single entry in the development of a national cinema. It featured a future star—really, secular saint—Pedro Infante, who as much as any other Mexican movie persona forged that cinema's relationship with the viewing public in ways that transcended Mexico's social diversity and geographic boundaries. (On this subject, see Anne Rubenstein's contribution to this volume.) Separate from the intertwined messages of the Mexican and U.S. governments, separate from the mission behind U.S. motion picture aid and the web of dependence it spun about Mexican producers, was the relationship between viewers and *their* movies. It is not likely that ¡*Mexicanos al grito de guerra!*, by itself at least, made many more pro-war or, for that matter, more pro-state, but the film's message was part of the price Mexican producers gladly paid (to U.S. and Mexican authorities) for their industry's wartime modernization and expansion.

But no matter how tied Mexican film producers were to the United States (*and* the Mexican state), audiences ultimately produced film culture. That relationship between audience and film transcends, of course, official objectives, just as it has outlasted the Golden Age of Mexican cinema. And the power of the popular nationalism, epitomized by Infante, has been recognized by official Mexico, which has scrambled to appropriate it ever since the star's untimely death in a 1957 aviation accident. His funeral, attended by the nation's leading political, cultural, and entertainment figures, laid the groundwork for his apotheosis as arguably the leading symbol of postwar Mexican popular culture. Into the 1990s, the anniversary of the star's death was commemorated annually by officially sanctioned public ceremonies, including gigantic outdoor projections of film clips and motorcycle demonstrations by fans clad in costumes reminiscent of *A toda máquina* at Mexico City's Monumento de la Revolución Mexicana. Such displays demonstrate how popular culture merges with official constructions of Mexican nationalism in the state's recognition of the power of Golden Age Mexican cinema's most enduring legend.

Rendering visible the transnational structure of the film system that created Infante renders visible as well transnational dimensions of postrevolutionary foreign policy and political economy. The products of that cultural infrastructure were designed to disguise that international logic, to distract from the rightist turn of national policy and reconfiguration of official rhetoric to support transnational structures of social and political power. In this way, in terms of image and ideology, Golden Age Mexican cinema conformed (at the level of production, if not necessarily reception) to the same limits imposed on its industrial development by the nation's political economy. U.S. hegemony alone did not set these limits; by 1945 Mexican elite aspirations were so bound up with U.S. ideological initiatives and transnationalized mass media that the two national projects cannot be easily extricated from one another for analytic purposes. That is, *together* they forged a cultural offensive vis-à-vis the Mexican masses, one which matured during the cold war and continues during the contemporary neoliberal epoch. As Roger Bartra points out in one of this essay's opening epigraphs, the conventionally formulated alternatives of either "'true' popular culture or the transnational invasion of the new mass culture" is a false dichtomy constructed to legitimize dialectically the Mexican state's political authority and its claim to be the representative of national culture. In fact, "current national culture is precisely the amalgam of these two options" which reveal themselves as complementary than oppositional.[82]

This offensive was, then, a hybrid project, combining U.S and Mexican messages, signs, and modes of dissemination, a more contemporary instance, we could say, of Mary Louise Pratt's transculturation.[83] This is not to occlude this system's relationship to the macrostructures of economic dependence, but rather to distinguish the power of culture from any instrumental formulation as a simple derivative of other international inequalities. As Néstor García Canclini has observed: "What we know today about the intercultural operations of the mass media and new technologies, and about the reappropriation that makes of them diverse receivers, distances us from the theses about the omnipotent manipulation of the big metropolitan consortia."[84] From its inception film was a precursor to Jameson's "cultural logic of late capitalism," characterized by semiautonomous (national) representational strategies operating within transnational economic structures.[85] In the case of *¡Mexicanos al grito de guerra!*, this took the form of a nationalist narrative in support of an internationalist ideology. This essay's other (much better) epigraph, the one uttered by Infante in *Los tres García*, alludes to this phenomenon. The Mexican star's sarcastic salute to Pan-Americanism reformulated the unequal terms of U.S.-Mexican socioeconomic integration and interstate collaboration (in no sector more apparent than postwar tourism, in no sector more concealed than postwar cinema) as a Mexican sign of international sexual conquest.

Luis Antonio García's joke at the expense of the United States, like Luis Sandoval's earlier defense against European imperialism, was produced by and reproduced Mexican cinema's transnational logic that pursued its own ideological and commercial objectives within limits imposed by the nation and the state's overall relationship with the United States. This system, which created considerable economic and representational space for national cultural production, exemplified neither cultural imperialism nor nationalism. As Prasenjit Duara put it in his analysis of how early-twentieth-century Chinese regimes captured and reconstructed transnational resources in domestic discourses, "Nationalist ideology develops strategy that will both deploy and overcome its own transnationality."[86] Infante, arguably the preeminent postwar (sex) symbol of Mexican national identity, was a product of such a system, which constructed the internationalist nationalism articulated by Luis Sandoval in *¡Mexicanos al grito de guerra!* as well as the nationalist internationalism expressed by Luis Antonio García in *Los tres García*.

In the cold war, official discourse would be reformulated, again, to support the Mexican state's rightist domestic agenda domestically by equating sociopolitical status quo with socioeconomic "progress" and opposition movements with externally controlled subversives whose rapacious activities undermine "development." Antifascist nationalism became anticommunist, still serving the convergent agendas of the Mexican state and U.S. foreign policy and facilitated by the persistence of industrial-level mass media (especially film) links between the two nations.[87] The logic of Mexican development since the 1940s has led toward the contemporary situation represented by transnational integration and political collaboration with the United States. As I have demonstrated for film, this has allowed room for growth, modernization, and semiautonomous mass cultural production, but within a hemispheric system dominated by the U.S. government and Hollywood.

The postage stamps discussed at this essay's outset (Figure 19), then, are at once ironic and logical; the state's invocation of nationalist nostalgia to distract from the cultural implications of its own neoliberal project depended on symbols themselves produced by a mass media system at the ideological and industrial center of Mexico's transnational political economy. Much like the Avila Camacho administration's simultaneous use of the juarista myth to both sell and conceal its own collaboration with the United States (embedded in *¡Mexicanos al grito de guerra!*'s production as well as displayed through its narrative), the Salinas administration invoked icons of Mexican film's Golden Age to distract from the latest scene in the movie of official U.S.-Mexican collaboration, which opened during World War II and continues today.

Official Mexico's production of mythological markers, of signs of cultural nationalism, reproduces a transnationalized system of production, of which Golden Age cinema is but a fragment. Rather than cultural imperialism, though, it is part of the ideological dialectic of the Mexican state, which depends on pseudo-anti-Americanism to fortify its own rule based on a half-century of elite collaboration with the United States. This "pantheon of myths," to borrow Sergio Aguayo's recent description of postwar Mexican nationalism and U.S.-Mexican relations,[88] is then a hybrid edifice. To return to García Canclini: "It is not simply a question of some forms of domination being superimposed on others and thereby being strengthened. What gives them their efficacy is the obliqueness that is established in the fabric."[89] Examining Golden Age Mexican cinema's hybridity shows transnational power as dialectical, diffuse, dense. *¡Mexicanos al grito de guerra!* is a remnant of that hybrid fabric, itself a part of the more extensive tapestry of Mexican development since the 1940s.

Notes

I thank Joanne Hershfield for her thoughtful comments at the initial Wilson Center presentation of this research, Ian Fletcher for his suggestions in response to that same earlier version, and Andrea Georgalis for her work to digitize the images presented here. All unattributed translations are mine.

1   *Los tres García*, film, dir. Ismael Rodríguez, prod. Rodríguez Hnos., 1946. 21:25–22:30. The epigraph reads: "Long live Pan-Americanism and the closeness of American women!"

2   In fact, Lupita turns out to be the García clan's half-Mexican cousin; her deceased mother was Mexican. Hence, in the end she is a symbol of U.S.-Mexican integration, one who returns to her Mexican heritage, more symbol of cultural reclamation than sexual reconquest.

3   This movement had an analogue in U.S. film (and later television) with the reemergence of the Latin lover as a new postwar stereotype which, I contend, unlike its earlier origins in Hollywood's silent feature film production, enters the United States from Mexican cinema after World War II. For example, a key scene in *March of Time*'s "Tomorrow's Mexico" (1946), 04:30–05:20, discussed (in a different context) later in this essay, reaches into Mexican cinema to produce a representation of a suave Mexican romancing a visiting gringa in a Mexico City nightclub. It is an important precursor to broader intercultural patterns of intertexuality. For a sensitive and original recent analysis of U.S. engagements with the Latin lover, see José Limón, *American Encounters: Greater Mexico, the United States, and the Erotics of Culture* (Boston: Beacon Press, 1998), 137–46.

4   Marcia Landy, *Cinematic Uses of the Past* (Minneapolis: University of Minnesota Press, 1996), 187.

5   For more on this coincidence between Infante's rise and Mexican popular culture in the 1940s, see Seth Fein, "Pedro Infante," in *Encyclopedia of Mexico: History, Society and Culture*, ed. Michael S. Werner (Chicago: Fitzroy Dearborn, 1997), 702–4.

6   I develop these ideas more fully in Seth Fein, "Everyday Forms of Transnational Collaboration: U.S. Film Propaganda in Cold War Mexico," in *Close Encounters of Empire: Writing the Cultural History of U.S.–Latin American Relations*, ed. Gilbert Joseph, Catherine LeGrand, and Ricardo Salvatore (Durham, NC: Duke University Press, 1998), 400–450; many of that volume's other essays also address these issues historically in timely ways. Among recent works particularly helpful in the development of my theoretical thinking about these matters are David Harvey, *The Condition of Postmodernity: An Enquiry into the Origins of Cultural Change* (Cambridge, England: Blackwell, 1990); William Roseberry, *Anthropologies and Histories: Essays in Culture, History, and Political Economy* (New Brunswick, NJ: Rutgers University Press, 1989); John Tomlinson, *Cultural Imperialism: A Critical Introduction* (Baltimore: Johns Hopkins University Press, 1991); Frederick Buell, *National Culture and the New Global System* (Baltimore: Johns Hopkins University Press, 1994); Néstor García Canclini, *Hybrid Cultures: Strategies for Entering and Leaving Modernity*, trans. Christopher L. Chiappari and Silvia L. López (Minneapolis: University of Minnesota Press, 1995); Octavio Getino, *Cine latinoamericano: Economía y nuevas tecnologías audiovisuales* (Mexico City: Trillas, 1990).

7   On the dilemmas posed to culture industries in the era of NAFTA, see Emile G. McAnany and Kenton T. Wilkinson, eds., *Mass Media and Free Trade: NAFTA and the Cultural Industries* (Austin: University of Texas Press, 1996).

8   See Seth Fein, "From Collaboration to Containment: Hollywood and the International Political Economy of Mexican Cinema after the Second World War," in *Mexico's Cinema: A Century of Films and Filmmakers*, ed. Joanne Hershfield and David Maciel (Wilmington, DE: Scholarly Resources, 1999), 123–64.

9   See Seth Fein, "Hollywood and United States–Mexican Relations in the Golden Age of Mexican Cinema" (Ph.D. diss., University of Texas at Austin, 1996) chap. 5, for detailed analysis of the everyday wartime intervention of the U.S. government and Hollywood in Mexican film production (at the studio level) and the role of the Mexican state, producers, and organized labor in that process.

10   Whitney backed David Selznick's *Gone with the Wind* (1939) and headed the Museum of Modern Art's Film Library in the 1930s, which was central to the Rockefeller Foundation's prewar visual education initiatives in Latin America. See ibid., 253–65.

11   See Blanca Torres, *Historia de la Revolución Mexicana, 1940–1952: México en la segunda guerra mundial* (Mexico City: El Colegio de México, 1979); Steven R. Niblo, *War, Diplomacy, and Development: United States–Mexican Relations, 1938–1945* (Wilmington, DE: Scholarly Resources, 1995), and *Mexico in the 1940s: Modernity, Politics, and Corruption* (Wilmington, DE: Scholarly Resources, 1999); María Emilia Paz, *Strategy, Security, and Spies: Mexico and the U.S. as Allies in World War II* (University Park: Pennsylvania State University Press, 1997).

12   See Fein, "From Collaboration to Containment," 137–42.

13   See Donald W. Rowland, *History of the Office of the Coordinator of Inter-American Affairs* (Washington, DC: U.S. Government Printing Office, 1947), for an overview of the OCIAA's work; see, too, J. Manuel Espinosa, *Inter-American Beginnings of U.S. Cultural Diplomacy, 1936–1945* (Washington, DC: Bureau of Educational and Cultural Affairs, U.S. Department of State, 1976). For a survey of the OCIAA's cultural work in Mexico, see José Luis Ortiz Garza, *México en guerra: La historia secreta de los negocios entre empresarios mexicanos de la comunicación, los nazis y E.U.A.* (Mexico City: Planeta, 1989).

14   George Messersmith to Laurence Duggan, 18 June 1942, National Archives Record Group 84 (NARG 84), Mexico City Embassy General Records (MCEGR), 840.6–MP.

15   For example, Fouce advised Hollywood on how to represent Mexico and Pancho Villa in the early 1930s, as several studios considered production of a feature about the *norteño* revolutionary; MGM finally made *Viva Villa!* (1934). See Seth Fein, "El cine y las relaciones culturales entre México y Estados Unidos durante la década 1930," *Secuencia* 34 (spring 1996): 161–62.

16   Nelson Rockefeller to George Messersmith, 5 March 1942, NARG 84, MCEGR, 840.6-MP-Breen and Fouce.

17   "Alstock Working out Helping Hand for Mexican Prodc'n," *Hollywood Reporter*, 2 April 1942.

18   Edward G. Trueblood to George Messersmith, 13 March 1942, NARG 84, MCEGR, 840.6-MP-Breen and Fouce.

19   "Visit of Messrs. Breen and Fouce, Motion Picture Executive, to Mexico City to Discuss Establishment of Local Motion Picture Industry," Guy Ray to State Department, NARG 84, MCEGR, 840.6-MP-Breen and Fouce.

20   Emily Rosenberg develops this concept, signifying government patronage of a particular private-sector concern in pursuit of strategic objectives, in *Spreading the American Dream: American Economic and Cultural Expansion, 1890–1945* (New York: Hill and Wang, 1982), 59–62.

21   "Summary of Plan to Stimulate Production of Motion Pictures by Mexican Industry in Support of War Effort," OCIAA, Motion Picture Division, Philip Bonsal, Division of the American Republics, to John Dreier, 23 May 1942, NARG 59, Central Files of the Department of State, 812.4061-MP/269.

22   In 1943, the United States "shipped 25,000,000 feet of raw film to Argentina, low enough so that Mexico could move into top place in the Latin field." See Florence S. Lowe, "Washington Hullabaloo," *Variety* (daily), 10 April 1944.

23   "Summary of Plan to Stimulate Production," NARG 59, 812.4061-MP/269.

24   On the general context of intraregional economic relations during the war, see Victor Bulmer-Thomas, *The Economic History of Latin America Since Independence* (New York: Cambridge University Press, 1994), 239–48; also Rosemary Thorp, "The Latin American Economies in the 1940s," in *Latin America in the 1940s: War and Postwar Transitions*, ed. David Rock (Berkeley: University of California Press, 1992), 45–53.

25   Two key works outlining Hollywood's non–Latin American collaboration with U.S. propaganda during World War II are Thomas Doherty, *Projections of War: Hollywood, Amer-*

ican Culture, and World War II (New York: Columbia University Press, 1993), which offers a comprehensive portrait of commercial and nontheatrical production; and Clayton Koppes and Gregory Black, *Hollywood Goes to War: How Hollywood, Profits and Propaganda Shaped World War II Movies* (Berkeley: University of California Press, 1990), which focuses on particular theatrical releases and the Office of War Information's interactions with major U.S. studios.

26 Transcript of unpublished 1972 oral history with Enrique Solís, conducted by Aurelio de los Reyes for the Instituto Nacional de Antropología e Historia, Archivo de la Palabra, Instituto Mora (Mexico City), PHO/2/8, 100–105.

27 Francis Alstock to Nelson Rockefeller, 26 May 1942, Rockefeller Archive Center, Pocantico Hills, New York, Record Group III-4-O, Box 7, Folder 56.

28 15 June 1942 Mexico City Agreement signed by Whitney, Alstock, Castillo, de Fuentes, and Solís, NARG 229, Records of the Office of the Coordinator of Inter-American Affairs, Motion Picture Division (MPD), Entry 77, Box 945, File MP-1332.

29 Ibid.

30 "Project of the Office of the Coordinator of Inter-American Affairs to Assist in the Development of the Mexican Motion Picture Industry in Support of the War Effort and Hemispheric Solidarity," 3 (15 June 1942, annex), enclosed with Neave to Fouce, 15 May 1943, NARG 84, MCEGR, 840.6-MP.

31 For a full discussion of how this international censorship and production machinery worked, see Seth Fein, "Transnationalization and Cultural Collaboration: 'Mexican' Cinema and the Second World War," *Studies in Latin American Popular Culture* 17 (1998): 105–28.

32 Fernando Coronil, *The Magical State: Nature, Money, and Modernity in Venezuela* (Chicago: University of Chicago Press, 1997), especially chap. 4.

33 On the early industry's production ties to the state and the state's struggle with Hollywood, see Fein, "Hollywood and United States–Mexico Relations," chaps. 2, 3. For a stimulating analysis of the connections between historical filmic representation and political power in 1930s Mexico, see John Mraz, "How Real Is Reel? Fernando de Fuentes's Revolutionary Trilogy," in *Framing Latin American Cinema: Contemporary Critical Perspectives*, ed. Ann Marie Stock (Minneapolis: University of Minnesota Press, 1997), 92–121.

34 See Fein, "El cine y las relaciones culturales entre México y Estados Unidos durante la década 1930," 155–95; on the transition to transnational propaganda production during World War II, see Fein, "La imagen de México: La segunda guerra mundial y la propaganda fílmica de Estados Unidos," in *México–Estados Unidos: Encuentros y desencuentros en el cine*, ed. Ignacio Durán, Iván Trujillo, Mónica Verea (Mexico City: IMCINE/UNAM, 1996), 41–59.

35 On the development of antifascist propaganda in Mexico during the later years of the Cárdenas administration, see Friedrich E. Schuler, *Mexico Between Hitler and Roosevelt: Mexican Foreign Relations in the Age of Lázaro Cárdenas, 1934–1940* (Albuquerque: University of New Mexico Press, 1998), 146–51.

36 On *Juarez*'s Mexican reception, see Fein, "United States–Mexico Relations," 265–76; see, too, Paul Vanderwood's analysis of the international relations surrounding the movie's

production in "The Image of Mexican Heroes in American Films," *Film-Historia* 3, no. 2 (1992): 221–44; and Ruth Vasey, *The World According to Hollywood, 1918–1939* (Madison: University of Wisconsin Press, 1997), 204.

37 Landy, *Cinematic Uses of the Past*, 67–106; citation is from 106. Notable are her conclusions about how European-U.S. relations and modern Italian history converged within the cinematic terrain of Sergio Leone's spaghetti westerns.

38 See "'¡Mexicanos al Grito de Guerra!' Será Producida por los Hermanos Rodríguez," *El Cine Gráfico* (21 June 1942): 2. In 1942, Rodríguez Hermanos submitted to the U.S. embassy a treatment by Gálvez y Fuentes carrying the same title for a film based on the sinking of the *Potrero del Llano*. Following some significant changes, especially in the way the story gendered U.S.-Mexican relations, it became the basis for *¡Espionaje en el golfo!* (1942), produced by Raúl de Anda; see Fein, "Transnationalization and Cultural Collaboration."

39 *¡Mexicanos al grito de guerra!*, dir. Ismael Rodríguez, prod. Rodríguez Hnos., 1943, 31:00–31:40.

40 See reports from RKO, Warner Bros., United Artists, and Columbia Pictures in "Reaction to Films" file, March and April 1941, NARG 229, Entry 1, Box 214.

41 A popular history of the himno first published in 1954 remains in print, available at Mexico City subway kiosks: J. Cid y Mulet, *México en un himno: Génesis e historia del Himno Nacional Mexicano*, 6th ed. (Mexico City: Costa-Amic Editores, 1994).

42 *¡Mexicanos al grito de guerra!*, 00:26.

43 Benedict Anderson, *Imagined Communities: Reflections on the Origins and Spread of Nationalism* (London: Verso, 1983). See Hobsbawm's introduction to Eric J. Hobsbawm and Terence O. Ranger, eds., *The Invention of Tradition* (Cambridge, England: Cambridge University Press, 1983).

44 See Alan Knight, "Racism, Revolution, and Indigenismo: Mexico, 1910–1940," in *The Idea of Race in Latin America, 1870–1940*, ed. Richard Graham (Austin: University of Texas Press, 1990), 71–113.

45 Jesús Martín Barbero, *Communication, Culture and Hegemony: From the Media to Mediations*, trans. Elizabeth Fox and Robert A. White (London: Sage Publications, 1993), 153.

46 *¡Mexicanos al grito de guerra!*, 17:11–19:20.

47 Ibid., 11:49–17:12.

48 Homi K. Bhabha, *The Location of Culture* (London: Routledge, 1994), 147.

49 Wartime censorship also expressed this irony; the Secretaría de Relaciones Exteriores prohibited production of a pro-war documentary-style film based on the petroleum nationalization, proposed by the politically influential Mexican film concern (España-México-Argentina) because, despite its intentions, it might have disrupted relations with the United States. See Fein, "Transnationalization and Cultural Collaboration," 120–21.

50 *¡Mexicanos al grito de guerra!*, 41:34–42:34.

51 Ibid., 45:20–53:00.

52 The film underlines this connection between national identity and cultural expression when the European powers intervene at Veracruz and France's minister, Conde Dubois, proclaims that Mexico has no national anthem because it is not a true nation. See *¡Mexicanos al grito de guerra!*, 1:01:37–1:02:40.

Golden Age Mexican Cinema 195

53 Ibid., 34:00–34:30.

54 Ibid., 1:00:35–1:01:38.

55 *Juarez*, dir. William Dieterle, prod. Warner Brothers, 1939. 08:26.

56 By thickly underlining the British commander's respect for Mexican sovereignty, the film rehabilitates Great Britain, a World War II ally, from negative images propagated after London's intransigent position in rejecting Mexican compensation following the 1938 expropriation of British oil holdings.

57 *¡Mexicanos al grito de guerra!*, 1:02:41–1:06:02.

58 "Tomorrow's Mexico," *March of Time* 12, no. 10 (1946): 09:57–12:59.

59 See Fein, "La imagen de México," 55–58.

60 *¡Mexicanos al grito de guerra!*, 22:00–24:32.

61 For a provocative gendered reading of film as international relations, see Emily Rosenberg, " 'Foreign Affairs' after World War II: Connecting Sexual and International Politics," *Diplomatic History* 18, no. 1 (winter 1994): 59–70; also see Julianne Burton-Carvajal, " 'Surprise Package': Looking Southward with Disney," in *Disney Discourse: Producing the Magic Kingdom*, ed. Eric Smoodin (New York: Routledge, 1994), 131–47; Ana M. López, "Are All Latins from Manhattan? Hollywood, Ethnography, and Cultural Colonialism," in *Unspeakable Images: Ethnicity and the American Cinema*, ed. Lester D. Friedman (Urbana: University of Illinois, 1991), 404–24; Chon Noriega, "Citizen Chicano: The Trials and Titillations of Ethnicity in the American Cinema, 1935–1962," *Social Research* 58, no. 2 (summer 1991): 413–38; and, for an encyclopedic source of images, Alfred Charles Richard Jr., *Censorship and Hollywood's Hispanic Image: An Interpretive Filmography, 1936–1955* (Westport, CT: Greenwood Press, 1993).

62 See Fein, "Transnationalization and Cultural Collaboration," "La imagen de México," and "Hollywood and U.S.–Mexican Relations," chaps. 4, 6. Also see David Edward Wilt, "Stereotyped Images of United States Citizens in Mexican Cinema, 1930–1990" (Ph.D. diss., University of Maryland, 1991).

63 *¡Mexicanos al grito de guerra!*, 56:54–57:59. The film rationalizes Ester's betrayal of France in a way reminiscent of Hollywood's depiction of (Nazi) Germany (although not Japan) in its World War II films; it equates the French intervention with Napoleon, his rightist faction (and their Mexican allies), rather than with the entire French nation.

64 *¡Mexicanos al grito de guerra!*, 45:20–53:00. Similarly, a carriage driver employed by Conde Dubois abandons the aristocrat when Ester explains that France intends to invade. Not only does he rush her to Puebla to warn Zaragoza of the impending attack, but the elderly commoner impulsively joins the liberal army (1:14:34–1:14:54).

65 Roberto Rodríguez to Manuel Avila Camacho, 25 June 1943, Archivo General de la Nación (AGN), Mexico City, Fondo Presidentes, Ramo Avila Camacho, 523.3/51.

66 See Florencia Mallon, *Peasant and Nation: The Making of Postcolonial Mexico and Peru* (Berkeley: University of California Press, 1995), 137–75.

67 *¡Mexicanos al grito de guerra!*, 1:00:31.

68 Ibid., 35:10.

69 This connection is further reinforced when General Zaragoza names General Porfirio

Díaz's forces after the Virgin of Guadalupe, as he concludes his grito with the assembled liberal troops before battle at Puebla (ibid., 1:15:38–1:16:59). This also resonated with widely available film images of Avila Camacho's grito from the balcony of the National Palace in May 1942 (in a ceremony of national unity in support of World War II) in which all of Mexico's living ex-presidents stood beside him.

70 See Marjorie Becker, *Setting the Virgin on Fire: Lázaro Cárdenas, Michoacán Peasants, and the Redemption of the Mexican Revolution* (Berkeley: University of California Press, 1995), 129–32.

71 Rodríguez to Avila Camacho.

72 *The Mad Empress*, featuring Jason Robards as Juárez, was a disaster on several levels. See Fein, "Hollywood and United States–Mexico Relations," 276–78.

73 Azcárraga, postwar founder of Televisa, was a key Mexican facilitator of OCIAA programs (which benefited the development of his own media empire). Building on his preexisting radio interests, he came to dominate Mexican mass culture as he entered film production as the partner of RKO in Estudios Churubusco, Latin America's most important postwar studio and also a site of transnational cold war propaganda production, as I have analyzed elsewhere. See Seth Fein, "Transcultured Anticommunism: Cold War Hollywood in Postwar Mexico," in *Visible Nations: Latin American Cinema and Video*, ed. Chon Noriega (Minneapolis: University of Minnesota Press, 1999), 82–111. On Azcárraga's radio relations with the U.S. government during the war, see José Luis Ortiz Garza, *La guerra de las ondas* (Mexico City: Planeta, 1992).

74 Alvaro Gálvez y Fuentes to Avila Camacho, 9 October 1943, AGN, Ramo Avila Camacho, 523.3/51.

75 Luis Medina, *Historia de la revolución mexicana, 1940–1952: Civilismo y modernización* (Mexico City: El Colegio de México, 1979), 5–6.

76 See Fein, "Imagen de México," 54–55.

77 Adalberto Menéndez, Assistant Manager, Films Mundiales, S.A., to Avila Camacho, 1 December 1945, AGN, Ramo Avila Camacho, 549.13/1.

78 Roger Bartra, *The Cage of Melancholy: Identity and Metamorphosis in the Mexican Character*, trans. Christopher J. Hall (New Brunswick, NJ: Rutgers University Press, 1992), 164.

79 See Octavio Getino, *Cine y dependencia: El cine en la Argentina* (Buenos Aires: Puntosur, 1990), especially chap. 3.

80 For a critical historical analysis of Galindo's nationalism, see Fein, "Transcultured Anticommunism."

81 Roger Chartier, *Cultural History: Between Practices and Representations*, trans. Lydia F. Cochrane (Cambridge, England: Polity Press, 1988), 41.

82 Bartra, *Oficio mexicano* (Mexico City: Grijalbo, 1993), 37.

83 See Mary Louise Pratt, *Imperial Eyes: Travel Writing and Transculturation* (New York: Routledge, 1992).

84 García Canclini, *Hybrid Cultures*, 206–63; quote appears on 259.

85 See Fredric Jameson, *Postmodernism, or, The Cultural Logic of Late Capitalism* (Durham, NC: Duke University Press, 1991), especially 279–96. For a compelling critique of Jame-

son's ideas regarding film, see Michael Walsh, "Jameson and 'Global Aesthetics'," in *Post-theory: Reconstructing Film Studies*, ed. David Bordwell and Nöel Carrol (Madison: University of Wisconsin Press, 1996), 481–500.

86 Prasenjit Duara, "Transnationalism in the Era of Nation-States: China, 1900–1945," in *Globalization and Identity: Dialectics of Flow and Closure*, ed. Bergit Meyer and Peter Geschiere (Oxford: Blackwell Publishers, 1994), 66.

87 See Fein, "Transcultured Anticommunism."

88 Sergio Aguayo, *El panteón de los mitos: Estados Unidos y el nacionalismo mexicano* (Mexico City: Grijalbo/El Colegio de México, 1998).

89 García Canclini, *Hybrid Cultures*, 259.

Bodies, Cities, Cinema:
Pedro Infante's Death as Political Spectacle
Anne Rubenstein

In 1992 the Museo del Palacio de Bellas Artes offered Mexico City museum-goers an exhibit on city life and popular culture in the twentieth century. It included thousands of artifacts of all kinds, but the crowds who made the show a surprise hit mostly came to see a single photograph: a snapshot of the singer and movie star Pedro Infante taking a shower. More charming than scandalous—soapsuds partially covered the great national hero—the photograph nonetheless created a sensation.[1] From the minute the museum opened every day until it closed, large groups of solemn museum-goers gathered before the photo, either keeping silent or conversing in respectful whispers, before politely giving way to the next group. And so it went for the entire run of the exhibit. Thirty-five years after his death, Pedro Infante's body still mattered.

Pedro Infante's Invisible Body

Pedro Infante sang on the radio, made records, acted in dozens of movies, grew famous, behaved scandalously and got his name in the papers, piloted airplanes and rode motorcycles, made and spent quite a lot of money for the time, and died young, in a plane crash, in 1957. At the time he was a contro-versial figure, notorious for a legal tangle with his first wife and, more gener-ally, as a womanizer. Infante was among the two or three most important male movie stars of the day, but hardly anyone would have predicted the lasting importance of his figure. In the days and decades following his sudden, shocking death, his reputation changed. Infante ceased to be a more or less charming rascal for whom few respectable persons would express admiration in public, and became a kind of secular saint. Along with the masked wrestler El Santo, Pedro Infante is now perhaps the most important male figure in the iconography of Mexican commercial culture, portraying moral and physical perfection as well as deep national pride.[2] He personifies several masculine ideals at once: the *charro* (cowboy) who is also a modern urban man, the macho with a tender heart, the working stiff and the rich guy too. But in all of his guises, Infante represents a living vision of what it might mean to be Mexican.

In the summer of 1998, every Mexican to whom I mentioned the topic I was researching—dozens of people—responded with the same line: "Oh? The death of Pedro Infante? Is he really dead?" This joke, or half-joke, reflected a rumor that has achieved the status of myth. Some people probably do believe that Infante lives on, but everyone believes that somebody believes it. In the 1970s the popular story ran that El Santo *was* Pedro Infante (which helped explain why the heroic wrestler never took off his silver mask).[3] Thus Infante lives on in Mexicans' imaginations.

Whether or not his fans truly are convinced that Infante is still alive, they do participate in maintaining a sort of posthumous existence for him. Fans visit Infante's grave and hometown (sometimes dressed in approximations of his outfits from one of his movie roles), buy video copies of his movies or watch them rerun on television, purchase new CDs of his old records, read books and watch documentaries about their hero, and listen to his songs on the radio. A few people have convinced themselves that they are Infante's mother, or one of his wives, or his child, or the idol himself; more make their living as Infante imitators.

The tale of Infante's life after death can be explained, at least in part, by the fact that his corpse was not displayed at his wake, for the accident that killed him had mangled his remains too badly: the invisibility of Infante's body allowed people to argue that he was not actually present at his funeral, that the whole sad series of events was instead an elaborate conspiracy. The manner of his death, including the violent public reaction to it, helped create the figure that Infante became only after the accident that claimed his life. And a careful examination of the events around Infante's death and burial can reveal much not only about the star's place in Mexican culture but also about the intersections of class and gender in Mexico City at the time—and today.

Funeral/Riot

On April 14, 1957, Infante was copiloting a flight from Mérida, Yucatán, where he had been vacationing at a house he owned near there, to Mexico City, where some urgent legal business awaited him. The four-engine plane (which belonged to a company Infante partially owned) fell from the sky shortly after takeoff, killing all its passengers. Within an hour, Infante's fans were crowding the streets near the accident site; by the next day, greater numbers had camped outside his house in Mérida and the city morgue; meanwhile, in Mexico City, thousands of people were flocking to his house, his mother's house, and his first wife's house, while across the country mourners gathered at movie theaters.

The next day a still larger group accompanied his body from the Mérida morgue to the airport, while somewhere between fifty thousand and a hundred thousand people met the plane carrying his remains at the Mexico City airport when it arrived, just before noon. Newspapers described these mourners, as they characterized all the crowds that gathered that week, as belonging to "the proletarian class," including "children of various ages, peddlers, workers, peasants."[4]

The police had to force their way through this mob to clear a path for the coffin to be carried from a plane to the waiting hearse by "frequently using their nightsticks. They did not strike only at particular persons. At times, they swung wildly, hitting whoever they could. Thus it was that women and children whose only crime was anxiety to attend the funeral of a much-loved actor, wound up driven to their knees on the pavement among screams of pain."[5] And the hearse could barely move through the crowd. (One of the injuries reported in this day's events was caused by this car actually running over one onlooker.)

Outside the airport, the streets too were clogged with mourning fans. That afternoon and throughout the night, perhaps fifty thousand people filed by his closed casket, and even more tried and failed to get into the theater where Infante lay. Some members of the crowd waited for more than twenty-four hours. They prayed, sang, wept, bought and sold snacks and souvenirs, suffered a few cases of sunstroke, and—ominously—resisted police attempts to create an orderly line.

The next morning, the day of Infante's funeral, thousands more were still waiting to pay their last respects to the fallen idol when the hearse arrived to bear his casket to the cemetery. Again, they tried to impede its arrival and

24. The crowd awaiting the arrival of Pedro Infante's body at the Mexico City airport, April 15, 1957. Díaz, Delgado y García archive of the Fototeca of the Archivo General de la Nación, Mexico City. Reprinted by permission.

25. Infante's coffin moves through the Mexico City airport, April 15, 1957. Díaz, Delgado y García archive of the Fototeca of the Archivo General de la Nación, Mexico City. Reprinted by permission.

26. Mourners beside Infante's coffin in the ANDA Teatro Jorge Negrete, April 15, 1957. Infante's mother is at the left of the picture, Irma Dorantes at the right. Note the portrait of Infante in charro regalia propped up against the coffin. Díaz, Delgado y García archive of the Fototeca of the Archivo General de la Nación, Mexico City. Reprinted by permission.

27. The funeral procession on the way to the Panteón Jardín, April 16, 1957. Díaz, Delgado y García archive of the Fototeca of the Archivo General de la Nación, Mexico City. Reprinted by permission.

departure, and again the police intervened violently. The multitude lining the route between the theater and the cemetery made the occasion "seem like a fair," and photos of the day show people hanging out of windows, standing on parked cars and sitting in trees; but, as Infante's body passed by, "an impressive silence fell."[6] Most of the hearse's roughly twelve-kilometer trip southwest from the theater passed peacefully.

Members of the crowd knew where to go to bid Infante farewell. They could assume that his coffin would follow the route taken three years earlier by the cortege of Infante's friend and rival, singer/actor Jorge Negrete. In any case, there was only one logical route southward from the theater where Infante had lain, which belonged to the actors' union ANDA, to ANDA's special section of Mexico City's finest cemetery. (As it happened, Infante was to be buried near but not in the ANDA plot of the Panteón Jardín. But it seems unlikely that many people were aware of this on the morning of his funeral; the newspapers did not report this fact until the next day.) Even those newcomers and visitors who lacked access to all this local knowledge could learn by radio where to go, how to get there, and when to be there; at least one station, the extremely popular XEQ, broadcast nonstop coverage of the events following Infante's death from the moment news of his plane crash reached them until the evening following his funeral, reporting that included detailed information on the sites where his coffin could be glimpsed. All over the city, in stores, restaurants, bars, and the courtyards of apartment buildings, people kept their radios playing to follow these events and join in the collective sorrow and excitement.[7]

The cortege was bearing Infante's body to the Panteón Jardín, where he would be buried in the center of the relatively new cemetery, just downhill from Blanca Estela Pavón, the actress who had costarred in his biggest hit, *Nosotros los pobres*, and its sequel, *Ustedes los ricos*. (Pavón, as all the papers remarked in their reporting on Infante's demise, may or may not have been Infante's lover; by morbid coincidence, she also had perished in a plane crash.) The cemetery, built in the late Porfirian era, suited the needs of Mexico City's dignitaries and wealthy elite. Designed for the public ceremonials of that era, its wide central boulevard led straight up a long hill from the grand, pillared fake-Greek entrance, with smaller paths branching off into neat rows of impressive tombs. But it was not nearly large enough to accommodate the huge numbers of mourners who had begun gathering there hours before Infante's casket was due to arrive. They clung to fences, trampled shrubbery, climbed trees, and even perched on tombstones to find

28. The funeral procession. Díaz, Delgado y García archive of the Fototeca of the Archivo General de la Nación, Mexico City. Reprinted by permission.

29. Infante's coffin passes through the cemetery. Díaz, Delgado y García archive of the Fototeca of the Archivo General de la Nación, Mexico City. Reprinted by permission.

30. Mariachi music accompanies the burial. Díaz, Delgado y García archive of the Fototeca of the Archivo General de la Nación, Mexico City. Reprinted by permission.

space for themselves. In the end, at least 150,000 people attempted to witness the burial in the cemetery, in addition to the people who had attended Infante's body from the airport to the wake, visited his body at the ANDA theater, and lined the route between the theater and the graveyard.

The police tried to keep a small space open for the official mourning party. These mourners included mariachi bands with whom Infante had sung; representatives of the motorcycle police with whom Infante had associated himself; various members of the Mexican film industry, some of whom had been Infante's close friends, others his long-term colleagues, and still others who barely knew him but needed the publicity. And, of course, his family all came: Infante's mother, all his living siblings, their various spouses and children, and some of Infante's young children. His legal spouse, María Luisa León de Infante, attended, but so did the woman whose marriage to Infante had only just been annulled by the Supreme Court as bigamous, Irma Dorantes. Infante's oldest living brother, Angel, carefully kept the two women on opposite sides of the grave.

The crowd knew all about the legal quarrel between Infante's wives, and they had chosen sides. Less than a week earlier, the popular tabloid *La Pren-sa*'s coverage of the bigamy trial had slanted heavily toward María Luisa León, with headlines shouting "Pedro Will Go to Jail" and "Pedro's Wife [meaning María Luisa] Willing to Forgive";[8] so this newspaper displayed particular disgust in reporting that the crowd at the funeral had clearly indicated their preference for Irma Dorantes. It gave an entire article over to the first wife's treatment by the funeral-goers, describing how "various women, above all those from humble backgrounds, besieged [María Luisa León] . . . as they considered her 'a usurper, and responsible for Pedro's problems.' As she walked into the cemetery, María Luisa León heard epithets that were lacerating and cruel. Many women shouted 'hypocrite' at her. Others, more daringly, called her 'shameless.'"[9] When President Ruiz Cortines sent a note of condolence on Infante's death, he sent it to neither Irma Dorantes nor María Luisa León, but to Infante's brother Angel; this, too, indicates the strength of public sentiment about Infante's two wives, its volatility, and its politicized nature.[10]

In response to the police shoving members of the crowd away from Infante's grave and the official members of the mourning party, a melee broke out while the service was still in progress. As a mariachi group continued playing and singing an Infante hit, the police began clubbing funeral-goers and shouting—and the funeral-goers hit back (see Figure 30). Soon enough, much of the crowd was fighting the police or each other. "Thousands of women, children, adults and old people tirelessly battled," according to newspaper accounts; others, attempting to flee, hurt each other in their panic.[11] The riot injured at least 140 people—some newspapers put the number as high as 210 injured funeral-goers—and caused seven people to be hurt seriously enough to require hospitalization. (Most, though, were treated at the scene by the Red Cross medics whom the mayor of Mexico City had requested to attend the funeral; these medics also attended to numerous people suffering from sunstroke and a number of young starlets who staged publicity-catching hysterical fits.) The worst injuries were caused by police nightsticks, but at least one policeman also suffered a beating "at the hands of the multitude."[12] The police arrested twenty-one people, accusing them of "delinquency" but also claiming that they were pickpockets and thieves.[13] Other would-be funeral-goers were "trampled" and "pushed into open graves" by the police or by people running away from the police.[14] The cemetery itself was badly damaged, as angry members of the crowd toppled gravestones and destroyed statuary and others knocked down fences and trampled gardens in their flight. Most newspapers referred to these events as a riot; one called it a "battle."[15]

Mexican elites expressed horror at these events. Perhaps expecting trouble, President Ruiz Cortines and his family and other high-ranking government officials had stayed away from the funeral, though ensuring an ample police presence. Afterward, Salvador Novo (a poet, playwright, and director whose weekly magazine column "Cartas a un amigo" gave voice to Mexico City's high society in this era) sourly punned "for almost a week, as you will have noticed, we all behaved like complete infants."[16] Novo usually marked the deaths of notables with long, emotional reminiscences in his column, so this comment—his only word on the death of Mexico's biggest star—was all the more remarkable. Similarly, *Tiempo* magazine, the Spanish-language edition of the conservative U.S. weekly *Time*, scolded: "At the moment that the coffin was lowered from the airplane . . . there began a demonstration of grief in which fervor, hysteria and mass emotion mixed to offer a spectacle that, if it was enormous in its magnitude, was not at all edifying in its results. . . . As the remains were being moved to the Panteón Jardín, there began fainting fits, inexplicably violent behavior and the excesses of the crowd, which was stirred up by collective hysteria. It was truly lamentable that an open display of grief . . . should degenerate into riot and disorder."[17] Four years later, when a fan magazine published an article on the anniversary of Infante's death, it made special note of the chaotic violence that marked his funeral and of the social status of those taking part in it: "The death of Pedro Infante moved all classes of society. But it was, especially, the masses who wept for him."[18]

Meanwhile, other people expressed rage and grief in more isolated ways. They wrote dozens of memorial songs and poems, for example. Some song lyrics bordered on hagiography, such as one that emphasized Infante's Christ-like "vocation as a carpenter" and promised him, "Heaven is waiting for you."[19] Many memorial ballads described Infante as the ideal Mexican, such as the one that praised his "noble Mexican heart," and a few glorified his status as a national representative to the world, underlining his "international fame."[20] Fans carried his picture around with them, put it in their family photo albums, or tacked it up on their walls.[21] In the most extreme reactions, in the week that followed Infante's death, at least two suicide notes claimed that the victims could not live without their idol.

Why did Infante's fans mourn him with such violence? To understand these strange, sad events requires a context: we have to understand what made Infante so important to those who mourned him, and who they believed Infante to be.

Pedro Infante's Real and Imaginary Life

Pedro Infante's fans knew his life story as well as they knew the biographies of the saints or of their neighbors. The story that fans knew may or may not have been entirely true—like fans everywhere, they probably did not always distinguish among the person himself, the publicity about the person, and the dramatic roles he played as a singer and an actor—but that need not concern us here. Informed by gossip columns, biographical photonovels, scandal sheets, movie magazines, and rumor as well as by Infante's movies and songs, audiences developed their own ideas about his life and character. These beliefs, in turn, made them into fans and motivated their intense emotions at his death.[22]

Pedro Infante was born to a large, poor, loving family in a small town in Sinaloa in 1917. He began working as a carpenter at an early age and, at the same time, studied with his father, a musician; he took a job as a drummer with a local dance orchestra at age fifteen. By 1937 he had migrated, like so many young people of the time, to Mexico City. He left a one-year-old daughter behind in Sinala. (By the time he died, he was supporting fourteen sons and daughters, children of four women; at least another three women would claim in the aftermath of his death that their children were Infante's.) In the city, Infante met and married his first wife, María Luisa León, who, depending on which version of the story fans decided to believe, either encouraged Infante to look for more lucrative work as a musician or shrewishly insisted on it. In either case, soon enough Infante joined a multitude of singers working in the booming radio business, with its insatiable demand for new voices. The most popular station in Mexico City, XEW, offered him a contract, beginning an association with the singer that culminated in their broadcast of his funeral, which earned extraordinarily high ratings.

The 200-kilowatt station, the most powerful in the Western Hemisphere when it began transmitting in 1930, reached well beyond the capital's boundaries; listeners tuned in all over the country and as far away as Havana. Station xew belonged to the U.S.-based rca network but carried very little network programming, partly because the technology of simultaneous transmission was not yet reliable enough to make networkwide broadcasting cheap or easy, but also because the Mexican government had promulgated laws between 1932 and 1936 that traded fifty-year concessions of the broadcast spectrum for a requirement that at least a quarter of all radio programming consist of "typically Mexican" songs. (At the same time, the government also was promoting national—if not nationalist—content in film and periodicals with price supports and controls on foreign media, among other measures.) Emilio Azcárraga Vidaurreta, xew's owner, made a virtue of necessity: by tirelessly advertising the station's *mexicanidad*, he helped call his audience into being. As new singers became xew regulars, they developed personas that fit within a relatively narrow range of possible "Mexican" roles: the urban bum, the fallen woman, the cheery rustic, and so forth. Pedro Infante quickly adopted the image of the charro, the heroic cowboy of the north, and specialized in *canciones rancheras*, the melodramatic ballads that fit the charro role.[23]

Ranchera songs can be understood as a socially conservative rebuke, both in their musical form and their lyrical content, to the more directly sexual boleros that were just as popular at the time. Boleros, most of all those by Agustín Lara, recorded the melodramas of urban life and modernity rather than those of the countryside and the mythic past. To oversimplify, the world of the bolero was the world of the city at night, populated by prostitutes, blind musicians, thieves, and murderers; boleros spoke of ruined lives. Ranchera music, though frequently sad, was set in the warmth, sunlight, and comfort of northern Mexico in some impossibly prosperous past; it spoke of ruined loves—with the implication that all parties would live to love another day—when it spoke of ruin at all.

Infante's audience certainly understood the political differences between song genres, because both the government and commercial culture had made a series of gestures to underline those differences. In 1936 the secretary of public education in the relatively radical administration of Lázaro Cárdenas made a conciliatory gesture to the right (after a long series of violent conflicts over the content of public education) by banning Lara's songs from being performed in Mexican schools. Ten years later, radio station xex, struggling to define itself in a market dominated by the Azcárraga family's network, hit on the notion of advertising itself as the clean alternative to racy popular music, an idea that soon did make XEX a huge success. The station distributed a list of songs, soon reprinted throughout the country, which it called "obscene" and vowed never to broadcast. Prominent among the blacklisted tunes were some of Lara's most popular compositions; none of Infante's hits appeared on this list.

Yet Infante did not make inoffensive or apolitical music. His biggest hits were love songs, but often they were not addressed to an individual woman. Frequently, they praised the land instead, or the nation, or a region of the nation. Sometimes they asserted the singer's manly mexicanidad by denigrating—in a jocular fashion—a former love. The songs he recorded in the five years before his death (not all of them rancheras, but all sharing the spirit and tone of the ranchera genre) often took a defiant, even boastful stance. In 1956 Infante's hit "Morir Soñando" proclaimed that "it's better to die while dreaming than to live in reality."[24] A year later another hit, "La Verdolaga," let Infante make much of his reputation as a Don Juan:

> I gave them love and money
> and then when it was least expected
> they got me into trouble
> that's why I live free
> without trusting in women. . . .
> Don't make commitments
> in matters of the heart.[25]

In 1953 another hit love song, "Ni por favor!" allowed Infante to sound both heartbroken and proud at the same time:

> If you don't love me, so what,
> Of love I will not die
> One suffers when one loves
> But one learns to forget, too. . . .
> If you think that because of my tender feelings
> I will have to come plead with you
> My love, you've made a mistake
> This I will not do, not even if you say please.[26]

Many of these songs were fast-paced and cheery, making a witty contrast with their sometimes glum or bitter lyrics. Others, including some whose words were gentle and loving, like "Te quiero así," sounded slow and sad. But all used Infante's untrained but pure tenor to great effect.[27] His instantly recognizable voice sounded as though he were singing from the heart, whether he was mourning the passing of a happier past, praising a new love, or declaring that his mother, his nation, or his northern region was the true object of all his affections.

In 1940 Infante entered the movies with a bit part for which another actor dubbed the words. Using the film business connections he had made through his work as a nightclub singer to help get himself better roles, and taking speech classes to modulate his strong northern accent, he quickly became a leading man. By 1943 he was a star, with a recording contract, weekly appearances on xew, and a series of hit movies. Many of these movies extended his charro persona: he made comedies like *Dicen que soy mujeriego* (1948), *Los tres García* and its sequel *Vuelven los García* (both 1946), and *Cuidado con el amor* (1954), but also melodramatic cowboy romances like *Los gavilanes* (1954). In them he sang the same, or similar, songs that radio listeners could hear him perform; he wore the same huge spangled sombrero, gunbelt, and tight, embroidered suit that he sported on his record covers and publicity photos; but the films put this static figure into action. They shifted the focus of audience attention from the elaboration of the myth of the rural past to the behavior (and thus the character) of the individual charro.

In his charro film roles Infante exuded authority through displays of physical ability; not only his strength and grace but also his talent as a singer and musician proved his masculinity (see Figure 31). Scenes that displayed him as irresistibly attractive to women—but not entirely conscious of his own power over them—underlined both his manly appearance and his good character. The conflicts that shaped these films' plots pitted loyalty to kin or (less frequently) male friends against romance, but as they were comedies, the screenwriters always found some way to end the story with Infante's relationships to friends, to lovers, and above all to family still intact, or strengthened: through virtue, luck, or effort, the hero protected all who depended on him.[28] So Infante's public persona came to include such traits as "his generosity without limits, [and] his enormous kindliness," as a photonovel written immediately after his death put it.[29] In the eyes of his audience, both before and after his death, Infante's appeal lay in the excellence, but also the ordinariness, of his character: the loyal son, the good father, the

31. Infante meets his fans on a southern Mexico City film set. Díaz, Delgado y García archive of the Fototeca of the Archivo General de la Nación, Mexico City. Reprinted by permission.

trustworthy friend, the devout Catholic, the happy drunkard. To be a charro, as Infante portrayed the role, was to be a Mexican that every Mexican could dream of being.[30]

Fans required and received constant reassurance that success had not changed Infante's humble, honest, hard-working, and loyal nature. So the press reported that as soon as he could afford to, Infante moved his mother and some of his ten brothers and sisters into a large new house in Mexico City. Meanwhile, the star built a huge new house for himself, but this well-publicized building included a gym and a carpentry workshop. Infante's daily exercise underscored his manliness and the difficulty of his job as a movie star. Movie magazines published a seemingly infinite number of publicity stills showing Infante lifting weights in his gym, and almost every movie he made after 1950 included at least one scene in which Infante displayed his unclothed torso, making visible the results of so much effort (see Figure 32).[31]

Fans were even more attached to the idea that Infante continued to prac-

32. This publicity still was part of a photo essay documenting Infante's new house; this photo was supposed to demonstrate the use of the modern gym. Díaz, Delgado y García archive of the Fototeca of the Archivo General de la Nación, Mexico City. Reprinted by permission.

tice carpentry, his first trade, as this indicated his humility and connection to his past. Thus, a biographical photonovel imagined that after death Infante would most want to be in his carpentry shop; every installment of the narrative was bracketed with scenes showing the star making toys for children at his workbench in heaven.[32] And it is not at all accidental that in three of his most popular movies—*Nosotros los pobres* (1947) and its sequels *Ustedes los ricos* (1948) and *Pepe el Toro* (1952)—Infante played a carpenter. In these melodramas, Infante moved from playing a rural to an urban figure, while still representing the height of masculine perfection in appearance, behavior, and character.[33]

In many of the last films he made, Infante played a character in the midst of this rural-urban transition, often one who was caught up in class mobility as well, but he played this role for laughs. Movies like *Escuela de vagabundos* (1954), *Escuela de música* (1955), *El Inocente* (1955), and *Escuela de rateros* (1956) were comedies of mistaken identity or double identity. In *El Inocente* Infante played a poor but honest singing automobile mechanic forced to act like a wealthy playboy to win the heart of the rich girl who married him by mistake. In *Escuela de vagabundos*, Infante played a successful rural songwriter who takes on the role of a butler to a rich urban family to win the heart of the spoiled daughter of the house. In *Escuela de música*, Infante played a humble but upwardly mobile urban businessman who can express himself only through song when he gets drunk enough to be possessed by the spirit of his irascible rural grandmother; this confusion of identities extends to a pretended engagement with a woman he does not like in order to provoke the jealousy of the woman he loves. And in *Escuela de rateros*, as a reviewer put it, "Pedro has two very different roles; the one is an unscrupulous type full of offensive vanity, and the other is a poor baker who, due to his surprising resemblance to the first, gets caught up in a horrible crime."[34]

As Gustavo García has written, scripts like these—along with the titles of other Infante movies like *El mil amores* (The man with a thousand loves, 1954) and *Cuidado con el amor* (Be careful with love, 1954)—seemed to make an ironic commentary on Infante's public image, particularly his long-standing legal first marriage to the "wrong" woman, María Luisa León.[35] But the multiplicity of Infante's public persona had other meanings, too.[36] Carlos Monsiváis has identified this ability to slide among cinematic archetypes, to knit them together into a single image of idealized Mexican manhood, as the source of Infante's power over the audience: "These multiple crossings . . . from the rural to the urban, from the machismo of the caudillo to a machismo able to cry, from the arrogant generosity of the social bandit to the sympathy of the humble carpenter . . . [demonstrate that] for the Mexican audience this actor-singer has been a bridge of understanding between the old and the new: his biography is the ideal of the collective."[37] Indeed, his audience seemed willing to forgive him almost anything. The charro role located the possibility of goodness in an imaginary rural past; so, as Infante took on film roles set in cities in the present day, as his wealth grew increasingly visible, and as he took up activities, especially motorcycle riding and piloting small planes, that symbolized a risky modernity, he was also putting his public persona at risk. But his roles as a barrio carpenter and as a motorcycle-riding traffic cop (in the hit comedy *A toda máquina*), like the songs he sang boasting of his romantic exploits, only increased his popularity.

Infante's public persona also slid between male archetypes: sometimes he seemed the devoted son and father, the happy stay-at-home husband, but sometimes he appeared as a rake, drinking with his male friends and flirting—at the least—with women to whom he was not married. He did marry twice and had well-known liaisons with at least three other women. He did this in an era when formal divorce was both a contentious political issue (its legalization had been one of the chief complaints of the Catholic Church against the revolutionary state from the 1920s through the 1950s) and exceedingly rare. Indeed, three days before his death the Supreme Court had ruled that Infante never had gotten a legal divorce from his first wife, so that his subsequent marriages were annulled. Headlines declaring the star a bigamist had made the front pages all over the country.

This marked the apparent end of a highly public legal battle among the star and his wives that began four years earlier, when María Luisa León opened her lawsuit. This had made Infante's womanizing public: gossip columns and cartoons referred to it constantly, men joked about it, and for a period before his death respectable women avoided mentioning their admiration for him.[38] Fan magazines even made oblique references to the rumor that the daughter María Luisa and Pedro had adopted was actually his child by another woman.[39] Apparently, all this had little or no effect on the sales of his records, nor did it make his movies less popular.

Newspaper coverage of the events surrounding Infante's death carefully described the appearance and behavior of María Luisa León de Infante, his first wife, and Irma Dorantes, his partner in his suddenly annulled marriage of the time. Newspapers hinted at the authenticity of Dorantes's grief and the tragedy of her plight. They reported that the young woman would be *forced* to work as an actress to support Pedro's baby daughter, while also noting approvingly that she had repeatedly exclaimed that Infante's death was "all my fault!" because he perished during a flight back to Mexico City, a trip intended to persuade Dorante to stay with him despite the sudden delegitimization of their marriage by the Supreme Court.[40] At the same time, the papers made León's sorrow seem phony, with constant references to her failed singing career and dramatic appearances at the public gatherings occasioned by Infante's death. Thus, the papers shifted the blame for the failure of Infante's first marriage and the subsequent legal tangle to his first wife, giving fans a means to forgive Infante even this. And the day before the funeral, the archbishop of Mexico City felt it necessary to issue a statement to the press reassuring parishioners that, due to the nature of his accident, Infante may not have died in a state of mortal sin even though he did not receive last rites: "Merely an instant of repentance, and the infinite goodness of God, would suffice for the pardon of sins."[41]

The constant emphasis after his death on the virtue of Infante's nature, despite all evidence to the contrary, is even more surprising considering the place of cinema in public life. Moviegoing was a relatively new form of behavior, and a highly contested one, though it was extremely popular.[42] Mexicans in the 1950s had not completely settled on proper movie house etiquette: one fan magazine reported on a 1956 controversy over whether or not to applaud, for example.[43] At the same time, the division of the cinema audience along class lines had long since been accepted. Different seats within the movie houses cost different amounts, creating a spatial gulf between poorer and richer viewers to match the economic gap between them. And the movie houses themselves each developed a kind of class identity, marked by location but also by the range of ticket prices, how recently the films shown at each theater had opened, and other factors. Salvador Novo even commented that he could tell who went to which Mexico City movie theater by the kinds of food sold outside each one, from *chicharrones* to the cuisine of Oaxaca and "a *menudo* worthy of a sonnet."[44]

But the pleasures of moviegoing could also be dangerous. Not only did many actors seem to be sinners, but movies themselves could threaten the soul and movie theaters were, famously, sites of transgressive behavior. The Catholic Church regarded cinema with such suspicion that it distributed leaflets at Sunday Mass that contained ratings of every movie showing in the diocese, sorted by the type and degree of sin visible in each picture. (This publication, *Apreciaciones*, often placed Infante's movies into such categories as "Reserved for those with well-developed moral standards" or even "Absolutely unadvisable for all" because of their "lack of respect for women, as is seen in movies from other countries," or their "scenes of drunkenness . . . [and] of vengence, acts of cruelty, seductions, and approval of dueling.")[45] Some parishes organized boycotts of movie theaters that persistently offered "immoral" films, and at least one town, Coyoacán, in the 1940s, set up an alternative neighborhood cinema to show "clean" pictures.

At secular cinemas, film sometimes seemed to be the last thing on anyone's mind. Movie houses were designed as architectural tributes to the ideas of modernity and the exotic. More prosaically, they were one of the rare locations in urban Mexico where young couples could find some privacy. In his recent memoir of the 1940s in Mexico City, journalist Manuel Magaña Contreras described this as a polite, decorous form of socializing: "How many of us who now have gray hair had the opportunity to enjoy movies of good quality with our girlfriends, in an atmosphere of good taste? Of course, the spectators . . . attended in our Sunday best, which in those days meant a suit and hat as well as an overcoat and perhaps gloves, and for the ladies a well-cut dress, gloves, hat and fur stole."[46] But many city-dwellers did not use moviegoing as a way to see and be seen by their peers, choosing instead to treat the cinemas as though couples could be alone together in them. (As humorist Abel Quezada put it in 1953, "You can learn a lot about love at the movies, as long as you don't watch the screen.")[47] Oscar Lewis quotes one of the "Sánchez" boys describing a date: "I took her to the movies where we could kiss and embrace." And that was not all that went on at the movies, according to Lewis. When a local gang, "the terror of the neighborhood," visited the local cinema, "they sat up on the balcony and smoked marijuana . . . and if the movie were a daring one, you could hear them saying dirty things."[48] Moreover, over the decades movie theaters housed union meetings and political rallies and were the site of parties, riots, demonstrations, and all kinds of disturbances.[49]

Mexicans came to associate moviegoing, and thus the movies themselves, with sinful or dangerous (but modern) behavior; they may also have seen a connection between going to movies—a foreign art form, and of course most movies available to Mexicans in 1957 were foreign, too—and opposition to the government in its more nationalist or puritanical phases.[50] All of these associations had to be considered, and rejected, in order for fans to see Pedro Infante as the perfect Mexican man.

The images and stories that Infante's life and art had produced hung in the air over the riot that marked his funeral. They gave meaning to his posthumous career, in which his movies seem to repeat constantly on television throughout the Spanish-speaking world and his records still play on radios and jukeboxes—a career that began immediately after his death with memorial newsreels and photonovels and continues into the present with the headline-producing announcement of Infante's primary director Ismael Rodríguez's plan to make a new movie memorializing the fallen idol.[51] Infante also had an imaginary, so to speak, career in transnational culture industries after his death. The stories went that he had been on the verge of signing contracts with Hollywood studios, of starring in plays with Broadway actresses, of cutting records in France or Germany. This was supposed to heighten the pathos of his loss: he had been on the verge of international stardom; he might have represented Mexico to the world.

Indeed, one way to understand the intensity of public response to Infante's death would be to describe it as a reaction to the sudden collapse of the Mexican film industry, which had been a source of national pride up through the middle of the 1950s. Another singing cowboy star, Jorge Negrete, had died, at a similarly young age, a few years earlier. At that point, Infante had become not only the most important male movie star of the day but the pillar on which the entire national entertainment industry rested. Fan magazines reported breathlessly on the progress of each new recording project, movie-making venture, and concert tour. Every week—in a few cases, every day—they detailed the sales of his records, of the sheet music for the songs he popularized, and of the tickets for his movies at home and abroad. Infante's success was the whole industry's success, and the industry's success was a point of Mexican honor. With Infante's death, the possibility of a Mexican cinema that could be at once nationalist, popular, competitive with Hollywood and European products, and aesthetically satisfying seemed to have reached a sudden, horrible end.

All of this suggests the context in which the riot at Infante's funeral might be understood, but none of it provides an explanation. I propose three angles from which this event might make more sense: a tension between the discourses of modernity and tradition, gender anxiety, and working-class fury. All of these emotional modes, I argue, were specific to Mexico City and its geography; all of them belonged to an overarching contest over the meaning of nation and citizenship in the postrevolutionary era.

Deadly Modernity, the Moving City, and Machismo's Double

The violence that marked public response to Pedro Infante's death grew from frustration, or so it seems to me; this riot can be understood as political speech in a situation where such speech was not otherwise possible. I read the events around Infante's death and burial as, specifically, an intervention in a long-standing national debate over citizenship and nation. To participate in this debate required the use of several voices. In one voice, the debate used words, metaphors, and ideas related to change (especially technological development) and stability. In another, the debate used words, metaphors, and ideas related to class identity and daily life, especially in Mexico City. And a third voice entered this debate as a series of arguments over gender roles. In this section, I suggest ways we can read Infante's funeral and the events surrounding it as intelligible speech in each of these three modes.

The difficult categories of "tradition" and "modernity" provided one language in which Infante's fans seemed to speak. Infante's movie career drew a kind of arc between the two sets of ideas. It began with his playing a character from an imagined past, an invented tradition of the rural north, but it ended in a series of comic and equivocal depictions of modern city life.[52] He associated himself specifically with the machinery of modernity through his well-publicized interest in motorcycles and airplanes. His last movies celebrated the possibilities of technological progress; in them, Infante played such roles as automobile mechanic, chauffeur, and, twice, motorcycle cop. In his last movies, viewers saw Infante singing into a telephone, kissing a girl in an airport, driving a tow truck, piloting a speedboat, and peddling bread from a bicycle.

But Infante's later movies—and, even more, the tension between his "modern" movies and the invented-tradition genres of the songs he continued recording until his death—recognized that few in his audience experienced technological change and modernity as an uncomplicated source of pleasure. The comedy in these films frequently relied on the untrustworthy nature of modern machinery: messages get garbled, buses break down, cars run out of gas. Even when machines worked, they could cause trouble: in

Escuela de rateros a clever thief uses a phonograph to aid his getaway from a jewelry store heist. Moreover, Infante frequently played a humble working man whose modern profession brought him into association with wealthy people, so the ultimate source of humor was not machinery but the class relations around machinery. And in his "real" life, Infante had as much wealth as any member of Mexico's elite and spent it very publicly on more modern machinery, from motorcycles and airplanes to kitchen gadgets.

In this context, Infante's slipping among roles—within his movies, between his movies, and between his movies and his "real" public life—helped reassure his audience about the possibilities of their own lives. Like most of them, he had left behind a rural life that looked happier in retrospect. Like most of them, he had enthusiastically adapted the styles and practices of urban, mechanized "modernity." Like the nation itself, he was inventing a past and a future as he went along. His films both celebrated the possibilities of these collective acts of invention and, however mildly, criticized their shortcomings. His artistic work seen in conjunction with his public persona did more: it suggested that Mexicans would not have to choose between being rural and urban, traditional and modern. They could be both at once.

Infante's death foreclosed that possibility by leaving his imagined body trapped forever in the modern. It was an airplane, his own airplane, that killed him, and on a flight from a distant, small provincial town to the booming capital city. It was another airplane that brought his body back, and from the moment he returned to the city Infante's body was accompanied by an honor guard of motorcycle policemen who claimed him as one of their own. Most of the sites in which Infante's fans mourned him implicated technological modernity in their idol's disappearance: the site of the plane crash, airports in Mérida and Mexico City, movie theaters, and the streets of the cities themselves. The minute-to-minute coverage of the whole sequence of events by radio, the flickering light of flashbulbs on the scene, and the obtrusive presence of newsreel cameramen all combined to call attention to mass media technologies in the midst of the mourning crowd. From there, it was a logical step to blame those responsible for modernity for the loss of the idol himself; thus, the crowd turned on the police, who were the nearest representatives of the state, in place of turning on the state itself. It was Mexico's "revolutionary" government, after all, that had most loudly and insistently demanded credit for the modernization of Mexico. Thus, as in other moments of national disaster, it would also have to take its share of the blame.

Urban space and social class provide the second mode of argument over citizenship and nation that emerges into view with the riot at Infante's funeral. If the federal government of Mexico had done much, beginning with the *cardenista* nationalization of the petroleum industry, to associate itself with modern technology, it also had begun more recently to assert itself as the ultimate authority in urban matters, particularly in Mexico City. In the 1950s, urban space began a long process of reorganization, with wealthy and powerful people migrating away from the centers of Mexican cities as poor migrants from the countryside crammed into them.[53] The state took several steps to supervise, control, and identify itself with this change; these steps included making huge physical changes in the cities themselves to support the reorganization processes, and making smaller gestures at ameliorating the worst effects of this process on the citizens left behind in the center of the cities.

President Adolfo Ruiz Cortines made a point of inviting citizens to address their complaints to him personally, and from 1952 onward a surprisingly large number of hopeful or desperate city-dwellers took him up on it. From the very neighborhood through which Infante's funeral procession had passed, one man wrote to the president complaining of a gang of thieves whom he suspected were "sons of policemen."[54] Other youth in a nearby neighborhood were, as another letter writer told the president, making it impossible for "people to live in peace . . . as they have formed more or less organized groups which create a scandal . . . [by] breaking windows and deliberately bothering us with their crude jokes and lack of respect."[55] Frequently, complaints about city life focused on conditions related to the crowding and anonymity of central Mexico City, where "decent families" might find themselves living uncomfortably close to "houses of assignation," overhearing "petty quarrels of the fallen women . . . gunshots, foul language," and worse.[56]

Complaints about vice, crime, and corruption frequently shaded over into complaints against mass media or popular culture. Brothels often called themselves dance halls, and some commercial institutions confused the matter even further by combining the two functions; thus, many people wanted to shut down dance halls, along with "cabarets, beer halls, etc.," because they were "centers of vice."[57] Even recorded music by itself could seem "infernal," as two Veracruz women told the president. They wrote that it was "worse than intolerable that . . . without the slightest scruple, without the least concern for any invalid, for any of those unfortunate families who happen to live close to a bar or pool hall, nor even for the exhausted working man who leaves his heavy labor wanting only to get some sleep to regain his strength to return eight hours later to his job, those JUKE BOXES, RECORD PLAYERS, AND RADIOS ... play at TOP VOLUME all night."[58] In other words, citizens might complain about Mexico's cities because of two spatial juxtapositions in them: first, the overlap of moral categories (home/ whorehouse, or policeman/thief), and second, the overlap of sonic categories (music/noise, decent talk/foul language, or uproar/peace).

The Mexican state rarely acted to address citizens' complaints directly.[59] Instead, and above all in Mexico City, it acted on policies designed to separate those spatial juxtapositions. In choosing where to dig sewers and place electric lines, which streets to pave, where to build new government office buildings, how to site new avenues and highways, and especially where to construct the huge, modern, new campus of the National Autonomous University, the government supported and encouraged an enormous change in the organization of the capital city. Mexico City's commercial and artistic hub moved rapidly southward, aided by all the new infrastructure the government provided, and leaving the center of the city to a combination of historical monuments and poor people's housing.[60] The government left the central barrios to molder, neglected, while it rapidly met the needs of the richer and better-connected citizens who had set themselves up just to the south.[61] Those left behind understood this process well, as newspapers and magazines depicted the elites' daring adaptations of the antique structures of Coyoacán and the sleek modernity of the new colony called Navarte.

Pedro Infante's life and death both rang with uncomfortable echoes of the spatial transformation of Mexico City. As a struggling young singer, Infante had come from the countryside to the very center of Mexico City. When he could afford to, he brought his mother and other relatives to live in a new house in Colonia Navarte, installing his first wife nearby. Eventually he moved even further south, to the very outskirts of the city. All these moves were, of course, well documented in the papers. Furthermore, as every fan knew, the movie studios where he worked were also well to the south of the city center. But Infante kept returning to central Mexico City, and again, this was well understood by his local fans. Not only were his movies showing there almost constantly, but also he performed live in theaters there, cut his records in studios there, and broadcast his radio shows from there. The center of the city remained his workplace, and so long as it did, Infante's fans could feel as though he still belonged to them.

When Infante died, his body came into the center from the east, where the airport was. This was where most of his fans first found him to bid farewell. They took him from there, relatively peacefully, into the central location of the ANDA theater. But all too soon, the motorcycle police arrived to take his body away from the crowd again. And when they did, they took it due south, for a very long trip along a relatively new and very prosperous thoroughfare, through some of Mexico's newer and richer sections, up to the cemetery. Thus, Infante's poor and working-class fans must have felt his loss as a double blow. Not only was Infante being removed from their midst forever, but he was being taken by the state along the same route that the prosperous had already fled, leaving his audience behind, while Infante entered an area they knew would never welcome them. Surely their objections to this spatial arrangement can be heard in the riot that ensued.

Gender is the last of the three languages in which I have suggested reading this event. There are two reasons why attention to gender categories helps us hear what the rioters were saying. First, and relatively straightforwardly, Infante's life and death both entangled themselves with contemporary debates over proper feminine behavior: he seemed to have the power to make women behave badly. Second, Infante's life suggested a new, syncretic style of Mexican manliness that the manner of his death seemed to contradict. Both of these factors, but especially the second, fueled the anger behind this riot and helped explicate its meaning.

The reports of Infante's funeral all imply, or explicitly state, that the majority of those in attendance (and thus, presumably, the majority of the rioters) were women, though photos reveal that, in fact, the majority of people attending the public events related to Infante's demise were male. So why did reporters seem to see the women in attendance more clearly than they could see the men? Perhaps because women in public at all, let alone women in crowds in the middle of the city, raising their voices and even fighting, were far more upsetting a sight than men when they did the same things (and this possibility might, in turn, help explain the strange erasure of this entire sequence of events from Mexican public memory). Perhaps, though, women seemed more likely to be there, and that was why those witnessing the events believed they saw them.

Women were supposed to be Infante's primary audience. Most of his songs were addressed to a group of admiring male friends (represented by the mariachi band backing him up on the record, or sometimes by a set of crooning male character actors in his movies' singing scenes), but his image, especially the photos and movie scenes that showed him shirtless, was supposed to be designed for female viewers. Furthermore, Infante rarely appeared in public, either as "himself" or in his movies, without a female partner of some kind. If not with one of his wives or his mother, his fans saw him in conjunction with such stars as Sylvia Pinal or María Félix. In an effort to improve his public image as the bigamy scandal began in 1953, Infante also made a point of his Catholicism. But rather than having himself pictured with a cross or kneeling in prayer, Infante portrayed himself as a devotee of the Virgin of Guadalupe. This enabled him to appear at once as a good Catholic, a Mexican nationalist, and a respecter of all womanhood.

Whereas his mother and the Virgin appear in fan magazine stories and song lyrics as good women, every other woman with whom Infante associated himself fit, sooner or later, into some pattern of stereotypically bad behavior: overly sexual, or domineering and shrewish, or faithless. But they fit these stereotypes in a very particular way, one that belonged more to the realm of bolero than ranchera songs. The women in Infante's story, as the public understood it, were like characters from a melodrama; they behaved badly *because they had no choice*. Like the essentially good women of the bolero lyrics, driven to prostitution from desperation, these women—both the real people as the public saw them, and the fictional characters in Infante's songs and films—were driven into unwomanly actions by their love for Infante. (The epitome of this was, of course, the long-drawn-out fight between two talented, beautiful women over who could claim the legal status of being Infante's wife.) No wonder that the women who did appear at Infante's funeral were expected to act in unusual, frightening, or immoral ways, or that those people who did riot at Infante's funeral would be portrayed as women.

In death and life, Infante's figure disturbed settled ideas about femininity. But even more urgently, Infante helped shape and reshape the meaning of masculinity in this era. The single word most frequently attached to Infante, both before and after his death, was *macho*. This most gendered of all terms described him pejoratively before his death and became, almost instantly, an affectionate characterization once he was gone. Machismo is a difficult word and a hotly debated subject. We could begin with an insightful observation made by Manuel Fernández Perera: macho behavior, which he writes is best exemplified by the charro cantantes like Infante, is "pure theater," a recently invented social fiction, a "twentieth-century myth."[62] Similarly, anthropologist Matthew Gutmann found recently that members of Mexico City's elite ascribe the characteristics of machismo to men of the working class, and vice versa: the word always describes somebody else.[63]

"Macho," in Gutmann's formulation, does not paint an altogether flattering portrait of the other. A macho is brave to the point of being foolhardy and commanding to the point of being violent; his uncontrolled (perhaps uncontrollable) appetites for women, alcohol, action, and emotion can cause terrible harm to the people around him. Perhaps the ultimate macho, at least in myth, was the revolutionary Pancho Villa. As Ilene O'Malley has pointed out, we can see the political uses of the macho stereotype in Villa's official rehabilitation during the 1950s, as the state appropriated his memory for its own purposes by shifting from describing him as a criminal to describing him as a real man and true patriot.[64] The valorization of the macho—perhaps even the construction of this stereotype—dates from this postrevolutionary period rather than the mythologized past from which this imaginary man was supposed to spring.

Interestingly, Mexican politicians of the 1940–1960 period were not eager, generally speaking, to see themselves described as macho men. Rather, they projected an image of calm self-control, as President Adolfo Ruiz Cortines did. Former president Manuel Avila Camacho makes an even better example of this countermacho identity. His persona—the self-contained, somewhat prudish family man, the good Catholic, the compromiser—deliberately made a sharp contrast with that of his pistol-waving brother, the General, with his exotic mistresses, horses, many out-of-wedlock offspring, powerful physique, and well-known ill fortune in his political career.[65] Power lay in rejecting the macho-as-charro stereotype and instead deploying a counterimage, the equally stereotypical postrevolutionary patriarch, the technocrat, the bureaucrat, the modern man. This iteration of the virtuous Mexican man is self-controlled, whereas the charro is impulsive; he is orderly, whereas the charro is unruly; he is celibate or monogamous, whereas the charro has many women (though perhaps only one true love); he is sober when the charro is drunk, and modest when the charro is boastful. The macho-as-technocrat, the countermacho, is also a mature man: he must rely on—and display—a certain authority that would sit oddly on the shoulders of a teenager. And this authority is both the essence and the political function of the stereotype.

This imagery, in turn, supported two related, central political aims of Avila Camacho's 1940–1946 presidency. He hoped to convince Mexicans that the Revolution was over (even in the relatively peaceful form it took in the Cárdenas years), and he had to show that his government was the legitimate heir to the Revolution. Thus, the figure of the charismatic General could be deployed to remind the citizenry that such macho-as-charro revolutionaries can also be unpredictable, violent, and dangerous: an admirable man, perhaps, but one best left slightly to the side of contemporary politics. The president's social and political conservatism, by contrast, looked modern (and safe). Yet the familial relationship and political partnership between the two men also reminded Mexicans of the connection between the two styles of politician, suggesting that this form of the postrevolutionary did draw from a Revolutionary heritage. The charro, in other words, is always receding into the past. Almost by definition he is a figment of a historicizing imagination. The countermacho, conversely, lives in the future, perhaps a revolutionary future of perfect justice, perhaps a modernized future of technological progress and material abundance.[66] So, as Infante added the trappings of a technological modernity to his persona—the motorcycles, the airplanes, even his famous, immense fortune—he also opened up the definition of machismo. Here Monsiváis's remark about the importance of Pedro Infante as a bridging figure takes on a deeper meaning. Infante, in his public persona and his film roles, enacted both the macho and the countermacho, the charro and the technocrat. He was both the womanizer *and* the devoted husband, both the self-contained businessman *and* the tearful drunk. Similarly, Infante's figure synthesized sets of opposed terms from the other two languages deployed in the debate over power and nation in Mexico. He was at once a hard-working northerner and an elite Mexico City dweller, the enthusiastic participant in modern technology and the old-fashioned cowboy. Up until his death, Infante was both a powerful and contradictory force in ordinary Mexicans' imagination because he suggested that the differences—the languages—that defined what it was to be Mexican (and thus, in the postrevolutionary world, to have political power) could be transcended. His death ended that possibility, as it ended so many others.

Thus, it was not only Infante's sudden, shocking death, but the manner of it—so soon after his legal defeat by the government in the matter of his divorce, far outside the capital city, and through the means of that most modern of all machines, the airplane—that created the despair and the rage that fueled the riot of April 17, 1957. Through these events, Infante had been removed from the future and from power, and placed in the same honored, heroic, and impotent past as Avila Camacho's brother, or as Pancho Villa. Infante's death closed off the possibility that "modernity" (the oldest of Mexican political goals) and "tradition" (a postrevolutionary construction) could be bridged in a way that made sense to his fans. It condemned them to remain in the decaying center of the cities while the elite margins thrived. It forced them to pick between opposing gender definitions, rather than pick and choose among them. The fans violently objected. In doing so, they told the police, and, by extension, the state and the entertainment industry that supported it, that they were growing tired of a national narrative in which they did not yet have a speaking part.

Notes

Thanks to Juan Rodríguez, Audrey Rohrer, and Barb Liggett for research assistance and to the Office of the Dean of Allegheny College for funding this research. Thanks, too, for advice from Julio Contreras Utrera, Gustavo García, Joanne Hershfield, Glen Kuecker, John Lear, Blanca de Lizaur, David Lorey, Verenice Naranjo, Jeff Pilcher, and Eric Zolov, to all of whom the author is very grateful. Unless otherwise noted, all translations are mine.

1   The photograph is reprinted in the catalogue of the exhibition: Alfonso Morales Carrillo et al., *Asamblea de ciudades* (Mexico City: Consejo Nacional para la Cultura y las Artes/Instituto Nacional de Bellas Artes, 1992), 210.

2   Verenice Naranjo has observed that "not every Mexican loves El Santo, and not every Mexican loves Pedro Infante, but every Mexican loves one or the other" (personal communication, 31 July 1998). Gustavo García, Infante's biographer, jokes that Infante is such an important national figure that he is "the Virgin of Guadalupe's husband" (personal communication, 15 August 1998).

3   García, personal communication.

4   "Duelo y Simpatía en Torno al Féretro del Actor Pedro Infante, Llorosa y Compacta Multitud en el Aeropuerto Central," *El Universal* 17 April 1957, 1B. Another newspaper article took the size and composition of these crowds as a sign that there were too many unemployed people in Mérida and Mexico City ("Recibimiento Puso de Manifiesto Grave Problema del Desempleo, Mucho Gente Faltó a su Trabajo, Pero la Mayoría Eran Cesantes," *El Excélsior* 17 April 1957, 1).

    In general, description of these events relies on reports from periodicals: the Mexico City papers *El Universal* and *El Excélsior*, along with the much less respectable tabloid *La Prensa*;

the provincial papers *Diario de Yucatán* and *La Opinión* of Veracruz; and the magazines *Revista de Revistas, Hoy, Siempre!, Tiempo, Cinelandia, Cinema Reporter, Jueves de Excelsior, Todo*, and *Melodías Mexicanas*. Except for differing estimates on crowd size and number of people injured or arrested, all these sources display a surprising degree of similarity: they tell exactly the same story.

Unfortunately, other sources for this event are hard to find. The records of the Mexico City police and other emergency services for the 1950s will not be available to historians for some years to come. Oral accounts seem even more difficult to obtain: in two research trips (summer 1998 and summer 1999) I made every effort to locate people who had attended Infante's funeral. Nobody I spoke to was willing to discuss it, not even a few whose family members assured me that they had been there. The general amnesia about this riot—which seems fairly memorable, from contemporary accounts—probably means something in itself, but it is impossible to determine what.

5   "Golpes y Destrozos por ver de cerca el Ataúd," *El Excélsior*, 17 April 1957, 12A.

6   "Tumultoso entierro fue el de Pedro Infante en la metropoli," *Diario de Yucatán* 18 April 1957, 1. The unpublished photographs are in the Hermanos Mayo and Enrique Díaz collections of fototeca of the Archivo General de la Nación, Mexico City. Some of them are reproduced here by kind permission of the Archivo General de la Nación.

7   "La Radio en el Duelo por la Muerte de Pedro," *La Prensa* 17 April 1957, 24.

8   "Pedro Infante Irá a la Cárcel," *La Prensa* 10 April 1957, 30; "La Esposa de Infanfe [*sic*] Dispuesta a Perdonar," *El Excélsior* 11 April 1957, 30.

9   "María Luisa León fue Objeto de Crueles Expresiones Populares," *La Prensa*, 17 April 1957, 3. This was not the first time that women "of the popular classes" had expressed disdain for Infante's first wife: four years earlier, at the beginning of León's bigamy suit against Infante, a gossip column reported that she had been accosted while trying to enter a radio station by a woman who yelled "Get out of here, now we know that you've been replaced by Irma Dorantes." See Enrique Rosado, "Cine mexicano," *Melodías mexicanas*, no. 75 (5 September 1953): 15.

10 For the family's polite response, in a telegram, see Angel Infante to Adolfo Ruiz Cortines, 24 April 1957, Expediente 132.1/305, Ramo Ruiz Cortines, Archivo General de la Nación.

11 "Con Canciones y Sollozos Despidió el Pueblo a Pedro Infante," *El Universal* 18 April 1957, 16.

12 Ibid.

13 "El Público se Amontinó e Intervino la Policía," *El Excélsior* 18 April 1957, 1.

14 Ibid.

15 "Con Canciones y Sollozos Despidió el Pueblo a Pedro Infante," 16.

16 Salvador Novo, "Cartas a un amigo," *Hoy*, no. 1055 (11 May 1957): 27; see also Salvador Novo, *La vida en México en el período presidencial de Adolfo Ruiz Cortines* (Mexico City: Consejo Nacional para la Cultura y las Artes, 1994), 3:83.

17 "Murió Trágicamente," *Tiempo* 30, no. 781 (22 April 1957): 25.

18 "Pedro Infante, Un Astro sin Ocaso," *Cine Novelas* May 1961, 59.

19 Lyrics of such songs appeared in the magazines that reprinted popular ballads, some written by professionals, others amateur efforts. This one is L. and M. de Juan Alcantara H., "Mi Pedro Infante," *Canciones de América*, no. 68 (11 May 1957): 4.

20 David González Martínez, "Tragedia de Pedro Infante," *Estrellas y canciones* (October 1957): 87; Ray Pérez y Soto, "Corrido a Pedro Infante," *Canciones de América*, no. 67 (27 April 1957): 4.

21 Advertisements for such photos, roughly wallet-sized, "to be put in your family photo album," were still running in movie magazines as late as 1961 (*Cine Novelas*, May 1961, 67). One fan magazine gave away a 3-D picture of Infante in his airplane pilot's outfit: "Pedro Infante en Tercera Dimensión," *Radiolandia* 16, no. 448 (26 September 1953): 2.

22 I am not making any claims of factual accuracy in this passage, but trying to come up with a general version of what a fan in 1957 might have believed to be true about Infante. Sources for this include photonovels (*La Vida y los Amores de Pedro Infante*, 1957–1958, and *Pedro Infante el Muchacho Travieso del Cine* 1955–1956); newspaper obituaries ("De Humilde Carpintero a Idolo del Pueblo," *El Excélsior* 16 April 1957, 1, 11A; "Pedro Infante pereció en un accidente," *El Dictamen* 16 April 1957, 1, 9; "La Carrera de Pedro Infante," *Diario de Yucatán*, 16 April 1957, 1; and "Los 2 Grandes Amores de Pedro Infante: Su Madre y la Aviación, De Aprendiz de Panadero a Estrella del Cine, la Radio y la Televisión," *El Universal*, 16 April 1957, 31); and other newspaper, movie magazine, and periodical coverage of Infante's death and funeral as cited for the previous section. Other important sources for this section were Infante's films and records, as mentioned in the text, and of course gossip repeated to me as I told people of my plans to write this essay.

23 The discussion in this paragraph is based on A. Rubenstein, "Mass Media and Popular Culture in the Twentieth Century," in *The Oxford History of Mexico*, ed. W. Beezley and M. Meyer (New York: Oxford University Press, 2000).

24 Lyrics reprinted in *Música y notas*, no. 9 (April 1956): 45.

25 Lyrics reprinted in *Música y notas*, no. 14 (March 1957): 47.

26 Lyrics reprinted in *Melodías mexicanas*, no. 68 (5 May 1953): 57.

27 Infante was a fine, well-trained violinist and guitarist, but he had received little singing instruction (in contrast to his friend and rival Jorge Negrete, who studied opera before beginning a film career). Sound recordist, editor, and composer Manuel Esperón recalled that of all the actors he had worked with in his long and distinguished career in Mexican cinema, Infante was the only true musician: "The only [actor] who actually played the violin in the movies was Pedro Infante, he played quite well." See unpublished transcript of an interview conducted by Martha Rocha, file PHO/2/49, Archivo de la palabra/Proyecto de historia oral, Instituto Nacional de Antropología y Historia (AP/INAH), 42.

28 Cartoonist Abel Quezada mocked the standard lead male role of this film genre in these words: "The guy is very drunk, but sings well . . . and sings well . . . and, once again, sings well." See Quezada, "Especialidades," *Cine Mundial*, 26 September 1953, 2.

29 *La Vida y los Amores de Pedro Infante*, no. 1 (29 April 1957): 1.

30 A similar analysis could be made of Infante's participation in historical dramas in which he did not play a charro, most of all *¡Mexicanos al grito de guerra!* (1943).

31 The excellence of Infante's body mattered so much to his fans that they objected vehemently when Gustavo's García's biography of their idol discussed his diabetic condition; this was a fact they preferred to deny for the sake of maintaining the image of Infante as physically perfect (García, personal comunication).

32 See, for example, *La Vida y los Amores de Pedro Infante*, 2–6.

33 The quality of these movies has been much debated. One critic holds *Nosotros los pobres* responsible for the subsequent "decadence of Mexican cinema." See Carmen de la Peza, *Cine, melodrama y cultura de masas: estética de la antiestética* (Mexico City: Punto de Fuga/Consejo Nacional para la Cultura y las Artes, 1998), 13.

34 Hamlet, "Sensacional estreno nacional," *Guía Cinematográfica* (Mérida, Yuc.), no. 27 (March 1958): 13. Most of these films are readily available on video; these four are also in the collection of the Filmoteca de la UNAM in Mexico City. For more complete plot summaries and production histories, see the indispensable chronology by Emilio García Riera, *Historia documental del cine mexicano*, vols. 6–9 (Guadalajara, Mexico: Universidad de Guadalajara, 1993).

35 Gustavo García, *No me parezco a nadie, la vida de Pedro Infante* (Mexico City: Editorial Clío, 1994), 3:7.

36 The movie that Infante was planning to make next at the time of his death, *El museo de cera*, would have wildly extended Infante's enactment of multiple roles, but does not appear to respond in any way to the public story of his love life. In the unmade film, he was to have played the curator of a wax museum while also starring in vignettes from the lives of the wax figures, including Juan Diego, Benito Juárez, Pancho Villa, Cuauhtémoc, and Christ.

37 Carlos Monsiváis, "Mythologies," trans. Ana López, in *Mexican Cinema*, ed. Paulo Antonio Paranaguá (London: British Film Institute, 1995), 125.

38 For example, a cartoon on the occasion of the May Day parade showed Infante as a revolutionary soldier on horseback followed by four bedraggled *soldaderas* on foot, with two children apiece (Abel Quezada, "Especialidades," *Cine Mundial*, 2 May 1953, 7); a gossip column in the same movie magazine gibed that Infante might not know exactly "how many ladies he finds himself married to at the moment" ("Ultima Hora!," *Cine Mundial*, 20 May 1953, 11).

39 As one put it, the little girl "looks extraordinarily like Pedro." See Hylda Pino Desandoval, "Confidencias de María Luisa León de Infante de mujer a mujer," *Cinelandia*, no. 8 (June 1957): 18.

40 One version even had Dorantes ascribing the blame for Infante's death both to herself and to "social prejudices." See Arturo R. Blanco, "Pedro Infante Murió en Aras del Amor," *Cinema Reporter* 26, no. 980 (1 May 1957): 8.

41 "Nadie Puede Asegurar que Infante Murió en Pecado, Declara la Mitra," *El Excélsior*, 17 April 1957, 1. The press release went on to remind Infante's fans of his enthusiastic support for the campaign to rebuild the Basilica of the Virgin of Guadalupe, implying ecclesiastic approval (if not guaranteeing salvation) to the star while borrowing a little of his prestige for the Church.

42 Ordinary moviegoers visited cinemas once or twice a week between the 1920s and the 1950s. For instance, in 1955 Salvador Novo described the "spectacle of the fat married couples who come to the center [of Mexico City] for the movies" every Sunday (*La vida en México en el período presidencial de Adolfo Ruiz Cortines* 2:133). But some fans, like film editor Gloria Schoemann's grandmother, went twice a day. See Schoemann's transcribed interview, by María Alba Pastor, PHO 2/26, AP/INAH, 3.

43 "Debe Aplaudirse en el Cine?" *El Cine Gráfico* 1, no. 216 (25 March 1956): 11.

44 Novo, *La vida en México*, 2:334.

45 "Cuando habla el corazón," *Apreciaciones* 43 (23 October 1943): 1; "El Ametralladora," *Apreciaciones* 40 (2 October 1943): 1.

46 Manuel Magaña Contreras, *Ciudad abierta: Los Años de Oro* (Mexico City: Análisis y Evaluación de Prensa, 1996), 167.

47 Abel Quezada, "Especialidades," *Cine Mundial*, 25 April 1953, 7.

48 Oscar Lewis, *The Children of Sánchez* (New York: Vintage, 1963), 31, 147. The continued use of cinemas as spots for illicit sexual behavior can be seen in Luis Zapata's novel of teenage street life during the 1970s in Mexico City, *El Vampiro de la Colonia Roma* (Mexico City: Grijalbo, 1979).

49 For protests and other disturbances in movie theaters, see A. Rubenstein, "Raised Voices at the Cine Montecarlo," *Journal of Family History* 23:3, (July 1998): 312–23; Eric Zolov, "*Rebeldismo* in the Revolutionary Family: Rock'n'Roll's Early Challenges to State and Society in Mexico," *Journal of Latin American Cultural Studies* 6, no. 2 (1997): 201–16; and "El Conflicto entre los estudiantes y la empresa 'Cines de Yucatán," *Diario de Yucatán*, 26 May 1955, 11 (thanks to Jeff Pilcher for this reference).

50 Material in this paragraph taken from Rubenstein, "Mass Media and Popular Culture in the Twentieth Century."

51 "Pedro volverá al cine," *La Nación*, 22 April 1997, B1. Rodríguez has already made two other documentaries in tribute to Infante.

52 His very last movie, *Tizoc* (released posthumously), actually returned to this imagined past, this time the late nineteenth century in central Mexico. But in *Tizoc*, Infante played an oppressed Indian and left the role of the heroic white would-be savior of the endangered white woman, who rides to her rescue at the very last minute, to the villain. For this and other reasons this eccentric film could have represented a whole new stage in Infante's career.

53 Mexico City had undergone many highly politicized transformations already, of course, beginning with the Spanish transformation of the newly conquered zone from a lake to swamp, and continuing with the pseudo-Parisian reforms that created the broad, magnificent Paseo de la Reforma in the nineteenth century. This was a new type of change in city space, however, in which the elite moved for the first time away from what they continued to perceive as the center of the city (and the nation.)

54 R. Sandoval to President Adolfo Ruiz Cortines, 20 September 1957, Archivo General de la Nación, Fondo Presidencial, Ruiz Cortines, (AGN/RC) vol. 44.94, exp. 128.

55 Gabriel Jiménez M. and 49 other signatories to Ruiz Cortines, 12 April 1957, AGN/RC vol. 444.94, exp. 12.

56 Arturo del Rio to Ruiz Cortines, 20 October 1957, AGN/RC vol. 425.3, exp. 26.

57 Alfonso R. Castrojón (and 38 others) to Ruiz Cortines, 6 June 1953, AGN/RC vol. 425.3, exp. 12.

58 Carmen Lindaly de Ruiz and Candelaria Delgado to Ruiz Cortines, 18 January 1956, AGN/RC vol. 415.1, exp. 29. Capitalization is in the original.

59 Action on such complaints addressed to the president was rare enough that it received front-page newspaper coverage when it did happen, and that such stories were carefully preserved in the president's files. See, for instance, "Las Autoridades cerraran el garito 'El

Emir' para impedir que se siga violando las leyes," *El Comentario* (Jalapa, Ver.), 7 March 1958, 1, in AGN/RC vol. 415.1, exp. 1.

60 This process was clear while it was going on to almost all concerned and to readers who did not live in Mexico City. For example, Salvador Novo's home and the theater he ran, both located in the southern neighborhood of Coyoacán, both benefited greatly from this process, and Novo recorded numerous examples of this change in his magazine column.

61 For complaints about decaying housing in central Mexico City in this era—including buildings without running water, buildings without connection to sewers, and whole blocks plagued by rats or regular floods—see AGN/RC vol. 424, exp. 13; vol. 425, exp. 1, 16, 17, 18, 28, 29; and vol. 424.1, exp. 162.

62 Manuel Fernández Perera, "El macho y el machismo," in *Mitos mexicanos*, ed. Enrique Florescano (Mexico City: Editorial Aguilar, 1995), 182.

63 M. Gutmann, *The Meanings of Macho: Being a Man in Mexico City* (Berkeley: University of California Press, 1996). Similarly, Alma Guillermoprieto describes macho behavior among Mexicans—specifically, groups of men getting together to get drunk and weep at parties—as a more or less self-conscious ritual of middle-class men who understand themselves to be playing a slightly ridiculous role. See *The Heart That Bleeds: Latin America Now* (New York: Knopf, 1994), 237–58.

64 Ilene O'Malley, *The Myth of the Revolution: Hero Cults and the Institutionalization of the Mexican State* (Westport, CT: Greenwood Press, 1986).

65 For the public image of the "gentleman president," see Magaña Contreras, *Ciudad abierta*, 213–16. On the contrast between the two brothers, see Enrique Krauze, *Mexico: Biography of Power* (New York: HarperCollins, 1997), 491–500.

66 Elsewhere I have argued that commercial culture embodied the countermacho in the figure of El Santo, the wrestler/photonovel character/movie star whose fame rivaled Infante's. See A. Rubenstein, "El Santo versus El Santos, or, Mediated Visions of Mexican Masculinity in the Post-Revolutionary Era," in *The Mexico Reader*, ed. G. Joseph (Duke University Press, forthcoming).

Discovering a Land "Mysterious and Obvious": The Renarrativizing of Postrevolutionary Mexico

Eric Zolov

The discursive lens through which most Americans viewed Mexico in the postrevolutionary period (c. 1920–1940) was one shaped by images of violent revolutionary turmoil and a later reformist zeal that targeted U.S. economic, political, and cultural influence.[1] Negative connotations of Mexico as a land plagued by social upheaval and moral degeneracy were not new, of course. Derogatory stereotypes about the Mexican "character" and the country's incapacity for social progress dated to the chaos of nineteenth-century caudillo-led revolts and were grounded in an ideological presumption of innate Latin American backwardness.[2] Beginning in the context of World War II, however, a noticeable change took place in the way Americans perceived and commented on Mexico or, perhaps better stated, on Central Mexico—Mexico City, in particular—and on such rising provincial tourist sites as Taxco, Guanajuato, and Acapulco. Certain deeply embedded prejudices did not necessarily disappear but, rather, were renarrated with an emphasis on the positive aspects of Mexican culture and society. During the period around 1950–1970 Mexico thus achieved a "new look," one that coincided with a sustained period of relative political stability, an unprecedented expansion of its middle classes, and a harmonious relationship with the United States.

This new look rested, on one hand, on the successful promotion of Mexico domestically and internationally as a modern, cosmopolitan nation, one that offered both comfort and a healthy return on foreign investment. At the same time, the new look also depended on marketing to visitors a friendly, exotic, folkloric charm not found at home. A number of factors helped bring about this transformation: a politico-military alliance with the United States born out of World War II and that extended into the cold war period; a shift in Mexico's development strategy away from a radical redistributionalism to a strategy of intensive capitalist accumulation (which now embraced foreign investment); a newfound political stability reflected in the rise of the Partido Revolucionario Institucional (PRI); the advent of mass communications and mass travel, and thus of mass tourism (especially by Americans, but also by Mexicans); and finally, a mutually reinforcing effort on the part of the Mexican and U.S. governments to forge cultural policies aimed at reframing popular perceptions of Mexican culture and of the country's revolutionary process. The post-1950 period, in other words, was the culminating moment in the refashioning of Mexican stereotypes of backwardness and danger, a narrative as well as political process that had concerned Mexican political elites since the prerevolutionary dictatorship of Porfirio Díaz.

Operating within a national and transnational framework, a complex cultural dialectic evolved in which referents of "cosmopolitan" progress and "folkloric" authenticity served as signposts for interpreting a new vision of Mexican nationhood. By the 1960s tens of thousands of tourists, largely from the United States, had traveled south of the border for a taste of what the *New York Times* touted as the "new Mexico," one that offered "not only picturesqueness but comfort."[3] The facility of travel, rising living standards in the United States, Mexico's political stability, and the appeal of experiencing a "premodern" culture without significant loss of luxury all factored into the decision to visit. Yet mainstream tourists were not the only ones traveling to Mexico. By the mid-1960s, scores of countercultural tourists (beatniks and hippies) also had crossed the border, drawn in no small measure by the same images of an authentic indigenous charm that now lured other tourists. One place in particular that hippies came to visit was the Mazatec Indian village of Huautla de Jiménez, located in the northern highlands of Oaxaca. In Huautla de Jiménez hallucinogenic mushrooms grew wild and were used by the local population in ritual healing practices; here indeed was an authentic indigenous experience! An unanticipated outgrowth of these countercultural tourists, moreover, was their impact on Mexican youth, who came to be known by the late 1960s as *jipitecas*. Ironically, foreign youth discovered in an indigenous Mexico an outlet for their quest for transcendence of their own modern selves, while Mexican jipitecas emulated the hippies for their embodiment of an authentic cosmopolitanism; this encounter ultimately led Mexican youth to a rediscovery of their own indigenous roots, an identity process that itself transcended the folkloric trappings of official Mexican culture.[4]

Arguably, at the heart of these different touristic experiences rested competing, though not entirely contradictory, notions of what "Mexico" signified. The cosmopolitan and the folkloric had become inextricably linked as key referents along a continuum of representation of the modern nation-state, a discursive and policy axis that directly shaped Mexican and foreign imaginings. Although accessing the imaginary has its perils,[5] this essay hopes to offer some insights into how a postrevolutionary narrative of Mexican progress became a central dimension of national development during this Golden Age of middle-class prosperity and U.S.-Mexican relations.

Forging a Cosmopolitan-Folklórico Discourse

Since the days of the dictator Porfirio Díaz (1876–1911), Mexico has faced the burden of exchanging an international reputation for banditry and backwardness (inherited from the chaotic dissolution of the nation-state following independence from Spain) for one of progress and civilization. During the Porfiriato (as the reign of Díaz is called), relative political stability and a surge in economic growth laid the foundations for a more favorable, even conceited outlook by Mexican elites and foreign observers. French, British, and U.S. cultural influence accompanied their economic investments and thus helped shape an impression of the capital, at least, as faithfully emulating the metropolises.[6] An incipient *indigenista* strategy—the glorification of Mexico's pre-Hispanic past, albeit in the context of a repression of Mexico's indigenous *present*—also shaped a nationalist discourse. Discussing the role of Mexican painting and architecture during the Porfiriato, for example, Mauricio Tenorio-Trillo writes that the Díaz regime "sought to order, classify, and civilize knowledge of the Indian past in such a way as to make it accessible and worthy of respect."[7] By linking an indigenista aesthetic with the regime's modernizing capitalist outlook, Díaz and his "wizards of progress" (as Tenorio-Trillo labels them) looked to establish a cosmopolitanism worthy of respect among the world's leading nations. In the course of the revolutionary violence from 1910 to 1920, this project effectively collapsed. Nonetheless, the prerevolutionary regime had established the basis for a postrevolutionary definition of nationhood in which the indigenous and the modern were inextricably linked.

From the ashes of revolutionary upheaval came a renaissance in artistic expression and folklore appreciation, a movement that not only valorized but romanticized indigenous culture (past *and* present) while elevating certain aspects of regional mestizo culture into iconic referents of national belonging.[8] The outcome of this nationalizing process was a more coherent sense of shared identity among Mexicans;[9] it also created a deeper respect (at times, even awe) by Americans for Mexican culture. Writing about the impact of a special exhibit of Mexican muralist art presented in the United States in 1930–1931, for instance, Helen Delpar notes that "instead of being a backward country full of bandits as many imagined, [Mexico] was now seen as a nation of culture."[10] The "vogue of things Mexican" that Delpar discusses reflected the beginnings of an important shift in the U.S. reception of Mexican nationalism (e.g., a valorization of the nation's indigenous present). It also pointed to the Mexican state's leveraging of representations of mestizo and Indian culture as a central component of its domestic and international diplomacy.

Still, most Americans continued to harbor grave doubts about Mexico. In large part this was because of the state's new, quasi-socialist domestic policies, epitomized by attacks on the Church and expropriations of private property in the name of revolutionary justice. Mexico thus continued to be viewed by Americans much as the rest of Latin America, "as lands inhabited by deviates from the norms of moral conduct."[11] These were images commonly reinforced by Hollywood and in popular literature, despite the later gloss of Good Neighborliness.[12] Those who did venture south of the border were mostly a hodgepodge of "drifters . . . writers, intellectuals, and artists," whom Fredrick Pike labels somewhat anachronistically as a "counterculture."[13] A deviant minority in their own right, this relatively small collection of bohemian adventurers and partisans of the Revolution took up residence in Mexico, believing to have found in the nation's revolutionary experiment the hope of a future utopia; for others, Mexico was a welcome refuge from anticommunist hysteria in the United States. Immersed in a radical restructuring of its society, postrevolutionary Mexico nevertheless undoubtedly struck most Americans as but a more threatening version of the old: xenophobic, socialist, and a direct challenge to U.S. hegemony in the circum-Caribbean "backyard."[14] Somewhat miraculously, however, in the post-1940 period this image changed. Through the exigencies of World

War II and the workings of a new Mexican president, Avila Camacho, perceived as pro-American, the terms of an earlier relationship marked by mutual mistrust and prejudice were soon transformed into a celebrated partnership.

Mexico became a key strategic ally of the United States during World War II, supplying oil, minerals, workers (*braceros*), and even a fighter squadron, which fought in the Pacific theater.[15] Because of the importance of Mexico and the rest of Latin America to the war effort, the U.S. government went to great lengths to influence public opinion at home and abroad of the necessity of the hemispheric partnership (itself an extension of an earlier Good Neighbor discourse). Under the auspices of the Office of the Coordinator of Inter-American Affairs (OCIAA), precursor to the U.S. Information Agency (USIA), the U.S. State Department took an active role in propagandizing America's newfound partnership with Mexico, part of a broader, pro-Allies cultural campaign waged throughout the Americas.[16] Among the many facets of these propaganda efforts was the production (often, coproduction with Mexican agencies) of documentary films showcasing this new relationship. These films were apparently distributed to schools and civic organizations in the United States. One such film, *Mexican Moods* (c. 1945), begins with a procession of Mexican soldiers marching in Mexico City under the respectful watch of U.S. officers, as the narrator trumpets: "Men are on the march [with] Mexico, too, proudly taking her place among the nations at war with the Axis." The film's direction then quickly shifts to scenes of a recently completed section of the Pan-American highway, an apt metaphor for the new U.S.-Mexican relationship and of the material and political advances Mexico was making: "These roads, well paved, well policed, are taking thousands of average United States folks into the heart of a neighboring country. Now that good roads run way down south of the border we Americans are more numerous, more truly representative of the United States and better liked in Mexico than ever before."[17] In addition to highlighting such clear signs of progress, *Mexican Moods* also features performative displays of the country's rich cultural heritage: its "folkloric" dances (featuring the Trio Mixteco), its colonial-era provinces (Taxco, "Where modern Mexico meets the look of Old Time Mexico"), its ancient Aztec civilizations ("This is undoubtedly how the ancient inhabitants of Mexico looked and acted on one of their holiest festive days"). Through such films, Americans were learning that Mexico was a land of progress and culture.

In another OCIAA film, *Mexico City* (c. 1946), narrated by Orson Welles and produced in direct collaboration with the Mexican Tourist Association, the viewer discovers a bustling metropolis where "the new and the old is [*sic*] always picturesquingly [*sic*] mixed." A tour of the capital includes modern downtown (whose "narrow streets open into broad avenues"), Indian Xochimilco (where long-braided women in dugout canoes sell "a great armful [of flowers] for a penny"), and the mysterious pyramids of Teotihuacán (imbued with "religious zeal behind the making of untold thousands of sculptures"). After a day's adventure into the unfamiliar, the film returns to the familiarity, comfort, and safety of reasonably plush accommodations: "The hotels are modern, down to the bellboy shining buttons. Whether you speak Spanish or not, you can get the best food you ever ate. Strange fish and exotic fruit. Then, worn out from trying to see everything at once, you can rest weary bones in rooms like these."[18] This lauding of Mexican modernity and the showcasing of its cultural richness reflected the culmination of a new vision of nationhood, one increasingly disseminated from both sides of the border.

During the 1950s scores of U.S. travelers and potential investors flocked to Mexico, eager to take advantage of an inexpensive vacation that promised comfort alongside the thrill of an encounter with the exotic. As one American observer noted in early 1953, "Politically, the country has never been more stable. The intense activity all around, the big building program and flourishing private enterprise point up a new era coming."[19]

The sense of progressive economic *movement*, moreover, had broader ramifications on foreign perceptions of a changing Mexican character. Slowly disappearing, for example, was the derogatory association of the Mexican "siesta" with sloth. Thus, whereas a *New York Times* article from 1946 referred to Mexico as a country "where the siesta spirit is prevalent,"[20] a decade later another writer felt confident in proclaiming that Mexico was "waking up after a long siesta": "Mexico proved herself a loyal ally in World War II. Mexico proved herself just as loyal a friend in the free world's defense against communism. . . . Mexico can no longer be caricatured as a poor peon, clothed in rags, having his mid-day siesta in the sun. Mexico is waking up!"[21] This discursive shift away from a deeply entrenched stereotype of laziness is also evidenced in cartoon narratives from the period. For example, in cartoon representations of Mexico dating from the mid-1930s, Mexicans are depicted as perpetually in siesta. This is true even as late as 1949, where "Señor Droopy" ("from Guadalupe") embodies the lackadaisical Mexican, who would rather rest in the shade than overexert himself.[22] But by 1959 the dominant archetype of Mexican character (at least for children) is "Speedy Gonzalez," a classic trickster with noble morals who goes on to join a pantheon of Looney Tunes figures on which generations of American youth would grow up.[23] The perception that the "siesta was over" had an important multiplier effect on Americans' willingness to reconsider their southern neighbor as a place suitable for a safe vacation, not to mention worthy of their investment dollars. As one Mexican editorialist wrote in 1964, at the high point of the Mexican Miracle, "A more precise knowledge of Mexico [by foreigners] has increased our commerce and multiplied our exports."[24]

Despite the newfound praise, however, Mexico still faced the burdensome realities of its underdevelopment, manifest in the inescapable presence of its poor, largely indigenous population. Failure on the government's part to manage *this* representation of Mexican reality threatened to subvert the new image of Mexico as a country "vigorously advancing along the path of progress at the same pace as the most advanced nations in the world."[25] One Mexican editorialist, for example, lamented the continued perception of the nation as dominated by "straw sombreros, serape blankets, guitars, pulque, poor *campesina* women traveling dusty roads with a child on their back, and Indians squatting indolently under a blanket," despite being "images quite distant from what Mexico really is today."[26] As the *New York Times* observed that same year (1957), these were the qualities of old Mexico: "things that have survived from earlier generations and that many Mexicans today would like to get rid of."[27]

What I suggest occurred by the 1960s was the evolution of an interpretative framework that located these decidedly *un*modern images within a discourse of the folkloric. This discourse was forged through the direct and indirect impact of government policy, artists and intellectuals, national and transnational cultural industries, and the participatory gaze of tourists themselves. A key outcome, I argue, was the emergence of a "folkloric vocabulary"—tropes gleaned from tourist advertisements and scripted performances of Mexican cultural identity—which helped translate the once unsettling imagery of underdevelopment into identifiable encounters with the Other. This "vocabulary"—in actuality, a repertoire of visual, aural, and other experiential-based references—aided in the codifying of tourists' everyday run-ins with the unfamiliar. A useful example of this process, before we continue further, is evidenced by a *New York Times'* travel description of the Mexican countryside from the late 1950s. Here the discussion seems almost to mimic a Diego Rivera mural, whose own romanticized depictions of everyday life were a staple referent for every visitor to Mexico: "This is picturesque Mexico, doing work by hand and by the sweat and pain of burden-carrying shoulders, using burros where trucks might more properly serve, taking refuge—outside the larger cities—in the daily siesta, celebrating with a kind of solemn gaiety on the market days and during the fiestas."[28] The article's quaint depiction of "premodern" social organization suggests a celebration of rural culture, whereas earlier, these same aspects would have been derided as signs of backwardness. Retold in this way, foreigners now saw virtue in the melding of "premodern" and "modern" society. This melding created an experience that was, in one writer's curious and revealing phrasing, both "mysterious and obvious."[29]

Stagings of the Folkloric

One of the key sites for the staging of Mexican culture was the Ballet Folklórico, which remains today a widely recognized trademark of Mexican cultural authenticity. Started by Amalia Hernández in 1952 with only eight students, by the 1960s the ballet had become an ideal ambassador for the Mexican state. According to Hernández, the concept of the ballet was to present "an articulation [through] dance of the history, customs, legends and personality of Mexico."[30] Interestingly, the origins of the dance troupe also lie in its sponsorship by the powerful mass media magnate, Emilio Azcárraga Milmo, who included the performance in a series of folklore programs designed for television. (Indeed, this fact suggests the more complicated dynamic that developed among the state, capitalist interests, and Mexican artists and audiences in the staging of national identity.[31]) In 1959 the ballet come under the direct sponsorship of the Instituto Nacional de Bellas Artes (INBA), an overarching state institution created under President Miguel Alemán (1946–1952), whose mission was to promote national artistic expression.[32] According to INBA's first director, the renowned classical music composer Carlos Chávez, the goals for the arts agency were nothing short of grandiose: "It is logical for the State to take under its protection all the fine arts, because of their transcendent importance; because the State is able to unify all things Mexican, including the arts. It is a duty to conserve both the arts of the past, especially the remains of the pre-Cortesian epoch, as also present-day works; and to aid in the creation of new works."[33] This commitment by the state to label and preserve "all things Mexican" underscored the problematic relationship of an authoritarian regime committed to cultural nationalism; by the late 1960s the regime's "monopoly" on cultural representation was widely denounced by students and intellectuals. Yet, for foreigners especially, the ballet and other aspects of nationalist cultural production (such as muralism) became key sites for the transference of a folkloric vocabulary, offering tourists the sights and sounds of an "authentic" Mexican experience.

The Ballet Folklórico's repertoire ranged from indigenous dance rituals to revolutionary corridos and *bailes típicos* from the nation's diverse regions. Though the notion of ballet embodied a European, cosmopolitan expression of "high art" (the home base for the ballet was the impressive, Italian-marbled Palace of the Fine Arts in Mexico City), the term "folklórico" at the same time dictated a surveyed narration of Mexican popular cultural history. The dances offered by the Ballet Folklórico provided an accessible, living image of the nation's indigenous and mestizo cultures. Removed from their original contexts and packaged for touristic consumption, what audiences witnessed was a distanced and conflated staging of local cultural traditions marketed as national folklore. These dances retained their exotic quality, yet at the same time became accessible; they remained unfamiliar, yet were nonthreatening. The Ballet Folklórico, in other words, presented a coherent, exportable picture of Mexican Otherness, allowing audiences to "get close" to Mexican culture via their own distanced participant-observation. From one widely used American tourist guidebook of the time, we learn that the ballet was the "best of its kind that you're likely to see and a stunning show in any terms": "Starting with the great hieratic dignity of ancient ritual and a solemn, hypnotic plume dance, it moves through the times and regions skillfully and imaginatively, accompanied by varieties of appropriate music: a chorus which sings the songs of the Revolution, a combination of *chirimía* and drum which make the thin, lonely sounds one still hears in remote churchyards, *mariachis* of good taste and musicianship, the nimble harp strings of Veracruz. The décor and costuming follow folkloric themes, bringing to life clay candelabra and primitive Spanish-Indian angels in bright crowns and wings, dancing around a stiff blue-and-gold Virgen de la Soledad."[34] Shortly after being absorbed by INBA the ballet was promoted through Mexico's Department of Tourism and a second, identical dance group was formed. While one act remained in the country performing several days a week at the Bellas Artes theater in Mexico City, the other traveled abroad as Mexico's "official representative."[35]

The success of the Ballet Folklórico can be measured, at least in part, by the attention and accolades it received in the United States. In August 1962 the troupe embarked on its first extended tour of the United States where they traveled up the West Coast and to Chicago, everywhere meeting with universal acclaim. For example, a reviewer in Seattle, Washington, described the group's performance as "a living travel folder" that "may very well spark a tourist boom for the land of the sun."[36] Indeed, through the Ballet Folklórico audiences learned how to *interpret* Mexican history and culture. "For two hours . . . we were shown the variety and richness of Mexico's cultural heritage," a Chicago reviewer wrote. She continued: "Our southern neighbor has several layers of civilization—Aztec, Mayan, Spanish conquistadores, Yaqui Indians. It is a land of mestizos and peons, primitive rites, and Christian holidays." In fact, it was the evident raw authenticity of the performance—the "primitive hand-made percussion and string instruments," "the ancient Indian dances [whose] robes, headdresses, and masks were wildly imaginative in design and were executed in gloriously raw and bright colors"—that clearly impressed audiences. As another reviewer described, in contrast to the Spanish—"who stamp in pride and arrogance"— the Mexicans came across as primitively charming: "[They] skip happily on bare feet or shuffle in sandals." Thus just as Amalia Hernández and the Mexican government clearly intended, the performances "evoke[d] the spirit of [the] nation and its people"; the Ballet Folklórico rapidly became a trademark of the country's new look. In 1965, the troupe performed live on the U.S. television variety show *The Hollywood Palace*, where their act ended with the host's (spontaneous?) cry of "Viva Mexico!"[37] References to the ballet were also featured in the numerous travel advertisements for Mexico (paid for by the Mexican Tourist Ministry) that proliferated in anticipation of the 1968 Olympic games (see Figure 33). A short promotional film entitled *Mexican Watercolor* (1965), produced by the J. C. Penney Corporation in collaboration with the Mexican Tourist Ministry, also highlighted the Ballet Folklórico's famed performance of the "Mexican Hat Dance."[38] Later in the decade, in response to a special function of the ballet arranged for the American Bar Association in Dallas, Texas, the president of the Dallas chapter of the bar wrote President Díaz Ordaz to thank him personally. The ballet, he explained, was presented "as the featured entertainment of the meeting so that our many visitors and guests could enjoy a portrayal of the cultures of Mexico." The performers of this "fine ballet troupe" returned for "innumerable curtain calls," and "in the minds and hearts of so many thousands the strong ties already existing between our countries and cultures were strengthened even more."[39]

Another important site for the transference of a folkloric vocabulary was the famed revolutionary murals found on various buildings throughout the capital, including several newly constructed hotels. The so-called muralist school of art was initiated in the early 1920s under the direct sponsorship of Mexico's first minister of education, José Vasconcelos. Initially associated with the regime's own revolutionary agenda, by the late 1950s the muralist school came to epitomize the stifling benevolence of official patronage; a new generation of artists and intellectuals increasingly regarded the movement with open disdain and cynicism.[40] Muralism's dramatic and often romanticized depictions of revolution, rural life, and pre-Hispanic civilizations were by now an integral element of the PRI's nationalist ideology and a celebrated feature of Mexican revolutionary culture. However, although a romanticized masking of the nation's history and of indigenous reality may have epitomized the regime's authoritarian character for some, for tourists the murals conveyed a primal authenticity. No wonder Alfaro David Siqueiros (one of the "tres grandes" of the muralism school and a defender of the PRI's commitment to the movement) commented that mural art had contributed "more than anything else . . . to the development of tourism."[41]

The Museum of Anthropology (completed in 1964) represented yet another important site for the staging of native cultures and became a famed location for foreigners seeking to "understand" indigenous Mexico. Widely celebrated in the U.S. press for its high-modernist architectural splendor ("deviationist," in one writer's phrase),[42] its educational dioramas depicting pre-Hispanic life, and an endless display of artifacts, the museum was a grandiose monument both to Mexico's cosmopolitan present and to its glorious Indian past. As Enrique Florescano later argued, here the country's pre-Columbian civilizations were celebrated as the "original substratum of the nation."[43] Yet the Indian *present* was virtually absent; dioramas instead focused on an imagined ideal existence before the time of the Spanish Conquest. Moreover, the sheer number of rooms and artifacts tended to have the effect of blurring an understanding of the historical differentiation between the cultures represented; in the vastness of their display, they all became "Mexican." Ignacio Bernal, founding director of the museum, inadvertently revealed this hidden hegemonic function in explaining the museum's mission as "producing not a series of more or less astonishing images, or which call attention to Mexico's pre-Hispanic past, but [rather] *a single image* which conveys the *basic homogeneity* of the country, out of that heterogeneity to which was referred."[44] Indeed, the one culture privileged in spatial and visual terms is the Aztec (Mexica). Néstor García Canclini elaborates on this ideological dimension in his important critique of the museum, noting that "the bringing together of thousands of testimonies from all over Mexico attests to the triumph of the centralist project, announcing that here [Mexico City] the intercultural synthesis is produced."[45] A visit to the museum thus offered not only a vicarious excursion to indigenous regions beyond Mexico City, it also conveyed to tourists, as did the Ballet Folklórico and the murals, a folkloric vocabulary used to interpret the "deeper" meanings of Mexican culture and history, minus the hindrance of actual Indians obscuring one's view.[46]

Encounters with the "Mexico of Tomorrow"

On the eve of World War II, with Western Europe closed off to U.S. travelers, Mexico's tourist sector rose to fourth place behind mining, food, and textile production as a contributor to economic growth.[47] Between 1938 and 1946, the numbers of foreign tourists arriving in Mexico—in their majority, clearly American—increased from 90,000 to over 300,000 and by 1960 that figure would more than double.[48] Indeed, in 1960 one article reported that "more American tourists go to Mexico than go to any other foreign country."[49] By 1968, income from tourist- and border-related transactions generated as much foreign exchange for Mexico as sales from goods.[50] This dramatic expansion in tourism was directly tied to a number of factors. One was the increase in road building across the American Southwest, which drew in more travelers from nonborder regions of the United States and modernized border crossings. A second factor was the development policies of President Miguel Alemán (1946–1952), who spurred private investment and channeled state resources toward tourist-related infrastructure. Part of Alemán's accomplishments in this regard was the completion of Mexico's section of the Pan-American highway in 1951. Thus, along with the expansion of air travel more generally, by the mid-1950s a trip to Mexico no longer implied a risky expedition made only by bohemian artists and intellectuals.[51] Finally, there were the changing perceptions of Mexico from that of a bandit-ridden country riven with danger to a "colorful" place with modern hospitality.

The first wave of U.S. tourists no doubt carried some of the cultural and political baggage of earlier U.S.-Mexican relations, but judging from published travel accounts and tourist letters discovered in the Mexican archives, many also seemed eager to embrace the new image of Mexico caught in the grips of an inexorable modernization. In one early travelogue, for example, we read that "Mexico is like an intricate, old and valuable rug that is constantly being mended and renewed."[52] The metaphor is quite revealing of the deeply ingrained assumptions behind U.S. hegemony in Latin America, for a rug adds color ("culture") but, more important, it cushions and protects (i.e., one's investments and interests). Reading into the metaphor still further, the Mexican "rug" has taken a beating from its revolutionary toil, but it is now "on the mend" and deserving of American support, especially since Mexico "cushions" the United States from other Latin American turmoil.

This eager reappraisal is found in numerous travelogues from the period. A prime example is a travel article from the mid-1950s entitled "On the Road to Utopia." From the start the author revels in Mexico's advances in infrastructure: "You may drive to this Never-Never Land . . . on good, paved roads, or go by plane, train, or bus."[53] With that one sentence decades of dark imagery of roadside bandits, rocky mule trails, and a nation beyond the pale are dispelled. Moreover, what awaits the traveler on arrival is of even greater surprise: "What I am about to report is strictly in the daydream department—except that it's true."[54] Among the author's discoveries: Mexico is surprisingly developed. Thus, the author refers to one provincial city as "a revelation in Mexico's modernization" and he is careful to note the various "sign[s] of Mexico's evolution."[55] The country also turns out to be more culturally authentic and *fascinating* than he apparently expected. He writes about villages "most tourists have not yet discovered," where "it's always spring. . . . Most are fairly close to metropolitan centers; a few are literally out of this world. All are excitingly 'foreign.'"[56] Interestingly, this narrative of a "foreignness within reach" became a major advertising slogan—"So foreign . . . yet so near"—used by the Mexican Tourist Department during the mid-1960s (see Figure 33).

Indeed, the appeal of "foreignness" is central to these tourist narratives. Visiting the country was "like poetry after prose," as one article phrased the experience, going on to say: "Mexico offers Americans the exhilaration of exotic images to vary the dull familiarity of the local scene; and since Mexico is a neighbor, the change is easily effected."[57] This reflection is also to be found in Kate Simon's popular guidebook, *Mexico: Places and Pleasures* (1962). Mexico, she writes, offers the prospect of progress and exotica both within easy reach: "In a world which is becoming homogenized with fearsome rapidity, Mexico is still a wonderful confusion and melding of disparate facts, eras, art, sociology, and mental climates. It is a country busily constructing dams, pulling roads out of the jungle, building and peopling automobile plants, and in the process, bringing to light its majestic antiquities."[58] Phrases such as "busily constructing," "pulling roads," and "bringing to light" all help convey a sense of industrial and technological *movement—* the wrenching of order from primitiveness. Yet Simon's language also celebrates the deep mystery (to her) of Mexican culture and society. The country is "a wonderful confusion . . . [of] mental climates," a description implicitly juxtaposed to the bounded, "homogenized" world at home. Mexico, in other words, was entering the popular imagination among travelers in the United States as an accessible and inviting frontier, at once "unbounded" yet sufficiently developed to offer a safe escape from the perception of a progressive standardization of life in the United States.[59]

We see this dualism expressed, for example, in yet another guidebook from the period, which talks about the "almost untouched" town of Tepotzlán. Here, the authenticity of an indigenous Mexico offered "sights and sounds not usually found in the tourists' circuit." Yet there is nothing threatening about the description; comfort, safety, and lodging are nowhere compromised: "There is a delightful American-managed hotel with all that you could desire in Mexico, but a few steps down the cobblestone streets will take you to the Plaza, where Nahuatl . . . is as frequently heard as Spanish, where English is almost nonexistent."[60] Both discursively and experientially, foreignness is constantly framed and contained through juxtaposition with a modern familiarity. Where once, for instance, the gabble of Indians speaking in Nahuatl might have been "read" as frightening, a folkloric vocabulary and the placement of that experience along the folkloric-cosmopolitan axis (where a modern hotel is reassuringly present) has helped reframe that experience as an adventuresome, romantic encounter. As an article in the *New York Times* expressed, Mexico was a country "strange and different" yet with surprising levels of "comfort and safety . . . [in] territory once occupied by a not so comfortable and not so safe, but infinitely lovely old Mexico."[61] Or, as another travelogue pointed out, "We hadn't known that Taxco is as safe for kids as Detroit if you follow a couple of simple rules about eating."[62] Moreover, Mexico was exceedingly cheap. Ameri-

cans openly marveled at the strength of the dollar (a fact that no doubt reinforced their own sense of superiority); this permitted even the traveler on a
moderate, budget to experience a certain fantasy of wealth. "In general we
lived at the top level of luxury" one author concluded, after describing his
"8-day, 2,000 mile excursion" with his family through Mexico. "It is no
wonder it has become a favorite American playground!"[63]

Thousands of U.S. travelers ventured "south of the border" during the
1960s, often for the first time and often by car, to discover the safe yet ac-
cessibly exotic "land of the pyramids and mariachis." Between 1960 and 1970
the number of foreign tourists, largely from the United States, more than
tripled, rising from 631,000 to 1,986,000.[64] In the first of what developed
into a series of tourist advertisements produced by the Mexican Tourist
Council in anticipation of the 1968 Olympics, the Mexican government
beckoned: "México, of course! . . . From the world-famed Folkloric Ballet
to the sophisticated night spots, it's cosmopolitan and gay. A lively country
on the move, incomparable relics of pre-historical and Hispanic cultures
grace it. In 1968 it will be host to the Olympic Games. Come for a pre-
Olympic view of this fabulous Mexico—so near, so modern and yet so
foreign."[65]

That Americans would feel comfortable traveling to Mexico in such numbers is a reflection of a new sense of familiarity with what the country had
to offer. The advertising phrase "so modern and yet so foreign" (later: "So
foreign . . . yet so near") thus neatly encapsulated tourists' anticipation of a
folkloric and cosmopolitan experience.

During this period of heightened cold war tension, when the "Third
World" emerged as the disputed terrain of superpower rivalries and Latin
America appeared on the brink of revolutionary upheaval, Mexico had also
become a model Latin American nation in the U.S. imaginary and a valued
strategic ally. Many Americans saw Mexico as a partner in progress, as a developing nation struggling to catch up to the United States and take its place
among the "First World." Though doubts briefly resurfaced when Mexico
refused to rupture relations with revolutionary Cuba (the only Latin American country to resist U.S. pressures to do so), the government's subsequent
repressive actions against "communist agitators" and a distanced association
with the Castro regime clearly belied the PRI's otherwise leftist rhetoric.
Americans were repeatedly assured that the new U.S.-Mexican strategic relationship was on firm ground. As one high-level government official in the

33. This advertisement (paid for by the Ministry of Tourism) was part of a series created in anticipation of the 1968 Olympics and clearly evidences the use of a folklórico-cosmopolitan discourse. *New York Times*, 3 September 1967, D29.

López Mateos administration (1958–1964) explained to a foreign reporter, "Mexico will not commit suicide for Castro."[66] Indeed, by the mid-1960s any doubts about Mexico's position in the cold war were firmly put to rest.

Interestingly, a number of Americans chose to convey their thoughts and impressions about Mexico by writing directly to President Díaz Ordaz (1964–1970). These letters, scattered as they are, provide a unique opportunity to glimpse the reactions of ordinary Americans to the "Mexico of tomorrow."[67] At one end of the spectrum, negative experiences with corrupt and arbitrary officials evidently reinforced preexisting racist stereotypes. This was the case with at least one letter writer, a man who charged that Mexico was "populated by men and women of questionable integrity and virtue who would steal at the slightest provocation, even if what they would steal is of no value to them."[68] A more humorous critique comes from a woman upset with Mexican cuisine. Irate at finding her favorite foods missing or Mexicanized beyond recognition, she demanded of the president: "Where are the club sandwiches? . . . On an expensive meal, where is the baked potato filled with creamcheese and chives? . . . Around the block from the hotel I was served a salad with lettuce, topped with tomatoes and then topped with green peas. I never heard of such a thing. Peas on top of tomatoes? And where were the hard-boiled eggs, split in half and then the yellow taken out and mixed with mayonnaise, etc."[69] What is interesting here is not simply her apparent disregard for traditional Mexican food, nor the implicit arrogance of her transformation of a trivial complaint into a point of dispute with the president of a foreign country. What should also strike the reader is the woman's own expectations of receiving a meal that was "familiar"; the exotic should be an option, not a requirement, and the familiar should be done right.

Most letters found in the archives, however, are more favorable. Indeed, their general tone reflects a dual fascination with Mexico's "modern progress" on one hand and the country's "colorful people" on the other. One writer, for example, noted that he or she (it is unclear in this case) has "watched with interest the encouraging progress of the Mexican nation in overcoming the major problems it has faced." Praising the country's economic and political stability, the writer offered that "Mexico has taken its place as a leader in the American community of nations."[70] In other letters, President Díaz Ordaz often received special praise as "a Great Leader and humanitarian."[71] This particular compliment came before the repression of students during the summer and fall of 1968, yet even afterward, support for Díaz Ordaz remained strong; a benevolent authoritarianism undoubtedly seemed to many Americans an apt political solution for Mexico's underlying conflicts.[72]

Mexico's modernization seems to reveal itself to these letter writers not only in terms of the nation's economic growth and political stability but also in a more abstract sense of "progress." As one woman wrote, "This past week my husband and I returned from a ten-day visit to your wonderful country. . . . Everywhere were signs of the great progress your country is making; industrially, economically, and socially."[73] Another man wrote encouragingly that, compared with earlier visits to the country, he and his wife felt that the "people [are] better dressed"; "We were most impressed with

the progress evident in the areas we visited . . . and what is even more important—a tremendous feeling of pride by the people in themselves and their
achievements!"[74] This same emotional intensity is conveyed in many of
these letters and seems suggestive of an ideological perspective that viewed
the *right* to an (unsolicited) American response as something natural and
beneficial for the president to receive.

Through the discourse of letter writers we also discover ways in which the
touristic imaginary has been shaped by expectations gleaned from myriad
sources, including advertisements, film, travelogues, scripted cultural encounters, and the language of experiences passed along by others, all of
which I argue provided an important framework for interpreting one's relationship with Mexico. For example, one woman wished to thank the president for her and her husband's "very wonderful trip to your exotic country,"
where "the people, the flowers, the climate were all wonderful."[75] As another woman summed up her impressions: Mexicans are "a happy people
. . . always a smile on their faces."[76] This romanticized idealization is repeated in many of the letters. "I have visited your country three times and I
have never been contented in the United States after my first visit," wrote
one woman; "your people have spirit."[77] In fact, many letter writers seemed
to project onto Mexico their own mounting anxieties and even disillusion-
ment with the United States, where racial, cultural, and political conflicts
were tearing the nation apart by the late 1960s. For example, one young
woman (describing herself as a "teenager") wrote: "The people are so real,
while with my country men [*sic*], they try to hide themselves and feelings
deep within them. The hatred and culty [*sic*] between the Negroes and the
whites is something I am ashamed of and I apologize. . . . Please never let
vanity, hatred or unhappiness enter the beautiful haven of Mexico. I just
wish my country could be just as proud of yours [*sic*] deserves to be."[78] Fredrick Pike identifies this idealization as "third world sentimentalism," an
emotional and ideological response he associates especially with the New
Left after 1959.[79] Yet we should also recognize how a folkloric vocabulary
helped channel tourists' reactive awe for the exotic toward more manage-
able tropes; Mexico becomes a land of "eternal springtime," with "colorful
folklore" and "prehistoric wonders," all of which were descriptions commonly used in tourist advertisements dating at least to the early 1950s.[80] In
a world wracked by social conflict, Mexico no doubt appeared to many
Americans (until the outbreak of student violence on the eve of the Olym-

pics) a paragon of political consensus, material advancement, and cultural authenticity.

At the same time, Mexican progress was regarded by these letter writers as inextricably linked with U.S. guardianship. Assumptions of benign tutelage ran deep. In one perhaps extreme example of this, the same woman who wrote about the lack of club sandwiches wrote another letter in which she was upset about the apparent misfortunes of a child caught in the trap of underdevelopment. Here, she describes how she spotted a young girl "about five years old . . . selling a small box of chiclets" outside the National University (UNAM) in Mexico City. Emphasizing the notion of a spiritually happy native, she described the child as "always smiling"; this part was underlined and circled. More important, the women saw it as her right as well as obligation to rescue this child and make her part of the woman's private, capitalist domain: "She looked exactly like my daughter and I would so much like to adopt her. I could give her everything in the world. . . . I want the child very much. Could you please locate her for me and ask her mother if I might adopt her. . . . Of course I would want to see a picture first to make sure it is the right child. Please do this for me as I fell in love with that little girl and will die if I cant [*sic*] have her."[81]

These letters, I suggest, reflect an ideological perspective influenced by hegemonic assumptions of U.S.–Latin American relations regarding the nature of "assistance," a rationale reinforced in this era by Alliance for Progress rhetoric. This same sense of benign imperialism comes through in another letter. Describing himself as someone who "always wanted to visit Mexico, but never had the funds to go," this letter writer nonetheless offered a neighborly solution to Mexico's problems: "I heard Mexico (some parts) are not doing so well. As you already know, America is extremely wealthy as compared to Mexico. You have the History, we (U.S.A.) have the wealth. Why don't you put in with the United States and become a part of the U.S.A.? . . . I am sure President Johnson would consider your request."[82] By the late 1960s U.S.-Mexican relations were stronger than ever before. The strategic partnership was never more valuable. It was a partnership, moreover, cultivated in diplomatic, economic, and cultural terms; few Americans felt the need to question the basic assumptions behind it. As U.S. Ambassador to Mexico Fulton Freeman stated in the spring of 1968, "The Mexican success story is not of interest only to U.S. traders and investors. Every American has a stake in the progress and development, the welfare and stability of Mexico."[83]

Countercultural Narratives

Coinciding with the development of an official tourism was a second, "unofficial" tourism: that of the beatniks and hippies. These counterculturalists (whose precursors were leftist and bohemian travelers in the 1920s and 1930s) were also attracted by images of a culturally authentic, indigenous Mexico. Yet they were more apt to disregard the staged, folkloric representations of native culture than to marvel at them. As Carl Franz, author of the famed countercultural guidebook *The People's Guide to Mexico* (1972), explained, "One of the reasons we used to go the Museum [of Anthropology] was to get clues about the areas we wanted to visit." The Ballet Folklórico was not even considered: "I thought it was completely hokey."[84] The beatniks and hippies instead ventured into the remote Mayan lowlands of the Yucatán peninsula, the highlands of Oaxaca (where hallucinogenic mushrooms became renowned), and secluded coastal towns along the Pacific coastline, where a *cabaña* with a hammock could be rented for literally pennies.[85] At first relatively few in numbers, by the mid-1960s the hippies' presence became widely noticed by Mexican authorities and in the press. Ironically these counterculturalists were lured at least in part by the same folkloric representations of Mexico that attracted mainstream tourists. Yet in their relentless pursuit of a "premodern" authenticity, they sabotaged the contained nature of that folklórico discourse. By their example, they helped influence the emergence of a Mexican countercultural movement (La Onda), whose impact was later profound.[86]

The story of the beatniks' travels to Mexico and other parts of Latin America during the 1950s is significant for at least two reasons. For one, the beatniks' interpretations of their experiences reveal a counternarrative to the discourse of tourists generally, one immortalized especially in Jack Kerouac's novel *On the Road* (1955).[87] Second, despite ideological claims to the contrary, in their actions and writings the beatniks often cast a touristic gaze not fundamentally different from the "straight" Americans they openly criticized. Indeed, their outbursts of neocolonial arrogance (frequently expressed in the published letters of such luminaries as Allen Ginsberg, Kerouac, and William Burroughs, though less explicitly in their fictionalized accounts), have led one author to characterize these bohemian adventurers as nothing short of imperialist. Thus, for Manuel Luis Martínez, the same ideology of rebellion that led the beatnik to regard himself as an "outlaw" in the United States translated to a posture of "conqueror" in

Mexico: "In both cases, the masculine subject is on the move."[88] Ginsberg discloses as much in a letter from southern Mexico from the 1950s in which he describes a trip into a mountain village struck by earthquakes: "Cant [*sic*] tell you how I enjoyed the situation—curious my psychology but it was a perfect set up [*sic*]—I was the leader, I organized and supplied the general power and intelligence—and I was deferred to, boys carried my *morale* (little bag) and my food, special indian coffee and eggs for me—the rest drank ground maize for lunch, they asked me questions, dozens of indians ready to run up and down mountains to get me horses or carry messages or perform any mysterious white man with beard wish."[89] Here, as Martínez argues, Ginsberg clearly "revels in the role of the great white explorer."[90] Mexico offered the possibility, as it had for travelers during the 1920s and 1930s, of an Other America, a premodern, Indian-centered world free from the hassles of modern, "straight" America. For the beatniks, Mexico represented "the fellaheen south [that] lies outside of time, at least outside of profane, historical time, and is now a sacred playground for the renewal of the northern civilized man."[91] Although, in a fundamental sense, the beatniks were attracted to Mexico by the same "magical" qualities that drew in other tourists, these counterculturalists delved behind the curtain of folkloric representation and eschewed the cosmopolitan comforts that were hallmarks of the "new Mexico," and behind which other tourists felt protected.

For the counterculturalists the framework of the folkloric was a fraudulent, empty vision. The beatniks were not interested in once-removed representations of culture prepackaged for ready consumption; those were for "the tourists." Instead, they searched out the roots of the "real" Mexico behind the stagings of native culture, disaggregating the very stereotypes the Mexican government sought in earnest to extirpate, reconstruct, and ultimately contain. "You have no idea what it is ten feet beyond that wire fence," Kerouac wrote to his friends Neal and Carolyn Cassady in describing his crossing of the Mexican border.[92] "Just across the street Mexico began," Kerouac writes in *On the Road*. "We looked with wonder. To our amazement, it looked exactly like Mexico. It was three in the morning, and fellows in straw hats and white pants were lounging by the dozen against battered pocky storefronts."[93] He continues: "Then we turned our faces to Mexico with bashfulness and wonder as those dozens of Mexican cats watched us from under their secret hatbrims in the night. Beyond were music and all-night restaurants with smoke pouring out of the door. 'Whee,' whispered Dean very softly. . . . We had finally found the magic land at the end of the road and we never dreamed the extent of the magic."[94] Even the beatniks' clothing styles reflect this search for transcendence. As Kerouac writes, wearing Mexican huaraches—"the silliest shoes in America"[95]—and working as a field hand alongside Mexican braceros and "Okies," Sal Paradise, Kerouac's alias in *On the Road*, imagines himself "a man of the earth." "They thought I was a Mexican, of course; and in a way I am," he writes.[96]

Mexico thus becomes the answer to the beatniks' pending boredom and sense of entrapment in the United States. Through their discovery that more adventure lies "south," the beatniks realize they can escape their tragic fate, as Todd Gitlin writes, of "hitchhikers upon a landscape already occupied."[97] As Sal Paradise describes the decision to go to Mexico: "It was no longer east-west, but magic *south*."[98] In an interesting way, Kerouac's narrative underscores Fredrick Pike's argument that U.S.–Latin American relations are premised on the value of Latin America as an extension of the western "frontier." Latin America not only provides material resources for an expanding U.S. economy, its "unsettled" expansiveness offers Americans the possibility of spiritual rejuvenation as well.[99] Thus Mexico, as Martínez writes, becomes "a site for a renewed creativity through symbolic conquest."[100] Certainly, the beatniks' writings are full of such references. For example, at one point in *On the Road* Dean and Sal find themselves in a remote mountainous village, surrounded by a group of children. The poverty of the area has a profound impact on Dean and he rummages through their car for a suitable gift. His choice is revealing. What he produces is an object that singularly symbolizes the triumph of capitalist relations: a wristwatch. In this act, Dean literally bestows Western Time upon a child, and thus by extension on an entire country. "He showed [the wristwatch] to the child. She whimpered with glee. The others crowded around with amazement. . . . Their mouths rounded like the mouths of chorister children. The lucky little girl squeezed it to her ragged breast-robes." Revealing the colonialist gesture implicit in the action, Kerouac writes: "They stroked Dean and thanked him."[101]

This ideology of symbolic conquest also contained a gendered expression of power relations. As Martínez again writes, "The supposed nobility of [the beatniks'] actions has to do with finding that which eludes the grasp of the modern American male: a sense of mission, patriarchal power, and primal freedom."[102] Indeed, Kerouac's "road" itself is a metaphor for endless movement, masculine prowess, virility, freedom, and technological know-how. It is the same road on which goods, services, and images will be transported into and out of Mexico and around the world. Despite an Eastern religion–based philosophy of "abandoning the ego" and of "losing oneself," the counterculturalists could not—any more than mainstream tourists might—evade associations with these imperialist relations that, as agents of the metropolis, they naturally embodied. As Kerouac writes in *On the Road*: "Then it was time to change our money. We saw great stacks of pesos on a table and learned that eight of them made an American buck, or thereabouts. We changed most of our money and stuffed the big rolls in our pockets with delight."[103] There was no escaping this basic fact of unequal power relations. The flow of persons across the border suggested as much; Mexican braceros and illegal immigrants searched for subminimum-wage jobs in the United States, jobs that, in turn, lowered the cost of goods for middle-class Americans. This further directly subsidized rising levels of consumption in the United States, thus allowing for leisure travel by mainstream tourists and counterculturalists alike back to Mexico. Still, I think it would be a mistake to dismiss *On the Road* and, by extension, the beatniks' and later hippies' actions as amounting to no more than "a misogynistic and neo-imperialist framework that undermines much of its acclaimed subversiveness," as Martínez argues.[104] Instead, one must be willing to recognize the impact of the beatniks on a *style* of countercultural rebellion that offered cultural appropriation as a strategy for the reinvention of selfhood. Such strategies of reinvention, undeniably imperialist as well as misogynist in many regards, worked to undermine repressive, patriarchal value systems in the United States and later, with the rise of La Onda, in Mexico as well.[105]

Following the trail blazed by the beatniks, a new wave of countercultural tourists—hippies—arrived in Mexico during the 1960s. What made the hippies' impact especially significant was not only their greater numbers but the fact that they arrived in the context of a global countercultural movement, of which Mexican youth were very much aware.[106] By the late 1960s, Mexican newspaper reports expressed increasing alarm at the infiltration of this foreign phenomenon under the guise of tourism. "The so-called 'hippies,'" editorialized the news magazine *Jueves de Excélsior*, "are shabby and ridiculous." They represented "a negative 'tourism,' in their majority undesirable and unproductive."[107] More alarming still was the influence the hippies seemed to have on Mexico's own middle-class youth. In fact, Mexico was experiencing a profound crisis of patriarchal values during the 1960s, of which the Mexican "hippies" (often written *jipis, jipitecas*, and even *xipitecas*) were but one manifestation. From a political standpoint the most significant challenge was posed by the massive student-led protest movement that erupted on the eve of the Olympic Games in the summer of 1968. Those protests were violently halted by a government massacre at the Plaza of the Three Cultures (Tlatelolco) on October 2 in Mexico City, barely two weeks before the start of the Olympics. In the massacre's wake, however, a Mexican countercultural movement, La Onda, filled the void for a youth movement whose protest energies had been squelched. By the early 1970s, Mexico's "hippie problem" indeed posed a significant threat to the state's nationalist project—not for its political challenge, but for its repudiation of the folklórico-cosmopolitan divide.

The rapid spread of La Onda reflected a number of transcultural influences, including that of foreign hippies. The latter embodied not only the psychedelic revolution occurring abroad but lifestyle changes appropriated in large part from the indigenous cultures they mined for experience. Ironically, for example, the hippies directly contributed to the popularization of *guaraches* (peasant sandals) and indigenous clothing among Mexican middle-class youth. As one youth commented on the influence of gringo travelers, "Before, no one used *guaraches*, and if someone put them on people would say: 'Oh no, you look like an Indian!' "[108] In emulating the hippies, Mexican jipitecas thus reappropriated a countercultural discourse grounded in their own indigenous roots yet dressed up as avant-garde. What is doubly ironic, moreover, is that the Mexican state facilitated this process by promoting an image of the nation abounding in indigenous culture. Although this official image of rural Mexico was narrated through a discourse of the folkloric, the hippies subverted this discourse (as the beatniks also had) in their pursuit of cultural "authenticity." This pursuit had an impact, in turn, on Mexican youth who also rejected folkloric imaginings of Mexican cultural identity in their rebellion against the PRI's stifling nationalist ideology. At a certain level then, the rise of La Onda suggested what might be seen as a "double-mirror effect"—Mexican youth observing American youth observing Mexico—of transcultural contact and reception, which played an important, though by no means singular, role in the subversion by Mexican youth of the state's hegemony.

Olympic Stagings of Progress and Culture

With the Mexican economic "miracle" of "stabilizing development" (low inflation backed by a stable peso) producing average annual growth rates of

34. By appropriating indigenous styles (note the use of guaraches and braided hair), these gringo hippies pursued an "authentic" Mexico beyond the folklórico construct offered by the regime. This crackdown on countercultural tourists in Huautla de Jiménez, Oaxaca, in July 1969, however, suggested the ideological threat of hippie influence on Mexico's own jipiteca youth. "Concentrados: Sobre 1303, 'Hippies [mugrosos gringos de la época],' July 1969," Hermanos Mayo Photo Archive, Archivo General de la Nación. Used by permission.

6–8 percent throughout the 1960s, the image of Mexico as the "land of 'Blood and Merriment,' of fighting cowboys and ragged Indians" had given way, according to the perspective of one Mexican editorialist, to a "more optimistic" image of the nation.[109] The selection of Mexico City as the site for the 1968 Olympics confirmed this, for it was the first time the Olympics were scheduled to be held in a "developing" country. Hosting the Olympics was of course an extremely important honor and clearly validated the state's decades-long efforts at nation building. For most Mexicans, the games clearly symbolized an important step up into the club of First Worldism. As one writer noted, "Mexico will be the point of observation for all the nations on Earth."[110]

Significantly, Mexico's folklórico image played an important role in this process. "Many factors have contributed and continue to contribute in providing an accurate image of our country abroad," the above writer continued to editorialize. "There is one factor, however, which is directly tied to this promotion and which at the same time presents one of the most favorable images of the nation. The artists, songs and regional costumes are perhaps those elements most applauded in other countries; furthermore, they constitute the most effective method of teaching our history, traditions, tastes and progress."[111] Special attention was in fact given to the dissemination of "Mexican folk and regional music," for example, in an international campaign led by the Mexican recording company Peerless. In negotiations with the Mexican Olympic Commission, Peerless received the government's backing to promote the theme of "native culture," which was disseminated on radio and television and via record sales. Peerless also planned the translation of "native music" into five different languages.[112] Following its lead, other record companies hoped to take advantage of the Olympic spotlight by "creating special packages exploring native music" aimed at the tourist market.[113]

Not surprisingly, the Mexican Tourism Ministry was a leading player in the promotion of the Olympics. In addition to the numerous advertisements taken out by the ministry in the mainstream press in the United States, slide presentations on such themes as Teotihuacán, the Museum of Anthropology, and indigenous Oaxaca were sent to embassies around the world. Available in Spanish, English, French, Italian, and German, the presentations were designed "to show the world the tourist attractions of our cities, museums, and archaeological zones" and were recommended for distribution to "travel agencies, area businesses, hotels, and many other entities directly connected with tourism."[114] Reflecting the coincidence of interests that a positive image of Mexican growth and stability had for the PRI as well as for U.S. companies, the Mobil Corporation collaborated with the tourist ministry to produce a 16-millimeter color documentary "to promote tourism toward Mexico and present the settings in which the XIX Olympic Games of 1968 will take place." Translated into six languages (including Japanese), the twenty-four-minute film was described by a marketing agency as "a beautiful product which presents pre-Hispanic Mexico and its cultures, its sports antecedents, colonial and present-day Mexico, with all of its color, its customs, folklore, dynamism, and progress." It was anticipated that over six million people would view the film through local showings, and, backed by the Mobil Corporation, it was screened "without any cost, on television."[115] Meanwhile a New York–based film company, Filmex, Inc., was contracted by the Mexican government to produce a series of three films in both Spanish and English for worldwide distribution. One film was entitled *Mexico: City of the 1970s*. Produced for pre-Olympic distribution, it "projects Mexico City as the Paris-Rome-London–New York of the next decade."[116] Mexico's cosmopolitan moment had surely arrived.

If the Olympic Games served to validate Mexico's claims to cosmopolitan accomplishments, the outbreak of student demonstrations and violent police repression cast a temporary pall over the pending Olympic ceremonies and raised doubts over whether Mexico was the appropriate site after all. Interestingly, the mainstream press in the United States reacted negatively to the regime's brutal crackdown and eventually adopted a more sympathetic viewpoint of the students' demands. The U.S. and Mexican mass media's unwavering support for President Díaz Ordaz, however, was never in question.[117] Letters by Americans to Díaz Ordaz during this period in fact reveal a certain longing for the toughness of character exhibited by his regime. These expressions came at a time when the domestic fabric of the United States itself seemed to be tearing apart. Comparing the Mexican situation to that in the United States, one woman wrote: "These acts [by student protesters] are perpetrated by the very same people—a merciless, radical rabble."[118] Still another American expressed his support of Mexican policies while underscoring how progress and anticommunism go hand in hand: "I just recently spent a vacation in Mexico City, Cuernavaca, Taxco, and Acapulco, and I 'Fell in Love' with Mexico and its people. I am now telling everybody I know to take their next vacation in Mexico! . . . We were AMAZED at the wide streets, the cleanliness, and the hospitality. MEXICO, SI—CASTRO, NO!!! . . . P.S. Why not use mace chemical on these anti-Mexican agitators, as well as police dogs. Give them the same treatment that Mayor Daley of Chicago did, multiplied many times. VIVA MEXICO!"[119] By the time this letter reached Mexico, Díaz Ordaz had already chosen to implement such a policy: the brutal massacre of unarmed protesters at Tlatelolco.[120]

The Mexican government went to great lengths in the days leading up to the opening of the Olympics to reassure foreigners that the social unrest was contained; momentary instability would not deter the nation's progress. Although small groups on the left in the United States condemned the repression, most Americans no doubt were simply thankful that the protests were finally over. In letters to Díaz Ordaz many Americans outright applauded the repression.[121] As one man wrote: "Sir, I have been reading about the riots in Mexico City and how you and your people handled them. I believe you sent troops in protection to control the mob in short thereby saving lives and property and preserving the Dignity of your Country. We need your type [of] riot control in American citys [*sic*]. Long live Mexico."[122] Another letter writer praised Díaz Ordaz in terms that clearly indicated his own frustrations with social protest in the United States: "You have recently made a move against the rebellious, lawbreaking anarchists and extremists that would destroy Mexico. These are the same people that have taken the processes of peaceful judiciary into the streets. I say that you have done a great service to the people of Mexico just as my fellow countryman Mayor Daley of Chicago has, and George Wallace will. My heart springs forth in joy. May it run with the blooded men [*sic*] that have gathered for the games in you[r] Federal City! Long live Mexico!"[123] A copy of the letter, he indicated, was sent to Mayor Daley and George Wallace.

In the wake of Tlatelolco the Mexican regime also stepped up its campaign against foreign hippies and Mexican jipitecas, seeking to manipulate public hostility toward long-haired youth and in turn shift attention away from the massacre. Deportations, jailings, beatings, and other repressive measures were unleashed against *los greñudos* (longhairs) in a strategy that conveniently sought to scapegoat "degenerate" youth as the moral instigators of social instability. Such youth were charged by the government and press as introducing "scandals, rising juvenile delinquency, and degeneracy in its crudest respect."[124] Many Mexican households in fact agreed that the rebelliousness of youth was the root cause of social instability in the country. But the Mexican crackdown on student demonstrators and hippie-jipiteca protesters also struck a chord of approval among Americans fed up with their own country's youth and their inability to do anything about it. As one woman wrote, "I am writing this letter to tell you that you and your police force are doing a magnificent job in clearing your country of the hippies. Your country's policy is one to be admired. You really show the hippies who is boss."[125] When the cancellation of a Mexican adaptation of the rock musical *Hair* (set for performance in Acapulco and produced by Alfredo Calles, grandson of the former president) made headlines in the United States, one woman wrote: "Congratulations to your Acapulco Mayor Israel Noquera—there should be more like him—we could use him in the U.S."[126] Mexico had thus ironically become a screen on which some in the United

States projected their own longings for a firmer government authority: "I wish our government had the backbone to take a stand against such un-Godly, trashy mess as you have," one writer summed up. "I believe we could put a stop to riots here, as you did when they tried to prevent the Olympics from being held in Mexico. I have never heard of any more riots in Mexico."[127]

Conclusions

The framing for foreign (and domestic) consumption of post-1940 Mexico as a nation full of cosmopolitan splendor and folkloric charm was a complex process. A dynamic of state-sponsored cultural activity, changing geopolitical relations, national and transnational capitalist ventures, and the impact of tourists' encounters together actualized the cosmopolitan-folklórico discursive framework I have outlined. By the 1960s it appeared that this dynamic had indeed succeeded. Foreign observers came to see and, more important, *believe* a narrative of Mexican progress, one that they read about and observed through the mass media, if not also experienced directly as tourists. As one couple wrote to the president following their recent trip to Mexico, "Everywhere we looked people were working—nobody shirking."[128] These perceptions were also shaped by a genuine belief in Mexico's partnership in progress with the United States and Americans' self-congratulatory role in the redemption of Latin American underdevelopment in general. Middle-class Americans, alongside middle-class Mexicans, wanted to view the Olympics as symbolic of the country's entry into the First World. In the United States, even the repression at Tlatelolco seemed to confirm this achievement; references to the students' demands and the repression that silenced them quickly faded from the mainstream press once the Olympics commenced, although the nation's unblemished glamour had clearly been dulled. In 1970, with Mexicans on the verge of electing a new president (Díaz Ordaz's former secretary of the interior, a man widely presumed responsible for the massacre at Tlatelolco), high officials in the U.S. government predicted little dramatic change in the U.S.-Mexican relationship.[129] They were wrong, for Echeverría unleashed a period of renewed populism and anti-Americanism that tapered off only with the rise of Salinas de Gortari.

Like the collapse of the mythical Revolutionary Family that Tlatelolco came to symbolize for many Mexicans, the shift toward a neopopulist radicalism under presidents Luis Echeverría (1970–1976) and José López Portillo (1976–1982), culminating in the debt-mired economic meltdown under President Miguel de la Madrid (1982–1988), undid the romanticization of Mexican "progress" in the mindset of most Americans. The usage of a cosmopolitan-folklórico discourse had not disappeared, but its representational power nevertheless receded as darker images of Mexico's economic and political turmoil came to the forefront. An important attempt to revive the credibility of this earlier discourse was made during the presidency of Carlos Salinas de Gortari (1988–1994), when, for example, the Mexican state, once more in conjunction with the mass media Azcárraga family, sponsored the traveling art exhibition "Mexico: Thirty Centuries of Splendor" and NAFTA became for symbolic purposes the Olympic Games of the 1990s.[130] By the end of Salinas's period in office, many Americans (and Mexicans, too, for that matter) seemed willing to reinvest their confidence, albeit tentatively, in a Mexican spiritual and economic recovery. But the nation's "barbarism" once again raised its head, this time in the ski-masked persona of Subcomandante Marcos and the bloody political infighting that broke out within the PRI itself. By the late 1990s increasingly negative associations of Mexico with corruption, drugs, poverty, political violence, and illegal immigration had more than overshadowed an earlier cosmopolitan-folklórico discourse. There was little praise for the Mexico of today, much less of "tomorrow." The dramatic collapse of the PRI in free elections in July 2000, however, now offers the opportunity to renew the lease on this discourse. The new government of President Vicente Fox faces a challenge not dissimilar to that of the postrevolutionary regime: to reassure foreigners that Mexico beckons, as an "exotic" land yet safe for travel and investment. Jorge Castañeda, at the time a part of Fox's transition team in charge of foreign policy, alluded to this opportunity just after Fox's victory. Castañeda noted the elections provided Mexico with an international image of "renewed vitality," something that "we haven't enjoyed for a long time."[131] What direct role the new regime will take in attempting to shape that image, for domestic and foreign consumption alike, still remains to be seen.

Notes

I wish to thank the Dean's Office of Franklin & Marshall College for research funding used to help complete this chapter as well as the History Department at Franklin & Marshall College for support and resources. Special thanks also go to Andrew Bergerson, Gilbert Joseph,

Anne Rubenstein, Mary Kay Vaughan, Carla Willard, and the Washington Seminar of Latin American Historians (November 1998) for their constructive commentary at various junctures. Unless otherwise noted, all translations are mine.

1   Throughout this essay I make an effort to avoid overuse of the term "American" (as both adjective and proper noun). I am fully aware of the questions the term raises, especially given the subject matter involved. However, avoiding its usage altogether is far too cumbersome to justify.

2   See John J. Johnson, *Latin America in Caricature* (Austin: University of Texas Press, 1993); Fredrick Pike, *The United States and Latin America: Myths and Stereotypes of Civilization and Nature* (Austin: University of Texas Press, 1992), chap. 1; Paul Vanderwood, *Disorder and Progress: Bandits, Police, and Mexican Development*, rev. ed. (Wilmington, DE: Scholarly Resources, 1992).

3   R. L. Ruffus, "Mexico Goes Modern, Unmodernly," *New York Times Magazine*, 29 September 1957, 45–61.

4   "Concentración de 'Hippies' Viciosos en la Procuraduría," *El Universal*, 12 July 1969, 1. Deportations, arrests, and censorship of countercultural activities all formed part of the government's efforts to stop the spread of *jipismo*. By the early 1970s, the government's anti-hippie policy involved not only the Ministry of the Interior (Gobernación) but the secretary of Foreign Relations as well. See "Archivo de Concentración," Secretaría de Relaciones Exteriores, 7 October 1971, v-1280–6. See also Eric Zolov, *Refried Elvis: The Rise of the Mexican Counterculture* (Berkeley: University of California Press, 1999), chaps. 3–4.

5   See the special issue of *Hispanic American Historical Review*, "Mexico's New Cultural History: ¿Una Lucha Libre?" (June 1999).

6   See, for example, Edward M. Conley, "The Americanization of Mexico," *Review of Reviews* 32 (1905): 724–25; Mauricio Tenorio-Trillo, "1910 Mexico City: Space and Nation in the City of the Centenario," *Journal of Latin American Studies* 28, no. 1 (February 1996): 75–104.

7   Mauricio Tenorio-Trillo, *Mexico at the World's Fairs: Crafting a Modern Nation* (Berkeley: University of California Press, 1996), 119. See also Alan Knight, "Racism, Revolution, and *Indigenismo*: Mexico, 1910–1940," in *The Idea of Race in Latin America, 1870–1940*, ed. Richard Graham (Austin: University of Texas Press, 1990), 71–113; Barbara Tenenbaum, "Streetwise History: The Paseo de la Reforma and the Porfirian State, 1876–1910," in *Rituals of Rule, Rituals of Resistance*, ed. William Beezley, Cheryl E. Martin, and William French (Wilmington, DE: Scholarly Resources, 1994), 127–50.

8   See Alex Saragoza's essay in this volume. Saragoza discusses the concept of *lo mexicano*, which is in many ways synonymous with my concept of the folklórico. To avoid confusion between the terms, however, I will stick to folklórico throughout my discussion.

9   For an excellent discussion of how a common, nationalist discourse of belonging was negotiated, see Mary Kay Vaughan, *Cultural Politics in Revolution: Teachers, Peasants, and Schools in Mexico, 1930–1940* (Tucson: University of Arizona Press, 1997).

10 Helen Delpar, *The Enormous Vogue of Things Mexican: Cultural Relations between the United States and Mexico, 1920–1935* (Tuscaloosa: University of Alabama Press, 1992), 146.

11 Pike, *United States and Latin America*, 244.

12 See Emilio García Riera, *México visto por el cine extranjero*, v. 1 and 3 (Guadalajara, Mexico:

Ediciones Era). For an interesting diatribe from the period, see Michael Kenny, *No God Next Door: Red Rule in Mexico and Our Responsibility* (New York: Hirtin, 1935). The first cartoon representation of Mexico is from 1934 (*Viva Buddy*), in which "Buddy, the Mexican troubadour, heads to the Cantina Del Moocher in time to awaken the sleeping and snoring locals from their siesta," later to be met by the "villain/revolutionary bandito . . . and his gang [who] ride into town, shooting everybody and everything in sight and laughing hysterically" (Jerry Beck and Will Friedwald, *Looney Tunes and Merrie Melodies: A Complete Illustrated Guide to the Warner Bros. Cartoons* [New York: Henry Holt, 1989], 32).

13   Pike, *United States and Latin America*, 245. See also Elena Poniatowska, *Tinísima*, trans. Katherine Silver (1995; New York: Penguin, 1998).

14   Among other diplomatic challenges to U.S. hegemony was Mexico's moral and diplomatic support for César Augusto Sandino, leader of Nicaragua's guerrilla forces, with whom the United States was locked in military conflict during the late 1920s.

15   Stephen R. Niblo, *War, Diplomacy, and Development: The United States and Mexico, 1938–1954* (Wilmington, DE: Scholarly Resources, 1995); María Emilia Paz, *Strategy, Security, and Spies: Mexico and the U.S. as Allies in World War II* (University Park: Pennsylvania State University Press, 1997).

16   See Gerald K. Haines, "Under the Eagle's Wing: The Franklin Roosevelt Administration Forges an American Hemisphere," *Diplomatic History* 1 (1977): 373–88.

17   United States Information Agency, *Mexican Moods*, c. 1945. Located in the Motion Picture and Sound Division of the National Archives and Records Administration, College Park, MD (MPSD-NARA), 306.3719. I wish to thank Seth Fein for first introducing me to these films in his seminar on U.S.-Mexican relations at the Instituto Mora (Mexico City) in 1993. See also the essay by Fein, "La imagen de México: la segunda guerra mundial y la propaganda fílmica de Estados Unidos," in *México-Estados Unidos: Encuentros y desencuentros en el cine*, eds. Ignacio Durán, Iván Trujillo, and Mónica Verea (Mexico City: Instituto Mexicano de Cinematografía, 1996), 41–58.

18   Office of the Coordinator of Inter-American Affairs, *Mexico City*, c. 1946. Located MPSD-NARA, 306.3577A.

19   Robert Scott Burns, "Simpatico, Senor! [*sic*]," *Travel* 99 (May 1953): 15.

20   Milton Bracker, " 'Beisbol' Hits a 'Jonron' Down Mexico Way," *New York Times Magazine*, 9 June 1946, 21.

21   "Mexico—Waking Up After a Long Siesta," *Scholastic* 68 (5 April 1956): 11. This was a reassessment that was also being extended to the rest of Latin America, as reflected in a U.S. government-produced guidebook for enlisted servicemen: "Latin American countries long ago were dubbed the 'lands of mañana' (tomorrow) to signify the leisurely tempo for which Latins have been noted for centuries. But in recent years the meaning has changed. Today, modern progress is transforming most of the countries south of the border and has made them truly 'lands of tomorrow.' " (Department of Defense, Departments of the Army, Navy, and Air Force, *South of the Border* [Washington, DC: Government Printing Office, 1958], 3).

22   *Señor Droopy*, Loew's, Inc., 1949. FEA 1330; located in Motion Picture, Broadcasting, and Recorded Sound Division, Library of Congress, Washington, DC (MPBRSD-LC). The earliest representation of Mexico in cartoons is *Viva Buddy* (see n. 12).

23 Speedy Gonzalez makes his first appearance in 1953 (*Cat-Tails for Two*), where he is depicted as "browner, lankier and rattier than his eventual incarnation, he wears no hat and has lots of imperfect teeth—one of them gold." Following this pilot cartoon, Speedy's character lay dormant for two years until he was revived in 1955 and redesigned "into his familiar form, bright-eyed, srubbed [*sic*] up and secure under his outsize sombrero." ("Unofficial Looney Tunes Website" run by Donnie Hoover, http://seagram.digitalchainsaw.com/speedy/speedy.htm [February 2000].) Between 1934 and 1953, Mexico served as the narrative backdrop for a total of only six cartoons. Between 1953 and 1969, however, there are forty-five Speedy Gonzalez cartoons alone, in addition to various others in which Mexico plays a narrative role (see Beck and Friedwald, *Looney Tunes*). In an interesting contemporary twist, Zapatista leader Subcommandante Marcos has reappropriated the figure of Speedy Gonzalez as a symbol of the Zapatistas' own wiliness (or, at least, that of Marcos). Thus, one of the Zapatista comuniqués was signed by Marcos: "Speedy Gonzalez. ¡Yepa! ¡Yepa! ¡Andale! ¡Arriba! ¡Arriba!" ("Speedy Gonzalez Lives!," *U.S. News & World Report*, 1 August 1998, 41–42); the cartoon character has also appeared on pro-Zapatista Web sites.

24 "Proyección de México," *Jueves de Excélsior*, 15 October 1964, 5.

25 Ruiz Cortínes, "Un Falso México," *El Universal*, 19 February, 1957, A3.

26 Ibid.

27 Ruffus, "Mexico Goes Modern," 45.

28 Ibid., 46.

29 "Strange Contrasts Make Mexico Mysterious and Obvious," *House and Garden* 102 (December 1952): 130. See also "Mexico: Old and New, Simple and Sophisticated," *Newsweek*, 31 December 1951, 32.

30 Cited from the original promotional tour pamphlet, *The Ballet Folklorico of Mexico: First American Tour* (New York: Newcastle Press, n.d.), author's personal collection.

31 See also the chapter by Omar Hernández and Emile McAnany in this volume.

32 The absorption of the Ballet Folklórico by INBA was part of a dramatic increase in state-sponsored cultural activities in general under the administration of President López Mateos (1958–1964). Between 1958 and 1959, for example, allocation in INBA's budget for "extraordinary activities," which included sponsorship of performances and exhibits abroad, increased nearly 400 percent. In 1958 the budget for Extraordinary Subsidies for Specific Activities was roughly U.S.$44,000; in 1959 this amount increased to U.S.$164,500. See Secretaría de Educación Pública, *Memoria del Instituto Nacional de Bellas Artes, 1958–1964* (Mexico: INBA, 1964); Stephen Niblo, *Mexico in the 1940s: Modernity Politics, and Corruption* (Wilmington, DE: Scholarly Resources, 1999), 55.

33 Quoted in Charles Poore, "Mexico Aids the Arts," *The Musician* (June 1947): 45.

34 Kate Simon, *Mexico: Places and Pleasures* (1962; New York: Dolphin Books, 1965), 120. Carl Franz cites Simon's book as his "favorite" among a list of "recommended reading" in the appendix to his countercultural guidebook *The People's Guide to Mexico* (Santa Fe, NM: John Muir Publications, 1972).

35 See Poore, "Mexico Aids the Arts." One troupe traveled abroad "at least eight months out of the year, performing daily," and a second troupe performed up to four days a week in Mexico City. A third troupe was in the process of being formed. See "Las Tareas de la Cul-

tura," *La Cultura en México* 134 (September 1964). A promotional pamphlet from the 1992 U.S. Tour, *40th Anniversary Tour: 500 Years of Dance*, is considerably scaled down from its original. Still, it presents the ballet as "The Original and Only! . . . Direct From the Palace of Fine Arts in Mexico City." Amalia Hernández continued to serve as director and choreographer. Friedson Enterprises and Latino Quality Productions, 1992, author's personal collection.

36 This and subsequent quotes in this paragraph are taken from a collection of newspaper clippings filed by the Palacio de Bellas Artes which can be found along with other correspondence on the Ballet's travels in the Archivo General de la Nación, Gallery 3, "Lopéz Mateos," (Ballet Folklórico).

37 *The Hollywood Palace*, 27 February 1965. The Museum of Television and Radio, New York City (T78:0597).

38 For a sample advertisement, see "México, of Course!" in *New York Times*, 22 January 1965, C55. For the J. C. Penney film, see *Mexican Watercolor* (J. C. Penney Co., 1965) located in MPBRSD-LC, FBA 4361.

39 Hugh Steger, letter to President, 30 December 1969. Located in uncatalogued boxes of the Díaz Ordaz papers, Gallery 3, Administración Pública, Archivo General de la Nación (AGN), Box 425.

40 See José Luis Cuevas, "The Cactus Curtain: An Open Letter on Conformity in Mexican Art," trans. Lysander Kemp, *Evergreen Review* 2 (1959): 111–20; Carlos Blas Galindo, "Nationalism, Ethnocentrism, and the Avant-Garde," *Latin American Art* (fall 1990): 38–43. By 1960 the muralist school had also lost two of its principal architects: Orozco died in 1949 and Rivera in 1956. Siquieros died in 1974.

41 Quoted in Leonard Folgarait, *So Far from Heaven* (Cambridge, England: Cambridge University Press, 1987), 27. See also Leonard Folgarait, *Mural Painting and Social Revolution in Mexico, 1920–1940: Art of the New Order* (New York: Cambridge University Press, 1998).

42 Horace Sutton, "Mexico and the Olympics," *Saturday Review*, 22 June 1968, 38.

43 Enrique Florescano, "La creación del Museo Nacional de Antropología y sus fines científicos, educativos y políticos," in *El patrimonio cultural de México*, comp. Enrique Florescano (Mexico City: Fondo de Cultura Económica, 1993), 161.

44 "Las Tareas de la Cultura," 16; emphasis added.

45 Néstor García Canclini, *Hybrid Cultures: Strategies for Entering and Leaving Modernity*, trans. Christopher L. Chiappari and Silvia L. López, foreword by Renato Rosaldo (Minneapolis: University of Minnesota Press, 1995), 123.

46 See Quetzil Castañeda's photo essay in this volume.

47 *Anuario Turístico de México* (Mexico: Asociación Nacional Automovilística, 1947), 104. The specific date for this statistic is 1940. The importance of tourism was reflected, moreover, in the formation of the Mexican Tourist Association in 1939, a club modeled after the American Automobile Association.

48 Ibid., 101–2. For figures after 1950, see Mary Lee Nolan and Sidney Nolan, "The Evolution of Tourism in Twentieth-Century Mexico," *Journal of the West* 27 (October 1988): 21. In 1948 a National Tourist Commission "with broad supervisory power over all phases of the industry" was created. The commission was entrusted with the goal of "insur[ing] the in-

dividuality of the Mexican scene against the ravages of time or the inroads of standardization." See "Mexican National Tourist Commission," *Bulletin of the Pan American Union* 82 (March 1948): 170. In 1961 the Department of Tourism was made a cabinet-level position, headed by former president Miguel Alemán.

49 Milton MacKaye, "Will Mexico Go 'Castro'?," *Saturday Evening Post*, 29 October 1960, 76.

50 Roger D. Hansen, *The Politics of Mexican Development* (Baltimore: Johns Hopkins University Press, 1974), 65.

51 Still, as late as the mid-1950s, the Yucatán Peninsula "could only be reached by train or air, so a journey to Mérida and the Mayan ruins was considered a grand expedition" (Nolan and Nolan, "Evolution of Tourism," 18).

52 "Mexico Is South," *House and Garden* 107 (February 1955): 13.

53 Don Eddy, "On the Road to Utopia," *American Magazine* 162 (July 1956): 37. I wish to thank the students in my Modern Mexico class at the University of Puget Sound (spring 1997) for bringing this magazine to my attention.

54 Ibid., 35.

55 Ibid., 77.

56 Ibid., 37. The trope of perpetual springtime became commonplace in travel advertisements and seems likely started by the Mexican Tourist Council. One early advertisement, for example, states: "Only a few hours to blossoming springtime in near-by Mexico. . . . In Mexico, where every month is June" (*Newsweek*, 3 March 1952, 72). I want to thank Randy Gibbs from my Latin American History II class at Franklin & Marshall College (spring 1999) for bringing this ad to my attention.

57 "Shuttling between Centuries," *House and Garden* 99 (March 1951): 114.

58 Simon, *Mexico*, xi.

59 See Pike, *United States and Mexico*. Mexico's "unboundedness" especially appealed to travelers eager to take advantage of the country's looser divorce laws, and servicemen on leave and other American youth continued to associate Mexico with the profligate border regions, where sex, marijuana, and alcohol were assumed to be free-flowing. Americans did not travel only as tourists, however. Many became expatriates, taking advantage of Mexico's even climate and low cost of living. During the repression of the McCarthy era, moreover, numerous U.S. citizens went to Mexico as political exiles (a pattern dating to the 1920s' "red scares"). See, for example, "Yanks Who Don't Go Home," *Life* 23 December 1957, 159–64; "Underground Railway for Reds Begins at U.S. Border," *U.S. News & World Report*, 7 November 1960, 82–84.

60 *Mexico: A Sunset Discovery Book* (1955; Menlo Park, CA: Lane Book Company, 1963), 64.

61 Ruffus, "Mexico Goes Modern," 45, 46.

62 Philip Spelman, "Taxco: Jewel City of Mexico," *American Magazine* 159 (March 1955): 108.

63 "Mexico for a Low-Cost Vacation," *Better Homes and Gardens* 30 (February 1952): 206, 205, 60.

64 Nolan and Nolan, "Evolution of Tourism," 21.

65 Advertisement, *New York Times*, 22 January 1965, C55. I want to thank M. Tucker Hemquist for locating this for me.

66 MacKaye, "Will Mexico Go 'Castro'?," 78; "Underground Railway for Reds"; Eric Zolov,

"Popular Perceptions and Official Concerns Toward Mexico, c. 1966–1968" paper delivered at the 10th Conference of Mexican and North American Historians, Ft. Worth, TX, 19–21 November 1999; Sergio Aguayo Quezada, *Myths and [Mis] Perceptions: Changing U.S. Elite Visions of Mexico*, trans. Julián Brody (La Jolla, CA: Center for U.S.-Mexican Studies, 1998).

67 The letters (around fifty) were all found in a series of uncatalogued boxes located in the Administración Pública wing of the Archivo General de la Nación in Mexico City during fall 1992. Around 70 percent of the letters are penned by men, with roughly 20 percent written by women (the remainder were sent by couples). The letters came from sixteen different U.S. states, suggesting a wide geographical dispersion; there were also several letters from Mexican Americans stationed in Vietnam.

68 Alexander Wilekin, letter to President, 19 September 1967. Uncatalogued boxes, Gallery 3, Administración Pública, AGN, Box 425. The writer was frustrated by local police in Veracruz who refused to act on the implicit meaning of a will left by deceased relatives who owned property in Mexico.

69 Cecilia Mopsik, letter to President, 11 July 1968. Uncatalogued boxes, Gallery 3, Administración Pública, AGN, Box 424. Mopsik's frustrations ironically were created in part by Mexicans' own desires to conform their eating habits to more "modern" sensibilities. In his discussion of food and national identity in Mexico, Jeffrey Pilcher describes the post-1945 period this way: "Housewives not only began making geometrically precise sandwiches instead of lush tortas compuestas; they also conducted bizarre experiments with mass-produced ingredients to create such hybrid dishes as shrimp and cornflakes, calf brains with crackers, macaroni and milk soup, and pork loin in Pepsi Cola." See *¡Que Vivan los Tamales!* (Albuquerque: University of New Mexico Press, 1998), 135. See also the essay by Pilcher in this volume.

70 K. R. Van Tassel, letter to President, 29 May 1968. Uncatalogued boxes, Gallery 3, Administración Pública, AGN, Box 422.

71 Leon Goldenberg, letter to President, 5 December 1966. Uncatalogued boxes, Gallery 3, Administración Pública, AGN, Box 422.

72 My current research project involves, in part, a further investigation of this issue. For a preliminary discussion, see Zolov, "Popular Perceptions and Official Concerns."

73 Ben and Fredrica Custer, letter to President, 12 November 1966. Uncatalogued boxes, Gallery 3, Administración Pública, AGN, Box 422.

74 John W. Gothard, letter to President, 16 March 1970. Uncatalogued boxes, Gallery 3, Administración Pública, AGN, Box 422.

75 Mrs. C. M. Zerr, letter to President, 16 May 1969. Uncatalogued boxes, Gallery 3, Administración Pública, AGN, Box 422.

76 Mrs. Francis Morgan, letter to President, 29 November 1966. Uncatalogued boxes, Gallery 3, Administración Pública, AGN, Box 422.

77 Jade Jones, letter to President, 3 December 1969. Uncatalogued boxes, Gallery 3, Administración Pública, AGN, Box 422.

78 Debbie Miller, letter to President, 26 July 1967. Uncatalogued boxes, Gallery 3, Administración Pública, AGN, Box 422.

79 Pike, *United States and Latin America*, 317.

80   See, for example, "México, of Course!," C55; for an earlier example, see ad cited in n. 56. Both advertisements were produced and paid for by the Mexican Ministry of Tourism.

81   Cecilia Mopsik, letter to President, 11 July 1968. In both letters, this woman identifies herself as a college graduate and former schoolteacher, now in the commercial real estate business with her family.

82   John L. Abbott, letter to President, 11 December 1966. Uncatalogued boxes, Gallery 3, Administración Pública, AGN, Box 425.

83   Quoted in "Mexico: Prospering Pacemaker," *Fortune Magazine* (May 1968): 83.

84   Quoted in Zolov, *Refried Elvis*, 147.

85   Robert Richter, "El Colón," *Tonantzín* (October 1990): 20–22.

86   Zolov, *Refried Elvis*, chaps. 3–4.

87   See also William S. Burroughs and Allen Ginsberg, *The Yage Letters* (1963; San Francisco: City Lights Books, 1975).

88   Manuel Luís Martínez, " 'With Imperious Eyes': Kerouac, Burroughs, and Ginsberg on the Road in South America," *Aztlán* 23, no. 1 (spring 1998): 41. Though females participated in the beatnik literary scene, the principal male figures remain the most representative.

89   Barry Gifford, ed., *As Ever: The Collected Correspondence of Allen Ginsberg and Neal Cassady* (Berkeley: Creative Arts Book Company, 1977), 174.

90   Martínez, " 'With Imperious Eyes,' " 38.

91   Ibid., 49. The Indians of Latin America appeared even more "soulful" than the blacks of the United States, who otherwise provided an important font of inspiration for the beatniks.

92   Carolyn Cassady, *Off the Road: My Years with Neil Cassady, Jack Kerouac, and Alan Ginsberg* (New York: Penguin, 1990), 180.

93   Jack Kerouac, *On the Road* (1955; New York: Viking Press, 1985), 224.

94   Ibid., 225–26.

95   Ibid., 26. ("My shoes, damn fool that I am, were Mexican huaraches, plantlike sieves not fit for the rainy night of America and the raw road night" [13].)

96   Ibid., 82. Kerouac, in fact, saw himself as a member of the " 'minority' races," a designation, as one author put it, "that was not altogether fanciful. His great-grandmother was one half American Indian and as a French Canadian he was one of the despised Canucks in his hometown of Lowell [Massachusetts]; he did not master English until he attended high school." See Ann Douglas, "On the Road Again," *New York Times Book Review* 9 April 1995, 21.

97   Todd Gitlin, *The Sixties: Years of Hope, Days of Rage* (New York: Bantam, 1987), 46.

98   Kerouac, *On the Road*, 217; italics in original.

99   Pike, *United States and Latin America*, chap. 5.

100   Martínez, " 'With Imperious Eyes,' " 39.

101   Kerouac, *On the Road*, 245.

102   Martinez, " 'With Imperious Eyes,' " 47.

103   Kerouac, *On the Road*, 225.

104   Martínez, " 'With Imperious Eyes,' " 46.

105   Zolov, *Refried Elvis*, especially chap. 3.

106 The following discussion is based on ibid., chaps. 3–4.

107 "Lo Efectivo y lo Negativo en la Industria Turística," *Jueves de Excélsior*, 18 April 1968, 23.

108 Quoted in Zolov, *Refried Elvis*, 137; see also chaps. 3–4; Álvaro Estrada, *Huautla en Tiempo de Hippies* (Mexico City: Grijalbo, 1996).

109 "Proyección de México."

110 "Promoción para México y las Olimpiadas," *Jueves de Excélsior*, 20 June 1968, n.p.; Ariel Rodríguez Kuri, "El otro 68: Política y estilo en la organización de los juegos olímpicos de la ciudad de México," *Relaciones* 76 (fall 1998): 109–29.

111 Ibid.

112 "Native Music to Swing at '68 Mexico Olympics," *Variety*, 16 February 1966, 1.

113 Eliot Tiegel, "Entertainment Fields Sparkle with Diversity!," *Billboard*, 16 December 1967, 4M.

114 20 March 1967, Secretaría de Relaciones Exteriores, Archivo de Concentración (SRE-AC), XV/820/(72:00)/2105. Unfortunately, I never was able to locate the actual slide material to which this document refers.

115 21 November 1967, SRE-AC, XV/821.7/(72)/1369.

116 "Filmex Doing Specials on Olympic Games for Mexican Government," *Variety*, 24 April 1968, 50. Of the other two films, one was a travelogue depiction of the country, and the other focused on the theme of the traditional lighting of the Olympic torch. The tone of celebrating Mexico's cosmopolitan splendor is also found in numerous articles published in the U.S. press in anticipation of the Olympics. See, for example, Sutton, "Mexico and the Olympics," 37–38, 81.

117 Zolov, "Popular Perceptions and Official Concerns"; Aguayo, *Myths and [Mis]perceptions*, chap. 12.

118 Mrs. Joseph W. Huddleston, letter to President, 28 September 1968. Uncatalogued boxes, Gallery 3, Administración Pública, AGN, Box 422.

119 H. S. Riecke Jr., letter to President, 23 September 1968. Uncatalogued boxes, Gallery 3, Administración Pública, AGN, Box 422. Although the Mexican government attempted to scapegoat the Mexican Communist Party for the student movement, the actual role of communists (Mexican or otherwise) was discounted by the State Department and downplayed by the U.S. press. See, for example, Bureau of Intelligence and Research, Department of State, "Student Violence and Attitudes in Latin America (working draft)," 15 November 1968. Located in the National Security Archives, George Washington University, Washington, DC.

120 New information about the army's role in the massacre suggests that the president's elite private guard, the Estado Mayor Presidencial, actually provoked the army into full-scale repression by firing on soldiers from within a building of the Tlatelolco housing complex, where student protesters had gathered. President Díaz Ordaz apparently sought a pretext to squash the demonstrations before the start of the Olympics, scheduled for 12 October. See Julio Scherer García and Carlos Monsiváis, *Parte de Guerra: Tlatelolco 1968* (Mexico City: Nuevo Siglo/Aguilar, 1999); Sergio Aguayo Quezada, *1968: Los archivos de la violencia* (Mexico City: Grijalbo/Reforma, 1998).

121 Of the many letters I found in the Archivo General de la Nación, only one spoke explicitly in favor of the students, and this was after 1968: "Perhaps one day we shall recognize that

we need not fear students. . . . Mr. President, I ask you, not as a citizen of the United States but as a human being, to free these political prisoners. The people of the world await your brave act. Free the students." See Bernard Smith, letter to the President, 11 May 1970. Uncatalogued boxes, Gallery 3, Administración Pública, AGN, Box 425.

122 Jesse Hughes, letter to President, 14 November 1968. Uncatalogued boxes, Gallery 3, Administración Pública, AGN, Box 422.

123 George R. Billard, letter to President, 15 October 1968. Uncatalogued boxes, Gallery 3, Administración Pública, AGN, Box 422.

124 "Gobernación y lo 'Jipis Alcinógenos,'" *Jueves de Excélsior*, 16 July 1970, 5.

125 David Jorgensen, letter to President, 29 July 1967. Uncatalogued boxes, Gallery 3, Administración Pública, AGN, Box 422.

126 Mrs. Wm. H. Haworth, letter to President, 9 January 1969. Uncatalogued boxes, Gallery 3, Administración Pública, AGN, Box 422. The letter included a copy of the UPI story "Mexican Police Order 'Hair' Cast Out of Country," printed in the *Tulsa World*, 6 January 1969, 11.

127 Elmer Belew, letter to President, 27 March 1970. Uncatalogued boxes, Gallery 3, Administración Pública, AGN, Box 422.

128 Charles and Corrine Marcotte, letter to President, 31 January 1970. Uncatalogued boxes, Gallery 3, Administración Pública, AGN, Box 422. This more positive projection of the Mexican work ethic is also revealed in the educational docudrama short *México: Sábado con Ramón*, which was likely shown in elementary schools and used in foreign-language classes in the United States (Solisburg Educational Media, Inc., 1969). MPBRSD-LC. FAA 9868.

129 Ambassador McBride to Assistant Secty. of State Meyer, 22 October 1969. Record Group 59, Box 2155, Pol. 13–2. National Archives and Records Administration, College Park, MD.

130 Roger Bartra, "Mexico Oficio: The Miseries and Splendors of Culture," *Third Text* 14 (1991): 7–15; Shifra M. Goldman, *Dimensions of the Americas: Art and Social Change in Latin America and the United States* (Chicago: University of Chicago Press, 1994), especially chaps. 19–20.

131 Rosa Elvira Vargas, "Crear el zar de las Fronteras, propone el equipo de Fox," *La Jornada*, 2 August 2000, 7.

Toiling for the "New Invaders": Autoworkers, Transnational Corporations, and Working-Class Culture in Mexico City, 1955–1968

Steven J. Bachelor

A century after
General Taylor and General Scott,
Come General Electric and General Motors,
As they are now known.

Through every border and every port,
And even by air,
Comes the invasion.
We all know very well,
The traitors of the past,
But do we know who are those of today?
—A. Martínez Camberos,
"The New Invaders," 1947, written
on the occasion of the Centennial
of the Defensa de Chapultepec

Lorenzo Ramírez, a recent arrival to Mexico City from the highlands of Puebla, had never before done industrial work, nor had he ever set foot in his country's capital.[1] But in 1963, not long after settling into the sprawling Mexican metropolis, the twenty-year-old son of *campesinos* found himself working for the world's largest corporation, the giant automaker General Motors. Before moving to Mexico City, Lorenzo had labored in a small sugar mill in his *pueblo*, where he and his father both manned sugarcane presses. When the mill shut down in the early 1960s, owing to its inability to compete with more technologically innovative mills, he was forced to find other employment. Sensing stronger prospects in the Federal District, Lorenzo, like tens of thousands of others leaving the countryside during these years, headed to the capital in search of work.[2] He hoped to land a job at one of the city's many factories, then sprouting up at unprecedented rates.[3] In a short time, an opportunity presented itself. Through his brother-in-law, a worker at the city's GM plant since its opening in 1937, Lorenzo learned the company sought to bring in hundreds of new workers as it began to implement a state-mandated project to create a new automobile manufacturing industry.[4] With the aid of his in-law's recommendation, Lorenzo was soon on the shop floor helping assemble cars for the enormous transnational corporation.

Lorenzo began working at GM at a time of massive industrial expansion and economic growth dubbed the Mexican Miracle. The state's import-substitution industrialization strategy, designed to spark domestic production of consumer and capital goods, had generated considerable employment opportunities for Mexico's masses, and thousands poured into the city's burgeoning factories. Like Lorenzo, many of these new workers had abandoned rural areas, where economic prospects had dwindled, and settled into industrial jobs and working-class communities in the capital. Still others hailed from the city's older *colonias populares*, such as Tepito and Santa Julia. All, however, had decided to stake their future on the industrial transformation and economic salvation promised by the country's ruling regime. Central to this state-advanced "modernization" strategy, government officials resolved to establish a domestic automobile manufacturing industry. Building such an industry, authorities maintained, would bring "progress" to Mexico and help catapult the country into the ranks of "modernity."[5]

Nurturing the Transnational Corporate Family

When Lorenzo Ramírez began at GM, he felt excited about having landed a job with the giant automaker. Hired as an unskilled, entry-level assistant, he started with a salary of 60 pesos a day, more than four times what he made while working briefly for the Mexico City government and far beyond what he earned in his Puebla village. In addition, his new employer offered generous benefits largely unknown to Mexican laborers, such as paid vacations, pension and profit-sharing programs, and *fútbol*, baseball, and bowling leagues.[6] Wage earners also had opportunities to attend night school and language classes sponsored by the firm.[7] Then only twenty years old, a bachelor, and living with his sister and brother-in-law virtually rent-free, Lorenzo felt "like I was rolling in the *lana* [money] and fortunate to have a job with a company like GM." "Granted," he continued, "the work was grueling

35. Workers at GM take a moment to enjoy refreshments with the director of personnel, Alberto Gómez Obregón (fifth from right, standing), and the president of GM
de Mexico, William Marr (third from right, standing), in 1963. Laborers recalled
that such convivial interludes shared by workers and managers largely disappeared
after the bitter strike of 1965. Courtesy of Ignacio Ceballos.

and left me exhausted at the end of each day." But, as he explained, he felt
"part of a family at the company. . . . It was so nice [*bonito*] at the factory. We
were all part of *la familia* General Motors."

This strong sense of family, a sentiment shared not only by Lorenzo but
by countless others at U.S. auto plants in Mexico, was hardly an accident.[8]
It grew out of distinct workplace cultures cultivated at the plants in the
1950s and 1960s. U.S. automakers heartily encouraged their Mexican wage
earners to view themselves as members of what could best be called a "transnational corporate family," an invented sense of belonging to a larger family
of employers and employees that would transcend differences of class and
national origin. As such, U.S. automakers attempted to construct for their
workers a new subjectivity, a distinct discursive category that would situate
autoworkers at the forefront of modernization and above the multitude of
Mexican wage earners who lacked the benefits employment at a transnational firm conferred. Executives held that this company-articulated ideology would help foster among workers a close, personal identification with
their employers and help wed working-class identities and social aspirations
to the belief that Mexican laborers and U.S. corporations together would

bring the fruits of industrial "progress" to Mexico. Company officials hoped that Mexican autoworkers, rather than regarding themselves as laborers toiling for profiteering gringos, would view themselves as privileged members of a larger Ford or GM family that allied them with fellow personnel in the United States and wherever else their employer's lengthy corporate arms may have reached.

A "New Model" Mexico

Bringing Mexican wage earners into the folds of this transnational family constituted only one facet of a much larger project elaborated by U.S. industrialists. Automakers sought to mold Mexican laborers into a class of efficient, well-paid, and reliable mass-production workers. Owing to the massive economic resources at their disposal, U.S. corporations like Ford and GM had a particularly strong hand in recasting Mexico's postrevolutionary working class and inculcating laborers with new work cultures and industrial discipline. Alan Knight has observed, "What the mines and plantations of the 1880s and 1890s had pioneered [in Mexico], the factories of Ford and General Motors would continue in the 1920s and 1930s."[9] One should note, however, that Ford and GM actually had relatively small operations in the 1920s and 1930s. Not until the 1950s and 1960s did automaking truly begin to transform the city's industrial landscape. By the beginning of the 1970s, automobile production had become Mexico's largest manufacturing industry.

From the automobile's earliest days in Mexico, U.S. automakers believed their operations would bring prosperity to the economically disadvantaged country. Even before establishing a plant in Mexico, Henry Ford bragged to government leaders that his enterprise would help calm the country's revolutionary waters and reduce rebels like Pancho Villa to mere "timekeepers" for industrial capitalism.[10] Corporate initiatives to shape Mexican men into a class of reliable autoworkers, in fact, closely resembled "Americanization" programs instituted at plants in the United States, where large numbers of foreign-born men occupied factory posts.[11] Programs there sought to drill immigrants in so-called American work habits and to eradicate cultural vestiges considered anathema to capitalism.[12] For Henry Ford, Americanizing foreign workers constituted nothing less than a social mission. "These men of many nations," he declared, "must be taught American ways, the English language, and the right way to live."[13] Several managers at

Ford's Mexican installation had personally worked with the company's founder, and all had been trained extensively in company ideologies and industrial strategies before being dispatched to Mexico. A number had even directly assisted the Dearborn industrialist with his various operations to Americanize the many Mexican immigrants who labored in Detroit-area auto plants in the 1930s.[14]

Although the revolutionary tides Ford promised to pacify had largely subsided, constructing a strong manufacturing sector and stable industrial proletariat remained a principal concern among the country's powerholders through the 1950s. Up to that point, Mexico's auto industry remained relatively small and confined to assembly operations—that is, the assembly of automobile kits manufactured in the United States. By the mid-1950s, automobile production showed great promise for growth, and in 1958 the López Mateos administration decided to put the industry at the center of its import-substitution industrialization strategy.[15] After much deliberation, in 1962 the government passed the Automotive Integration Decree. The act mandated that, by the end of 1964, all automobiles sold in the country would have to be manufactured in Mexico.[16]

With its vast backward and forward linkages, the auto industry seemed the perfect candidate to spearhead the nation's push toward modernization. Anticipating an economic takeoff following on the heels of the Integration Decree, state authorities were confident that motor vehicle manufacturing would propel a "second industrial revolution," one built around mass-production industries.[17] On an even greater level, they maintained, the industry would usher in a new era for the country. Automobile manufacturing would serve, in the words of GM president Frederick Donner, as a "testament to the rapid and visible progress of Mexico."[18] Henry Ford II, who took over the reins of the corporation founded by his grandfather, similarly vowed that his company's plants would bring "social progress" to the country's backward masses.[19]

Advertisements, too, reflected this firm faith in the connection between automobiles and the country's march toward modernity. Newspaper ads taken out by Ford and GM in the late 1950s and early 1960s frequently pictured light-skinned *capitalinos* posed alongside sleek automobiles and dressed in elegant attire that could easily have come from Brooks Brothers or Bloomingdale's. Marking a sharp contrast with images of Mexico of yore, the vehicles were often photographed on cobblestone streets in front of colonial-style homes in well-preserved colonial-style neighborhoods such as San Angel and Coyoacán. The obvious implication was that automobiles would carry their owners into a new era of progress, which would entail the adoption of new cultural orientations and consumer desires. Progress—that elusive goal the Mexican elite had long assured the populace was just within reach—would finally be at hand with the beginning of full-scale motor vehicle manufacturing. At least this was what such leading newspapers as *El Universal* proclaimed on the day GM opened its new factory in January 1965, only a few weeks after Ford and Auto-Mex/Chrysler (a company partially owned by the U.S. automaker) inaugurated new plants of their own.[20]

Corporate Representations,
Or, Image Isn't Everything, but It Sure
Means Something When Millions Are on the Line

Of course, not everyone pinned their hopes on transnational auto firms. Ford and GM were also regular targets of derision, disparaged as agents of U.S. domination. One need not venture too far into the recesses of popular consciousness in Mexico to locate instances of the two corporations being likened to gringo imperialists exploiting Mexican labor and carting the booty back to the homeland. Even a casual perusal of labor periodicals reveals numerous depictions. The poem "The New Invaders," which begins this essay, is simply one of the more imaginative examples, drawing a striking parallel between U.S. military generals of the war between the United States and Mexico and the contemporary captains of industry, General Motors and General Electric. Granted, verbal attacks against U.S. corporations have long abounded in Mexico, and casting such fiery aspersions has often figured as little more than rhetorical flourishes intended to stoke nationalist passions. Even in the headiest days of the 1910 revolution, *anti-yanquismo* never reached the frenzied proportions some scholars would have us believe.[21] Nevertheless, corporations such as Ford and GM—whose executives, particularly Henry Ford, were wont to expound on their own country's supposed superiority—remained potent symbols of Yankee presence in the postrevolutionary period. Although popular hostility against U.S. corporations found expression far more frequently in words than in deeds, there nonetheless existed in Mexico an underlying nationalist sentiment that served as a taproot for popular hostility against U.S. companies.[22] Indeed, as Alex Saragoza points out in his contribution to this volume, anti-

U.S. sentiment in the postrevolutionary years remained embedded "in the bedrock of Mexican nationalist feelings."

Powerful corporations such as Ford and GM came to cast an even longer shadow as the U.S. presence in Mexico's economy reached new heights during the López Mateos administration. By the close of the 1950s, U.S. investments in Mexico neared $800 million, a nearly 100 percent increase in less than a decade. By then, U.S. investments accounted for over 73 percent of all total foreign investments in the country.[23] Labor leaders seemed especially concerned about the presence of transnational firms, which several viewed as potential threats to national sovereignty and labor's political standing. Rafael Galván, who then headed a large federation of electrical workers and would later lead the dissident Tendencia Democrática labor movement, warned, "Mexico cannot be governed by big foreign monopolies. . . . It has to be led by authentic, sincere, and genuine representatives of *national* interests."[24]

Automakers expressed extreme unease about what they saw as negative attitudes toward U.S. corporations. They feared such hostility could jeopardize their massive investments and possibly even provoke nationalization of the industry, as the federal government chose to do with the electricity industry in 1962.[25] To counter such views, automobile manufacturers took great pains to underscore the ample benefits they brought to Mexico and its people. In the words of executives at GM, workers and company officials were "marching together to produce more and better to benefit *our* national economy."[26] At Ford, executives considered it necessary to concentrate on improving the company's image as a way to overcome what they discovered to be "unfavorable attitudes" toward the firm.[27] This decision came after conducting opinion polls in the late 1950s, which revealed a high degree of ill will directed toward the company. Executives agreed to redouble their efforts to enhance the company's image by highlighting what they called "Ford's corporate good citizenship."[28] Ford officials also decided to create a new management position, manager of civic affairs, and tellingly filled the post with a Mexican, Eduardo de Villafranca. His job primarily consisted of calling attention to Ford's "good corporate citizenship" and spreading the word on how the company's advancement went hand in hand with national advancement. This suggestion bore a remarkable resemblance to the notion advanced by GM president Charles Wilson in his famous adage, "What's good for General Motors is good for the United States"; only now, U.S. firms were further maintaining that the various companies' windfall would blow into Mexico as well. Not surprisingly, Frederick Donner, who succeeded Wilson at GM and took particular interest in promoting operations in Mexico, echoed similar sentiments, offering a promising vision for transnational corporations. "Multinationals," he explained, "represent a new kind of capitalism," one in which firms like GM and Ford would create a stable, well-paid working class and help bring industrial progress to developing countries like Mexico.[29]

Turning Workers into Transnational "Family" Members

In the early 1960s, as the auto industry shifted gears into full-scale manufacturing, automakers drew on the working-class communities surrounding the plants to fill their expanding ranks. Nearby neighborhoods had swelled, barely able to hold the thousands who had left the countryside and settled in the expanding metropolis. The city was quickly becoming, in the words of Octavio Paz, "a monstrous inflated head, crushing the frail body that holds it up."[30] Indeed, it has been estimated that, in the 1960s alone, some 1.8 million people flocked to the capital.[31]

The neighborhood that absorbed most of those who went on to work in the auto industry in the early 1960s was Santa Julia. A ragged and densely populated barrio north of the GM and Auto-Mex/Chrysler factories, Santa Julia was the destination of hundreds of would-be autoworkers. Lorenzo Ramírez, for instance, settled in Santa Julia when he arrived in the city in 1963.[32] Like Lorenzo, Angel Taboada, the son of campesinos from a small village in Tlaxcala, also established roots in Santa Julia, only blocks from the GM plant where he was soon working.[33] José Juan Hernández, the child of peasants from Michoacán, moved to Santa Julia and learned from a neighborhood *cuate* (friend) of employment opportunities at the nearby auto plant, where he subsequently took a job.

Located in the northwest part of the capital, Santa Julia was home to much of the city's industry. Although only two miles northeast of Chapultepec Park, site of former Emperor Maximilian's palace, and two miles northwest of the posh Zona Rosa (Pink Zone), where by the 1960s elegant shops displayed the latest high-priced goods from Europe and the United States, Santa Julia nonetheless seemed a world apart.[34] Its poorly paved roads—that is, those that were paved—were sliced with railroad tracks on which arrived raw materials for the neighborhood's various factories. Smokestacks towered high above the community's ramshackle dwellings, and the din of industrial production served as a constant companion for area residents. Among the neighborhood's many plants were large sites owned by GM, Auto-Mex/Chrysler, Singer, General Popo Tires, and Cervecería Modelo. Extending nearly two miles around, the GM complex acted as a symbolic border separating Santa Julia from Polanco, the affluent neighborhood to the south where diplomats and government dignitaries lived in luxurious homes. Residences on the Santa Julia side of the divide, in contrast, were tightly squeezed onto small lots and appeared to be in an endless state of construction. As families multiplied and newcomers spilled in from the countryside, inhabitants added rooms on top of or alongside existing structures, often using cast-off lumber and tin.

The community also boasted a tough, raucous reputation, which it had earned over the decades. The scene of several riotous antigovernment demonstrations stretching back well into the Porfiriato, the neighborhood was infamous for being a haven for roughnecks, robbers, and ruffians.[35] Writing of Santa Julia in the 1960s, Paco Ignacio Taibo II described it as the type of neighborhood where one would go to hire thugs who rough up others for money, or just for kicks.[36] One resident recounted, exaggeratedly but no less tellingly, "Walking through the neighborhood you had to look over your shoulder to keep from being accosted from behind, but you also had to look down to keep from tripping over a dead body."[37] In short, Santa Julia typified what elite and middle-class capitalinos referred to as a *ciudad perdida* (lost city).[38]

The community, however, was far more than simply a "lost city," a term that fails to convey the degree of cultural creativity that blossomed in such neighborhoods. Residents there became part of a new urban culture taking root in working-class barrios like Santa Julia in the late 1950s, as newcomers from the countryside spilled into the capital. Like many settling in Santa Julia, future autoworker Salvador Navas, an emigrant from the village of Joquicingo in the state of Mexico, "tired of life in the *campo*" and journeyed to Mexico City "to be part of a new culture, to have a new way of being."[39] According to Carlos Monsiváis, Santa Julia exemplified the cultural worlds of working-class life in Mexico City and helped give birth to "the mass presence that now defines Mexico City" and Mexican culture.[40] The barrio was especially known for its well-attended weekend *carpas* (tent shows), where members of the popular classes would converge for low-budget (and often low-brow) entertainment. From these weekend carpas emerged several highly celebrated figures of Mexican cinema and working-class favorites, including Adalberto Martínez Resortes and Cantinflas, the famed comic and perennial working-class underdog.[41]

Even more, neighborhoods like Santa Julia served as the birthplace of a new cultural type emerging at the end of the 1950s: the *naco*. A derogatory term derived from Totonaco, the name of an indigenous group in the northern highlands of Puebla and Veracruz, naco became the quintessential epithet used by the cosmopolitan elite and middle classes to refer to the working poor and those of Indian ancestry, the latter of whom were generally discursively associated with low socioeconomic standing.[42] In the words of cultural critic Monsiváis, nacos were "of Indian or *mestizo* heritage . . . [who were] uneducated, [living in] slum homes with cement floors, [and who had] a recent agrarian past." In the eyes of middle- and upper-class capitalinos, nacos were the "alienated, manipulated, and economically devastated" who poured into barrios like Santa Julia in the late 1950s and early 1960s.[43]

Those who flocked to Santa Julia and found work in the auto industry epitomized the image of the naco, although few ever used the term to identify themselves. They hailed from the countryside, had rarely gone beyond *primaria* (elementary school), were economically downtrodden, and sought factory jobs to improve their lot in life.[44] As word passed through Santa Julia in the early 1960s that the nearby automobile plants were opening their doors to hundreds of new workers, barrio inhabitants traversed to the various plants to solicit work.[45] One resident who "sought to make a better life" for himself found a line of some six hundred men stretching around the factory gate the day he went to apply for work.[46] Another prospective employee, Angel Daniel Ruiz, a native of Oaxaca, worried that his inexperience and the fact that he lived in Santa Julia would hinder his chances of landing a job at GM. Men from Santa Julia, he confided, "were known to be hardheaded and defiant workers."[47] Despite the neighborhood's reputation, residents of Santa Julia continued to make up the bulk of the industry's workforce through the early 1960s.

Like Ruiz, few of the incoming autoworkers had previous factory experience. To those signing on with one of the transnational automakers in the 1950s, the factory seemed like another world, far different from the previous workplaces they had known. Few had ever before done mass-production work, and certainly not for the world's largest corporations. Not surprisingly, employment at transnational corporations took on great importance and profoundly reshaped their cultural and political lives. For these new industrial workers, the auto factory became a cauldron where laborers fashioned a new political consciousness and social identity built around their position as privileged members of a transnational corporate family. One-time campesinos and rural dwellers took great pride in being at the forefront of national progress and modernization. As one autoworker declared, summing up a widely held opinion, "I took real pride in saying I worked for General Motors. . . . I was helping industrialize my country."[48]

Those who did have previous work experience tended to have been employed in small *talleres* (workshops). Not surprisingly, workers found life at transnational firms far different from that at the talleres. For one thing, workers' wages, as long as they kept their jobs, were secure. As former *tallerero* Ignacio Bobadilla explained, "When I worked at the taller, the owner frequently wouldn't pay me because he didn't have the money. Working for a giant automaker like GM, I knew I would always have money to buy food for that week."[49] What is more, wages in the automobile industry remained significantly higher than those found in nearly every other economic sector.[50] Even those who knew next to nothing about the nature of the firms were aware of their high wages. Marcelino Sánchez, who started working in small talleres at the age of eight, applied for a job at GM after his neighbor mentioned that the company was hiring and providing excellent wages. When he arrived, Marcelino could barely believe his eyes. He had thought GM was an auto repair shop, not an assembly plant.[51] Similarly, Rafael Castro had heard from his uncle that GM was hiring. At the time, Rafael held a job in a blacksmith's shop where he earned 4 pesos an hour; GM then paid entry-level workers more than twice that wage. Rafael met with the director of the plant, Fraine Rhuberry (soon to head of Ford de México), who told him that, at the moment, the company was hiring only custodial workers. Rafael explained that he had nearly completed middle school (*secundaria*) and was qualified to do much more than custodial work; he eventually reconsidered and accepted the job because the pay and benefits far surpassed what he could find elsewhere.[52]

In addition to cultivating a loyal workforce, executives hoped high wages would, in time, help build a body of consumers for the products they assembled. This endeavor closely paralleled efforts in the United States to establish a consumer base for the thousands of automobiles that rolled off the line each year. Indeed, an abiding faith in the buying power and expanding consumer desires of working people remained one of the hallmarks of the phenomenon known as Fordism.[53] In Mexico, however, few industrial workers had the means to purchase any of the 25,000 new cars (spread across 44 makes and 117 models) sold each year by the late 1950s.[54] In fact, by the end of the decade, scarcely 15 percent of Mexico's population could afford to purchase new automobiles.[55] And this remained the case even as government decrees extended strong incentives for manufacturers to keep vehicles priced below $1,920 and prohibited retail prices from exceeding $4,400.[56] In an attempt to broaden its base of customers, in 1964 GM doubled its annual advertising budget to 16 million pesos and enlisted the services of the country's leading ad agency, Noble y Asociados, to mount a massive campaign illustrating the joys of car ownership.[57] Though automakers could hardly expect single-handedly to create a well-paid working and consuming class, they hoped at least that their employees would eventually become purchasers of their products. To this end, on top of the high wages, auto firms made sizable discounts on their various models available to employees. But if automobile ownership remained uncommon among younger wage earners in the 1960s, a number of veteran autoworkers took advantage of such discounts and joined the ranks of Mexico's burgeoning, yet still small, population of car owners.[58]

Company largesse went even further in furnishing benefits few Mexican firms granted. For example, U.S. automakers provided paid vacations and pensions to their permanent workers. Pensions encouraged wage earners to entrust their long-term security to the company and instilled the idea that the corporation would care for its workers after a lifetime of loyalty. Autoworkers also had opportunities to take classes and receive training, all at company expense. Ford and GM both advanced money for employees to attend night classes to complete secundaria, which few workers had done.[59] Firms also provided training for laborers to learn additional trades and ran apprenticeship programs in which workers' children could, at the age of sixteen, begin to master skills that would garner them a permanent position at the plant.

U.S. automakers also tried to forge a close bond through the numerous functions and festivities they held. Company newsletters, which served to connect workers spread across large industrial facilities, were filled with stories of factory celebrations and the good cheer shared between employers and employees. Nary a mention of discontent could be found in their pages, which abounded with pictures of smiling workers shaking hands with their U.S. supervisors.[60] One festivity that offered several such photo opportunities was the annual Mother's Day celebration, held on what is a national holiday in Mexico. Each May 10, plants would halt production and open their doors to workers' families. Mother's Day festivities gave U.S. executives splendid opportunities to reach out to Mexican workers and solidify a sense of family at the factories. As part of the merriment, family members toured the factories, received presents, listened to live music, and dined with executives. Similarly, according to Rafael Castro, during the Christmas season, families were again invited to the plants, where in addition to presenting workers their traditional holiday bonuses, companies staged a giant gift giveaway for employees' children.

Workers' lives outside the factory also closely swirled around the corporation. The demands of work, however, left little time for leisure activities that did not revolve around the company. As one laborer recalled, "I would work eight-hour days and then would usually do three hours of overtime each weekday, and then play fútbol after work on three of those days. Then on Saturdays, I would often go in for an eight-hour shift. On Sundays, I would usually collapse."[61] What leisure time laborers did have tended to center around company-sponsored activities, particularly company sports teams (see Figure 36). Workers actively participated in company baseball, fútbol, basketball, and bowling leagues, and followed the various teams' standings with great interest. Many of the fútbol teams, which were generally organized around factory work sections, received coverage in the city newspapers, especially in the late 1950s, when several GM workers qualified for a national soccer team to compete against Guatemala in a match held in that country's capital. In fact, as residents of Santa Julia overwhelmingly took up employment at the nearby GM and Auto-Mex/Chrysler plants, a number of neighborhood teams became absorbed by those sponsored by the automobile companies. Squads from Santa Julia's other industrial firms—including General Popo Tires, Cervecería Modelo, and Oxxo—regularly played against one another at neighborhood soccer and baseball fields, with residents filling the bleachers and cheering on their favorite teams. Despite the long days autoworkers spent inside the plants, many nonetheless found the time—not to mention the energy—to throw themselves headlong into the company sports leagues. Guillermo Alvarez, known by fellow GM workers as El Estrella (the Star) because of his skills on the soccer field, remembered, "We played on Mondays, Wednesdays, Thursdays, and Fridays. We didn't play on Tuesdays because that's when we went bowling."[62] Workers also often socialized and shared drinks after the games. As Marcelino Sánchez, a regular player, put it, "We had just as many teams who played *jaibol* [enjoyed cocktails] as we did who played fútbol."

36. Mario "El Caballo" Reynoso with his wife after a company baseball game, held at a field near the GM factory. Company sports leagues, first established by auto industry executives to help build solidarity between U.S. employers and Mexican laborers, by the 1970s had become closely associated with union life and ultimately served to connect workers at GM with those at other automobile manufacturing firms who waged similar rank-and-file campaigns to democratize their unions and participate in company decision making. Courtesy of Mario Reynoso.

The close bond shared by employees was further reinforced by the multitude of marriages that occurred between male workers and female staff, the latter of whom held clerical positions or posts in the company cafeteria. Automakers sponsored bridal showers and devoted extensive space in company newsletters to engagements and marriages between employees, prominently displaying photographs of the various celebrations. Bulletins also proudly announced the birth of children, typically calling the newborns additions to the Ford or GM family. And of course, when the children reached the appropriate age, they were encouraged to apply for company scholarships to attend university. Each year, Ford and GM awarded several scholarships that covered all school expenses, even tuition at the much costlier private universities. Moreover, company officials placed no restrictions on the type of career students could pursue, but they did hope that recipients would study industrial engineering and come to work for the firm upon graduation. José Luis Vargas, who himself left school after the sixth grade, put all three of his children through university with the help of GM fellowships; two of them eventually went on to work for the company in the 1970s.[63]

To further its goal of cultivating a transnational family, management also took great pains to convey a pristine image of all things North American. Company officials held up the United States as a model country, one where the working class had "succeeded" and virtually joined the ranks of the middle class. To give their workers a sense of North American life, automakers from time to time sent their laborers to plants in the Detroit area so they could experience industrial progress firsthand. Firms also conducted English classes for those interested in learning the language. Executives believed that such lessons would foster better communication between Mexican wage earners and U.S. bosses, many of whom had very limited Spanish-speaking skills. Several U.S. supervisors also set aside time from their busy schedules to converse with workers in English, helping them practice what they were learning in their language courses.[64]

Finally, U.S. bosses also took considerable care not to show any discriminatory treatment toward Mexican wage earners. While nationwide polls done in the United States in the 1940s revealed that nearly half of all U.S. respondents considered Latin Americans "lazy" and "backward," U.S. bosses strove not to let any such sentiments show—even if they shared them.[65] In fact, most workers believed that the U.S. bosses treated them more kindly than Mexican managers. As Pedro Barajas explained, "The North American bosses were better than the Mexicans. The ones from here were slave drivers [*negreros*]; the whole world knows that. North Americans would always stop, say 'Hi,' and try to talk to us in Spanish."[66] José Luis Vargas struck a similar chord, remembering, "North Americans had a very special manner of being. . . . I never saw any friction between North Americans and Mexicans. U.S. bosses would always ask for things and say 'please,' but never the Mexican bosses." Salvador Navas, who spent time at both Chrysler and GM, found even more fault with Mexican managers: "Mexican bosses never served us; they were exploiters. North American *jefes* were far better than Mexicans."[67]

The favorable opinion held of U.S. supervisors was, to a large degree, the product of the bosses' own design. Personnel from the United States, who occupied the highest offices within the companies, delegated actual disciplining and enforcement to lower-level assistants, all of whom were Mexican. Occasions when workers did have contact with U.S. managers tended to be when bosses toured the factories, or at parties, celebrations, and large company events, such as Christmas parties or the Mother's Day fiestas. Thus, workers associated U.S. executives with company benevolence rather than shop-floor despotism.

The same, however, could not be said of Mexican supervisors and engineers. Workers frequently protested that Mexican managers meted out authority in arbitrary ways. (It should be noted that foremen who had come from the ranks of the workforce were typically spared such scorn.) Ignacio Bobadilla, expressing a widely shared opinion about Mexican supervisors, maintained that "the worst enemies of the Mexican working class are Mexican bosses. They make outrageous demands because they know we are at their mercy." Another worker recalled bitterly, "The boss said I had to set up a rendezvous between him and my wife in order to get a promotion. I absolutely refused. The next thing I knew, I was mounting tires in the 'pit' [a particularly onerous work assignment]. I stayed there for years without ever being promoted."[68]

Turning Around the Transnational Family

As the Integration Decree, which called for full-scale automobile production, neared passage, manufacturers began to expand their workforces at unprecedented rates. Up to that point, the auto industry had grown very slowly. Between 1947 and 1957, for instance, the workforce at GM had increased by only 17.5 percent, from 837 to 1,056 workers. The next three years, during which time the López Mateos administration announced its plans to make the industry the centerpiece of its import-substitution industrialization strategy, saw GM's workforce expand by 33 percent. The true explosion for the company, however, came between 1960 and 1965, when the workforce tripled in size, soaring from 1,480 to 4,330. Similarly, during these same five years, employment at Ford went from 1,029 to 3,931, and at Auto-Mex/Chrysler the workforce jumped from 1,024 to 2,411.[69]

Veterans at the GM plant quickly sensed the coming changes. In 1961, management began "replacing" older workers with younger, ostensibly stronger laborers.[70] Men such as Arcadio Morón and Edmundo Castillo, both of whom had given nearly twenty-five years to the firm and been among those first hired at the plant in 1937, found themselves terminated without cause. Workers protested these actions and launched formal grievances in the national labor court, but management maintained that veterans had passed their prime and could be "retired" at the company's will.[71]

Production demands increased at such a tremendous rate that management resorted to putting apprentices to work on the assembly line, a practice that violated the existing labor contract. Apprentices, most of whom were between sixteen and eighteen years of age, accepted the appointments on the assumption that the company would teach them a skill. These positions, which were filled by the sons of permanent laborers, drew half the wages of the lowest-paid unskilled worker. But now, compelled to do unskilled labor, apprentices failed to learn their promised trade. Autoworkers had little trouble grasping the company's aims: by utilizing their services, firms gained the labor of line workers at half the cost.

Workers began to protest the increasingly stringent production demands as GM geared up for the implementation of the 1962 decree. They complained that "the bosses [were] demanding more work than ever."[72] Responding to such complaints, Jorge Abarca, an autoworker and Santa Julia resident who would soon emerge as a vocal member of a coalescing rank-and-file labor movement at GM, advised laborers, "When a jefe demands work beyond the normal pace, go immediately to the union office."[73] Once aware of the possible contract violation, Abarca would make his way to the assembly line and measure its velocity with a stopwatch to determine whether the speed fell within the parameters of the collective contract. As we shall see, Abarca's proposal hinted at the new role autoworkers were envisioning for their union, an organization that had previously avoided challenging management on most production-related issues.

During this time, the company also began introducing new bosses. Previously, foremen, who had gotten promoted out of the ranks of the union, oversaw workers. Over the previous decade, laborers had grown accustomed to working closely with these men, who themselves had once been fellow workers with many of the same concerns. Obviously, this was not the case with all bosses, but nonetheless, many shared a common understanding of the demands of autowork and empathized with workers' toils. As one laborer explained, "We were all cuates who got along."[74]

But beginning in the mid-1960s, engineers from technical schools—*los ingenieros*, as workers would refer to them with a noticeable tone of disdain—increasingly occupied supervisory positions. Workers asserted that engineers knew very little about the minutiae of autowork, yet served as the ones making all the key decisions. In the words of one worker, "They sat in their offices eating sandwiches, and then would come over and bark orders at us. And with their titles and degrees, they still didn't know how to do the work."[75] As engineers came to occupy these posts, laborers found working closely with them increasingly difficult. In 1964, one particularly disliked engineer, Romero Beltrán, who had previously been employed at the plant but was let go "due to incompetence," returned to GM to oversee the upholstery department. Workers soon complained that he had come back with "a new mission to push us as hard as he can."[76] Management even started awarding monthly prizes, such as weekend trips to Acapulco, to the bosses whose departments recorded the highest productivity.[77] The bonuses seem to have succeeded in convincing bosses to prod their workers as much as they could. Even with hundreds of newcomers entering the factories, productivity per laborer soared.[78]

The work environment, most agreed, was becoming more demanding. Assembly line velocity jumped from fifteen inches to twenty-five inches per minute, and workers went from assembling around forty units to seventy units per shift.[79] Laborers frequently complained about the pace, prompting bosses to slow it momentarily, but soon thereafter the line would resume its earlier speed.[80] A wage earner in the engine department, considered one of the most forbidding work areas, remembered that demands in 1964 became so unbearable that one day he broke down on the shop floor and cried.[81] From then on, his workmates, in ridicule rich with gender-encoded meanings we shall examine presently, took to calling him *La Llorona*, after the legend of the long-suffering "Weeping Woman" in Mexican oral tradition.

As workers saw it, they were increasingly bearing the brunt of these shop-floor changes. In one respect, new methods and technologies made their labor less physically onerous. Working on engine blocks, for instance, employees no longer needed to push the unwieldy units to the next work station; now an overhead conveyor moved the blocks through the department. On the other hand, laborers no longer established their own pace; conveyor belts and overhead chains—and, by extension, the bosses who controlled their velocity—determined it.

It was more than simply the strenuous pace of the work that laborers disliked. Few workers complained about the hard work; in fact, it remained something of a badge of honor, an affirmation of one's masculinity.[82] As one worker recalled, "I had nothing against working hard. I worked really hard, like a donkey. No kidding, *un pinche burro*."[83] In earlier times, of course, bosses had supervised laborers, ensuring that they did not slacken in their duties. Nonetheless, workers thought nothing of running to the bathroom for a quick smoke, as long as they continued to do their work well. With engineers closely watching over workers' shoulders, however, such jaunts to the restroom became increasingly rare. Bathroom breaks were still permitted, but with an incessantly moving assembly line, bosses often refused to excuse their workers, a circumstance that laborers took as a personal affront to their dignity and their manhood. One laborer vividly recounted that his boss never allowed him to visit the restroom, something that embittered the veteran autoworker. Finally, one day in 1964, as both an act of rebellion (using the one weapon he had at hand) and because nature called, he proceeded to urinate in a corner where his jefe usually stood.[84]

With heightened pressure placed on productivity, laborers had inadequate time to do their work as skillfully as they desired. This problem struck directly at the heart of the social identity workers had constructed for themselves. Although many outside the industry may have an image of autoworkers as mindless drones or automatons, laborers took tremendous pride in their toil and proudly defined themselves in terms of their work. Autoworkers put their labor at the core of the social identity they carved for themselves and infused their work with significance far beyond what one typically assigns to mass-production labor. One autoworker, in a saying he was fond of repeating, nicely captured this widely shared sentiment: "First God, then my work, then the company. In that order."[85] Reflecting this commitment to elevate only the holy spirits higher than autowork, autoworkers made certain that each factory section had its own reliquary dedicated to the Virgin of Guadalupe, who would protect them from the always looming prospect of life-threatening accidents. Wage earners took their work seriously not only because a slight mishap could suddenly spell the loss of an appendage but also because their work reflected a part of them. Work remained one of the fundamental ways wage earners could demonstrate their moral worth.[86] Many, in fact, considered their work a form of art, an expression of themselves, something through which they derived aesthetic satis-

37. Autoworkers developed a strong sense of camaraderie on the shop floor, owing in large part to the intensely collective nature of autowork. But life at the factory consisted of more than just work; here men from GM's paint department take a break to snap a lighthearted photograph. Courtesy of Mario Reynoso.

faction. In the words of Perfecto Rodríguez, whose first name suited his artisanal perfectionism, "I felt like I was an artist at my work. I was always very proud of my work and the knowledge and skill I had in doing it."[87]

In constructing this identity, autoworkers sharply distinguished themselves from those *en la calle* (on the streets), who worked in the informal sector and lacked training and technical skills. It mattered little, however, that many autoworkers themselves had once been en la calle and without a trade. Now part of a major corporation and enjoying company welfare programs that held them up as members of an exclusive corporate family, autoworkers created an identity for themselves as privileged *trabajadores con oficio* (workers with a trade). But this identity they constructed, although heavily influenced by U.S. company ideologies and practices, bitterly clashed with the realities of life on the shop floor. As production demands multiplied, autoworkers had great difficulty performing their work at the level of craftsmanship that they, as trabajadores con oficio, demanded of themselves. Voicing a widely held complaint, Mario Reynoso explained, "The bosses would push me to go faster, and I'd get angry because I didn't have enough time to do the work the way I wanted it done." Workers pointed out that bosses, at least rhetorically, called for quality but seemed interested primarily in quantity. "The company asks for quality . . . but the demands of work prohibit it," expounded Mario Reyes, a worker in Romero Beltrán's department, in the late months of 1964, just as the company completed overhauling the upholstery division.[88]

Laborers' pride in their work was also closely associated with their identity as men. With its drudgery and exhausting pace that the men maintained only they could endure, autowork was inextricably tied to laborers' own vision of their masculinity. During these years, only men participated in automobile manufacturing and assembly. Not until the early 1980s did women come to hold production jobs in the industry. Prior to this, female employees held either clerical jobs or positions as food servers and cooks in the company cafeterias. Autoworker Fernando Córdoba explained the absence of women on the shop floor: "Women in Mexico have a great fear of taking on production jobs; they have a fear of taking charge. Mexican women were not adequately prepared to be autoworkers."[89] Not surprisingly, female cafeteria workers saw things entirely differently: "The men marginalized us. . . . We would say something, and no one would listen because only men's opinions mattered. We had to keep quiet at the factory."[90]

A good number of employees met their future spouse at the factory. Cafeteria jobs offered women the chance to meet many of the workers at the plant. The majority of female cafeteria staff began at GM at a young age, often around sixteen years old. Those women who did wed autoworkers tended to leave the company on tying the knot. Autoworkers' high wages allowed the men to remain the primary breadwinners and to have their wives stay at home. The corporation, in fact, encouraged their male employees to marry, reasoning that a household's sole wage earner would be a more reliable worker and less likely to support salary-threatening activities like labor walkouts.[91] Autoworkers' high wages also afforded them the opportunity to establish *casas chicas* (literally "small houses," the term refers to both a mistress and the site of extramarital liaisons). Having *aventuras* (affairs) further bolstered men's claims to masculinity.[92] Although it remains difficult to gauge how widespread this practice was, the fact that several autoworkers boasted of having casas chicas speaks volumes about the significance men ascribed to them. One worker, Carlos Guerrero, who presided over the GM union in the late 1950s (when, in the words of workers a decade later, the union was ineffectual and had "legs of saliva"), was known for having a number of mistresses and securing jobs in the cafeteria for several of them.[93]

Autoworkers based their masculinity primarily on their capacity to do factory labor. It is not surprising, therefore, that workers in the engine department would dub the man who began to sob on the shop floor La Llorona. The worker acquired the name for more than simply shedding tears. Equating physical weakness with femininity, laborers in the engine department rechristened their workmate after the female figure because of his inability to endure the travails of autowork. At the center of workers' specific notion of masculinity were two crucial and highly coveted characteristics: craftsmanship and physical endurance. Indeed, the two traits represented the core of autoworkers' identity as workers and as men. Not surprisingly then, as production rhythms intensified and supervisors began to privilege quantity over quality, laborers saw their bosses' behavior as a direct attack on their identity as both workers and men.

Despite the increased demands, laborers tried to work at a pace they found acceptable, especially when engineers stood behind them with stopwatches and conducted time-motion studies. In May 1964, for example, a recent hire for GM's second shift began doing his work much faster than the others in his section. His workmates quickly chastised him, saying, "Hey, what is your problem? Slow down. We've got to work together." The newcomer soon slowed his pace, but for the rest of his career with the company, which spanned the next thirty-one years, he was known to all as *El Campeón* (the Champion).[94] Reflecting this esprit de corps, laborers applauded those who stood up to the bosses to defend their own pace and preserve their high level of craftsmanship. Language used to describe such individuals was imbued with connotations of manliness and fortitude. Clemente Zaldívar, a line worker from Santa Julia who would gain notoriety for his labor militancy, was revered as a "worker with *huevos* [balls]," who always acted *por sus pantalones* (literally, "by the pants," here meaning "on one's own authority").[95] Nicknames assigned to laborers further illustrate this gender-steeped language. For instance, autoworkers called Daniel Espinosa *El Tiburón* (the Shark) because he was a tough worker and fierce union leader who prided himself on never backing down from a fight. Another admired laborer was christened *El Caballo* (the Horse), a name closely associated with endurance (not to mention sexual endowment), because he was considered a strong, tireless laborer who could work like a horse. Nor were bosses spared from such nicknaming practices. Workers dubbed Salvador Maldonado *El Gallo* (the Rooster, a name also steeped in sexual connotations) because he was judged to be one of the toughest, most obdurate supervisors at the plant. More frequently, however, workers gave bosses disparaging *apodos*. Laborers took to calling one supervisor who spoke with a strong lisp *Tejuites*, because when workers would return to their duties after sneaking off for a few moments, he would always ask, "Muchacho, cabrón, ¿dónde 'te juites'?" ("Hey bastard, where did you go? [*dónde te fuiste*]").[96]

Raising a Rank-and-File Family

Although changes in consciousness are difficult to chart day by day, by the end of 1964, workers at GM had reached the conclusion that the company had betrayed them. The corporation had asked laborers to entrust it with their future, but, as workers explained, "They are deceiving us. They made us think they would solve our problems, but they will not. We will never again allow this to happen."[97] The company's vision of employer and employees joining hands as members of a transnational family was crumbling. Workers increasingly recognized that company paternalism and welfare programs did very little to dampen the harsh reality of work and changing class relations on the shop floor as GM shifted to full-scale automobile manufacturing. Speaking at a well-attended meeting, rank-and-file worker Armando Pérez captured a sentiment shared by many: "We gave all of our support to the company, and now it is betraying us. We never thought it would deceive us, but now we are aware that it has."[98]

Workers began condemning what they called "the absurd conduct of the bosses." The only way to remedy the treatment, laborers declared, would be to "exert pressure against the company as a union." This, they realized, would bring workers far greater strength than they would have making individual demands through paternalistic labor channels. For instance, the union collectively called for the dismissal of engineer Romero Beltrán, who, according to men in his department, "will not let us stop for a single second." But their complaints hardly ended there. "The worst," they agreed, "is that he is not the only one; there are many."[99] Having lost faith in the promises of the company to address laborers' rising concerns, workers appropriated for their union the familial vision originally elaborated by the corporation. At a well-attended meeting in mid-1964, union members declared, "The GM family does indeed exist, and we—the union—are that family."[100]

Workers began articulating demands that hinged on a new vision for the role their union should take in the company's industrialization efforts. The GM union had been in place since 1937, but as was the case with many unions in Mexico, few of its members considered it an effective agent to represent them. Indeed, many felt that it had done very little for workers since the 1950s, when Carlos Guerrero completed three successive terms as union head, in defiance of provisions prohibiting the reelection of the secretary general. Now, however, with Guerrero gone and a new host of men drawn from the rank and file making up the leadership committee, union members began to give their organization teeth in battles against management and to imbue it with new significance. Foremost, the union demanded a role in determining how industrial expansion would take place at GM factories and how the transition to automobile manufacturing would be undertaken. In 1964, management embarked on an enormous project to overhaul entire factory sections and to begin integrating production routines into a single manufacturing system. One such department scheduled for refurbishing was the engine department, which laborers deemed among the most arduous at the plant. Union members worried that the engineers' plans would fail to take into account the department's already burdensome work load and would leave assignments even more onerous. Workers called on engineer Luis Jiménez, the superintendent of production, to let the union help draft the designs. Workers stressed that they knew the minutiae of the various departments better than the engineers, and thus should play a part in deciding how industrial production would be reconfigured.

The union also asserted a right to direct how company profits would be distributed. Union leaders accused management of taking funds earmarked for employee profit-sharing programs and using that money to invest in new technologies and production facilities. Workers charged the company with lying about its profits from previous years so that it would not have to contribute as heavily to employee profit-sharing accounts. In response, the union established a committee that drafted its own plan to disburse profits, manage profit-sharing programs, and invest capital into new production facilities. The union's plans were premised on the notion of incorporating workers' voices into running the firm, of establishing an industrial arrangement in which all members of the corporate family, not simply GM executives, would decide the company's future. Not surprisingly, given the implications of such demands, management roundly rejected the proposals, judging such areas to be completely outside the purview of the union, no matter how vocal and aggressive it had become. Workers, however, disagreed. As Clemente Zaldívar, the union member who headed the committee, explained to fellow laborers, "It's only logical that all those who work for the company should decide how the profits are divided."[101]

What is more, the union also demanded the right to contract the workforce at the company's new plant in Toluca (about sixty miles outside of Mexico City), which was scheduled to open in January 1965. Having a labor organization comprising workers at both plants would allow the revitalized union an unparalleled opportunity to build a larger, stronger labor movement within the industry that could bring even greater pressure to bear against management. The labor contract shared by workers had previously stipulated that the Mexico City GM union had the right to organize at all facilities the company might construct in the future, regardless of management's potential desires to establish an open shop or a union local affiliated with the Confederación de Trabajadores de México (CTM).[102] But in 1961, in a move GM workers would condemn for the next thirty-five years, the secretary general of the Mexico City local, Raul Sánchez del Castillo, agreed to remove the important provision from the contract. In return, he secured a modest salary increase for union members, the promotion of about 150 temporary workers to permanent status, and (as soon became evident) a handsome monetary kickback and cushy management job. Most egregious was Sánchez del Castillo's acceptance of these new contract provisions without putting the changes to a vote of the membership, a point that union members insisted made the agreement null and void. Workers correctly recognized that, if they hoped to sustain any semblance of negotiating strength vis-à-vis management, they had to prevail in organizing the workforce at the Toluca facility.

Rumors had already begun to circulate that within a few years GM would close its Mexico City plant and transfer all of its operations to the new factory in Toluca, where the minimum wage was a third of that in the capital and fully 70 percent less than what entry-level GM workers in Mexico City earned.[103] Information also surfaced that GM executives had recently held meetings with a corrupt labor boss in Toluca, asking him to create a *sindicato fantasmo* (phantom union) at the new facility that would do management's bidding. The phantom union, affiliated with the Fidel Velásquez–led CTM, was "organized" before a single worker at the Toluca plant had even been hired—hence the name "phantom union." When workers in Mexico City caught wind of this, they proclaimed, "We declare war. We will not let foreign interests do this. . . . We Mexicans are not going to permit any more foreign conquests."[104] Interestingly, suggesting the gravity of the situation, this was one of the only occasions in which GM workers made explicit, politically charged use of their employers' foreign status. Much more typically, union members alluded to the company's U.S. origins in a highly favorable light, casting U.S. corporations as far more benevolent than their Mexican counterparts.

Faced with the impossibility of organizing the Toluca plant under its own auspices, union members in Mexico City had only one option short of striking: switching their affiliation to the CTM and creating a union made up of wage earners at both plants. Not surprisingly, the move was strongly encouraged by GM managers, who would have greatly preferred dealing with the more conservative CTM hierarchy. But as opponents of the CTM put it, joining Velásquez's confederation would mean submitting to "venal leaders who rob their workers."[105] Union members recognized that management "would much rather talk to CTM leaders than to workers" and thus rejected this unsavory alliance, vowing that "we should fight for ourselves rather than become involved with the CTM." Ultimately, unionists concluded, "We are better off being alone than being poorly accompanied."[106]

In the first week of January 1965, formal contract negotiations between union and management commenced. The company refused to cede ground on any of the union's primary demands, specifically those that would give workers a hand in deciding the company's industrialization undertakings. Management did, however, assent to a 5 percent wage increase, which the union's negotiating team called "pure nonsense."[107] Twelve days into the talks, both sides still refused to budge. As the head of the union, Carlos Castañón, emphasized, "To accept the conditions of the negotiations would be to lose the gains of the last twenty-eight years. . . . No agreement will be possible as long as the company is intransigent."[108] Workers vowed that if an acceptable agreement was not reached by midnight, January 20, they would strike. Learning of a possible work stoppage, the company moved quickly to post bulletins around the plant threatening swift action against anyone who joined the walkout.[109] Few workers, however, were dissuaded (see Figure 38).

The General Motors Strike of 1965

The next morning, residents of the tony neighborhood of Polanco awoke to what must have struck them as an odd scene, but one that would become

38. A scene from the front of the GM factory during the momentous 1965 strike, the first strike in the company's history in Mexico. The men to the left are eating food that employees' wives prepared for the picketers. As one female GM wage earner recalled of the walkout, "The men expected us cafeteria workers to fix them food, but we refused because we were on strike too." Courtesy of Ignacio Ceballos.

ever more common over the next fifteen years as labor conflicts at the plant multiplied.[110] The General Motors plant stood surrounded by a sea of red and black flags. Large banners hung down the walls, and lines of workers guarded the factory gates, keeping anyone from gaining entrance into the plant.[111] For the first time in its nearly thirty-year history in Mexico, GM was being struck.[112]

If the scene seemed odd, it would take on an even stranger cast when the next day snow began falling on the city. Striking workers nonetheless braved the cold as they continued to guard the gates. Perhaps even stranger than the snowfall, Fidel Velásquez had already publicly endorsed the strike, proclaiming his support for it within twenty-four hours of workers first taking to the picket lines. Considered by many to be the person most responsible for defanging the country's labor movement, Velásquez promised that he would do everything he could to help strikers break free from the clutches of what he called their "yellow union."[113] Although workers appreciated the attention Velásquez brought to their cause, they politely declined his assistance.

With work at a standstill during a crucial time in the company's production schedule, executives wasted little time in condemning the strike, calling it "regrettable and unnecessary."[114] Richard Ehrlich, president of GM-

Mexico, considered the conflict entirely an economic issue, one of employees simply wanting higher wages. He failed to grasp (or, if he grasped, refused to acknowledge) any of the larger concerns voiced by workers. Management also hinted that the strike movement was being led by outside agitators who had been "erroneously informed" about the labor situation at the plant.[115] The company had long prided itself on having impeccable labor relations and one of the best contracts in the country, with excellent wages and benefits. Thus, in management's eyes, laborers had little reason to strike.[116]

General Motors proved unable to resolve this conflict as it had settled many others elsewhere (especially in the United States), by quickly granting wage increases as a way to convince laborers to resume production.[117] According to workers, the strike centered around issues more important than pay raises. Behind the scenes, management had offered the head of the union, Carlos Castañón, 100,000 pesos to sabotage the strike.[118] He declined and quickly informed union members of the plot, which seemed only to strengthen their resolve. With the bribe unsuccessful, executives hoped at least that talks, which were being mediated by an official from the Junta Central de Conciliación y Arbitraje, the nation's labor court, would soon lead to an acceptable agreement. The great importance the company commanded garnered the union immediate attention from the labor board—a rarity for many unions, whose grievances could languish for months before being heard.[119] Although their position as GM employees brought them immediate attention, most agreed that the company and the nation's labor court "played on the same team."[120]

Workers, however, had no intention of ending the strike as long as GM refused to respond to their demands. But laborers could last only as long as their limited means would allow. This being their first strike, workers had never before established a strike fund; thus, they had few resources with which to wage a long-term battle against the world's largest corporation. Moreover, workers had the added disadvantage of never having participated in a strike against the company. Unfortunately for them, they would have to learn as they went along.

Meanwhile, the strike struck a nerve among the city's working people. Several unions lent moral and economic support as *sindicatos hermanos* (union brothers).[121] In the words of one worker, the union and the strike had "gained the attention of the world."[122] Though this was undoubtedly an exaggeration, the conflict had nonetheless moved to the fore in a burgeoning national debate about the role of transnational corporations in the country. President Gustavo Díaz Ordaz, known for his support of foreign investment, had already come under fire for concentrating on economic expansion at the expense of much-needed social programs.[123] Comics had begun to appear in popular newspapers harshly criticizing the government's "modernization" efforts.[124] Even mainstream periodicals such as *Siempre* editorialized in favor of the strike. One front-page article, in particular, criticized tax exemptions the government awarded to GM to entice them to expand operations, only to have the "company turn against Mexican workers." The article further argued that the company was "not creating new industry but, rather, taking advantage of new labor in new places."[125]

A week into the strike, Díaz Ordaz appeared at the Fifteenth National Council of the Confederación Revolucionaria de Obreros y Campesinos, the government-allied labor confederation to which the GM union belonged. Inside, several delegates from the union listened to the Mexican president, while hundreds more stood outside protesting and drawing attention to their struggle. Speaking before the assembly, Díaz Ordaz acknowledged that "sometimes there will be disorders because of evolution," but urged workers to "demand all of your rights and comply with all of your obligations."[126] In the past, the president had made comments that bolstered workers' faith in their movement, but on this occasion it was difficult to know precisely what Díaz Ordaz meant by his words.[127] Workers took his guarded remarks to indicate that they were welcome to strike, but that they should not expect any support from his administration, especially against a massive corporation like GM. And, indeed, no support came. Not wanting to jeopardize GM's hefty investments in the country, state authorities refused to intervene, believing that the actual implementation of the motor vehicle industrialization project should be left in the hands of corporate managers.

On February 6, workers brought down the flags and ended the walkout. Quite simply, they had run out of resources with which to fight the giant automaker. As one participant lamented in the days immediately following the strike, "The company held all the cards from the beginning."[128] As much as workers attempted to put a positive spin on the strike, they knew it had culminated in defeat. Although the company agreed to a 13 percent wage increase (which was considerably higher than what executives offered before the walkout), the promotion of 250 temporary workers to permanent positions, and the payment of 55 percent of the wages they lost during the strike, management ceded no ground on the substantive issues. Union leaders warned members returning to work the next day to carry their labor contracts with them in their overalls: management would be looking for any and all infractions, even fabricating them if necessary, as a way to take reprisals against the strikers.[129]

But the conflict hardly ended there. Within days, management stepped up the pace of work like never before to "teach us never again to disobey the bosses."[130] Clemente Zaldívar, who headed the committee that drafted plans to distribute GM profits, refused to sit by idly as the company violated the labor contract. When workers complained that the assembly line was advancing beyond the permissable rate, Zaldívar threw off one of the power switches and shut down the assembly line, bringing the factory to a halt. Management immediately dispatched company police to haul him out of the plant; he was thrown out of the factory and promptly fired. Though he never again set foot in the factory, he remained active in the union (as a compañero emeritus, one might say) and received money collected by fellow members to supplant his lost wages.

In the wake of the strike and Zaldívar's bold act of defiance, the company accused the movement's leaders of being communists, a fairly common authorial practice at the time. In statements released to the press, officials declared that Zaldívar had taken money from communists to stir up trouble at the plant and turn workers against the company—a charge they knew would catch the attention of the "cold warriors" who populated the federal branches of power.[131] Due to Zaldívar's supposed agitation, executives suggested, workers had followed his lead against the company and into the waiting arms of communism. Company officials proved unable to substantiate any of their claims, which most workers saw as facile attempts at red-baiting. In the words of one worker, expressing a widely shared view, "Our consciousness didn't come from the outside," brought in by communist rabble-rousers. "Our ideas came from *la vivencia* [our experiences]."[132] Most important, autoworkers' new political consciousness grew out of their transnational encounters on the shop floor toiling for U.S. corporations.

Finding the National in Transnational

At the heart of autoworkers' emerging political consciousness was the insistence that they should have a role in deciding the course of corporate and state modernization projects. This became readily apparent as GM workers demanded collectively to set production quotas, control the pace of production, standardize wage rates, hire and fire workers, control promotions, and set the percentages of the total workforce employed in different wage categories. As members of the firm's transnational family, workers contended they had a right to participate in determining the direction the company would take in industrializing Mexico. Union members hardly considered this a radical proposition, as management did. Rather, autoworkers deemed their goals to be the fulfillment of the promises—or at least their interpretation of such promises—implicit in company-advanced ideologies and ideals. From their first days at the factory, laborers had been taught to regard the company as a transnational family in which the interests of employees went hand in hand with those of their foreign employers. "Good workers," the company instructed, were those who joined with management and "united their collective forces for the greater good of all."[133] Management constantly sang the refrain that the company's "guiding fundamental principle is the spirit of collaboration" that thrived between workers and bosses.[134] To a large degree, such company-promoted ideals took hold among autoworkers. Company welfare programs and U.S. corporate ideologies spurred autoworkers to see themselves as privileged transnational family members at the forefront of modernization. And collectively they gave credence to the corporation and President Díaz Ordaz's claim that "modernization is an economic necessity, not a pretext for cracking down on working conditions."[135] But as GM shifted to full-scale manufacturing, autoworkers discovered the company to be "treating us like beasts" and "making us beg for alms . . . like so many laborers at *other* firms have to do."[136] Resorting to such behavior went squarely against the privileged position in which employment at GM had placed autoworkers. Finding themselves without a voice in the company's industrialization initiatives, workers saw little evidence of the "spirit of collaboration" that executives asserted flourished at the plant. Ultimately, they concluded that "the company is going against its own words. . . . Now we see that their promises were all lies." "All of their promises," reiterated another, "remain in the supervisors' inkwells."[137]

With "the strike movement having revitalized *sindicalismo* within our organization," the union began to take over many of the company-sponsored welfare programs.[138] The labor organization began steering its own training program, in which experienced workers "taught their labor skills and passed down their knowledge of struggle" to succeeding generations of wage earners.[139] The union also started to publish its own newspaper, *El Eco*, designed to counter the limited and sanitized focus of the company newsletter. In addition, the union proposed—and, a few years later, built—a cooperative union store, where workers could buy goods below prevailing retail prices. The union also came to dominate many of the company sports leagues. Team sports like baseball and fútbol became closely tied to the union and served to forge solidarity on the sports field, which in turn reinforced solidarity on the shop floor. Clemente Zaldívar, for example, was recognized as much for his ball handling on the soccer field as for his huevos on the factory floor. Bosses who had previously competed on baseball and fútbol teams abandoned them in favor of the bowling league, which became the recreational domain of the *batudos* (bosses) and wage earners considered *barbero* (cuddly) with them. Playing baseball and soccer against teams from the Ford and Chrysler plants further helped the union forge pivotal ties to the workforces at other plants, tilling the ground for the cultivation of a larger, national movement of autoworkers in the years to come.

Interestingly, autoworkers harbored little ill will toward U.S. executives at the firm. Even at the height of the 1965 strike, union members attributed the company's intransigence to lower-level executives having misled Richard Ehrlich, the head of GM-Mexico.[140] Workers insisted that Ehrlich would right all of the company's wrongs, if only he were truthfully informed about workers' concerns.[141] In this context, union members displayed little of the doctrinaire anti-yanquismo associated with most strains of "revolutionary nationalism," particularly the brand of "official" nationalism espoused by the Mexican state in the 1960s and 1970s. As Eric Zolov has shown, the ruling regime effectively advanced a "state-guided" nationalism that condemned the propagation of state-designated "foreign" values and influences, even as it welcomed vast sums of foreign capital into the country and projected the image of a modern, cosmopolitan Mexico.[142] In the process, the ruling regime succeeded, at least partially, in co-opting nationalist discourses that could threaten state and corporate modernization projects.

Evincing few of the anti-gringo sentiments found among many sectors of Mexico's laboring classes, workers at GM faced a barrage of criticism, some even coming from groups that, at one time, expressed support for the strike. A number of unions, primarily those of a "revolutionary nationalist" bent, denounced GM workers for having been made *agringados* ("gringified") by their U.S. employers.[143] Since the Porfiriato, Mexicans who were considered to have forsaken their "national" culture for the trappings of gringo life have served as objects of scorn.[144] In some respects, the charge leveled at GM workers was accurate. Employment at the U.S. corporation put GM workers in an enviable position, one in which they were treated to benefits few of Mexico's popular classes enjoyed. Moreover, company projects designed to cultivate a transnational family had largely succeeded in persuading GM workers to regard the U.S. working class as a model to emulate. But this hardly meant that workers had turned their backs on their compañeros in Mexico. Not long after their own strike, laborers at GM contributed generous amounts of money to unions at General Electric and Euzkadi Tires to help them sustain their own walkouts and awaken sindicalismo in other industrial sectors.

In solidifying ties to other unions, GM workers looked well beyond their immediate environs toward the "Colossus of the North," the United States.[145] The head of GM-Mexico maintained that at least part of the explanation for Mexico's poverty lay in its workers' lacking a "better incentive to reach for social and economic progress."[146] To this end, GM executives urged their Mexican workers to pattern themselves after the company-projected image of a prosperous, loyal, and compliant U.S. working class. To Mexican autoworkers, however, the prosperity U.S. workers enjoyed bespoke not labor's compliance, but labor's strength. High wages, home and car ownership, and democratic representation, Ignacio Bobadilla surmised, "could only have come from workers' own *conquistas* [conquests]." No doubt contemporary line workers in Detroit would have disputed Mexicans' rosy assessment of U.S. factory life.[147] Mexican autoworkers, after all, were peering at an invented image of the U.S. working class, an example of the social construction Arjun Appadurai has dubbed the "nation of make-believe Americans."[148] Yet, although this was a message originally propagated by the company, workers interpreted the image in novel ways, reinscribing it with new meanings that led them in unintended directions. Thus, interpreting U.S. workers' accomplishments to be the result of union efforts and not of company generosity, GM workers looked to their working-class counterparts in the United States for signposts to help them guide their new union movement.

In looking to the U.S. working class, GM workers sought to forge ties to U.S. labor organizations—something their position at the transnational firm made far easier. During the course of their strike, union members established links to one of the largest labor organizations in the United States, the United Auto Workers (UAW). At the time, Walter Reuther, the head of the UAW, was organizing a world automobile council, which he hoped would bring together unions at transnational auto firms around the globe. The labor leader, himself a veteran of several pitched battles against GM, took great interest in the Mexican union. In particular, Reuther hoped to focus organizing drives in Mexico, where he was well aware of the country's concerted industrial push. Mexico held special importance in his view because of the growing practice of "wage dumping" done by transnational firms there, an activity he reasoned would intensify with time. Only by bringing workers' wages in Mexico more in line with those in the United States, he figured, would the practice ever diminish. Such an effort would bolster the labor movement in Mexico as well as in the United States, where—some thirty years before the North American Free Trade Agreement—labor leaders were already beginning to take notice of the far-reaching implications of transnational firms relocating to low-wage countries. As Reuther argued, "We have to find a rational way to bring to bear the maximum power of international solidarity, or we will be isolated and divided, weak and defenseless in the face of the growing power of international capital to exploit us separately."[149]

The Mexican union used its ties to the U.S. organization to strengthen its hand at the plant and within the auto industry more broadly. During the 1965 strike, the union local received economic support from the UAW's amply endowed International Solidarity Fund, which had over $30 million in its coffers. The money helped boost the union's paltry strike fund, which had been established only two days before the walkout commenced. Mexican workers also assisted the UAW in assembling a massive database of the wages paid at GM factories around the world. In addition, they participated in a research project that studied virtually every collective bargaining agreement signed by the auto giant. From these undertakings, Mexican workers learned of the wages and concessions the company had awarded elsewhere in the world. This made them even more keenly aware of how far their wages lagged behind those in other countries, especially the United States. As one worker succinctly put it at the time, "Wages are cheaper in Mexico; the company is taking all the profits to the 'other side' [the United States]."[150]

Inspired by the example of the UAW, wage earners at GM set out to establish a similarly organized national union of autoworkers. They hoped to bring together laborers at Ford, Auto-Mex/Chrysler, Nissan, and Volkswagen into a single, federal union that could skirt the authority and predominance of the state-backed CTM.[151] At the time, unions at these plants remained affiliated with and under the firm control of the state-allied labor confederation, which imposed union leaders from above and from outside the ranks of the workforce. As evidence of this influence, as well as the success of company welfare programs in discouraging unionism, a survey at the Ford factory in the mid-1960s revealed that 30 percent of the workforce were unaware they belonged to a union—and this at a plant with a closed shop![152] Confident of the encumbrances autoworkers would face in forming a labor federation outside the channels of the CTM, Jesús Yurén, one of the federation's directors, scoffed at the GM workers' efforts and derided them for having "a union that in its twenty-seven years of existence has never been combative or aggressive."[153] To help mount their campaign, unionists at GM sought the assistance not only of the UAW but also the Switzerland-based International Metalworkers Federation (IMF), a worldwide labor organization founded at the turn of the century to which the UAW belonged.[154] With the support of the UAW, the GM union joined the IMF and began participating in its numerous conferences on international labor organizing. In early 1966, the workforce at GM selected ten of its members to attend an IMF-sponsored conference in Venezuela on training workers to organize national auto unions throughout Latin America. These ten men, all drawn from the rank and file, went on to play important roles in the labor battles that would rock Mexico City in the 1970s.[155]

After launching a campaign to make organizational inroads into the CTM-affiliated workforces at the other auto firms, unionists quickly found labor leaders at the various facilities to be a significant obstacle. At Auto-Mex/Chrysler, where a rank-and-file movement was beginning to challenge the plant's "yellow" union, workers encountered stiff opposition from the head of the company-controlled union, a Velásquez appointee and career labor official named Luis Quijano. Workers at Chrysler caustically nicknamed the labor boss "Porfirio Díaz," in reference to the long-ruling Mexican dictator, because of the firm hand he exercised at the plant. Quijano, who had occupied his post for several years, had also secured for his two brothers high-ranking administrative positions within the company. Similarly, the head of the "yellow" union at Ford, Joaquín del Olmo, brooked no opposition from the rank and file and seemed to enjoy the benefits that presiding over a union at a major automaker could bring. Workers could not help but notice the new cars del Olmo always seemed to be driving and the other accoutrements of affluence that no autoworker could afford. Union members at GM rightfully wondered, "How can these men who accept bribes from the company expect to defend workers?"[156] Laborers at Ford and Auto-Mex/Chrysler were beginning to ask themselves the same question. They expressed strong enthusiasm for the campaign to form a national union, although stiff opposition came almost immediately from CTM officials, who had close ties to management and had at their disposal the union dues deducted from autoworkers' paychecks. In the face of the obstacles thrown up by the CTM, workers' efforts met with limited immediate success. They did, however, prevail in establishing the National Automotive Council, composed of several of the industry's unions. Launched in January 1967 at an inauguration attended by Walter Reuther and members of the UAW and IMF, the council fought to regularize wages at the various factories and bring them more in line with salaries in the United States.

Nacos No More

Throughout this period, the influence GM had on its workers extended well beyond the factory gates and into working-class communities, where laborers' social identities and cultural lives were thoroughly transformed. As members of a massive transnational corporation, workers at GM developed new aspirations and sought, as employee Salvador Navas put it, to "make for ourselves a new culture." Although many of those starting at GM in the mid-1960s hailed from the countryside and had settled in the barrio of Santa Julia, their position at the company ushered in new opportunities to "make a new life for ourselves, to better ourselves," as Melitón Hernández explained. Standing at the forefront of modernization and national progress, few autoworkers wanted to be identified with their rural roots. Granted, even after migrating to Mexico City, many autoworkers still preserved significant ties to their pueblos and rural communities.[157] One is reminded, for instance, of autoworker Gonzálo Robledo, who went by the nickname Zacatecas. He founded a club made up of fellow *zacatecanos* at the GM plant who would meet once a month in Chapultepec Park to drink *mezcal* brought back from the *patria chica* and to reminisce about life in the homeland.[158] Nevertheless, autoworkers hoped to create a new culture and new cultural orientations, ones distinguishable from the naco characteristics they sought to leave behind.

As such, workers at GM took to adopting U.S.-influenced cultural forms and orientations, which had largely remained limited to Mexico's upper and middle classes. Unlike most working people, Mexico's upper classes had the economic means to afford products from the United States (many of which had high tariffs) and to follow the latest styles and consumer trends, including U.S. rock music. For instance, in the years prior to the massacre at Tlatelolco in 1968 (after which time it became associated with student radicalism), rock music symbolized the cosmopolitan aspirations and modernizing impulses of Mexico's upper classes.[159] As Eric Zolov has shown for 1960s Mexico City, class was "located within a complex set of cultural, social, racial, and topographic (i.e., neighborhood) characteristics," and appropriating "Americanized" cultural forms was viewed as an indicator of class and worldliness.[160]

For Mexican autoworkers, this cultural transformation took root in their employment at transnational firms. The high wages provided by GM gave autoworkers significantly more income than most laboring people, offering them the opportunity to buy products few fellow *proletarios* could afford. Their salaries, coupled with the two weeks of paid vacation granted annually, allowed many autoworkers to travel to places such as Acapulco, bastion of sun-worshiping, largely middle- and upper-class tourists. Employee discounts on GM products allowed several workers to purchase automobiles by the early 1970s. Company-sponsored night classes afforded many the opportunity to finish secundaria, and scholarships awarded by the company helped numerous laborers send their children to university, which most other working people of their generation were unable to do. And language courses at the plant taught a number to speak English (or at least some English), just like the *fresas* (the "beautiful people" more commonly associated with Americanized culture) in Polanco and the Zona Rosa. Thus, autoworkers were able to share in several of the cultural trappings associated with both upper- and middle-class, not to mention North American, life. After their work shifts, some GM wage earners even took to frequenting the quintessentially Mexican bourgeois hangout, Sanborn's, after one was built a block away from the plant. They did so, however, with a decidedly tongue-in-cheek air. As one of the regulars, Angel Daniel Ruiz, recalled of the visits, "The fresas would all look over at us as we walked in. We'd look back at them and shout, '¡Ya estamos!' [Now we're here!]."

Enjoying cocktails at the local Sanborn's, however, hardly meant that laborers hoped to join the ranks of the fresas, who remained the object of considerable ridicule among working people. But neither did it mean that the cultural choices autoworkers made were neutral or without meaning.

Rather, workers' changing cultural orientations formed part of a larger process of cultural transformation taking place among the industrial working class in Mexico City in the mid- and late 1960s. During this time, autoworkers actively drew new lines of cultural demarcation, constructing for themselves a social identity that sharply distinguished them from los nacos, *los pobres* (the poor), and the most recent arrivals from the countryside. As autoworkers saw it, their position at transnational firms—and all the benefits their employment brought them—placed them above these more economically disadvantaged groups, even though they shared very similar roots. By developing new cultural orientations, shaped in large measure by their experiences at the U.S. auto giant, autoworkers came to define themselves in marked contrast to los nacos.

One of the most telling examples of this was the effort among GM workers to move out of the poor barrio of Santa Julia, where so many of them lived. Union members who resided in Santa Julia struck on the idea of establishing their own neighborhood, to be called Colonia General Motors, where workers would all live together. The project nicely captured the new significance with which workers had imbued their union. Before the 1965 strike, workers on several occasions had petitioned the company for loans to help them purchase houses. Wage earners at several large corporations had made similar requests of their employers, even pushing, unsuccessfully, for legislation that would have required firms with more than one hundred employees to provide housing provisions.[161] As migrants arrived weekly by the thousands, housing was quickly becoming one of the most pressing concerns in the city. Workers soon discovered that, whereas the government was slow to respond to the housing shortage, most employers simply shunned such requests. Executives at GM at first had entertained thoughts of loaning funds to establish a company colonia, but never moved beyond verbal promises. In the wake of the 1965 walkout, which drove a thick wedge between labor and management, workers elected to direct the housing project themselves, without the participation of company authorities.

After discovering that land prices in the nearby neighborhood of Polanco were far beyond their means, workers at GM selected the municipality of Naucalpan, in the state of Mexico, as the site for their colonia. Naucalpan seemed ideally suited for the type of neighborhood workers hoped to construct. It lay in an undeveloped area of high rolling hills and offered abundant space for lots and sweeping views of the capital to the south. Some ten miles northwest of the capital's *centro histórico*, the area was far enough away from downtown Mexico City to escape its pollution and bustling crowds. The region also bordered Ciudad Satélite, Mexico City's first satellite city and a model bedroom community. Developed for middle-class Mexicans fleeing the irruption of rural poor into the capital, Ciudad Satélite displayed little of the urban decay that the well-to-do claimed was beginning to characterize the erstwhile City of Palaces. Naucalpan's proximity to middle-class Satélite gave workers access to amenities and cultural trappings not available in neighborhoods such as Santa Julia. Although much of the area remained undeveloped, by the time autoworkers moved there, it already boasted a Lion's Club, a U.S.-style supermarket, and a Boy Scout troop. And for those with a fondness for U.S. fast-food chains, the area also claimed Pizza Hut, Shakey's, Denny's, Tastee Freez, and Kentucky Fried Chicken franchises.

Workers' plans called for the construction of single-family, unattached homes on large lots, complete with front and back yards, two-car garages, and neighborhood greenbelts. Their homes stood in marked contrast to the makeshift structures and *tugurios* (slum homes) of Santa Julia and the ramshackle dwellings being built by *paracaidistas* (squatters) in settlements on the industrial periphery of the city. The designs also differed immensely from the enormous, densely populated, high-rise housing developments—such as the Unidad Habitacional Popular Loma Hermosa, only a few miles north of the GM plant, and the Alliance for Progress–inspired Unidad John F. Kennedy—sponsored by the government to house the city's burgeoning working class and, even more, lower middle classes.[162] In contrast to these immense, tightly packed housing projects, Colonia General Motors was patterned after suburban residences in the United States, with yards, garages, and greenbelts. Many area residents, in fact, considered the neighborhood and its spacious homes to be much nicer than most middle-class communities and houses in the capital.[163] Each house cost 55,000 pesos, a price much steeper than most working-class homes. By comparison, residences in the Unidad Loma Hermosa—considered to be a very nice, "upper"-working-class and lower-middle-class development—sold for 20,000 pesos, a price nearly 65 percent less.

In March 1966, two hundred families moved into the colonia. As this was one of the first union local-led housing projects of its kind, the press arrived to cover the ribbon-cutting ceremony.[164] Also in attendance were GM executives, who, according to workers, "attempted to take credit for the project."[165] Union members reminded those present that the colonia was the result of workers' own efforts. Interestingly, residents opted not to name the neighborhood Colonia General Motors, although it would go by that name informally for years to come. Instead, guided by their own sense of transnationalism and high regard for North America, workers dubbed the community Colonia Las Americas. In keeping with that spirit, streets in the neighborhood bore such names as California, Canada, Washington, and North America.

Life in the neighborhood, however, proved more challenging than residents anticipated. For one thing, the colonia lacked many municipal services and utilities. A year after settling into the community, residents still suffered through long stretches without water, electricity, and waste disposal services. This particularly raised the ire of neighborhood women, who, while their husbands labored at the GM plant, were expected to do household labor without the benefit of utilities—which made doing the unwaged labor all the more burdensome. As one female resident explained, "During the day, when temperatures got the warmest, all the trash collecting out on the street would really begin to stink."[166] On several occasions, wives petitioned municipal authorities, but each time their requests went ignored. Residents suspected that officials refused to take the complaints seriously because women were lodging them.

Tired of the municipal government's neglect, the women resolved to do something that would capture the authorities' attention: they decided to march through the community to the Palacio Municipal carrying huge bins of trash.[167] In March 1967, almost a year to the day after moving into the neighborhood, approximately one hundred women met one morning on Washington Street. Each brought with her a large container filled with the rankest refuse she could find. When they arrived at the Palacio Municipal, the women forced their way into the office of the municipal president. There, throughout his office and especially all across his desk, they scattered their rubbish. This seemed to have the desired effect; a few days later, trash trucks began passing through the colonia picking up garbage. The birth of this neighborhood movement was made easier by the connection its members already shared through GM. Several of the women had spent time together as cafeteria workers at the plant, where political life in the union was severely circumscribed for them. Still other women, who had not worked for the corporation, had come to know one another through the rich social life GM workers and their families shared—a life that centered around the company and the union. Thus, for both male and female residents of the colonia, the cultural worlds of the transnational factory and the working-class neighborhood had become tightly interwoven.

The changing cultural orientations among GM workers and their families sparked criticism from various quarters, especially from state-affiliated labor bosses, who charged them with *malinchismo*. Derived from the name given to Hernán Cortés's indigenous interpreter and mistress, La Malinche (Doña Marina), the term referred disparagingly to the emulation of "foreign" cultures.[168] Labor leaders like Jesús Yurén, a high-ranking official in the CTM, claimed that GM workers had long ago capitulated to foreign interests and had never struggled in the true tradition of revolutionary nationalism, which the CTM putatively epitomized.[169] In a sense, the charge was not surprising. Looking to the United States and its labor movement figured as a practice over which state-affiliated labor leaders could exercise little control and that could lead to demands that fell outside "official" unionism and the state-controlled lexicon of nationalism. Nationalism had long been a state-dominated idiom, and appropriating "foreign" influences that crossed the boundaries of that idiom could pose a danger to the state-controlled labor movement, of which the GM union technically formed a part. Patterning themselves after the U.S. labor movement threatened to undermine the state's monopoly over national identity and the legitimacy of the "official" labor movement. State-allied labor bosses no doubt knew they could not deliver what North American workers had gained for themselves. Thus, CTM leaders sought to combat rank-and-file movements like the one at GM by equating such transnational influences with a rejection of one's *mexicanidad*.

During these years, the cultural terrain became charged with new political significance, as the signs and practices associated with mexicanidad changed under the weight of transnational influences.[170] The very lines of what it meant to be Mexican were being redrawn from below, by workers' own cultural choices and efforts at self-representation, over which the state could maintain only limited control. In this context, the Mexican state labored to rearticulate a sense of mexicanidad, etching a line between "national" cultural forms and "foreign" influences.[171] The GM workers, however, saw little contradiction between appropriating foreign cultural forms and their own sense of mexicanidad. As one autoworker succinctly put it, "We were no less Mexican for wanting what gringo workers had."[172] Noted cultural critic Néstor García Canclini has argued that transnational influences did not necessarily have denationalizing consequences; they could just as likely lead to reformulations of national identity.[173] Rather than malinchista behavior, GM workers believed their efforts in the workplace and in their colonia to be fulfilling the promise of modernization; they saw themselves building an industrialized Mexico, with factories and neighborhoods that were in keeping with *their* vision of a modern industrial working class.

Unlike the automobile modernization project envisioned by the Mexican state, which left most authority over its implementation in the hands of transnational corporations, autoworkers maintained that such a project needed to involve working people in determining how industrialization would be carried out. Thus, autoworkers fought to secure for themselves a portion of the "fruits of progress" that authorities pledged modernization would bring and battled to assert at least a measure of control over the powerful social forces industrialization unleashed at the factories and in working-class neighborhoods. Ironically, the very project the Mexican state pursued to shape a new industrial working class also helped spawn a reinvigorated movement of autoworkers. During these years, however, their efforts saw few attempts to link with other politically engaged sectors outside of the industrial working class, such as university students or squatter groups. Instead, they sought alliances with comrades in the United States and, even more, struggled on their own to realize at least part of the promise of the Mexican Miracle.

Lorenzo Ramírez, who went on to spend over thirty years at the GM factory, remembered being "part of a new generation of workers in Mexico City . . . that spawned a new culture and new political ideas." Fueling much of the economic expansion that brought campesinos like Lorenzo to the Federal District in the 1950s and 1960s, transnational corporations played a profound role in reshaping Mexico City's working class. Those who spilled into the city's auto factories encountered distinct company programs to mold them into a class of well-paid and loyal workers. As employees at U.S. firms, autoworkers enjoyed benefits and developed cultural orientations that set them apart from many of Mexico's masses. In the course of this process of class formation, autoworkers drew new lines of social demarcation, sharply delineating between rural and urban life, work en la calle and at U.S. corporations, and naco cultural attributes and the new urban culture being forged by industrial workers. In so doing, laborers at GM faced stiff criticism, coming primarily from state-affiliated "revolutionary nationalists," for having succumbed to U.S. "cultural imperialism."

Autoworkers, however, saw things differently, in a manner that belied facile charges of having surrendered to "cultural imperialism." Whatever aims executives may have originally envisioned, laborers utilized U.S. corporate initiatives in novel, unintended ways. Company-projected images of U.S. autoworkers, which Mexicans were encouraged to emulate, depicted a class of laborers whose participation in company affairs and whose virtual membership in the middle class had all but made labor activism unnecessary. This company-advanced image, however, flew directly in the face of the realities of Mexico's rapid industrialization. Finding little of the "spirit of collaboration" that ostensibly guided U.S. corporate practices, Mexican autoworkers concluded that their collective interests would be best pursued through union struggle. By organizing a strong, democratic union (like those they believed North Americans to have), Mexican laborers fought to secure for themselves what U.S. workers already enjoyed. Moreover, with the transnational contacts they had, wage earners at GM launched a campaign with the UAW to form their own transnational "family" of union members to level the great inequalities between Mexican and U.S. autoworkers. These popular initiatives took root on the factory floor, but they also extended into working-class neighborhoods, where laborers sought to exert control over the rampant urban growth that industrial expansion spurred. Ironically, autoworkers' position at U.S. firms provided them, to a large degree, with the resources to mount a challenge to state and corporate modernization schemes, one in which workers would have a role in determining the course transnational corporations took in industrializing Mexico.

Notes

1 Lorenzo Ramírez, interview by author, Mexico City, 26 May 1997. All unattributed translations are mine.

2 The mechanization of commercial agriculture, together with an acute shortage of new cultivable land and government manipulation of agrarian reform plots, put intense pressure on rural employment opportunities and served to push thousands of landless into urban areas, primarily into Mexico City, during the 1960s and 1970s. See Jorge Martínez Ríos, "Los campesinos mexicanos: Perspectivas en el proceso de marginalización," *El perfil de México en 1980*, vol. 3 (Mexico City: Siglo XXI, 1972). Rodolfo Stavenhagen has concluded that there was a 74 percent increase in the number of landless agricultural workers in Mexico between 1960 and 1970; see "Social Aspects of Agrarian Structure in Mexico," in *Agrarian Problems and Peasant Movements in Latin America*, ed. Rodolfo Stavenhagen (Garden City, NY: Doubleday Anchor Books, 1970), 225–70. Luis Unikel has estimated that between

1950 and 1970, approximately 4.5 million individuals migrated from rural to urban locations; in the 1960s alone, 1.8 million migrated to Mexico City; see *La dinámica del crecimiento de la Ciudad de México* (Mexico City: Fundación para Estudios de la Población, 1972), 24. Also see Wayne Cornelius, *Politics and the Migrant Poor in Mexico City* (Stanford, CA: Stanford University Press, 1975).

3 On Mexico's economic growth during these years, see Roger D. Hansen, *The Politics of Mexican Development* (Baltimore: Johns Hopkins University Press, 1971); Timothy King, *Mexico: Industrialization and Trade Policies Since 1940* (New York: Oxford University Press, 1970); Clark Reynolds, *The Mexican Economy: Twentieth Century Structure and Growth* (New Haven: Yale University Press, 1970).

4 Until 1962, when the Automotive Integration Decree was passed, all automobiles sold in Mexico were either imported wholly assembled or as "completely knocked-down" units (or CKDS) manufactured in the United States and then assembled in Mexico. The CKDS were transported by railroad to Mexico City, brought on lines that led directly to the Ford, GM, and Auto-Mex/Chrysler plants. For a full description of this process, see Steven J. Bachelor, "At the Edge of Miracles: Postrevolutionary Mexico City and the Remaking of the Industrial Working Class, 1934–1982" (Ph.D. diss., Yale University, 2001).

5 Such ideas were not at all uncommon among economists at the time; for a perceptive critique of the model of "modernization" theory as it was conceptualized during the 1950s and 1960s, see Arturo Escobar, *Encountering Development: The Making and Unmaking of the Third World* (Princeton, NJ: Princeton University Press, 1995).

6 Profit-sharing programs were formally guaranteed in the 1917 constitution but were rarely extended to workers and unenforced by the government. Not until 1963 did President López Mateos finally act on working people's demands for such programs to be implemented, an act many saw as an attempt to make amends after the president's brutal crackdown on the national railroad strike of March 1959. On this decision, see Susan Kaufman Purcell, *The Mexican Profit-Sharing Decision: Politics in an Authoritarian Regime* (Berkeley: University of California Press, 1975).

7 English courses at GM were held, ironically, at the nearby Instituto de la Patria, which was across the street from the GM plant. Most often, courses were taught by the Institute's teachers, but on occasion managers from the company or their bilingual secretaries would lead the classes. See, for instance, *Noticiero GM* 4, no. 5 (1955); *Noticiero GM* 5, no. 3 (1956).

8 Michael David Snodgrass, "The Birth and Consequence of Industrial Paternalism in Monterrey, Mexico, 1890–1940," *International Labor and Working-Class History* 53 (spring 1998): 115–36; and Kenneth Maffitt, "Bringing the Global Worker to Light: Labor in Transnational and Electrical Products Firms in Mexico City, 1970–1985" (Ph.D. diss., University of California, San Diego, 2000), have both found similar evidence of efforts to forge a sense of "family" at the workplace in their respective research. Nor were such efforts confined to Mexico; see Lisa M. Fine, "'Our Big Factory Family': Masculinity and Paternalism at the Reo Motor Car Company of Lansing, Michigan," *Labor History* 34 (spring/summer 1993): 274–91; and Jacquelyn Dowd Hall et al., eds., *Like a Family: The Making of a Southern Cotton Mill World* (Chapel Hill: University of North Carolina Press, 1987).

9 Alan Knight, "The United States and the Mexican Peasantry c. 1880–1940," in *Rural Revolt in Mexico and U.S. Intervention*, ed. Daniel Nugent (La Jolla, CA: Center for U.S.-Mexican

Studies Monograph Series no. 27, 1988), 59. Knight was trained enough in the tradition of E. P. Thompson not to be suggesting here that workers themselves did not have a hand in their own making.

10 Quoted in Dennis Nodín Valdéz, "Perspiring Capitalists: Latinos and the Henry Ford Service School, 1918–1928," *Aztlán* 12 (autumn 1981): 229; originally cited in Jonathan Norton Leonard, *The Tragedy of Henry Ford* (New York: G. P. Putnam's Sons, 1932), 154. Secretary of State Robert Lansing in 1918 made similar comments when he suggested that building U.S.-owned auto plants in Mexico "may very well lead to a solution of the entire Mexican problem" (cited in Robert Freeman Smith, *The United States and Revolutionary Nationalism in Mexico, 1916–1932* [Chicago: University of Chicago Press, 1972], 132.)

11 Warren C. Whatley and Gavin Wright, "Employee Records of the Ford Motor Company [Detroit Area], 1918–1947" (Ann Arbor, MI: Computer File, ICPSR version, Warren C. Whatley and Gavin Wright [producers], 1994).

12 On "Americanization" programs at Ford's Detroit-area plants, see Zaragoza Vargas, *Proletarians of the North: A History of Mexican Industrial Workers in Detroit and the Midwest, 1917–1933* (Berkeley: University of California Press, 1993); and Stephen Meyer III, *The Five Dollar Day: Labor Management and Social Control in the Ford Motor Company, 1908–1921* (Albany: State University of New York Press, 1981).

13 Quoted in Meyer, *The Five Dollar Day*, 151.

14 Vargas, *Proletarians of the North*. For further discussion of this, see Bachelor, "At the Edge of Miracles."

15 On the auto industry and import-substitution industrialization, see Douglas C. Bennett and Kenneth E. Sharpe, *Transnational Corporations Versus the State: The Political Economy of the Mexican Auto Industry* (Princeton, NJ: Princeton University Press, 1985). Bennett and Sharpe nicely reveal the various negotiations that went into the promulgation of the Integration Decree. At first, the U.S. corporations balked at the plans outlined by the Mexican state. Not until the Mexican government granted several concessions to the U.S. automakers did they agree to the necessary large-scale capital investments.

16 *Diario Oficial de la Federación*, 25 August 1962; 1 September 1962. After much heated negotiation involving the U.S. State Department, automakers succeeded in persuading the Mexican government to write the decree such that only 60 percent of the value-content of the automobiles would need to be manufactured in the United States. This allowed Ford, GM, and Auto-Mex/Chrysler to continue importing body stampings (hoods, door panels, etc.) from the United States, where they enjoyed economies of scale.

17 This was, of course, an era during which Walt W. Rostow's *The Stages of Economic Growth: A Non-Communist Manifesto* (Cambridge, England: Cambridge University Press, 1961), which placed great emphasis on economic "takeoffs," enjoyed enormous popularity among economic policy advisors in North and South America. Although this work appeared in 1961, Rostow's research in general, and that of many other "modernization" theorists, was already widely publicized and being widely followed.

18 Quoted in *El Universal*, 14 January 1965.

19 *Accension* 74–18056, International File, Ford Industrial Archive, Dearborn, MI [hereafter cited as FIA].

20 *El Universal*, 1 January 1965.

21 Here I am referring to John Mason Hart's much-debated argument that the revolution of 1910 represented a war of national liberation to free Mexico from its gringo exploiters; see *The Coming and Process of Revolution in Mexico* (Berkeley: University of California Press, 1987). Alan Knight, *The Mexican Revolution*, 2 vols. (Cambridge, England: Cambridge University Press, 1986) took strong issue with Hart, claiming that the revolution was many things, but not a war of national liberation.

22 Knight, *The Mexican Revolution*, I: 560 n. 422; also see Knight, "Nationalism, Xenophobia and Revolution: The Place of Foreigners and Foreign Interests in Mexico, 1910–1915" (Ph.D. diss., Oxford University, 1974), 258–68.

23 These data are adapted from Van R. Whiting Jr., *The Political Economy of Foreign Investment in Mexico: Nationalism, Liberalism, and Constraints on Choice* (Baltimore: Johns Hopkins University Press, 1992), 31, 66; and David P. Glass, "The Politics of Economic Dependence: The Case of Mexico" (Ph.D. diss., University of California, Berkeley, 1984). The statistics are in 1992 U.S. dollars.

24 Quoted in Florencio Zamarripa M., *Díaz Ordaz: Ideología y perfil de un revolucionario* (Mexico City: Editorial Futuro, 1964), 15. Who these "genuine representatives" were remains unclear.

25 There were real fears of nationalization among automakers, especially after the upheavals of 1968; see "Yanqui Companies Are Feeling the Heat," *Business Week*, 29 November 1969.

26 *Noticiero GM* 4, no. 5 (1956); the emphasis is mine.

27 *Accension* 67–6, box 2, International File, FIA.

28 Ibid; Ford de México, *Apuntes para una historia de la industria automotriz* (Mexico City: Ford de México, c. 1976).

29 Quoted in Victor G. Reuther, *The Brothers Reuther and the Story of the UAW: A Memoir* (Boston: Houghton Mifflin, 1976), 401.

30 Quoted in the interview entitled "Return to The Labyrinth of Solitude," in Octavio Paz, *The Labyrinth of Solitude, The Other Mexico, and Other Essays* (New York: Grove Press, 1985), 344.

31 Unikel, *La dinámica del crecimiento de la Ciudad de México*, 24.

32 Chrysler did not actually have its own factories in Mexico at the time. They had a distribution agreement with Fábricas Auto-Mex, which oversaw the assembly of Chrysler automobiles in the country. In 1959, Chrysler purchased one-third of Fábricas Auto-Mex's equity, and in 1971 purchased the remainder.

33 Angel Taboada, interview by author, Mexico City, 23 May 1997.

34 For an illuminating description of the Zona Rosa around 1967, see Carlos Monsiváis, "Cuevas en la Zona Rosa," in *Días de guardar* (Mexico City: Biblioteca Era, 1970), 78–90.

35 William Beezley has described the neighborhood's frenzied Judas-burning in 1908, which exhibited a strong antigovernment current, complete with torched effigies of the aging dictator Porfirio Díaz; see *Judas at the Jockey Club and Other Episodes in Porfirian Mexico* (Lincoln: University of Nebraska Press, 1987), 115–16. The community also served as the namesake for the famed "Tiger of Santa Julia," Jesús Negrete, a notorious bank robber and womanizer who was sheltered from authorities by residents of the community; see John Robert Lear, "Workers, Vecinos, and Citizens: The Revolution in Mexico City, 1909–1917"

Steven J. Bachelor

(Ph.D. diss., University of California, Berkeley, 1993). The police, in fact, refused to patrol the area because of the animosity residents had toward them; see Laurence John Rohlfes, "Police and Penal Correction in Mexico City, 1876–1911: A Study of Order and Progress in Porfirian Mexico" (Ph.D. diss., Tulane University, 1983), 87–88.

36 Paco Ignacio Taibo II, *Una cosa fácil* (Mexico City: Leega, 1989), 89.

37 Armando Trejo, interview by author, Mexico City, 11 February 1997.

38 Beezley, *Judas at the Jockey Club*, 115.

39 Salvador Navas, interview by author, Estado de México, 13 June 1997.

40 Carlos Monsiváis, *Escenas de pudor y liviandad* (Mexico City: Grijalbo, 1981), 241.

41 See the forthcoming study of Cantinflas by Jeffrey Pilcher, to be published by Scholarly Resources.

42 R. Douglas Cope, *The Limits of Racial Domination: Plebeian Society in Colonial Mexico City, 1660–1720* (Madison: University of Wisconsin Press, 1994), nicely traces the historical roots of the conflation of class and race in colonial Mexico. Steve Stern, *The Secret History of Gender: Women, Men, and Power in Late Colonial Mexico* (Chapel Hill: University of North Carolina Press, 1995), similarly shows the historical imbrication of race and class, something he calls the "class-color order."

43 Monsiváis, *Escenas de pudor y liviandad*, 238. Also see Claudio Lomnitz, "Fissures in Contemporary Mexican Nationalism," *Public Culture* 9 (1996): 55–68.

44 Monsiváis, *Escenas de pudor y liviandad*, 238–39.

45 Ads were taken out in several of the city's newspapers calling on prospective workers to apply; see, for example, the large ad that ran in *Novedades*, 14 February 1965.

46 Melitón Hernández, interview by author, Mexico City, 8 July 1997.

47 Angel Daniel Ruiz, interview by author, Mexico City, 3 June 1997.

48 "El Huevón," interview by author, Mexico City, 24 June 1997.

49 Ignacio Bobadilla, interview by author, Mexico City, 30 May 1997.

50 Jeffrey Bortz, "Industrial Wages in Mexico City, 1939–1975" (Ph.D. diss., University of California, Los Angeles, 1984).

51 Marcelino Sánchez, interview by author, Mexico City, 22 February 1997.

52 Rafael Castro, interview by author, Mexico City, 21 February 1997.

53 Henry Ford firmly believed that workers should be paid wages and have leisure time that would sufficiently allow them to "find out what is going on in the world." See "The 5-Day Week in Ford Plants," *Monthly Labor Review* 23 (December 1926): 10–14. Elsewhere he said, "There should be leisure, music and poetry, the five-day week, the old-fashioned dance, and the hospitable inn beside the road" (quoted in David Montgomery, *The Fall of the House of Labor: The Workplace, the State, and American Labor Activism, 1865–1925* [Cambridge, England: Cambridge University Press, 1987], 252; originally cited in H. Dubreuil, *Robots or Men? A French Workman's Experience in American Industry*, trans. Frances Merrill and Mason Merrill [New York: Harper and Brothers, 1930], 152). Also see Antonio Gramsci's seminal discussion of Fordism, "Americanism and Fordism," in *Selections from the Prison Notebooks*, trans. Quintin Hoare and Geoffrey Nowell Smith (New York: International Publishers, 1971), 279–318.

54 Data from the Asociación Mexicana de la Industria Automotríz; these data also appear in

Bennett and Sharpe, *Transnational Corporations*, 52–53. Frank Brandenburg shows that by 1964 annual sales of automobiles in Mexico had jumped to 60,000; see *The Making of Modern Mexico* (Englewood Cliffs, NJ: Prentice-Hall, 1964), 297.

55 Bennett and Sharpe, *Transnational Corporations*, 53–54.

56 Brandenburg, *The Making of Modern Mexico*, 53.

57 *The News* (Mexico City), 7 January 1965.

58 Although few working people during these years were able to purchase new automobiles, there did emerge a new car culture, closely associated with notions of "modernity," not unlike the craze surrounding bicycles during the Porfiriato, which William H. Beezley has effectively described. See his essay, "The Porfirian Persuasion: Sport and Recreation in Modern Mexico," in *Judas at the Jockey Club*, 11–66. Although automobile ownership remained confined to the middle class and well-to-do during most of the postrevolutionary period, the government did embark on a large-scale road construction program, which established paved roads throughout the republic; see Wendy Waters, "Re-Mapping the Nation: Road Building as State Formation in Post-Revolutionary Mexico, 1925–1940" (Ph.D. diss., University of Arizona, 1999).

59 In the 1970s workers much more commonly had completed secundaria.

60 This is based on a reading of the company newsletters *Noticiero GM* and *Boletín Ford*.

61 Francisco Díaz, interview by author, Mexico City, 12 June 1997.

62 Guillermo Alvarez, interview by author, Mexico City, 4 July 1997.

63 José Luis Vargas, interview by author, Mexico City, 27 February 1997.

64 Marcelino Sánchez, interview.

65 Hadley Cantril, ed., *Public Opinion, 1935–1946* (Princeton, NJ: Princeton University Press, 1951), 502. Based on a careful reading of the *New York Times*, Sergio Aguayo Quezada, in *Myths and (Mis)Perceptions: Changing U.S. Elite Visions of Mexico* (La Jolla, CA: Center for U.S.-Mexican Studies, 1998), has found similar attitudes among North American elites in the 1950s. Eric Zolov, however, in his contribution to this volume, argues that by the time of the 1968 Olympics in Mexico City, attitudes among North Americans were undergoing considerable changes as Mexico attempted to modernize.

66 Pedro Barajas, interview by author, Mexico City, 21 March 1997.

67 Contrast these opinions with those held by copper miners at the El Teniente mine in Chile, where workers deemed U.S. bosses to be far worse than their Chilean counterparts. See Thomas Miller Klubock, *Contested Communities: Class, Gender, and Politics in Chile's El Teniente Copper Mine, 1904–1948* (Durham, NC: Duke University Press, 1998); and Gilbert M. Joseph, Catherine LeGrand, and Ricardo Salvatore, eds., *Close Encounters of Empire: Writing the Cultural History of U.S.–Latin American Relations* (Durham, NC: Duke University Press, 1999).

68 José Cruz Rincón, interview by author, Mexico City, 18 June 1997.

69 Secretaría del Trabajo y Previsión Social, Registro de Asociaciones [STPSRA], exp. 10/6298, leg. 3; unpublished data from Asociación Mexicana de la Industria Automotríz; Kevin J. Middlebrook, "Union Democratization in the Mexican Automobile Industry," *Latin American Research Review* 24 (spring 1989): 69–93.

70 STPSRA, exp. 10/6298, leg. 4.

71 Eventually, two of these workers settled with the company and received pensions, and an-

other two succeeded in regaining their positions at the firm (STPSRA, exp. 10/6298, leg. 4). Though they would listen to workers' grievances in the labor courts (usually after considerable stalling), state authorities often showed unease about entering into labor conflicts at major transnational corporations. This is not surprising, considering the awkward position in which it put government authorities. On the one hand, if the state sided with the corporation, state legitimacy could be called into question; on the other hand, if state authorities sided with workers, the state could jeopardize foreign investments. The state often tried to stand above such conflicts, deeming them the domains of capital and labor and rarely in need of government intervention. Many workers argued that this was simply another way of saying that the government would not interfere with capital accumulation, as the strategy assumed that there existed a level playing field between employers and workers. President López Mateos neatly summarized his administration's position the following way: "All labor-management problems are being solved in an atmosphere of understanding and harmony. Both employees and workers are willing to compromise to solve their differences, knowing that a satisfactory solution will mutually result." See *The News* (Mexico City), 29 June 1957.

72   STPSRA, exp. 10/6298, leg. 4.

73   Ibid. For a detailed examination of how this rank-and-file movement took shape, see Bachelor, "At the Edge of Miracles."

74   Ignacio Ceballos, interview by author, Mexico City, 5 June 1997.

75   Mario Reynoso, interview by author, Mexico City, 22 May 1997.

76   STPSRA, exp. 10/6298, leg. 4.

77   Ignacio Ceballos, interview.

78   This was happening more generally in all mass-production industries at the time. A government study showed that productivity had jumped from 5.7 to 8.3 units per worker between 1965 and 1971. See *Bandera Roja*, June 1975. Their data came from the government records.

79   Isidro Trevilla, interview by author, Mexico City, 4 June 1997.

80   Melitón Hernández, interview.

81   "La Llorona," interview by author, Mexico City, 1 June 1997. This bears a striking resemblance to an incident Peter Winn found at the Yarur textile mill in Chile. See "A Worker's Nightmare: Taylorism and the 1962 Yarur Strike in Chile," *Radical History Review* 58 (spring 1994): 4–34.

82   On notions of masculinity during these years, see Anne Rubenstein, "Mediated Styles of Masculinity in the Post-Revolutionary Imagination, or, El Santo's Strange Career," paper presented at the conference Representing Mexico: Transnationalism and the Politics of Culture Since the Revolution, Woodrow Wilson Center, Washington, DC, 7–8 November 1997; also see her book, *Bad Language, Naked Ladies, and Other Threats to the Nation: A Political History of Comic Books in Mexico* (Durham, NC: Duke University Press, 1998). Additionally, see the provocative essays by Carlos Monsiváis in *Escenas de pudor y liviandad*. For an excellent discussion of contemporary notions of masculinity, many of whose arguments also ring true for the 1960s, see Matthew C. Gutmann, *The Meanings of Macho: Being a Man in Mexico City* (Berkeley: University of California Press, 1996). For an excellent discussion of masculinity among laborers elsewhere in Latin America, see Klubock,

Contested Communities; and Heidi Tinsman, "Unequal Uplift: The Sexual Politics of Gender, Work, and Community in the Chilean Agrarian Reform" (Ph.D. diss., Yale University, 1996). For a provocative analysis of masculinity among manual workers in Britain, see Gary Willis, "Shop Floor Culture, Masculinity, and the Wage Form," in *Working-Class Culture: Studies in History and Theory*, ed. John Clarke, Chas Chritcher, and Richard Johnson (London: Hutchinson, 1979), 185–98.

83 Emilio Flores, interview by author, Mexico City, 2 June 1997.

84 Name withheld by request, interview by author, Mexico City, 18 June 1997.

85 Juan Roberto Chávez, interview by author, Estado de México, 3 March 1997.

86 Kathryn Marie Dudley, *The End of the Line: Lost Jobs, New Lives in Postindustrial America* (Chicago: University of Chicago Press, 1994), 45.

87 Perfecto Rodríguez, interview by author, Estado de México, 11 June 1997.

88 STPSRA, exp. 10/6298, leg. 4.

89 Fernando Córdoba, interview by author, Estado de México, 21 February 1997.

90 Irma Vargas, interview by author, Mexico City, 13 June 1997.

91 STPSRA, exp. 10/6298, leg. 3, 4.

92 For an excellent discussion of *casas chicas* in Mexico City, see Gutmann, *Meanings of Macho*, 138–41.

93 José Mena Torres, interview by author, Estado de México, 19 June 1997.

94 "El Campeón," interview by author, Mexico City, 23 May 1997.

95 Alfonso Nabor, interview by author, Estado de México, 21 February 1997.

96 Mario Reynoso, interview; Lorenzo Ramírez, interview.

97 STPSRA, exp. 10/6298, leg. 4.

98 Ibid.

99 Ibid.

100 Ibid.

101 Ibid.

102 Contrato Colectivo, Sindicato de Obreros y Empleados de General Motors de México, S.A. de C.V., 1953, in the personal archives of Jorge Martínez.

103 STPSRA, exp. 10/6298, leg. 4; Instituto Nacional de Estadística, Georgrafía e Informática, *Estadísticas históricas de México*, 2 vols. (Mexico City: Secretaría de Programación y Presupuesto, 1985), 1:170.

104 STPSRA, exp. 10/6298, leg. 4.

105 Ibid.

106 Ibid.

107 Ibid.

108 Quoted in *La Prensa*, 19 January 1965; Jorge Anguiano Romero (a member of the union's negotiating committee), interview by author, Estado de México, 27 August 1997.

109 STPSRA, exp. 10/6298, leg. 4.

110 For a discussion of these future labor conflicts, see Bachelor, "At the Edge of Miracles."

111 For newspaper accounts leading up to the strike, see *El Día*, 19 January 1965; *La Prensa*, 19 January 1965; *The News*, 20 January 1965.

112 There had been an attempt to launch a strike as early as 1947, but conflict was averted before a strike call was issued.

113   *El Día*, 22 January 1965.

114   *The News*, 15 January 1965; *El Universal*, 14 January 1965; *Novedades*, 15 January 1965; *El Heraldo de Toluca*, 14 January 1965; *El Dia*, 15 January 1965. The auto industry had one of its best years ever in 1964; see *The News*, 7 January 1965.

115   *The News*, 22 January 1965; *La Prensa*, 22 January 1965; *The News*, 23 January 1965; STPSRA exp. 10/6298, leg. 5.

116   *Novedades*, 21 January 1965.

117   See, e.g., Nelson Lichtenstein, *The Most Dangerous Man in Detroit: Walter Reuther and the Fate of American Labor* (New York: Basic Books, 1995); Nelson Lichtenstein and Stephen Meyer, eds., *On the Line: Essays in the History of Autowork* (Urbana: University of Illinois Press, 1989); Robert Asher and Ronald Edsforth, eds., *Autowork* (Albany: State University of New York Press, 1995).

118   STPSRA exp. 10/6298, leg. 5; Carlos Castañón, interview by author, Estado de México, 30 August 1997.

119   Kevin Middlebrook, *The Paradox of Revolution: Labor, the State, and Authoritarianism in Mexico* (Baltimore: Johns Hopkins University Press, 1995), 199. Middlebrook shows that in one extreme case, a worker waited from 1944 to 1967 for his case to be decided.

120   Jorge Martínez, interview by author, Mexico City, 28 January 1997. Such a view was not uncommon among workers in the city; see *Acción Sindical*, 15 July 1963, where workers complain that the "Junta operates like a mafia."

121   Tellingly, workers used the highly gendered term *hermanos* to refer to union comrades, coding union membership as decidedly "male."

122   STPSRA, exp. 10/6298, leg.4.

123   Although the data he utilizes stop just before the Díaz Ordaz administration, James W. Wilkie shows that federal social expenditures declined in the years just prior to Díaz Ordaz taking office. Díaz Ordaz went on to reduce social spending to even lower levels than López Mateos; see *The Mexican Revolution: Federal Expenditure and Social Change Since 1910* (Berkeley: University of California Press, 1970).

124   See, for example, the cartoon in *El Día*, 25 January 1965, in which a worker who is about to collapse is shown carrying an enormous block on his back. Behind him trails a wealthy man in tuxedo and tails carrying a large basket of money. Written on the block are the words "The Weight of Economic Development."

125   *Siempre*, 10 February 1965.

126   *El Universal*, 26 January 1965.

127   See, for instance, *Acción Sindical*, no. 94 (July 1964).

128   STPSRA, exp. 10/6298, leg. 4.

129   Ibid.

130   Ibid.

131   Richard Ulric Miller, "The Role of Labor Organizations in a Developing Country: The Case of Mexico" (Ph.D. diss., Cornell University, 1966), 190–91; STPSRA, exp. 10/6298, leg. 4; *The News*, 6 February 1965; *El Día*, 5 February 1965. John Womack noted at the time that authorities commonly labeled independent movements communist as a tactic to discredit them; see "Unfreedom in Mexico," *New Republic*, 12 October 1968, 27–31.

132   Raúl Villegas, interview by author, Mexico City, 17 June 1997.

Toiling for the "New Invaders"   323

133 *Noticiero GM*, January–February–March 1955.

134 In a widely disseminated document, the company's personnel director, José Ignacio Echeagaray, expounded on what the company viewed as the defining characteristics of the type of discipline they hoped to instill in workers; see José Ignacio Echeagaray, "Fundamento y Características de la Disciplina," Archivo de General Motors de México, S.A. de C.V., Mexico City. This document also appeared in the company newsletter, *Noticiero GM*.

135 *Acción Sindical*, no. 64 (July 1964).

136 STPSRA, exp. 10/6298, leg. 4.

137 Ibid. This is an example of what James C. Scott has found to be the "most common form of class struggle," that which "arises from the failure of a dominant ideology to live up to the implicit promises it necessarily makes." As he goes on to show, dominant ideologies provide subalterns with the means, symbolic tools, and ideas for a critique of dominant ideologies. See *Weapons of the Weak: Everyday Forms of Peasant Resistance* (New Haven: Yale University Press, 1985), 338. Also see Nicholas Abercrombie, Stephen Hill, and Bryan S. Turner, *The Dominant Ideology Thesis* (London: Allen and Unwin, 1980), 149, where the authors note that workers may support general elements of the dominant ideology but accept opposing values that correspond to their everyday experiences. Moreover, it is quite clear that workers can appropriate elements from dominant ideologies, develop their own interpretations, and use them to their own advantage.

138 STPSRA, exp. 10/6298, leg. 4.

139 Jorge Martínez, interview.

140 STPSRA, exp. 10/6298, leg. 4.

141 Ibid.

142 In their essays in this volume, Eric Zolov and Seth Fein make similar points. Also see Eric Zolov, "Containing the Rock Gesture: Mass Culture and Hegemony in Mexico" (Ph.D. diss., University of Chicago, 1995), 75, 121; and his book, *Refried Elvis: The Rise of the Mexican Counterculture* (Berkeley: University of California Press, 1999).

143 STPSRA, exp. 10/6298, leg. 4; Ignacio Bobadilla, interview. On *agringación*, see Claudio Lomnitz-Adler, "Nationalism's Dirty Linen: On the Geography of 'Contact Zones,'" paper presented at the conference on Mexican Popular Political Culture, 1800–2000, Center for U.S.-Mexican Studies, University of California, San Diego, 24–25 April 1998.

144 Carlos Monsiváis, *Mexican Postcards*, trans. John Kraniauskus (London: Verso, 1997), 110–11.

145 For a discussion of earlier attempts to forge cross-national ties among working people, see Gregg Andrews, *Shoulder to Shoulder? The American Federation of Labor, the United States, and the Mexican Revolution, 1910–1924* (Berkeley: University of California Press, 1991).

146 STPSRA, exp. 10/6298, leg. 4.

147 A classic study of autoworkers in Detroit during these same years shows the variety of complaints U.S. autoworkers did have; see Dan Georgakas, *Detroit, I Do Mind Dying: A Study in Urban Revolution* (New York: St. Martin's Press, 1975).

148 Arjun Appadurai, "Disjuncture and Difference in the Global Cultural Economy," *Public Culture* 2, no. 2 (spring 1990): 3.

324 *Steven J. Bachelor*

149   Quoted in Lichtenstein, *The Most Dangerous Man*, 339.

150   STPSRA, exp. 10/6298, leg. 4.

151   Federal unions and unions operating in federalized industries (which the auto industry became in 1975) had their disputes settled in the Junta Federal de Conciliación y Arbitraje rather than in the Junta Local.

152   Miller, "The Role of Labor Organizations," 186 n. 29.

153   STPSRA, exp. 10/6298, leg. 4.

154   On the IMF (which in Mexico is known as the FITIM [Federación Internacional de Trabajadores de la Industria Metalúrgica], see Fritz Opel, *Seventy-five Years of the Iron International, 1893–1968* (Geneva, Switzerland: International Metalworkers Federation, 1968); Everett M. Kassalow, "The International Metalworkers' Federation and the Latin American and Asian Automotive Industries," in *International Labor and the Multinational Enterprise*, ed. Duana Kujawa (New York: Praeger, 1975); Norris Willatt, *The Multinational Unions* (London: Financial Times, 1974), 101–5. On the institutional arrangement made between the FITIM and auto unions in Mexico, see Kevin J. Middlebrook, "International Implications of Labor Change: The Automobile Industry," in *Mexico's Political Economy: Challenges at Home and Abroad*, ed. Jorge I. Domínguez (London: Sage Publications, 1882), 133–70.

155   On labor conflict in the industry in the 1970s, see Bachelor, "At the Edge of Miracles."

156   STPSRA, exp. 10/6298, leg. 4.

157   Wayne Cornelius, *Politics and the Migrant Poor in Mexico City*, notes the importance ties to one's pueblo could still have for the urban poor in Mexico City.

158   Gonzálo Robledo, interview by author, Mexico City, 10 June 1997.

159   This is fully analyzed in Zolov, "Containing the Rock Gesture," and *Refried Elvis*.

160   Zolov, "Containing the Rock Gesture," 286; Bernard Cassen, "La lengua inglesa como vehículo del imperialismo cultural," *Comunicación y Cultura* 6 (February 1979): 77.

161   To alleviate the housing shortage at the time, workers called on all companies with more than one hundred employees to build houses for their workers, a demand they maintained was outlined in the Ley Federal del Trabajo. They charged that companies were not addressing the collective and social concerns of their employees; see *Expresiones* (Estado de México), 4 March 1965.

162   See *La Voz de la Unidad Kennedy* (Mexico City), December 1965, the inaugural issue of the newspaper serving the housing complex.

163   Workers who still live in Colonia Las Americas are quick to point out that whenever anyone moves out of the area, the homes are quickly purchased and fetch nice prices. One worker noted that a famed *telenovela* actor lives next door to him.

164   *El Día*, 10 March 1966.

165   Manuel Palafox, interview by author, Estado de México, 16 June 1997.

166   Esther Pérez, interview by author, Estado de México, 16 June 1997.

167   This resembles findings made by Matthew Gutmann on the role of women in *colonias populares*; see *Meanings of Macho*.

168   Octavio Paz wrote one of the most widely known formulations of the so-called malinche complex; see "The Sons of La Malinche," in *Labyrinth of Solitude*, 65–88. There have since been many efforts to rethink La Malinche, including a number from various feminist per-

spectives. For a good introduction, see Sandra Messinger Cypess, *La Malinche in Mexican Literature: From History to Myth* (Austin: University of Texas Press, 1991).

169 STPSRA, exp. 10/6298, leg. 4.

170 This point is argued very provocatively in Carlos Monsiváis, "La nación de unos cuantos y las esperanzas románticas (Notas sobre la historia del término 'Cultura Nacional' en México)," in *En torno a la cultura nacional*, ed. Héctor Aguilar Camín (Mexico City: Instituto Nacional Indigenista, 1989), 159–221. It is also taken up in Zolov, "Containing the Rock Gesture." Also see Alan Knight, "Revolutionary Project, Recalcitrant People: Mexico, 1910–1940," in *The Revolutionary Process in Mexico: Essays on Political and Social Change, 1880–1940*, ed. Jaime E. Rodríguez (Berkeley: University of California Press, 1990), 261, where he argues that "mass culture" eventually supplanted the Mexican state's revolutionary cultural project. For a perceptive analysis of Americanization in Latin America more broadly, see William Roseberry, "Americanization in the Americas," in *Anthropology and Histories: Essays in Culture, History, and Political Economy* (New Brunswick, NJ: Rutgers University Press, 1989), 80–121.

171 Zolov notes that Monsiváis has called the government's construction of mexicanidad "state control over the signification of [what it means] to be Mexican" ("Containing the Rock Gesture," 12; originally cited in Carlos Monsiváis, "Muerte y resurreción del nacionalismo mexicano," *Nexos* 109 [1987]: 13–22).

172 Armando Montes, interview by author, Mexico City, 2 July 1997.

173 Néstor García Canclini, *Hybrid Cultures: Strategies for Entering and Leaving Modernity* (Minneapolis: University of Minnesota Press, 1995). For the United States, Lizabeth Cohen makes the argument that mass consumer culture, rather than eroding working-class culture, actually became the "common ground" on which industrial laborers constructed a new working-class culture. She reveals, for example, that phonograph recordings of Caruso singing Italian operas helped keep a sense of Italian culture alive in the United States. See *Making a New Deal: Industrial Workers in Chicago, 1919–1939* (New York: Cambridge University Press, 1990). Michael Denning has similarly argued that the expansion of the culture industries in the 1930s United States allowed for a massive flowering of politically engaged working-class cultural forms, which he has termed "the Cultural Front"; see *The Cultural Front: The Laboring of American Culture in the Twentieth Century* (London: Verso, 1996).

El Santos and the Return of the Killer Aztecs!

Jis y Trino

Guadalajara artists Jis y Trino have drawn cartoons and illustrations for many Mexican publications, but are best known for a series of surreal adventures featuring the antihero El Santos. El Santos parodies and pays homage to the beloved wrestler and movie star El Santo. Like El Santo, Santos collaborates with the police (his best friend, the Chief, warns him about the Killer Aztecs in this strip). His antagonists are just as strange as those of El Santo in his movies (El Santos fights the Zombies and Killer Peyote, but El Santo wrestled with the Diabolical Hatchet and the Television Murderer). And they dress alike. Poor Santos is just an ordinary guy, though: he entirely lacks the strength, courage, and technical skills that always gave El Santo the victory. Jis y Trino use this comic reversal to record and comment on what lies beneath the surface of Mexico's most cherished national myths. Here, for example, the reference to a widely held belief that Mexicans sell each others' organs for transplant into the bodies of ailing U.S. citizens—in itself a metaphor for Mexican cultural/economic subjugation to the United States—has added meaning because it appears in a U.S.-produced volume that describes (or sells?) Mexico to an English-speaking audience, and gets even more complicated because the organ dealers are Aztecs, representatives of *México profundo*, frightening mythic figures from history and present-day oppressed, impoverished Nahuatl speakers. Who is exploiting whom here?

ONE DAY EL SANTOS WAS SCRATCHING HIS CROTCH...
UUH! THAT'S THE SPIRIT!
...WHEN SUDDENLY...
SANTOS! THE KILLER AZTECS ARE COMING FOR YOU!
WHAT?
THEY WANT TO TAKE YOUR HEART OUT!
OH YEAH? WELL I'M NOT AFRAID!
OH!
MUY MACHO, EH?
¡GULP!
GASP!
WAIT, THAT'S NOT MY HEART!
WE'LL SEE ABOUT THAT!
AAAA!!
OOPS, SORRY!
TUNK!
TUNK!
THAT'S ONE OF MY BALLS!
RELAX, YOU HAVE ANOTHER!
DON'T WORRY, IT'S STILL ALIVE!

Masked Media: The Adventures
of Lucha Libre on the Small Screen

Heather Levi

The first person I met in the world of professional wrestling in Mexico was the man who became my wrestling teacher, Luis Jaramillo Martínez. On a November afternoon in 1996 I found myself in a gym in the city center, explaining that I wanted to train with him as part of my research on *lucha libre* (the Mexican version of professional wrestling). He offered me a seat on one of the weight benches, and gave me the following speech (which I was to hear several times in different versions over the subsequent year and a half). "Lucha libre," he said, "is not the clown show [*payasado*] you see on TV, with the ones from the Triple-A [a wrestling *empresa* that I discuss below].[1] If you want to learn the real lucha libre, you have to learn it step by step. First falling, tumbling, then Olympic wrestling, Greco-Roman wrestling, intercollegiate wrestling, locks from jiujitsu, strikes from karate. Only then can you learn *professional* wrestling. If you're willing to learn the real lucha libre, then I will teach you. I am a great professor, many people know and respect me, but I had a greater teacher behind me and he had others behind him."

His speech laid out a paradox central to Mexican lucha libre, for it would not have sounded strange coming from a kung fu teacher: "This is an old art with dignified traditions that has been vulgarized by the mass media. If you really want to know its secrets, then I will teach you within the tradition that I myself was taught." He was not, however, offering to teach me a purportedly ancient secret fighting art, but professional wrestling, a practice that is widely considered inherently vulgar and unworthy of respect. As Sharon

Mazer has pointed out, wrestling is "the one sport in which participants lose legitimacy when they move from 'amateur' to 'professional.'"[2] Many do not consider it a sport at all. In the United States, the World Wrestling Federation itself went so far as to call it "sports entertainment" instead of sport to avoid a state tax on sporting events. Yet my teacher (who certainly considered lucha libre a sport) was sincerely worried about its degeneration, and as my research continued, I met many others in the wrestling world who shared his concern. They, as did my teacher, connected the economic and aesthetic decline of "real Mexican lucha libre" to televised broadcast of the sport.

Why did it make sense for certain wrestlers, wrestling fans, reporters, and others to worry about the loss of authenticity of a performance widely regarded as wholly inauthentic? How did they come to defend on nationalist grounds a genre that everyone agrees was imported to Mexico from the United States in the 1930s? Finally, why did they see television, in particular, as a threat to lucha libre?

The answers lie in the specific history of professional wrestling in Mexico, and in particular its relationship to mass mediation, processes of urbanization, and the state. Lucha libre was televised in Mexico during the early 1950s, but was taken off the air by the middle of the decade. It returned to television in 1991 (and is still televised as of this writing). In both instances, lucha libre's alliance with television proved to be highly controversial, provoking or exacerbating tensions and rivalries within the "wrestling family" and drawing lucha libre into conflicts between and among owners of the mass media and functionaries of the state. These conflicts were connected with broader demographic, cultural, and political changes in Mexico City after the consolidation of the postrevolutionary state. As I will show, disputes over televisualization of lucha reflected, sometimes to the point of parody, broader struggles in Mexican politics, even as lucha libre itself dramatizes and parodies the idea of struggling for power.

Television and Professional Wrestling

Professional wrestling is a transnational entertainment form, performed all over the Americas, Asia, Europe, and the Anglophone South Pacific, but most popular in the United States, Japan, and Mexico. Wherever it is found, it follows a particular set of conventions: it is a struggle between two or more wrestlers, in which a wide range of techniques, including some that are forbidden in amateur wrestling, are considered legitimate. These include many holds, but also hitting, running away, bouncing or jumping off the ropes surrounding the ring, and more. But the central difference between amateur and professional wrestling is that the latter is a morality play. Wrestlers compete not as themselves but as characters that they (or their promoters) invent and that are morally coded. On one side is the "clean wrestler, in that he follows what are supposed to be, and what are perceived by the audience as, the rules"; on the other side is "the wrestler who breaks these supposed rules in order to gain what the audience should consider an unfair advantage."[3] (In Mexico, these roles are called *técnico* and *rudo*, respectively.) The matches are overseen by referees who often are seen as unwilling or unable (out of ineptitude or corruption) to enforce the rules against the bad guys. A wrestling match typically reminds its audience that there is a difference between right and wrong, but that for right to prevail in an unjust world, the good must never trust in authority or the rules.

Professional wrestling developed out of saloon entertainments and circus sideshows in the United States and Europe during the mid- to late nineteenth century. European exhibition wrestlers adopted the "catch-as-catch-can" style that was popularized in the United States in the 1920s.[4] The conventions that now define professional wrestling—ethically coded stage personae in particular—probably evolved at that time. Exhibition wrestling continued to grow in popularity in the United States during the 1920s and by 1931 "routinely attracted sell-out crowds" to Madison Square Garden.[5] Soon thereafter, its popularity declined sharply, not to recover until the arrival of television at the end of the 1940s.[6] Television and wrestling turned out to be a perfect match: networks in search of highly visual, easily understandable material to use in the new medium revitalized the moribund performance genre. For the next five decades, American pro wrestling would still be organized in regional touring circuits, but it would be disseminated primarily as a category of television show.

In Japan, professional wrestling's third "capital," the association between television and professional wrestling was even stronger because both arrived at the same time. Japanese professional wrestling did not exist as a live performance prior to its televised broadcast in the mid-1950s (although there were, of course, exhibitions of indigenous wrestling styles, such as sumo and judo). The association of professional wrestling and television was so strong that in the late 1950s the two were nearly synonymous for many Japanese.[7] In neither the United States nor Japan did wrestlers or promoters question the expediency of televised broadcast. Indeed, in both countries, the genre came to be defined through its association with television.

La Lucha Libre

In contrast to the United States and Europe, where professional wrestling developed gradually, lucha libre is considered to have debuted on a specific date: September 21, 1933. It was brought to Mexico by a promoter named Salvador Lutteroth after he saw a match in Texas during a trip to the United States. He and a partner, Francisco Ahumado, decided to promote wrestling events in the Mexican capital and hired four wrestlers to come back to Mexico with them. Mexico City had hosted several exhibitions of Greco-Roman wrestling in the late nineteenth and early twentieth centuries, and there was one exhibition of "lucha libre" (catch-as-catch-can) in 1922.[8] Unlike their predecessors, however, Lutteroth and Ahumado incorporated as the Empresa Mexicana de Lucha Libre (EMLL) to promote wrestling events in the city on a regular basis. The 1933 event thus inaugurated the Mexicanization of professional wrestling—the birth of lucha libre per se. During 1933–1934, the EMLL organized events in the rundown Arena Modelo in the neighborhood of Doctores, and the Arena Nacional, just south of the Alameda. In 1934, the empresa was able to purchase Arena Modelo, which they renamed Arena México. In 1943, the EMLL built a second arena in Mexico City, the Arena Coliseo in the neighborhood of La Lagunilla, in back of the Zócalo.

The EMLL began by promoting wrestlers from the United States but soon recruited a stable of its own wrestlers, most of them Mexicans. The wrestlers would fight in the empresa's arenas in the Federal District and tour the provincial circuit. Monterrey, Guadalajara, Pachuca, and other cities welcomed Mexico City's wrestling stars, and by the early 1940s were producing their own local heroes. The EMLL, however, remained the only empresa in the capital with both its own arenas and its own stable of wrestlers. The genre began to take on elements specific to its Mexican version, most notably, the use of wrestling masks. In the 1930s, two wrestlers, La Maravilla Enmascarada (The Masked Marvel) and El Murciélago Velásquez ("Bat" Velásquez), appeared in the arenas wearing masks.[9] A novelty during

40. *Rudo* Gori Guerrero delivers a flying kick to masked rival Blue Demon, while his partner El Santo moves in to assist. Courtesy of Colección Hermanos Mayo, Fototeca of the Archivo General de la Nación, Mexico.

lucha libre's first decade, the wrestling mask became a common feature of costuming by the 1950s, eventually coming to symbolize the sport itself (see Figure 40).

Although the EMLL maintained its position as Mexico's preeminent wrestling empresa, it did not have a monopoly on the sport. Other promoters organized matches at the Arena Ferrocarríl Cintura Roma-Mérida as early as 1934.[10] In the late 1930s and early 1940s, wrestlers would perform at arenas Venustiano Carranza, Plan Sexenal, 18 de Marzo, Libertad, and Vencedora.[11] Another promoter, Jesús Garza Hernández, organized events well northwest of the city center at the Frontón Metropolitano and the Cine Politeama.[12]

Many of the people who formed lucha libre's early audience were drawn from the social class developing in Mexico City out of the unprecedented migration that followed the revolution. Between 1920 and 1950, the population of the Federal District increased by nearly 500 percent.[13] By far the largest part of this increase came from peasants and artisans from all over Mexico who moved to the capital to settle in the neighborhoods of the center and in ever expanding peripheral zones. The majority of lucha libre's fans may have been from the *clase popular*, but not all. The writer Salvador Novo confessed to being an *aficionado*, attending regularly in the early 1940s, even exchanging his Friday night season tickets to the ballet for Tuesday night tickets so that he could be free to attend the luchas. In a piece he wrote in 1940 entitled "Mi lucha (libre)" he said little about the class makeup of the audience, although he strongly implied that they were not of the elite. He did, however, shed light on what drew lucha libre's fans to the arenas.

One attraction (then as now) was the way lucha libre minimized the distance between performers and spectators, constituting both as participants. As in other sports, spectators respond actively to the performance, cheering their heroes and booing their opponents. Spectator participation in lucha libre, however, is even more intense, for the match is both a sporting event and a melodrama. Fans do not cheer their home team, but the forces of good against the forces of evil (or for supporters of the rudos, the tricksters, and *chingones* [badasses] against the smarmy hypocrites). Finally, lucha libre allows, indeed demands, physical and verbal interaction between the spectators and the wrestlers: fans touch the wrestlers as they enter the arena; rudos exchange insults with the técnicos' supporters; wrestlers, thrown from the ring, fall onto whoever is sitting in the front row. Salvador Novo gleefully described the blurring of the roles of performer and spectator that took place in the arena, relating how "each rheumatic and bald master of a two peso ticket at ringside loses the kilos and years necessary to transform himself, during a quarter of an hour, into Jimmy el Apolo, and with equal ease, find in El Hombre Montaña or in Alberto Corral his enemies scattered about the world—the landlord, the section chief, his own father-in-law—and contributes from his seat to exterminate them, to kick them, to throw them out of the ring."[14]

Another interesting feature of lucha libre was that it attracted a large female following. The EMLL offered a monthly Thursday "ladies night" when women could enter for free, but Novo noted that Sunday afternoons were "the days in which the Arena appears more full of those of the fair sex who know how to pay for their tastes." Of their vociferous participation, he wrote that it constituted a "happy and probatory expression of the existence of the collective unconscious that Jung discovered, that is able to remember words that haven't been used for centuries when confronted with an adequate stimulus."[15] The participation of women as lucha libre spectators was significant, considering that some kinds of public space, notably the cantina, were formally closed to women until the 1970s, and the gendering of other public spaces, such as the cinema and the rock concert, was sometimes subject to violent contestation.[16]

Mass mediation: The 1950s

In the early 1950s, lucha libre became enmeshed in networks of mass media. In 1954, the biweekly wrestling fanzine *Lucha Libre* (which is still published as *Box y Lucha*) was founded. El Santo, a wrestler who wore a silver mask and was already on his way to becoming Mexico's most famous wrestler, became the protagonist of a long-running comic book by José G. Cruz (even though he was still wrestling as a rudo). And in addition to its adoption by the print media, lucha libre entered into wider circulation via television and cinema.

As in the United States and Japan, professional wrestling was one of the first offerings of Mexican television. The first televised wrestling matches were broadcast from the EMLL's Arena Coliseo on Rómulo O'Farril's Channel 4 in November 1950. Two years later, O'Farrill's rival at the time, Emilio Azcárraga, began to broadcast matches on his television network, Televicentro (the precursor of the media conglomerate Televisa). Rather than deal with the EMLL, the network put up a ring in the new Televicentro studios on Avenida Chapultepec (about two blocks north of Arena México). He recruited Jesús Garza Hernández, the owner of Lucha Libre Internacional, to run an empresa owned by the television station. Using a mix of wrestlers from Lucha Libre Internacional and stars enticed away from the EMLL, Televicentro began to broadcast lucha libre directly from their studio. During 1953, broadcasts took place four times a week, as competition between the two networks intensified.[17]

The broadcasts had a number of effects, some intended, others perhaps not. Television opened new spaces and practices of reception for lucha libre, even as lucha libre was supposed to draw a broader audience to the medium. Few Mexicans could afford their own television set, but in popular barrios, the owners of bars and *fondas* invested in the devices to attract clients. Lower-class Mexicans who managed to buy a set would charge their neighbors to watch, perhaps providing drinks and snacks with the price of admission. Watching lucha libre on television, then, was a collective activity, even if the interaction between audience and performers was lost.

The audience for lucha libre in this era was not, moreover, limited to the popular classes. I have interviewed several middle- and upper-class Mexicans who remember watching lucha libre on television when they were children. Their families were able to afford their own set, and they too described watching lucha libre as a collective experience, one that crossed generational

41. Lucha libre audience, c. 1954. Courtesy of Colección Hermanos Mayo, Fototeca of the Archivo General de la Nación, Mexico.

and class lines as it brought the extended households together, from the grandparents to the servants. One man told me that his upper-middle-class family would invite their friends over to watch lucha libre one week, opera the next. The live performance also drew a middle-class (and possibly upper-class) element, as photographs of the audience at events in the Televicentro studios (and possibly Frontón Metropolitano) reveal the front rows to be full of well-dressed, stylish men and women (see Figure 41).

Another mode by which lucha libre was disseminated to the Mexican public and the star system reinforced was film. The year that Televicentro brought lucha libre to television, four different directors released movies that featured wrestlers. Over the subsequent four decades, the Mexican film industry produced hundreds more such films. The wrestling movie, in the words of Nelson Carro, "was always a parasitic genre—of melodrama, of comedy, of horror and of science fiction. At no time did it look to be autonomous—on the contrary, in mixture, in pastiche, in anachronism, one finds much of its power."[18] What distinguished wrestling films from other movies was the insertion of one or more scenes of lucha libre into the narrative. The wrestlers would spend most of their screen time battling evil, solving mysteries, or untangling domestic complications, the plot interrupted by gratuitous lucha libre matches tucked into the narrative like awkward dance numbers. Despite (or perhaps because of) their notably low production values, the movies were wildly popular. Roughly two hundred of them were produced between 1952 and 1983, and El Santo alone acted in fifty of them.

The Office of Public Spectacles

In contrast to film, television contributed little to the dissemination of lucha libre in the long run, because the move from the arena to the small screen brought lucha libre under the scrutiny of the state, and it was pulled off the air a few years after its debut. For all its novelty and apparent informality, lucha libre was incorporated into the organization of the Mexican state fairly early in its history, around 1938, when it was placed under the authority of the Comisión de Box y Lucha Libre (Commission of Boxing and Lucha Libre), a division of the Oficina de Espectáculos Públicos (Office of Public Spectacles), which oversaw all manner of public entertainments, from opera and theater to cinema and sports. In 1953, Rafael Barradas Osorio was appointed as the secretary of lucha libre. Barradas Osorio was an acquaintance of the recently elected president Adolfo Ruiz Cortines. He had worked in the movies before and hoped to parlay his relationship with the president and his acting experience into a position in the Office of Public Spectacles. The president did send him to see the head of the office, Adolfo Fernández Bustamante, who did not give him the position he expected (in the division that oversaw cinema), but put him in charge of lucha libre (much to his surprise).[19] When the controversy over televised lucha libre began, he was still new to the job.

Opposition to televised lucha libre seems to have begun with the Televicentro broadcasts. Before putting up the Televicentro ring, Azcárraga solicited authorization from the Secretary of Communications and Transportation (which was in charge of television), but he neglected to consult the Commission of Boxing and Lucha Libre. In response, Fernández Bustamante took Televicentro to court to block the broadcasts.[20] Once it reached the courts, however, the argument over lucha libre broadcasts was reframed as one over the safety of underage viewers. The object of control, moreover, shifted from the television studios to the live events, and the court began to consider the question of whether minors should be permitted to go to the arenas. The judge in charge of the case granted the Televisa empresa a stay and ruled that minors could continue to attend the luchas. But he also issued a strong condemnation of the behavior of the rudo wrestlers and ordered the commission to "clean up" the event. Barradas Osorio, the EMLL, and the head of the wrestlers union were charged with negotiating a list of rules for lucha libre performance that made it impossible to perform the rudo role at all. And really, without the rudos, there is no lucha libre.[21]

Meanwhile, the government's attention shifted from the issue of minors entering the arenas back to the question of televised matches. This time, the city's regent, Ernesto Uruchurtu, prohibited the transmissions by fiat because many parents had, allegedly, complained that their children had been injured while attempting to imitate the wrestlers.[22] Rafael Barradas later justified the ban in his memoirs, recounting: "It was said that even though little ones attended events, in those cases they were accompanied by adults who very probably explained to them what the wrestlers were doing, and that didn't happen in the intimacy of the homes where the wrestlers were seen by children to whom no one explained what was happening on the television screen, and from there came the danger that was involved with televising wrestling."[23] Children were also barred from attending the live event because they would try to approach their heroes during the match and might be squashed by rudos fighting outside the ring (in violation of commission directives). Veterans of the era—wrestlers, officials, and journalists—do not challenge Barradas Osorio's account and agree that lucha libre was taken off the air to protect children. Yet, as José Agustín has suggested, the reasons behind the prohibition were probably more complex.[24]

First, the ban on televised lucha libre should be seen in the overall context of the administrations of President Ruiz Cortines and Regent Ernesto Uruchurtu. The early 1950s were marked by attempts by both the national and the municipal governments to exercise control over cultural expressions and social geography in Mexico City. For example, the boleros of Agustín Lara, which celebrated fallen women and the men who loved them, were banned from the radio, and independent vendors were pushed off the streets and into formal, state-constructed markets.[25] In what could be seen as a brilliant containment of dissent, the government and the right-wing opposition worked together to tighten control over the content of comic books.[26] Seen in this context, the campaign to limit lucha libre's audience was unusual in that other campaigns (over comic books, music, film, and public education) were often articulated in terms of protecting young women from *moral* dangers. The campaign to control lucha libre, however, sought to protect little boys from physical dangers. And although there was no attempt to control adult female spectatorship of lucha libre, women were prohibited from working as wrestlers in the Federal District.[27]

Second, there was already a certain ambivalence within the wrestling "family" over the effects of televised broadcast of their sport. Some were concerned that ticket sales at the arenas would drop. Others worried about the effect that increased government scrutiny would have on performance. One journalist viewed the court case and the judge's ruling as evidence of television's deleterious effect on lucha libre performance—allowing, as it did, for the interference of government officials who misunderstood the spectacle. Another journalist suggested that the entire epoch had been nothing more than an unfair move on the part of Jesús Garza Hernández, writing that "99% of the fans know that the Médico Asesino was a product of the era of television, with an eye on the part of his promoter to compete with El Santo, when the reign of the Lutteroth family felt, more than ever, like it was trembling and about to go down. This was the main goal of the creation of Médico Asesino: to do away with the empresa of La Coliseo and start a new reign in which Chucho Garza Hernández alone would rule."[28]

Lucha libre's retreat from television reestablished the authority of the commission over the sport. Barradas Osorio discarded most of the rules controlling the performance but set up three "dispositions": no fighting outside the ring, no acts of aggression toward the referee, and no acts of aggression toward the audience.[29] On the other hand, according to his own account and that of many veterans, Barradas insisted that the rules be enforced. All lucha libre events in Mexico City were (and still are) attended by representatives of the commission, who would stop the match or levy fines if, in their opinion, the wrestlers were in violation of a commission directive.

With the end of televised wrestling, Jesús Garza Hernández thus lost the (semivirtual) space of the Televicentro studios and returned to the Cine Politeama and the Frontón Metropolitano. According to Barradas, he resisted the directive prohibiting the entrance of minors and so attracted the attention of the commission. His wrestlers drew so many suspensions and fines (for various violations), that they became unwilling to work for him. Within a few years he was driven out of business. The EMLL, meanwhile, "voluntarily" stopped allowing children into their arenas and were able to continue unchallenged as the major empresa in Mexico City.[30]

The effect of the ban on televised broadcast was not to suppress lucha libre but to reconfigure its public. As the center filled with growing numbers of self-employed artisans and peddlers and underemployed construction and service sector workers who made up (and continue to make up) the bulk of the population of Mexico City, the middle class began a migration to the south and west of the city. By the time lucha libre was taken off the air, much of the city's middle class had moved to the suburbs of Narvarte, Coyoacán, and Pedregal—far away from neighborhoods like Doctores and the Center, where the principal EMLL arenas were located. By 1957, lucha libre's stars could be seen at the EMLL arenas in Doctores and La Lagunilla. The only other venues for the spectacle were minor arenas, temporary spaces on the provincial circuit, and the movies.[31]

Live performance of lucha libre maintained its autonomy relative to the movies. Banished from both the airwaves and middle-class spaces of the city, it became closely connected with the *colonias populares* where the arenas remained. It was precisely in this context that lucha libre had what veterans and long-time fans call its "golden era." During the 1960s, the only sport to draw more spectators than lucha libre was soccer.[32] In 1956, the EMLL demolished the old Arena México and opened a new arena in its place with almost 18,000 seats. They opened a third arena in the Federal District in the early 1960s, the Pista Arena Revolución, as well as several arenas outside the capital. In addition, minor empresas affiliated with independent arenas sprang up around the city. Their wrestlers might appear in star position in the small, neighborhood-based arena, or contract out to the EMLL to appear in one of the opening matches in one of their shows. As new neighborhoods or whole cities sprang up in the expanding peripheries of the city, new arenas opened to serve them.[33] In the 1970s one empresa, Lucha Libre Internacional (unrelated to the Garza Hernández enterprise of the same name), organized events in the bullring Toreo Cuatro Caminos on the outskirts of the city limits, taking advantage of the expanding northeast suburbs. Owned by a promoter from Hidalgo, Francisco Flores, and run by his partner, Carlos Maynez, it became the second-largest empresa in the metropolitan area.

The restriction of lucha libre spectatorship to the colonias populares coincided with a shift in the way that their residents were perceived by the middle and upper classes and represented in the mass media. These neighborhoods included both descendants of a proletariat and a subproletariat who had lived in Mexico City for generations, and ever more immigrants from the countryside and the smaller cities. To the extent that these new urbanites constituted a social class, they were not explicitly accounted for by the ideology or institutional structure of the postrevolutionary state. The governing party was originally organized "explicitly as a class alliance" between labor, *campesinos*, and a "popular" sector, which "was to be the home of the Revolutionary elements of the middle class; its base was in the civil-service unions, which were probably kept out of the labor sector to limit its power."[34] Thus, at the formal, institutional level, the self-employed artisans and peddlers and underemployed construction and service sector workers who made up (and continue to make up) the bulk of the population of Mexico City were not differentiated from the middle class.

They were, however, distinguished culturally, in both intellectual discourse and mass-mediated representations, where they were denigrated as *pelados*. The term pelado, which literally means "baldie" or "stripped," identifies the poor (man) with (his) lack: of possessions, of culture, of everything. The essayist Samuel Ramos described the pelado thus: "His name defines him quite well. He is a person who carries his soul uncovered, with nothing to hide his most intimate urges. He cynically holds on to elemental impulses that other men try to dissimulate. The '*pelado*' belongs to the lowest categories of social fauna, and represents the human detritus of the big city. In the economic hierarchy he is less than the proletarian, and in the intellectual, a primitive. Life has been completely hostile to him, and attitude toward life is one of black resentment."[35] In the 1930s, the figure of the pelado began to circulate in public discourse as a kind of Every-Mexican. On the one hand, the comedian Cantinflas developed his character, the *peladito*, a "wise fool," who unintentionally ridicules the pretensions of the Mexican elite as he struggles through his misadventures. The circulation of the image of the innocuous peladito coincided with the pelado's entrance into intellectual discourse with the publication of *Profile of Man and Culture in Mexico*, in which Ramos used the pelado as a metonym for the Mexican condition. The pelado thus emerged as the predominant image of both the urban popular classes and the problematic of Mexican national culture.

In the 1950s, however, the term pelado began to be displaced as the key term of class denigration by the word *naco*. Naco is said to be a contraction of Totonaco (the name of an indigenous ethnic group) or of *chinaco* (a derogatory term for the soldiers of Zapata, who briefly occupied parts of Mexico City during the Revolution). Claudio Lomnitz has argued that between the 1950s, when it first appeared, and the mid-1970s, the word underwent an important shift in meaning. In the 1950s, it "was used as a slur against Indians or, more generally, against peasants or anyone who stood for the provincial backwardness that Mexico was trying so hard to dispel." In the mid-1970s, he continues, "naquismo came to be recognized as a characteristically *urban* aesthetic . . . a special kind of kitsch [that] is considered vulgar because it incorporates aspirations to progress and the material culture of modernity in imperfect and partial ways."[36] But the naco is not only an aesthetic but (like the pelado) a member of a specific class of urban people. And whereas the pelado was defined by his lack—of resources, of culture—the naco was defined by excess of culture. The nacos never leave their Indian roots entirely behind, or rather, their Indian roots never leave them. By the end of the 1950s, lucha libre was available only to the middle and upper classes in the form of the campy, laughably low-budget, fun but admittedly ridiculous wrestling movies. But the live performance, with its participatory catharsis, its spaces for parody, its corporal elegance, became the exclusive and unmediated property of *la clase naca*.

The fact that lucha libre developed as a live rather than mass-mediated genre had several implications for both the institutional structure supporting lucha and the style of performance. In the United States, where television was a significant factor in the organization of professional wrestling, events took place in venues normally used for other events. In Mexico City, however, events regularly took place in spaces used solely or primarily for lucha libre. The power of individual promoters depended on their access to (preferably ownership of) an arena and their affiliations with wrestlers, the state (via the commission), and the wrestlers union, rather than their connections with the mass media.

Moreover, the needs of the camera and the dispersed public did not condition the development of the performance style. Wrestling events in Mexico came to follow a different format from events in the United States. Matches are longer: each match lasts until one side wins two pins out of three (in the United States the match ends as soon as one wrestler gets a pin). But in addition to greater length, the Mexican style never depended on verbal displays, such as the pre- and postmatch interviews so important in the United States. Instead, it developed as a style that depends on agility and acrobatics. *Luchadores* (wrestlers) played to the third balcony instead of the camera. Lucha libre remained and evolved as a fundamentally gestural performance.

It developed, moreover, as (to paraphrase Clifford Geertz) a story that Mexicans (of a certain historically constituted class position) told themselves about themselves (and about the world they inhabited).[37] In the interactions between apparently suffering técnicos and apparently underhanded rudos, lucha libre dramatized and parodied common understandings of the postrevolutionary system and their place within it. It reflected a political system in which people who appear to be opponents are really working together. It paralleled an electoral system in which electioneering took place behind closed doors and elections ratified decisions that had already been made. Ongoing dramas in the ring demonstrated that loyalty to kin and friends is more important than ideology, and that arbiters of authority are not necessarily on the side of the honest and honorable. By its very name, lucha libre (which not only means "free wrestling" but "free struggle") resonated with the widely held and fundamental philosophy of the Mexican popular classes: life is struggle. This struggle was ritually enacted every week in the ring (see Figure 42).[38]

Revalorization and Appropriation

The ban on televised broadcast of lucha libre separated its actual performance from its mass-mediated circulation. It situated lucha libre as a neighborhood-based and class-specific practice, separate from, albeit related to, the version that disseminated through films (the consumption of which crossed class as well as spatial boundaries).[39] In 1991, however, Televisa began to broadcast lucha libre again. Its return to television was not accepted willingly by all, or perhaps even most, wrestlers. Instead, televised broadcast became the focal point of conflicts in the world of lucha libre that continue to this day. Several changes occurred during the decade of the 1980s that facilitated lucha libre's return to the small screen and simultaneously laid the groundwork for resistance to televised broadcast. Two such changes were a loosening of commission control over the spectacle and a revalorization of lucha libre by artists and organizers associated with the left opposition to the ruling party.

In the dominant discourse of postrevolutionary Mexico, the locus of authentic popular culture was ambivalently imagined to be the Indian, campesino sphere.[40] Indigenous Mexicans were portrayed as backward and suffering but the repository of a rich and colorful cultural tradition,

42. Maravilla López and Super Can enter the ring in the flamboyant style of the Mexican técnico. Courtesy of Deportivo Los Galeanos, September 1997.

awaiting the modernizing and civilizing efforts of the *mestizo* national subject. This formulation constituted "an argument about the individuality of the Mexican process: the soul of Mexican culture is Indian and its political body is destined to be ruled by *mestizos* against the Europeanizing process of the lackeys of foreign imperialism."[41] But if the sphere of the rural and Indian stood for the realm of the authentic and popular as well as a site for state intervention, the culture of the urban poor constituted a different problematic in official (state) and unofficial discourse—for the residents of the colonias populares were neither quite Indians nor quite the modernizing subjects. Instead, they were simultaneously modern and backward, inauthentic and provincial—in short, naco.

In the 1970s and early 1980s, lucha libre came to the attention of a number of artists and intellectuals who, in the aftermath of 1968, were engaged in a cultural project in opposition to the official nationalism of the Mexican state. As Eric Zolov puts it, "The larger theoretical paradigm of what now constituted 'popular culture' was itself being challenged by a new level of critique that questioned the validity of a narrowly defined notion of cultural imperialism. The very term *cultura popular* underwent a transformation from its exclusively rural orientation into one that embraced all levels of urban cultural expression."[42] In a sense, the participants in the "neopop" movement discovered lo naco as the locus of the authentically Mexican.

Although those engaged in the neopop project did not regard mass-mediated cultural expressions as inherently imperialistic, they did regard them as alienating and alienated—separated from local cultures. While the *telenovela*, for example, might be of cultural significance to the people of the barrios, they had little or no direct contact with its production. In lucha libre, however, those involved in the neopop movement discovered something uniquely precious: an expression of popular modernity that escaped being defined through the mass media.

The first neopop use of lucha libre imagery was a performance piece by Felipe Ehrenberg. In 1973, the artist had several men, dressed as (masked) wrestlers, walk around the Bellas Artes building with flashlights. They were supposed to circle the building until the batteries ran out, but the police intervened first.[43] By the early 1980s, other artists, notably the photographer Lourdes Grobet and the painters Marisa Lara and Arturo Guerrero, started spending time at the arenas, hanging out with the wrestlers, and becoming part of the wrestling subculture. Lucha libre was, for them, a revelation. In the words of Grobet, "In *lucha libre* we discovered *urban Mexico* . . . Prehispanic Mexico, indigenous Mexico, but urbanized. . . . There's the whole presentation, the play of the mask, the masked wrestler, the modernity in the ritual mask, in the costume, the characters. . . . All that the Mexican culture carries, all of the values of Mexican culture are found there."[44]

In addition to visual artists, essayists like Carlos Monsiváis and José Joaquín Blanco, dramatists like José Buíl, novelists like Paco Ignacio Taibo II, and others wrote about it. These high-culture uses of lucha libre imagery constituted an argument about continuities between urban and rural cultural spaces. Those continuities, they contended, distinguished an essential Mexican culture whose fundamental quality was a love of ritual. With its masks, its moral text, the importance of gesture, the intimacy between performers and audience, the infinite play of secrecy and revelation, lucha libre figured as urban ritual par excellence.

In the 1980s, lucha libre imagery was appropriated by grassroots political organizers as well. In 1983 a group of activists organizing tenants in a building behind Arena Coliseo hit on the idea of having one of their members dress as El Santo to confront the landlord when he came to evict tenant families.[45] Four years later, the episode inspired the creation of Superbarrio Gómez, spokeswrestler for the *asemblea de barrios*, an umbrella organization of groups that were formed to address the concerns of those left homeless or inadequately housed after the disasterous earthquake of 1985. Superbarrio

Gómez was the first (along with Ecologista Universal, who appeared in Veracruz the same year) of a number of "social wrestlers," people who dress as (masked) wrestlers to represent particular causes.[46] Though the man behind Superbarrio's mask was a retired wrestler, Superbarrio himself was the product of the collective imagination of the asamblea membership.[47]

Superbarrio was intended as a novelty, to be used in a demonstration that took place on June 12, 1987. Soon after, the asamblea membership discovered that his mask made him a surprisingly effective representative in their dealings with politicians. Marcos Rascón Bandas explains:

> A very common way that demonstrators arrive at public offices is to send a commission. Now, in this transition, where the commission enters the office of the functionary, there's a change of attitude. They start ready to do battle and . . . as soon as four or five enter, there's a guy behind a desk, who says "What is your problem?" You arrive, and everything is a sanctuary, with photographs of the president . . . and someone suddenly wants to know "What do you want?" You have to express yourself well. . . . In that terrain, in that little parcel, many movements are left humiliated, we might say, no? But when suddenly Superbarrio enters the struggle [*lucha*], and Superbarrio appears in the office, the functionary behind his desk feels absolutely disoriented, out of order. He's the one who starts to stutter, who stumbles and knocks things over. . . . Because he knew by the presence of Superbarrio that we were mocking him.[48]

Superbarrio's mask made him, first of all, incorruptible—it's impossible to co-opt a fictional character. Second, he functioned as a Brechtian device, disrupting the rituals of the state through his surreal (or perhaps hyperreal) presence. In addition, social wrestlers like Superbarrio took advantage of the semantic flexibility of the word lucha, to associate lucha libre with the lucha *social*. They (and their creators) treated lucha libre as a symbol of the popular, of their constituencies. By hiding their faces, the masked social wrestlers could claim to represent (in both senses of the word) their followers in a way that other leaders could not. In the words of the Veracruzan Ecologista Universal, "The mask makes you visible, but it also makes it easier to present the struggle as universal, rather than personal; a way to say 'I am the people, I exist and I do not agree with what's going on.'"[49]

Artistic and political reappropriation of lucha libre resignified the genre. In its early years, before the ban on televised broadcast, lucha libre was (like television, movies, soccer, and comic books) a sign of modernity, of Mexico's progressive trajectory. After the ban, outside of its public, lucha libre signified the impossibly naco. In the 1980s, artists would immerse themselves like anthropologists in the lucha libre world, in search of urban popular authenticity. Luchadores welcomed them and enjoyed their legitimating attentions. This collaboration reached its zenith with the 1992 exhibit on lucha libre at the Museo de Culturas Populares in Coyoacán.

But by 1992, the lucha libre "family" was embroiled in a new struggle. In the 1970s, the Azcárraga family's Televicentro absorbed other private networks into the media conglomerate Televisa, which then held a monopoly on commercial television until the 1990s. In 1991, the media giant brought lucha libre back to the small screen. Felipe Ehrenberg has suggested that the attention paid to lucha libre by artists and the press (because of the social wrestlers) was one of the reasons that Televisa executives reconsidered televised lucha libre.[50] The embrace of lucha libre by the neopop movement coincided, however, with a boom in professional wrestling in the United States. Vince McMahon's reorganized World Wrestling Federation (WWF) succeeded in bringing professional wrestling from regional networks to national networks and cable.[51] Perhaps Televisa saw a lucrative model in the revamped WWF.

Many wrestlers and promoters saw televised lucha libre as an opportunity to increase their profits and expand their audience. Other members of the world of wrestlers, promoters, journalists, and dedicated fans that make up lucha libre's subculture saw the revival of televised lucha libre as a disaster. The broadcasts were not accepted passively by the wrestling community. Instead, televisualization of lucha libre became a battleground of conflicts over labor rights, aesthetics, and cultural integrity.[52]

The Return of the Televised Wrestler

Televisa's interest in lucha libre came after a decade of reorganization as well as resignification of the genre. In the mid-1980s, the Commission of Boxing and Lucha Libre began to loosen its control over the sport. In 1985, the EMLL was granted permission to allow children into the arenas.[53] Later that year Luis Spota, president of the commission since 1957, died, and in 1986 Rafael Barradas retired. The commission itself was reorganized. Lucha libre and boxing were administratively separated, and the administration of the former was placed in the hands of a string of retired *luchadores*.

The commission was not the only institutional structure organizing lucha libre. Wrestlers belonged to unions, most belonging to the CTM-affiliated Sindicato Nacional de Luchadores, which was headed by a retired wrestler named Manny Guzmán. Some belonged to the smaller, CROC-affiliated Asociación Nacional de Luchadores, Referís y Retirados.[54] The Association was founded by retired wrestler and waiter Juan Alanís as an alternative to the Sindicato.[55]

In 1985, the Association leadership decided to work for the repeal of the prohibition against luchadoras (women wrestlers) working in the Federal District. In the process, they discovered that the ban had never existed on paper. They further discovered that the commission had never been granted legal authority, and that lucha libre had no binding regulation.[56] Thus by 1990, when Televisa began to reconsider lucha libre, the commission's authority over the spectacle had diminished.

The EMLL, however, maintained its hegemony in the Federal District. It was the largest, oldest, and most prestigious empresa. The second largest, Carlos Maynez's Lucha Libre Internacional, operated mostly from the Toreo Cuatro Caminos, which is just over the border from the Federal District, in the State of Mexico. In the spring of 1991, Televisa signed a contract with the "serious and stable" EMLL to tape performances in Arenas México and Coliseo and broadcast them on Saturday afternoons. They later switched to Sundays.

From the start, many wrestlers and promoters expressed concern over the economic impact of television. Some veterans of the 1950s remembered that arena attendance dropped sharply when it was broadcast by Televicentro. One journalist, echoing accusations leveled against the Garza Hernández Lucha Libre Internacional forty years before, called televised wrestling an underhanded attack on Carlos Maynez's Lucha Libre Internacional by the EMLL.[57] Other wrestlers did not oppose televised broadcast as such, but were worried about its terms, especially the scheduling of the broadcasts. The two biggest shows at the arena are Friday nights and Sunday afternoons, and many feared that Sunday broadcasts would compete directly with the arenas. Hence, televised broadcast immediately raised a host of concerns.[58] During the next year, Guzmán was in charge of representing the wrestlers' interests in the EMLL's negotiations with Televisa, but in the spring of 1992 several disgruntled wrestlers broke with the Sindicato, publicly accusing Guzmán of selling out the membership. They were immediately blackballed by the union.

The deal between the EMLL and Televisa was brokered by the former's director of programming and public relations, Antonio Peña. Peña, whose duties included scouting new talent and developing new characters, was known for making changes to the live event. He had added several foreign wrestlers to the EMLL stable who had never trained as wrestlers before their recruitment.[59] Notable among these were Conan el Bárbaro, a Cuban American recruited from the streets of Miami, and Vampiro Canadiense, a tall, muscular rock'n'roller from Canada.[60] In addition, Peña added a number of new elements to lucha libre performance—musical themes and scantily clad female escorts for the wrestlers, and special lighting for the arena—which some thought innovative but others thought degrading.

As the controversy over the broadcasts continued, rumors began to circulate that Peña was leaving the EMLL to start his own empresa. The rumors proved to be true, and on June 7 he left, taking a group of about thirty wrestlers, among them some of the empresa's biggest stars, to whom he promised higher pay and more exposure. He gave the empresa the rather dry name of Asistencia, Asesoría y Administración (Assistance, Accounting and Administration, but better known as the Triple A). In the weeks following the announcement, journalists wondered in print how he was going to support an empresa with no reliable access to arenas. He wouldn't have use of the EMLL arenas, and it was unlikely that smaller arena owners would want to antagonize the empresa by letting him use theirs.

Peña retorted that his empresa would bring stars of lucha libre to the provinces and "internationalize" lucha libre through his connections with the WWF in the United States. His goal, he said, was to "bring innovation to the spectacle by creating new characters, and to elevate the dissemination of this rough discipline not only at the national level, but in places like South America, Europe and the United States. We will make it so that the public of the provinces has access to the great stars."[61] But it soon came out that the owner of the new empresa was not Antonio Peña, but Televisa itself. The stable, dependable space of the Triple A would not be in any arena, but in the virtual space of Channel 9. Like its precursor Televicentro in 1952, Televisa seized control of the spectacle by going around the EMLL and sponsoring a network empresa. Triple A stars would appear in independent arenas outside the Federal District (and thus outside the jurisdiction of the Federal District commission), where their performances would be taped for broadcast.[62]

From the point of view of the EMLL, this was an act of base treachery on the parts of both Televisa and (especially) Peña. They closed ranks with Lucha Libre Internacional and the Sindicato against the Triple A, and warned that their wrestlers were free to go with Peña but might not be free to come back if things didn't work out.[63] Guzmán announced that the Sindicato, as "the only legitimate holder of the national collective contract for wrestlers," could legitimately demand the suspension of all Triple A functions, but would graciously refrain from doing so. Any union member who participated in a Triple A function, however, would be expelled from the Sindicato.[64] In addition, he negotiated an agreement in the State of Mexico with the Commission of Lucha Libre and the owners of the major arenas to prohibit the entrance of new empresas (allegedly to protect the public from fraudulent advertising by fly-by-night promoters).[65]

Some wrestlers followed Peña. The wrestler "Justiciero" took over as head of a new Triple A–affiliated union to represent the now blackballed wrestlers.[66] Meanwhile, the Sindicato, still led by Guzmán, suddenly changed its position to oppose televised broadcast. The movement against televised lucha libre climaxed in June 1993, when the Sindicato went on strike. The strike culminated in a march on the presidential residence of Los Pinos by a group of about three hundred wrestlers, many wearing their masks. The strikers hoped to get an audience with President Salinas de Gortari to ask for his intervention in the matter, but the president was unavailable and the strike fell apart.[67]

In the end, the Sindicato lost most of its influence. One group of wrestlers, fed up with Guzmán, left to join Juan Alanís's alternative union; others reached an accord with the EMLL to form an in-house union. Televisa agreed to continue to broadcast EMLL events. The strike failed to stop the televised transmission of lucha libre or to wrest its control from the media conglomerate.

The victory of Televisa and the Triple A had a number of consequences for the practice and reception of lucha libre. First, television changed the rhythm of the wrestling event. Rather than show a series of five matches in one arena, the broadcasts show a number of events from different arenas around the republic.[68] The action, moreover, is not confined to the ring (and the space surrounding it), but includes areas separated in space and time from the arena (the locker rooms, the parking lot, the promoter's office before the event, etc.). The broadcast audience is separated from the wrestlers, and even spectators in the arena are separated from the ring and the wrestlers by movable barricades. Where live (unbroadcast) lucha libre problematizes the difference between participants and observers, televised lucha libre reinforces it. In the words of Ecologista Universal, "Television kills the relationship between the wrestlers and the audience."

Perhaps more significant, the Triple A and televised wrestling in general promoted a shift in the composition of the wrestling audience, for once again, the broadcast of lucha libre brought the sport/spectacle to a new audience of middle-class children and youth. During the golden era, when lucha libre was enmeshed in a particular class culture, the class composition of the live audience was secured not only by middle-class disdain of the genre but by the actual and perceived risks of going to an arena. In addition to the real and imagined dangers associated with entering neighborhoods in the center, or settlements like Ciudad Nezahualcóyotl, many middle-class Mexicans were (and are) wary of the behavior of the lucha audience, which they imagine to be far more unruly than it is. For example, several middle-class Mexicans told me that they didn't want to go to the arenas because people in the balcony throw cups of urine onto the ringside seats—an apparently widespread (and erroneous) belief.[69] Broadcast of lucha libre meant that an emerging middle-class fanship could watch from their homes, where many developed a taste for the Triple A version of the sport. In general, middle-class Mexicans with whom I spoke identified lucha libre with its mass-mediated manifestations: television during the 1950s and the movies from the 1950s through the 1970s. As far as they were concerned, lucha had been dormant since the decline of the wrestling movie (or even since it was taken off the air in the 1950s), and the new televised version represented its revival.

Television thus took the place of cinema as the main means of dissemination of lucha libre to middle-class and provincial audiences. But unlike cinema, which had relatively little impact on the form of the live event, televised wrestling generated changes in the genre itself. There has always been a tension in lucha libre between spectacularity and the display of wrestling skill. Retirees whose careers spanned the 1950s and 1960s told me that even then there were those who disparaged the more acrobatic wrestlers for being *maromeros* (tumblers). In the late 1960s, when lucha libre started to include more aerial moves than before, sportswriters and veterans complained that the changes would degrade the sport to mere circus.[70] However, in those years, at least according to nostalgic veterans, wrestlers in the Federal District first had to be conversant in standard wrestling techniques and be able to display that knowledge in the ring. Thus, lucha maintained its character of being, first and foremost, an exhibition of skill in a specific physical discipline.

Televised events, on the other hand, make more use of the broad pantomime that typified pro wrestling in the United States. There is less exchange of locks and more hitting. Elements of action that used to be used sparingly—bloodletting, obvious use of props as illegal weapons, and so on—are used liberally in lucha's televised incarnation. That, in turn, changed the expectations of spectators of the live event, and wrestlers now must accommodate those expectations to be successful. Triple A–affiliated wrestlers and their fans portrayed the empresa's innovations as progress: both aesthetic (asserting that "lucha libre is always evolving") and in terms of expanding lucha libre's audience. Fans from lucha libre's traditional public, and many veterans of the lucha world, rejected the discourse of progress for one of degeneration. When Vampiro Canadiense would appear in the ring, his young fans cheered wildly, but more committed aficionados taunted him with cries of "El Vampiro doesn't know how to wrestle."[71] They said that it might be *libre*, but it wasn't *lucha*.

Third Round: PromoAzteca

In 1994, in line with the neoliberal policies of the Salinas administration, the state-owned Corporación Mexicana de Radio y Televisión, which ran TV Channels 7 and 13, was privatized, ending Televisa's monopoly on commercial broadcast television in Mexico. It was sold to Ricardo Salinas Pliego, who named the new network TV Azteca. The Azcárraga family, who had long been active supporters of the PRI, vigorously protested the sale, which they probably saw as a betrayal. They accused the president's brother Raúl Salinas de Gortari of selling the station at a loss to a relative. The government denied the charges, insisting that Salinas Pliego was not related to the Salinas de Gortaris.[72]

In 1995, Pedro Ortega, then secretary of the Commission of Lucha Libre, and Raúl Reyes, a promoter who owned a few arenas on the outskirts of the Federal District, approached Salinas Pliego with the idea of starting a wrestling empresa sponsored and broadcast by the new network, TV Azteca. He agreed, but Reyes was forced out of the organization before the contract was signed.[73] Shortly thereafter, in the fall of 1996, a group of wrestlers from the Triple A, led by Conan, Peña's director of international relations, and including stars like Vampiro Canadiense and Máscara Sagrada, left to join the new empresa.

The errant wrestlers accused Peña of corruption and unfair labor practices. Conan accused Peña of breaking (unspecified) promises and of docking his pay when he was working in the United States. Juventud Guerrera charged Peña with having his U.S. visa canceled when he left to join PromoAzteca (the new empresa). Máscara Sagrada complained that Peña was promoting droves of spurious Máscara Sagrada spinoffs (Jr.s, IIs, etc.) without his consent.[74] In language that was often used (at that time) to criticize the PRI, they described the Triple A as a corrupt monopoly, a "dinosaur."[75] In response, Peña and his allies portrayed the PromoAzteca wrestlers as a group of disloyal stooges, led astray by perfidious foreigners (Conan and Vampiro). Peña accused the fleeing wrestlers of "lack of gratitude toward the house which saw their birth," and Perro Aguayo, speaking for the wrestlers staying with the Triple A, avowed that it was "a shame that a foreigner could offend and fool the public and that a TV station that carried the name of an ancient Mexican culture, the Aztec, could be used for this."[76]

All of the parties in the dispute positioned themselves in ways that reflected then current political discourse and paralleled the conflict between the two networks. In 1991, Peña portrayed the Triple A as an innovative, internationalizing enterprise that would maximize employees' earnings—in other words, an enterprise in line with Salinas de Gortari's discourse of neoliberal modernization. When the PromoAzteca wrestlers broke away, they echoed the terms that people used to condemn the president and the PRI, claimed the discourse of modernization for themselves, and condemned Peña's corruption and monopoly of power. The PromoAzteca wrestlers' accusations of corruption were met with countercharges of unpatriotic xenophilia.

The New Traditionalists

This time, however, there were no strikes and no organized opposition to the saturation of the airwaves with even more lucha libre. During 1997 and much of 1998, lucha libre was broadcast twice a week: once by TV Azteca and once by Televisa, which broadcast four hours of Triple A and EMLL wrestling on Sundays. The relationship between the broadcasts and arena attendance is not well documented, but attendance had fallen. Most luchadores, trainers, and administrators outside of PromoAzteca and the Triple A agreed that it was the fault of televised broadcasts coupled with the economic crisis that followed the 1994 crash of the peso. During the period of research, there was a great deal of free-floating discontent in the wrestling world over the decline of live lucha libre. There was, however, one novel response to the perceived crisis: the formation of a wrestling empresa dedicated to the reformation and renovation of Mexican lucha libre.

The new empresa, called Renovación 2000, was formed in an alliance between associates of Juan Alanís's union (the Association), Raúl Reyes (the disenfranchised cofounder of PromoAzteca), and a number of other promoters and wrestlers who were left out of televised lucha libre. Reyes was named president of the new empresa, which also had the support of the EMLL.[77] Renovación 2000 was, like the Triple A and PromoAzteca, critical of both the labor and aesthetic practices of their competitors. Their critique, however, differed radically from those of the other two. When Peña and his followers left the EMLL, they criticized the empresa's failure to maximize the exposure and income of their wrestlers. PromoAzteca condemned the Triple A for failure to deliver on its promises. Renovación 2000, however, contended that the problem was that too few wrestlers could earn a living wage. They repeated criticisms that already circulated at the time of the first 1991 broadcasts: that lucha libre was suffering from *estrellitis* (star-itis), and that television limited the number of opportunities for wrestlers so that only a few carefully managed stars could find enough work to support themselves. Television, they argued, took work away not only from wrestlers but from the cleaners, ushers, and concessionaires who worked in the arenas. Empresas, they implied, like the government, have a social obligation to provide jobs for the people—an obligation that the major empresas ignored.

Many of the associates of Renovación 2000 participated in the protests of 1993, and their economic analysis of television was much like the one in circulation at that time. But they linked their criticisms to an aesthetic vision that recast lucha libre as a traditional practice. In other words, the leadership (and some of the rank and file) embraced the discourse of the neopop movement to claim lucha libre as a popular art form, part of Mexico's national patrimony, therefore deserving the protection of the state.[78] Their position, which was by no means limited to wrestlers working with Renovación, was that the Triple A had not only disrupted the economic base of lucha libre but was bringing about its aesthetic degradation. The Renovación project thus was one of cultural renovation: to define and promote the real, traditional lucha libre Mexicana. Naturally, defining traditional lucha entailed defining what it was not.

The Real Mexican Lucha Libre

Renovación 2000 members (and those who shared their point of view) complained about a number of practices of the televised empresas, especially the Triple A. Their most frequently voiced objection was the same one that outsiders often make about professional wrestling in general: it isn't really wrestling. They complained that televised wrestling involved too much indiscriminate use of props and novelties, and that *ya no hay llaveo* (nobody really wrestles anymore). But their critique of televised wrestling went further, to define an aesthetic and ethical vision of lucha libre that they were ready to defend on several grounds.

One site where the traditionalists criticized the Triple A and PromoAzteca was in relation to gender and performance. The luchador, they insisted, should embody virility. Yet they did not consider the presence of luchadoras problematic (although many individual luchadores disapprove of women wrestlers). Renovación's traditionalists accepted luchadoras as part of the Mexican lucha libre tradition. Indeed, women have wrestled in Mexico since the late 1940s. In many conversations with wrestlers and others in the wrestling world, both inside and outside of Renovación, I was told that the participation of women in lucha libre was just another example of their participation in the workforce: there are women cab drivers, women police officers, so why not luchadoras? No one challenged the right of women to engage in paid employment, and only some questioned the appropriateness of wrestling as woman's occupation.[79]

Renovación 2000 militants disapproved of mixed (male versus female) matches and were critical of the relationship between the rudo Killer and his escort, Miss Janet, who sometimes comes to his aid in the ring or helps him cheat against an opponent. They found both examples disturbing because they believed mixed wrestling to endanger and degrade the luchadora and to elicit dishonorable and inappropriate behavior from the male luchadores. But, unsurprisingly, given its affiliation with the union that won luchadoras the right to wrestle within city limits, they did support women in wrestling as long as luchadoras wrestled only each other.

The gendered degeneration of lucha libre was not personified by the Triple A's support of women in the ring (which was not notable), but by its promotion of a group of wrestlers known as the Exóticos.[80] Male wrestlers who work in drag, the Exóticos wrestle in frilly bathing suits under floral robes, in very 1970s bell-bottomed jumpsuits, or whatever they choose. As they enter the ring, they deliver kisses to their opponents, the referees, and male members of the audience. When they wrestle, they use a flamboyantly campy style, mincing and slapping, acting out a parody of femininity. Despite their small frames and effeminate personae, they often win their matches, putting their conventionally masculine opponents into a feminized position in the final pin. Their detractors regarded them as a symptom of the lucha libre's degeneration at the hands of the television industry.

Yet there is nothing novel about effeminate (male) wrestlers. In fact, exóticos have participated in lucha libre almost as long as have women. The first wrestlers to enter the arena as "exóticos" played a role closer to that of dandy than of drag queen. Gardenia Davis and Lalo el Exótico, whose careers peaked in the 1950s, had valets who would help them comb their hair, put on perfume, and spray cologne on the canvas and the audience just before the match.[81] During the 1980s, another exótico, Rudy Reynosa, carried the act a little further, harassing his opponents in the ring with kisses and flirtatious gestures. He, however, denied that his exótico style was anything more than an act.

Reynosa was also a trainer, and while he worked as an exótico, he also recruited and mentored two young men who would perform with him as a team called Los Exóticos. These two, May Flowers and Pimpernela Escarlata, represented an interesting shift in the exótico role, for, unlike their predecessors, they publicly embraced a gay identity. They made it clear in interviews that they were gay, and that in playing the role of exótico, they were doing what came to them "naturally." According to Pimpernela Escarlata, taking another role would have been an act of fraud, impossible to pull off in front of a discerning audience. In an interview with Lola Fascinetto, he recounts: "I used the mask on three occasions, *m'hija*. When I started in *lucha libre* I began wrestling as a man with the title 'Vans,' but later the people figured out that I wasn't a man, because they know, they aren't stupid, 'that's a *joto!*' they shouted. It made me ashamed, and in order to throw them off the scent, I put on another mask of a man with another name: El Playboy. But sincerely, I couldn't do it, *m'hija*. So I put away the men's masks, and I went out camping it up [*joteando*] as an *exótico*."[82]

The Exóticos changed the exótico style from a representation of a tendency to a representation of a social category. Instead of separating their wrestling personae from their personal identities, they presented themselves as "homosexual" (their term, sometimes interchangeable with gay) role models: ambassadors from the liberated capital to the closeted provinces. As Pimpernela Escarlata recounted to an interviewer, when they went to Villahermosa, Tabasco: "We gave advice to the gays there, because many of them, for x problems with the family, with work, school, were ashamed and went pretending that they weren't gay, but when they see us up in the ring, photographed in magazines and they know about us from the news reports, then it's like they feel like they have more freedom to be themselves."[83]

For the Renovación 2000 contingent, this had different implications for the sport than did the participation of women (who do not, after all, wrestle against men). The Exóticos, unlike women, undermined the representation of masculinity on display in the arena. Perhaps if the trio played their role as only a role, the traditionalists might have seen them as the latest version of an older form. Instead, the Exóticos presented their role as a social identity and so the Renovacionistas saw them as a degeneration of the lucha libre tradition by promoters who will do anything to gain a television audience.[84]

The complaint that I heard most frequently from associates of Renovación 2000, however, had to do with bodies. The wrestler, they said, was supposed to represent something. If a wrestler walked down the street, people were supposed to know it. Even if he fought incognito, they should be able to say, "Ah, there goes a wrestler." Thus, the physical development of the (male) wrestler was supposed to be directed to the formation of a thick, muscular physique. Even though the Mexican style emphasizes agility over size, the wrestler was not supposed to look like a soccer player or a bicyclist. His physique was supposed to be on display in the arena, and thus certain types of costume were preferable to others.

In the early days of lucha libre, most wrestlers wore a pair of boots, a pair of trunks and, in some cases, a mask. The typical wrestling mask was a smooth piece of fabric that completely covered the face and head with trim around the eye, nose, and mouth holes, and perhaps some discreet insignia. To this basic costume might be added tights, knee pads, and/or a tank top. The overall effect called attention to the wrestler's musculature, especially his bare (or nearly bare) torso and arms. Traditionalists were thus critical of a style of costume promoted by Antonio Peña that featured ever more elabo-

43. Novice wrestlers, bodies fully covered, wrestle at the Arena Caracol in the State of Mexico, November 21, 1997. Photo by author.

rate covering of the body. The costumes, worn by some of the Triple A wrestlers, consisted of boots, tights, briefs, a jersey that completely covered the arms, and elaborate masks with horns, beaks, or other extensions (see Figure 43). The physique of the wrestler was obscured by the costume, a physique, traditionalists complain, that was not meaty enough to be convincing as a wrestler's body.[85]

Behind their aesthetic critique (which I also heard from aspiring wrestlers planning their costumes) lay questions about labor conditions and copyright, for the fully covered body has the power to disrupt the ambiguous relationship between the wrestler and the character. That disruption lay at the root of Máscara Sagrada's conflict with the Triple A. Prior to the current round of televised wrestling, ownership of the wrestler's character was assumed to reside with the wrestler. Antonio Peña, however, made a point of copyrighting the characters that he promoted (and says he developed).[86] In promoting the Máscara Sagrada spinoffs, Peña asserted ownership of the character, a character fully alienable from the wrestler who embodies it. When the original Máscara Sagrada left, he simply put another wrestler into the costume. Thus, in 1997 there were two Máscara Sagradas in circulation, one belonging to the Triple A and the other (the "original") still with Pro-moAzteca. Even more disturbing to my informants was the case of the wrestler Pentagón, who was disabled by a neck injury sustained in the ring in 1994. Many wrestlers were unnerved when Peña hired another wrestler to wear the Pentagón costume without consulting the original or explicitly marking (with Jr. or II or other indicator) the fact that it was a different man.[87]

The question of costume, therefore, is enmeshed in discourses about tradition, embodiment, and labor rights. A traditionally masked wrestler hides the face to better display the body. In concealing his or her identity, he or she heightens the identification between wrestler and character. A fully covered, elaborately masked wrestler, on the other hand, cannot embody the physical ideal and becomes interchangeable with others in the same costume. For wrestlers and others in the world of lucha libre, the idiosyncrasies of performance (the fixed ending, the right of the rudos to cheat) do not constitute fraud, but the interchangeability of wrestlers does. The shift in costume style, in their analysis, spoke directly to questions of authenticity.

But beyond such aesthetic matters, the main concern of the Renovación 2000 partisans was the decline in attendance at lucha libre functions with the advent of televised wrestling. As predicted in 1991, arena revenues fell. Many neighborhood arenas closed down (Raúl Reyes, for example, shut down three of his four arenas), and in July 1997 even the EMLL had to close the smallest of its three arenas in the Federal District, the Pista Arena Revolución (which used to operate three days a week). Some wrestlers outside of the televised empresas complained to me that they had gone from working several days a week to a few days a month.

In the eyes of the Renovación 2000 group, this decline was not due to televised broadcast per se, but to the fact that the televised empresas had abandoned their public. The problem, some argued, was not that potential spectators wanted to see more blood or more acrobatics, but that the true aficionados of real lucha libre did not want to have to leave their neighborhoods and could no longer afford ticket prices at the remaining arenas.[88] Others blamed the decline in attendance to generalized malaise, resulting from overuse of novelties (blood, props, disrespect to referees and audience, etc.) and a subsequent decline in the quality of wrestling available to spectators. The Renovación traditionalists tried to address both of these issues. They held events in gyms, dance halls, and other spaces in marginal neighborhoods, charging "popular prices" (5 or 10 pesos). The functions would feature several matches between novices recruited by Alanís and ending with a match between stars of the EMLL. Reyes would attend the events and stop the matches if the wrestlers did something, such as hitting another wrestler with a chair, that violated the empresa's directives. He acted, in other words, as commissioners were said to do in lucha libre's golden age. But the Renovacionistas did not believe that their efforts would save lucha libre. Its recovery, in their analysis, depended on reestablishing the control of the Commission of Lucha Libre over the content of the spectacle.

During 1997, when the term of acting secretary Luis González was about to end, various discontented parties (including Renovación 2000, the Association, independents like my teacher, and some members of the wrestling press) began to demand increased intervention in lucha libre by the *state*, in the form of a strengthened commission. As noted before, in the 1980s, Association militants discovered that lucha libre had no formal regulation. The commission had no legally binding authority and thus no formal power to authorize or prohibit functions in the Federal District. That authority lay, instead, with the political delegation of the neighborhood where the match was to take place.[89] In the eyes of the traditionalists, that meant that wrestlers had no recourse against those who would degrade their art. As Hara Kiri complained: "Even if the secretary or president of the commission was to put forward a very complete plan to regulate the spectacle, if the promoter already complied with his documentation, it would mean nothing. That's why lucha libre has degenerated. Because if the gentleman has complied with the requisites of the corresponding state, municipality, and delegation, and they authorized the function, the gentleman could put a person in to wrestle with a lion. . . . And if the gentleman says to a wrestler 'You're going to dress like a monkey and swing from the lights,' that's it."[90]

The Renovación wrestlers with whom I worked lived in areas of the city that were, by then, strongholds of support for the Partido de la Revolución Democrática (PRD), the leftist opposition party that won the municipal elections that July.[91] Some had worked with the asamblea de barrios and with Superbarrio since the late 1980s. They hoped to use those connections to ask the new government to "return" lucha libre to the control of the commission by granting it the legal authority to regulate the spectacle—to regulate not only work conditions, but to determine what could or could not count as real Mexican lucha libre.

Conclusion

Professional wrestling may not seem a likely site to play out conflicts over neoliberal economics or cultural authenticity, yet lucha libre has been the locus of just such struggles, particularly in relation to questions of mass mediation. Both times that the sport was televised, it precipitated a crisis that reconfigured relationships among participants in the sport and between the sport and the state.

Lucha libre underwent a complex series of resignifications after its arrival in 1933. It started as a ritual of modernization, linked to processes of migration and urbanization centered in the Federal District. This set of associations might have been reinforced or changed in other ways in the 1950s had its run on television lasted longer. Instead, the exposure that television gave it brought it under greater scrutiny by the state. That scrutiny strengthened the hand of the commission and reinforced the links between state institutions and the occupational subculture of the wrestlers.

As a further result, lucha performance was confined to spaces that, in that moment, were strongly marked as popular, or even naco. The ban on broadcast guaranteed that it would continue as a class-specific, neighborhood-centered performance. This eventually made the genre reconfigurable as a quasi-artisanal practice to the artistic and political avant-garde. Artists and organizers came to view it both as a source of imagery and as an exemplary nonalienated ritual of lived urban reality. Thus resignified, it gained a measure of respectability that carried it out of its niche.

Its return to television in the 1990s precipitated another crisis. In many ways it paralleled the conflicts of the 1950s: Televicentro/Televisa challenged the hegemony of the EMLL in their attempts to control the spectacle, and the competition, conflicts, and alliances between rival empresas became enmeshed in competition among rival broadcasters. In the 1950s, the conflict between empresas and networks was resolved by the actions of the state in ways that seem to have benefited the EMLL (at the expense of its biggest rival) and kept lucha libre independent of the exigencies of television.

In many ways, the conflicts of the 1990s echoed those of the 1950s. First, the decision to televise lucha libre proved controversial in both cases. Second, the broadcasts led to a complex set of alliances and enmities between and among wrestling impresarios, broadcasters, and politicians. The antagonism between Televisa and TV Azteca, for example, went well beyond "competition," and was part of a larger set of conflicts playing out between different factions of the PRI. The rivalries among the EMLL, the Triple A, and PromoAzteca reflected those of their sponsoring networks.

In the 1990s, the success of televised broadcast imposed a different structure on the event and a different relationship between performers and spectators. A conflation of labor and aesthetic issues then led wrestlers, fans, and reporters to ask what constitutes lucha libre. Are promoters, as the name implies, free (*libre*) to make of it whatever the market demands? Can or should the conventions of its performance be regulated by the state? The response of Renovación 2000 made sense within this context and clarified stakes of the EMLL–Triple A conflict. Lucha libre's transition to a televised genre was implicated in the shift from an economic and ideological complex based on import substitution to one based on neoliberal globalization.[92]

The traditionalists saw television alienate lucha libre from the space of the arenas and the communities in which the arenas were located. Lucha's traditional audience, less able to afford tickets, is now more likely to bypass the arenas and watch at home, while a new, young, middle-class audience has learned to enjoy the imagery without the gestalt of the arena.[93] Many luchadores welcomed the return to television, eager for the level of celebrity it could offer those lucky enough to succeed (even as the broadcasts made fewer jobs available). But those displaced by televised lucha libre embraced and resignified the assessment of the artists who celebrated the genre in the 1970s and 1980s. In what is, in effect, a critique of the neoliberal stance of the large empresas, they make a claim: that lucha libre, a practice that many believe to be intrinsically vulgar, intrinsically corrupt, is instead a popular tradition worthy of the state's protection from corruption and vulgarization.

Epilogue

Renovación 2000's candidates for president and secretary of the commission were passed over in 1998. Rafael Barradas was reappointed to the commission as secretary, the wrestler Fantasma was appointed as president, and Renovación 2000 fell apart shortly thereafter. TV Azteca decided not to renew its contract with PromoAzteca. The latter still functions as an empresa, but now there are rumors that it had been secretly co-owned by Antonio Peña all along. Yet another empresa, the Grupo Revolucionario Internacional de Lucha Libre (based in Naucalpan in the State of Mexico), now broadcasts matches on Friday nights on ESPN2. Televisa continues to offer four hours of lucha libre a week. Although the arenas are often half empty, the live event continues to attract its public. They come week after week to cheer on the técnicos and curse the rudos (or vice versa).

If Antonio Peña was really a partner in PromoAzteca, perhaps the entire episode was just a lucha libre metamatch—where, despite the appearance of implacable hostility, rudos and técnicos are always working together behind the scenes. So perhaps the last word belongs to the wrestler Canek.

Canek is a star, one of the few wrestlers affiliated with Lucha Libre Internacional who can always get work on his own terms. I spoke to him one day when I was in a wrestling gym, interviewing the patrons. When I asked other wrestlers there what they thought of the changes of the past decade, all responded eagerly, recounting the damage that had been done to the sport and the community of professional wrestlers by the Triple A and Televisa. Finally, I went to talk to a dark, muscular, and taciturn wrestler I knew to be the famous Canek. He agreed to the interview reluctantly, just before starting his daily weight routine. Finally, I asked him what *he* thought of the changes lucha libre had undergone since his debut in the 1970s. Turning to the weight bench, he growled laconically, "There haven't been any changes. It's like Mexican history: it never changes."

Notes

1 Lucha libre is organized by empresas, which are private enterprises minimally consisting of a promoter and a stable of wrestlers. An empresa might or might not own its own arena(s). A "promoter" may be an owner of an empresa, or an agent for individual wrestlers, or an arena owner. An empresa without an arena is in an inherently unstable position, as is an arena owner without wrestlers. All translations are my own unless otherwise noted.

2 Sharon Mazer, *Professional Wrestling: Sport and Spectacle* (Jackson: University of Mississippi Press, 1998), 4.

3 Susan Birrell and Alan Turowetz, "Character Workup and Display: Collegiate Gymnastics and Professional Wrestling," in *Sport and the Sociocultural Process*, ed. M. Hart and S. Birrell (New York: William C. Brown, 1984), 589. For most observers, the main difference between professional and amateur wrestling is that the outcome of professional matches is arranged in advance. There used to be some disagreement over whether this was, in fact, the case and whether the audience was aware of it. When the World Wrestling Federation argued that it should be exempt from taxes on sporting events, it was on those grounds: because the ending was fixed, it was not a sport. Thus, the fixed ending can no longer be considered a secret, even an open secret, in the United States. This has not happened in Mexico. Because I trained in lucha libre and interacted with the people in the wrestling world in good faith, I am not comfortable with stating, publicly and in print, that the endings are prearranged

(although I would not be the first person in the wrestling world to do so). However, because the fixed ending has become common knowledge in the United States, it seems absurd to pretend that it is a secret. I hereby resolve this dilemma by stating that the endings are, in fact, predetermined, even though much of what happens in the course of a match is improvised—but I am burying that fact in a footnote.

4   Charles Morrow Wilson, *The Magnificent Scufflers: Revealing the Great Days When America Wrestled the World* (Brattleboro, VT: Brattleboro Press, 1959); Athol Oakley, *Blue Blood on the Mat: The All In Wrestling Story* (London: Paulie, 1971). Wilson traces catch-as-catch-can to a wrestling style popular in rural Vermont called "collar-and-elbow." In the Greco-Roman style that was popular in European exhibition wrestling before the 1920s, contact below the waist is forbidden, and a wrestler can win only by pinning both an opponent's shoulders to the mat. In collar-and-elbow and catch-as-catch-can, a wrestler can use legholds and can win by pinning an opponent or by putting the opponent in a submission hold. Both collar-and-elbow and catch-as-catch-can depend on skill and speed more than size, and thus make it possible for wrestlers of different sizes to wrestle each other.

5   Jeffrey Mondak, "The Politics of Professional Wrestling," *Journal of Popular Culture* 23, no. 2 (1989): 144.

6   The A&E video *The Unreal Story of Professional Wrestling*, produced by Steve Allen and Chris Martensen (New York: A&E Home Video, 1998) attributes the decline to the Depression and to the 1932 publication of *Fall Guys: The Barnums of Bounce* by Marcus Griffin, a tell-all account by a disgruntled journalist, who revealed that the endings were fixed. Charles Murrow Wilson (*The Magnificent Scufflers*) blames radio, observing that it encouraged the development of sports such as baseball that lend themselves to linear narrative at the expense of more visual spectacles like wrestling. Mondak ("The Politics of Professional Wrestling") claims, to the contrary, that professional wrestling was popular throughout the 1930s. He argues that, in the United States, its popularity follows cyclical peaks that correlate with periods of intensified isolationist sentiment. He claims that the 1930s, 1950s, and 1980s are three such periods.

7   Lee Austin Thompson, "Professional Wrestling in Japan: Media and Message," *International Review for the Sociology of Sport* 21 (1986): 65–81. At first, promoters brought foreign wrestlers to wrestle each other, but they soon recruited Japanese talent as well. In one important sense, Japanese wrestling closely followed the U.S. model. U.S. wrestlers usually assume characters that represent national, ethnic, or social types (this is not as common in Mexico). The stock villains are enemy foreigners: Germans before and after World War II; Russians during the cold war; Arabs, Iranians, and Iraqis in the 1980s and 1990s. Likewise, in Japan, promoters staged matches as dramas about the recuperation of national pride after the war, with Japanese good guys ultimately defeating nefarious, usually American, foreigners.

8   EMLL press packet; *Excélsior*, 31 May 1922, section 2, 6.

9   The first wrestling mask used in Mexico was designed by Antonio H. Martínez, a shoemaker and wrestling fan, at the request of a North American wrestler, Cyclone Mackay. He asked Martínez to design a mask that would be "like a hood, like for the Ku Klux Klan," so that he could tour as the Masked Marvel (Victor Martínez, personal communication, 14 May 1997). Antonio Martínez's son, Victor, took over the business when his father died and remains Mexico's premier maker of custom-made wrestling masks.

The Masked Marvel character was first used in the United States by a wrestler named Mort Henderson in 1915. Several other wrestlers later appeared as the Masked Marvel, among them Ray Steele, Bulldog Bill Ganon, and Rebel Bob Russel. The Masked Marvel thus appears to have worked as a shtick rather than a regular character in U.S. wrestling. See Joe Jares, *Whatever Happened to Gorgeous George* (Englewood, NJ: Prentice Hall, 1974), 95.

10 "Doña Vicky" Aguilera, a woman who became know as lucha libre's most loyal fan, saw her first match in 1934 at the Ferrocarríl Cintura Arena Roma Mérida ("Doña Virginia, Toda una Existencia Dedicada a La Lucha Libre," *La Jornada*, 13 February 1989, 21).

11 Salvador Novo nostalgically recalls going the rounds of these arenas before 1943 in *México en el Período Presidencial de Manuel Avila Camacho* (Mexico City: Empresas Editoriales, 1965), 35.

12 The Frontón Metropolitano was a venue for watching and gambling on jai alai, located in a neighborhood to the north of the Bosque de Chapultepec. Jai alai spectatorship had long been a pastime of Spanish-identified elites, but was falling out of fashion in the 1940s (Anne Rubenstein, personal communication May 15, 1998.)

13 B. R. Mitchell, *International Historical Statistics: The Americas 1759–1993* (New York: Stockton Press, 1994), 4–44. Between 1950 and 1990, the population of the Federal District continued to grow at an even faster rate, and the metropolitan area absorbed several areas of the State of Mexico.

14 Salvador Novo, "Mi Lucha (Libre)," in *México en el Período de Lázaro Cárdenas* (Mexico City: Consejo Nacional para Cultura y las Artes, 1994), 600.

15 Ibid., 602.

16 See Anne Rubenstein, "Raised Voices at the Cine MonteCarlo," *Journal of Family History* 23:3, July 1998: 312–23; Eric Zolov, *Refried Elvis: The Rise of the Mexican Counterculture* (Berkeley: University of California Press, 1999), 47–49.

17 Fernando Mejía Barquera, "Televisión y Deporte," in *Apuntes para una historia de la Televisión Mexicana II* (Mexico City: La Revista Mexicana de Comunicación, 1999), 202–3; Rafael Barradas Osorio, *Fuera Máscaras* (Mexico City: Mi Lucha para Limpios y Rudos, n.d.), 148. For some reason, none of the veterans that I interviewed (including Rafael Barradas) ever mentioned the O'Farrill–EMLL broadcasts. The 1950s are remembered as "the era of Televicentro," when there was no competition among television stations or empresas (in contrast with the conflict-ridden present; see below).

18 Nelson Carro, *El Cine de Los Luchadores* (Mexico City: Cineteca de la UNAM, 1993), 47. Wrestling movies were still made in the 1990s, but they were far less popular than they used to be, and they were turned out at a much slower rate.

19 Barradas Osorio, *Fuera Máscaras*, and personal communication, 24 February 1997.

20 Mejía Barquera, "Televisión y Deporte," 203.

21 Manuel Seyde, "La Lucha por la Vida," *Revista de Revistas*, 4 April 1953, 74. Barradas Osorio, *Fuera Máscaras*, 149.

22 Up to 1997, the regency (mayoralty) of Mexico City was a presidential appointment and was considered an important federal post.

23 Barradas Osorio, *Fuera Máscaras*, 149. It is interesting that Barradas imagined viewing to take place in an isolated, individualized context, which is quite different from the context that viewers remember.

24 José Agustín, *Tragicomedia Mexicana* (Mexico City: Editorial Planeta, 1990), 1:136–37.

25 John Cross, *Informal Politics* (Stanford, CA: Stanford University Press, 1999), 160–87.

26 Anne Rubenstein, *Bad Language, Naked Ladies and Other Threats to the Nation* (Durham, NC: Duke University Press, 1998), 96–99.

27 According to veteran luchadora Irma González, women began wrestling in Mexico in the 1940s (personal communication, 16 December 1997).

28 *Lucha Libre* (1 April 1954): 5. Médico Asesino wore a white mask, similar to the silver mask worn by El Santo (see below). Chucho is a diminutive form of Jesús.

29 The interesting thing about the three "dispositions" is that they are about maintaining the boundaries among performers, the public, and the representative of (state) authority. Indeed, as Barradas explained: "Of the twenty eight rules . . . I left three—of order, nothing more—not to wrestle below [the ring], to prevent accidents with the public; not to hit the referee, because he is an authority; and not to insult the public. They must be respected because their ticket makes the spectacle possible" (personal communication, 24 February 1997). The rules were always unevenly enforced (in fact, at present they are never enforced) and are not really the only rules of performance. There are, for example, rules defining the parameters of the event—the size of the ring, and so on—not to mention the rules of the sport itself. In addition, the prohibition against women wrestling within the Federal District remained in effect until 1986.

The most important power of the commission, however, was (and remains) that of licensing wrestlers and referees to work in the Federal District.

30 Barradas Osorio, *Fuera Máscaras*, 149.

31 Outside of the Federal District, lucha libre remained (for the most part) a traveling show that was relatively unregulated. Townspeople of all social classes attended the periodic events that often included displays by luchadoras (women wrestlers) as well as (or even instead of) male wrestlers.

32 My source is the *Anuario Estadístico de Los Estados Unidos Mexicanos*, vols. 31, 33, 34 (Mexico City: Secretaría de Industria y Comercio, Dirección General de Estadística, Talleres Gráfico de la Nación, 1993, 1967, 1971). In 1959, the *Anuario* lists two venues for lucha libre, three for soccer, and one for bullfighting. The number of tickets sold is listed as 460,000 (lucha libre), 727,000 (soccer), and 418,000 (bullfight). In 1965 (when Arenas México, Coliseo, and Pista Arena Revolución were all open) it lists one venue for lucha libre (1,011,000 tickets sold), one venue for soccer (2,911,000), and one venue for the bullfight (695,000), so these figures cannot be taken literally, but they do indicate the relative popularity of lucha libre. Baseball, in contrast, attracted only 141,000 ticket holders in 1959, and 164,000 in 1965.

33 In 1969, Ciudad Nezahualcóyotl, the largest of the "mushroom cities" that grew up around the Federal District, seemingly overnight, already had three wrestling arenas and a bullring that was often used for lucha libre events. See Carlos G. Velez-Ibañez, *Rituals of Marginality* (Berkeley: University of California Press, 1983).

34 Martin C. Needler, *Mexican Politics: The Containment of Conflict* (Westport, CT: Praeger, 1995), 14.

35 Cited in Carlos Monsiváis, *Escenas de Pudor y Liviandad* (Mexico City: Grijalbo, 1981), 89.

36 Claudio Lomnitz, "Fissures in Contemporary Mexican Nationalism," *Public Culture* 9 (1996): 56.

37 Clifford Geertz, "Deep Play: Notes on the Balinese Cockfight," in *The Interpretation of Cultures* (New York: Basic Books, 1973), 412–54.

38 For a summary of the "classical" Mexican political system, see Needler, *Mexican Politics*; see also Agustín, *Tragicomedia Mexicana*; Claudio Lomnitz and Ilya Adler, "The Function of the Form," in *Constructing Culture and Power in Latin America*, ed. Daniel Levine (Ann Arbor: University of Michigan Press, 1993), 357–402.

Even the terms técnico and rudo echo a political discourse that emerged in the 1970s. Técnico marks one side of two traditionally opposed tendencies within the PRI: the técnicos (technicians or technocrats) versus the *políticos* (politicians). It is a split between a politics based (in theory) on rational management, and one based on negotiation of personal loyalties. Although the técnicos may be seen as a tendency within the PRI, that tendency (which privileges efficiency and modernization) has been important in the ideological justification of the PRI's rule, for the party has consistently portrayed itself as a force for rational modernization regardless of the use of tactics that could be seen as militating against such rationality. In a sense, then, support for the técnico wrestler could be read as a kind of support for the government, or at least for a vision of modernization that the Mexican state has endorsed. *Rudo* also has a range of meanings beyond that of "crude." One of its connotations, at least in Mexico City, is that of an urban tough: someone from the city, with little formal education but plenty of street smarts, both product and master of the urban environment. In a sense, then, luchadores portrayed a contest between opposed models of urban comportment. I discuss the moral economy of lucha libre performance in detail in my dissertation (forthcoming).

39 Although very few middle-class Mexicans told me that they have been to a wrestling match, I have yet to hear anyone from Mexico City claim that he or she has never seen an El Santo movie.

40 The term *popular culture* has come to mean very different things in Anglo and Latin contexts; in Great Britain and the United States, it usually refers to television, rock music, fan magazines, and other products of the "culture industry." In this usage, popular culture (whether reviled or celebrated) is basically coterminous with mass-mediated culture. In Italian, French, and Latin American usage, however, popular culture is the culture of the subaltern classes. It may be imagined as a site of authenticity and resistance, in contrast to inauthentic and/or hegemonic mass (-mediated) culture.

41 Claudio Lomnitz Adler, *Exits from the Labyrinth: Culture and Ideology in Mexican National Space* (Berkeley: University of California Press, 1992), 2.

42 Zolov, *Refried Elvis*, 258.

43 Felipe Ehrenberg, personal communication, 9 November 1996.

44 Lourdes Grobet, personal communication, 3 May 1999.

45 Marcos Rascón Bandas, personal communication, 10 March 1997.

46 Ecologista Universal is a wrestler who appeared in Veracruz to protest the construction of the Laguna Verde nuclear power plant the same year that Superbarrio appeared to represent the asamblea de barrios. Ecologista advocates for the integration of environmental concerns with a broader program of social justice. Other social wrestlers include SuperAn-

imal, Mujer Maravilla, and SuperNiño, who advocate for the rights of animals, women, and street children, respectively.

47 Marcos Rascón Bandas, one of Superbarrio's "intellectual authors," remembers the moment of his creation thus: "At one moment we found out that there was going to be a demonstration against an eviction, with a lot of people. Two thousand people got up to defend a girl over in one of the buildings in La Merced, and on the way back . . . when we got back, we remembered what we wanted to do in 1983, [now that it was] four years later. And so we got the idea of giving the asemblea de barrios SuperBarrio. We began to talk, and the SuperBarrio thing came out. And from there, with the ladies who came to the meetings, some went to get the tights, others the trunks, others to find the mask" (personal communication.)

48 Ibid.

49 Ecologista Universal, personal communication, 18 January 1996.

50 Felipe Ehrenberg, personal communication, 9 November 1996.

51 Jeffery Mondak has argued that pro wrestling in the United States peaks in popularity during cyclical waves of nationalist, xenophobic sentiment, and the Reagan era was one such period. During the jingoist fervor of the mid-1980s, the World Wrestling Federation, under the direction of Vince MacMahon Jr., began to emphasize the theatrical, verbal aspects of the spectacle. It proved a successful strategy that brought professional wrestling back to mainstream television.

52 Description of these events relies primarily on articles that appeared in the newspaper *Afición* and the wrestling magazine *Box y Lucha* from 1992 to 1993 and from 1996 to 1998 and interviews, conversations, and gossip with members of Renovacíon 2000, the Asociación Nacional de Luchadores, Referís y Retirados, and unaffiliated wrestlers. Many thanks to all, and my special and affectionate thanks to Irma González, Irma Aguilar, and Hara Kiri for their generous assistance.

53 The change in policy came about after the secretary of tourism polled children in a number of schools about what sporting event they would like to see in honor of the U.N. Year of the Child. Unsurprisingly, 75 percent wanted to see the forbidden lucha libre. The commission, together with the EMLL, organized a special, "clean" event in Arena Coliseo, and because nothing bad happened, the empresa was given permission to continue to allow minors into the arena (Barradas Osorio, *Fuera Máscaras*, 153).

54 CTM (Confederación de Trabajadores Mexicanos) and CROC (Confederación Revolucionaria de Obreros y Campesinos) are both confederations of labor unions. CROC was founded in 1952 as an alternative to the more powerful CTM, which was under the firm control of labor leader Fidel Velázquez (Agustín, *Tragicomedia Mexicana*, 1:122–29).

55 Juan Alanís also worked for the CROC-affiliated waiters union. The two unions (waiters and wrestlers) share offices and, to some extent, resources.

56 Juan Alanís, personal communication, 15 May 1997. The ban on luchadoras was probably a verbal order given by Ernesto Uruchurtu, regent of the Federal District, at some point in the 1950s.

57 "The EMLL wants to do away with their antagonists from El Toreo [Cuatro Caminos], or, the same thing, they want to liquidate (promotorily) [*sic*] Don Carlos Maynez and all of the small *empresas*, so that they are left with nothing more than to accept the servitude of

the EMLL" ("*La EMLL Coarta La Libre Expresion*" *Suplemento de Lucha Libre* [31 October 1991]: 2). Lucha Libre Internacional broadcast on the public television station Imevisión for a few months, but the quality of the broadcasts was very low, and they did not develop an audience. See "Espaldas Claras," *Box y Lucha* (15 March 1992): 29; "Yo Mejoraría las Transmisiones de los Independientes Cambinado de Canal y Locutores: Dr. Wagner Jr., *Box y Lucha* (1 May 1992): 26.

58 "Manny Guzmán es un Líder Nefasto: Justiciero," *Afición*, 3 April 1992. According to some of my informants, the return to television happened at a moment when the Sindicato was particularly unstable. Around 1990, under the leadership of union president Manny Guzmán, the Sindicato began to charge arena owners a 50 peso per wrestler insurance fee. This represented a significant expense for smaller arena owners, compromising their ability to hire more than a few wrestlers per night. During the same period, wrestlers who approached the union to collect their pensions or other compensation were told that the organization was bankrupt (Irma González and Hara Kiri, personal communication, 20 December 1997).

59 Peña's job included acting as promoter. Promoters of individual wrestlers are not only responsible for managing the appearances of their clients but are usually the masterminds behind the personae adopted by the wrestlers. Wrestlers thus owe their promoter not only their support in getting into the arenas but their professional identity.

60 Barradas Osorio, personal communication, 24 February 1997. For the interview with Conan, see Lola Miranda Fascinetto, *Sin Máscara ni Cabellera* (Mexico City: Marc Ediciones, 1995), 29. Conan the Barbarian is currently working in the United States with the WCW (World Championship Wrestling).

61 "Inicia Actividades la Nueva Empresa Luchística," *Afición*, 1 March 1992, 28.

62 Despite the blows to the commission's legitimacy in the mid-1980s, wrestlers still regard the Federal District commission as a more active and authoritative body than other, regional commissions.

63 "La EMLL Da a Conocer su Postura ante la Nueva Competencia," *Afición*, 7 May 1992, 25.

64 "No Habrá Oposición a las Funciones de la 'AAA': SNL," *Afición*, 15 May 1992, 25.

65 "Pugnarán Promotores del Edomex por Evitar Funciones de Intrusos," *Afición*, 15 May 1992, 25.

66 "Nace un Nuevo Sindicato Pancratista, Afiliado a la C. O. M.," *L'Afición*, 8 May 1992, 29. Justiciero had already been blackballed from the Sindicato Nacional in April.

67 "El S.N.L Realizó Marcha en Contra de las Transmisiones de Luchas Por TV," *Box y Lucha* (25 June 1993): 9.

68 One implication of televised wrestling is that the most prestigious matches may take place outside the jurisdiction of the Federal District commission.

69 Wrestling audiences can be very aggressive toward wrestlers, but I've never seen (or heard of) audience members becoming seriously aggressive toward one another.

70 Juanito Díaz, personal communication, 6 April 1997.

71 Insulting wrestlers is an important part of fan participation, but the case of Vampiro Canadiense is unusual. First, his detractors don't break down along rudo/técnico lines. Second, insults are usually not about technical skill. More common are cries of *matonero* (gang-uper), *metiche* (busybody), *maricón* (faggot), and others. The closest thing to "x doesn't know

how to wrestle" that one usually hears in the arena is "No puede" ("x can't do it") or "Sólo así puede" ("x can only do it that [dishonest or cowardly] way"), which is quite different.

72 TV Azteca summarized and responded to Televisa's charges in a two-page advertisement in *La Jornada* ("Las 20 Mentiras de Emilio Azcárraga y Ricardo Rocha," 4 November 1996, 26, 39).

73 An anonymous source gave me the following account. Pedro Ortega knew Ricardo Salinas Pliego because he gave massages to the latter's father (like many wrestlers, he was also a part-time chiropractor/massage therapist). He approached Raúl Reyes with the idea of collaborating on a function to be broadcast by TV Azteca. The event was broadcast, and was well received. Reyes authorized Ortega and their lawyer to sign the contract, naming them as president and secretary, respectively, but Ortega cut Reyes out of the deal. Later, he was invited to join the new empresa Renovación 2000 in the capacity of president (see below).

74 Jr.s, IIs, and sons-of are ideally sons or nephews of veterans, but the relationship is often spurious. Even when the Jr. (or whatever) is not related to the original, the connection is worked out with the cooperation and sometimes remuneration of the original.

75 Interview with group of thirteen wrestlers from PromoAzteca, *En Caliente*, Channel 13 (29 October 1996). The use of the term "dinosaur" resonates particularly with a then current derogatory term for old-style PRI militants who had come up through party ranks and were associated with corruption and stagnation.

76 "Konnan [*sic*] Engaña al Público, Afirma Perro Aguayo," *La Jornada*, 7 November 1996, 52.

77 Although the EMLL fully participated in the televisualization of lucha libre, the empresa allied itself with Renovación 2000 partly to make common cause against Peña and the Triple A, and partly because it promoted itself as the "serious and stable" empresa, defenders of "real" lucha libre (as opposed to the Triple A).

78 This was a radical departure from the neopop agenda, which looked to lucha libre as a cultural performance that had evaded state co-optation.

79 Irma González, one of the first luchadoras, encountered a great deal of harassment from male colleagues when she started wrestling in the late 1940s. Luchadores would accuse the women of taking their jobs, and play tricks on them, such as gluing their shoes to the dressing room floor (Irma González, personal communication, 20 December 1997). Luchadoras who started in the 1980s and 1990s, on the other hand, did not report incidents of overt harassment by male colleagues. Nevertheless, there are many luchadores who do not believe that women should wrestle. In the best of cases, women's place in lucha libre is still marginalized, as they are almost never positioned as the main event.

80 Although the term *exótico* is clearly related to the term *raro*, a commonly used word that roughly translates as "queer," I've never heard exótico used to describe gay or transgendered males outside the context of lucha libre. In general, exótico is used to describe a male wrestler who cross-dresses or displays mannerisms usually coded as female. Capitalized, Los Exóticos refers to a particular team of three exóticos, May Flowers, Pimpernela Scarlata, and Casandra, who are the best-known (but not the only) exóticos presently active. I discuss exóticos in greater detail in Heather Levi, "Lean Mean Fightin' Queens: Drag in the World of *Lucha Libre*," *Sexualities* 1, no. 1 (August 1998): 275–85.

81 These wrestlers were contemporaries of the American wrestler Gorgeous George. Garde-

nia Davis was a wrestler from the United States who worked in Mexico. His shtick, handing out orchids to irritate the audience, was one of the inspirations for the Gorgeous George character. See Jares, *Whatever Happened to Gorgeous George*.

82 Quoted in Fascinetto, *Sin Máscara Ni Cabellera* 188.

83 Quoted in ibid., 192.

84 Ironically, Televisa banned Los Exóticos from performing in drag on the air. Instead, the three wrestlers appear on television as members of the "Vatos Locos," made up to look like members of the rock band Kiss. They wrestle as exóticos only in live performances that are not taped for broadcast (May Flowers, personal communication, 15 March 1999).

85 Despite the criticisms of full-body costumes that I often heard expressed by Renovación associates, many of their younger wrestlers wore the very costume styles that their spokespeople regarded with suspicion.

86 At the time of the research, several wrestlers contested Peña's claim to having created their characters. Other wrestlers credit Peña with inventing their characters, but I do not know whether he created all of the ones he copyrighted.

87 Wrestlers who complained about the use of Pentagón's costume also claimed that the Triple A had failed to make expected disability payments to the injured wrestler. Again, I do not know if the charges were warranted or not.

88 The remaining venues included centrally located arenas like the EMLL arenas and irregular, relatively expensive venues like the Toreo Cuatro Caminos. Ticket prices at Arena México usually ranged from about U.S.$2 to 7, and tickets at the Toreo cost from about U.S.$7 to 15 at the time of research (prices varied according to the event and the seat). A movie, by comparison, cost U.S.$1–3. There were, in fact, still a number of small arenas where Renovación and other minor empresas would charge less (U.S.$1.50–2).

89 Mexico City is divided into delegations, each consisting of several colonies (neighborhoods). A political delegation is an administrative body in charge of a given delegation and has the power to give out or deny permits, levy fines, and so on.

90 Hara Kiri, personal communication, 20 December 1997.

91 The person behind Superbarrio's mask was elected to the Camera de Deputados in the same election.

92 It is this shift that Claudio Lomnitz argues is at the root of the phenomenon of lo naco. See "Fissures in Contemporary Mexican Nationalism," 55–68.

93 Another factor that may have facilitated lucha libre's return to television was a change in patterns of cultural consumption in Mexico that Néstor García Canclini and his associates documented at the beginning of the 1990s. See Néstor García Canclini et al., "Mexico: Cultural Globalization in a Disintegrating City," *American Ethnologist* 22, no. 4 (1995): 743–55. In a survey of 1,500 homes in Mexico City in 1993, they found a trend toward domesticization of cultural consumption. Over 40 percent of their sample had not been to see a movie in over a year, and almost 25 percent reported that their major leisure activity was watching television. Presumably, attendance at lucha libre events would have been affected by this trend, whether it was televised or not.

Corazón del Rocanrol

Rubén Martínez

Mexico City, December 1990

Under a zinc-colored sky, a block away from the railroad tracks and next to a buzzing electrical substation, a young man with hair immaculately slicked back, wearing an oversize gray jacket, a starched white shirt, a fat 1940s tie, and black baggies with fob swinging low, takes giant strides as he leads me down the asphalt corridor toward the crowd ahead. "Now, you're going to see the true history of Mexican *rocanrol!*" he calls back over his shoulder, flapping along through the warm, smoggy breeze.

I scramble after him as we dive into the marketplace. Throngs of Mexico City youth in all manner of *rockero* regalia surround us: *chavas* in leather miniskirts or torn jeans, *chavos* wearing Metallica T-shirts, James Dean leather jackets, or Guatemalan-style *indígena* threads. We walk past stall after rickety stall, scraps of splintered wood and twine holding up faded blue tarpaulins, where vendors—young *punkeros* or *trasheros* (thrash fans), leathered heavy *metaleros*, Peace and Love *jipitecas*, and the working-class followers of Mexican raunch-rock heroes El Tri known as *chavos banda*—sell cassettes, CDS, LPS and singles, bootlegs and imports, as well as posters, steel-toed boots, skull earrings, fan mags, spiked bracelets and collars, incense, and feathered roach clips. Ghettoblasters blast Holland's Pestilence, Mexico's El Tri, Argentina's Charly García, Ireland's U2.

"*¡Tenemos punk, tenemos heavy metal, tenemos en español y en inglés, tenemos al Jim Morrison y El Tri!*" yells a young vendor, exactly as any one of Mexico's army of street vendors hawk rosaries or Chiclets. His is but one voice among hundreds at El Chopo, as the sprawling swap meet is known.

It's a Saturday afternoon, some ten years after this institution was born, and the vendors tell me that the crowd of about three thousand is on the light side. "What's *chingón* is that there's no divisions here between the different *rockeros*," proclaims Ricardo, a high school kid in a T-shirt emblazoned with the logo of the punk band Lard, a Vision Streetwear beret, and hip-hop hi-tops. "It doesn't matter whether you're hardcore or *trashero*."

Mexican authorities haven't distinguished among styles either: all are equally suspect. El Chopo is often raided by police eager to club skinheads and longhairs alike, Ricardo and his young punk friends say, as a jipiteca strolls by with a gleaming white Fender Precision bass, telling everyone that he'll let it go for one million pesos.

It isn't long before my zoot-suited guide is recognized. "Don't you play with La Maldita?" kids inquire, before asking for autographs. Roco, the lead singer of Maldita Vecindad y los Hijos del Quinto Patio (roughly, The Damned Neighborhood and The Sons of the Tenement), greets all comers effusively. "And don't forget to make the gig tonight! At LUCC, about midnight! *¡Órale, hijo!*"

We're already hopelessly late for a meeting with Maldita's manager on the other side of the city (a trip that takes about an hour and a half by subway and bus), but Roco is intent on getting me freebies. Already I'm loaded with copies of *La Pus Moderna*, one of city's underground magazines, along with more than a dozen LPs and cassettes by groups with names like Atóxxxico, Sedición, Psicodencia.

"It's the craziest city, *hijo*," Roco says, standing in place for a rare moment before a stall featuring a lithograph of Marilyn Monroe hanging next to another of Che Guevara. "Anything can happen here."

"We've received influences from all over," he adds, the words spilling out rapid and vowel-twisted, in classic Mexico City, or *chilango*, slang. "From the North, from the South, from Europe. It might be true that rock began in the North, but now it's all ours."

"Rock *en español*," reads the publicity slogan, "Music for a New Generation." Since the mid-1980s, in Mexico, Argentina, and Spain, *rocanrol* has been billed as the perpetual Next Big Thing. Record labels, mostly the Spanish and Latin American subsidiaries of majors like BMG, Sony, and WEA, signed dozens of bands. Stadium gigs drew huge crowds at most of the big capitals in Latin America.

Key groups lived up to the advance publicity: Mexico's Caifanes, a dark-pop band reminiscent of The Cure, sold a respectable 100,000 copies of their first album; a subsequent *cumbia* rock single, "La negra Tomasa," moved half a million. Other acts, such as Radio Futura and La Unión from Spain, Los Prisioneros from Chile, and Miguel Mareos and Soda Stereo from Argentina, sold well and garnered airplay throughout Latin America.

Impresarios also looked toward the United States and its relatively un-tapped Latino youth market; there have been impressive Latin-rock gigs in Los Angeles and other major U.S. cities since 1988. "L.A. is a meeting ground for rock from Latin America and Spain," says Enrique Blanc, a dee-jay at Rancho Cucamunga's KNSE, one of the few Spanish-rock supporters in the States. "And there are plenty of people with money who are inter-ested." Marusa Reyes, a transplanted *chilanga* producer living in Los Ange-les who handles both Caifanes and Maldita Vecindad, succeeded in convinc-ing Jane's Addiction to book a few shows with a special added attraction: none other than Maldita Vecindad y los Hijos del Quinto Patio.

Roco and the Chopo crowd want to shake Mexican culture to its very roots. But these heavier rockeros are still on the margins—and not because they necessarily like it there. It's the pop rockers like Menudo that have be-come megastars. As one veteran of the Mexico City rock wars put it, "The joke here has always been that *this* is the year real *rocanrol* is going to make it—and we've been saying it for thirty years."

In the summer of 1985, a group of chavos from different Mexico City bar-rios began holding jam sessions: a piano player, a vocalist, and six percus-sionists (water bottles, pots and pans), but nothing experimental about it. "Either we waited to save up and buy equipment, or we played with what we had," recalls Roco, his leg bouncing nervously up and down on the bar stool.

The city around them was on its knees, again, enduring the worst eco-nomic crisis since the revolution of 1910. A profound malaise contaminated all areas of life. Then, on the morning of September 19, 1985, Mexico City lurched over its liquid foundation, the ancient volcanic lake it was built on.

"It was total devastation, *cabrón*," Roco says, leaning into me and yelling over UB40's "Red Red Wine." "Whole *barrios* darkened, without electricity, water running everywhere, people carrying coffins, looking for their loved ones. The people of the *barrio* had to organize themselves to survive. All of a sudden, people I'd seen my entire life but didn't know, I knew."

Citizens' committees organized relief efforts much better than the gov-ernment, which had spurned international aid for the first two days after the quake, claiming it had "everything under control," until a second devastating *terremoto* made it clear that nobody controlled anything.

The city was transformed by the experience. Out of the rubble there arose all manner of new populist political personalities, including Superbarrio, a masked wrestler, whom the earthquake turned into an activist/performance artist who to this day shows up in his yellow cape and red suit wherever slumlords do their foul deeds. Cuauhtémoc Cárdenas nearly tossed the ruling PRI (Partido Revolucionario Institucional) dynasty out of office. In the midst of this upheaval, Maldita Vecindad y los Hijos del Quinto Patio were born.

The other members of La Maldita join Roco and me at our table, weaving through a crowd whose attire would fit in well in New York's East Village or on L.A.'s Melrose Avenue. These *niños bien* have paid 50,000 pesos (about U.S.$17) for Maldita's *tocada*, their gig. We're in the Zona Rosa, the Pink Zone, at Rockstock, a club whose logo bears a suspicious resemblance to the Hard Rock Café's.

In comes Pato, curly locks peeking out from under his trademark gray fedora, a veteran of several vanguard Mexican bands. Sax, at twenty-two the youngest of the group, is leaning toward a U2 look with long, straight hair and loose, gauzy white shirt. He's Maldita's purest musical talent, and moonlights with mariachi bands in the famous Garibaldi Plaza. Lobo, a dark, leathery rockero, is the quiet one who batters the congas. Elfin-smiling and clean-cut Aldo, born in Argentina but now a full-fledged Mexico City boy, is on bass. And Pacho, the oldest at twenty-nine, with head shaved close on one side and exploding curly on the other, is the drummer, an intellectual who studied anthropology at Mexico's finest university, UNAM. (Roco, too; he's finishing his degree in journalism.)

La Maldita huddle close together sipping Coronas and smoking Marlboros in Rockstock's cagelike no-smoking section. Their look—resonances of James Dean, Tin Tan (a Mexican comedic great of the 1940s and 1950s, who popularized a Chicano/Pachuco swing style), U2, and the Mexico City barrio kids of Buñuel's *Los Olvidados*—clashes wildly with that of the surrounding scenesters. Roco's wearing a pair of mammoth black work boots. He notices me eyeing them.

"They're just like my father's, *cabrón*," he says, lifting his foot up and inviting me to tap the steel toe. "They cost sixty thousand pesos, *cabrón*—not like those European ones that all the *niños bien* wear, that sell for three hundred thousand here in the Zona Rosa."

Maldita and other young bands, like Café Tacuba, Santa Sabina, and Tex Tex, lash out at the Americanization of the Mexican middle class, a tendency led by media giant Televisa. This corporation prides itself on nationalism, a tune that's made it millions and that the PRI government has also used to help keep itself in power for the past seventy years. It's a bastion of national pride, but Televisa is also accused of promoting *malinchismo*, a term that goes back five hundred years to La Malinche, Hernán Cortés's Aztec translator, the most famous traitor of Mexico's history.

Televisa's is a no-lose strategy: by backing both national and gringo, mainstream and underground, it's cornered all markets. But somehow, the Americanized acts always seem to fill the screen. Pato tells the story of the time Maldita did *not* meet Madonna at L.A.'s trendy Club Vertigo. Seems that somebody told somebody that Madonna was in the club the night of the band's first L.A. appearance. Though the band members swear they never met her, tabloid headlines hit home instantly: the blonde goddess had given the sons of Mexico her blessing. Upon returning to Mexico City, the band was deluged with press queries about their all-night party with Madonna.

"They wanted to know about her, nothing about us," recalls Aldo. Horrified, the band called a press conference to set the record straight. "But it made no difference," Aldo says, finishing his beer before he heads backstage. "They still ask us about her all the time."

When Maldita bounds on stage, they start without so much as a hello. They play with a precise fury, styles merged, overturned, and burned. Ska gives way to funk, funk to rap, rap to *son veracruzano*, to *danzón*, to cumbia and mambo on one of their anthemic numbers, "Bailando":

> No tengo ni puta idea porque quiero hoy salir
> lo último de mis ahorros me lo gastaré en ti
> en la fábrica dijeron, "Ya no nos sirves, Joaquín"
> para no perder dinero nos corrieron a dos mil
> hoy es viernes por la noche todos salen a bailar
> yo me apunto en el desmoche tengo ganas de gritar:
> ¡Ya no aguanto mas, quiero bailar![1]

A few kids sing along, some skitter perfunctorily about the dance floor. It seems the niños bien don't want to risk tearing a thread. But Roco doesn't care: he's bouncing up and down, spraying his legs like Elvis being chased

44. Maldita Vecindad y
los Hijos del Quinto
Patio. Publicity photo-
graph. Courtesy of Mal-
dita Vecindad/BMG
Records.

by *la migra*, diving down and nearly kissing the floor with the mike stand. His face flashes a grin, a sneer; now he jerks his head back repeatedly, as though he's being slapped by interrogators, while rapping his way through "Apañón," a song about police abuse of barrio youth:

> En un sucio callejón, despiertas sin recordar
> nada de lo que pasó, te duelen hasta los pies
> no traes dinero no traes zapatos y ya no traes pelo
> sales de ese callejón, ¡ODIANDO!²

Jesus, I'm thinking, Maldita have blasted on the wind of free-jazz sax past decades of balding trios, put the lie to the World Beaters by merging mambo, danzón, R & B, ska, and rap—within each song—exploding it all on stage with the rage and rapture of boys possessed by the most sacred of rock demons, and these kids (black-stockinged *chicas*, Mel Gibson *chavos*) aren't seriously dancing?

When Maldita's roadies begin to break down the equipment, UB40's

"Red Red Wine" again blares through the speakers. Suddenly, five hundred Zona Rosa kids are singing along in English, dancing so cool.

While the niños bien pride themselves on their Americanized hipness at Rockstock, elsewhere in the city a bunch of long-haired, wannabe gringo kids from Tampa, Florida, are playing before another crowd, having been billed as death-metal heroes from the North. On Televisa, surely, there is a fake blonde reading the news off a prompter. And all across the city on billboards and posters hung in liquor stores, buxom blondes are tonguing beer bottles, sucking cigarettes. Looks like La Malinche is alive and well and as sexy as she was five hundred years ago.

> Yo no soy un rebelde sin causa
> ni tampoco un desenfrenado
> yo lo único que quiero
> es bailar rocanrol[3]

The battle for the cultural soul of Mexican youth may well be as old as La Malinche. And Mexico City intellectuals are only half joking when they say that postmodernism actually originated here five hundred years ago, with the Conquest and its clash of radically different sensibilities. The tango, swing, and mambo have each arrived from distant lands and transformed the city's style. Even so, most of what was promoted on radio, vinyl, and the silver screen through the first half of the century was the sacred *cultura nacional*: mariachis and romantic balladeers like Augustín Lara and Pedro Infante.

When the first leather jackets and Elvis pompadours appeared on the streets of the barrios, the over-forty guardians of culture, nervous that Mexico City youth would arm themselves with switchblades and roar Harleys through elegant Zona Rosa establishments à la Marlon Brando in *The Wild One*, mounted an all-out assault. Films like *The Blackboard Jungle* were pulled from movie theaters and newspapers apprised the populace of the dangers of *rocanroleando*: gang violence, lax morality, and, especially, the destruction of *la cultura nacional*. Maybe the single thing the government, the Catholic Church, and the Marxist left could all agree on was that Mexican youth were imperiled by the Protestant, decadent, and individualistic North. But bandas like Los Locos del Ritmo, Los Apson Boys, Los Hooligans, Los Crazy Boys, and Enrique Guzmán y los Teen Tops all had avid followers.

Most songs from the early years were covers sung either in English or

45. During the early 1960s scores of Mexican rocanrol bands emerged throughout the country performing Spanish-language covers (*refritos*) of imported hits. Here we see Los Rebeldes del Rock during a live Radio Mil presentation in the capital, c. 1962. From Federico Arana, *Guaraches de ante azul*, vol. 1 (Mexico City: Posada, 1985), 187. Used by permission.

awkwardly translated into Spanish ("Hotel Descorazonado," "Rock de la cárcel," "Pedro Pistolas," "Un gran pedazo de amor"). Gradually, however, the translated covers of American hits became more than literal adaptations; Mexican rockeros began rewriting the lyrics. "Under the Boardwalk," for example, became "En un café." Though these tunes were often fluff, the feel of the songs was subtly shifting toward a Mexicanness that, many years later, would come to exemplify the best of the country's rock.

Lest the Old World version of cultura nacional be forever buried, the *oficialistas* made one final attempt to crush the rockeros. Elvis Presley, undisputed king in 1957, was their weapon. In what was probably an unsubstantiated story, Elvis was quoted in a border newspaper as saying, "I'd prefer to kiss three Negro women than one Mexican."

Headlines across the country: "¡INDIGNACION POR INSULTO A LAS MEXICANAS!" "¡INICIA FUERTE BOICOT CONTRA EL INSOLENTE ARTISTA!" Radio stations sponsored massive public record-shatterings. "Love Me Tender" was yanked from playlists. But, as Federico Arana, Mexico's premier rock historian, points out in his *Guaraches de ante azul* (Blue Suede *Guaraches*), the conspiracy was bound to fail. "The best that you can do for a person or group to reaffirm their ideals is to persecute them and surround their lives with prohibitions," writes Arana. "The story of the three kisses actually helped Mexican rocanrol."[4]

> Ayer tuve un sueño, fue sensacional
> los pueblos vivían en paz
> nunca había soñado nada igual[5]

In the late sixties and early seventies, rock reached into every corner of Mexico and Central and South America as more bands bypassed covers and explored the peace and love idealism of the time, with original songs in Spanish. In Mexico, rock had become a solid underground christened *la onda*, or "the wave" (a term that survives today in all manner of colloquial speech: "*¿Qué onda?*"; "*¡Que buena onda!*").

In 1971 at Avándaro, on the outskirts of Mexico City, anywhere between one hundred thousand (government figure) and half a million (rockero version) chavos de la onda attended a two-day festival featuring bands like Three Souls in My Mind, Love Army, and El Ritual. The spectacle was a mirror image of Woodstock, right down to one of the organizers stepping up to the mike and warning the kids about a bad batch of LSD. The authorities braced for a predicted riot, but the rockeros camped out peacefully under the rain with little food or warm clothes and, yes, plenty of pot and acid.

"The fact that so many kids got together in one place really scared the government," recalls Sergio Arau, who later formed Botellita de Jerez, one of the most important bands of the eighties. The government had every reason to be nervous. It was the first large gathering of youth since 1968, the year the army massacred several hundred protesting students in the Tlatelolco district of Mexico City. Since Avándaro, the Mexican government has rarely granted permits for large outdoor rock concerts.

For Carlos Monsiváis, one of the Mexican left's best-known essayists, la onda still seemed more of an imitation of the North's hippie culture than an authentic national discovery, except in one important regard. "*La onda* was the first movement in modern Mexico that, from an apolitical position, rebelled against institutionalized concepts [of culture]," he writes in *Amor perdido*, a collection of essays on the sixties in Mexico. "And it eloquently revealed the extinction of cultural hegemony."[6]

Throughout the early seventies, jipitecas wearing *guaraches*, loose sandals with auto-tire soles, hitchhiked across Mexico on hallucinogenic pilgrimages, a tattered copy of *Las enseñanzas de don Juan* stuffed into their rucksacks. Even Joaquín Villalobos, a top commandante of El Salvador's FMLN guerrilla army, admitted that there is room for rocanrol in *la revolución*. Probably half the cadres of any given guerrilla army listened to groups like Los Pasos in the mid-1970s, not to mention Pink Floyd and Led Zeppelin. Salvadoran Marxist friends have boasted to me of sneaking a few tokes of pot and listening to rock on battered tape recorders, breaking away from clandestine military training on El Salvador's remote beaches.

By the early eighties, however, Mexican rock was on the verge of extinction. Only a handful of Mexican bands survived the doldrums of the late seventies—punk hadn't arrived to save rocanrol here as it had in the North—and El Tri, formerly Three Souls in My Mind, was the only solid draw. The battle between English and Spanish, North and South, had been virtually conceded to the gringos. The city had a bad case of Saturday Night Fever.

After generations of rockeros had done their best to overthrow the cultura nacional by singing in English and bleaching their hair, it took a few radicals to discover the obvious: that they didn't need to go north to take back rock'n'roll. Botellita de Jerez announced the birth of a new sound: *guácarock* (*guaca* as much a reference to *guacamole*, the sacred national snack, as to *guácatelas*, an onomatopoeic term for vomiting). Botellita reclaimed popular traditions like the *norteña* and cumbia, as they ridiculed American rock megaheroes and el PRI. Mexico City youth were joining their cultural roots with the heart of rock'n'roll.

Considering how well these worlds merged, one begins to wonder whether rock is really foreign to Mexico City at all. Ask Roco, and he'll say that the blues could have begun only here, what with the city's deep ties to Afro-Caribbean culture, its long-standing love affair with death. And rock itself? Where else could it have exploded into being other than in the biggest city in the world, where soot and sex and social unrest are legendary? Even rap: Roco claims the music actually originated in Mexico with Tin Tan and fellow golden era comedian El Piporro. "Just listen to the raps on the streets of the city," he says. "The vendors are the best rappers in the world!"

After Botellita, frenetic movement ensued: hardcore punk (Atóxxxico, Masacre '68), industrial disco rap (Santa Sabina), roots rock (the perennial El Tri and younger bands like Tex Tex), dark pop (Caifanes), straight pop

(Neón, Fobia, Los Amantes de Lola), and bands like Maldita and Café Tacuba, with their crazy blends of styles from North and South—all churning out Spanish-only product.

"There was an explosion," says Luis Gerardo Salas, executive director of Nucleo Radio Mil, a network of seven radio stations in Mexico City, one of which is dedicated full time to rock. "Everyone in Mexico seemed to want to be a *rocanrolero*. People discovered that there was rock in Spanish with the same quality as in English."

The *hoyos fonquis*, underground clubs that spontaneously appeared in poor neighborhoods, were the heart of the new scene. Bands would set up in the middle of the street, running electricity straight from somebody's living room. "All of a sudden, you'd see smoke rising around the stage," says Lalo Tex, lead singer of Tex Tex. "But it wasn't from a smoke machine. It was the dust being kicked up by the kids dancing on the asphalt."

A childlike awe overwhelms me as we pull up to the block-long monolith that houses the biggest media conglomerate in Latin America. We walk past the security checkpoint and wait in an antiseptic hallway. I glance at a pair of memoranda on the wall: one says you'll be fired if you're fifteen minutes late, the other urges employees to attend a seminar entitled "How to Enhance Your Image." Tonight Maldita enters Televisa's domain for a live appearance on Galavisión, a cable infotainment network.

To be inside the monster, finally! After nearly three decades of watching it in my Mexican grandmother's bedroom in Los Angeles: all those macho heroes and child stars, Jacobo Zabludowsky, the dour-faced anchor with the Mickey Mouse earphones, and Raúl Velasco, variety show host with the sweet "This is our glorious national culture" voice. Zabludowsky and Velasco are among the most powerful men in Mexico, friends of presidents and corporate executives the world over.

Though it is often considered synonymous with el PRI, Televisa may be more powerful than the party. It is one tentacle of the country's most powerful business cartel, the Monterrey Group, which owns over 90 percent of television outlets, numerous radio stations, an important record label, and, to boot, the country's biggest brewery. If you want to reach the masses, Televisa is the only way.

Maldita lounge about smoking cigs, antsy to get the performance over with. "Our real audience is in the *barrios*, at the universities," Pacho says, a little defensively. So entering into the realm of Televisa is a contradiction, right? "We aren't just going to do Televisa's bidding—we aren't about that," he scoffs.

The Marxist youth of the sixties and seventies would never have walked through Televisa's glass doors—except with machine guns. Even today, some look on rockeros like Maldita and Caifanes (who have been on several Televisa shows) as *vendidos*, sellouts. Maldita insist that reaching the mass audience is crucial. But what will happen on the day they decide to sing a song, say, about political prisoners on a Televisa program? Or burn the Mexican flag? Or use profanity on a single?

While the anchors read the news off prompters a few feet away, the band takes its place on the pristinely waxed stage before elegant bronze urns gushing water. The newscast breaks for a commercial and, a few seconds later, on a talk show set at the other end of the studio, entertainment hosts Rocío Villa García and Mauricio Chávez (she an aging, tall, fake blonde in a red dress, he a light-complected innocent in preppy sweater and black tie) shuffle papers and listen to the countdown. "And now, with us tonight is a group of fine young men . . . " The studio fills with a loud recording of the only song that's gotten airplay, "Mojado," the tale of a father who makes the perilous journey to the United States but dies along the border "like a pig, suffocated in a truck." These tragic lyrics are set, somewhat bizarrely, to a blend of highly danceable tropical and flamenco rhythms.

Televisa staffers crowd the plate-glass windows that seal off the newsroom, watching the band make an only half-serious effort to lip synch to the recording. Restrained at first, Roco begins jumping tentatively, but it's not until the second song, the Veracruz-style "Morenaza," that the band really loosens up. Sax spreads his arms and snaps his fingers, twirls about. Pato sneers, scratching ska-ishly at his guitar. Pacho and Lobo are bashing away on percussion—which, apparently, you're not supposed to do when lip-synching: you can hear the skins being pummeled even above the deafening monitors. Aldo plucks his bass with a vengeance. And Roco is now all over the waxed floor, collapsing his legs, flailing them outward in a leap, skidding and sliding. This image is being seen live all over Latin America and Europe, I'm thinking, but twenty minutes from now, it'll be back to the soap operas and wheezing professors discussing the Aztec legacy. And then I notice it: from the moment he hit the stage, Roco's black work boots (just like his father's) have been scuffing the Televisa floor like jet tires on a runway. Rocío Villa García is drop-jawed in horror. Technicians are making exaggerated hand signals, trying to settle Roco down. But no! Roco is blind to the world, on the verge of knocking himself out dancing as the song slowly fades.

Out bounds Villa García, all smiles for the interview. "Roco," she bubbles, "just how is it that you can dance around with those *heavy* boots?" Roco looks down at them, and for the first time notices the dozens of black streaks radiating out from his mike. Before he can answer, Villa García is already into her next question.

"Now just what is this about Madonna showing up at your concert in Los Angeles?"

In the late 1980s, encouraged by the success of such Argentine rockeros as Soda Stereo and Charly García, as well as by the birth of guácarock in Mexico, the labels began signing again. BMG's Ariola led the way, producing Mexican acts Los Caifanes, Maldita Vecindad, Fobia, Neón, and Los Amantes de Lola. A suspiciously supportive Mexican government also helped by allowing a few rock acts from Argentina to stage large outdoor gigs. At the Plaza de Torros in 1987, twenty-five thousand rockeros attended the biggest rock en español gig since Avándaro.

In 1998, the hit that promoters, label execs, radio program directors, and rockeros had all been waiting for arrived: "La negra Tomasa" by Caifanes. The song was a slightly electrified, cumbia-style cover of an old Cuban standard, and it sold over half a million copies—more than any other Mexican single in the thirty-year history of rocanrol. It seemed as if rock's Latin hour had finally come.

Not quite. No other band came close to matching the sales of "La negra Tomasa": most acts topped out at well under 50,000 units. Maldita barely managed 25,000. "There was a crash," says Jorge Mondragón, a Mexico City rock promoter. "People were saying that *rock en español* had only been a fad."

The reasons cited for the crash were familiar: bad label promotion, unscrupulous concert promoters, conservative radio, government censorship. "Let's face it," says Giselle Trainor, an Ariola label manager. "It's not as easy to sell this concept as it is to sell Lucerito." The teen star's voice is nonexistent, but her long legs and fair hair have made her a Televisa darling. "And if other labels don't start supporting rock, it's going to collapse."

Soon after the initial boom, pop rockers like "Mexican Madonna" Alejandra Guzmán (daughter of Enrique Guzmán of Los Teen Tops, the rock-ero heroes of the sixties) achieved stardom, propelled by Televisa's massive promotional machine.

"Rock was taken over by people who aren't *rockeros*," says Nucleo Radio Mil's Gerardo Salas. "Sometimes I think that the whole *rock en español* move-ment was planned and promoted in such a way that pop rockers like Timbi-riche and Menudo would end up winning."

Pop rock, one Televisa promoter told me, is most successful with the mid-dle class, Mexico's strongest consumer force, and the bulwark of the PRI. Working-class *chavos de banda*, who are more likely to listen to the under-ground, are not part of the equation. "They're dirty, violent," I was told by the promoter, who complained about violence at hoyos fonquis and at some of the few larger-scale concerts (a violence, rockeros say, that is usually pro-voked by the authorities). "The underground may just as well roll over and die. We don't want to have anything to do with that crowd, and we never will."

Bouncing around El LUCC, a dingy concrete vault light years away from Rockstock in the south of the city, Roco has his arm around Saúl Hernán-dez, lead singer of Los Caifanes, slurring: "Come on, *cabrón*, admit it. You guys sound like The Cure. *Ya no mames, güey*." And Saúl comes back, rock-ing back and forth on his heels: "Not everything has to be so obvious like in your songs. There's an interior landscape, too, *cabrón*."

By the time Maldita stumbles onto the stage, the walls of the club are sweating. Everyone's hair is pasted onto their foreheads in the dripping-wet air. I inch my way through the crowd, slipping on stray bottles on the un-seen floor below. The balconies seem on the verge of collapse, dozens of kids hanging over the railing.

The sound coming from the stage convulses, lurches: Roco, Sax, Pato, Aldo, and Lobo are floating away on tequila-inspired riffs (they've been partying since early afternoon), steamrolling crazily toward a great abyss, drunk boys daring each other as they look down into the darkness and laugh. The anarchy doesn't perturb the crowd in the least. On the dance floor a thousand bodies match Maldita's wild energy leap for leap.

Roco loses his breath during the melodramatic held note on "Morenaza." Sax stumbles through solos, barely keeping up with the rushed rhythms, flapping across the stage in his loose shirt, waving his arms, giggling. Lo-

46. During the 1970s and 1980s, Mexican rock percolated in the barrios where it was transformed by lumpen proletariate culture into a forceful expression of marginalized angst. By the mid-1980s nationally recognized groups with appeal to the middle classes had reemerged from this milieu, but the significance of rock for barrio culture remains strong. Here, a chavo banda (punk rocker) stage-dives at a concert in the outskirts of Mexico City, 1993. Note the piñatas (at top) and jipiteca-style youth (center). Photo by Eric Zolov.

bito is oblivious to everything but his own private torpor, slamming away at bloodied congas (he ripped his hand open during the second song).

Punkish youths leap on stage and tumble back into the crowd. Now Roco himself takes a diving leap of faith into the mass of steaming bodies. Now Sax. Now Roco is pushing Pato, guitar and all, into the pit.

The band launches into "Querida," a hardcore cover of pop megastar Juan Gabriel's hit. Roco leaps skyward so high that he bangs his head on the red spotlight overhead. Saúl Hernández suddenly climbs onto the stage in all his tall, dark elegance, plays with a microphone-become-penis between his legs, hugs Roco like a long-lost brother, throws his head back, closes his eyes, and then without warning he too dives out onto the dance floor, where the slamming youths edge ever closer to absolute madness.

As the crowd files out afterward—punks, ex-hippies, ex-Marxists, kids from the barrios—Lobo is nursing his hand, bleary-eyed in the arms of his girlfriend. Aldo is downing more beer at the bar. Pacho, the only one who played the gig straight, is talking with a small group of fans. Roco is nowhere to be found. Sax is back behind the percussion section, weeping into a friend's arms—in a few minutes he'll make a bizarre attempt at taking off his pants and pass out.

Tonight, Maldita have fallen apart. Tomorrow they'll wake up, hungover as hell, in the city where rocanrol never quite dies.

Notes

1 "I don't have a fucking idea why I want to go out tonight/but I'll spend the last of my savings on you/at the factory they said, 'We don't need you anymore, Joaquín'/they fired two thousand so as not to lose any money/it's Friday tonight, everyone's going out to dance/sign me up in the madness, I really want to scream:/I can't stand it anymore, I want to dance!" All translations are by the author.

2 "In a dirty alley, you wake without remembering/anything about what happened, even your feet hurt/you don't have a jacket, you don't have money you don't have shoes and you don't even have hair/you leave that alley, HATING."

3 "I'm not a rebel without a cause/nor a hoodlum/the only thing I want to do/is to dance rock & roll."

4 Federico Arana, *Guaraches de ante azul*, v. 1 (Mexico City: Posada, 1985), 115.

5 "Yesterday, I had a dream, it was great/all the nations lived in peace/I'd never dreamed anything like it."

6 Carlos Monsiváis, *Amor Perdido* (Mexico City: Biblioteca Era, 1977), 235.

Cultural Industries in the Free Trade Age: A Look at Mexican Television

Omar Hernández and Emile McAnany

Latin American Cultural Industries Today

At the dawning of a new century, of a new millennium indeed, the industrialization of culture seems like a taken-for-granted development, a rather natural state of affairs with few or none of the paradoxical overtones the term "culture industries" had when it was first coined by Horkheimer and Adorno more than half a century ago (1944).[1] As transnational capitalism flourishes, so do a number of powerful cultural industries that comprise large-scale processes of production, distribution, and consumption and operate at an increasingly global level, participating in international trade and global financing deals to pursue higher profits. At the same time, the cultural goods thus produced must still have relevance at the local or national level where they are ultimately to be consumed. To put it differently, audiences have to appropriate and make their own cultural products created under tremendous pressure to have both massive national *and* global appeal. This is the dilemma facing cultural industries everywhere today: the manufacturing of products that can have relevance at specific localities yet are also universally appealing. In Mexico, during the period when television first flourished and became perhaps the dominant expression of Mexican culture in the sixties and seventies, there was little concern about pleasing a global audience. It has only been in the past fifteen years that a push toward the export of television programming has become a conscious focus for most producers, not only in Mexico but in the Latin American region as a whole.

Latin American cultural industries are obviously affected by the logic of production that characterizes today's globalizing atmosphere. Two factors tend to accentuate even more the "international" aspect of Latin American cultural producers: the first is the growing perception in recent years of Latin America as a highly desirable market for many transnational producers eager to find new export destinations; the second is that regional cultural industries have been exporting their products, especially *telenovelas*, quite successfully throughout Latin America for approximately two decades, and for a decade and a half to countries beyond the region. Thus, the globalizing "push" of large transnationals at present is joined by the notion of Latin America as a hot "emerging market"; added to this is a set of cultural producers within the region who have already been exporting for some time. On the other hand, we should keep in mind that the perceived promise of millions and millions of new eager consumers of cultural products (and of the consumer goods that TV advertising promotes) is a vision yet to be realized, because most Latin Americans fall far short of the income levels required to perform successfully as "desirable consumers." Similarly, the exporting dimension of Latin American producers developed almost serendipitously, particularly when we consider that their quintessential export item, the telenovela, was always (and, arguably, continues to be) a product created for, and thanks to, a national market.

In any case, Latin America is home to large media companies, such as Brazil's Rede Globo and Mexico's Grupo Televisa, which can by now be rightfully considered veteran exporters of their own productions. Although the various cultural producers of the region have developed under the particularly unique historical circumstances of their respective countries of origin, they share certain common features that make it possible to talk about a Latin American context where the expansion of transnational cultural industries has been taking place. In the second half of the past century we have seen steady regional efforts to promote development and raise the standard of living of a population overwhelmingly poor. The U.N.'s Economic Commission on Latin America and the Caribbean (ECLAC) generated a set of strategies designed to boost these countries' internal production primarily for the purpose of alleviating their dependence on imported goods. The main goal of these import-substitution industrialization (ISI) policies was the consolidation of national production to satisfy national demand, with the state playing a central role in this process, which could be seen throughout the region during the sixties and seventies. The external debt crisis of the early eighties, coupled with the emphasis on market economic principles ushered in during the Reagan era in the United States, contributed to the demise of the ISI model and to a reorientation of the Latin American economies toward an increasingly laissez-faire situation capable, at least according to this formulation, of creating export-led growth. Production for export, then, has been the region's guiding light over the past decade and a half.

This overall regional economic context coincides with the previously described globalizing trends present in the cultural industries: they both point in the direction of greater outward orientation as a model for development. Indeed, Latin America as a whole appears to be on the verge of profound economic and political transformations driven by trade liberalization, massive privatization of state sectors, and regional economic integration, as exemplified by the North American Free Trade Agreement (NAFTA) and the Southern Common Market (MERCOSUR). The liberalized trade environments brought about by such commercial agreements do have an impact on the ways cultural industries plan, finance, and implement their efforts to explore and tap into new markets, and on the establishment of international partnerships and joint ventures in foreign countries.[2]

Related to the subject of increased regional integration is the recent emergence of Miami as "the cultural capital of Latin America" (or "the Hollywood of Latin America," as the *New York Times* has called it).[3] The convergence of music, film, and television companies, along with their supporting postproduction institutions, in this South Florida city during the past decade or so has fostered a valuable financial, technological, and creative support network for Latin American cultural producers, the likes of which cannot be found anywhere else. Miami, in other words, is emblematic of what an internationally oriented Latin American cultural producer requires: in addition to the production facilities, the various national populations from Latin countries represented in the area, the ease of traveling to and from any regional destination, and the effective provision of every possible cultural industry service (talent, skilled workforce, technology, attorneys, finance, etc.), the city offers invaluable business *opportunities* simply because everybody is there.[4] That is, it seems that most media companies doing significant business at an international level in Latin America either have moved their headquarters to Miami or have at least opened an office there. Perhaps there is no better proof of the importance Miami has acquired for the transnational business in cultural products for this part of the world than the sheer agglomeration of companies found today in the South Florida area.[5]

Although the tendencies toward a global or international orientation on the part of Latin American cultural producers are undeniable, we must keep in mind that industries such as television developed firmly within national boundaries and thanks to national audiences, with their specific cultural, social, and political circumstances. In fact, the very product on which the whole business of exporting regional cultural goods is based, the telenovela, is itself one whose conception, production, and exhibition depended almost entirely on its financial success with domestic audiences. If the telenovela is the primary export product of globalizing cultural exporters like Globo and Televisa, it is the domestic audiences that remain the bedrock of this strategy. Against this background, then, we now turn to examine recent developments in the Mexican television industry, which will serve both to illustrate some of the general tendencies mentioned as well as the particular situations unique to a specific industry in a specific country.

Cultural Competition at the End of an Era

As we have seen, free market ideology and practices reign supreme over the region these days, and Mexico is no exception. But the organic nature of the PRI's power has left a deep imprint on many aspects of the country's culture, far beyond the political arena. It is not our intention to discuss the relative merits of either the ideological system or its respective consequences; instead, we are merely pointing out that the way of doing things in Mexico during the past six or seven decades, not only politically but economically as well, has been marked profoundly by the institutionalized practices that had their origins in and derived their legitimacy from the revolutionary period. The modus operandi prescribed by the globalizing free market tendencies of the nineties is substantially different from and largely incompatible with the corporativist style that has prevailed in Mexico for so long. In consequence, we should expect changes to take place.

And changes we are seeing. Though the effect of these changes remains to be seen, there is absolutely no denying that they are taking place. The 1997 election of opposition leader Cuauhtémoc Cárdenas as mayor of Mexico City and the no less significant loss of control by the PRI of the national legislature were stunning political developments that would have been unthinkable just a few years ago. But these events pale in comparison to the July 2000 election of the Partido Acción Nacional (PAN) candidate Vicente Fox, to the presidency. The once almighty PRI is finally having to relinquish that which for so long it considered to be its exclusive domain: political power. An old ally of the PRI is now facing a similar situation: Televisa, the country's preeminent television network (thanks in part to its cozy relationship with the governing party), has seen the emergence of an upstart television network, TV Azteca, which in a very short time has begun to challenge its previously uncontested domination of the Mexican airwaves.[6] The point to keep in mind is that market forces can have unforeseen political and cultural consequences. Thus, the new playing field in Mexican open television was made possible in the first place by the privatization efforts of the Salinas de Gortari administration, and the commercial interests of the market have been the main factors in shaping it to this day.

It could be argued that Mexico was transformed with the passage of NAFTA at the end of 1993. It was not so much that the lives of average Mexicans were changed on January 1, 1994, when the treaty became law (though some would argue that the Zapatistas signaled the change more eloquently than the treaty itself), but that the passage of NAFTA indicated to the outside world that Mexico was now a promising location for investment and trade and, furthermore, that the way Mexico was ruled politically would become of greater concern to outside interests investing in the country. The remainder of that year and certainly the years building up to NAFTA were times of dramatic increases in both trade and investment. This was certainly the case for entrepreneurs like Emilio Azcárraga Milmo, head of Televisa, although he had been thinking in global terms since the early 1980s.[7] However, the difference between the global expansion of the eighties and early nineties and what begins to take place after the passage of NAFTA is that political change becomes a tangible possibility in this last period.

As the peso crash of 1995 and the slow recovery in 1996 and 1997 indicated, the opening up of Mexico's economy had dangers not only for businesses but for the average Mexican as well. One business that seemed to weather the peso squeeze reasonably well was one of Mexico's largest corporations, Televisa, which had gone public in 1991. Yet in the economic recovery of 1997, all was not well at Televisa. This section examines the trajectory of Mexico's most powerful cultural conglomerate to better understand how both internal and external changes have made life increasingly difficult for a monolithic organization like Televisa and opened possibilities for challenges from smaller but more agile competitors.

To begin the story at the end rather than the beginning, we need to note the death of Azcárraga Milmo, head and chief architect of Televisa in its current global form, on April 17, 1997. The importance of his death is twofold. First, his ability to see and take advantage of a changing global landscape in cultural production and distribution will be sorely missed at Televisa.[8] Second, the problem of succession in a family-owned corporation in transition to a publicly owned one may be particularly relevant to other major Latin American media businesses (with special reference to Rede Globo in Brazil, where the privately held giant is still dominated by the patriarch, Roberto Marinho, now in his mid-nineties). But Televisa's problem is not just life without its storied leader; after all, his son and new president of the company, Emilio Azcárraga Jean, has acquitted himself rather well in his first three years at the helm, and has even garnered praise from investors for restructuring company finances and streamlining its operations.[9] Perhaps the central problem for Televisa in this new era comes in the form of an entirely new experience for the giant broadcaster: genuine competition for a national television audience.

Televisa had been formed out of several mergers over the decades between the 1950s and the 1970s, but its emergence as a major player beyond Mexican borders began after its merger with a competitor in 1973 and the death in 1972 of its founder, Emilio Azcárraga Vidaurreta. The son, Emilio Azcárraga Milmo, began to build an international company that, by the time he died in 1997, was one of Mexico's largest and wealthiest, with revenues of almost u.s.$2 billion in 1994.[10] For all the success that Televisa experienced over the past three decades, it could not sustain its one great advantage into the NAFTA era: that of being a virtual national monopoly in the sharply expanding global media market.

Carlos Salinas de Gortari was the president who carried the national sell-off of government businesses and assets to its high point. In 1993 he put up for bid a series of audiovisual companies from the government-owned and -operated Imevisión television system. It is worth noting that, at this point in time, Imevisión was the only nationwide broadcaster in Mexico besides Televisa, and that this last one was the only *commercial* broadcasting network in the country. The package put up for sale included two national television channels, 169 stations, other television assets and theater chains; it was valued at about u.s.$500 million. Televisa was excluded from the bid, but many other national and international media companies were involved. Most were surprised when, in April 1993, the government announced that retailing magnate Ricardo Salinas Pliego (no relationship to Salinas de Gortari) had won the bid for u.s.$640 million, the highest bid by more than $100 million. What were the consequences for Televisa, and for Mexico, of this sale?

First, for Mexico, it seemed that the new entity, called Televisión Azteca, was not much of a change from the status quo, where Televisa had from 90 to 95 percent of advertising revenue and about 85 percent of audiences in competition with Imevisión. Moreover, Salinas Pliego was a businessman who made no political claims of competing with Televisa by countering any of its notorious pro-PRI news coverage. Rather, Salinas Pliego outlined his plan for making money and not waves in his new venture.[11] Second, Televisa, and most of the early commentary by analysts, saw Azteca as David trying to pelt Goliath with a few stones. Moreover, Salinas Pliego vowed not to get into a production war with Televisa, which had dominated all the important news and entertainment categories for years on end, but suggested he would rather distribute lower-cost imported programming and concentrate on selling cut-rate ads to gradually lower Televisa's dominant audience share.[12]

A little more than two years later, Salinas Pliego's scenario had changed and Azteca had, indeed, gotten into high-cost production competition with Televisa.[13] And the surprising thing for all of those who had alluded to the David and Goliath analogy was that David's stone had landed squarely between the giant's eyes in the name of both a popular telenovela as well as in the national news program that reported an occasional critique of the PRI and a more objective form of news reporting. By the end of 1996, what had changed were factors both internal to Mexican politics and economics, but also international ones that affected cultural production and export.

It seems that Salinas Pliego quickly recognized Televisa's strategy for success and its weaknesses, and took advantage of its much larger and better-capitalized competitor. As Azteca's vice president, Adrian Steckel, put it most bluntly: "We are doing what Televisa is doing—they are a terrific model."[14] The strategy Televisa has followed successfully for many years was to produce large numbers of television programs (mainly telenovelas) to capture large national audiences to sell to national and international advertisers, and then export these programs, which were already paid for in a national context, to the United States (through Univisión), Latin America, and other global markets (dubbed versions of Televisa novelas can be seen in Morocco, Israel, Russia, and the Philippines, to name only a few of the approximately ninety countries that currently import them). According to some estimates of Televisa's foreign sales (which make up close to half of its revenues), these are roughly equally divided among U.S. Hispanic audiences, the Latin American market, and Europe and Asia.[15] With all the changes in technology (such as the use of direct-to-home television by digital satellite) and other ventures (such as development of portals to the World Wide Web) Televisa has pursued in recent years, telenovela production and export continue to account for over half of its revenue and constitute its most steady source of income.[16]

But what about the strategies that TV Azteca has used to become competitive? Before tackling that question, there is a prior question we need to pose: To what extent can we say that Azteca has managed to compete in a market dominated so long by Televisa? As mentioned above, Televisa's control of the Mexican television scene was nearly absolute. In fact, IBOPE Mexico's ratings for the top twenty TV programs in the period July–November 1993 (the time of Azteca's creation) showed that *all twenty* were aired by Televisa's Canal 2, El Canal de las Estrellas.[17] Therefore, any accomplishments that Azteca may have managed have to be viewed from this perspective of total Televisa domination. Which is precisely why it is so remarkable that in December 1996, Azteca's *Nada Personal* surpassed Televisa's *Sentimientos Ajenos* and *Tú y Yo* as the number one telenovela in the nightly prime-time block by more than two full rating points.[18] Perhaps more significant, however, are Azteca's achievements in terms of overall audience share and ad revenues. It was well known that Salinas Pliego had all kinds of difficulty "overcoming advertisers' skepticism that he would ever reach his goal of 25% audience share."[19] An equally skeptical reception awaited his plans regarding the advertising marketplace: he was reported to have "ambitious goals" when he announced, shortly after his purchase of Grupo Azteca in 1993, that he planned to reach "24% of the television ad market by his fourth year of operation."[20] Four years later, *Variety* reported that "Azteca, with just two stations to Televisa's four, captured 25% of viewers."[21] An analysis by Valores Finamex, a Mexico City brokerage firm, confirms that Azteca held a 25 percent share of the nationwide audience, and Merrill Lynch analyst Pablo Riveroll says that "TV Azteca was able to get about 31% of the ad market in the first half of the year [1997]. That's pretty good."[22] Actually, this is really better than "pretty good": Azteca not only attained but in fact exceeded the goals that even Salinas Pliego himself must have considered "ambitious" when he announced them four years before, and that were generally received with skepticism by industry observers and the specialized press. In light of all this, we can probably answer our initial question positively: yes, Azteca has managed to compete effectively and to a significant extent on what everyone considered to be, simply put, Televisa's own turf.

Now we can truly ask *how* this happened. What kinds of strategies did TV Azteca use to become competitive? The first point to mention is neither specific nor strategic, has little to do with any action by Azteca itself, and tends to be easily overlooked, yet is absolutely crucial for understanding all the changes taking place in Mexican television. The overarching ideological atmosphere, which includes the economic and political currents that allowed the formation of Azteca in the first place, already provided a nurturing environment where the new network, *as long as the right business moves were made*, could flourish. Although this may seem obvious, we only need to look at the skepticism with which most experts received the notion of the new network as real competition for Televisa to realize that few understood it. It is hard to see how the climate that allowed this large and unthinkable change to actually take place (the formation of a second national commercial network in Mexico) could have the potential influence to help actualize what, even at that point, appeared as even more unlikely; that this second network could some day—let alone in just four years—effectively compete.

Let us then look into those "moves" Azteca did make: the strategies at both national and international levels adopted by the network to raise itself from the single-digit ratings bog where its previous government-owned and -operated incarnation, Imevisión, dwelled for so long. Near the top of this list would have to be the delivery of *credible* news, which, at first glance, might be considered something fairly easy to do, given the circumstances. The circumstances were such that "credible news" could be taken to simply mean "anything other than what Televisa was doing." In other words, the Mexican audience in general was so fed up with the blatantly PRI-friendly way in which information was presented in *24 Horas*, Televisa's main national news program, that one could easily expect that any other source of TV news would be immediately welcome. In addition, Televisa's coverage of the Zapatista uprising of January 1994 was so one-sided in its pro-government stance that it shocked an audience already accustomed to biased reporting into buying record numbers of newspapers and magazines to get at even the most basic information on this national crisis.[23] It seemed that even the timing of this event was favoring the emergence of the recently created Azteca *noticiarios* as a viable alternative to Televisa's tiresome "prinformation." But nothing of the sort happened, and Azteca's main news program, *Hechos*, continued to command consistently low ratings (five points or below) until mid-1995.

The reasons for this lack of support are not hard to figure out, if one is willing to grant Mexican television viewers a little bit of credit as a discerning audience. Channels 7 and 13 might have been sold off into private hands, but they were still very much Channels 7 and 13. And this meant Imevisión, the government network, including a news department that for many years delivered the official party line. It takes time to reshape the orientation in which television news is conceived and presented, and even longer to put together a team of journalists and other professionals capable of generating and delivering a different news product. The mere fact that 7 and 13 had changed hands did not mean that now their news would be instantly credible and worthy of being watched. And the initially low ratings for Azteca's noticiarios reflected this. If the new network wanted to lure viewers away from *24 Horas* to its news shows, it would have to produce something different to earn their attention.

TV Azteca did just that when in August 1995 it launched *Ciudad Desnuda*, a reality news show that so unabashedly set out to report the everyday violence found in Mexico City that its producers claimed that "blood would drip from the TV sets."[24] The show caught on quickly and in little over a year it was pulling ratings consistently in the high teens; perhaps more significantly, *Hechos*, Azteca's national news program, began getting ratings comparable to those of *24 Horas* by the middle of 1996.[25] Although there is no denying that the success of the sensationalist *Ciudad Desnuda* helped the ratings of its neighboring *Hechos*, we must note that TV Azteca carried out a major reorganization of its news division with the creation in 1996 of Fuerza Informativa Azteca (FIA), an area within the company charged not only with the creation of news products but with the development of capable personnel to generate and deliver such products. To head FIA, Azteca hired Sergio Sarmiento, a veteran journalist of solid reputation as an independent voice and famous for his well-read opinion column, *Jaque Mate* (Checkmate).[26] The program *La Entrevista con Sarmiento* is a good example of how FIA has met with success by doing things well: the show started a few weeks before the July 1997 elections as a space for the kind of political reflection necessary during such times, with the implicit understanding that it would constitute a financial loss for TV Azteca and thus would not extend much beyond the election. However, the program met with much greater success than expected and is now enjoying its fourth year on the air. As Sarmiento himself said only a few months after the show was launched, "The program has good ratings and it makes money."[27] We can see from this evidence, therefore, that the rise in the acceptance of Azteca's news programs was, in large measure, the result of well-conceived strategies of production coupled with a keen eye for the successful adaptation to the Mexican scene of show formats that have done well in other countries.

Azteca demonstrated an international awareness practically from its inception. Less than a year after its formation, in May 1994, Azteca announced a deal with the U.S. network NBC in the hopes of gaining some management and programming expertise, the better to compete with Televisa. The alliance, signed by officials from both companies in late July at the residence of Mexican President Carlos Salinas de Gortari, was hailed by Azteca's chairman Salinas Pliego as "one of the first concrete results of the North American Free Trade Agreement." Salinas de Gortari, for his part, described this partnership as a reaffirmation of his administration's commitment to free expression and the positive result of Mexico's economic opening, adding that it "strengthens competition in the television market." This last remark was unusually prescient, but perhaps the clearest vision in that summer ceremony was that of Robert Wright, president and chief executive of NBC, who stated plainly that "Azteca has the greatest growth potential of any Latin American broadcast entity."[28]

Just a few years later, this potential has developed into a concrete and very significant share of the Mexican television audience, although the actual contribution of the NBC-Azteca alliance to this development has been, at best, rather limited. In fact, the partners began quarreling over the three-year option NBC had in which to buy up to a 10 percent stake in Grupo Azteca. The U.S. network had backed away because of concern for the consequences of the 1995–1996 peso crash; by the time they recognized that Azteca had bucked the downturn and was indeed a good investment, the relations between the two companies had turned sour and a binational legal battle was underway. In April 1997, Azteca sought to void the contract between them in an attempt to block NBC from exercising its 10 percent option, claiming that NBC had forfeited its right to buy the shares because it failed to deliver services agreed on in the original deal, in spite of repeated requests by the Mexican network. The U.S. network countered that Azteca owed them money and maintained that the latter's success was due in large measure to their strategic alliance, a statement that Azteca called "false and tendentious," saying instead that its own productions had been the key to its rapid growth in popularity among viewers.[29] The dispute was eventually taken before the International Chamber of Commerce in Paris, and was finally settled in May 2000, three full years after the conflict arose.[30] At any rate, the interesting point here is that this alliance showed Azteca's awareness of itself as a company belonging to an industry with an increasingly international scope. This willingness to readily cross national borders has been confirmed by Azteca's recent efforts to push its telenovelas in various Latin American markets and by its purchase of two small networks in Chile and El Salvador.[31] In addition, Azteca has continued to seek favorable international strategic associations, such as the agreement with the U.S. Spanish-language network Telemundo to coproduce telenovelas that would do well in both markets.[32] Out of this alliance came *Nada Personal*, Azteca's first hit against Televisa and an excellent example, as we shall see in the next section, of how the new kid on the block managed to get respect.

Entre Tú y Yo, No Hay Nada Personal

So goes the beautiful theme song that the legendary Mexican composer Armando Manzanero wrote for this telenovela, and which he sang in a duet with Chanteuse Lisette at the beginning of each episode. The words seemed to echo the sentiment that Salinas Pliego claims to have had toward Televisa: no attacks, no bad blood, nothing personal—he just wanted to go about his business of making television. However, this "business," in and of itself, is something that *El Tigre*, Emilio Azcárraga Milmo, would see as an intensely personal affront, for he considered television in Mexico to be his own private domain. At any rate, in the first couple of years of Azteca's existence, its relation with Televisa was rather quiet. But things started being less congenial once Azteca began to gain ground and, beginning in 1996, their behavior toward each other started to get downright nasty, *muy personal* indeed.

The ugliest episodes took place in June and July 1996, right after allegations surfaced charging that Raúl Salinas de Gortari, brother of the by then ex-president Carlos Salinas, had transferred u.s.$29 million to a company owned by Salinas Pliego just a few days before the latter bought the government media package that became Grupo Azteca S.A. What ensued was a media war conducted through the two networks' main news programs, which retarnished the image of Mexico's tv journalism, an image that had slowly but steadily been improving.[33] Televisa drew first blood by featuring the news about the loan prominently and often, and having Ricardo Rocha, conductor of *Detrás de la Noticia*, a news analysis program, devote several shows to discussing potential irregularities in the bidding process for the privatization of Imevisión. The afternoon daily *Ovaciones*, published by the anchorman of *24 Horas* and long-time Televisa power Jacobo Zabludovsky, splashed on its front page the headline "Salinas + Salinas = 7 + 13," making their insinuation crystal clear. Azteca retorted by saying that "the defamation campaign is a reaction to [our] success."[34] Salinas Pliego himself appeared on the air and called Rocha *un cobarde* (a coward), stressing again that Televisa's personal attacks against him were due to Azteca's gains both in terms of ratings and advertising revenue.[35] Then came the revelation that Abraham Zabludovsky, son of Jacobo and anchorman of Televisa's afternoon news, had been one of Raúl Salinas's "most important business partners" in the previous *sexenio*. Abraham appeared on his father's *24 Horas* program insisting that he was not a crook, but the scandal was too much even for Televisa: Abraham was fired as the afternoon's news anchor in early July, only to be rehired the next day, but for a lower-profile position.[36] One thing was clear from all this bickering: TV Azteca had become a contender and even Televisa was acknowledging it. And all this was happening just as Azteca was delivering its best punch yet, *Nada Personal*, which was airing at the time.

In 1998 Televisa celebrated forty uninterrupted years of telenovela production. The success of this genre could hardly be exaggerated. After all, who could have predicted, back in the late fifties and early sixties, that the melodramas produced in Mexico City studios would break audience records in places like Russia, Indonesia, Morocco, and the Philippines, to name just a few? And Televisa, quite rightly, considers itself the pioneer and leading exponent of the genre. Thus, when in 1996 TV Azteca, with barely three years of existence and practically no experience in telenovela production, rose to the top of the ratings with *Nada Personal*, the shock was generalized. But after the even greater success of *Mirada de Mujer* in 1997–1998, Azteca proved that this was not some sort of fluke or lucky strike and that it was capable of sustaining a high level of interest with its productions. In fact, *Nada Personal* can be better described as emblematic of many of the strategies that have allowed Azteca to become a bona fide competitor so quickly on the Mexican television scene. It provides us with a unique opportunity to illustrate how the upstart network operates and takes advantage of the production and distribution conditions it finds at both the national and international level.

Perhaps the best place to start when talking about *Nada Personal* is by referring to its producer, Epigmenio Ibarra. After spending fifteen years as a war correspondent in places like El Salvador, Nicaragua, Panama, Colombia, Guatemala, Iraq, and Bosnia, Ibarra decided, in the early nineties, to try something different and began producing shows with reports and interviews focused on Mexico City's cultural sphere for small local and cable channels. Eventually he was hired by Azteca to produce *Expediente 132230*, a reality news magazine that was immediately well received and could be considered the predecessor of *Ciudad Desnuda*. This early success led to an offer by Salinas Pliego to develop both a police-type series and a telenovela, efforts that led to the creation of *Nada Personal*.

It was obvious from the start that there was something different about this novela. In the first episode, a top Mexican police official, Col. Fernando Gómez, appropriately nicknamed El Aguila Real (played by former Televisa actor Rogelio Guerra), is shown lighting a cigarette as he looks down at the dead body of his best friend, anticorruption crusader Raúl de los Reyes, who had just been gunned down right before being named the nation's attorney general. El Aguila Real, who had overseen the assassination on orders from the highest levels of power, puffs on his cigarette and tells his dead friend, in a voice that sounds almost sad, *"No es nada personal, hermano . . . nada personal."* To put it simply, it would have been completely out of the question for anyone in Televisa to even conceive of doing something like this at the time. We must remember that Azcárraga Milmo was a staunch supporter of the PRI and once even called himself a "soldier" of the Salinas presidency.[37] But in the Mexico of 1996, after over two years of one political scandal after another, including the 1994 assassinations of the PRI's presidential candidate Luis Donaldo Colosio and the PRI's secretary general José Francisco Ruiz Massieu, as well as the gunning down of the Archbishop of Guadalajara, people were, in the words of Carlos Monsiváis, "totally convinced that they were governed by gangsters."[38]

It would be a gross understatement to say that the Mexican audience was ready to welcome a telenovela with an openly political theme.[39] Ibarra and Venezuelan scriptwriter Alberto Barrera were only too eager to portray this bleak vision of Mexico, which closely resembled the shattered credibility of national institutions and the political leadership. Azteca was capitalizing on a wonderful opportunity, but at the same time taking the risk of doing something that had never been done on Mexican television. It is important to remark, once again, that those changes in the Mexican political and economic atmosphere that made the formation of TV Azteca possible are also partly responsible for allowing a public climate in which a story like *Nada Personal* could succeed on a massive scale. However, Ibarra was quite aware that politics, corruption, and intrigue are not enough to carry a telenovela; thus, the plot included a classic romantic triangle and even the customary secrets involving a lead character's true identity. Still, clever plot innovations went beyond the overtly political theme and the references to actual events that had clouded the Mexican public sphere. One of the heroes of the novela was Luis Mario Gómez, son of El Aguila Real and a handsome journalist bent on exposing the web of official corruption. He conducted his idealistic crusade against the government on a television network called (you guessed it!) TV Azteca. Not the most inventive name, one might say, but rather blatantly obvious (and who knows how effective?) as a self-promotional tool.

The innovative theme and plot twists in *Nada Personal*, where one could also find the classic elements necessary in a telenovela, can be considered definite factors in its success.[40] But there were other ingredients in the mix. For one thing, the Mexican audience has by now become used to the star system implanted by Televisa and is always expecting the names and faces of familiar actors and actresses to embody the various characters of the telenovelas. Azteca did not have any stars of this type because it did not have a system in place that could produce them.[41] The obvious solution to this problem was to lure well-known actors from Televisa to come over and star in Azteca's productions. This, of course, was no easy matter, for Televisa demanded exclusivity from its corpus of actors. They were kept under a permanent contract, even when they were not working, that prohibited their appearance anywhere else in television. Breaching this contract (or, for that matter, antagonizing Televisa in any other way) had long meant blacklisting, which, given the monopolistic nature of the Mexican television system at the time, would have been a fatal blow to anyone's career.

How could Azteca, then, convince anyone to take such an enormous risk? The answer, says Ibarra, is that Azteca offers them the opportunity to participate in "television made with dignity and high quality, because they are hungry for good products."[42] To this we might add that many Televisa actors were unhappy just waiting for their turn to work in the next telenovela. Over the years, the number of actors on the Televisa payroll had grown tremendously, whereas the network could have only three or four novelas in production at any given time. This meant that the opportunities to play lead roles were few relative to the number of actors waiting for their turn. The same was true for veteran *artistas*, whose chance to play a really interesting character in a strong supporting role was quite slim, not only because of the "ratio of actors to novelas" problem but also because such roles, in the staple Televisa productions, were few and far between. In this respect, Ibarra may be quite right in his assertion that many in the television acting community "are hungry" for quality roles.

Azteca, once again, took advantage of this opportunity and built up Argos Producciones, headed by Ibarra, as a semi-independent production company charged with conceiving, developing, casting, and finally producing telenovelas on a project-by-project basis. Argos offered actors specific roles in a specific telenovela, an arrangement significantly different from Televisa's long-term contractual obligations and more in keeping with global industry standards set within the competitive context of Hollywood. Although the security of a regular monthly paycheck is forsaken, being cast in an Argos telenovela means that actors are free to pursue whatever interesting project may arise next. Of course, at first this meant being ostracized from Televisa, a seemingly heavy price to pay. But a veteran actor like Guerra was only too glad to have the opportunity to interpret a role such as El Aguila Real, even if Argos had not yet proven itself at all as a competent producer of novelas. It was a risk that paid off, as it did for Demian Bichir, Lupita Ferrer, and even for Ana Colchero, the fiery leading lady who actually abandoned the novela just a few weeks before production ended on the grounds that her character was being manipulated away from how it was originally conceived. She sued Azteca and Azteca sued her back, but perhaps the most significant development in this impasse was that rumors began circulating about a possible return to Televisa (rumors fueled when Televisa did an extensive interview with Colchero in her own home), which tended to allay the fears that working with Azteca meant eternal banishment from Mexico's number one network.[43] At this point, the list of Televisa actors who have switched to Azteca is long and includes such established stars as Lucía Méndez, Fernando Ciangherotti, Rocío Banquells, Rafael Sánchez Navarro, Ari Telch, Claudia Ramírez, Angélica Aragón, María Rojo, Humberto Zurita, and Christian Bach, among others.[44]

Colchero's lawsuit included a complaint that her image was used without her approval on the cover of the *Nada Personal* album. This album was released by the newly created label Azteca Music, and quickly sold over 100,000 copies in its first couple of weeks on the market. The new label also released a "greatest hits" collection of ex-Televisa star Rocío Banquells's recordings, as well as the debut albums of new artists being promoted in Azteca's musical shows. Grupo Azteca also ventured into the realm of publishing with the launching of its first magazine, *Secretos*. This new publication, which came out in September 1997, is devoted mainly to gossip about and interviews with television and music stars, and includes lots of photographs as well. Both these developments, the recording label and the publishing venture, are patterned after Televisa's successful model for cross-promotion of its products. In this sense, we can say that Azteca has been able to adopt and adapt old strategies with a proven track record, in addition to implementing new and creative ideas, all as part of a well-orchestrated effort to become more competitive.

Azteca's status as the underdog may have facilitated its willingness to take risks with its program acquisition strategies. A prime example of such risk taking is the decision to purchase and prominently feature two shows that many in the industry considered "too American" to do well in the Mexican market. Overlooking these naysayers, Azteca found itself with two shows that soon became favorites with Mexican audiences: *The Nanny* (*La Niñera*) and *Los Simpsons*. Furthermore, the new network's readiness to innovate and its awareness of the increasingly international characteristics of this business are exemplified by the already mentioned coproduction alliance with Telemundo. By strategically allying with Azteca, Telemundo has the opportunity to offer the U.S. Spanish-language audience (of which about 70 percent are of Mexican origin)[45] a product with Mexican actors, themes, and flavor, which is already receiving an enthusiastic acceptance by audiences in Mexico. This bodes well for its potential reception in the United States. Azteca, for its part, gets a partner to share the added costs of increasing both the number and the quality of its telenovela productions, which it needs to do to fight the Televisa juggernaut. Thus, this partnership is guided by fairly well-defined goals marked by a clear understanding of each partner's target audience.[46] Moreover, Azteca has the opportunity to offer its own products in the international market, as the agreement calls for each partner to keep international distribution rights to half of the telenovelas they produce jointly.[47]

One last strategy worth mentioning is Azteca's handling of its advertising clients. Salinas Pliego quickly recognized that Televisa could charge whatever it pleased for its advertising slots because it was, quite simply, the only game in town. Its French Plan required advertisers to sign on for a whole year and pay in advance, and dissenters and renegades could suffer blacklisting and be effectively banished from advertising to large audiences on TV. Azteca once again sought to take advantage of this virtual tyranny by offering discount ads and a contract period of only three months. This lured some advertisers, but they were mostly, at first, companies who previously did not even bother to promote their products on TV. As Azteca's ratings grew, larger companies began to take an interest in announcing with the new network and to lose the fear of Televisa's intimidation practices. The ensuing surge in Azteca's share of the advertising pie appears to have come as a result of its decision to link ad rates directly to the ratings. As Azteca's sales VP Gustavo Guzmán responds when asked to describe the key to their success: "Great planning and the fact that we've based our ad rates directly on ratings points."[48]

The Current Scene in Mexican Television

From an economic perspective, Televisa continues to have an enormous advantage in deep pockets over its smaller rival, but Salinas Pliego has capitalized on weaknesses Televisa has suffered as it grew nationally and globally. In mid-1997, the issue of leadership was of great concern. Emilio Azcárraga Milmo foresaw his own exit and created a structure in March 1997 for his son, Emilio Azcárraga Jean, only twenty-nine at the time, to codirect the company with a trusted financial officer, Guillermo Cañedo White.[49] But the rule by committee ended in July of the same year, when Cañedo White resigned along with his two brothers, fellow Televisa executives Pablo and José Antonio. Wall Street analysts worried where Televisa would turn next for stable leadership, although a recapitalization scheme announced in September of that year injected a healthy dose of capital (about U.S.$400 million) and strengthened the position of the new chairman, who now owns directly a full 52 percent of the stock and has secured allegiance of three quarters of the voting members of the board. In addition, the return of the chairman's cousin, Alejandro Burillo Azcárraga, a still young but more seasoned Televisa hand, as the chairman's personal advisor, president of international affairs, and VP of the Board, served to add a measure of stability in the post-Cañedo era.[50]

Second on the list of problems that Televisa must face while it competes with Azteca is a large debt burden of more than U.S.$1 billion. Although it had begun to downsize its workforce and sell off nonessential businesses (including a 40 percent share in PanAmSat), the process was far from complete when Azcárraga Milmo died.[51] However, Azcárraga Jean's successful restructuring of corporate debt and his streamlining of the operations (he has shaved off more than 30 percent of the total number of employees he inherited) seem to have significantly alleviated this problem. Finally, how the Azcárraga family, with its absolute majority of stock and company control, will decide to run things without the commanding presence of its seasoned leader calls into question the setting of new strategies for survival and growth in a very changed Mexico. All of this is taking place in the context of a Mexico in political transition. The situation seems to have helped Azteca more than Televisa, as the former is far more flexible and less tied to old structures of power than the latter. However, the young Azcárraga has gone out of his way to declare the political independence of Televisa and has clearly tried to distance himself from his father's autocratic style of management by claiming he is running the company as a "directed democracy."[52] In any case, no one seems to know where all the changes taking place in the country will lead, and effective leadership in Mexico has traditionally involved more than financial maneuvering and skillful administration.

We also need to note that Televisión Azteca is not without problems of its own. For starters, it may be difficult to continue its telenovela success against a shrewd and mighty competitor like Televisa. It should not take long for veteran company producers to figure out how changes in the novela genre best appeal to audiences, and then to implement such changes with much larger assets than Azteca can currently muster, as exemplified by the long-running hit *Tres Mujeres* (1999–2000). Other audience hits like Pedro Damián's *Mi Pequeña Traviesa* (1997) and *Preciosa* (1998), as well as the tremendously successful remake of the old classic *La Usurpadora* (1998), attest to the fact that Televisa continues to be a powerhouse when it comes to telenovela production.[53] The financial challenge for Azteca to compete in production became evident in 1996, when Salinas Pliego borrowed U.S.$100 million from his publicly owned retailing company to bolster Azteca's growth.[54] Needless to say, stockholders in Elektra were not pleased.

The successful incursion of *Nada Personal* into the political world was followed by the even more successful thematic innovation of *Mirada de Mujer*, which explored the emotional needs and desires of a middle-aged wife estranged from her cheating husband. But the next risky subject tackled by Azteca and Ibarra did not fare well at all. Indeed, *Tentaciones*, which told the story of a handsome priest whose religious vocation is endangered when he falls in love with a woman who turns out to be his half-sister, proved too much for a country that can still be described as largely conservative, particularly when it comes to religion. Curiously, however, it was not the low ratings that brought about the premature end of this novela, but rather the pressure exerted by the Catholic Church and other influential groups. Initially planned for two hundred episodes, *Tentaciones* was abruptly ended after seventy-seven. Of these, forty had to be reshot to accommodate the concerns raised by the main commercial sponsors, Bimbo and Pond's, whose "intervention" was prompted in turn by Catholic groups.[55] These "adjustments" caused production costs to soar, yet still were not enough to placate the ire of those who considered it anathema. In other words, this telenovela was doomed from the start and, besides being a financial disaster, served as a reminder that there are certain topics and treatments that are clearly off limits for this type of massively consumed cultural product.[56]

Speaking of audience appeal, even though we argued that the coproduction success of *Nada Personal* was the result of carefully implemented strategies, trying to please several audiences in Mexico and the United States with the same production is a balancing act that is difficult to sustain, as coproducers in Europe have recognized over the past twenty years. Televisa has had a different and easier strategy up to this point: please large national audiences and pay for the telenovela at home, then ship it to the United States, Latin America, and the rest of the world for profit. Azteca is still a novice in international markets, but it has recognized that it must sell products like telenovelas outside Mexico if it is to grow. There may be some evidence that the most universal themes of family relationships and stereotyped romance sell better internationally than the more nationally appealing political realism of telenovelas like *Nada Personal* in Mexico or *Por Estas Calles* in Venezuela.[57]

Finally, adding to problems on Azteca's agenda is the already mentioned squabble with NBC, which ended with the former having to pay u.s.$46 million to the latter. At the time there were fears that the suit might threaten the initial public offering planned by Azteca for late 1997, but the company entered the international financial markets by raising a healthy u.s.$605 million.[58] Still, the fact that Azteca is at odds with a giant corporation like

General Electric (owner of NBC) is cause for concern among Wall Street investors—not a good sign for a company that requires steady access to capital to fuel the growth necessary to compete against Televisa.

Conclusion

We may be coming to the end of an era in Mexico when a single institution like Televisa could establish the cultural context for national consciousness. With the expansion of the television audience from the 1950s to the 1980s, Televisa so dominated the national information and entertainment agenda that it was possible to focus on its messages as cultural and political voices of power. But in today's more fragmented and postmodern age, a single dominant voice may not be feasible. Nevertheless, Azteca's success in capturing audiences in Mexico gives it a certain amount of power to influence the national debate in a critical time of transition. More than just the audience ratings, Azteca has managed to capture a certain momentum from a discredited Televisa and has made economic gains that were unimaginable before.

One must be careful to distinguish the economic success of an enterprise like Azteca from the wielding of political power that Televisa consciously exercised. Azteca's appearance on the scene at a critical juncture in Mexico's civic evolution does not mean that Salinas Pliego or his enterprise are political reformers. The mass media could undoubtedly be a source of power for those who control them, but their economic success in capturing audience attention is not the same as the exercise of political power. Media are commercial institutions whose products have ideological consequences, but the owners and operators of media may not consciously promote the ideology they carry. This was clearly *not* the case with Azcárraga Milmo's Televisa, whose allegiance to the PRI was beyond question and at times was even expressed by El Tigre himself. In the case of Azteca, and perhaps even in the post-Tigre Televisa, we have cultural industries that claim to operate outside the realm of politics and ideology but whose products of necessity convey certain ideas and attitudes. The difference now is that these ideas are not necessarily monolithic anymore and may be, albeit unintentionally, a critical factor in the transformations currently taking place in Mexico.

At the end of our story about the recent changes in Mexican television, what can we say about globalization and cultural industries in Mexico? First of all, Televisa can no longer be seen as the singular voice of Mexican popular culture. TV Azteca was able to politicize the most popular of television's cultural forms, the telenovela, but this change was in turn made possible by the convergence of internal political change, the globalizing pressures of external forces, and a transformed Mexican society. This last factor could well be considered the crucial element in the market-oriented atmosphere of the times: Mexican audiences were a ripe market for what Azteca offered them. In this sense, the nineties marked a political and cultural transition that seems much more obvious in hindsight than when it was stirring a decade ago. Even Azteca had a blurry vision at the very start, thinking that it could make money as a transnational funnel of cheaply imported foreign products into Mexico. It soon recognized that, in order to grow, it needed to turn the funnel around and work on national content that would play well at home and then could be exported abroad. It needed, in its own way, to emulate the successful model developed by Televisa. That the turnaround in Azteca's thinking was so swift simply indicates that this is a business created in a decade when the pace of change in the global media was even more stunning. We need only to glance in the direction of the recent megamerger between the "old" content provider, the once dominant Time-Warner, and the agile young upstart, AOL, to get an idea of the speed at which changes in the industry are developing these days.

Another concluding thought suggests that, even though Azteca has succeeded in catching on to Televisa's strategy, it still must prove its capacity to make the strategy work on a continued basis by keeping national audiences with captivating local material that is also appealing to audiences outside of Mexico, including the Mexican diaspora. Azteca was shrewd in adapting an old genre to new and exciting local realities in Mexican society, but how to market this cultural product to others is the dilemma now faced by the new network.

Regardless of whether Azteca succeeds in its globalizing strategy, it has certainly marked a cultural change internally. For Mexican audiences, this change meant that many political and social discourses that had few outlets until the mid-1990s now had their most public expression in the nation's most popular medium. This did not mean that Mexican television culture was politicized in the transformative sense of promoting more participation in the political process. That remains to be seen. What did happen was the opening for public discussion of themes that had usually been limited to a few high-cultural sources and to elite audiences. For instance, political elites had long discussed corruption among themselves in the pages of a few Mexico City newspapers and magazines. After *Nada Personal* and *Mirada de Mujer*, however, mass audiences could talk about political corruption or *machista* behavior as part of the daily conversation about what happened on the latest novela episode the night before. This is perhaps the most critical contribution of Azteca to the current Mexican public sphere, even though it was an unintended effect on the part of a company whose leadership saw their enterprise as a strictly commercial cultural industry.

Notes

1   Max Horkheimer and Theodor W. Adorno, "The Culture Industry: Enlightenment as Mass Deception," in *Dialectic of Enlightenment* (1994; reprint New York: Continuum, 1982). All translation are the authors' unless otherwise noted.

2   Emile McAnany and Kenton T. Wilkinson, *Mass Media and Free Trade: NAFTA and the Cultural Industries* (Austin: University of Texas Press, 1996).

3   Larry Rohter, "Miami, the Hollywood of Latin America," *New York Times*, 18 August 1996.

4   Daniel Mato, "Miami en la transnacionalización de la industria de la telenovela: Sobre la territorialidad de los procesos de globalización," paper presented at Latin American Studies Association, Miami, March 2000; Kevin Baxter, "Miami: El 'Hollywood Latino,'" *El Norte*, 9 September 1998, 20.

5   Sharon Strover, Omar Hernández, and Patrick Burkhart, "Transnational Media Industries in Latin America," paper presented at the SCOLAS conference, University of Texas at Austin, February 1997; Sharon Strover, "Spatialization and International Communication Industries: The Case of Miami," *Javnost: The Public* (November 1998): 35–45.

6   Barbara Belejack, "Aztec Time," *Latin Trade* (July 1998): 46–50.

7   Claudia Fernández and Andrew Paxman, *El tigre: Emilio Azcárraga y su imperio Televisa* (Mexico City: Grijalbo, 2000).

8   *San Antonio Express News*, "Businessman Started Small and Became Media Giant," 20 April 1997, 11A.

9   Julia Preston, "A Firm Grip on Mexico's Dial: New Generation Executive Controls Top Broadcaster," *New York Times*, 25 April 2000, C1.

10 Hoover's Company Profiles, *Grupo Televisa* CD-ROM (Austin: Hoover's, 1997). Televisa's revenues for 1998 have been reported at U.S.$1.7 billion; see Andrew Paxman, "Variety 94th Anniversary: The Global 50-Televisa Group, Rank 34," *Variety*, 23 August 1999, A62. Though it appears that the company's revenues are diminishing, once we consider that the Mexican peso lost about two thirds of its value against the U.S. dollar as a result of the 1995 crisis, the fact that Televisa's revenues for 1998 are at nearly the same level (in U.S. dollars) as they were before the devaluation is indeed remarkable. The overall corporate value of the Televisa empire has recently been estimated at U.S.$9 billion; see Preston, "A Firm Grip on Mexico's Dial."

11 Joel Russel, "Free Markets Help Business Too," *Business Mexico* (December 1993): 45.

12 Ibid.

13 Mary Sutter, "Home-grown Programming Takes Off: Azteca and Televisa Expand Production for Export," *Business Mexico* (August 1996): 12–15.

14 Ibid.

15 Ibid.

16 Elizabeth Malkin and Mark Landler, "Will a *Yanqui* Partner Make TV Azteca a Player?," *Business Week* (May 1994): 56; Claudia Villegas, "Mexico TV Giant Sets Sights on U.S. Latin Markets," *Reuter Business Report* (June 1996).

17 The top three programs, by the way, were telenovelas, led by the extremely popular *Dos Mujeres, Un Camino*, which topped the chart at 39.1 points; see *Adcebra, la revista mexicana de mercadotécnica, publicidad y comunicación* (1993). IBOPE stands for Instituto Brasileño de Opinión Pública, and is a Brazilian ratings company that operates in Mexico.

18 IBOPE/Grupo Delphi ratings show that both *Sentimientos Ajenos* and *Tú y Yo* topped at 18 whereas *Nada Personal* totaled 20.2 points; see *Adcebra* (1997).

19 Malkin and Landler, "Will a *Yanqui* Partner Make TV Azteca?"

20 Elizabeth Jensen, "NBC Creates Broad Alliance with TV Azteca," *Wall Street Journal*, 16 May 1994, A3.

21 Mary Sutter, "Televisa Heir Plays Down Family Drama," *Advertising Age International*, 15 September 1997, I24.

22 Quoted in Mary Sutter, "Mexican Acquisition Executives Are Looking in Part to Mipcom," *Variety*, 22 September 1997, M58.

23 Carlos Monsiváis, keynote speech at the conference Mass Media and Free Trade: NAFTA and the Cultural Industries, University of Texas at Austin, March 1994.

24 Adriana Garay, " 'Escurrirá sangre' por la TV," *Reforma*, 23 August 1995, 7.

25 *Adcebra* (1997)

26 Adriana Garay, "1996 es el año de TV Azteca," *Reforma*, 30 December 1996, 7.

27 Quoted in Hugo Lazcano, "Sergio Sarmiento llega a las 100," *Reforma*, 23 October 1997, 3.

28 *Dow Jones News Service*, "NBC Formalizes Alliance with Mexico's TV Azteca," 26 July 1994.

29 An interesting twist in the dispute is the rumor that the reason for NBC's delay in exercising the option to buy (they expressed intent in April 1997, barely a month before the three-year period expired) was the alleged relation between Salinas Pliego and Raúl Salinas de Gortari, the by-then jailed brother of ex-president Carlos Salinas de Gortari; see Roberto Aguilar and Jesús Ugarte, "Pelean acciones TV Azteca-NBC," *Reforma*, 1 May 1997, 21. It is also worth noting that certain investment banking firms have concluded that the long-running dispute is likely to have "an adverse financial impact on the Mexican network"; see *Hollywood Reporter*, "Report: Disputed with NBC will cost Azteca," 13 April 1999, 69.

30 *PR Newswire*, "Televisa Sees $80 Million Layoff Charge for Restructuring," 21 May 1997.

31 Belejack, "Aztec Time."

32 Claudio di Persia, interview by Omar Hernández, Hialeah, Florida, 4 February 1997.

33 In fact, Televisa itself had recently aired video footage that revealed a police cover-up in a massacre of peasants in the state of Guerrero, a revelation that led to the resignation of the state's PRI governor. It must be noted, however, that this action, though it might have somewhat improved Televisa's image as a news provider, caused tremendous turmoil in-

side the network and prompted the firing of Azcárraga Milmo's own nephew, Alejandro Burillo Azcárraga, who had authorized the controversial broadcast; see Sutter, "Mexican Acquisition Executives."

34 Howard LaFranchi, "Mexican TV Stations Crow over Each Other's Links with Raúl Salinas," *Christian Science Monitor*, 9 July 1996, 7.

35 Garay, "1996 es el año de TV Azteca."

36 LaFranchi, "Mexican TV Stations Crow over Each Other's Links."

37 Ibid.

38 Mary Beth Sheridan, "Corruption Makes for a TV Hit in Mexico," *Los Angeles Times*, 14 December 1996, A12.

39 As a point of comparison, Brazilian producers had been making telenovelas with social and political themes for well over two decades, and Colombian and Venezuelan producers had been doing so since at least the mid-1980s.

40 The performance of *Nada Personal* in the transnational market has been mixed. Although it has not sold particularly well, we must keep in mind that it was the very first novela that Azteca tried to distribute internationally—a big handicap in a business where an established clientele and a proven track record are crucial. Given this, the fact that *Nada Personal* did well in novela-savvy countries like Venezuela and Colombia, coupled with the MIDIA (Mercado Iberoamericano De la Industria Audiovisual) award it received in the summer of 1997 as the best Spanish-language telenovela of the year, prompt us to conclude that this novela performed reasonably well beyond Mexico's borders.

41 Briefly, Televisa's star system works on a couple of different levels. Some would-be telenovela stars are converted singers whose fame as performers already gives them high name recognition, immediately useful to boost interest in any new production. Their participation in novelas also helps their musical careers, as many theme songs become huge hits (at other times, already-famous hit songs are used as theme songs for novelas). Just as often, young telenovela actors and actresses are launched as singers through Televisa's musical shows, such as *Siempre en Domingo*. In this way, their names and faces are more easily kept in the public's eye, an objective also met via Televisa's own network of print magazines that specialize in gossip about the artists (*revistas de farándula*). Finally, new stars are usually developed in steps, beginning as supporting characters and, once they've gained popularity, moving on to leading roles.

42 Quoted in Garay, "1996 es el año de TV Azteca."

43 Ibid.

44 Zurita and Bach have their own production company, ZuBa, which has already produced several novelas for TV Azteca, including *La Chacala* (a story incorporating elements of magical realism), *Azul Tequila* (a Revolution-era historical piece), and *El Candidato* (an explicitly political drama).

45 Di Persia, interview.

46 It should be noted that the initial partnership between Azteca and Telemundo did not work out as smoothly as planned, particularly because the latter underwent a change of ownership in 1998, in a protracted deal that was approved by the FCC a full eight months after it was first announced. The network has been acquired by a consortium led by Sony and Liberty Media. See Vicente Guerrero, "Yo también soy católico-Salinas Pliego," *El*

Norte, 23 May 1998, 3; Andrew Paxman, "FCC Approves Telemundo Takeover," *Variety*, 10 August 1998, 22. However, under this new ownership, Telemundo and Azteca have agreed to a new coproduction venture for telenovelas; see *Dow Jones News Service*, "Mexico's TV Azteca, Telemundo Reach Co-Production Pact," 17 June 1999.

47 Di Persia, interview.

48 Quoted in *Adcebra* (1997)

49 Leslie Crawford, "Televisa Chief Hands Control to His Son," *Financial Times*, 4 March 1997.

50 Sutter, "Mexican Acquisition Executives."

51 *Reuter Business Report*, 21 May 1997.

52 Preston, "A Firm Grip on Mexico's Dial."

53 Adriana Garay, "Pintan la pantalla de colores," *Reforma*, 28 August 1998, 4.

54 Joel Millman, "Mexican Retailer's Move Pummels Stock," *Wall Street Journal*, 10 April 1996, A15.

55 Arturo García Hernández, "Mala experiencia, no fracaso," *La Jornada*, 24 July 1998, 45, 49.

56 As a curious note, we must indicate that *Tentaciones* ended on the same night (July 24, 1998) as Televisa's popular remake of *La Usurpadora*. On Monday, July 27, Televisa's new offering, *El Privilegio de Amar*, began. This is a story that begins with a young would-be priest in a Catholic seminary who falls in love (and in bed) with a beautiful young woman. Though *Privilegio*'s producer, Carla Estrada, claims her production is "completely different" from Azteca's *Tentaciones*, it is hard to ignore the obvious coincidence and to refrain from making at least the following two comments: first, that Televisa seems to be paying close attention to what Azteca is doing; and second, that Estrada's reluctance to draw any comparisons between the two novelas is quite understandable. See Ethel Alvarez, "Carla Estrada no acepta comparaciones," *Reforma*, 9 July 1998.

57 Omar Hernández, "Transnational Cultural Products and National Production of Cultures: The Effects of Globalization on Latin American *Telenovelas*," Ph.D. diss., University of Texas at Austin, 2000.

58 Belejack, "Aztec Time."

Cablevision(nation) in Rural Yucatán: Performing Modernity and *Mexicanidad* in the Early 1990s

Alison Greene

Cablevision came to Pustunich, a small town in the *municipio* of Ticul, Yucatán, in August 1991, exactly one year before I arrived to conduct fieldwork there. Brought by a Ticul businessman and political leader of one of the two factions of the PRI, cable service was offered for an initial installation charge followed by a monthly service fee. Four satellite dishes were installed on the two highest roofs in the town center. Some advocates of this businessman's political faction viewed subscription to cable service as an act of solidarity. At least several members of the rival PRI faction viewed the issue similarly and acknowledged that they were contributing to this entrepreneur's already sizable wealth by subscribing. However, they were unwilling to forgo participation in cable technology. The great majority of households signed up for the service immediately, regardless of political orientation. One key reason for this instant marketing success is that no one was required to pay much of anything up front.[1]

The immediate effects of the installation of cable were not very dramatic. Most households had televisions and VCRs prior to cable, and the majority of residents already had a long-established taste for regular viewing. The most direct and immediate effect was that the half dozen or so households that had made small amounts of money by running video rental businesses out of their homes were immediately driven out of business. New movies were now available several times a day via cable. Reception was much clearer and there was now much, much more to receive. Cable initially simply intensified local involvement in broadcast television. Still, internationally produced programming available through Univisión, Telemundo, CNN, and ESPN was also a significant novelty. The local televisual world had instantaneously become global.[2]

Television viewing was not originally one of my topics of investigation, but it pressed itself into my view. In my study of economic change and women's work, I was committed to attend to everyday life and to the local meanings attached to the experience of dramatic socioeconomic and cultural change. Watching television was one significant, if not defining feature of everyday life. Hence I began to record and analyze people's talk about television in general, patterns of television watching (what was interesting to whom), and uses made of material from TV. Because of my interest in women's changing lives, I was, perhaps inevitably, drawn into involvement with the *telenovelas* popular in the village in 1992 and 1993. What was happening on television in general and in these serials particularly formed at least part of my conversations with all women, almost every day. In my study of Pustunich, interpreting television talk and other social uses of television directed me to issues of great importance to women in town and provided insight into the senses in which they view themselves as "Mexican" women.

In this essay I present ethnographic material about the reception and social uses made of television in this particular place to demonstrate the strong connections between participation in television and local conceptions of "modernity" and *mexicanidad*.[3] The appropriation of televisual material into the practice of everyday life is an important means by which people in this small town come to experience mexicanidad and to incorporate it into their own lives as a feature of complex and constantly changing identities. Following Ana López, I show that participating in television creates the nation as "imagined community" at the local level in significant ways, and to a lesser extent fosters identifications with a transnational Latin American world.[4]

Finally, I take the analysis a step further and describe more general changes in daily practice that are being wrought partly through engagement in television. In her own study of the production and reception of soap operas in Egypt, Lila Abu-Lughod has commented that "careful ethnographic work might reveal significant transformations . . . in social life, . . . the nature of experience itself, . . . [and] the facilitation of new identifications and affiliations" that have been produced through engagement with television.[5]

I argue that the significance of participation in television goes well beyond the fostering of national and even transnational identification, through the creation of a relatively open social space in which, in novel daily practices, new forms of social relationships and new subjectivities are emerging.

Analytical Approach, Theoretical Concerns: Identities/Identifications, Modernity and Mexicanidad, and the Role of Television

The central project of this essay is to show with ethnographic description and story how practices of television viewing contribute to nation building at the local level and processes of sociocultural transformation in general. First, however, I briefly define the central terms of the argument and make plain my theoretical orientation and analytical approach. Then I provide a short historical sketch of Pustunich in its relation to the Mexican state to provide a context for interpretation before turning to the ethnographic material.

The concept of identity is fundamental to my analysis. Although I agree with critiques of essentialist conceptions of identity, questions of identities and identifications and their production were absolutely central to the work of understanding local responses to profound economic reorganization. Stuart Hall notes that the concept of identity will not go away because it is crucial "to the question of agency and politics." Hall writes, "It seems to be in the attempt to rearticulate the relationship between subjects and discursive practices that the question of identity recurs—or rather, if one prefers to stress the process of subjectification to discursive practices, and the politics of exclusion which all such subjectification seems to entail, the question of *identification*."[6] People in Pustunich frequently explained their strategies for dealing with new circumstances ultimately by reference to the demands of their own *formas de ser* (ways of being), or "selves."[7] Specific identifications and performed identities strike me as component parts of such "selves."[8]

When I refer to "identities" I do not mean to imply any sort of fixed essence, but rather the conglomeration of images and discursive forms that people marshal to (re)present themselves in daily social practice. I am interested in the ways people build "identities," through attraction to and identification with particular stories and forms and through ongoing social negotiation in particular and multiple contexts. The following exploration of national and transnational identifications and the production and performance of modern, Mexican identities focuses on the readings and appropriations of television into daily practice by particular persons. It does not, however, require a theoretical return to the Cartesian "unitary subject" or "lone thinker." Television viewing in Pustunich is a profoundly social activity, as are the procedures involved in appropriating forms from television into daily life.

Modernity and mexicanidad (essential Mexicanness) are two key issues in local productions and presentations of identities. Though these terms have general currency, what concerns me here is specifically local readings of these concepts and the ways they are deployed in local social fields. The importance of modernity in local identity constructions is immediately obvious because a dichotomy between *lo moderno* (the modern) and *lo tradicional* (the traditional) is daily re-created and reinforced in village discourse (regardless of how thoroughly discredited this dichotomy is in critical intellectual circles).[9] Virtually everyone in town views modernity as an important issue, regardless of how they position themselves in relation to it. In conversations every day, young people of Pustunich invoke the "modern" as desirable and appropriate, and dismiss whatever practice they deem "traditional" as belonging properly to a "time that has already passed." On the other hand, many older people in Pustunich describe themselves using terms that are understood to oppose them to lo moderno, including *tradicional, más o menos tradicional, pobres, gente humilde*, and *campesinos* (traditional; more or less traditional; poor people; humble people; peasant farmers).

All young people in Pustunich wish at some level to participate in modernity as it is locally construed, and to be considered modern by others. The problem is that modernity is neither a transparent nor a closed category. Hence, multiple "struggles of classification" are taking place in daily discourse surrounding the definition of modernity and its attributes in practice.[10] For instance, individuals often compare their own habits and tastes to those of specific neighbors to claim modernity for themselves and to question tacitly their neighbors' status as modern. Habits that are commonly brought up in such comparisons include hygiene and health practices, ways of eating, and manners of speaking. Tastes in food, entertainment, and clothing styles are also held to indicate traditional or modern character. Young people constantly make such efforts to be identified as modern, *nonethnic*, urbane individuals, and to distance themselves from their rural, poor, Maya roots.[11]

In contrast to lo moderno, mexicanidad is not often invoked in daily conversation. However, this lack of discussion does not mean that mexicanidad is insignificant in local social practice. The definition of mexicanidad is not a point of active contention, in part because there is general familiarity with and agreement on the ideal forms and contents of Mexican national character. Furthermore, as I argue in the following section, although Pustunicheños consider themselves Yucatecos first, all participate to some extent in the Mexican nation and culture and accept the participation of their neighbors as a given. Therefore, everyone in town already possesses mexicanidad in some measure, and there is not much to discuss.

Defining mexicanidad or lo mexicano became an interest of Mexican intellectuals and statesmen beginning with Independence.[12] Around the turn of the twentieth century, Justo Sierra elaborated an extremely influential version of lo mexicano that would become the core of later portrayals. According to Sierra, the Mexican people were in the process, begun by the Conquest, of evolving from the mixture of two "races," the Spanish and the indigenous.[13] Thus, mestizos were the only true Mexicans.[14]

After the 1910 revolution, defining and disseminating mexicanidad was institutionalized as a key facet of many state-led efforts at nation building, including myriad development initiatives, the extension of public education, and, not least, through state support for the development of a national-(ist) cinema and later television.[15] This situation continues to the present day. Postrevolutionary representations of mexicanidad have continued to center on the figure of the mestizo, whose indigenous heritage is valorized but submerged. Machismo defines the character of the mestizo, and is expressed in the endeavor to defend patriarchal honor, the family, and *la patria*. Furthermore, the mestizo is not a static form, but is caught up in a teleological evolution paralleling the development of capitalist society, moving away from its indigenous, rural roots and toward the urban and "civilized."[16] Despite this clearly identifiable core figure, portrayals of mexicanidad, regardless of genre or medium (e.g., from intellectual essay to film melodrama), have always joined multiple and contradictory discourses in the attempt to engage all sectors of Mexico's diverse and highly stratified society.[17]

Daily life in Pustunich has been and continues to be profoundly affected by many kinds of state programs aimed at nation building. Film, radio, and television, however, have been by far the most successful purveyors of locally appealing images of mexicanidad.[18] Based on hundreds of conversations with informants about Mexican music, films, and television pro-grams, I argue that this corpus provides a set of relatively open and evolving, yet clearly recognizable, archetypal characters, styles, and discursive forms that constitute mexicanidad in the rural imaginary.[19]

Modernity and mexicanidad become linked in local image and practice. Common practices such as the adoption of styles recognized as distinctly modern *and* specifically Mexican reveal that mexicanidad features promi-nently in local identity productions. Francine Masiello argues that con-sumption from media resources has a long history that is bound up with processes of state formation in Latin America. Masiello writes, "The accou-trements of gender—cosmetics, dress, and pose—are treated as commodi-ties to be bought and sold in the image-making service of the nation. In effect, from the time of the nineteenth-century independence wars through the recent transition to democracy, patterns of dress and sexuality have formed part and parcel of the Latin American political imagination. . . . Fashion thus strengthened the projects of the modern state; it also endorsed a mode of citizenship related to sales and commerce."[20]

In the local field, practices of style consumption were not usually con-nected with the nation or citizenship in conversation. However, these prac-tices were seen as directly involved in the ongoing process of presenting self-as-modern and staking claims in local social terrain for recognition of this status.[21] It is my contention that local people view the adoption and per-sonal tailoring of mexicanidad as the most appropriate and easiest entrance into modernity. In other words, mexicanidad serves as the most desirable variety of modernity.

In their study of the Golden Age of Mexican cinema, Carlos Monsiváis and Carlos Bonfil argue that cinema gained immense popularity with masses of rural and urban poor Mexican people, partly because through engagement with specifically national melodrama, such subaltern people learned how to be modern and Mexican.[22] This situation persisted with the proliferation of broadcast television. Monsiváis claims that melodrama, the central discursive form of Mexican film and television serials, has thus acted as a major vehicle of cultural modernization in Mexico. According to Mon-siváis, melodrama "became a secular form of catechism: modernity con-densed, made consumable and simple."[23]

My own research on television viewing confirms and extends this inter-pretation. However, though I found residents of Pustunich to be avid con-sumers of melodrama and other televisual material, I am not advancing an argument of transparent media imperialism: that all people simply absorb and are transformed by melodrama and whatever else is broadcast by the hegemonic culture.[24] Nor do I wish to imply that the residents of Pustunich are unschooled and innocent *güiros* (hicks or country bumpkins) who are forced by the poverty of their own traditions and social positions to take advice on becoming civilized wherever they can get it. On the contrary, the current political and economic situation in rural Yucatán has given every rural family a practical impetus to use material from television in preparation for urban-based working lives. It has become possible and even common for young people to find jobs in tourist zones and for a minority to obtain education for relatively secure, urban professions, including elementary school teaching, nursing, and engineering. These opportunities are perceived as open to all people as long as they successfully disguise or discard marks of their rural, Maya history.

The social mechanics of practical learning from television begin at the viewing site. As family groups watch TV, many conventional practices of social positioning, comportment, and the content and style of speech are temporarily suspended as participants talk about what they are viewing, joke loudly, and imitate what occurs on the screen. Roger Lancaster argues that play, partly because it is recognized as superfluous, "embodies practice at its freest and most creative." After a careful consideration of the key features of play, Lancaster asks rhetorically, "Is it such a far step to ask whether what social constructionism attempts to describe is also a kind of play? Would it really be so outlandish to suggest that play is the 'matrix of identity,' that very surplus of activity whose consequences entail 'subjects,' 'selves,' and 'groups?'"[25]

In my observations of the social uses of television in Pustunich, this suggestion does not seem at all outlandish. In this small town in rural Yucatán, television creates a space for identity play within the household. Furthermore, when and wherever stories from television are discussed (with the important exception of news stories),[26] a playful social atmosphere is recreated. The social flexibility of this atmosphere permits the testing of unconventional practices.

The alterations of social practice allowed for by television are particularly noteworthy for women. Although verbal play is a highly developed and greatly appreciated tradition in Yucatec Maya culture, an almost extreme verbal reticence is valued in public conversation across the region.[27] Women in particular are hesitant to talk much in public, and the negative term *chis-*

mosa (gossipy) is applied to women by others who consider them morally suspect. A good woman, daughter, or wife *no platica mucho* (doesn't chat much). Although in domestic settings, especially in groups of female kin or with classmates, girls and women engage in lively conversation about all kinds of issues, women are generally not accustomed to expressing their opinions individualistically. During my interviews about educational and economic plans and aspirations, most women couched their responses in terms of "responsibility to family." In the context of discussing television programs, however, women expressed pleasure and a wide range of emotions, voicing more strong opinions and detailed aspirations than they ever did during structured research interviews focusing on their experiences of economic change. As Marie Gillespie found in her ethnographic study of television, ethnicity, and culture change, "TV talk, though it may often seem esoteric and trivial, is an important form of self-narration and a major collective resource through which identities are negotiated."[28]

In summary, the social power accorded to television is demonstrated by the alterations in practice that television viewing is allowed to engender. This power arises from the prior identification of television and all its products with modernity and is augmented by the context of rapid economic change. To put it most simply, televisual material and television viewing practices provide indispensable resources in local productions and performances of modern, Mexican identities.

Context: The State of the Nation in One Small Town

Pustunich is a small town of about three thousand residents in the southern Puuc zone of the state of Yucatán. Classified as a *comisario*, Pustunich is politically and economically subordinate to Ticul, the large industrial town next door. Through the 1960s, *milpa* agriculture was the basis of survival, and Yucatec Maya was the principal language in town.[29] Almost all adult men were campesinos first and foremost. Almost all women were peasant farmers' wives and wore traditional Maya dress. Over the course of thirty years, Pustunich has been transformed into a primarily Spanish-speaking town that depends principally on wages earned in construction and service work in tourist zones.

As has been amply documented, the entire Yucatán peninsula long remained a relatively marginal zone of the nation, arguably until the development of tourism on the Caribbean coast in the 1970s.[30] Certainly, residents believe that their town is a marginal place from any urban point of view. Nonetheless, primary place identification in Pustunich is first local, and then regional.[31] To outsiders, people generally describe themselves as Yucatecos rather than Mexicanos or any term signifying the nation.[32] Also indicative of a continuing sense of separation from the nation is the practice of designating people from other parts of Mexico with the Yucatec Maya term *huach*.[33] Local people insist this word simply indicates people who originate outside of the Yucatán peninsula and is not pejorative. Still, the common use of the term communicates the prevalent local sense that there is an essential difference between native Yucatecos and everybody else.

Despite these continuing signs of provincialism in outlook, Pustunicheños have long been caught up in the politics of the region, and by extension the nation. Typical of the region, the town also has a long history of engagement in transnational capitalism. Although Pustunich always maintained physical independence, villagers participated in the early-nineteenth-century production of sugar at the neighboring plantation, Tabí, and later in the production of henequen on numerous haciendas. Located at the southern tip of the henequen zone, village independence had to be actively protected during the nineteenth-century henequen boom.[34] During my fieldwork in the early 1990s, there were still several old men who had personal memories of the final years of the *época de esclavitud*, the period of debt peonage associated with prerevolutionary henequen production.[35]

Many local residents retain vivid memories of the revolutionary era. Throughout the 1920s the village was divided into factions of "liberals" and "socialists." The sometimes violent struggles between these groups are remembered and at times replicated in current factional political fights. In this period, Yucatán's socialist governor, Felipe Carrillo Puerto, made several visits to the village and gained much support for his projects among locals on the socialist side.

The Mexican Revolution made a big difference in Pustunich, notwithstanding its failures. The revolutionary period was described by several local older men as the point at which relations between national government and rural citizens were transformed. For the first time campesinos felt invited to participate.[36] Since the Revolution, residents of Pustunich have been actively and continuously involved in national politics, participating through the fractious local arena of the municipio of Ticul. A majority of men and

many women vote in every election, although the rewards for such participation appear to be few and complaints about the ineffectiveness, un-
fairness, and corruption of all levels of government are frequently heard.

Since the Revolution, Yucatán has frequently been the object of development initiatives directed by the Mexican state. Many such programs have
affected Pustunich directly.[37] For example, the extension of public education was extremely significant in Pustunich. Though a secondary school was
opened in town only in 1993, Pustunicheños enjoyed unprecedented access
to educational programs outside of town beginning in the late 1950s.
Through a stroke of luck, the first primary school teacher from Pustunich
was hired to work in the state office of the Secretaría de Educación Pública.
He became an effective conduit, channeling promising local primary school
students into the rapidly expanding national system of normal schools.

By the early 1990s, former residents of Pustunich were teaching all over
Mexico, and fifty teachers from Pustunich daily left home to teach in rural
schools in nearby towns. Schoolteachers have thus formed a significant sector of the local population since the late 1970s. Until the decentralization of
the education system in 1993, primary school teachers or members of their
families occasionally had to travel to Mexico City to conduct bureaucratic
business with their employers. A trip to the national office of the Secretaría
de Educación Pública was often required, for example, to arrange a position
transfer or to receive back pay.

With regard to economic activities, townspeople participated in both formal development projects and informal income-generating strategies. For
example, beginning in the 1950s, Pustunich was included in state-directed
efforts to develop irrigated citrus production for export. Furthermore,
through the late 1970s, many residents of Pustunich engaged in petty commodity production and "putting-out work" for a number of industries.[38] In
the late 1970s, the participation of local people in wage labor began to increase due to the growth of the regional tourist industry.

Residents of Pustunich became avid consumers of radio and film in the
late 1950s. By the early 1960s almost every family had a transistor radio, and
a local merchant operated an extremely popular open-air cinema on the lot
behind his store.[39] Almost all adult residents of Pustunich have seen most if
not all of the classics of Mexican cinema. Many local people developed tremendous affection and appetite for Mexican music and film quite early on
in the local history of electronic media. One family, whose attachment to
Yucatecan traditions and Maya practices is still well known, started naming

their pet dogs after film stars (e.g., Negrete) in the early 1960s. At the time, one of their daughters, who had a nice singing voice, quickly learned songs from the radio; her mother made her a *charro* costume, and she earned money for the family by singing northern Mexican music at parties in Ticul.[40] Thus, to a great extent, local people adopted musical and filmic products of national culture as their own.

Regardless of the scant success of perhaps most development projects and income-generating strategies, the potential opportunity of each successive development scheme since the late 1950s has drawn most residents of Pustunich into common contact with government agencies. At the same time the consumption of national(ist) music, movies, and most recently television has provided pleasure and entertainment, a sweet side to entanglement with the nation-state. Through this history of involvement in political process, cultural productions, the educational system, economic development projects, and extraregional industries, residents have become well aware of the importance in their own lives of events in Mexico City. Pustunicheños are Mexican citizens in practice and are highly cognizant of this fact. Furthermore, local sensibilities are distinctly Mexican as well as Yucatecan.

The development of Cancún in 1975 as a hotspot of international tourism dramatically accelerated the changes in daily life that were already underway. Their history of long-standing involvements with the state and global economy alongside continuing relative isolation and independence demonstrates amply that residents of Pustunich are full-fledged participants in modernity, at least from an outsider's perspective.[41] This historical context must be kept in mind in the following discussion of the readings and uses of television, because it shapes current orientations of residents of Pustunich to television.

Gustando: General Patterns

In Pustunich and throughout Yucatán, people use the verb *gustar* (to taste, to try) in its uncommonly used active form to refer to the activity of using television, rather than the standard verb *mirar* (to look at, to watch). The standard phrase for watching television is *gustando* with or without the addition of the understood object, *la tele*. Although I don't know the specific historical depth of this phrase, because the term is almost universally used it seems likely to have been established in the era of outdoor cinema in rural areas. To my outsider ears, the use of a verb that in its active form refers to consumption and eating, and in its more common reflexive form indicates pleasure and having a liking for the subject, seems extremely apt because the general orientation to television and its uses is overwhelmingly positive.

People in town are interested in many kinds of programming. Kids watch cartoons before and after school. National and international sports programs (especially baseball and soccer/*fútbol*) are popular with men and boys, and *lucha libre* (championship wrestling) matches captivate whole families. Movies (mostly reruns of Mexican classics and dubbed U.S.-made films—horror and adventure genres are most popular), both Mexican and "transnational" talk shows such as *Cristina* on Univisión, and a few dubbed U.S. serials (I couldn't seem to escape *Friday the 13th*, the serial) are all common fare. *Shows de Auditorium* (*Sábado Gigante* and *Siempre en Domingo*) dominate weekend evening viewing. Advertising, national and especially international (on Telemundo and Univisión), is a popular genre in itself.[42] National and international news shows (Mexican network and CNN broadcasts), although the object of intense interest for a small minority, are sprinkled throughout daily programming and precede evening programs, so that few people go through whole days without hearing at least parts of news broadcasts. Finally, Mexican-made telenovelas are by far the most important type of television program in their great popularity and the amount of time that goes into watching and discussing them.

Although everyone consumes, women are more deeply involved in television than men. Certainly, if fathers or older sons have a preference for a particular program, the entire family defers to their wishes. However, at least in my presence, men tended not to express strong opinions about or preferences for television programs. Perhaps this is because in the local social milieu, men have customarily had a wider range of leisure options and are free to leave the house as they please. Proper women and girls, on the other hand, stay at home in the evening after a family outing to the park. In practice, choice of television programming is by and large the province of women.[43]

Social Uses of Television

Although some older people clearly preferred life without television (one grandmother in her sixties told me that it gives her a headache), the great majority of people enjoy television. Almost all households possess at least one color set (I estimate that fewer than a dozen of over two hundred households do not have televisions). Furthermore, almost every household with a television has cable service. Television now forms a common audiovisual backdrop to many parts of daily practice. Many of my interviews were conducted with the television on. In short, it would be difficult to overstate the immense impact of television viewing on the practice of daily life in Pustunich.

Television is, perhaps first and foremost, entertaining. While they watch television together, family groups and groups of friends comment on and sometimes imitate pieces of the action. Stories from television are related later to those who did not see them. Jokes, slapstick routines, songs, dance moves, and dramatic interactions are later repeated in living rooms, school yards, and the town park. One group of young people, the Club of the Eighties, used telenovela plots and characters as the basic structure for humorous plays they wrote and performed in town. Interactions during broadcasts and later repetitions of televisual material are typically playful and relatively free of social constraint.

On the other hand, television is regarded by many as a tremendous resource for authoritative information and knowledge. One elderly campesino was genuinely interested in national and international news. In his view, television brought a type of empowerment through increased knowledge of the wider world. He told me that before they had cablevision, it wasn't that they weren't interested in larger issues and world events, it was just that they had no idea what was happening. World news seemed to provide some town residents with a sense that they could evaluate their own position in the world in a more positive, informed, and objective way. They might be poor, but they were positively rich and lucky compared to Bosnians and Somalians, not to mention people from rural Chiapas.[44]

In all kinds of conversations every day television is used as a source of authority and legitimation, an impartial purveyor and arbiter of the modern, urban, and civilized. One man underlined his disdain for the misplaced sense of superiority exhibited by priests that served the village by quoting a priest that he had heard interviewed on a television talk show. The priest on television reportedly stated that he was just one man before God and that he knew it was not his place to judge other men or tell them how to live their lives. The television priest exposed and confirmed the hypocrisy of local priests that this man perceived; television undermined whatever shred of authority they might have exercised over him.

People take all kinds of things directly from television into their own lives and then claim the provenance of these things as a built-in justification.

Televisual materials give impetus and form to emergent practices in town. For instance, the local novelty of young women engaging in calorie counting, jogging, and aerobic dance to lose weight was fueled by talk and fitness shows. The proper conduct of romantic relationships is often the subject of talk shows and has become a popular topic of conversation among young women. Furthermore, young women frequently copy styles directly from television programs. These are just a few examples of the local riot of consumption from television.

In summary, television in Pustunich is generally viewed as an important information resource, an extralocal and impersonal source of authority, and a tremendous repository of models of modernity. The combination of these authoritative features with the nonserious and playful aspects of televisual involvements makes television an extremely potent force in social and cultural change. Interpreting the role of television in observed changes is, however, no simple affair. The following observation by my village landlady provides a cautionary note regarding this reading of television use. A widow in her early sixties who was deeply involved in the administration of the local Catholic church, she frequently expressed the view that "television gives excellent models for a good religious life." However, she would then continue, "Unfortunately, people here are so bad, they overlook all of the good on television and take only the worst examples."[45] Television tastes, readings, and uses are by no means homogeneous in town. In fact, the selection of television programs and their interpretation provide one distinct arena for local interpretive struggles over the meaning and proper content of modernity.

In the following sections, I turn first to a consideration of the social practices associated with viewing telenovelas and then provide an ethnographic case that illustrates how local participation in Mexican telenovelas qualifies as an "everyday form of state formation."[46] I then examine a negative route to national identifications available through engagement with national and international broadcasts. Local identifications with and commitments to the Mexican state are forged partly through oppositions to gringos and the United States. Finally, I argue briefly that particularly nationalistic identifications, fostered positively through engagements in telenovelas, are mediated by transnational Hispanic programming that is also consumed in town via cable. Transnational television works in these social milieux to produce additional identifications that conflict at some points with specifically nationalist identities.

Telenovelas and Positive Constructions of Nation Identification

Ana M. López argues that many studies of Latin American telenovelas have misunderstood the nature of the power of these programs by analyzing them outside of the social contexts of reception. She claims that it is important to understand how telenovelas are "inserted into daily life." This approach avoids the skewed conclusions reached by studies utilizing media imperialism theory, which construed telenovelas as the "alienating guest" that supposedly were intended to globalize the culture of the household. This focus on daily social practices also eschews conclusions reached by adherents to the opposing theory of "reverse media imperialism." This theory cast telenovelas as "saviors" of national culture. López proposes an intermediate image, the "welcomed guest," which takes account of the interpretive role of viewers in assessing the practical effects of telenovelas. López states, "Thus refigured as a 'welcomed guest' rather than an alienating poacher or a national savior, the telenovela can be understood as an agent for and participant in the complex processes of Latin American modernization, nation-building, and increasing transnationalization."[47] In my analysis of specific responses to telenovelas, I attempt to show several ways that telenovelas become active "sites of mediation."[48]

According to López, the telenovela is a form of melodrama that emphasizes dialogue (over visual staging and action) and narrative closure and consistently uses melodramatic devices (e.g., returns from the past, reversals of fortune, painful confrontations) to structure stories. Most important, López argues, "the telenovela exploits personalization—the individualization of the social world—as an epistemology. It ceaselessly offers its audience dramas of recognition and re-cognition by locating social and political issues in personal and familial terms and thus making sense of an increasingly complex world."[49] Finally, López notes that telenovelas change form over time and in different national contexts. In comparison with telenovelas produced in other nations, "Mexican telenovelas are notorious for their weepiness, extraordinarily Manichaean vision of the world, and lack of specific historical referents."[50]

I learned that local residents are highly cognizant of the predictable specificity of the Mexican telenovela in a conversation one afternoon with a seamstress, Martina, her younger sister, Amalia, and their friend and neighbor, Lucía. Three of us sat on the double bed while Martina worked at her sewing machine. They recounted the story of a popular telenovela that had been broadcast the previous year. Not far into their description I interrupted. I admitted confusion, because the story they were telling sounded just like a telenovela that was currently being broadcast. No, they assured me, this was an entirely different telenovela. I protested that the two sounded exactly alike. Martina responded, "Yes, they are all the same," in a tone that suggested that this fact was completely irrelevant. Then the three young women produced a verbal composite sketch of the standard Mexican telenovela: The main character is a good woman who falls in love with a man, who, if he can't be called good, is for some reason desirable; this good woman has all kinds of difficulties, usually experiencing danger or personal tragedy at the hands of one or more bad women (greedy, mean, and/or sexually voracious women, in my understanding); despite the difficulties, in the end, the good girl gets the guy; during the last episode, they marry in a religious ceremony, *a lo mejor* in the Basilica of Guadalupe in Mexico City.

This admission of a standard pattern did not preclude their interest. The three women avidly absorbed the particular details of each successive telenovela and relished guessing outcomes of the multiple subplots.[51] They looked for favorite actors and actresses who appeared in telenovela after telenovela and occasionally read about them in the magazine *TV y Novela*. There is no question that they recognized the telenovelas as Mexican. After all, the writers, many or most of the actors, the symbols (e.g., the Virgin of Guadalupe), and the settings are Mexican. They were also aware of the great popularity of these telenovelas all over the country.[52] Occasionally, telenovelas produced in other parts of Latin America become popular in town, but generally, Mexican telenovelas are much preferred. Familiarity in this case breeds not contempt but strong identification.

The fact that Mexican telenovelas have a distinctive Mexican form that is recognized by local people and that works to constitute the nation in living space, as I argue below, does not exhaust the images and discursive forms contained in them or the meanings attached to these images and forms. Alongside the main characters, who embody and enact the struggle of good and evil, are more ambiguous characters. Multiple contradictions emerge in the combination of subplots. Mexican telenovelas are also characterized by "contending discourses."[53] Regardless of the intents of writers and producers, local consumers of Mexican telenovelas take all kinds of messages from them.

In her study of the reception of nationalist soap opera in Egypt, Abu-Lughod cautions that responses to soap operas are not predictable and that viewers may well ignore patriotic content intended by serial writers or readings that might be assumed to be predictable by outsiders. In Abu-Lughod's interviews concerning an extremely popular and overtly nationalistic serial, "when asked what they liked about the serial, several poor women who work as domestic servants in Cairo volunteered not the serious political or social messages, but the character of Nazik Hanem, the aristocratic, conniving, magnificently dressed *femme fatale* who plays the leading female role."[54] In Pustunich too, telenovela materials are subject to all sorts of readings and put to all kinds of uses, and none of these multiple uses has transparent meanings. They cannot be understood without reference to the complex social fields in which they are deployed.

For example, during my stay in the community, two baby girls were named after characters in current telenovelas.[55] One of the infants was born to a young married couple who were following tradition and living and working with the young man's father, a respected town leader. They named their baby Cassandra after a supporting character in a telenovela about a band of gypsies. The gypsy women were portrayed as beautiful but passionate, willful, and wild, hardly desirable characteristics for a girl in town circles. Nonetheless, this first case did not provoke much of a response in village conversation. Perhaps the couple's secure social position buffered them from criticism.

Around the same time, however, another baby was named Aidé, after the *mala* of noble birth in an ostensibly historical telenovela. Many women semiprivately registered negative judgments about this choice. Much of this negative judgment undoubtedly arose from the fact that, in the second case, the mother was single and the baby's father was said to be married to someone else. Still, several women specifically viewed this name choice as confirmation of the mother's and even the grandmother's apparent sense of superiority, unfriendly demeanor, and antisocial character. Even some close relatives of the baby seemed uncomfortable with the choice and called the baby by a diminutive form of her mother's name.

Multiple valences contained in telenovela stories themselves are multiplied as pieces of stories are brought into the complex and intersecting social fields of daily life by actors with all kinds of motivations. Furthermore, conflicts in interpretation emerge in conversations and in evaluations of particular instances of appropriations from telenovelas. Finally, the use of telenovela materials can have results that are not always consciously intended. There is always a surplus of meanings in appropriations of television, beyond any specific deployments or their explanations. Despite these complexities, engagement with telenovelas produces observable effects in practice. In the following section, I describe the nation-building effects of local participation in one particular telenovela in Pustunich.

María Mercedes

María Mercedes (para servirle a Ud.) was the most popular telenovela broadcast during my fieldwork in 1992 and 1993, and the story was already in full swing when I arrived. Although initially I kept to myself, retiring to my little house at night without cable or even TV, I soon noticed that something was going on. The town's central park was lit up at night and usually full of people from a little after sunset until 8:45 P.M. Then (on weeknights) everyone would quickly drain away, and the center of town remained deserted and quiet. When I commented on this to my landlady, she laughed and told me that everyone had to get inside to see the telenovela *María Mercedes*. She was an organizer of many activities at the Catholic church at the center of town, and she said that no meetings could successfully be scheduled to overlap with *María Mercedes*; no one would show up. She then admitted that she was glad enough to be free of her church responsibilities by default, because she too absolutely adored *María Mercedes*, the story and the character.[56] There is no doubt that watching *María Mercedes* was a significant and regular source of pleasure in town.

María Mercedes is the story of a poor but exceptionally beautiful and virtuous girl in Mexico City (played by the popular Mexican actress and singer Thalía). Her mother abandoned the family years before the action starts, and her father is wheelchair-bound, alcoholic, and unable to support the family. Because of this, María Mercedes is forced to earn money to take care of her father and younger brothers and sisters. She walks the streets of Mexico City, selling lottery tickets. All who meet her are struck by her innocence and beauty, including a very rich man who is terminally ill.

This rich man is aware that his already wealthy relatives (his wife, Malvina, and her son, Jorge Luis, and daughter, Digna) can barely contain their eagerness to see him in his grave so that they can have his money too. Before he dies, he changes his will and states that Jorge Luis will inherit all his money only if he marries the poor lottery ticket salesgirl. Not surprisingly, Malvina and Jorge Luis think the match a preposterous idea, but they are determined to get the money. Hence they scheme to get María Mercedes to marry Jorge Luis, and then plan to get rid of her somehow, after they have secured the riches.

Things don't go smoothly for these bad guys, because María Mercedes is so irresistibly good. In her innocence, she actually falls in love with Jorge Luis. Jorge Luis finds himself attracted to her and pulled by her sheer goodness away from his life of vice. Still, his mother's influence is strong, as is the influence of Mística, a temptress who tries repeatedly and successfully to divert Jorge Luis from his increasing love for María Mercedes. María Mercedes marries Jorge Luis in a civil ceremony and instantly becomes pregnant with their future son.

Jorge Luis is unfaithful; María Mercedes is miserable; and Malvina is dead set against her as a legitimate daughter-in-law. Surrounded by enemies, María Mercedes is faithful and works hard to keep her man. All the while she remains completely ignorant of the money at stake. She physically fights with Mística and tries to show Jorge Luis true love. Finally, good and virtue win out over evil, greed, and immoral sensuality. In the last episode of the telenovela, María Mercedes gets her just reward when Jorge Luis marries her in the Basilica of the Virgin of Guadalupe with her baby son in her arms.

María Mercedes (para servirle a Ud.) was an archetypically Mexican telenovela. The form of this telenovela however, was in many respects unique. *María Mercedes* was a self-conscious spoof, one that exaggerated and caricatured the specifically Mexican telenovela form, while at the same time locating itself squarely within that form. The names of many of the characters were directly linked to their essential natures. María Mercedes is the young virgin (closely linked in imagery to the Virgin Mary); the evil mother-in-law is Malvina (people in Pustunich pronounced this as two words, *mala-vina*, bad vine); the sister-in-law is Digna (in this case a tongue-in-cheek assessment of an obedient mouse who always did her mother's bidding); and the sexy temptress is named Mística (pronounced *X'Mística* by the women of Pustunich),[57] portrayed as a witch who suddenly appears on the scene and then leaves by vanishing.

Viewers in Pustunich were not put off by this exaggeration of the story in form. If anything, they enjoyed the high relief of the moral roles portrayed and the classic main story line. Men, women, and children watched *María Mercedes*, but women were most deeply involved. Many women would watch a repeat broadcast of the previous evening's episode in the morning if they could manage it at the same time they did their housework. María Mercedes seems to have been a universally appealing character, but older women seem to have found her particularly irresistible because of her absolute innocence. My landlady commented that María Mercedes was so good, such a good daughter, such a hard worker; this was evident in the way she spoke, in the innocent things she said. Her life reminded my landlady of her own life, her innocence and illusions right before marrying. In this recognition of herself in the heroine, my landlady's memory of her own life was brightened. She also invoked the character of María Mercedes as a fine example of Catholic morality in talks she gave at the church. Thus, in my landlady's case, the character of María Mercedes served as a model for the past, present, and future.

Individual women identified with different pieces of the *María Mercedes* story, depending on their own experiences. One morning, while I was hanging up my laundry, my quite serious and traditional neighbor rushed out her back door and excitedly called me in to watch: "*Ven acá, Doña Alicia, ven! María Mercedes está reclamando su esposo*" (Come here, Doña Alicia, come on! María Mercedes is reclaiming her husband). I hurried in to watch the scene in which María Mercedes gets into a knock-down, drag-out fight with Mística. I was deeply impressed and puzzled by the extreme pleasure this scene gave this sweet, self-sacrificing grandmother. I later recalled that one of the most difficult parts of my neighbor's life had been her husband's frequent and obvious affairs with other women. For my neighbor, watching *María Mercedes* was a cathartic experience.

The latest events in María Mercedes's life were an important topic of conversation every day in any place where women gathered. For example, women in Pustunich knew María Mercedes was pregnant even before she herself did. All of the women in the marketplace were engaged in a lively discussion of María Mercedes's symptoms the morning after the first hints of a pregnancy were dropped.[58] This motherly sense of knowing (created so simply and so consciously by writers and directors) seems to have increased women's attraction and attachment to María Mercedes. Furthermore, the discussion of María Mercedes's pregnancy was much more detailed than decorum would have allowed in a public discussion of any resident woman's pregnancy. Thus, the telenovela provided an opportunity for a group of women to express themselves forthrightly in public on issues of general significance, including pregnancy and marital relations. Almost everyone shared the interest in *María Mercedes*, and everyone was entitled to an opinion. Among more intimate groups of women, pieces of the telenovela story were broached in direct or indirect reference to real-life events.[59] Because such discussions of telenovelas take place in private and public settings on a daily basis, they serve a community-building function.

Furthermore, discussion of events in the telenovela were not separated from discussions of local social, political, and economic events, and were no less intense.[60] Certainly, local people were able to distinguish between telenovela stories and real-life events; the fact that they did not do so in conversation attests both to the social importance of telenovela talk in town and to the close relationship between telenovela forms and themes and the practice of everyday life. The relatively slow tempo of telenovela narrative fit easily into local patterns of discourse.[61] Five days a week, bits and pieces of the multiple stories in *María Mercedes* emerged and were processed in local talk. Furthermore, the personal, moral themes of melodrama generally paralleled local concerns and ways of viewing the world.[62]

Women's strong personal and collective engagements with *María Mercedes* demonstrate that the viewing of telenovelas in Pustunich is far from passive reception. The deep level of daily involvement in the story would be hard to overemphasize. And the significance of these engagements goes well beyond identifications with particular characters and individual catharsis. Mexican telenovelas like *María Mercedes* generally do not contain overtly nationalistic messages for viewers to absorb and accept or resist and reject. The local, televisual nation-building process is more subtle. Town residents daily and actively participated in this self-consciously and particularly Mexican melodrama by discussing it eagerly and openly with each other. Again as López states, "The telenovela has served to create a televisual 'national' in which the imagined community rallies around specific images of itself. Following in the footsteps of radio and cinema, television increasingly makes 'living' the nation a tangible and daily possibility."[63]

In summary, this oblique process of nation building takes place at multiple levels. First of all, most popular telenovela stories are recognized as essentially Mexican. Apart from this, women frequently strongly identify with specific characters or pieces of the stories. Furthermore, the daily discussion of telenovelas is one of the central unifying practices of social life in town. Finally, local people are aware that this active engagement in telenovelas is occurring in towns and cities all over Mexico. Hence, through active participation in the archetypal national story, locals experience mexicanidad, and the "nation" is created locally.

Negative Receptions: Gringos, Gringo Society, and the United States

Identifications are always partly constructed by negative reference.[64] The contentious relationship between Mexico and the United States has always informed Mexican nationalism. Though few Pustunicheños concern themselves with many details of national history, all are aware of this relationship and of important points of conflict between the two countries.[65] Currently, engagement with a wide range of television programs, including, significantly, television that is produced in the United States and received via cable, reinforces Mexican national identification through oppositions to U.S. society.

People in rural Yucatán are widely known for their generous hospitality to strangers, including foreigners, most of whom are gringos.[66] No doubt the reasons for this are complex. Certainly there is interest in gringo lifestyles and habits, which is fueled by observations in tourist zones.[67] There is also a widespread desire for many items available for sale in the United States. This interest in gringo life experience in the abstract, and the openness and generosity with which visiting gringos are treated, is combined with a distinctly negative overall image of U.S. culture and gringo character.

Rural people gather information about gringos and their culture and society from a wide variety of sources. Personal experience with gringo anthropologists and tourists is not at all rare. Furthermore, relatives and friends who have had contact with gringos in tourist zones provide numerous anecdotes for those whose personal experience is more limited. These stories get passed around town and incorporated into general local knowledge. The most important televisual sources of information about gringos and gringo society include national and international news programs, international advertising, and, to a lesser degree, U.S. television programs. Through dozens of comments and stories, I gradually gathered a rough composite view of local images and impressions of gringos. It is impossible to separate fully the sources of information that compose the following images. In daily conversation, bits of televisual materials, hearsay, personal experiences, and the reports of kin and friends are brought together on the topic and sources often get confounded.

During my fourteen continuous months of fieldwork, local people told me three times that they had heard news of *mi tierra*, North Carolina. The three news stories addressed (1) a series of terribly destructive tornadoes that hit the state; (2) a group of North Carolina witches shown conducting a (satanic?) baptism of a baby; and (3) a resident of North Carolina reported to have attempted suicide by eating pins and needles. I didn't see or hear any of these stories directly, and I know that reporting always entails some odd miscommunications. Still, I am primarily interested in the reception of these stories, not what was actually broadcast. These stories became a part of local understanding of gringo life, experience, and character. They served both to reinforce previously held views and to add new dimensions to previous images. The composite impact of these three stories might not have been very significant, but it could not have been very salutary with regard to local images of my place of origin.

News programs produced in Mexico constantly invoke the nation, and international news programs structure reports around nations and international relations. Local readings of national and international news stories repeatedly confirm the view that North American society is violent, gun crazy, and extremely racist, with perhaps a special racist hatred of Mexican people. Particular news stories that were held to reinforce the last view were frequently broadcast during my stay and became the subject of daily discourse. The broadcast of debates over NAFTA included all manner of anti-Mexican statements from U.S. citizens. Ross Perot gained brief local notoriety as a chief enemy of Mexican people as his anti-NAFTA comments were transmitted and excoriated by television news analysts. Even more upsetting, a Mexican national was executed in a Texas prison despite the efforts of the Mexican government to have him returned to Mexico. Though most of the time people were extremely gracious to me, these particular stories provoked such outrage that several people in town expressed anger and frustration to me about the reported events. In these encounters, Pustunicheños considered themselves affronted Mexican citizens, and I was viewed as a representative of the United States.

From the perspective of many Pustunicheños, people from the United States appear to lack devotion to their families. Gringos do not seem to honor their parents and seem deeply ambivalent about children. Television accounts broadcast during my stay that were seen to support this view included an international news exposé showing elderly people in U.S. rest homes who had been abused by staff personnel. There were also a number of reports of egregious cases of child abuse and neglect.

Furthermore, gringas seemed to avoid pregnancy; some local women concluded that they "feared" childbirth. Of course, very few obviously pregnant gringas toured Yucatán or appeared on television shows. Still, it was assumed that most gringas would eventually want to bear children. Televised stories about the seemingly incredible medical technologies that were used to help older gringas and others with reproductive problems have babies fascinated numerous local women of child-bearing age and older whom I interviewed. This interest in the infertility problems of gringas was not simply a matter of idle curiosity; gringa infertility was thought to have potentially ominous consequences locally. Many locals believed that some gringos kidnap children in Mexico and other countries.[68]

In addition to news stories that chronicle crimes and U.S. actions toward Mexico, cable television has provided views of supposedly more daily experiences through advertising, talk shows, and U.S.-produced serials. In advertisements from the Miami-based Telemundo, happy people are shown shopping for, buying, and enjoying everything imaginable from gargantuan stores and engaging in all kinds of leisure activities, many of which are unfamiliar to Pustunicheños. The anonymous, satisfied gringos of advertisements are also shown eating fast food at chain restaurants or processed foods that are prepared instantly. These bright and pleasant images do not, however, necessarily translate into positive evaluations of gringos. Early on in my stay, people frequently asked me what I was accustomed to eating back home. On one such occasion, my neighbor's son interjected, "*Puro de lata, y hamburguesa—de McDonald*" ([They eat] exclusively canned food, and hamburgers—from McDonald's). Such foods are known to be expensive (there are McDonald's in Mérida and Cancún), and beyond that, not very appealing and certainly not healthful.

Because of all the wealth and privilege that television proves gringos enjoy, it is clear they don't have to work very hard to make a living. In the course of television news discussions of NAFTA, wage-rate differentials between Mexico and the United States were discussed. By local standards, gringos seem to earn astronomical wages. Pustunicheños also know from television, however, that there are many poor people in the United States. But that fact just does not seem explicable. Several locals expressed the view that people who are poor in the United States must be lazy. Although very few people from Pustunich have gone to work in the United States, there is a lot of information on the subject available from national and international television news, the reports of the few experienced people, friends, and friends of friends. For example, it is widely believed that most Mexicans who go to the United States to work temporarily can save enough money to buy a new truck within a year or two. And this is in spite of the well-known fact that Mexican migrants in the United State face discrimination, work harder, and are paid far less for their work.

Despite their privilege, from the perspective of Pustunicheños, gringos as a group don't seem very savvy. In fact, they seem perverse. Endless examples from television, reports from tourist zones, and other contacts with gringos combine to make this point. For one thing, gringos are known to waste money with abandon and to pay far more for goods and services than they are worth. Many local residents pay attention to the prices mentioned in international cable television advertisements. One family asked me how much I had paid for my athletic shoes. I admitted with embarrassment that I had paid u.s.$50. After quickly calculating the amount in pesos, they were chagrined that I had spent so much money unnecessarily. They told me that they had seen Kmart advertisements, and that athletic shoes are available for u.s.$10. They also knew, however, that it was possible to pay much more, because they had heard television news stories about kids in the United States killing each other for athletic shoes that cost u.s.$200.

The images of gringos chronicled in the preceding paragraphs by no means exhaust the local imaginary on the subject.[69] However, such views of gringos and gringo society are quite widespread, and they are supported by the historically adversarial relationship between Mexico and the United States. This underlying structure is built on by countless reports detailing observed practices and televisual images and stories about gringos. The constant reinforcement of a negative view of the United States and its gringo residents encourages identifications with the Mexican state.

Telemundo, Univisión, and Transnational Identifications

Identification with the nation through participation in television is more complex than might appear in the preceding discussion, first because such participation and identifications are not isolated in any way from the rest of daily experience. Many members of local families now work for foreign-owned businesses in Cancún or other spots in the Caribbean tourist zone of Quintana Roo. The social milieu in the Caribbean is dominated by tourists from the United States, but workers also come into contact with Canadian, European, and Latin American tourists, as well as Mexican tourists and workers from many other regions of the country. These cosmopolitan contacts can work to limit identifications with Mexico. For example, one man in town (now a teacher) worked for a time in hotels on the Caribbean and Gulf coasts and had many positive interactions with Canadian tourists. He is very drawn to Canadian culture and society and thinks he would like living in Montreal. He corresponds with a number of Canadian friends there and hopes at least to visit someday.

Furthermore, televisual messages are complex and can be read in more than one way at once. In addition to identifications with the nation, identifications with a relatively amorphous transnational Hispanic "imagined community" are also fostered through engagements with television, particularly through programming on Telemundo and Univisión that became available only with cable technology.[70] Weekend evening variety shows (*Sábado Gigante* and *Siempre en Domingo*) introduce to town residents celebrities from all over Latin America. On *Cristina*, the most popular talk show broadcast in Pustunich (hosted by a Cuban, Cristina Saralegui), all sorts of issues of "modern" life are broached, usually from the points of view of residents of Miami or urban centers of Latin America. Miami, because it is frequently featured on international television, seems to have emerged as the capital of an imagined Latin transnation. More than one person told me they found it odd that Miami was a part of the United States.

Identifications with this transnational Hispanic world mediate specific identifications with the Mexican nation. It is true that Pustunicheños are Mexican citizens in practice, and they greatly prefer Mexican styles, music, telenovelas, and other cultural products, but they cannot be said to be complacent and satisfied citizens. In most cases, they are highly critical of and frustrated by the performance of government at all levels, and they are also often critical of various aspects of their society. Many local people feel at least somewhat culturally kindred (at least through ties of language) to other Latin American societies. There is general interest in the varying customs and histories of different Latin American countries. Under the influence of Telemundo and Univisión, mexicanidad becomes one of numerous possible forms of participation in the Latin world. Through increasing local awareness of a broader Latin world, local commitments to mexicanidad may be strengthened at the same time that specific commitments to the Mexican nation are weakened.

Engagements with television have significance well beyond the issue of national identification. Television is having a clear impact on the "nature of experience" in Pustunich partly because myriad televisual images are now imprinted in the local imaginary.[71] These images become source material for performances of self and interactions with others. The following three ethnographic vignettes point to the deeper significance of televisual involvements in the practice of everyday life. It is important at this point to remember that until the 1970s, Pustunich was known as a farming village. Most women in town were housewives, wore traditional Maya dress, and spoke Yucatec Maya most of the time. Now most families rely on income earned by members in construction and service jobs in tourist zones. The changes have been particularly dramatic for women. No young women wear traditional dress or speak Yucatec Maya, and many are pursuing professions outside the home and town.

The first vignette has to do with recent changes in romantic relationships in Pustunich. I asked many women specifically about their experiences of courtship and marriage. Most women who had been married for a decade or more by the early 1990s had talked very little with their *novios* by the time they got married. One woman recounted, "Oh yes, we had been novios for over five years by the time we got married. And I suppose I knew that we would get married someday, because when I would come home to visit [from her job as a domestic servant in Mérida], he would come visit me. But still, by the time we got married, we had barely exchanged five words." Active communication between novios or marriage partners has certainly not been emphasized in practice in the village in the past.

The current situation provides a sharp contrast. The proper conduct of romantic relationships is a popular topic of conversation with young women and such relationships are often the subject of talk shows. When explaining to me her reasons for breaking up with her village boyfriend, one young woman complained that this fellow never wrote or called her when they were away working at different migration destinations.[72] Furthermore, when reunited in town, he didn't tell her much of anything about what was happening in his life or evince much interest in how she was doing. In concluding her story, she said that she agreed with something she had heard on a talk show about love relationships. "Communication is the main thing," she said. "Don't you agree?"

The second story has to do with the fairly common practice of imitating styles seen on television. One particularly noteworthy case of style copying occurred over the course of several years in the late 1980s. A group of fifteen to twenty young girls who were attending secondary school began to gather socially. They were united by their general lack of interest in schooling, an active interest in sports (they formed a basketball team coached by one of their fathers and played in a Ticul-based league), and by common tastes in clothes, music, and television programs. In the late 1980s, Televisa invented a girl's pop music group, the Chicas Flans, who had their own show. Members of this local girl's group became big fans of the show and gradually adopted the style of the Chicas Flans.

The Chicas Flans wore spandex shorts partly covered by flowing babydoll tops, and the local girls group did too. Soon people in town began referring to the local group as the Chicas Flans. The girls liked this recognition, and deepened their involvement in and mimicry of the television Chicas. They began to perform dance routines to Chicas Flans songs at local youth entertainment events. They gleaned whatever information they could find about the Chicas Flans in the most widely read publication in town, *TV y Novelas*. Through detailed imitative play of the TV Chicas Flans in combination with their other activities, the local Chicas carved out a distinctive and relatively free space for themselves in town social life. In village circles they succeeded in defining themselves as a particular type of modern woman: attractive, athletic, nonintellectual, romantic, and sexy—in short, ideal marriage material.[73]

The last story is a case of self-modeling using telenovela material. One young woman, Landy, directly copied the style of a mala from a popular telenovela. With the help of her aunt Lilia, a skilled seamstress, the two women produced exact copies of a number of the mala's outfits. They made sketches from the television, and then Lilia constructed paper patterns, combining the drawings with Landy's measurements. In Mérida, they searched for and found similar fabrics in identical colors. These outfits, skirt suits and dresses, became important pieces of Landy's wardrobe. She wore them to a school entrance exam and job interviews, and now wears them to the office job she eventually took in Cancún.

On a trip we took together to Mérida, Landy openly pondered the meaning of her attraction to the style of a woman who was morally reprehensible. "The things she did were terrible, but I still *really liked* everything she wore," she mused. In her own view, this identification with a mala contrasted sharply with (at least most) other aspects of her own self-image as a devoted Catholic, a hardworking daughter, and a trustworthy keeper of her family's honor. In making these clothes with her aunt, Landy decided not to let concerns about the mala's character get in the way of her desire to adopt the style. However, her adoption of this style has social consequences, even if they are subtle or unintended. When Landy, dressed as the mala, emerges from the combivan in a Mérida park or takes the bus to her current job in Cancún, it is a certainty that many people recognize the mala. At the very least, these clothes add contradiction and complexity to Landy's daily public and private performance of self.

Conclusions

Using ethnographic examples, I have illustrated how, in one small town in Yucatán, involvements with national and international television broadcasts work in two opposite ways to create identifications with the Mexican nation. I have also suggested that these nationalist identifications are now being complicated by overlapping identifications with an imagined transnational Latin community through increased televisual connections with other regions of Latin America. Televisual involvements are a central feature of the experience of increasing connection to the global economy in small towns such as Pustunich.

New practices are emerging through the free play allowed locally in connection with television. "Television talk" among women is a relatively new form of expression in town and an important example of these new practices; it is more individualistic, more opinionated, often louder, and usually more dramatic in expressive form than other typical forms of talk in town. Television talk and other novel practices are transforming patterns of interaction and social relationships. The anecdote about the woman who broke up with her boyfriend because he was uncommunicative is just one of many examples of transformations in traditional local forms of social relationships. Many young women in Pustunich are choosing to remain unmarried, and some are even consciously opting for single motherhood, partly through reference to televisual stories. These and other important changes in fundamental social practices of everyday life indicate that new types of subjectivities are being constructed. These novel subjectivities, though locally and socially constructed, are less constrained by local histories and social conventions partly because of deep involvements in national and transnational television. Finally, the emergence of these novel forms of subjectivity is of greater significance to the nation than any specific nationalist identifications. These novel subjectivities are urban-focused, constructed through the consumption of images and goods, and fundamentally committed to a development-as-progress model of modernity.

Notes

1 No payment was required prior to installation: having cable implied a commitment to pay the stated installation and service fees. Households were allowed to pay these fees in small, unspecified increments, as they were able to part with bits of cash. A couple of local schoolteachers (men) were hired to serve as collectors. It was their job to keep up the pressure for payment. All unattributed translations in this chapter are mine.

2 I do not mean to suggest here that Yucatecan television viewers were unfamiliar with global media products prior to the installation of cable television. Foreign-made television shows and movies had frequently been broadcast by Mexican television stations. However, in my view, the tremendous increase in volume of foreign programming available, and the fact that this programming was available from extranational stations, created a significant shift in the character/quality of the televisual universe from the perspective of rural viewers.

3 *Mexicanidad* translates roughly as "Mexicanness," or "the state or nature of being Mexican." I use this term interchangeably with *lo mexicano*, "that which is Mexican."

   Although the politics, economics, and social and technological mechanics of broadcast television, as well as the intentions of writers for television are important to overall understandings of televisual impacts and processes of globalization, this essay focuses almost exclusively on local reception because of the nature of my ethnographic research project. For insight into recent trends in telenovela production, see Omar Hernández and Emile McAnany's essay in this volume.

4 I borrow the now well-worn phrase "imagined community" from Benedict Anderson, *Imagined Communities: Reflections on the Origin and Spread of Nationalism* (London: Verso, 1983). This essay owes much to Ana M. López, "Our Welcomed Guests: Telenovelas in Latin America," in *To Be Continued . . . : Soap Operas around the World*, ed. Robert C. Allen (London: Routledge, 1995), 256–75. López's chapter on telenovelas and nation building clarified many questions that were unanswerable in fieldwork about the history and mechanics of the production of Latin American television, especially telenovelas. López's comprehensive analysis (of both sides of the television equation: production and reception) draws conclusions similar to those I was forming in my analysis of field notes on telenovela viewing and use. Hence, this ethnographic case supports much of what López has argued.

5 Lila Abu-Lughod, "The Objects of Soap Opera: Egyptian Television and the Cultural Politics of Modernity," in *Worlds Apart: Modernity through the Prism of the Local*, ed. Daniel Miller (London: Routledge, 1995), 190–210.

6   Stuart Hall, "Introduction: Who Needs 'Identity'?," in *Questions of Cultural Identity*, ed. Stuart Hall and Paul du Gay (London: Sage Publications, 1996), 2.

7   The *forma de ser* is equivalent to a moral self. Conceived as essential, the forma de ser is a fairly constant referent in local discourse. It is a key consideration in the production and performance of identities. I have many examples of forma de ser talk in my field notes. Such stories often began by citing the practices of others that the teller has found personally unsuitable, for example, "My neighbor is really smart [*lista*], she is always ready to take advantage of a chance to earn a profit. She gathers her eggs and goes around selling them door to door for x [high] price. That might be smart, but I just cannot do it, it is not my forma de ser. I sell my eggs to the poor little kids who come by for [next to] nothing" (field interview, March 1993).

8   Hall, "Introduction: Who Needs 'Identity'?," 1–17. Following Hall, I use the terms identification and identity almost interchangeably because the line between them is vague. However, identification refers more directly to practices and process, whereas identity/identities more directly invokes subjects-in-relationship and particular positions.

9   Alison Greene, "Huipiles and Spandex: The Cultural Politics of Dress in Pustunich, Yucatán," paper presented at the annual meeting of the American Anthropological Association, Atlanta, GA, 1994.

10 Pierre Bourdieu, *Distinction: A Social Critique of the Judgment of Taste*, trans. Richard Nice (Cambridge, MA: Harvard University Press, 1984), 479–81. Bourdieu writes, "What is at stake in the struggles about the meaning of the social world is power over the classificatory schemes and systems which are the basis of the representations of the groups" (479). This conception of "struggles of classification" works well to describe local debates over the meaning and content of modernity and the daily practices appropriate to "it" (479–81). For a related discussion, see Alison Greene, "Performing Social Transformation in Rural Yucatán: An Analysis of a Regional Drama," *FOLK: Journal of the Danish Ethnographic Society* 38 (1996): 5–31.

11 This rejection of the Maya past is extremely pronounced in Pustunich relative to other villages in the same subregion. I analyze this situation in Alison Greene, "Varieties of Maya Ethnicity," paper presented at the annual meeting of the American Anthropological Association, Washington, DC, 1997.

12 Henry C. Schmidt, *The Roots of lo Mexicano: Self and Society in Mexican Thought, 1900–1934* (College Station: Texas A&M University Press, 1978), 20–37.

13 Ibid., 43–45.

14 Outside of Yucatán, the term *mestizo* refers to people of mixed Spanish and indigenous heritage. It is in this standard sense that I am using the term here. In Yucatán, however, the term refers to people who participate in Maya cultural practices and who are thought to be of more purely indigenous heritage.

15 Frederick C. Turner, *The Dynamic of Mexican Nationalism* (Chapel Hill: University of North Carolina Press, 1968); Schmidt, *The Roots of lo Mexicano*; Mary Kay Vaughan, *The State, Education, and Social Class in Mexico, 1880–1928* (DeKalb: Northern Illinois University Press, 1982), 239–66; Joanne Hershfield, *Mexican Cinema/Mexican Women, 1940–1950* (Tucson: University of Arizona Press, 1996).

16 Hershfield, *Mexican Cinema/Mexican Women*, 27, 38, 48–51, 57.

17 Ibid.; see also Vaughan, *The State, Education, and Social Class in Mexico*, 255; Carlos Monsiváis, "All the People Came and Did Not Fit onto the Screen," in *Mexican Cinema*, ed. Paulo Antonio Paranaguá (London: British Film Institute, 1995), 145–51, especially 149–50. Vaughan points out fundamental contradictions in the commitments and expressions of participants in the "movement of cultural nationalism" of the revolutionary era. Monsiváis lists many contradictory features of the early Mexican cinema, which was instrumentally involved in nation building.

18 See Carlos Monsiváis, "Mythologies," in *Mexican Cinema*, ed. Paranaguá, 117–27. According to Monsiváis, this has long been the case across Mexico: "Between 1935 and 1955 (as always, approximately), this cinema, more than any other cultural form, modernised tastes and prejudices, and refashioned the idea of the nation by transforming nationalism into a big spectacle" (127).

19 It is important to note here that although the construction of mexicanidad in films and government documents shares important features with local receptions and deployments of the concept, the two are not identical. Mexicanidad is reformulated as it is translated by locals for the specific social milieu. Henceforth in this essay, I use mexicanidad to refer to an essential character of Mexico and its people *only* as it is locally perceived. This reflects a basic theoretical commitment that agency and social position or point of view importantly affect the "text" through the act of reception/reading.

20 Francine Masiello, "Gender, Dress and Market: The Commerce of Citizenship in Latin America," in *Sex and Sexuality in Latin America*, ed. Daniel Balderston and Donna J. Guy (New York: New York University Press, 1997), 219–233, quote on 220.

21 In several cases, women told me they suspected that others in town considered shocking particular styles they had copied from television. Their general response to this suspicion of criticism was to state something to the effect that those who didn't like such styles were either unconcerned with or uninformed about lo moderno.

22 Carlos Monsiváis and Carlos Bonfil, *A través del espejo: El cine Mexicano y su público* (Mexico City: Ediciones El Milagro, 1994).

23 Quoted in John Kraniauskas, "Critical Closeness: The Chronicle-Essays of Carlos Monsiváis," in *Mexican Postcards*, by Carlos Monsiváis, ed., trans., introduced by John Kraniauskas (London: Verso, 1997), xviii. Latin American media scholars are in general agreement about the tremendous importance of the melodramatic genre. A great deal of scholarship analyzing the forms and functions of melodrama was inspired by Peter Brooks's foundational work, *The Melodramatic Imagination: Balzac, Henry James, Melodrama, and the Mode of Excess* (New Haven: Yale University Press, 1976). Brooks defined melodrama as "a mode of conception and expression, as a certain fictional system for making sense of experience, as a semantic field of force" (xiii). Most important, Brooks identified the "melodramatic mode as a central fact of the modern sensibility" (21). The struggle between good and evil within individuals, the family, and the social world at large is the fundamental theme and organizing principle of melodrama.

24 Though I agree that melodrama has had and continues to have great social and political significance, I wish to avoid portraying the genre as a powerful historical agent in itself. Melodrama is produced, broadcast, and consumed in specific social and historical con-

texts. In the following analysis, I emphasize the specific points of attraction to and engagements in telenovela melodramas in the local field, rather than the effects of the genre as a whole.

25 Roger N. Lancaster, "Guto's Performance: Notes on the Transvestism of Everyday Life," in *The Gender/Sexuality Reader: Culture, History, Political Economy*, ed. Roger N. Lancaster and Micaela di Leonardo (New York: Routledge, 1997), 569. Lancaster's discussion has become integral to my own thinking about the social uses of television in Pustunich and the relationship between participation in television and "identities."

26 News stories are generally read as the reporting of serious, authoritative facts, except in cases where viewers have independent knowledge of the situation being reported (e.g., events in state politics, economic conditions in Cancún). Viewing and recounting television news stories do not foster playful behavior.

27 See Allan F. Burns, *An Epoch of Miracles: Oral Literature of the Yucatec Maya* (Austin: University of Texas Press, 1983). Despite the many rich and multilayered forms of verbal practice that people use in particular circumstances, the following conversational exchanges are standard in everyday speech in Yucatec Maya and have been carried into Spanish in Pustunich: "How are you?" "So-so" or "Same as usual"; "What are you doing?" "Nothing"; "What do you say?" "Nothing"; "Where are you going?" "Nowhere"; etc.

28 Marie Gillespie, *Television, Ethnicity and Cultural Change* (London: Routledge, 1995), 205.

29 *Milpa* agriculture is a form of slash-and-burn subsistence farming centered on the production of corn and beans, with the addition of some combination of tomatoes, chiles, and a great variety of herbs and vegetables. For centuries, most rural people across the Yucatán peninsula have survived by "making milpa." See Irwin Press, *Tradition and Adaptation: Life in a Modern Yucatán Maya Village* (Westport, CT: Greenwood Press, 1975). In Pustunich until the 1970s, making milpa was of great social significance and value. According to Press, it was the "*sine qua non* of male identity" (59).

30 See Gilbert M. Joseph, "Rethinking Mexican Revolutionary Mobilization: Yucatán's Seasons of Upheaval, 1909–1915," in *Everyday Forms of State Formation: Revolution and the Negotiation of Rule in Modern Mexico*, ed. Gilbert M. Joseph and Daniel Nugent (Durham, NC: Duke University Press, 1994), 135–69. Perhaps originally because the region was devoid of natural resources that were widely desired in the formation of the colony, and the peninsula was on the way to nowhere, Yucatán long remained geographically isolated. Joseph notes that lines of communication with the nation's center were long undeveloped: "There were no roads connecting Yucatán with central Mexico until well after World War II" (158).

31 Local people use the term *mi tierra* (my land) to refer to the village and even sometimes, more specifically, to that part of the village that belongs to their relatives and where they were born and raised. One man told me that he had worked away from "his land" for seventeen years. He was never comfortable doing so, and finally he returned home to work. I asked him where he had worked, and to my surprise he responded Oxkutzcab, a town that is a fifteen-minute ride down the road that runs through Pustunich.

32 *Mexicanos* are understood specifically as residents of Mexico City's Federal District.

33 Although I have read and heard many possible interpretations and translations of this term, I have not personally been convinced that any one of them is definitive and correct.

34 See Joseph, "Rethinking Revolutionary Mobilization," 145–46. Joseph notes that "on the fringes of the henequen zone, along the southern range of stunted hills known as the Puuc . . . independent small holders stubbornly guarded their lands against the incursions of local *hacendados* and Molinista *jefes políticos*." Pustunich is located squarely in the Puuc zone. Joseph goes on to show how pueblos in this zone became centers of revolutionary mobilization (135–69). He refers to Santa Elena, a neighboring comisario in the *partido* of Ticul, as a "prime staging area of revolutionary violence during the Madero period" (146 n.19). Currently, Pustunicheños resent their pueblo's political subordination to Ticul and express pride in their history as an independent and self-sufficient village. When discussing local history with me, residents frequently remarked, "It is said that Pustunich is older than Ticul."

35 One ninety-four-year-old man (in 1993; since deceased) described how his older brother had become indebted to a neighboring hacendado by seeking sponsorship for his wedding without asking their father for permission. The whole family put aside their subsistence labor to work alongside this indebted son/brother, so that he would not sink into permanent indenture. Partly because of this experience, this man became an avid socialist. He remembered hearing Madero speak in Ticul, and later became an active supporter of Yucatán's socialist governor, Felipe Carrillo Puerto, who visited Pustunich at least twice.

36 I derive this interpretation from conversations with a number of men across a variety of age groups who were politically active. In my experience, women were loath to comment on political history except as asides to more personal kin-based histories.

37 The schoolmaster has a picture of himself standing beside Lázaro Cárdenas, taken when the president stopped to conduct a town meeting in Pustunich concerning government plans for local development during his 1937 tour of the region.

38 Using locally harvested palm fronds, many local families participated in the production of a low-cost version of the Panama hat that was sold in national and international markets. Men's dress shirts, women's shoes, and various machine-embroidered goods were produced. In this "putting-out work" system, companies in Ticul and Mérida provided materials, and Pustunicheños returned finished products. Payment was made by the piece.

39 See Press, *Tradition and Adaptation*.

40 See Monsiváis, "Mythologies," 118. Monsiváis identifies one of the principal box office formulas of the Golden Age of Mexican cinema as "the Mexican *fiesta* filled with *charros* and *chinas poblanas* (folkloric types)." This formula obviously appealed to many in Pustunich and Ticul.

41 See also Abu-Lughod, "The Objects of Soap Opera," 207.

42 See Noreene Janus, "Transnational Advertising: Some Considerations on the Impact on Peripheral Societies," in *Communication and Latin American Society: Trends in Critical Research, 1960–1985*, ed. Rita Atwood and Emile G. McAnany (Madison: University of Wisconsin Press, 1986), 127–42. Janus argues that although "the patterns of production determine, to a significant degree, the patterns of consumption," and advertising has played a major role in the transnationalization of consumption, all advertising is subject to unpredictable local reinterpretations and resistance (132).

43 This situation contrasts sharply with the findings of James Lull, "The Social Uses of Televi-

sion," *Human Communications Research* 6, no. 3 (1988): 198–209; and David Morley, *Family Television: Cultural Power and Domestic Leisure* (London: Routledge, 1991). In these studies of television reception in Britain and the United States, men clearly dominated viewing choices in the families studied.

44 In the summer of 1993, there were some hints of the coming storm in Chiapas (the EZLN revolt of January 1, 1994) in television news stories of unexplained military exercises in highland Chiapas, in which Maya villagers claimed abusive treatment.

45 One specific example of the misuse of television cited by this grandmother was the great popularity of a telenovela aired in 1993, *Dos Mujeres, Un Camino* (Two Women, One Road). "I've never even watched it. I don't want to hear about it. I know from the name that I wouldn't like it." She suspected correctly that the telenovela told the story of two women who loved one man and gave sympathetic treatment to both women. In her opinion, this telenovela was an example of the "trash" available on television for those who made poor choices.

46 I take this phrase from Joseph and Nugent, *Everyday Forms of State Formation*.

47 López, "Our Welcomed Guests," 256, 257. For a related discussion, see Adriana Estill, "Closing the Telenovela's Borders: *Vivo por Elena*'s Tidy Nation," *Chasqui* (forthcoming).

48 Jesús Martín Barbero has referred to the telenovela as a "a site of 'mediations,' a place where the interaction between the forces of production and reception are crystallized" (quoted in López, "Our Welcomed Guests," 257). It can also be seen as a site of mediation between the state and the local that works to construct the nation.

49 López, "Our Welcomed Guests," 261. López here cites Jesús Martín Barbero and Sonia Muñoz, eds., *Televisión y melodrama* (Bogotá: Tercer Mundo Editores, 1992), 26–28.

50 López, "Our Welcomed Guests," 261.

51 See Gillespie, *Television, Ethnicity*, 161. In her analysis of soap opera reception in an Asian neighborhood in London, Gillespie finds that the central attraction for viewers lies in the soap opera narrative itself. She concludes, "*What* is revealed may be of great fascination in itself, but it is the *process of revelation* which constitutes the most important source of pleasure. In soaps, multiple enigmas are initiated, developed and resolved at different rates, so the viewer's curiosity is in a constant state of arousal." That seems to be the case among telenovela viewers in Pustunich.

52 Local residents learn that telenovelas are popular all over the country from a variety of sources, including the magazine *TV y Novela*, televised interviews with telenovela stars, their own travels around the country, and reports of friends and relatives who have traveled.

53 See Jacky Bratton, "The Contending Discourses of Melodrama," in *Melodrama: Stage, Picture, Screen*, ed. Jacky Bratton, Jim Cook, and Christine Gledhill (London: British Film Institute, 1994), 38–49. Bratton argues that, because English melodrama is characterized by "contending discourses," it is "heteroglot," using the term that Mikhail Bakhtin applied to the novel (39).

54 Abu-Lughod, "The Objects of Soap Opera," 200.

55 People also commonly name children after celebrity singers and actors. This is a common practice around the world, but in Yucatán, with its history of discrimination against rural

and Maya people, the juxtaposition of television character or celebrity names with Maya surnames is apparently jarring. Such names are often considered comical or even ridiculous by rural people themselves, and are common joke material.

56 See also Daniel Miller, "The Consumption of Soap Opera: *The Young and the Restless* and Mass Consumption in Trinidad," in *To be Continued*, ed. Allen, 213–33.

57 X' is a Yucatec Maya feminine prefix, pronounced "sh," that denotes at least mild disrespect. It is commonly and playfully attached to women's names in conversations among older women in town.

58 These hints had been too subtle for me, so in the conversation in the marketplace I protested that it was too soon after the civil marriage ceremony for it to be plausible that María Mercedes was pregnant. I didn't sway the views of a single participant in the conversations. I think, partly based on the knowing looks the women gave each other, that they were thinking that because I had never been pregnant, I had no idea of what I spoke. Turns out to have been true.

59 See also Gillespie, *Television, Ethnicity*, 147.

60 This phenomenon has been noted by ethnographers of television use in other world regions, including Miller, "The Consumption of Soap Opera"; and Gillespie, *Television, Ethnicity*, 145. Gillespie writes, "It is the interweaving of fiction and real experiences that perhaps most of all characterises the nature of soap talk."

61 Miller, "The Consumption of Soap Opera," 232. Miller notes that soap opera's "foundation in a form of 'real-time' narrative structure makes it far more amenable to consumption through means of displaced gossip than other television genres."

62 Gillespie, *Television, Ethnicity*, 143. Gillespie identifies a "homology between the form of soap narration and gossip as a social speech form." I specifically use "local discourse" rather than "gossip" because in Pustunich, gossip (*chisme*) is a negatively sanctioned form of discourse and is not the same as telenovela talk. Furthermore, though discussions of telenovelas tend to focus on family and personal issues, they are not strictly limited to these themes.

63 López, "Our Welcomed Guests," 262.

64 Hall, "Introduction: Who Needs 'Identity'?," 4. Hall writes, "Directly contrary to the form in which they are constantly invoked, identities are constructed through, not outside, difference."

65 For example, cardenista populist nationalism made a deep impression in Pustunich, perhaps most importantly because President Cárdenas made a personal visit to town. This visit is an important point in local popular memory. See also Alex Saragoza's essay in this volume. Saragoza points out that "cardenismo possessed an implicit antiforeign sentiment, witnessed perhaps most dramatically in the emotional, massive response to the expropriation of the foreign-controlled oil industry in March of 1938."

66 *Gringo* is an epithet originally used in Mexico to refer specifically to citizens of the United States. In current practice in Pustunich, people use the term both to indicate anyone from the United States and more generally Canadians and Europeans (i.e., foreigners who are not African, Asian, or Latin American).

67 See Saragoza, this volume. Saragoza argues, "Tourism served to magnify the difference between 'Mexican' and 'foreign.'"

68 I am not aware of any television programming that directly informs this common and strongly held belief. Nonetheless, much televisual information about U.S. society is interpreted to support this idea.

69 People express their views about gringos point by point. I never heard anyone give a thorough description of gringo character. The composite picture I have produced here is thus artificial simply because the images are placed together. Furthermore, I do not mean to suggest that no one ever has anything good to say about gringos. Positive comments, however, tend either to refer to individual gringos whom local people have met, or to the supposedly beautiful physical characteristics typical among gringos, including fair hair and skin and blue eyes.

70 For a related discussion of the transformation of the telenovela genre in the pan-national Latin context, see López, "Our Welcomed Guests," 270.

71 Abu-Lughod, "The Objects of Soap Opera," 205–6.

72 The practice of women initiating breakups with boyfriends is becoming more common in Pustunich. Although a certain number of romantic relationships have foundered in every generation, there has always been pressure on women to avoid choosing to break up. Young women who were known to have rejected boyfriends suffered damage to their reputation because they were seen as fickle, at the very least.

73 It would be more accurate to modify the above statement referring to the Pustunich Chicas as "ideal marriage material." Clearly, group members wished to be viewed in this way. However, in 1993, there were only about eight Chicas Flans still practicing as such. When I asked members of another informal youth group what had happened to the rest of the local Chicas, they looked at each other and then told me, "*Todas se escaparon*" (They all escaped) and laughed with some embarrassment. "Escaping" means running off with your boyfriend without parental consent. If such unions last, they become recognized as common-law marriages. Escaping is, however, the least desirable way to marry, and girls who escape are seen as morally weak and, at least for a while, are considered to have "cheated" their families. By escaping, the local Chicas Flans became victims of their own romanticism.

The Aura of Ruins

Quetzil E. Castañeda

Walter Benjamin describes the concept of aura as "the unique phenomenon of distance no matter how close it may be." In the age of mechanical reproduction, he claims, the aura of authentic originals, which he likens to ruins, withers away due to the proliferation of copies—identical copies and authentic copies—that appropriate and ruin the aura of the original.[1] They ruin ruins. Such replicas and replication thereby gives rise, through film and photograph, to a new kind of original, a ruined original.

Ruins and originals. These concepts—derived from Latin *ruina*, a falling down, from *ruere*, to rush, and *origo*, source, from *oriri*, to rise—entail movements in opposing directions: a "falling down" and a "rising up." Mysteriously, the science of archae-logos has made these two contrary movements live harmoniously together in original ruins.

The White City of Chichén Itzá

The ruins of Chichén, under construction by archaeologists and Maya, appear as white spots rising up from a green carpet. The photo in Figure 47, taken from the southeast in the late 1920s, is unique for the distance of the

47. "The White City of Chichén Itzá." Photo by Fairchild Aerial Surveys, Inc. N.Y.C. Courtesy of the Peabody Museum Photographic Archive, Carnegie 7023, Box 20-29, slide S11984.

approach to the ruins and for capturing the Western imagining of the savage monotony of the jungle. Identifying with this ironic mystery of civility in savagery, George Lucas used analogous aerial shots of Tikal temples emerging from the jungle to create the cinemagraphic approach to the renegade hideout in *Star Wars*.

Empty Ceremonial Center, a Mecca of Travel

In 1974, Luis Arochi identified, if not discovered, "The Phenomenon of Light and Shadow," which is "an incredible solar phenomenon [that] occurs in Chichén Itzá" during the spring and fall equinoxes on 21 March 21 and 23 September 23. Scientifically calculating the building of the pyramid, the Maya used the setting sun to cast shadows from the platform bases on which triangles of light formed on the balustrade in a symbol of the rattlesnake and epiphany of K'uk'ulcan, or Feathered Serpent. In 1984, the state of Yucatán began to organize a vernal celebration the Maya and K'uk'ulcan with music, dance, poetry, speeches, and theatrical performances. Today, tens of thousands come rushing to witness this phenomenon, whose meaning is intensely debated by archaeologists, archaeoastronomers, ethnographers, Maya, gnostics, the state, and New Age spiritualists (see Figure 48).

48. Empty ceremonial center, Mecca of Travel. Photo by author.

49. Maya building Maya ruins, an American Mecca. Photo by CIW staff photographer. Courtesy of the Peabody Museum Photographic Archives, CIW, Ethnology, Chichén Itzá Drawer 46-1-107.

Maya Building Maya Ruins of Chichén Itzá

The kind of image shown in Figure 49 is rare, first, for showing the *process of building ruins*, versus images of the results revealed by excavation and restoration, and, second, for showing Maya *workmen at work*, versus posing them as human measuring sticks by which the Westerner could perceive the scale of buildings and artifacts. This type of image of Maya building Maya ruins has been kept in the archives and virtually absent from publications created for both professional and broader public audiences. Even the Maya of Pisté, among whom are siblings, children, and grandchildren of archaeological workers, are surprised to see images of familiar buildings and scenes made unfamiliar and strange by the presence of their relatives and neighbors busy building a Tourist Mecca.

Ruining Ruins

In 1923 a ten-year renewable contract was signed between the Carnegie Institution of Washington (CIW) and the Mexican Secretaría de Educación Pública (SEP). This granted the CIW permission to conduct archaeological, physical anthropological, epigraphic, linguistic, climatological, medical, faunal, botanical, geological, historical, sociological, and ethnological studies of the Maya civilization of Yucatán. Sylvanus G. Morley directed these investigations, which were organized under the umbrella of Project Chichén. The Mexican Monumentos Prehispánicos, precursor to the Instituto Nacional de Antropología e Historia (INAH), also excavated and restored buildings under the initial direction of José Erosa Peniche, a Yucatec archaeologist and writer of the first tourist guidebook to Chichén Itzá. Together these projects transformed Yucatán into a laboratory and Chichén into a factory of knowledge.

In eighteen years of cutting, chopping, digging, sifting, drawing, measuring, writing, painting, photographing, and cleaning, the archaeologists—Mexican, Anglo, and Yucatec North Americans—literally peeled back the jungle growth to carve out of, and inscribe in, *puro monte* their vision of the Maya. With hundreds of Maya workmen—who were mostly from the nearby community of Pisté but also from Campeche, Chan Kom, and Oxkutzcab—the archaeologists created ruins, ruins in ruins, and ruined ruins. This "foundation act" was the ritual and originary reenactment of the scientific cosmovision of early-twentieth-century archaeology that created—out of the chaos of the profane and "undifferentiated" space of the everyday, that is, out of earth, stone, paper, and ink—the sacred and ordered space of modern ruins.

Taking the debris—the ruins—of an ancient city that had collapsed on its own remaining remnants, the archaeologists and Maya workmen selectively and strategically constructed buildings and architectural spaces according to their imagining of the past. This work, which is called without any sense of irony "restoration" and "reconstruction," is known by archaeologists to destroy information about the past that is not "restored" and to preclude as well the possibility of alternative interpretations of the past. Obliterating—or ruining—each specific historical moment of an architectural artifact, whose "life" spanned hundreds of years, the work of restoration nonetheless creates, through a mechanical process of re/production, a ruin of the ruined building that represents its essence and testifies to all of the different phases, uses, and meanings that it has experienced in its history.[2] Like a photograph, as Benjamin noted, the archaeologically restored and reconstructed ruin is simultaneously both a copy and an original. It is a copy of an original that never existed. Restored to authenticity by the genius of modern science, ruins are original copies: authentic inventions of modernity.

In his first annual report as director of the CIW-sponsored research projects, Alfred V. Kidder, a most prominent Americanist archaeologist, wrote, "If Chichén Itzá can be kept both interesting and beautiful, it will without question become a *Mecca of Travel* and incidentally, a most valuable asset for archeology which, like every other science, needs its 'show-windows.'"

Seventy years later, approximately half a million tourists a year visit Chichén to celebrate what the Carnegie archaeologists called the Maya "genius." Despite Kidder's stated desire, most do not seem to recognize that the life-size model replica of a ruined original was built for tourists to marvel at the aura of the modern science of archaeological reproduction.

Documenting Performance

During the production of a video documentary on the phenomenon of the equinox event, visual anthropologist and filmmaker Jeff Himpele (to the left in Figure 50) was photographed while videographing the ritual of a group of New Age Maya visitors. The ritual included placing sticks and stones on the ground to form a hieroglyph around which the group danced, sang, prayed, and burned incense in anticipation of the epiphany of the "Feathered Serpent" or K'uk'ulcan, who appears in the form of seven or eight isosceles triangles of light on the north balustrade of the pyramid, at the foot of which is a six-foot tall carved serpent's head (left staircase in the photograph; further to the left, the colonnade, connected to the Temple of the Warriors, can be seen). After this group hug shown in the photo, one woman, with her arms in the air and her body akimbo, approached ecstatic trance and fell in altered state to the plaza floor of the ruined city. While many of the international tourists—including Yucatec students on high school field trips from Mérida, visiting Maya from neighboring towns, and ethnographers—joined in the performance of the ritual by participating through observation, one tall, clean-cut European tourist rushed into the subsequent hand-holding circle with a big smile; after his companion took a quick picture of his ritual activity, the man just as quickly separated him-

50. Documenting performance. Photo by author.

51. The Mexican Revolution visits Chichén Itzá. Photo taken by Tomás Burgos for the author.

self from the group and continued on his tour of Chichén. Others turned to approach the pyramid and awaited the arrival of K'uk'ulcan.

The Mexican Revolution Visits Chichén Itzá

In celebration of the seventy-fifth anniversary of the beginning of the Mexican Revolution, the government sent the Revolutionary Bell and related icons with a brigade of soldiers to visit every town of the republic. In August, the entourage arrived at Chichén. Clearing everyone off the main pyramid, soldiers stationed themselves on the corners of the nine platforms and at temple openings. Having been displaced from the Castillo by the soldiers, I ran to the Ball Court, where Tomás Burgos, a tour guide and Pisté resident reporter for the *Diario de Yucatán*, also climbed up to take some photographs. He offered to take a picture of me with my camera: following the architectural lines of the Upper Ball Court Temple on which I lean, one's eye is led to the mountainous temple, whose proximity is perceived despite the distance of the main plaza that lies like a valley between the pyramids (Figure 51). In solemn silence, the bell was then brought to the west staircase and symbolically raised to the top of the pyramid. Meanwhile, a platform was assembled on which a brief jarana, a tradition of Yucatán, was danced. Within twenty minutes the Revolution continued its tour to the next town in this "land apart."

Modernity in Ruins

New Age Maya is a heterodox theology conceived and practiced as an eclectic spiritualism by a variety of Anglo North Americans. The White Brotherhood of Quetzalcoatl, in contrast, is a Mexican spiritual and political *indigenismo*, as Judith Friedlander discussed thirty years ago, that was created by urban *mestizos*; it is a political-countercultural movement based in Central Mexico and on a "revindication" of ancient Mexican, specifically Aztec, not Maya, culture. Though both are spiritual movements with significant historical legacies, the distinctly (hermispherically) American utopianism centered on non-Indian redemption through the Indian would properly, and profitably, place them among the "new social movements" that seek alternative paths to sociopolitical change and democracy in the Americas. Both deploy highly polarized gender conceptions based in notions of complementary dualism, as does a third spiritualism, gnosticism, which spread to Mexico from its roots in Europe through transnational masonic cults and popularized literatures. In Mexico, as in all that comes from Europe, and especially in Yucatán, gnosticism has been transculturally nativized to and with Mesoamerican beliefs and symbols. All three, but especially Mexican gnosticism, find appropriate ideas from a variety of Oriental religious sects and spiritualisms with which to further hybridize. Cancún, in particular, is a hotbed of spiritual syncretism and hybridized religiosity; on any given day, any number of the major resort hotels will be the scene of a religious workshop of spiritual awakening and improvement for the Mexican middle classes and resident *gabachos*.

Adalberto Rivera A. is an interesting figure of this transcultural hybridity. A Central Mexican resettled in Yucatán, he sought his initial career in tourism as an archaeoastronomer. Entering into the bull ring of touristic interpretation of the Maya with José Díaz Bolio, Luis Arochi, and others, he also became a "discoverer" of some heretofore unrevealed and unknown aspect of the equinox: that K'uk'ulcan is actually Quetzal-Kan, and the existence of the Serpent of Shadow that is projected on the plaza floor (as opposed to the Serpent of Light that is projected on the staircase). His connections in Mexico City and elsewhere gave him an advantage in this fraught market, and he successfully courted the state government, which granted him the role of providing the official explanation of the Equinox Phenomenon of Light and Shadow that it sponsors. Like many persons employed in public, mid- to upper-level positions in the tourist industry of Yucatán, and especially in Pisté, he was a "closeted" practitioner of his Maya gnosticism. But things changed after his involvement with the political movement of the town of Pisté—the Lucha 107 (1989–1993).

When Pisté lost its gambit, Rivera in turn lost the honorable and prestigious role of official narrator of the equinox and moved to Cancún. At first, he began to sell, on a daily basis, his explanation to charter groups using a six-foot miniature replica of the Pyramid of Quetzal-Kan that he had constructed near the Plaza Caracol in the Hotel Zone of Cancún. His book, which blended gnosticism, spiritualism, Maya numerology, and miscellaneous symbols from Eastern religions, with a *strong* masculinist spin, gave him an entry into organizing his own spiritual group or cult of Maya gnostics. At the nationally organized ritual event of 23 March 1997, he arrived, in the muggy heat of an overcast spring day, sporting the standard white clothing with red sash, a staff of power, and a full gray beard to pray with the priests of the White Brotherhood of Quetzalcoatl.

"Façade du chateau à Chichén"—Désiré Charnay
at the Feathered Serpent Column Entrance
to Temple of K'uk'ulcan

Compare the photographic image in Figure 52 with the description on page 342 of Désiré Charnay's *The Ancient Cities of the New World*:

52. "Façade du chateau à Chichén"—Désiré Charnay at the Feathered Serpent Column entrance to the Temple of K'uk'ulcan. Photographer for D. Charnay. Courtesy of the Peabody Museum Photographic Archives, Charnay Box 20-18:AB.

Pisté, where we arrive, stands on the extreme [eastern] border of the state [of Yucatán]; it has been so often sacked and burnt by the revolted natives, that the only building left is the church, occupied by a company of twenty-five men. It looks a forsaken, God-forgotten place, a veritable exile for the small garrison quartered here in turn for three months in the year; not that there is any immediate danger, for the natives, who first rose to conquer their liberties, fell to massacring from a spirit of revenge, and now only take the field for the sake of plunder. We have nothing to tempt their cupidity, consequently our escort of fifty men [and twelve Winchesters] is a measure of prudence rather than of necessity. . . . The ruins of Chichén are two miles east of Pisté, and were used as pasture for the cattle of the inhabitants, who at stated periods had the woods cut down, when the monuments were easily distinguished. It was a favorite place, to the prejudice of the palaces and sculptures, which were made the butt by the visitors to shoot at; but since the destruction of Pisté, nature again reigns supreme; every sign of the buildings has disappeared, and the jungle has become so impassable, that twenty men were required to open the old path. This was not

my first visit to Chichén, nevertheless my emotion was profound on be-
holding again the gigantic outline of El Castillo, which we had decided
beforehand should be our headquarters, as from its elevated position
it offered many strategical advantages, which would secure us against
surprise. It was with considerable difficulty that we climbed the steps,
which are steep and completely invaded by a vigorous vegetation; as for
our great quantity of baggage, none but the nimble, sure-footed natives could have succeeded in hauling it up on to the platform of the
monument.[3]

Becoming-Maya, Becoming-Intense

Following in a rich tradition of heterodox religions and religious practices
that include mesmerism, hydrotherapy, and Mormons, late-twentieth-cen-
tury Anglo North Americans began to turn to Mexico and Mexican Indians
for spiritual regeneration, transcendence, and reinvention. Spurred by Carlos Castañeda, Yaqui Indians, Joseph Campbell, and more mainstream cultural nationalisms based in Aztlán, one California Chicano, José Argüelles,
began a journey into discovering the Maya and transforming standard an-

53. Becoming-Maya, becoming-intense. Photo by author.

thropological interpretations (based on the CIW and related research) into a New Age theology. The Harmonic Convergence on 17–18 August 1989 marks the transnationalization of this theology and the inauguration of a New Age Maya heterodoxy. Based on an eclectic appropriation of practices and symbols from a multitude of religions and cultures, initiates enter a path of knowledge that "comes from" the Ancient Maya in order to become "Maya"—that entails purification of the "Inner Self/Light Child" to attain the Higher Vibrational Frequency and Oneness of the Galaxy. In Figure 53 three New Age Maya dressed in white await the equinoctial approach of Hunab Ku K'uk'ulcan at the Feathered Serpent Column entrance to the Temple of K'uk'ulcan. Each came separately but were joined by others, and, moments after this photograph was taken, a group of seven formed spontaneously in the inner chamber of the temple that began "a ritual of love" and "purification" of Self/Universe through "toning."[4]

In the Aura of Ruins

After events of recidivism in Central Mexico and elsewhere in the decades after Conquest and mass conversions, the Spanish Crown sought to put a stop to missionary inquiry into the history, society, and religion of their Indian subjects. Censorship of publications had a material and symbolic double in the way tens of thousands of Indian cities—those on which Spanish towns had *not* been built—were in the course of centuries covered over by jungle, "lost" both in sociogeographic space and in knowledge. In turn, the Indian peoples were lost, or displaced from their origins, and "deindigenized," or transformed into not-native natives who thereby could not legitimately claim rights as people over territory. The historical struggle to create independent nations at the beginning of the nineteenth century stimulated efforts to convert lost cities and lost peoples into primordial origins of these emergent nation-states. The opening of Spanish America and then Latin American nations to foreign traveler-scientists, beginning with Humboldt, oriented this conversion of Lost Cities into fables of Lost Civilizations. This is clear from the European traveler-antiquarians and protoanthropologists who endeavored to re/present these ancient societies as civilizations and thus as patrimony within the Eurocentric vision of World Civilization, or what is today juridically organized as Patrimonio de la Humanidad by UNESCO. By approaching the ancient indigenous peoples as objects of knowledge within the framework of cultures and civilization, U.S. North American and European national and capitalist interests could appropriate the hemisphere in parts and as parcel.

In Yucatán, the Criollo intelligentsia needed and used these foreign travelers, such as Stephens and Charnay, and their travelogues about the Maya to transform Yucatecan understanding from fearful hating and denial to celebratory approach and appropriation. Playing off the construction of the Maya as patrimony–primordial origin by Anglo and Eurocentric narratives (and material discursive practices, such as archaeology) of Civilization-Humanity, the Yucatecos folklorized the slippery images, things, and communities of the Maya in moves parallel to those deployed by European countries. Yucatán used the trinity of history, literature, and ethnography to folklorize the Maya as a contemporary vestige and "vanishing" minority. Given Mexico's interest in Central Mexican Indians—"Aztecs"—versus the Indians of this "land apart," Yucatecan intellectuals, such as Mediz Bolio, could compose, with tranquility, eulogies to the Maya in genres typical of Latin American regionalist modernities.

Mal Imagen: Third World Invasion of Chichén Itzá

The first "invasion" of Chichén by local artisans and vendors, from 1983 to 1988, was a low-intensity campaign of sporadic violence, complicated subterfuge, and espionage. Conflict occurred not only between state authorities and private capital on one side, and artisans and vendors on the other, but among the vendors, who fought each other to control every centimeter of space along paths and in the plazas between ruins. Feuds developed between families of the INAH workers, who sought to expel the vendors, in part, for reasons of personal economic interests, and the vendors who claimed Chichén as collective property by both a customary right of proximate residence in Pisté and by juridical right that places the ruins in the *ejido* land grant. The invasion was illicit not only because it threatened ruining the ruins but because it provided a *mal imagen*, a "bad image" to the visiting tourists. This rhetoric and motivation propelled the state to sweep Chichén, and other sites of archaeological patrimony, clear of invading vendors. The *ambulantaje* (itinerant vending) of the artisans and food vendors, with their manifest poverty in the eyes of the gringo, were clear signs of Mexico's under- and uneven development in the age of the 1980s debt crisis. In 1997, dur-

54. *Mal imagen*: Third world invasion of Chichén Itzá. Photo by author.

ing the *third* invasion, the man in Figure 54, a veteran Maya artisan from Pisté and an old friend, allowed me to take his portrait under the shadows of a Maya Mecca of Travel.

"How Did You Get One Without Any People?" ("How *Did* You?")

The first to observe the angular lines that are produced on the western balustrade of the north staircase of the principal pyramid at Chichén Itzá was Arcadio Salazar, who worked there as a stonemason in 1928. Salazar, father of the current custodian of the ruins, told me eight years ago: "I worked on the reconstruction of the staircase and, one day, when the sun set, I saw a line of luminescent angles that was projected on the balustrade. I reported this to Miguel Angel Fernández, who worked at Chichén for the government, and the next day he saw what I told him I had seen. Miguel Angel Fernández, who was a good archeologist and drawer, published an article about it, in a journal that he sent

55. "How did you get one without any people?" ("How *did* you?") Photo by author.

me a copy of, but that I lost years later." When I asked him about the name of the journal, Salazar told me that he could not remember. Fernández was a contributor to the journal of the INAH, and it would be worthwhile to find out if that was the journal in which the phenomenon with which we are concerned was discussed. His archeological drawings are uniquely good and it is possible that he copied this column of angles in black and white.[5]

Ruined Ruins

Aura is never entirely separated from its ritual function. In other words, the unique value of the "authentic" work of art has its basis in ritual, the location of its original use value . . . for the first time in world history, mechanical reproduction emancipates the work of art from its parasitical dependence on ritual. To an even greater degree the work of art reproduced becomes the work of art designed for reproducibility. From a photographic negative, for example, one can make any number of prints; to ask for the "authentic" print makes no sense. The instant the criterion of authenticity ceases to be applicable to artistic reproduction, the total function of art is reversed. Instead of being based on ritual, it begins to be based on another practice—*politics*.[6]

One day in the mid-1970s, Don Vincente Chablé, a native of Oxkutzcab employed by the INAH as a custodian of the archaeological zone, was inspired to carve stone and wooden idols in the image of ancient Maya gods to sell to tourists. He took as his inspiration images from Maya hieroglyphic books and the carvings of Chichén. Chablé, not seeking to make reproductive replicas nor to copy other, and older, Yucatec styles of folkloric representations of the natural world, developed a primitivist aesthetic using common tools that he adapted from agricultural work. At first he guarded his products, but curiosity and envy compelled a flood of young boys and some adults to secretly observe and copy his techniques and artwork as a way to explore economic alternatives to the unstable subsistence farming of corn. This first generation of artisans were known as *chac mooleros* because of the statue they most typically carved. This became a term of deprecation not only because of the crude quality of the craftsmanship that mass-produced these but for the manner in which profits were mostly consumed in the purchase of alcohol and for the typically aggressive tactics of selling and ambulantaje.

Second and third generations of artisans refined old and created new figures and forms as they dramatically improved technique and tools. As well, the strong competition for the Chichén market, which was booming in the 1980s due to Cancún, propelled the evolution of this work into a unique handicraft tradition, *arte pisteleño*. Entirely originating in the context of tourism, the invasion of Chichén, and the anthropological construction of Maya Meccas of Travel, this Pisté artwork has never been legitimated by state agencies such as Culturas Populares, Instituto Nacional Indigenista, or the Casa de Artesanía. Emergent from this cottage industry that massproduces for the tourist market, some artisans in the 1990s have developed techniques, styles, and aesthetics—but not the cult of the artist—that transgress the devaluing categories of tourist kitsch, native replica, and folkloric handicraft that constitutively situate the artwork. Invented in the horizon of the anthropological and touristic fascination of the Maya, arte pisteleño is an autoethnographic "art writing" that reappropriates the Maya. As well, this approximation of ancient Maya art is an ethnographic writing of the Western Other and the latter's fascination with the Maya. In repeatedly approaching the ruins, however, these invading Maya artisans and transgressing artists are continually swept aside by the multiple agencies of the state, its allies in the private sector, anthropologists, and tourists, both secular and sacred, who assert their own visions of Maya ruins.

Notes

1 Walter Benjamin, "The Work of Art in the Age of Mechanical Reproduction," in *Illuminations* (New York: Harcourt, Brace and World, 1968), 221.

2 Ibid.

3 Désiré Charnay, *The Ancient Cities of the New World; Being Travels and Explorations in Mexico and Central America from 1857–1882*, trans. J. Gonino and Helen S. Conant (London: Chapman and Hall, 1887), 322–24.

4 See Jeffrey Himpele and Quetzil E. Castañeda, *Incidents of Travel in Chichén Itzá*, videocassette, 90 mins., 1997.

5 José Díaz Bolio, *La serpiente de luz de Chichén Itzá* (Mérida, Mexico: Area Maya, 1982), 1.

6 Benjamin, "The Work of Art," 221, 223–24; emphasis added.

III

FINAL

REFLECTIONS

Transnational Processes and the Rise
and Fall of the Mexican Cultural State:
Notes from the Past

Mary Kay Vaughan

In the twentieth century, no other state in the Western Hemisphere invested as much in the creation and promotion of a national culture as the
Mexican central government. This investment began in 1921 in education,
the plastic arts, music, archaeology, and museums. By the 1930s, it expanded
to radio, film, comic books, newspapers, roads, and tourism. By the 1950s,
it embraced dance and television. Whether directly controlled, as in the case
of public education, museums, and archaeological sites, or regulated
through subsidization and censorship, few areas of modern cultural production in the print and electronic media have until recently escaped the
state's gaze. Nor did any regime in Latin America enjoy a greater payoff for
its investment than that of the Partido Revolucionario Institucional.

These rich, colorful, and penetrating essays bring new insights and perspectives to our understanding of this production. Most important, they
provide new ways for understanding the rise and fall of the Mexican state as
cultural producer. They show that post-1940 Mexican developments cannot
be seen exclusively as the result of PRI patron-clientelist politics and economic modernization. Both politics and economics had important discursive, representational dimensions that shaped, enabled, and mediated them.
Moreover, the essays bring a transnational dimension to cultural analysis
that complicates traditional approaches of political economy. Without ne-
gating the debilitating, disciplining, and culturally homogenizing influence that growing U.S. penetration had in Mexico after 1940, these essays

also demonstrate its democratizing, enabling, and culturally differentiating effects. While transnational forces empowered the PRI state and helped at critical junctures to underwrite its cultural activity, they also challenged and weakened these.

What do the essays in this volume tell us about national cultural production in Mexico after 1940 in relation to past production, transnational processes and historical junctures, regime and citizen politics, and the formation of subjectivity among Mexicans? What do they tell us about historical shifts or periodization during the underresearched years after 1940? Toward what paths for future research do the essays point?

There is a tendency in recent scholarship to speak of a postrevolutionary state cultural project as if it had been systematically planned and implemented from a central government-unified command post in Mexico City. It is frequently assumed to have a unitary character, often located in the antireligiosity exhibited in the late 1920s and early 1930s. Certain essays in this volume suggest a unity around the figures of striking workers and armed and angry peasants who populate the murals of Diego Rivera, in part because these contrast with apolitical representations of national culture after 1940. On the contrary, the postrevolutionary state's cultural politics are better understood as an improvised, multivalent, accumulative process that grew through interaction between state and society. The Constitution of 1917 spoke of land reform, workers' rights, and economic nationalism, not culture. Except to attack the Church as an educating institution inappropriate to secular modernization and to express their moral concerns about gambling, drinking, and prostitution, constitutional delegates had little to say about culture. In 1921, those dimensions of state cultural production most relevant to this essay—representation of national culture in the plastic arts, music, crafts, history, and historical preservation—took shape with the creation of the central Ministry of Education. The Secretaría de Educación Pública (SEP) brought together Mexico City, provincial, and local intellectuals in the orchestration of literacy crusades and cultural nationalist production: teachers, musicians, composers, artists, photographers, poets, anthropologists, archaeologists, physicians, hygienists, and folklorists. All were inspired by the popular upheaval of revolution. Many elite intellectuals sought to control and civilize the masses through art and schools. Others, like muralist Diego Rivera, sought to goad them on to greater acts of class struggle. Thousands of schoolteachers sought to impart to them the tools of modernity while sharpening their weapons of political action.

Because the Mexican Revolution had destroyed the Porfirian state, a new one had to be forged in the midst of widespread social mobilization and fragmented, regionally based military and civilian power. Official cultural representation and performance became critical to the process of state formation. Had they been simply top-down impositions, they could never have played such a role. Rather, the cultural initiative was an interactive one. Just as the figures of striking workers and armed peasants in Rivera's murals stemmed from his imagining what workers and peasants actually did in the Revolution, so in the early 1930s accelerating pressure from peasants to redress grievances, material and religious, led the central government to induct the figure of the agrarian revolutionary, Emiliano Zapata, into the pantheon of patriot heroes. Over time, a plethora of cultural talent gathered up local and regional artistic materials, selected, synthesized, and repackaged them for dissemination through schools, the emerging media of radio and cinema, and, above all, for use by the official party in formation, the future PRI. Through "folkloric" and "indigenous" representations in song, dance, costume, sport, and crafts—and historical "monuments," as Alex Saragoza so well documents in this volume—local and regional cultures in their popular representations became national culture—or part of a national culture that in its synthesis empowered the local and the regional. The process signified more than the centralization of state power, its enhanced capacity for manipulation, the dominion of Mexico City, and the flattening of regional cultures through their absorption into a national culture. Rather, in the intense, multilevel negotiations necessary to consolidate the postrevolutionary state, notions of lo mexicano as nation, region, village, and subject were mutually inscribed in the actors of the time in diverse but meaningful ways, the more so because notions of the national affirmed distinctly regional, local, and individual identities and enabled their articulation in a new national synthesis. This process was especially intense in the 1930s, when it was associated with land redistribution, worker mobilizations, and the oil nationalization carried out during the regime of Lázaro Cárdenas.[1]

Essays in this volume by Eric Zolov, Alex Saragoza, Seth Fein, and Anne Rubenstein suggest—to this student of the pre-1940 period—the amount of cultural capital acquired by the central government by 1940: in personnel, infrastructure, experience, knowledge, and equipment. They show how cleverly this cultural capital was deployed at a particular transnational juncture. Mexican collaboration with the Allies in World War II provided the regime with the opportunity, funds, skills, and markets to massify national culture through the electronic media.[2] In dire need of hemispheric support for the war effort, the U.S. government turned to the Mexican film industry for propagandistic production because it was competent, on the one hand, and because Mexican audiences had rejected Hollywood's version of Latin American culture as denigrating and pro-Yankee. The Mexican film *¡Mexicanos al grito de guerra!* so perceptively analyzed here by Fein, impresses not only because of its tactical brilliance as a tool in securing domestic support for the regime's unpopular decision to join the Allied cause, but because of its narrative, which could not have been written without the accumulated cultural experience of postrevolutionary state formation. It may seem manipulative that the composer of the national anthem was inspired by the tune of a poor woman singing in the street, but it was consistent with the postrevolutionary production of national culture. The great Mexican composers of the twentieth century—Carrillo, Chávez, Moncayo, Revueltas—drew on a rich repertoire of traditional, popular music. The story's association of liberalism with national defense and conservatism with European imperialist decadence and upper-class privilege was not new. This interpretation could be found in government-approved school textbooks of the late nineteenth century. What was new was the inclusive populist mantle in which liberalism could now be cloaked.

However, in 1940, on the eve of the war, the Mexican government was not particularly strong or popular. The 1930s had been fraught with violence and class and religious strife. The oil expropriation had temporarily united the nation around the government, then disunited it under the burdens of back-breaking debt obligations, a retreat from social spending, cries of corruption and communism from the right and betrayal from the left. Most believe the PRM, predecessor of the PRI, lost the elections of 1940, or rather stole them, through fraud. It was World War II and the intervention of the United States that gave the PRM/PRI state the capacity to mobilize the nation. By joining the Allied war effort, the government seized the moral high ground from Catholic conservatives, now tainted by their identification with fascism, and from the left, obliged to submit to a wartime pact of class unity. Capital accumulated in trade with the United States during the war and a subsequent influx of U.S. investment gave the Mexican state and the private sector the material wherewithal to accelerate economic growth, opening new areas of employment and increasing the state's capacity to meet some social demands.

These essays make clear the critical cultural dimensions of regime consolidation and consensus building. The Avila Camacho government (1940–1946) seized on the cultural/political opening between Mexico and the United States to intensify the cultural and political use of radio and film begun in the Cárdenas period. The president promoted, identified with, and broadcast icons of popular culture: movie stars María Félix and Jorge Negrete, composer-musicians Agustín Lara and Carlos Chávez, comedians Tin Tan and Cantinflas. The cultural policy helped eclipse political opposition while focusing attention on Mexico City and the president, to whom it brought prestige and a touch of celebrity status.[3] The regime of Miguel Alemán pursued the more commercial dimensions of cultural policy, especially the development of tourism. Zolov and Saragoza describe how Acapulco emerged as a resort of the rich, famous, and sexy—an object and center of modern desire and fantasy. As John Mraz writes here, state regulation of the press increasingly promoted presidentialism by giving the president excessive publicity in every aspect of his public life. At the same time, it elaborated on and reiterated a discourse justifying Alemán's repression and domestication of militant and independent sectors of the labor movement. This discourse had transnational components in cold war anticommunism as well as national ones (the militants were "traitors to the *patria*" and corrupt demagogues misleading the workers).

How did national, state-associated cultural production in the 1940s and 1950s differ from that of the 1930s? As schooling expanded under increasingly centralized administration, the SEP turned its attention from rural to urban areas. The official curriculum discarded class struggle and history textbooks that made workers and peasants the primary agents of Mexican history in their pursuit of liberation and social justice. Instead, SEP programs subordinated individual and group rights to membership in a collective national effort led by the government and directed toward achieving modern development, material well-being, and freedom within a postwar world of "united (noncommunist) nations." In a general proliferation of mass media production in the private sector, subsidized and regulated by the state, comic books boomed from the mid-1930s, outstripping the standard press in readership and circulation.[4] As these essays make abundantly clear, U.S. officials and entrepreneurs became far more engaged in the film industry, the promotion of tourism, and advertising for new consumer goods. However, in each case, the strength of the accumulated national cultural repertoire, self-consciously manipulated by state, market, and society, was such that U.S. involvement was concealed beneath a flourishing—indeed, what Saragoza has called a massification — of Mexican national identity.[5] In tourism, as Saragoza and Zolov show, Mexico was sold to foreigners and Mexicans as simultaneously modern (new hotels and resorts, burgeoning cities, new highways, new technologies) and traditional and folkloric. The crafts, archaeological sites, museums, colonial architecture, cuisine, dance, costume, and song, recovered and officialized after 1921, proliferated through commercialization. Advertising "Mexicanized" the American Dream by integrating consumption into a national narrative of progress and improvement and deploying Mexican images, contexts, and subjects to sell predominantly U.S. products.[6] Consumer goods were selected and appropriated for explicitly Mexican uses and even spawned Mexican industries, as Jeff Pilcher shows here for national cuisine.

In cinema, the stylized, moralistic renderings of class struggle and social justice characteristic of the Cárdenas period (*Las redes*) yielded to more apolitical but more popular and seductive national stereotypes: the strutting masculinity of mariachi musicians and the singing cowboys (Pedro Armendáriz, Jorge Negrete, and Pedro Infante), motherhood (Sara Garcia), dangerous and alluring female sexuality (Dolores del Río and María Félix), and everyman's clever streetwise comics, Cantinflas and Tin Tan.[7] Rather than trying to reform popular culture through prohibitions against drink, saints, womanizing, and blood sports, post-1940 cinema embraced these. Personal and family melodrama substituted for political epics. Glamorous movie stars and singers dwarfed the public images of politicians and labor leaders. The formal politics of class struggle became the social politics of unity around *mexicanidad*, simultaneously traditional and modernizing. Further, whereas official cultural production in the 1930s had given enormous attention to the countryside, post-1940 production in the mass media was more urban and Mexico City–oriented. As Zolov argues here, in representation, the countryside lost its politically active and revolutionary character. In comics, film, and advertising, it became a backdrop for migration to the cities. In the movies, it was portrayed as a backwater of corruption, *caciquismo*, and want, or idealized to affirm traditional patriarchal and religious values threatened by city life.[8] In tourism, as Zolov, Saragoza, and Castañeda show, rural sites became quaint, folkloric, and archaeological places to visit.

In the 1940s, the face-to-face, oral, "live," and participatory nature of official cultural performance was complemented by mass communications: visual, audible, readable, but distant and externally produced. Interaction and participation took on new but more anonymous and depoliticized forms. As Anne Rubenstein has written elsewhere, readers actively participated in the narratives of the booming comic book industry.[9] Michael Miller has recounted how comic book romance took to the radio waves in 1945 with XEW's *Colegio de Amor*: young men called in to propose marriage to their sweethearts and husbands to explain why they had "left for cigarettes years ago and never returned."[10] In her depiction of the funeral of Pedro Infante in this volume, Rubenstein describes the intimate engagement of Mexico City audiences with the on- and off-screen lives of movie stars— an engagement that appears to have taken on dimensions of a "national romance." This is not to suggest a decline in live entertainment. Heather Levi well describes the growing popularity of *lucha libre* in Mexico City. Cheap and expensive cabarets featured the musicians who sang over the airwaves and in the movies. Movie theaters were themselves sites for audience performance and interaction. In rural areas, the fiesta system, secured for the government and party in the 1930s, continued to function as an arena where aesthetic, ritualized performance of music, dance, sports, and words served to affirm local social and political unity; to articulate and negotiate interests; and to dispense goods, services, and patronage within what Claudio Lomnitz has called the hierarchical pyramid of state power.[11] The urban counterpart of the rural fiesta flourished in massive civic celebrations: the Grito de Independencia issued by the president from the balcony of the National Palace to cheering crowds in the Zócalo, the May Day parades where the president and union leaders reviewed contingents of hundreds of organized workers carrying red-and-black flags.

The essays focusing on the 1940s and 1950s suggest the importance of a new political category in Mexico: that of social citizenship. Scholars of commodity culture and mass communications (among them, Rubenstein and Alison Greene in this collection) emphasize their transformative potential.[12] Consumption of modern goods and mass communication messages does not simply confirm existing values. It can create new values, experiences, and aspirations. In short, in modern society consumption is a potent force shaping identities and subjectivities. It generates social citizenship. It becomes a critical dimension of an imagined national community and an arena for democratization. It makes available material and cultural goods formerly accessible only to a minority. It creates desires. It is an area for the exercise of choice and the right to self-fulfillment and self-development, implicitly and explicitly included in modern political discourse. Though it is an arena that agents of the state and marketplace seek to manipulate and regulate in order to shape citizenship, their messages may be contradictory.[13] The ways consumers read and acted on them cannot be predicted.[14]

Each essay in this book speaks to the extension of Mexican citizenship to consumption and the marketplace after 1940 and to the cultural, discursive, and identity-generating aspects of this process. It is not facile to wager that for the middle and working classes in formation in post-1940 Mexico, the act of consumption—or the hope to consume, as inspired by state and market discourses—may have substituted to some degree for the practice of formal political rights. It is not facile when one considers how socially transitional and transformative the years between 1940 and 1960 were. In this period of rapid urbanization, representations of Mexican national identity were infused with a notion of modernity conflating science and technology, consumption, and individual freedom and gratification. Surely, this discourse and the possibility of acting within it went far to heal the fissures between the Catholic and secular middle classes cut by the government's attack on the Church between 1926 and 1936. It probably served to absorb into the middle class new entrants of more popular and humble origin. The latter could own their new class identities because they could assume them through work and consumption, rather than the more narrow, ascriptive, behavioral, and educational categories that had regulated membership in the past. For another in-between group—the thousands of migrants pouring into Mexico City from the countryside—Rubenstein, Carlos Monsiváis, Michael Miller, and others have argued how important were comic books and movies in teaching new behaviors and ways of navigating the tricky and dangerous urban environment.[15] They have pointed as well to the mass media's role in the formation and acquisition of voice and social space by two other emerging groups: women and youth.

In her analysis in this volume of Pedro Infante's funeral, Rubenstein shows us how the mutual construction of the mass media and social citizenship created notions of membership, entitlement, and inclusion that could spill over into proto-political expressions of social frustration. Thus she reads the battling between crowds and police in Mexico City as an expression of anger against increasing social stratification and political exclusion manifest in a reorganization of urban space that moved power, culture, and wealth southward and left the central city poor and neglected—by implication, a part of the past rather than the media-generated promissory future.

Rubenstein's essays and others in the volume whet our appetite for more information on consumer reception and appropriation of mass media messages. Most essays assume a primarily Mexico City audience. We also want to know about provincial cities and the countryside. We need to know about differential access to radio, cinema, television, the print media, and advertising and the material capacity of people and communities to absorb and participate in a world of modern consumerism. Evidence can be gleaned from ethnographic studies like those of Oscar Lewis and the classical microhistory of the period, Luis González y González's *Pueblo en vilo*, to show that radio, movies, and some consumer goods reached particular villages.[16] However, we suspect that messages and goods were selected and appropriated within a dense local framework of practice and meaning shaped by peasant agriculture, its economic limitations, its social hierarchies, and its politics. The revolutionary process had not so much unleashed a desire for modernity in rural Mexico as it had shored up *campesino* traditions through agrarian reform and cultural struggle. On the other hand, the appropriation of modern consumer goods and messages could introduce change, and particularly seems to have opened new possibilities for women and youth.[17]

We need systematic, ethnographic studies of communities between 1940 and 1960 such as those in this volume by Steve Bachelor and Greene for later periods. Such ethnographies need to examine the interaction of new cultural production with other messages emanating from family, school, church, work, community, and differentiated social groups. In fact, we need these studies for provincial cities and Mexico City as well. For Mexico City, essays in this book present us with a plethora of contradictory models for gendered behavior, appropriate in their complex multiplicity to a period of rapid and intense social change. Women are at once presented as saintly, abnegating mothers, *indias bonitas*, and *charras*, modern Catholic ladies who act as moral policewomen of the dangerous and vice-ridden city, serious students of science in preparatory school, sexy, independent film stars, and aggressive fans of movie stars and lucha libre. Men are presented as sober, virtuous, desexed technocrats, traditional protective patriarchs, irresponsible but handsome lovers, humorous but subversive *pelados*, and modern daredevils revving up airplanes and motorcycles. We need to know how and if people of different social classes, neighborhoods, genders, and ethnic groups read and selected from this menu of possibilities.

We need to know as well how the messages of the mass media intersected with more explicitly political language and action. Whereas the Alemán pe-

riod (1946–1952) was one of severe repression of labor and agrarian movements, the 1950s gave rise to major organized protests in Mexico City and
elsewhere. We need to know how languages of dissent and negotiation constructed in the more openly militant and populist 1930s were deployed and
transformed under new political conditions and how these meshed with
cultural representation. Pedro Infante's funeral took place just months before Mexico City became a battlefield in a near civil war. In May 1958, the
historically militant railroad workers' union mobilized throughout the
country for wage increases and union democracy. President Ruíz Cortines
met their wage demands. However, when the Ministry of Labor refused to
recognize the new union leadership elected by the rank and file, 80,000
railworkers nationwide walked off their jobs. As the army and police occupied the railroad workers' union halls, 7,000 telegraph operators and 15,000
teachers stopped work in solidarity. University students declared a strike
and took to the streets to protest bus fare increases. Trade and commerce
came to a halt in what was called the most important strike movement in
Mexican history.[18] To resolve the crisis, President Ruíz Cortines had to re-
tire government troops from the union halls and accept worker demands
for new elections, freedom of arrested workers, and job and wage restitu-
tion.

Fernando del Paso's novel *José Trigo* describes the daily life and consciousness of the railroad worker families who inhabited the camps of Nonoalco-
Tlatelolco in the northern quarter of the city next to the old Buenavista Railroad Station.[19] Del Paso is a novelist with his own particular strategy, but
his fictional ethnography is suggestive and should give us pause. He paints
a portrait of a culture unpermeated by the mass media or Sears Roebuck–
marketed consumer goods. It was a neighborhood of old Mexican-owned
factories: beer, soap, glass, soft-drink bottling plants. Families lived in box-
cars they had painted green; they covered the holes in the roof with banana
leaves and hung tin-can flowerpots from the windows. Inside, there might
be an oil stove, an old aluminum bathing tub, a plastic-covered table, and
above the beds, the images of the saints. There were no radios or televisions.
In the wagons, women cooked, watered plants, made coffee, soap, love, and
babies. They held their husbands' cigarettes while the men bathed and toler-
ated the time they passed in brothels. The world of women was confined to
the home, their *comadres*, the *carnicería*, the *tortillería*, and the church. They
ritually pleaded with their husbands not to strike, then distributed leaflets
in support of the movement. After a strike in 1927, the men had stopped

reading the national newspapers: "Ever since then, the newspapers called us reds and there was nothing we could do." They had their own press and oral traditions they passed on to their sons as they passed on their jobs. Theirs was a *gremial* culture of corporate, familial solidarity. This culture had colonial artisan origins; through the Mexican Revolution, it had acquired dimensions of class consciousness and rights. What the workers remembered and talked about on the boxcar stoops, in the *ostionerías* and *cantinas* were past and present strikes, their skill at repairing the trains, the women they had loved and conquered, and the benefits their collective organizing had won them: vacations, rail passes, medical coverage, and accident indemnification. As one worker put it, "Our struggle is very old—*más vieja que tú, madre.*"

The state eventually repressed the railroad workers' movement and jailed the leaders. The transnational automobile industry and highways eclipsed railroad transport. The government bulldozed the camps at Nonoalco and built a massive popular housing project nearby at Tlatelolco. In the 1960s, children of the railroad workers attended the new technical preparatory school at Tlatelolco that would send hundreds of youthful militants into the student movement of 1968, which once again turned Mexico City into a battlefield. As essays in this volume make abundantly clear, the 1960s mark a profound cultural, ideational shift in Mexico City with important political implications. The state did not forfeit its production or regulation of national culture; however, it lost its monopolistic control and its own messages were increasingly deployed against it by a burgeoning and rapidly differentiated population whose demands for inclusion it had difficulty meeting.

In agreement with Monsiváis and Agustín, acute observers of the Mexico City cultural scene, Zolov and Bachelor tell us in their essays that the shift involved a decline in the efficacy of state-related production of national identity and historical narrative (at least for the capital's intellectual elite and middle classes) simultaneous with the arrival of huge multinational corporations, primarily U.S.-based.[20] A new generation of writers noted the regime's growing dependence on the United States and the government's worsening habit of punishing those it claimed to represent. The Cuban Revolution inspired them. In the hopes raised by its youthful and unproven promise, the real consequences of its much older Mexican counterpart looked shabby and its leadership decidedly bourgeois. Carlos Fuentes debunked the populist heritage of the Mexican Revolution in *The Death of Ar-*

temio Cruz.[21] In *José Trigo*, del Paso demonized the repressive government and its alliance with the CIA and reclaimed the Revolution's heritage for the workers. The capital's middle class had lost interest in Mexican music and film and were increasingly attracted to foreign, particularly U.S., goods and messages. Many of their children had turned James Dean and Marlon Brando into icons of youth rebellion. They took up rock music and, by 1964, were listening to the Beatles. They pushed against the uninspiring authoritarianism, corruption, and materialism of the adult world in search of self-expression. In Agustín's words, the only thing they asked was "Let Us Be."[22] They avidly devoured an emergent literature that gave voice to alienated youth: the novels of Agustín himself (twenty years old in 1964), José Emilio Pacheco, and Parmenides García Saldana—the Mexican counterparts, as it were, of J. D. Salinger's *Catcher in the Rye*. Zolov vividly describes a new generation of transnational tourists—the hippies—for whom the traditional, indigenous rural, and dirty "Other" Mexico was preferable to the "modern," so uncontestable to their parents. Young Mexican *jipitecas* joined them. A transnational youth culture was beginning to emerge.[23]

In 1968, on U.S. university campuses, in Paris, Mexico City, Turin, and elsewhere, youth rebelled against the post-1945 Pax Americana and its national variations. In Mexico and the United States, they shredded the historical narrative that had provided moral agency to their parents and to themselves. The Mexican generation of 1968 not only demanded democracy and denounced the government's irresponsibility toward the poor, it rewrote the history of the Mexican Revolution as a manipulation of the masses by an all-powerful bourgeois state. The state these young adults and sprouting scholars had grown up with became mistakenly but understandably the central government of 1921, and it appeared not as an enabler or a negotiator but as a repressive manipulator. By the early 1970s, in response to the student movement, the government granted considerably more freedom to the press and universities. Higher education was decentralized and more critical journalism and intellectual production enjoyed greater national circulation.

In his essay on the GM workers of Naucalpan in the 1960s, Bachelor shows how transnational processes empowered a new generation of industrial workers to seize on nationalism to challenge their employers and the PRI. Mexican workers had long used the revolutionary nationalism constructed in the Cárdenas era to negotiate with the state and stake their claims; what was novel here was its use by a new sector of the labor force working for transnational firms and allying with an emerging transnational labor movement. Bachelor's ethnographic approach helps us see how, through transnational processes, the GM workers invigorated a language and practice of Mexican working-class culture not dissimilar to that of the railroad workers of Nonoalco. New languages and practices were mediated by older forms in ways that transformed both.

Bachelor shows the vulnerability of the Mexican state and transnational capital at a particular conjuncture in the early 1960s. Stung by its handling of the railroad workers' strike, the government passed a number of measures favoring organized labor and nationalized the electricity industry. The transnational automobile industry had to demonstrate good citizenship to avoid nationalization and overcome worker hostility to gringo bosses. Thus, it offered to the GM workers of Naucalpan generous wages and a panoply of benefits—educational, recreational, monetary—to win them over to the GM family as privileged workers who were playing a vanguard role in the industrialization of their country. Even though workers were new migrants from rural areas, the actions and values they described to Bachelor strongly resembled the gremial traditions articulated by the railroad workers: dignity and pride in masculine work skills and craftsmanship, patriarchal familialism, the right and pleasure of sexual conquest and promiscuity, and a notion of worker control that had become part of militant trade union practices in the 1920s and 1930s. When GM instituted a massive speed-up of the production line that stunned and dishonored them, the workers demanded the right to participate in production and management decisions. This demand shocked GM, for worker control was in no way part of U.S. industrial culture. The GM workers became new leaders in the Mexican trade union movement through distinguishing themselves as privileged workers, through acts of solidarity other workers showed toward them, and through their association with the transnational labor movement: the U.S. United Auto Workers and the International Metalworkers Confederation. Thus, they injected new fire into the Mexican movement.

They also become self-conscious modern consumers, taking Acapulco vacations, purchasing cars, and sending their children to university. It was a gremial, familial culture they created in their union (sports, welfare, and training programs, newspapers, union stores) and in their homelife in Las Americas, the *colonia* they built with its U.S.-style single-family homes with yards and garages lining streets called California, Canada, Washington, North America. When, to secure garbage collection for their Americanized colonia, their wives marched to the office of the municipal president and littered it with rubbish, these women acted on long-standing traditions of female political action in the city—actions that became increasingly generalized in the exploding metropolis.

In the 1970s and especially after 1981, the postrevolutionary state's cultural project—understood as the official production and regulation of national culture to secure regime hegemony and modernization—unraveled under the twin pressures of popular, domestic demands and the politics of global economics. Import-substitution industrialization linked to the United States brought the Mexican state and economy deeper into debt and increasingly unable to sustain an inclusive project of state-led, national modernization. In 1981, a fall in international oil prices brought the economy to a halt. The Mexican state became a captive of its foreign creditors: Wall Street, the International Monetary Fund, and Washington. Bowing to their neoliberal demands for market-driven modernization, the PRI state divested itself of social and cultural spending as well as its subsidization and regulation of the economy. Lomnitz has argued that its loss of capacity fostered the growth of opposition political parties and obliged it to surrender control over the last of its cultural spaces: the political ritual that in the past had unified nation, community, party, and state.[24] No longer the *Estado Educador, Protector*, or *Constructor*, the PRI government acquired the image of a narrow Americanized technocratic elite, a "freefloating crust of predators" without moorings in Mexican society, plunderers "who take the jewels from the temple at the top of the pyramid and deposit them in Switzerland."[25] Mexico City lost its centrality to economy, culture, and politics. Industrialization took place outside the capital. The countryside no longer lived from agricultural production and government subsidies, but from the earnings of millions of migrants who went to the United States to make a living and acquire new cultural and technical knowledge. Television came to prevail as the major educating and entertaining medium.[26] While national television diversified somewhat and to a degree replaced state-sponsored production of national history and culture, transnational cable —as Greene so vividly describes in this volume—spawned new identifications with an imagined trans–Latin American/Latino community with its capital in Miami and Cristina, Latin America's Oprah Winfrey, as its president.

It is ironic that the two essays in this volume that treat cultural production outside of Mexico City deal with the present period, when Mexico City has lost its centrality and agriculture is no longer the mainstay of regional economies. Thus youth in Pustunich, Yucatán, use the television to shed rural customs and behaviors as quickly as they can in order to seek jobs and training elsewhere. Transnational tourism—the beach resort at Cancún and the archaeological site of Chichén Itzá—grows as a magnet for employment. Greene and Castañeda examine the contestatory creative dynamics of the local within the national and their interaction with transnational processes. Although such dynamics are operative in most places in Mexico, they have particular historical roots in Yucatán. Castañeda shows how Chichén Itzá was the joint creation of the U.S. government, the Carnegie Institute, the Yucatecan and Mexican governments, Yucatecan and U.S. archaeologists, and the Mayas who cleared the bush and created the now ruined site in the first place. Though Chichén belongs to the Mexican National Museum, Castañeda portrays it as an intensely local and regional space, empowered in large part by transnational tourism and archaeology. For Yucatecans and Mayas, Chichén creates their "land apart" from Mexico, generates their struggles to keep the space clear of "foreign" (i.e., Mexican) commodities, and allows them to create a tourist narrative containing only faint traces of Mexico. Greene shows how identity in Pustunich is local, then regional: "Mexicans" are derogatively referred to as *huach*. Yet, despite traditions of local distinctiveness and the seductive new world of transnational television and tourism, sentiments of mexicanidad persist. They are stirred through *telenovelas* of personal romance, sports competitions, and international news. Learning about the rest of the world becomes a way of recognizing what is Mexican. In local banter, the United States continues to be "Othered" as a metaphor for the dangers of modernity: of class and race discrimination, guns and crime, fast food, family disintegration, and heartless abandonment of elders, children, and the poor.

As a student of the postrevolutionary Mexican state's cultural work between 1921 and 1940, I gained rich insights from this volume into the state's role as cultural producer and regulator after 1940. It convinced me that after 1940, neither education nor politics nor the economy can be looked at independent of mass media production. It strengthened my conviction that penetrating historical analysis comes through integrating macro and micro approaches linking local ethnography to larger political, economic, and cultural phenomena. It points as well to the need to supplement traditional written sources with oral, visual, and auditory ones. And it provides new, surprising, and challenging perspectives on the intersection of transnational, national, and local processes.

Notes

1 I have so argued in *Cultural Politics in Revolution: Teachers, Peasants, and Schools in Mexico, 1930–1940* (Tucson: University of Arizona Press, 1997), and "Cultural Approaches to Peasant Politics in the Mexican Revolution," *Hispanic American Historical Review* 79, no. 2 (1999): 291–97. Alex Saragoza makes a similar argument in this volume with a focus on historical monuments and tourism.

2 See Michael Nelson Miller, *Red, White, and Green: The Maturing of Mexicanidad, 1940–1946* (El Paso: Texas Western Press, 1998).

3 Ibid., 7, 87, 99, 139.

4 See Anne Rubenstein's important and entertaining book, *Bad Language, Naked Ladies, and Other Threats to the Nation* (Durham, NC: Duke University Press, 1998).

5 Alex Saragoza, "The Selling of Mexico: Tourism and the State, 1946–58," paper presented at the conference Representing Mexico: Transnationalism and the Politics of Culture Since the Revolution, Woodrow Wilson Center, Washington, DC, 6–8 November 1997, pp. 4, 13, 19.

6 Julio Moreno, "Constructing the Mexican Dream: Consumer Culture in Mexico City and the Reconstruction of Modern Mexico in the 1940s," paper presented at the conference Representing Mexico: Transnationalism and the Politics of Culture Since the Revolution, Woodrow Wilson Center, Washington, DC, 6–8 November 1997.

7 See Saragoza, "The Selling of Mexico: Tourism and the State, 1946–1958," 14; for a recent collection on Mexican film in English, see Joanne Hershfield and David R. Maciel, eds., *Mexico's Cinema: A Century of Film and Filmmakers* (Wilmington, DE: Scholarly Resources, 1999).

8 See Rubenstein in this volume, and Miller, *Red, White, and Green*, 87–89.

9 Rubenstein, *Naked Ladies*, 41–74.

10 Miller, *Red, White, and Green*, 112.

11 See Claudio Lomnitz, "Ritual, Rumor and Corruption in the Constitution of Polity in Modern Mexico," *Journal of Latin American Anthropology* 1 (1965): 20–47, and "Fissures in Contemporary Mexican Nationalism," *Public Culture* 9 (1996): 55–68.

12 In this volume, the methodology for examining the consumer dimension of modern cultural production is best laid out by Alison Greene. For analysis of the transformative dimensions of modern consumption, see, among others and in addition to those cited by Greene, Jean Baudrillard, *Selected Writings*, ed. Mark Poster (Stanford, CA: Stanford University Press, 1988); Simon Bonner, ed., *Consuming Visions: Accumulation and Display of Goods in America, 1880–1920* (New York: Henry Francis Du Pont Winterhur Museum, 1989); Roland Marchand, *Advertising the American Dream: Making Way for Modernity, 1920–40* (Berkeley: University of California Press, 1985); Thomas Richards, *The Commodity Culture of Victorian England: Advertising and Spectacle, 1851–1914* (Stanford, CA: Stanford

University Press, 1990); Victoria de Grazia with Ellen Furlough, eds., *The Sex of Things: Gender and Consumption in Historical Perspective* (Berkeley: University of California Press, 1996); and Michel de Certeau, *The Practice of Everyday Life* (Berkeley: University of California Press, 1988).

13 See Francine Masiello, "Gender, Dress and Market: The Commerce of Citizenship in Latin America," in *Sex and Sexuality in Latin America*, ed. Daniel Balderston and Donna J. Guy (New York: New York University Press, 1997), 219–33.

14 This is the major point of Certeau in *The Practice of Everyday Life*.

15 Rubenstein, *Naked Ladies*; Miller, *Red, White, and Green*; Carlos Monsiváis, "Mythologies," trans. Ana López, in *Mexican Cinema*, ed. Paulo Antonio Paranaguá (London: British Film Institute, 1995), as cited by Rubenstein in this volume. See also Carlos Monsiváis, *Mexican Postcards*, trans. John Kraniauskas (London: Verso, 1997), 88–105, 106–18.

16 Luis González y González, *Pueblo en vilo: Microhistoria de San José de Gracia* (Mexico City: El Colegio de México, 1972); Oscar Lewis, *Life in a Mexican Village: Tepoztlan Revisited* (Urbana: University of Illinois Press, 1963).

17 See essays in Heather Fowler Salamini and Mary Kay Vaughan, eds., *Creating Spaces, Shaping Transitions: Women of the Mexican Countryside, 1850–1990* (Tucson: University of Arizona Press, 1994).

18 Antonio Alonso, *El movimiento ferrocarrilero en México, 1958–59* (Mexico City: Era, 1972), 118–30; Mario Gil, *Los ferrocarrileros* (Mexico City: Editorial Extemporáneos, 1971), 170.

19 Fernando del Paso, *José Trigo* (Mexico City: Siglo XXI, 1966).

20 See, for example, Carlos Monsiváis, "La nación de unos cuantos y las esperanzas románticas: Notas sobre la historia del término 'Cultura Nacional' en México," in *En torno a la cultura nacional*, ed. Héctor Aguilar Camín (Mexico City: Instituto Nacional Indigenista, 1989), 159–221; "Muerte y resurreción del nacionalismo mexicano," *Nexos* 109 (1987): 13–22; José Agustín, *Tragicomedia mexicana: La vida en México de 1940 a 1970* (Mexico City: Planeta, 1990), 143–252.

21 Carlos Fuentes, *La muerte de Artemio Cruz* (Mexico City: Fondo de Cultura Económica, 1962).

22 Agustín, *Tragicomedia*, 149–50.

23 For a full account of this aspect of emerging Mexican youth culture, see Eric Zolov, *Refried Elvis: The Rise of the Mexican Counterculture* (Berkeley: University of California Press, 1999).

24 Lomnitz, *Fissures*, 64.

25 Ibid., 65.

26 Ibid., 62.

Contributors

STEVEN J. BACHELOR is Assistant Professor of History at Roosevelt University. He recently completed his dissertation, entitled "At the Edge of Miracles: Postrevolutionary Mexico City and the Remaking of the Industrial Working Class, 1934–1982," at Yale University. He has held fellowships from the Andrew W. Mellon Foundation, the Fulbright Commission, and the Whiting Foundation. From 1997 to 1999, he was a Visiting Research Fellow at the Center for U.S.-Mexican Studies at the University of California, San Diego, and prior to that was a Visiting Research Scholar at El Colegio de México. He has written widely on working-class culture and politics in Mexico and is currently completing an edited volume entitled *Postrevolutionary Mexican Politics: The Rise and Fall of an Authoritarian Regime, 1940–2000*.

QUETZIL E. CASTAÑEDA has taught anthropology at the University of Houston and Lake Forest College and is currently teaching Latino and Latin American cultural studies in the Spanish Language and Literatures Department at the University of Hawai'i. He has been doing historical ethnography and fieldwork in Yucatán since 1985. In addition to his book on transnational anthropology in relation to Maya communities at Chichén Itzá (*In the Museum of Maya Culture*, 1996) and the award-winning film on tourism and the state (*Incidents of Travel in Chichén Itzá*, 1997) that he coproduced, Castañeda has organized an annual exhibition of modern Maya art in Yucatán (beginning in 1997) and curated an international exhibition with the participation of Pisté Maya artists in the United States (29 November–11 December 1999). He is currently writing on the theory and practice of experimental ethnography that he has been conducting since 1997 in the community of Pisté, Yucatán.

SETH FEIN is Assistant Professor of History at Yale University, where he teaches U.S. international and transnational history. He has been Invited Research Professor at the Instituto Mora in Mexico City. Among his publications are essays in the books *Visible Nations: Latin*

American Cinema and Video (2000), *Mexico's Cinema: A Century of Films and Filmmakers* (1999), *Close Encounters of Empire: Writing the Cultural History of U.S.-Latin American Relations* (1998), *Horizontes del segundo siglo: investigación y pedagogía del cine mexicano, latinoamericano y chicano* (1998), and *México-Estados Unidos:encuentros y desencuentros en el cine* (1996). His articles have appeared in *Studies in Latin American Popular Culture, Secuencia, Historia y grafía*, and *Film Historia*. He is completing a book entitled *Transnational Projections: The United States in the Golden Age of Mexican Cinema*.

ALISON GREENE is completing her Ph.D. in anthropology at the University of North Carolina in Chapel Hill. Her dissertation, entitled "Huipiles and Spandex: Refashioning Gender in the Global Economy of a Town in Yucatán," is based on ethnographic fieldwork and examines practices producing novel forms of female gender in the midst of rapid economic and social change in the 1990s. She plans to continue working in Yucatán, Mexico and to develop similar research with Latin American immigrants in the United States.

OMAR HERNÁNDEZ received his Ph.D. from the Department of Radio-TV-Film at the University of Texas at Austin. His research focuses mainly on the relationship between Latin America's televisual culture, exemplified primarily by telenovelas, and the national public sphere in countries such as Mexico and Venezuela. He is also interested in the flow of television programming across countries within the region, as well as beyond Latin America, and continues to study Latino culture in the United States. He currently teaches at the Instituto Tecnológico y de Estudios Superiores de Monterrey, in Monterrey, Mexico.

JIS (JOSÉ IGNACIO SOLÓRZANO) AND TRINO (JOSÉ TRINIDAD CAMACHO) are both from Guadalajara, Mexico. There they joined the local avant-garde punk/performance/visual art scene of the 1980s, before starting professional careers as cartoonists with the weekly full-page strip "El Santos Contra la Tetona Mendoza" in the Mexico City daily *La Jornada* in 1989. The strip, now collected in three volumes from Editorial La Jornada, ended in 1996 but has been followed by others made by the team Jis & Trino and by Jis and Trino individually. These new strips have appeared in the newspapers *Siglo XXI* and *La Jornada*, and the humor magazine *El Chamuco*, as well as in new collections of their work. Trino's animated cartoons and videos have also appeared on television in Guadalajara and nationally.

GILBERT M. JOSEPH is Farnam Professor of History and director of Latin American Studies at Yale University and editor of the *Hispanic American Historical Review*. He is the author of *Revolution from Without: Yucatán, Mexico, and the United States, 1880–1924* (rev. ed., 1988; Spanish ed., 1992), *Rediscovering the Past at Mexico's Periphery* (1986), *Summer of Discontent, Seasons of Upheaval: Elite Politics and Rural Insurgency in Yucatán, 1876–1915* (with Allen Wells, 1996), and numerous articles on modern Mexico and U.S. involvement in Latin America. His edited collections include: *Everyday Forms of State Formation: Revolution and the Negotiation of Rule in Modern Mexico* (with Daniel Nugent, 1994), *Close Encounters of Empire: Writing the Cultural History of U.S.-Latin American Relations* (with Catherine LeGrand and Ricardo Salvatore, 1998), and *Mexico's New Cultural History: Una Lucha Libre?* (Special Issue of the *Hispanic American Historical Review*, with Susan Deans-Smith, 1999). He is currently completing a study of rural strategies of survival and protest in nineteenth- and twentieth-century Latin America with cultural anthropologist Patricia Peassar that is based on research in Mexico, Guatemala, Brazil, and the Dominican Republic.

HEATHER LEVI teaches anthropology at Wagner College on Staten Island. Her articles have been published in the journals *Social Text* and *Sexualities* and in the collection *SportCult* (1999).

EMILE G. MCANANY is the Walter E. Schmidt, S.J. Professor of Communication and Chair of the Department of Communication at Santa Clara University. He previously taught for eighteen years at the University of Texas at Austin and also at Stanford University. He is the author and editor of nine books, including *Mass Media and Free Trade: NAFTA and the Cultural Industries* (1996). He has spent most of his professional life doing research on communication media content and technologies in Latin America. He is currently coediting a book on the social and cultural impact of Brazilian telenovelas.

RUBÉN MARTÍNEZ is a journalist, poet, and staff writer at *L. A. Weekly*. His chapter on rocanrol is taken from his book, *The Other Side: Fault Lines, Guerrilla Saints and the True Heart of Rock 'n' Roll* (1992).

JOHN MRAZ is Research Professor at the Instituto de Ciencias Sociales y Humanidades, Universidad Autónoma de Puebla (Mexico), and has been named National Researcher II by the Secretaría de Educación Pública. He considers himself an "historiador gráfico," and has published widely on the uses of photography, cinema, and video in recounting the histories of Mexico and Cuba. Among his recent books are *Nacho López y el fotoperiodismo mexicano en los años cincuenta* (1999), *La mirada inquieta: nuevo fotoperiodismo mexicano, 1976–1996* (1996, English translation, 1998), and *Uprooted: Braceros in the Hermanos Mayo Lens* (1996). He has been Guest Editor of monographic issues for several journals: *Cinema and History in Latin America* (*Film Historia*, 1999), *Visual Culture in Latin America* (*Estudios Interdisciplinarios de América Latina*, 1998), and *Mexican Photography* (*History of Photography*, 1996). He directed the award-winning documentary videotapes *Innovating Nicaragua* and *Made on Rails: A History of the Mexican Railroad Workers*, and curated several international exhibits of photography. He has been a visiting professor at Oxford University, Dartmouth College, Universidad de Barcelona, University of Connecticut, University of California at Santa Cruz, San Diego State University, and the Fototeca del INAH.

JEFFREY M. PILCHER is Associate Professor of History at The Citadel. He is the author of *Cantinflas and the Chaos of Mexican Modernity* (2000) and *¡Que vivan los tamales! Food and the Making of Mexican Identity* (1998), which won the Thomas F. McGann Prize of the Rocky Mountain Council for Latin American Studies. Currently he is writing a history of the Mexico City meat supply and editing a volume titled *The Human Tradition in Mexico*.

ELENA PONIATOWSKA is a prominent and prolific Mexican journalist and novelist who has written over twenty books, including a recent biography of Mexican poet Octavio Paz. Many of her books have also been translated into English, including *Massacre in Mexico* (about the 1968 student movement in Mexico City), *Nothing, Nobody* (on the 1985 earthquake), the historical novel *Tinísima* (based on the life of Tina Modotti), and the testimonial narrative *Here's to You, Jesusa!*

ANNE RUBENSTEIN is Assistant Professor of Latin American History at York University. She is the author of *Bad Language, Naked Ladies, and Other Threats to the Nation: A Political History of Comic Books in Mexico* (1998). Her current research focuses on film spectatorship and the consumption of other forms of media in postrevolutionary Mexico.

ALEX M. SARAGOZA is Professor of History in the Department of Ethnic Studies at the University of California Berkeley, where he has served as Chair of the Center for Latin American Studies and as Director of the University of California Mexico Studies Center located in Mexico City. He is the author of the *Monterrey Elite and the Mexican State, 1880–1940* (1988) and *The Media and the State in Mexico: The Origins of Televisa* (forthcoming). His current research focuses on the development of Acapulco as a tourist site from the 1930s to the 1980s.

ARTHUR SCHMIDT is Professor of History at Temple University. He teaches courses in Latin American, third world, and global economic history. He is the author of *The Economic and Social Effect of Railroads in Puebla and Veracruz, Mexico, 1867–1911* (1987); cotranslator (with Aurora Camacho de Schmidt) of Elena Poniatowska's *Nothing, Nobody: The Voices of the Mexico City Earthquake* (1995); and editor of the English-language edition of Mario Lungo's *El Salvador in the Eighties: Counterinsurgency and Revolution* (1996). He has contributed to the *Encyclopedia of Mexico: History, Society, and Culture* (1998) and also published several articles, including "Mexicans, Migrants, and Indigenous Peoples: The Work of Manuel Gamio in the United States," in *Strange Pilgrimages: Travel, Exile, and Foreign Residency in the Creation of Latin American Identity* (2000). Presently he is at work on a popularly accessible history of the world economy since World War II.

MARY KAY VAUGHAN is Professor of History at the University of Maryland, College Park. She is the author of *The State, Education and Social Class in Mexico, 1880–1928* (1982) and *Politics in Revolution: Teachers, Peasants, and Schools in Mexico, 1930–1940* (1997), winner of the Herbert Eugene Bolton Prize of the Conference on Latin American History and the Bryce Wood Award of the Latin American Studies Association. She has written extensively on themes of education, women, and gender in modern Mexico. She is coediting a volume with Steve Lewis on the formation of national memory and identity in Mexico from 1920 to 1940. Her current project focuses on citizenship and education in the Mexican generation of 1968.

ERIC ZOLOV is Assistant Professor of History at Franklin & Marshall College in Lancaster, Pennsylvania. He is the author of *Refried Elvis: The Rise of the Mexican Counterculture* (1999), and *Latin America and the United States: A Documentary History* (with Robert Holden, 2000), and a contributor to the *Encyclopedia of Mexico: History, Society, and Culture* (1998), *Student Protest: The Sixties and After* (1998), and *The Human Tradition in Mexico* (forthcoming). He is also a coeditor and contributor to a forthcoming collection of essays, *Rockin' Las Americas: The Global Politics of Rock in Latin America*. His current research explores diplomatic and cultural relations between the United States and Mexico during the 1960s, for which he was awarded a National Endowment for the Humanities fellowship (2001-2002).

Contributors 491

Index

Library of Congress Cataloging-in-Publication Data
Fragments of a Golden Age : the politics of culture in Mexico since 1940 /
edited by Gilbert M. Joseph, Anne Rubenstein, and Eric Zolov.
p.   cm. — (American encounters/global interactions)
Includes index.
ISBN 0-8223-2707-4 (cloth : alk. paper) — ISBN 0-8223-2718-x (pbk. : alk. paper)
1. Mexico—Cultural policy.   2. Popular culture—Mexico—History—20th century.
   I. Joseph, Gilbert M.   II. Rubenstein, Anne.   III. Zolov, Eric.   IV. Series.
   F1210.F72 2001   972.08'2—dc21   2001018784

March of Hunger   p 127   > 1951

Humlder   p. 142   1954

Illustrated Magazine poked fun at powerful
                      + appealed to middle class
                      audiences.

showed
/State sanctioned pol
violence agint indep
workers on May Day
melee

creator of Telesistema media empire 1955, p. 10